Mean square within

$$MSW = \frac{SSW}{dfw}$$

Mean square between

$$MSB = \frac{SSB}{dfb}$$

F ratio

$$F = \frac{MSB}{MSW}$$

CHAPTER 11

Chi square

$$\chi^2 \text{ (obtained)} = \sum \frac{(f_o - f_e)^2}{f_e}$$

CHAPTER 13

Phi

$$\phi = \sqrt{\frac{\chi^2}{N}}$$

Cramer's V

$$V = \sqrt{\frac{\chi^2}{(N)(\text{Minimum of } r - 1, c - 1)}}$$

Lambda

$$\lambda = \frac{E_1 - E_2}{E_1}$$

CHAPTER 14

Gamma

$$G = \frac{N_s - N_d}{N_s + N_d}$$

Spearman's rho

$$r_s = 1 - \frac{6 \sum D^2}{N(N^2 - 1)}$$

CHAPTER 15

Least-squares regression line

$$Y = a + bX$$

Slope

$$b = \frac{N \sum XY - (\sum X)(\sum Y)}{N \sum X^2 - (\sum X)^2}$$

Y intercept

$$a = \overline{Y} - b\overline{X}$$

Pearson's r

$$r = \frac{N \sum XY - (\sum X)(\sum Y)}{\sqrt{[N \sum X^2 - (\sum X)^2][N \sum Y^2 - (\sum Y)^2]}}$$

CHAPTER 17

Partial correlation coefficient

$$r_{yx.z} = \frac{r_{yx} - (r_{yz})(r_{xz})}{\sqrt{1 - r_{yz}^2} \sqrt{1 - r_{xz}^2}}$$

Least-squares multiple regression line

$$Y = a + b_1X_1 + b_2X_2$$

Partial slope for X_1

$$b_1 = \left(\frac{s_y}{s_1}\right)\left(\frac{r_{y1} - r_{y2}r_{12}}{1 - r_{12}^2}\right)$$

Partial slope for X_2

$$b_2 = \left(\frac{s_y}{s_2}\right)\left(\frac{r_{y2} - r_{y1}r_{12}}{1 - r_{12}^2}\right)$$

Y intercept

$$a = \overline{Y} - b_1\overline{X}_1 - b_2\overline{X}_2$$

Beta-weight for X_1

$$b_1^* = b_1\left(\frac{s_1}{s_y}\right)$$

Beta-weight for X_2

$$b_2^* = b_2\left(\frac{s_2}{s_y}\right)$$

Standardized least

$$Z_y = b_1^*Z_1 + b_2^*Z_2$$

Coefficient of m

$$R^2 = r_{y1}^2 + r_{y2.1}^2(\quad_{y1})$$

Statistics

A TOOL FOR SOCIAL RESEARCH

First Canadian Edition

Joseph F. Healey

Christopher Newport University

Steven G. Prus

Carleton University

NELSON / EDUCATION

NELSON / EDUCATION

**Statistics: A Tool for Social Research,
First Canadian Edition**

by Joseph F. Healey and Steven G. Prus

**Associate Vice President,
Editorial Director:**
Evelyn Veitch

Editor-in-Chief, Higher Education:
Anne Williams

Executive Editor:
Laura Macleod

Executive Marketing Manager:
David Tonen

Developmental Editor:
Lily Kalcevich

Permissions Coordinator:
Natalie Barrington

**Senior Content Production
Manager:**
Anne Nellis

Production Service:
Integra

Copy Editor:
Michael Kelly

Proofreader:
Integra

Indexer:
Integra

**Production
Coordinator:**
Ferial Suleman

Design Director:
Ken Phipps

**Managing
Designer:**
Franca Amore

Cover Design:
Peter Papayanakis

**Cover
Image:**
© iStockphoto.com/Dale Hogan

Compositor:
Integra

**Library and Archives Canada
Cataloguing in Publication**

Healey, Joseph F., 1945–
    Statistics : a tool for social research /
Joseph F. Healey, Steven
G. Prus.—1st Canadian ed.

Includes index.
ISBN 978-0-17-644253-8

1. Social sciences—Statistical methods.
2. Statistics. I. Prus, Steven G. (Steven Gerald),
1967– II. Title.

HA29.H42 2009   519.5
C2008-907400-9

ISBN-13: 978-0-17-644253-8
ISBN-10: 0-17-644253-7

BRIEF CONTENTS

DETAILED CONTENTS

PREFACE TO THE FIRST CANADIAN EDITION

Sociology and the other social sciences (including political science, social work, public administration, criminal justice, urban studies, and gerontology) are research-based disciplines, and statistics are part of their everyday language. To join the conversation, you must be literate in the vocabulary of research, data analysis, and scientific thinking. Knowledge of statistics will enable you to understand the professional research literature of your discipline as well as the research reports you encounter in everyday life. Knowledge of statistics will enable you to conduct quantitative research and to contribute to the growing body of social science knowledge. Statistical literacy will move you closer to reaching your full potential as a social scientist.

Although essential, learning (and teaching) statistics can be a challenge. Students in statistics courses typically have a wide range of mathematical backgrounds and an equally diverse set of career goals. They are often puzzled about the relevance of statistics for them, and, not infrequently, there is some math anxiety to deal with.

This text introduces statistical analysis for the social sciences while addressing these challenges. The text makes minimal assumptions about mathematical background (the ability to read a simple formula is sufficient preparation for virtually all of the material in the text), and a variety of special features help students analyze data successfully. The text is sufficiently flexible to be used in any program with a social science base.

The text is written at a level intermediate between a strictly mathematical approach and a mere "cookbook." We have not sacrificed comprehensive coverage or statistical correctness, but theoretical and mathematical explanations are kept at an elementary level, as is appropriate in a first exposure to social statistics. For example, we do not treat formal probability theory per se. Rather, the background necessary for an understanding of inferential statistics is introduced, informally and intuitively, in Chapters 5 and 6 while considering the concepts of the normal curve and the sampling distribution. The text makes no claim that statistics are "fun" or that the material can be mastered without considerable effort. At the same time, students are not overwhelmed with abstract proofs, formula derivations, and mathematical theory, which can needlessly frustrate the learning experience at this level.

GOAL OF THE TEXT

The goal of this text is to develop basic statistical literacy. The statistically literate person understands and appreciates the role of statistics in the research process, is competent to perform basic calculations, and can read and appreciate the professional research literature in his or her field as well as any research reports he or she may encounter in everyday life.

Statistical literacy is developed in this text through both computation and interpretation of statistics, with particular emphasis placed on the latter. The latter method will be apparent in several ways. For example, a feature called "Interpreting Statistics," which is a non-computational section included in about half the chapters, presents detailed examples of "what to say after the statistics have been calculated." The sections contain real data and research situations within a Canadian context to illustrate the process of developing meaning and understanding, and they exemplify how statistics can be used to answer important questions. The issues addressed include changes in average income and income inequality over time, the gender gap in income, and the correlates of crime in Canada. Also, and in recognition of the fact that modern technology has rendered long, tedious hand calculation obsolete, interpretation of statistics is made through the application of the Statistical Package for the Social Sciences (SPSS), a state-of-the-art computerized statistical package, to real data. SPSS exercises are available at the end of each chapter, and they provide students the opportunity to produce and interpret the statistics presented in the chapter. Detailed instruction on using SPSS for each exercise is also provided. Indeed, this book has been designed so that SPSS can be taught at a basic level without the aid of an SPSS supplementary text.

MAIN FEATURES OF THE TEXT

The text provides various features to facilitate the process of learning statistics and to develop statistical literacy. We have grouped the main features of the text into three categories for the ensuing discussing:

1. An Appreciation of Statistics.   A statistically literate person understands the relevance of statistics for social research, can analyze and interpret the meaning of a statistical test, and can select an appropriate statistic for a given purpose and a given set of variables. This textbook develops these qualities, within the constraints imposed by the introductory nature of the course, in the following ways:

- *The relevance of statistics*. Chapter 1 includes a discussion of the role of statistics in social research and stresses their usefulness as ways of analyzing and manipulating data and answering research questions. Each example problem is framed in the context of a research situation. A question is posed and then, with the aid of a statistic, answered. The relevance of statistics for answering questions is thus stressed throughout the text. This central theme of usefulness is further reinforced by a series of boxes labelled "Application," each of which illustrates some specific way statistics can be used to answer questions.

   Almost all end-of-chapter problems are labelled by the social science discipline or subdiscipline from which they are drawn: SOC for sociology, SW for social work, PS for political science, CJ for criminology and criminal justice, PA for public administration, and GER for gerontology. By identifying problems with specific disciplines, students can more easily see the relevance of statistics to their own academic interests. (Not incidentally, they will also see that the disciplines have a large subject matter in common.)

- *Interpreting statistics.* For most students, interpretation—saying what statistics mean—is a big challenge. The ability to interpret statistics can be developed only by exposure and experience. To provide exposure, we have been careful, in the example problems, to express the meaning of the statistic in terms of the original research question. To provide experience, the end-of-chapter problems almost always call for an interpretation of the statistic calculated. To provide examples, many of the answers to odd-numbered computational problems in the back of the text are expressed in words as well as numbers. The "Interpreting Statistics" sections provide additional, detailed examples of how to express the meaning of statistics.

- *Using statistics: Ideas for research projects.* Appendix E offers ideas for independent data-analysis projects for students. The projects require students to use SPSS to analyze a data set. They can be assigned at intervals throughout the semester or at the end of the course. Each project provides an opportunity for students to practise and apply their statistical skills and, above all, to exercise their ability to understand and interpret the meaning of the statistics they produce.

2. Computational Competence. Students should emerge from their first course in statistics with the ability to perform elementary forms of data analysis—to execute a series of calculations and arrive at the correct answer. To be sure, computers and calculators have made computation less of an issue today. Yet, computation and statistics are inseparable, and since social science majors frequently do not have strong quantitative backgrounds, we have included a number of features to help students cope with these challenges:

- *Step-by-step computational algorithms* are provided for each statistic.

- *Extensive problem sets* are provided at the end of each chapter. Most of these problems use fictitious data and are designed for ease of computation.

- *Cumulative exercises* are included at the end of each part to provide practice in choosing, computing, and analyzing statistics. These exercises present only data sets and research questions. Students must choose appropriate statistics as part of the exercise.

- *Solutions* to odd-numbered computational problems are provided so that students may check their answers.

- *Analysis* of real data uses SPSS for Windows to give students access to the computational power of the computer. This feature is explained in more detail below.

3. The Ability to Read the Professional Social Science Literature. The statistically literate person can comprehend and critically appreciate research reports written by others. The development of this quality is a particular problem at the introductory level since (1) the vocabulary of professional researchers is so much more concise than the language of the textbook, and (2) the statistics featured in the literature are more advanced than those covered at the introductory level. To help bridge this gap, we have included a series of boxes labelled "Reading Statistics" beginning in Chapter 1. In each box, we briefly describe the reporting style typically used for the statistic in question and try to alert students about what to expect when they approach the professional literature. These inserts include excerpts from the Canadian research literature and illustrate how statistics are actually applied and interpreted by social scientists.

Additional Features. A number of other features make the text more meaningful for students and more useful for instructors:

- *Readability and clarity.* The writing style is informal and accessible to students without ignoring the traditional vocabulary of statistics. Problems and examples have been written to maximize student interest and to focus on issues of concern and significance. For the more difficult material (such as hypothesis testing), students are first walked through an example problem before being confronted by formal terminology and concepts. Each chapter ends with a summary of major points and formulas and a glossary of important concepts. A list of frequently used formulas inside the front cover and a glossary of symbols inside the back cover can be used for quick reference.

- *Organization and coverage.* The text is divided into four parts. Overview sections have been included with each of the four parts of the text. These provide a "road map" of the material that follows and help students see why the chapters are organized as they are. Most of the coverage is devoted to the first three parts of the text: descriptive statistics, inferential statistics, and bivariate measures of association. The distinction between description and inference is introduced in the first chapter and maintained throughout the text. In selecting statistics for inclusion, we have tried to strike a balance between the essential concepts with which students must be familiar and the amount of material students can reasonably be expected to learn in their first (and perhaps only) statistics course, while bearing in mind that different instructors will naturally wish to stress different aspects of the subject. Thus, the text covers the full gamut of the usual statistics, with each chapter broken into subsections so that instructors may choose the particular statistics they wish to include.

- *Flow charts*. Flow charts that help students select appropriate statistics are provided in the text. The flow charts (the first of which appears on p. 23) depict the selection process in more general terms at the beginning of each of the four parts of the text and in more detailed form at the beginning of each chapter.

- *Learning objectives*. Learning objectives are stated at the beginning of each chapter. These are intended to serve as "study guides" and to help students identify and focus on the most important material.

- *Review of mathematical skills*. A comprehensive review of all of the mathematical skills that will be used in this text (Appendix H) is included. Students who are inexperienced or out of practice with mathematics may want to study this review early in the course and/or refer to it as needed. A self-test is included so that students may check their level of preparation for the course.

- *Statistical techniques and end-of-chapter problems are explicitly linked*. After a technique is introduced, students are directed to specific problems for practice and review. The "how-to-do-it" aspects of calculation are reinforced immediately and clearly.

- *End-of-chapter problems are organized progressively*. Simpler problems with small data sets are presented first. Often, explicit instructions or hints accompany the first several problems in a set. The problems gradually become more challenging and require more decision making by the student (e.g., choosing the most appropriate statistic for a certain situation). Thus, each problem set develops problem-solving abilities gradually and progressively.

- *Computer applications*. To help students take advantage of the power of the computer, this text integrates Version 16 of SPSS for Windows, though Versions 10 through 17 are completely compatible with the book. SPSS is the leading social science statistical package. A student version of SPSS is available as a supplement to this text. Alternatively, students can download a full working evaluation copy of SPSS for Windows. This free 14-day trialware can be downloaded after registering at https://www.spss.com/registration/login/auth_login009.cfm.

  The last part of each chapter, labelled "SPSS for Windows," offers demonstrations and exercises in using SPSS to produce the statistics presented in the chapter. All SPSS outputs from the demonstrations are shown in the text, and are unedited. Students choosing to replicate the demonstration will see the same output on their computer screen. SPSS exercises are provided below the demonstrations and give students the opportunity to actually use SPSS to compute statistics. Furthermore, Appendix E provides additional SPSS exercises, and Appendix F gives a general introduction to SPSS.

Overall, detailed instructions and demonstrations on how to use SPSS for each exercise are provided in this book. SPSS can be taught at a basic level from this text without the aid of an SPSS supplementary text.

- *Realistic, up-to-date data.* Three databases for SPSS application give students a wide range of opportunities to practise their statistical skills on "real-life" Canadian data: 1) a shortened version of the 2004 Canadian General Social Survey (labelled *GSS.sav*); 2) a shortened version of the 2001 Census of Canada (*Census.sav*); and 3) the full version of the 2001 Census of Canada (*CensusFull.sav*). The databases are described in Appendix G and are available in SPSS format (i.e., the ".sav" file format) on the website for the text.

- *Companion website.* The website for this text includes additional material and some less frequently used techniques, additional end-of-chapter problems, supplements containing a detailed discussion of probability and measures of association, and various other features.

- *Instructor's Manual/Testbank.* The Instructor's Manual includes chapter summaries, a test item file of multiple-choice questions, answers to even-numbered computational problems, and step-by-step solutions to selected problems. In addition, the Instructor's Manual includes cumulative exercises (with answers) that can be used for testing purposes.

- *Study Guide.* The Study Guide contains additional examples to illuminate basic principles, review problems with detailed answers, SPSS projects, and multiple-choice questions and answers that complement but do not duplicate the test item file.

CHANGES IN THE EDITION

This edition of the text remains focused on developing the skills necessary for students to become statistically literate. It is written for students with varying levels of mathematical proficiency, providing an accessible yet comprehensive examination of statistics. With this in mind, the following changes were made in this edition:

- There is more emphasis on interpretation.

- Flow charts that help students select appropriate statistics have been included. The flow charts depict the selection process in more general terms at the beginning of each part and in more detailed form at the beginning of each chapter.

- Tables and figures throughout the text help clarify and illustrate underlying conceptual relationships and help students make decisions. For example, Table 7.2 helps clarify how to choose the appropriate formula for constructing confidence intervals and Figure 8.1 illustrates the logic of hypothesis testing.

- Several new sections have been added. Section 6.5 provides an example to help clarify the differences between the sample, sampling, and population distributions. Section 15.7 explains how to read a correlation matrix. Other sections have been expanded or rewritten to enhance clarity, including the treatment of probability in Chapter 6 and the explanation of bivariate tables in Chapter 11.

- Several new statistics have been added. These include percentage change (Chapter 2) and the maximum difference (Chapter 12). Other statistical techniques have been moved from the website back into the text. These include finding real limits (Chapter 2), computing the median, mean, and standard deviation for grouped data (Chapters 3 and 4), and the goodness-of-fit test (Chapter 11).

- More applications boxes—providing examples of the computation and interpretation of statistics—have been added throughout the text.

- Overview sections have been added to each of the four parts of the text. These provide a "road map" of the material that follows and help students see why the chapters are organized as they are.

- Throughout the text, there is an increased use of real data to help underline the relevance and importance of statistics. Also, consistent with the growing importance of comparative research, there is a new emphasis on cross-national examples and problems. In particular, many problems use comparative data from Canada and the United States.

This edition also exposes students to statistics from a uniquely Canadian perspective. Statistics are applied to contemporary social issues in Canada, and students learn to read and interpret statistics in a variety of Canadian settings. In this regard, the most important changes in this edition include:

- Computation and interpretation of statistics in each chapter occur within a Canadian context.

- Tables, figures, and application boxes in each chapter have been completely "Canadianized" to help underline the relevance and importance of statistics to understanding Canadian society.

- Several new sections have been added and other sections have been expanded:
  - New graphs have been added to Section 2.7 (stem-and-leaf plot), Section 4.3 (boxplot), and Section 7.5 (error bar graph).
  - Section 3.3 now illustrates how to calculate the median for aggregate data in a frequency distribution, and Section 3.5 and Section 4.5 include a similar illustration for the mean and the standard deviation respectively.
  - Section 6.5 has been expanded to show how to construct the sampling distribution from hypothetical data to help clarify the relationships

between the sample, sampling, and population distributions, and Section 6.6 has been added to illustrate these relationships in a real (GSS) data set.

- Section 7.9 has been added to show how to determine an appropriate sample size for a given project.
- Section 8.8 and Section 9.5 have been added to illustrate how to test hypotheses through confidence intervals.

- End-of-chapter problems have been made more relevant to Canadian society.

- End-of-chapter "SPSS for Windows" demonstrations and exercises use two Canadian surveys: the 2004 General Social Survey and the 2001 Census. Appendix G has been rewritten to describe these two new data files, including dealing with issues of sampling design and missing data.

- Detailed instruction on how to use SPSS Version 16, though Versions 10 through 17 are entirely compatible with this instruction and with the text, including:
  - All end-of-chapter "SPSS for Windows" sections have been thoroughly updated.
  - Appendix F has been enhanced to provide a detailed introduction to SPSS for Windows, including the new Section F.5 (computing and recoding variables), Section F.6 (editing output), and Section F.7 (pasting and exporting output).

Ancillaries. The instructor and student resources for *Statistics*, First Canadian Edition, have been adapted for use in Canadian classrooms by the co-author of the text, Dr. Steven Prus.

STUDENT RESOURCES

The **Study Guide (0176440321)** includes Learning Objectives, Chapter Summaries, and 15 multiple-choice questions per chapter. In addition, Work Problems and SPSS Work Problems test students' knowledge, with detailed answers so they can verify that they've understood and solved the problems accurately.

SPSS Datasets for *Statistics* can be found at www.healeystatistics.nelson.com. Instructions are provided on the student page for obtaining a password to access SPSS datasets prepared for this text. These datasets were written for use with Version 16 of SPSS, but Versions 10 through 17 are completely compatible.

 The *Statistics* website at www.healeystatistics.nelson.com is a comprehensive, resource-rich location for students to find pertinent information. As well as SPSS Datasets, they'll find additional review and study materials, including quizzes, glossary flashcards, a basic math review, tables of frequently used formulas and random numbers, and more!

InfoTrac® College Edition is automatically bundled FREE with every new copy of this text! InfoTrac College Edition is a world-class online university library that offers the full text of articles from over 5000 scholarly and popular publications—updated daily and going back as far as 20 years. Students (and their instructors) receive unlimited access for four months.

INSTRUCTOR RESOURCES

The **Instructor's Resource CD (017644016X)** gives instructors the ultimate tool for customizing lectures and presentations. These ancillaries include:

- *Instructor's Manual.* The Instructor's Manual contains a chapter Summary, a guide to changes in the Canadian edition (providing useful transition notes for users of the U.S. edition), answers to even-numbered end-of-chapter problems, detailed answers to selected text problems, and answers to even-numbered text cumulative exercises.

- *Test Bank.* The Test Bank consists of multiple-choice, problem, and essay questions. Correct answers and page references are provided for more than 650 multiple-choice questions. Answers are also provided for the problems and essay questions. Files are provided in rich text format for easy editing and printing with all common word-processing formats.

- *ExamView.* All Test Bank questions are included in the ExamView computerized version. The easy-to-use software is compatible with Microsoft Windows and Mac. Create tests by selecting questions from the question bank, modifying these questions as desired, and adding new questions you write yourself. You can administer quizzes online and export tests to WebCT, Blackboard, and other formats.

- *PowerPoint Lecture Presentation.* The PowerPoint Lecture Presentation enables instructors to customize your own multimedia classroom presentations. Key concepts from each chapter are presented in an average of 20 slides per chapter. Material can be modified or expanded for individual classroom use. PowerPoints are also easily printed to create customized transparency masters.

- *Day One.* Day One—Prof InClass is a PowerPoint presentation that instructors can customize to orient their students to the class and text at the beginning of the course.

- *SPSS Datasets.* For the convenience of instructors, the SPSS datasets created for the text are available on the Instructor's Resource CD. (They are also downloadable from a password-protected page in the student resources of the website.) These datasets were written for use with version 16 of SPSS, but versions 10 through 17 are completely compatible.

The instructor's page of the Statistics website at www.healeystatistics. nelson.com contains downloads for the Instructor's Manual, PowerPoint, SPSS datasets, and Day One—Prof InClass presentation. For security reasons, the Test Bank is not offered as a download; contact your Nelson Education sales representative to obtain a copy of it on the Instructor's Resource CD.

ACKNOWLEDGMENTS FOR THE CANADIAN EDITION

I would like to acknowledge the extraordinary assistance of Mohsen Haghbin, to whom I am truly grateful for his steadfast support and insightful feedback during the preparation of this book. I also wish to thank Emre Uckardesler for his assistance and valuable comments. I would like to especially thank Dr. Stephen Gyimah, Queen's University and Dr. Michael Weinrath, University of Winnipeg for their in-depth comments and practical guidance in writing this book. The book has greatly benefitted from their direction and help.

The reviewers of this book provided many invaluable suggestions. Along with others who prefer to remain anonymous, they include:

Gerald Bierling, *McMaster University*
Jonah Butovsky, *Brock University*
Stephen Obeng Gyimah, *Queen's University*
David A. Hay, *University of Saskatchewan*
Robert Hiscott, *University of Waterloo*
Nikolaos Liodakis, *Wilfrid Laurier University*
William Marshall, *University of Western Ontario*
Michael Weinrath, *University of Winnipeg*

Lily Kalcevich and Lesley Mann at Nelson Education provided the utmost effort and dedication to this project, and I am very thankful for their support. I also wish to thank Michael Kelly, Tintu Thomas, and Cara Yarzab for their help at various stages in this project. Finally I want to acknowledge the support of my family. My parents, Gerry and Tina Prus, have provided constant inspiration, support, and love over the years. Above all I would like to thank my adoring wife, Deborah Prus, and my three wonderful children, Laura, Mandy, and Michael. I dedicate this book to them.

We lastly acknowledge and are grateful to the Literary Executor of the late Sir Ronald A. Fisher, F.R.S., to Dr. Frank Yates, F.R.S., and to Longman Group Ltd., London, for permission to reprint Appendixes B, C, and D from their book *Statistical Tables for Biological, Agricultural and Medical Research* (6th ed., 1974). We are also grateful to SPSS Inc. for providing an advanced copy of SPSS Version 16 to accommodate the timing of publication for this book, as well as to the many people at Statistics Canada, namely Belia Velho, Judy Cotterill, Sandra McIntyre, and Marie-Josée Lalonde, for providing the General Social Survey and Census data sets used in this book.

Steven G. Prus

1

INTRODUCTION

LEARNING OBJECTIVES

By the end of this chapter, you will be able to

1. Describe the limited but crucial role of statistics in social research.
2. Distinguish among three applications of statistics (univariate descriptive, bivariate descriptive, and inferential) and identify situations in which each is appropriate.
3. Distinguish between discrete and continuous variables and cite examples of each.
4. Identify and describe three levels of measurement and cite examples of variables from each.

1.1 WHY STUDY STATISTICS?

Students sometimes approach their first course in statistics with questions about the value of the subject matter. What, after all, do numbers and statistics have to do with understanding people and society? In a sense, this entire book will attempt to answer this question, and the value of statistics will become clear as we move from chapter to chapter. For now, the importance of statistics can be demonstrated, in a preliminary way, by briefly reviewing the research process as it operates in the social sciences. These disciplines are scientific in the sense that social scientists attempt to verify their ideas and theories through research. Broadly conceived, **research** is any process by which information is systematically and carefully gathered for the purpose of answering questions, examining ideas, or testing theories. Research is a disciplined inquiry that can take numerous forms. Statistical analysis is relevant only for those research projects where the information collected is represented by numbers. Numerical information is called **data,** and the sole purpose of statistics is to manipulate and analyze data. **Statistics,** then, are a set of mathematical techniques used by social scientists to organize and manipulate data for the purpose of answering questions and testing theories.

What is so important about learning how to manipulate data? On one hand, some of the most important and enlightening works in the social sciences do not utilize any statistical techniques. There is nothing magical about data and statistics. The mere presence of numbers guarantees nothing about the quality of a scientific inquiry. On the other hand, data can be the most trustworthy information available to the researcher and, consequently, deserve special attention. Data that have been carefully collected and thoughtfully analyzed are the strongest, most objective foundations for building theory and enhancing understanding. Without a firm base in data, the social sciences would lose the right to the name *science* and would be of far less value.

Thus, the social sciences rely heavily on data analysis for the advancement of knowledge. Let us be very clear about one point: it is never enough merely to gather data (or, for that matter, any kind of information). Even the most objective and carefully collected numerical information does not and cannot speak for itself. The researcher must be able to use statistics effectively to organize, evaluate, and analyze the data. Without a good understanding of the principles of statistical analysis, the researcher will be unable to make sense of the data. Without the appropriate application of statistical techniques, the data will remain mute and useless.

Statistics are an indispensable tool for the social sciences. They provide the scientist with some of the most useful techniques for evaluating ideas, testing theory, and discovering the truth. The next section describes the relationships among theory, research, and statistics in more detail.

1.2 THE ROLE OF STATISTICS IN SCIENTIFIC INQUIRY

Figure 1.1 graphically represents the role of statistics in the research process. The diagram is based on the thinking of Walter Wallace and illustrates how the knowledge base of any scientific enterprise grows and develops. One point the diagram makes is that scientific theory and research continually shape each other. Statistics are one of the most important means by which research and theory interact. Let's take a closer look at the wheel.

Because the figure is circular, it has no beginning or end, and we could begin our discussion at any point. For the sake of convenience, let's begin at the top and follow the arrows around the circle. A **theory** is an explanation of the relationships between phenomena. People naturally (and endlessly) wonder about problems in society (like prejudice, poverty, child abuse, or serial murders), and in their attempt to understand these phenomena, they develop explanations ("lack of education causes prejudice"). This kind of informal "theorizing" about society is no doubt very familiar to you. One major difference between our informal, everyday explanations of social phenomena and

FIGURE 1.1   THE WHEEL OF SCIENCE

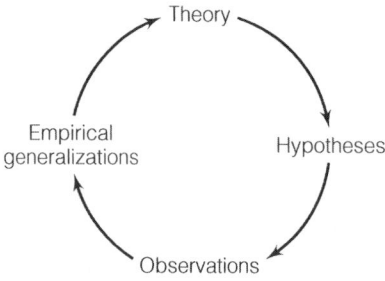

Source: Adapted from Wallace, Walter. 1971. *The Logic of Science in Sociology.* Copyright © 1971 by Transactions Publishers. Reprinted by permission of the publisher.

scientific theory is that the latter is subject to a rigorous testing process. Let's take the problem of health inequality as an example to illustrate how the research process works.

Why do people differ in their health? One possible answer to this question is provided by the *materialistic hypothesis*. This theory was stated over 25 years ago in the groundbreaking "Black Report," named after the physician Sir Douglas Black, on health inequalities in the United Kingdom. It has been tested on a number of occasions since that time.*

According to the materialistic hypothesis, health is affected by social class. We often think that it is the individual who chooses whether to have a healthy diet, participate in leisure-time exercise, protect one's own health and prevent illness (e.g., annual physical, flu shot), and so on. The materialist hypothesis asserts that such "individual choices" are constrained by one's social class. Social class is linked to health by one's access to items such as nutritional foods; health care; preventative health care information and services; and safe housing, living, and working conditions that are necessary to maintain and improve health.

The materialistic hypothesis is not a complete explanation of health inequality, but it can serve to illustrate a sociological theory. This theory offers an explanation for the relationship between two social phenomena: (1) health inequality and (2) social class. People who have lower social class will have poorer health, and those with higher social class will have better health.

Before moving on, let us examine theory in a little more detail. The materialistic hypothesis, like most theories, is stated in terms of causal relationships between variables. A **variable** is any trait that can change values from case to case. Examples of variables would be gender, age, ethnicity, or political party affiliation. In any specific theory, some variables will be identified as causes and others will be identified as effects or results. In the language of science, the causes are called **independent variables** and the effects or result variables are called **dependent variables.** In our theory, social class is the independent variable (or the cause) and health is the dependent variable (the result or effect). In other words, we are arguing that social class is a cause of health condition or that an individual's level of health depends on his/her social class.

So far, we have a theory of health, and an independent and a dependent variable. What we do not know yet is whether the theory is true or false. To find out, we need to compare our theory with the facts—we need to do some research. The next step in the process would be to define our terms and ideas more specifically and exactly. One problem we often face in conducting research is that scientific theories are too complex and

---

*Source: Townsend, P. and Davidson, N. (eds). 1982. *Inequalities in Health: The Black Report.* Harmondsworth, UK: Penguin Books.

abstract to be fully tested in a single research project. To conduct research, one or more hypotheses must be derived from the theory. A **hypothesis** is a statement about the relationship between variables that, while logically derived from the theory, is much more specific and exact.

For example, if we wish to test the materialistic hypothesis, we have to say exactly what we mean by social class and health. There has been a great deal of research on the effect of social class on health, and we would consult the research literature to develop and clarify our definitions of these concepts. As our definitions develop and the hypotheses take shape, we begin the next step of the research process during which we will decide exactly how we will gather our data. We must decide how cases will be selected and tested, and how the variables will be measured. Ultimately, these plans will lead to the observation phase (the bottom of the wheel of science), where we actually measure social reality. Before we can do this, however, we must have a very clear idea of what we are looking for and a well-defined strategy for conducting the search.

To test the materialistic hypothesis, we would begin by considering people from all sections of society (rich, poor, healthy, unhealthy, and so on). Then, we need to decide what our measures of social class and health status are. In other words, we need to operationalize the concepts of social class and health status. For example, we may decide to use those measures used in the "Black Report:" occupation and chronic illness as measures of social class and health respectively. We would then administer a survey that asked each person, "What is your current main occupation?" and "How many long-term or chronic medical conditions diagnosed by a health professional do you have?" Our goal would be to see whether people with higher occupational status have fewer chronic illnesses.

Now, finally, we come to statistics. As the observation phase of our research project comes to an end, we will be confronted with a large collection of numerical information or data. If our sample consisted of 2,000 people, we would have 2,000 completed surveys measuring social class and health. Try to imagine dealing with 2,000 completed surveys. If we had asked each respondent five questions about their health, instead of just one question, we would have a total of 10,000 separate pieces of information to deal with. What do we do? We need to have some systematic way to organize and analyze this information; at this point, statistics will be very valuable. Statistics will provide us many ideas about "what to do" with the data, and we will begin to look at some of the options in the next chapter. For now, let us stress two points about statistics.

First, statistics are crucial. Simply put, without statistics, quantitative research is impossible. Without quantitative research, the development of the social sciences would be severely impaired. Only by the application of statistical techniques can mere data help us shape and refine our theories and understand the social world better. Second, and somewhat paradoxically, the role of statistics is rather limited. As Figure 1.1 makes clear, scientific research proceeds through several mutually interdependent stages, and statistics become directly relevant only at the end of the observation stage. Before any statistical analysis can be legitimately applied, the preceding phases of the process must have been successfully completed. If the researcher has asked poorly conceived questions or has made serious errors of design or method, then even the most sophisticated statistical analysis is valueless. As useful as they can be, statistics cannot substitute for rigorous conceptualization, detailed and careful planning, or creative use of theory. Statistics cannot salvage a poorly conceived or designed research project. They cannot make sense out of garbage.

Conversely, inappropriate statistical applications can limit the usefulness of an otherwise carefully done project. Only by successfully completing *all* phases of the process can a quantitative research project hope to contribute to understanding. A reasonable knowledge of the uses and limitations of statistics is as essential to the education of the social scientist as is training in theory and methodology.

As the statistical analysis comes to an end, we would begin to develop empirical generalizations. While we would be primarily focused on assessing our theory, we would also look for other trends in the data. Assuming that we found that social class was linked to health in general, we might go on to ask if the pattern applies to males as well as females or to older respondents as well as younger. As we probed the data, we might begin to develop some generalizations based on the empirical patterns we observe. For example, what if we found that social class was linked to health for older respondents but not for younger respondents? Could it be that material advantages and disadvantages have an accumulative effect on health, and thus the social class-health link does not emerge until old age? As we developed tentative explanations, we would begin to revise or elaborate our theory.

If we change the theory to take account of these findings, however, a new research project designed to test the revised theory is called for and the wheel of science would begin to turn again. We (or perhaps some other researchers) would go through the entire process once again with this new—and, hopefully, improved—theory. This second project might result in further revisions and elaboration that would (you guessed it) require still more research projects, and the wheel of science would continue turning as long as scientists were able to suggest additional revisions or develop new insights. Every time the wheel turned, our understandings of the phenomena under consideration would (hopefully) improve.

This description of the research process does not include white-coated, clipboard-carrying scientists who, in a blinding flash of inspiration, discover some fundamental truth about reality and shout, "Eureka!" The truth is that, in the normal course of science, it is a rare occasion when we can say with absolute certainty that a given theory or idea is definitely true or false. Rather, evidence for (or against) a theory will gradually accumulate over time, and ultimate judgments of truth will likely be the result of many years of hard work, research, and debate.

Let's briefly review our imaginary research project. We began with an idea or theory about social class and health. We imagined some of the steps we would have to take to test the theory and took a quick look at the various stages of the research project. We wound up back at the level of theory, ready to begin a new project guided by a revised theory. We saw how theory can motivate a research project and how our observations might cause us to revise the theory and, thus, motivate a new research project. Wallace's wheel of science illustrates how theory stimulates research and how research shapes theory. This constant interaction between theory and research is the lifeblood of science and the key to enhancing our understandings of the social world.

The dialogue between theory and research occurs at many levels and in multiple forms. Statistics are one of the most important links between these two realms. Statistics permit us to analyze data, to identify and probe trends and relationships, to develop generalizations, and to revise and improve our theories. As you will see throughout this text, statistics are limited in many ways. They are also an indispensable part of the research enterprise. Without statistics, the interaction between theory and research would become extremely difficult, and the progress of our disciplines would be severely retarded. *(For practice in describing the relationship between theory and research and the role of statistics in research, see problems 1.1 and 1.2.)*

1.3 THE GOALS OF THIS TEXT

In the preceding section, we argued that statistics are a crucial part of the process by which scientific investigations are carried out and that, therefore, some training in statistical analysis is a crucial component in the education of every social scientist. In this section, we will address the questions of how much training is necessary and what the purposes of that training are. First, this textbook takes the point of view that statistics are tools. They can be a very useful means of increasing our knowledge of the social world, but they are not ends in themselves. Thus, we will not take a "mathematical" approach to the subject. The techniques will be presented as a set of tools that can be used to answer important questions. This emphasis does not mean that we will dispense with arithmetic entirely, of course. This text includes enough mathematical material so that you can develop a basic understanding of why statistics "do what they do." Our focus, however, will be on how these techniques are applied in the social sciences.

Second, all of you will soon become involved in advanced coursework in your major fields of study, and you will find that much of the literature used in these courses assumes at least basic statistical literacy. Furthermore, many of you, after graduation, will find yourselves in positions—either in a career or in graduate school—where some understanding of statistics will be very helpful or perhaps even required. Very few of you will become statisticians per se (and this text is not intended for the preprofessional statistician), but you must have a grasp of statistics in order to read and critically appreciate your own professional literature. As a student in the social sciences and in many careers related to the social sciences, you simply cannot realize your full potential without a background in statistics.

Within these constraints, this textbook is an introduction to statistics as they are utilized in the social sciences. The general goal of the text is to develop an appreciation—a "healthy respect"—for statistics and their place in the research process. You should emerge from this experience with the ability to use statistics intelligently and to know when other people have done so. You should be familiar with the advantages and limitations of the more commonly used statistical techniques, and you should know which techniques are appropriate for a given set of data and a given purpose. Lastly, you should develop sufficient statistical and computational skills and enough experience in the interpretation of statistics to be able to carry out some elementary forms of data analysis by yourself.

1.4 DESCRIPTIVE AND INFERENTIAL STATISTICS

As noted earlier, the general function of statistics is to manipulate data so that research questions can be answered. There are two general classes of statistical techniques that, depending on the research situation, are available to accomplish this task, and each is introduced in this section.

Descriptive Statistics. The first class of techniques is called **descriptive statistics** and is relevant in several different situations:

1. When the researcher needs to summarize or describe the distribution of a single variable. These statistics are called *univariate* ("one variable") descriptive statistics.
2. When the researcher wishes to describe the relationship between two or more variables. These statistics are called *bivariate* ("two variable") or *multivariate* (more than two variables) descriptive statistics.

To describe a single variable, we would arrange the values or scores of that variable so that the relevant information can be quickly understood and appreciated. Many of the statistics that might be appropriate for this summarizing task are probably familiar to you. For example, percentages, graphs, and charts can all be used to describe single variables.

To illustrate the usefulness of univariate descriptive statistics, consider the following problem: Suppose you wanted to summarize the distribution of the variable "family income" for a community of 10,000 families. How would you do it? Obviously, you couldn't simply list all incomes in the community and let it go at that. Imagine trying to make sense of a list of 10,000 different incomes! Presumably, you would want to develop some summary measures of the overall income distributions—perhaps an arithmetic average or the proportions of incomes that fall in various ranges (such as low, middle, and high). Or perhaps a graph or a chart would be more useful. Whatever specific method you choose, its function is the same: to reduce these thousands of individual items of information into a few easily understood numbers. The process of allowing a few numbers to summarize many numbers is called **data reduction** and is the basic goal of univariate descriptive statistical procedures. Part I of this text is devoted to these statistics, which allow you to report, clearly and concisely, essential information about a variable.

The second type of descriptive statistics is designed to help the investigator understand the relationship between two or more variables. These statistics, called **measures of association,** allow the researcher to quantify the strength and direction of a relationship. These statistics are very useful because they enable us to investigate two matters of central theoretical and practical importance to any science: causation and prediction. These techniques help us disentangle and uncover the connections between variables. They help us trace the ways in which some variables might have causal influences on others; and, depending on the strength of the relationship, they enable us to predict scores on one variable from the scores on another. Note that measures of association cannot, by themselves, prove that two variables are causally related. However, these techniques can provide valuable clues about causation and are therefore extremely important for theory testing and theory construction.

For example, suppose you were interested in the relationship between "time spent studying statistics" and "final grade in statistics" and had gathered data on these two variables from a group of university students. By calculating the appropriate measure of association, you could determine the strength of the bivariate relationship and its direction. Suppose you found a strong, positive relationship. This would indicate that "study time" and "grade" were closely related (strength of the relationship) and that as one increased in value, the other also increased (direction of the relationship). You could make predictions from one variable to the other ("the longer the study time, the higher the grade").

As a result of finding this strong, positive relationship, you might be tempted to make causal inferences. That is, you might jump to such conclusions as "longer study time leads to (causes) higher grades." Such a conclusion might make a good deal of common sense and would certainly be supported by your statistical analysis. However, the causal nature of the relationship cannot be proven by the statistical analysis. Measures of association can be taken as important clues about causation, but the mere existence of a relationship can never be taken as conclusive proof of causation.

In fact, other variables might have an effect on the relationship. In the example above, we probably would not find a perfect relationship between "study time" and "final grade." That is, we will probably find some individuals who spend a great deal of time studying but receive low grades and some individuals who fit the opposite pattern. We know intuitively that other variables besides study time affect grades (such as efficiency of study techniques, amount of background in mathematics, and even random chance). Fortunately, researchers can incorporate these other variables into the analysis and measure their effects. Part III of this text is devoted to bivariate (two-variable) and Part IV to multivariate (more than two variables) descriptive statistics.

Inferential Statistics.   This second class of statistical techniques becomes relevant when we wish to generalize our findings from a **sample** to a **population.** A population is the total collection of all cases that the researcher is interested in and wishes to understand better. Examples of possible populations would be all Canadian adults, senior citizens, unemployed youth in the greater Toronto area, or university students in British Columbia.

Populations can theoretically range from inconceivable in size ("all humanity") to quite small (all professional hockey players currently residing in downtown Ottawa) but are usually fairly large. In fact, they are almost always too large to be measured. To put the problem another way, social scientists almost never have the resources or time to test every case in a population. Hence the need for **inferential statistics,** which involve using information from a sample (a carefully chosen subset of the population) to make inferences about a population. Because they have fewer cases, samples are much cheaper to assemble, and—if the proper techniques are followed—generalizations based on these samples can be very accurate representations of the population.

Many of the concepts and procedures involved in inferential statistics may be unfamiliar. However, most of us are experienced consumers of inferential statistics—most familiarly, perhaps, in the form of public-opinion polls and election projections. When a public-opinion poll reports that 36 percent of the Canadian electorate plans to vote for a certain political party, it is essentially reporting a generalization to a population (the "Canadian electorate," which numbers about 23 million people) from a carefully drawn sample (usually about 1,500 respondents). Matters of inferential statistics will occupy our attention in Part II of this book. *(For practice in describing different statistical applications, see problems 1.3 and 1.7.)*

1.5 DISCRETE AND CONTINUOUS VARIABLES

In the next chapter, you will begin to encounter some of the broad array of statistics available to the social scientist. One aspect of using statistics that can be puzzling is deciding when to use which statistic. You will learn specific guidelines as you go along, but we will introduce some basic and general guidelines at this point. The first of these concerns discrete and continuous variables; the second, covered in the next section, concerns level of measurement.

A variable is said to be **discrete** if it has a basic unit of measurement that cannot be subdivided. For example, number of people per household is a discrete variable. The basic unit is people, a variable that will always be measured in whole numbers: you'll never find 2.7 people living in a specific household. The scores for a discrete variable will be zero, one, two, three, or some other whole integer. Other discrete variables include number of siblings, children, or cars. To measure these variables, we count the number of units for each case and record results in whole numbers.

A variable is **continuous** if the measurement of it can be subdivided infinitely—at least in a theoretical sense. One example of a continuous variable would be time, which can be measured in minutes, seconds, milliseconds (thousandths of a second), nanoseconds (billionths of a second), or even smaller units. In a sense, when we measure a continuous variable, we are always approximating and rounding off the scores. We could report somebody's time in the 100-metre dash as 10.7 seconds or 10.732451 seconds, but, because time can be infinitely subdivided (if we have the technology to make the precise measurements), we will never be able to report the exact time elapsed. Since we cannot work with infinitely long numbers, we must report the scores on continuous variables as if they were discrete.

The distinction between these two types of variables relates more to measuring and processing the information than to the appearance of the data. This distinction between discrete and continuous variables is one of the most basic in statistics and will constitute one of the criteria by which we will choose among various statistics and graphic devices. *(For practice in distinguishing between discrete and continuous variables, see problems 1.4–1.8.)*

1.6 LEVEL OF MEASUREMENT

A second basic and very important guideline for the selection of statistics is the **level of measurement** or the mathematical nature of the variables under consideration. Variables at the highest level of measurement have numerical scores and can be analyzed with a broad range of statistics. Variables at lower levels of measurement have "scores" that are really just labels, not numbers at all. Statistics that require numerical variables are inappropriate, and often completely meaningless, when used with non-numerical variables. When selecting statistics, you must be sure that the level of measurement of the variable justifies the mathematical operations required to compute the statistic.

For example, consider the variables age (measured in years) and income (measured in dollars). Both of these variables have numerical scores and could be summarized with a statistic such as the mean or average (e.g., "The average income of this city is $43,000." "The average age of students on this campus is 19.7.").

However, the mean or average would be meaningless as a way of describing gender or area codes, which are variables with non-numerical scores. Your personal area code might *look* like a number but it is merely an arbitrary label that happens to be expressed in digits. These "numbers" cannot be added or divided and statistics like the average cannot be applied to this variable: the average area code of a group of people is a meaningless statistic.

Determining the level at which a variable has been measured is one of the first steps in any statistical analysis, and we will consider this matter at some length. We will make it a practice throughout this text to introduce level-of-measurement considerations for each statistical technique.

The three levels of measurement, in order of increasing sophistication, are nominal, ordinal, and interval-ratio. Each is discussed separately.

The Nominal Level of Measurement.   Variables measured at the nominal level have "scores" or categories that are not numerical. Examples of variables at this level include gender, area code, province of residence, religious affiliation, and place of birth. At this lowest level of measurement, the only mathematical operation permitted is comparing the relative sizes of the categories (e.g., "there are more females than males in this residence"). The categories or scores of nominal-level variables cannot be ranked with respect to each other and cannot be added, divided, or otherwise manipulated mathematically. Even when the scores or categories are expressed in digits (like area codes or street addresses), all we can do is compare relative sizes of categories (e.g., "the most common area code on this campus is 221"). The categories themselves are not a mathematical scale: they are different from each other but not more or less, or higher or lower than each other. Males and females differ in terms of gender but neither category has more or less gender than the other. In the same way, an area code of 621 is different from but not "more than" an area code of 221.

Although nominal variables are rudimentary, we need to observe certain criteria and procedures in order to assure adequate measurement. In fact, these criteria apply to variables measured at all levels, not just nominal variables. First, the categories of nominal-level variables must be mutually exclusive so that no ambiguity exists concerning classification of any given case. There must be one and only one category for each case. Second, the categories must be exhaustive: a category—at least an "other" or miscellaneous category—must exist for every possible score that might be found.

Third, the categories of nominal variables should be relatively homogeneous, that is, our categories should include cases that are comparable. To put it another way, we need to avoid categories that lump apples with oranges. There are no hard and fast guidelines for judging if a set of categories is appropriately homogeneous. The researcher must make that decision in terms of the specific purpose of the research. Categories that are too broad for some purposes may be perfectly adequate for others.

Table 1.1 demonstrates some errors of measurement in four different schemes for measuring the variable "religious affiliation." Scale A in the table violates the criterion of mutual exclusivity because of the overlap between the categories Catholic and Christian and Protestant and Christian. Scale B is not exhaustive because it does not provide a category for people who belong to religions other than the eight listed or for people with no religious affiliation (None). Scale C uses a category (Non-Catholic) that would be too broad for many research purposes. Scale D represents the way religious affiliation is often measured in Canada, but note that these categories may be too general for some research projects and not comprehensive enough for others. For example, an investigation of issues that have strong moral and religious content (assisted suicide, abortion, or capital punishment, for example) might need to distinguish between the various Protestant denominations (e.g., United Church, Presbyterian, Lutheran, Anglican, Baptist, Jehovah's Witnesses, Pentecostal, Mormons, and so on), and an effort to document religious diversity would need to add categories for other Eastern or Christian religions (e.g., Bahai, Greek Orthodox, and so on). Likewise, Scale D does not capture the variety within Islam, Judaism, and other non-Christian religions.

Numerical labels are often used to identify the categories of variables measured at the nominal level. This practice is especially common when the data are being prepared for computer analysis. For example, the various religions might be labelled with a 1 indicating Protestant, a 2 signifying Catholic, and so on. Remember that these numbers are merely labels or names and have no numerical quality to them. They cannot be added,

TABLE 1.1   FOUR SCALES FOR MEASURING RELIGIOUS AFFILIATION

Scale A (not mutually exclusive)	Scale B (not exhaustive)	Scale C (not homogeneous)	Scale D (an adequate scale)
Catholic	Catholic	Catholic	Catholic
Protestant	Protestant	Non-Catholic	Protestant
Christian	Other Christian		Other Christian
Jewish	Jewish		Jewish
Muslim	Muslim		Muslim
Buddhist	Buddhist		Buddhist
Hindu	Hindu		Hindu
Sikh	Sikh		Sikh
Other religions			Other religions
None			None

subtracted, multiplied, or divided. The only mathematical operation permissible with nominal variables is counting and comparing the number of cases in each category of the variable.

The Ordinal Level of Measurement.   Variables measured at the ordinal level are more sophisticated than nominal-level variables. They have scores or categories that can be ranked from high to low so that, in addition to classifying cases into categories, we can describe the categories in terms of "more or less" with respect to each other. Thus, with variables measured at this level, not only can we say that one case is different from another; we can also say that one case is higher or lower, more or less, than another.

For example, the variable socio-economic status (SES) is usually measured at the ordinal level. The categories of the variable are often ordered according to the following scheme:

4. Upper class
3. Middle class
2. Working class
1. Lower class

Individual cases can be compared in terms of the categories into which they are classified. Thus, an individual classified as a 4 (upper class) would be ranked higher than an individual classified as a 2 (working class) and a lower-class person (1) would rank lower than a middle-class person (3). Other variables that are usually measured at the ordinal level include attitude and opinion scales such as those that measure prejudice, alienation, or political conservatism.

The major limitation of the ordinal level of measurement is that a particular score represents only position with respect to some other score. We can distinguish between high and low scores, but the distance between the scores cannot be described in precise terms. Although we know that a score of 4 is more than a score of 2, we do not know if it is twice as much as 2.

Because we don't know the exact distances from score to score on an ordinal scale, our options for statistical analysis are limited. For example, addition (and most other mathematical operations) assumes that the intervals between scores are exactly equal. If the distances from score to score are not equal, $2 + 2$ might equal 3 or 5 or even 15. Thus, strictly speaking, statistics such as the average or mean (which requires that the scores be added together and then divided by the number of scores) are not permitted with ordinal-level variables. The most sophisticated mathematical operation fully justified with an ordinal variable is the ranking of categories and cases (although, as we will see, it is not unusual for social scientists to take some liberties with this strict criterion).

READING STATISTICS 1: Introduction

By this point in your education you have developed an impressive array of skills for reading words. Although you may sometimes struggle with a difficult idea or stumble over an obscure meaning, you can comprehend virtually any written work that you are likely to encounter.

As you continue your education in the social sciences, you must develop an analogous set of skills for reading numbers and statistics. To help you reach a reasonable level of literacy in statistics, we have included a series of boxed inserts in this text labelled "Reading Statistics." These will appear in most chapters and will discuss how statistical results are typically presented in the professional literature. Each installment will include an extract or quotation from the professional literature so that we can analyze a realistic example.

As you will see, professional researchers use a reporting style that is quite different from the statistical language you will find in this text. Space in research journals and other media is expensive, and the typical research project requires the analysis of many variables. Thus, a large volume of information must be summarized in very few words. Researchers may express in a

word or two a result or an interpretation that will take us a paragraph or more to state.

Because this is an introductory textbook, we have been careful to break down the computation and logic of each statistic and to identify, even to the point of redundancy, what we are doing when we use statistics. In this text we will never be concerned with more than a few variables at a time. We will have the luxury of analysis in detail and of being able to take pages or even entire chapters to develop a statistical idea or analyze a variable. Thus, a major theme of these boxed inserts will be to summarize how our comparatively long-winded (but more careful) vocabulary is translated into the concise language of the professional researcher.

When you have difficulty reading words, your tendency is (or, at least, should be) to consult reference books (especially dictionaries) to help you identify and analyze the elements (words) of the passage. When you have difficulty reading statistics, you should do exactly the same thing. We hope you will find this text a valuable reference book, but if you learn enough from this text to be able to use any source to help you read statistics, this text will have fulfilled one of its major goals.

The Interval-Ratio Level of Measurement.* The categories of nominal-level variables have no numerical quality to them. Ordinal-level variables have categories that can be arrayed along a scale from high to low, but the exact distances between categories or scores are undefined. Variables measured at the interval-ratio level not only permit classification and ranking but also allow the distance from category to category (or score to score) to be exactly defined.

Interval-ratio variables have two characteristics. First, they are measured in units that have equal intervals. For example, asking people how old they are will produce an interval-ratio level variable (age) because the unit of

---

*Many statisticians distinguish between the interval level (equal intervals) and the ratio level (true zero point). We find the distinction unnecessarily cumbersome in an introductory text, and since most statistical analysis that is appropriate for interval variables is also appropriate for ratio variables we will treat these two levels as one.

TABLE 1.2   BASIC CHARACTERISTICS OF THE THREE LEVELS OF MEASUREMENT

Levels	Examples	Measurement Procedures	Mathematical Operations Permitted
Nominal	Sex, race, religion, marital status	Classification into categories	Counting number of cases in each category of the variable; comparing sizes of categories
Ordinal	Social class (SES), attitude and opinion scales	Classification into categories plus ranking of categories with respect to each other	All above plus judgments of "greater than" and "less than"
Interval-Ratio	Age, number of children, income	All above plus description of distances between scores in terms of equal units	All above plus all other mathematical operations (addition, subtraction, multiplication, division, square roots, etc.)

measurement (years) has equal intervals (the distance from year to year is 365 days). Similarly, if we ask people how many siblings they have, we would produce a variable with equal intervals: two siblings are one more than one and thirteen is one more than twelve.

The second characteristic of interval-ratio variables is that they have a true zero point. That is, the score of zero for these variables is not arbitrary: it indicates the absence or complete lack of whatever is being measured. For example, the variable "number of siblings" has a true zero point because it is possible to have no siblings at all. Similarly, it is possible to have zero years of education, no income at all, a score of zero on a multiple-choice test, and to be zero years old (although not for very long). Other examples of interval-ratio variables would be number of children, life expectancy, and years married. All mathematical operations are permitted for data measured at the interval-ratio level.

Table 1.2 summarizes this discussion by presenting the basic characteristics of the three levels of measurement. Note that the number of permitted mathematical operations increases as we move from nominal to ordinal to interval-ratio levels of measurement. Ordinal-level variables are more sophisticated and flexible than nominal-level variables and interval-ratio-level variables permit the broadest range of mathematical operations.

Level of Measurement and Discrete Versus Continuous Variables.   The distinction made earlier between discrete and continuous variables is a concern only for interval-ratio-level variables. Nominal- and ordinal-level variables are discrete, at least in the way they are usually measured. For example, to measure marital status, researchers usually ask people to choose one category from a list: married, living common law, widowed, and so on. What makes this variable discrete is that respondents can place themselves in a single category only; no subcategories or more refined classifications are permitted.

The distinction is usually a concern only for interval-ratio-level variables, of which some are discrete (number of times you've been divorced) and others are continuous (income or age). Remember that because we cannot work with infinitely long numbers, continuous variables have to be rounded off at some level and reported as if they were discrete. The distinction relates more to our options for appropriate statistics or graphs, not to the appearance of the variables.

Level of Measurement: A Summary. Remember that the level of measurement of a variable is important because different statistics require different mathematical operations. The level of measurement of a variable is the key characteristic that tells us which statistics are permissible and appropriate.

Ideally, researchers would utilize only those statistics that were fully justified by the level-of-measurement criteria. In this imperfect world, however, the most powerful and useful statistics (such as the mean) require interval-ratio variables, while most of the variables of interest to the social sciences are only nominal (race, sex, marital status) or ordinal (attitude scales). Relatively few concepts of interest to the social sciences are so precisely defined that they can be measured at the interval-ratio level. This disparity creates some very real difficulties for social science research. On one hand, researchers should use the most sophisticated statistical procedures fully justified for a particular variable. Treating interval-ratio data as if they were only ordinal, for example, results in a significant loss of information and precision. Treated as an interval-ratio variable, the variable "age" can supply us with exact information regarding the differences between the cases (e.g., "Individual A is three years and two months older than Individual B"). Treated only as an ordinal variable, however, the precision of our comparisons would suffer and we could say only that "Individual A is older (or greater than) Individual B."

On the other hand, given the nature of the disparity, researchers are more likely to treat variables as if they were higher in level of measurement than they actually are. In particular, variables measured at the ordinal level, especially when they have many possible categories or scores, are often treated as if they were interval-ratio because the statistical procedures available at the higher level are more powerful, flexible, and interesting. This practice is common but researchers should be cautious in assessing statistical results and developing interpretations when the level-of-measurement criterion has been violated. Level of measurement is a very basic characteristic of a variable, and we will always consider it when presenting statistical procedures. Level of measurement is also a major organizing principle for the material that follows, and you should make sure that you are familiar with these guidelines. *(For practice in determining the level of measurement of a variable, see problems 1.4–1.8.)*

SUMMARY

1. Within the context of social research, the purpose of statistics is to organize, manipulate, and analyze data so that researchers can test their theories and answer their questions. Along with theory and methodology, statistics are a basic tool by which social scientists attempt to enhance their understanding of the social world.
2. There are two general classes of statistics. Descriptive statistics are used to summarize the distribution of a single variable and the relationships between two or more variables. Inferential statistics provide us with techniques by which we can generalize to populations from random samples.
3. Two basic guidelines for selecting statistical techniques were presented. Variables may be either discrete or continuous and may be measured at any of three different levels. At the nominal level, we can compare category sizes. At the ordinal level, categories and cases can be ranked with respect to each other. At the interval-ratio level, all mathematical operations are permitted. Interval-ratio-level variables can be either discrete or continuous. Variables at the nominal or ordinal level are almost always discrete.

GLOSSARY

Continuous variable. A variable with a unit of measurement that can be subdivided infinitely.

Data. Any information collected as part of a research project and expressed as numbers.

Data reduction. Summarizing many scores with a few statistics. A major goal of descriptive statistics.

Dependent variable. A variable that is identified as an effect, result, or outcome variable. The dependent variable is thought to be caused by the independent variable.

Descriptive statistics. The branch of statistics concerned with (1) summarizing the distribution of a single variable or (2) measuring the relationship between two or more variables.

Discrete variable. A variable with a basic unit of measurement that cannot be subdivided.

Hypothesis. A statement about the relationship between variables that is derived from a theory. Hypotheses are more specific than theories, and all terms and concepts are fully defined.

Independent variable. A variable that is identified as a causal variable. The independent variable is thought to cause the dependent variable.

Inferential statistics. The branch of statistics concerned with making generalizations from samples to populations.

Level of measurement. The mathematical characteristic of a variable and the major criterion for selecting statistical techniques. Variables can be measured at any of three levels, each permitting certain mathematical operations and statistical techniques. The characteristics of the three levels are summarized in Table 1.2.

Measures of association. Statistics that summarize the strength and direction of the relationship between variables.

Population. The total collection of all cases in which the researcher is interested.

Research. Any process of gathering information systematically and carefully to answer questions or test theories. Statistics are useful for research projects in which the information is represented in numerical form or as data.

Sample. A carefully chosen subset of a population. In inferential statistics, information is gathered from a sample and then generalized to a population.

Statistics. A set of mathematical techniques for organizing and analyzing data.

Theory. A generalized explanation of the relationship between two or more variables.

Variable. Any trait that can change values from case to case.

PROBLEMS

1.1 In your own words, describe the role of statistics in the research process. Using the "wheel of science" as a framework, explain how statistics link theory with research.

1.2 Find a research article in any social science journal. Choose an article on a subject of interest to you and don't worry about being able to understand all of the statistics that are reported.
  a. How much of the article is devoted to statistics per se (as distinct from theory, ideas, discussion, and so on)?
  b. Is the research based on a sample from some population? How large is the sample? How were subjects or cases selected? Can the findings be generalized to some population?
  c. What variables are used? Which are independent and which are dependent? For each variable, determine the level of measurement and whether the variable is discrete or continuous.
  d. What statistical techniques are used? Try to follow the statistical analysis and see how much you can understand. Save the article and read it again after you finish this course and see if you do any better.

1.3 Distinguish between descriptive and inferential statistics. Describe a research situation that would use both types.

1.4 Below are some items from a public-opinion survey. For each item, indicate the level of measurement and whether the variable will be discrete or continuous. *(HINT: Remember that only interval-ratio-level variables can be continuous.)*
  a. What is your occupation? _____
  b. How many years of school have you completed? _____
  c. If you were asked to use one of these four names for your social class, which would you say you belonged in?
    _____ Upper   _____ Middle
    _____ Working   _____ Lower
  d. What is your age? _____
  e. In what country were you born? _____
  f. What is your grade point average? _____
  g. What is your major? _____

  h. The only way to deal with the drug problem is to legalize all drugs.
    _____ Strongly agree
    _____ Agree
    _____ Undecided
    _____ Disagree
    _____ Strongly disagree
  i. What is your astrological sign? _____
  j. How many brothers and sisters do you have? _____

1.5 Below are brief descriptions of how researchers measured a variable. For each situation, determine the level of measurement of the variable and whether it is continuous or discrete.
  a. **Sex.** Respondents were asked to select a category from the following list:
    _____ Male   _____ Female
  b. **Honesty.** Subjects were observed as they passed by a spot on campus where an apparently lost wallet was lying. The wallet contained money and complete identification. Subjects were classified into one of the following categories:
    _____ Returned the wallet with the money.
    _____ Returned the wallet but kept the money.
    _____ Did not return the wallet.
  c. **Social class.** Subjects were asked about their family situation when they were 16 years old. Was their family:
    _____ Very well off compared to other families?
    _____ About average?
    _____ Not so well off?
  d. **Education.** Subjects were asked how many years of schooling they and each parent had completed.
  e. **Sex integration on campus.** Students were observed during lunchtime at the cafeteria for a month. The number of students sitting with students of the opposite sex was counted for each meal period.
  f. **Number of children.** Subjects were asked: "How many children have you ever had? Please include any that may have passed away."
  g. **Student seating patterns in classrooms.** On the first day of class, instructors noted where

each student sat. Seating patterns were remeasured every two weeks until the end of the semester. Each student was classified as

_____ same seat as last measurement;

_____ adjacent seat;

_____ different seat, not adjacent;

_____ absent.

h. Physicians per capita. The number of practicing physicians was counted in each of 50 cities, and the researchers used population data to compute the number of physicians per capita.

i. Physical attractiveness. A panel of 10 judges rated each of 50 photos of a sample of males and females for physical attractiveness on a scale from 0 to 20 with 20 being the highest score.

j. Number of accidents. The number of traffic accidents for each of 20 busy intersections in a city was recorded. Also, each accident was rated as

_____ minor damage, no injuries;

_____ moderate damage, personal injury requiring hospitalization;

_____ severe damage and injury.

1.6 For each of the first 20 items in the General Social Survey (see Appendix G), indicate the level of measurement and whether the variable is continuous or discrete.

1.7 For each research situation summarized below, identify the level of measurement of all variables and indicate whether they are discrete or continuous. Also, decide which statistical applications are used: descriptive statistics (single variable), descriptive statistics (two or more variables), or inferential statistics. Remember that it is quite common for a given situation to require more than one type of application.

a. The administration of your university is proposing a change in parking policy. You select a random sample of students and ask each one whether he or she favours or opposes the change.

b. You ask everyone in your social research class to tell you (1) the highest grade he or she ever received in a math course and (2) the grade on a recent statistics test. You then compare the two sets of scores to find out whether there is any relationship.

c. Your aunt is running for mayor and hires you (for a huge fee, incidentally) to question a sample of voters about their concerns in local politics. Specifically, she wants a profile of the voters that will tell her what percent belong to each political party, what percent are male or female, and what percent favour or oppose the widening of the main street in town.

d. Several years ago, a country reinstituted the death penalty for first-degree homicide. Supporters of capital punishment argued that this change would reduce the homicide rate. To investigate this claim, a researcher has gathered information on the number of homicides in the country for the two-year periods before and after the change.

e. A local automobile dealer is concerned about customer satisfaction. He wants to mail a survey form to all customers for the past year and ask them if they are satisfied, very satisfied, or not satisfied with their purchases.

1.8 For each research situation below, identify the independent and dependent variables. Classify each in terms of level of measurement and whether or not the variable is discrete or continuous.

a. A graduate student is studying sexual harassment on university campuses and asks 500 female students if they personally have experienced any such incidents. Each student is asked to estimate the frequency of these incidents as either "often, sometimes, rarely, or never." The researcher also gathers data on age and major to find out whether there is any connection between these variables and frequency of sexual harassment.

b. A supervisor in the Solid Waste Management Division of a municipal government is attempting to assess two different methods of trash collection. One area of the city is served by trucks with two-person crews who do "backyard" pickups, and the rest of the city is served by "high-tech" single-person trucks with curbside pickup. The assessment measures include the number of complaints received from the two different areas over a six-month period, the amount of time per day required to service each area, and the cost per tonne of trash collected.

c. The adult bookstore near campus has been raided and closed by the police. Your social research class has decided to poll the student body and get their reactions and opinions. The class decides to ask each student if he or she supports or opposes the closing of the store, how many times each one has visited the store, and if he or she agrees or disagrees that "pornography is a direct cause of sexual assaults on women." The class also collects information on the sex, age, religious and political philosophy, and major of each student to see if opinions are related to these characteristics.

d. For a research project in a political science course, a student has collected information about the quality of life and the degree of political democracy in 50 nations. Specifically, she used infant mortality rates to measure quality of life, and the percentage of all adults who are permitted to vote in national elections was the measure of democratization. Her hypothesis is that quality of life is higher in more democratic nations.

e. A highway engineer wonders if a planned increase in speed limit on a heavily travelled local avenue will result in any change in number of accidents. He plans to collect information on traffic volume, number of accidents, and number of fatalities for the six-month periods before and after the change.

f. Students are planning a program to promote "safe sex" and awareness of a variety of other health concerns for university students. To measure the effectiveness of the program, they plan to give a survey measuring knowledge about these matters to a random sample of the student body before and after the program.

g. Several provinces have drastically cut their budgets for mental health care. Will this increase the number of homeless people in these provinces? A researcher contacts a number of agencies serving the homeless in each province and develops an estimate of the size of the population before and after the cuts.

h. Does tolerance for diversity vary by race, ethnicity, or gender? Samples of males and females from various racial and ethnic groups have been given a survey that measures their interest in and appreciation of cultures and groups other than their own.

SPSS

Introduction to the Canadian General Social Survey, Census of Canada, and SPSS

The Problems exercises at the end of chapters in this text have been written so that they can be solved with just a simple hand calculator. We've purposely kept the number of cases involved unrealistically low so that the tedium of mere calculation would not interfere unduly with the learning process. To provide a more realistic experience, actual social science data from two Canadian social surveys, the Census of Canada (Census) and the Canadian General Social Survey (GSS), are used in the SPSS for Windows computer exercises, also located at the end of chapters.

The GSS is an annual public-opinion poll, administered by Statistics Canada, of a representative sample of Canadians. It has been conducted since 1985, and explores a broad range of social issues. Each year the survey collects information on specific aspects of society relevant to social policy. Since survey topics are often repeated every few years, GSS data can also be used to track trends and changes in these characteristics over time. The GSS has proven to be a very valuable resource for testing theory, for learning more about Canadian society, and for informing public debates.

The 2004 version of the GSS is supplied and used in this text. It collected information on the nature and extent of criminal victimization in Canada and perceptions of crime and the criminal justice system, including the police, criminal courts, and prisons. With the 2004 GSS data students can describe how Canadians feel about crime or their personal safety, as well as their satisfaction with the criminal justice system. Students can further examine if variables such as gender, age, province of residence, and so on are associated with opinions and assessments of crime and justice in Canada.

The 2004 GSS includes hundreds of variables for a sample of 25,000 Canadians. It was not possible to provide this complete version of the GSS for distribution with the text due to licensing issues. The version supplied with this text, named *GSS.sav*, has been limited to about 50 of these variables and 1,500 randomly selected Canadians. While limited in number of variables and cases, the *GSS.sav* file still contains actual "real-life" data, so you have the opportunity to practise your statistical skill in a more realistic context.

The Census provides information on the demographic, social, and economic characteristics of a random sample of Canadians. The Census is conducted by Statistics Canada every five years. The 2001 Census is provided here. Using Census data, students can describe and explain many aspects of Canadian society, including family composition, labour force activity, income, and poverty.

The 2001 Census contains dozens of variables for a sample of hundreds of thousands of Canadians. We are able to provide the complete version of the Census (*CensusFull.sav*) containing the original random sample of 640,526 cases. We also provide a shortened version (*Census.sav*) with 1,500 randomly selected cases.

The three databases (*GSS.sav*, *Census.sav*, and *CensusFull.sav*) and the user's guide for the 2004 GSS (*GSS_guide.pdf*) and 2001 Census (*Census_guide.pdf*) can be downloaded from our website at http://www.healeystatistics.nelson.com. The user's guides provide a detailed description of each survey; however, for quick reference, a list of the variables in each database is shown in Appendix G.

One of the problems with using "real-life" data to practise your statistical skills is that the data often contain too many cases to be solved with just a simple hand calculator. This brings us to the second purpose of this section: computers and statistical packages. A statistical package is a set of computer programs for the analysis of data. The advantage of these packages is that, since the programs are already written, you can capitalize on the power of the computer with minimal computer literacy and virtually no programming experience.

This text utilizes the Statistical Package for the Social Sciences (SPSS). Version 16 of SPSS is used, though Versions 10 through 17 of SPSS are completely compatible with the text. In the SPSS for Windows sections, we will explain how to use this package to manipulate and analyze the GSS or Census data, and we will illustrate and interpret the results.

There are two versions of SPSS: a full version and a student version. The student version, created for classroom instruction, is, in essence, the full version of the SPSS base software package but is limited to a maximum of 50 variables and 1,500 cases. Hence, the student version is compatible with the *GSS.sav* and *Census.sav* data files. Be sure to read Appendix F, which gives a general introduction to SPSS, before attempting any data analysis.

Part I Descriptive Statistics

Part I consists of four chapters, each devoted to a different application of univariate descriptive statistics. Chapter 2 covers "basic" descriptive statistics, including percentages, ratios, rates, frequency distributions, and graphs. It is a lengthy chapter, but the material is relatively elementary and at least vaguely familiar to most people. Although the statistics covered in this chapter are "basic," they are not necessarily simple or obvious and the explanations and examples should be considered carefully before attempting the end-of-chapter problems or using them in actual research.

Chapters 3 and 4 cover measures of central tendency and dispersion, respectively. Measures of central tendency describe the typical case or average score (e.g., the mean), while measures of dispersion describe the amount of variety or diversity among the scores (e.g., the range or the distance from the high score to the low score). These two types of statistics are presented in separate chapters to stress the point that centrality and dispersion are independent, separate characteristics of a variable. You should realize, however, that both measures are necessary and commonly reported together (along with some of the statistics presented in Chapter 2). To reinforce the idea that measures of centrality and dispersion are complementary descriptive statistics, many of the problems at the end of Chapter 4 require the computation of a measure of central tendency from Chapter 3.

Chapter 5 is a pivotal chapter in the flow of the text. It takes some of the statistics from Chapters 2 through 4 and applies them to the normal curve, a concept of great importance in statistics. The normal curve is a type of line chart or frequency polygon (see Chapter 2), which can be used to describe the position of scores using means (Chapter 3) and standard deviations (Chapter 4). Chapter 5 also uses proportions and percentages (Chapter 2).

In addition to its role in descriptive statistics, the normal curve is a central concept in inferential statistics, the topic of Part II of this text. Thus, Chapter 5 serves a dual purpose: it ends the presentation of univariate descriptive statistics and lays essential groundwork for the material to come.

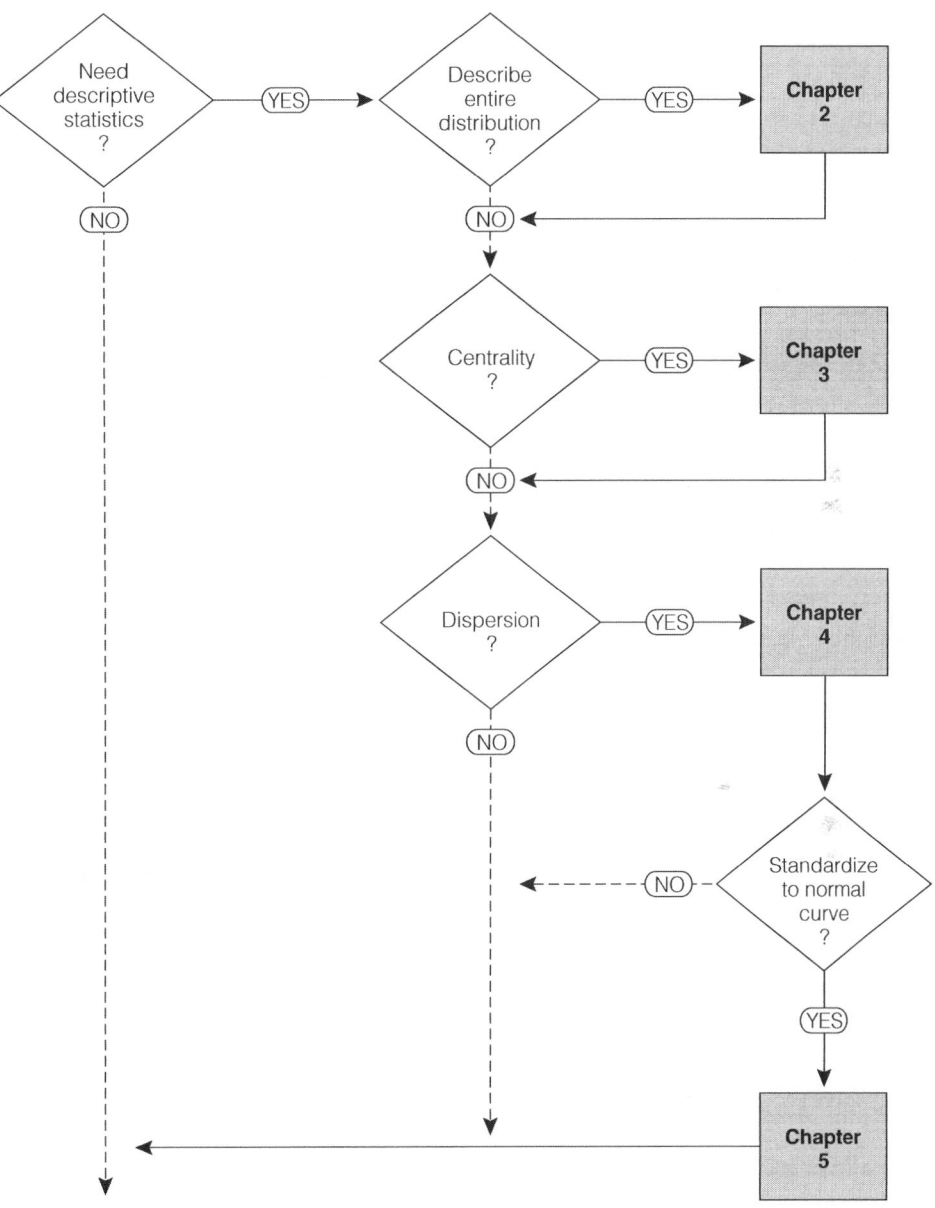

2

BASIC DESCRIPTIVE STATISTICS
PERCENTAGES, RATIOS AND RATES, TABLES, CHARTS, AND GRAPHS

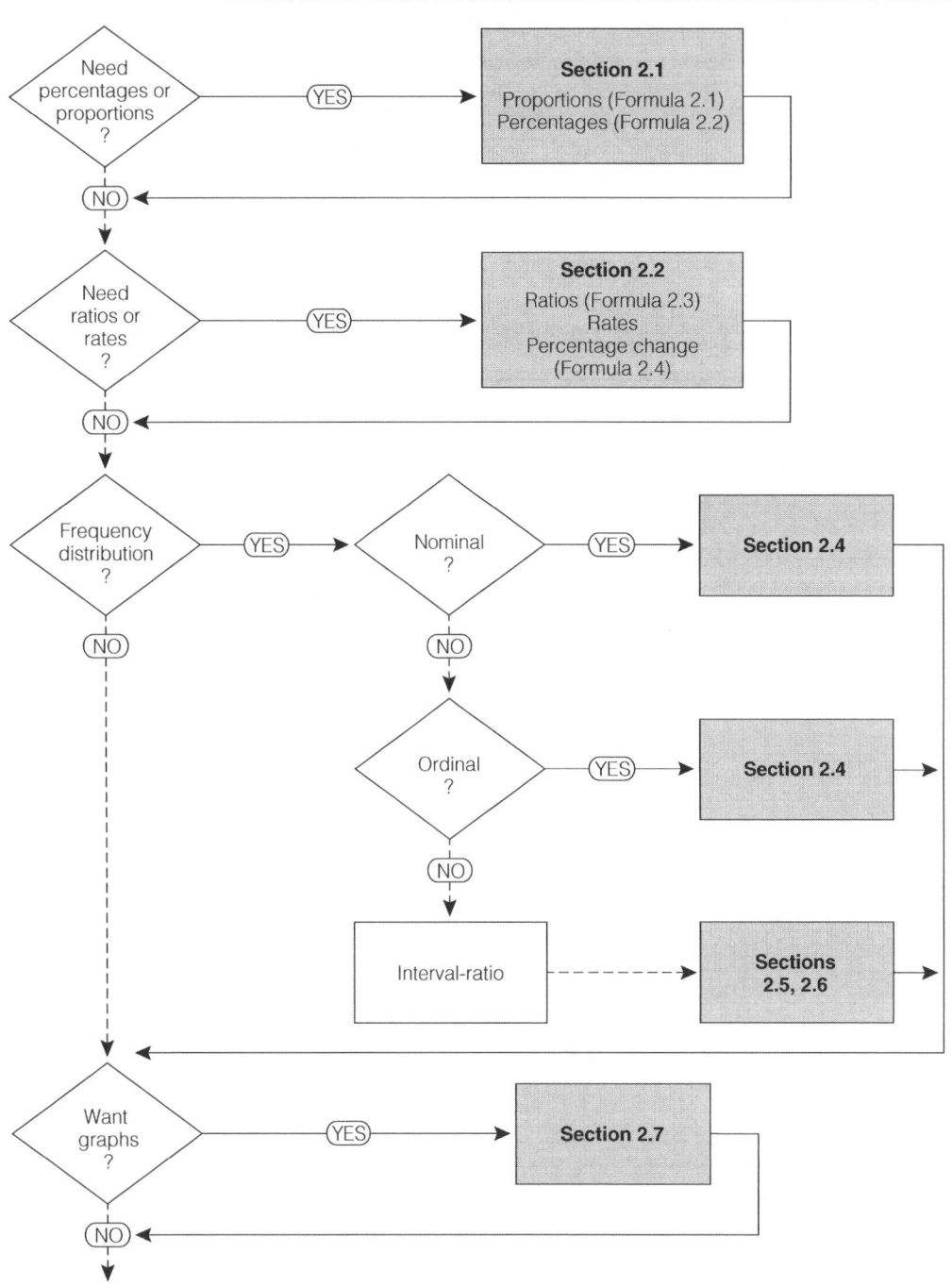

LEARNING OBJECTIVES

By the end of this chapter, you will be able to

1. Explain the purpose of descriptive statistics in making data comprehensible.
2. Compute and interpret percentages, proportions, ratios, rates, and percentage change.
3. Construct and analyze frequency distributions for variables at each of the three levels of measurement.
4. Construct and analyze bar and pie charts, histograms, stem-and-leaf plots, and line charts.

Research results do not speak for themselves. They must be organized and manipulated so that whatever meaning they have can be quickly and easily understood by the researcher and by his or her readers. Researchers use statistics to clarify their results and communicate effectively. In this chapter, we will consider some commonly used techniques for presenting research results: percentages and proportions, ratios and rates, percentage change, tables, charts, and graphs. Mathematically speaking, these univariate descriptive statistics are not very complex (although they may not be as simple as they appear at first glance), but, as you will see, they are extremely useful for presenting research results clearly and concisely.

2.1 PERCENTAGES AND PROPORTIONS

Consider the following statement: "Of the 781 survey respondents who plan to celebrate St. Valentine's Day, 312 will go out to a restaurant." While there is nothing wrong with this statement, the same fact could have been more clearly conveyed if it had been reported as a percentage: Of those who plan to celebrate St. Valentine's Day, almost 40% will go out to a restaurant.

Percentages and proportions supply a frame of reference for reporting research results in the sense that they standardize the raw data: percentages to the base 100 and proportions to the base 1.00. The mathematical definitions of **proportions** and **percentages** are

FORMULA 2.1

$$\text{Proportion: } p = \frac{f}{N}$$

FORMULA 2.2

$$\text{Percentage: } \% = \left(\frac{f}{N}\right) \times 100$$

where f = frequency, or the number of cases in any category
N = the number of cases in all categories

To illustrate the computation of percentages, consider the data presented in Table 2.1. How can we find the percentage of cases in the first category (going to a restaurant)? Note that there are 312 cases in the category ($f = 312$) and a total of 781 cases in all ($N = 781$). So,

$$\text{Percentage (\%)} = \left(\frac{f}{N}\right) \times 100 = \left(\frac{312}{781}\right) \times 100 = (0.3995) \times 100 = 39.95\%$$

TABLE 2.1 MOST POPULAR WAYS FOR CANADIANS TO CELEBRATE ST. VALENTINE'S DAY

Ways to Celebrate	Frequency (f)	Proportion (p)	Percentage (%)
Going to a restaurant	312	0.3995	39.95
Romantic evening at home	110	0.1408	14.08
Giving a gift/card/flowers/chocolate	92	0.1178	11.78
Going on a trip	22	0.0282	2.82
Going out dancing	7	0.0090	0.90
Other	74	0.0947	9.47
Don't know	164	0.2100	21.00
	$N = 781$	1.0000	100.00

Source: Leger Marketing. 2007. *Canadians and St. Valentine's Day.* http://www.legermarketing.com/documents/SPCLM/070212ENG.pdf.

Using the same procedures, we can also find the percentage of cases in the second category:

$$\text{Percentage (\%)} = \left(\frac{f}{N}\right) \times 100 = \left(\frac{110}{781}\right) \times 100 = (0.1408) \times 100 = 14.08\%$$

Both results could have been expressed as proportions. For example, the proportion of cases in the third category is 0.1178.

$$\text{Proportion } (p) = \frac{f}{N} = \frac{92}{781} = 0.1178$$

Percentages and proportions are easier to read and comprehend than frequencies. This advantage is particularly obvious when attempting to compare groups of different sizes. For example, Table 2.2 provides actual data collected by the Student Financial Survey (a survey sponsored by the Canada Millennium Scholarship Foundation) on program-of-study of post-secondary students from across Canada during the 2001–2002 academic year. Based on the program-of-study information presented in the table,

TABLE 2.2 DECLARED MAJOR FIELDS OF STUDY FOR MALE AND FEMALE UNDERGRADUATE UNIVERSITY STUDENTS

Major	Male	Female
Business	101	112
Natural sciences*	156	192
Social sciences†	156	246
Engineering	69	26
Other	106	122
	$N = 588$	$N = 698$

*Includes computer science, health, and medicine.
†Includes fine arts, education, humanities, and law.
Source: Data from *Making Ends Meet*, 2001–2002 Student Financial Survey, Canada Millenium Scholarship Foundation, March 2003.

Application 2.1

Not long ago, in a large social service agency, the following conversation took place between the executive director of the agency and a supervisor of one of the divisions.

> *Executive director:* Well, I don't want to seem abrupt, but I've only got a few minutes. Tell me, as briefly as you can, about this staffing problem you claim to be having.
>
> *Supervisor:* Ma'am, we just don't have enough people to handle our workload. Of the 177 full-time employees of the agency, only 50 are in my division. Yet, 6,231 of the 16,722 cases handled by the agency last year were handled by my division.
>
> *Executive director (smothering a yawn):* Very interesting. I'll certainly get back to you on this matter.

How could the supervisor have presented his case more effectively? Because he wants to compare two sets of numbers (his staff versus the total staff and the workload of his division versus the total workload of the agency), proportions or percentages would be a more forceful way of presenting results. What if the supervisor had said, "Only 28.25% of the staff is assigned to my division, but we handle 37.26% of the total workload of the agency"? Is this a clearer message?

The first percentage is found by

$$\% = \left(\frac{f}{N}\right) \times 100 = \frac{50}{177} \times 100$$

$$= (.2825) \times 100 = 28.25\%$$

and the second percentage is found by

$$\% = \left(\frac{f}{N}\right) \times 100 = \left(\frac{6231}{16{,}722}\right) \times 100$$

$$= (.3726) \times 100 = 37.26\%$$

which sex has the higher relative number of business majors? Because the total enrollments are much different, comparisons are difficult to make from the raw frequencies. Computing percentages eliminates the difference in size of the two groups by standardizing both distributions to the base of 100. The same data are presented in percentages in Table 2.3.

TABLE 2.3   DECLARED MAJOR FIELDS OF STUDY FOR MALE AND FEMALE
UNDERGRADUATE UNIVERSITY STUDENTS

Major	Male	Female
Business	17.18	16.05
Natural sciences*	26.53	27.51
Social sciences†	26.53	35.24
Engineering	11.73	3.73
Other	18.03	17.47
	100.00%	100.00%
	(588)	(698)

*Includes computer science, health, and medicine.
†Includes fine arts, education, humanities, and law.
Source: Based on data from *Making Ends Meet*, 2001–2002 Student Financial Survey, Canada Millenium Scholarship Foundation, March 2003.

Application 2.2

In Table 2.2, how many male social science majors are there compared to male business majors? This question could be answered with frequencies, but a more easily understood way of expressing the answer would be with a ratio. The ratio of male social science to business majors would be

$$\text{Ratio} = \frac{f_1}{f_2} = \frac{156}{101} = 1.54$$

For every male business major, there are 1.54 male social science majors.

The percentages in Table 2.3 make it easier to identify both differences and similarities between the sexes. We now see that a greater percentage of males than females study business at Canadian universities, even though the absolute number of female business majors is more than that of male business majors. How would you describe the differences in the other major fields? *(For practice in computing and interpreting percentages and proportions, see problems 2.1 and 2.2.)*

Some further guidelines on the use of percentages and proportions:

1. When working with a small number of cases (say, fewer than 20), it is usually preferable to report the actual frequencies rather than percentages or proportions. With a small number of cases, the percentages can change drastically with relatively minor changes in the data. For example, if you begin with a data set that includes 10 males and 10 females (i.e. 50% of each gender) and then add another female, the percentage distributions will change noticeably to 52.38% female and 47.62% male. Of course, as the number of observations increases, each additional case will have a smaller impact. If we started with 500 males and females and then added one more female, the percentage of females would change by only a tenth of a percent (from 50% to 50.10%).

2. Always report the number of observations along with proportions and percentages. This permits the reader to judge the adequacy of the sample size and, conversely, helps to prevent the researcher from lying with statistics. Statements like "two out of three people questioned prefer courses in statistics to any other course" might impress you, but the claim would lose its gloss if you learned that only three people were tested. *You should be extremely suspicious of reports that fail to state the number of cases that were tested.*

3. Percentages and proportions can be calculated for variables at the ordinal and nominal levels of measurement, even though they require division. This is not a violation of the level-of-measurement guideline (see Table 1.2). Percentages and proportions do not require the division of the *scores* of the variable (as would be the case in computing the average

score on a test, for example) but rather the *number of cases* in a particular category (f) of the variable by the total number of cases in the sample (N). When we make a statement like "43% of the sample is female," we are merely expressing the relative size of a category (female) of the variable (gender) in a convenient way.

2.2 RATIOS, RATES, AND PERCENTAGE CHANGE

Ratios, rates, and percentage change provide some additional ways of summarizing results simply and clearly. Although they are similar to each other, each statistic has a specific application and purpose.

Ratios.   **Ratios** are especially useful for comparing categories of a variable in terms of relative frequency. Instead of standardizing the distribution of the variable to the base 100 or 1.00, as we did in computing percentages and proportions, we determine ratios by dividing the frequency of one category by the frequency in another. Mathematically, a ratio can be defined as

FORMULA 2.3

$$\text{Ratio} = \frac{f_1}{f_2}$$

where f_1 = the number of cases in the first category
f_2 = the number of cases in the second category

To illustrate the use of ratios, we will use actual information from the 2006 Canadian Election Study, which is an interuniversity project that regularly conducts a survey of Canadian voters on a variety of political issues. Canadians were asked about their feelings toward the federal sponsorship scandal that involved the misappropriation and misdirection of government funds. Of those polled, 3,351 people said that they were angry about the sponsorship scandal, while 630 said that they were not angry.* What is the relative size of these two groups? To find the ratio of "angry" Canadians (f_1) to "not angry" Canadians (f_2), divide 3351 by 630:

$$\text{Ratio} = \frac{f_1}{f_2} = \frac{3351}{630} = 5.32$$

The resultant ratio is 5.32, which means that for every Canadian who is not angry about the sponsorship scandal, there are 5.32 Canadians who are angry about the scandal.

Ratios can be very economical ways of expressing the relative predominance of two categories. That "angry" Canadians outnumber "not angry" Canadians in our example is obvious from the raw data. Percentages or proportions could have been used to summarize the overall distribution (e.g., "84.17% of Canadians were angry about the sponsorship scandal, and

*Source: 2006 Canadian Election Study.

Application 2.3

In 2005, there were 337,856 births in Canada, within a population of 32,270,507 persons. In 1972, when the population of Canada was only 22,218,475, there were 351,256 births. Is the birth rate rising or falling? Although this question can be answered from the preceding information, the trend in birth rates will be much more obvious if we compute birth rates for both years. Like crude death rates, crude birth rates are usually multiplied by 1000 to eliminate decimal points. For 1972:

$$\text{Crude birth rate} = \frac{351,256}{22,218,475} \times 1,000 = 15.81$$

In 1972, there were 15.81 births for every 1,000 people in Canada. For 2005:

$$\text{Crude birth rate} = \frac{337,856}{32,270,507} \times 1,000 = 10.47$$

In 2005, there were 10.47 births for every 1,000 people in Canada. With the help of these statistics, the decline in the birth rate is clearly expressed.

Source: Data from Statistics Canada, CANSIM, Tables 051-0001 and 051-0004.

15.83% were not"). In contrast to these other methods, ratios express the relative size of the categories: they tell us exactly how much one category outnumbers the other.

Ratios are often multiplied by some power of 10 to eliminate decimal points. For example, the ratio computed above might be multiplied by 100 and reported as 532 instead of 5.32. This would mean that, for every 100 Canadians who are not angry about the sponsorship scandal, there are 532 Canadians who are angry about it. To ensure clarity, the comparison units for the ratio are often expressed as well. Based on a unit of ones, the ratio of "angry" Canadians to "not angry" Canadians would be expressed as 5.32:1. Based on hundreds, the same statistic might be expressed as 532:100. *(For practice in computing and interpreting ratios, see problems 2.1 and 2.2.)*

Rates. **Rates** provide still another way of summarizing the distribution of a single variable. Rates are defined as the number of actual occurrences of some phenomenon divided by the number of possible occurrences per some unit of time. Rates are usually multiplied by some power of 10 to eliminate decimal points. For example, the crude death rate for a population is defined as the number of deaths in that population (actual occurrences) divided by the number of people in the population (possible occurrences) per year. This quantity is then multiplied by 1000. The formula for the crude death rate can be expressed as

$$\text{Crude death rate} = \frac{\text{Number of deaths}}{\text{Total population}} \times 1000$$

In 2005, a total of 234,645 deaths were registered in Canada. With a population of 32,270,507, Canada's crude death rate for that year was*

$$\text{Crude death rate} = \frac{234,645}{32,270,507} \times 1000 = (0.00727) \times 1000 = 7.27$$

Or, for every 1,000 Canadians, there were 7.27 deaths in 2005.

Rates are often multiplied by 100,000 when the number of actual occurrences of some phenomenon is extremely small relative to the size of the population, such as homicides in Canada. Canadian police reported 658 homicides in 2005, hence the homicide rate was**

$$\text{Homicide rate} = \frac{658}{32,270,507} \times 100,000 = (0.00002039) \times 100,000 = 2.04$$

Or, for every 100,000 Canadians, there were 2.04 homicides in 2005. *(For practice in computing and interpreting rates, see problems 2.3 and 2.4a.)*

Percentage Change.   Measuring social change, in all its variety, is an important task for all social sciences. One very useful statistic for this purpose is the **percentage change,** which tells us how much a variable has increased or decreased over a certain span of time.

To compute this statistic, we need the scores of a variable at two different points in time. The scores could be in the form of frequencies, rates, or percentages. The percentage change will tell us how much the score has changed at the later time relative to the earlier time. Using death rates as an example once again, imagine a society suffering from a devastating outbreak of disease in which the death rate rose from 16.00 per 1,000 population in 1995 to 24.00 per 1,000 in 2000. Clearly, the death rate is higher in 2000, but by how much relative to 1995?

The formula for the percentage change is

FORMULA 2.4

$$\text{Percentage change} = \left(\frac{f_2 - f_1}{f_1}\right) \times 100$$

where f_1 = first score, frequency, or value
f_2 = second score, frequency, or value

In our example, f_1 is the death rate in 1995 (16.00) and f_2 is the death rate in 2000 (24.00). The formula tells us to subtract the earlier score from the later and then divide by the earlier score. The value that results expresses the size of the change in scores ($f_2 - f_1$) relative to the score at the earlier time (f_1). The value is then multiplied by 100 to express the change in the form of a percentage:

$$\text{Percentage change} = \left(\frac{24 - 16}{16}\right) \times 100 = \left(\frac{8}{16}\right) \times 100 = (.50) \times 100 = 50\%$$

---

*Source: Statistics Canada. 2006. *Annual Demographic Statistics 2005.* Catalogue no. 91-213-XIB.
**Source: Statistics Canada. 2006. *Crime Statistics in Canada, 2005.* Catalogue no. 85-002-XIE.

The death rate in 2000 is 50% higher than in 1995. This means that the 2000 rate was equal to the 1995 rate *plus* half of the earlier score. If the rate had risen to 32 per 1,000, the percentage change would have been 100% (the rate would have doubled) and if the death rate had fallen to 8 per 1,000, the percentage change would have been −50%. The negative sign means that the death rate has decreased by 50%. The 2000 rate would have been half the size of the 1995 rate.

An additional example should make the computation and interpretation of the percentage change clearer. Suppose we wanted to compare the projected population growth rates for various nations over the next 40 years.

The necessary information is presented in Table 2.4. Casual inspection will give us some information. For example, compare China and Mexico. China is projected to add more than twice as many people (about 76 million for China and 35 million for Mexico), but because China's 2010 population is approximately 10 times the size of Mexico's population, its percentage change will be much lower. Calculating percentage change will make these comparisons more accurate. Table 2.4 shows the projected population for each nation in 2010 and 2050. The "Increase/Decrease" column shows how many people will be added or lost. The right-hand column shows the percentage change in projected population for each nation. These values were computed by subtracting the 2010 population (f_1) from the 2050 population (f_2), dividing by the 2010 population (f_1), and multiplying by 100.

Although China is projected to have the largest population in 2010, it will grow at the slowest rate among these six nations (5.68%). India, which will have the second largest population in 2010, has the highest growth rate; it will add the most people and its population will increase in size by over 50%. This means that, in 2050, the population of India will be the largest in the world. The United States and Mexico will increase by just over 30% (in 2050, their populations will be about one-third larger than in 2010), and Canada will grow by about one-fifth. Italy's population will actually decline by over 13%. *(For practice in computing and interpreting percentage change, see problem 2.4b.)*

TABLE 2.4   PROJECTED POPULATION GROWTH FOR SIX NATIONS, 2010–2050

Nation	Population, 2010 (f_1)	Population, 2050 (f_2)	Increase/ Decrease ($f_2 - f_1$)	Percent Change $\left(\dfrac{f_2 - f_1}{f_1}\right) \times 100$
China	1,347,563,498	1,424,161,948	76,598,450	5.68
India	1,184,090,490	1,807,878,574	623,788,084	52.68
United States	309,162,581	420,080,587	110,918,006	35.88
Mexico	112,468,855	147,907,650	35,438,795	31.51
Italy	58,090,681	50,389,841	−7,700,840	−13.26
Canada	34,252,514	41,429,579	7,177,065	20.95

Source: U.S. Bureau of the Census. http://www.census.gov/ipc/www/idb/.

Application 2.4

The demographic composition of students in Canadian universities has been changing over the past decades. One major change has been an increase in the number of women pursuing university education. For example, in the 1972–73 academic year, 37% of all full-time university students were female. In the 2001–02 year, this figure was 57%. How large has this change been?

It is obvious that in the 2001–02 academic year the percentage is much higher and calculating the percentage change will give us the exact magnitude of the change. The 1972–73 academic year percentage is f_1 and the 2001–02 figure is f_2, so

$$\text{Percentage change} = \left(\frac{57 - 37}{37}\right) \times 100$$

$$= \left(\frac{20}{37}\right) \times 100$$

$$= (0.54054) \times 100$$

$$= 54.05\ \%$$

Between the 1972–73 and 2001–02 academic years, women's share of full-time university enrollment increased by 54.05%. (Note that at 57%, women today make up the majority of full-time students in Canadian universities.)

Source: Statistics Canada. 2006. *Women in Canada: A Gender-based Statistical Report.* Catalogue no. 89-503-XIE.

2.3 FREQUENCY DISTRIBUTIONS: INTRODUCTION

Frequency distributions are tables that summarize the distribution of a variable by reporting the number of cases contained in each category of the variable. They are very helpful and commonly used ways of organizing and working with data. In fact, the construction of frequency distributions is almost always the first step in any statistical analysis.

To illustrate the usefulness of frequency distributions and to provide some data for examples, assume that the counselling centre at a university is assessing the effectiveness of its services. Any realistic evaluation research would collect a variety of information from a large group of students, but for the sake of this example, we will confine our attention to just four variables and 20 students. The data are reported in Table 2.5.

Note that even though the data in Table 2.5 represent an unrealistically low number of cases, it is difficult to discern any patterns or trends. For example, try to ascertain the general level of satisfaction of the students from Table 2.5. You may be able to do so with just 20 cases, but it will take some time and effort. Imagine the difficulty with 50 cases or 100 cases presented in this fashion. Clearly the data need to be organized in a format that allows the researcher (and his or her audience) to understand easily the distribution of the variables.

One general rule that applies to all frequency distributions is that the categories of the frequency distribution must be exhaustive and mutually exclusive. In other words, the categories must be stated in a way that permits each case to be counted in one and only one category. This basic principle applies to the construction of frequency distributions for variables measured at all three levels of measurement.

TABLE 2.5 DATA FROM COUNSELLING CENTRE SURVEY

Student	Sex	Marital Status[1]	Satisfaction with Services[2]	Age
A	Male	Single	4	18
B	Male	Married	2	19
C	Female	Single	4	18
D	Female	Single	2	19
E	Male	Married	1	20
F	Male	Single	3	20
G	Female	Married	4	18
H	Female	Single	3	21
I	Male	Single	3	19
J	Female	Divorced	3	23
K	Female	Single	3	24
L	Male	Married	3	18
M	Female	Single	1	22
N	Female	Married	3	26
O	Male	Single	3	18
P	Male	Married	4	19
Q	Female	Married	2	19
R	Male	Divorced	1	19
S	Female	Divorced	3	21
T	Male	Single	2	20

[1]Married includes persons legally married, legally married and separated, and persons living in common-law unions.
[2]Measured on a scale from 1 (very dissatisfied) to 4 (very satisfied).

Beyond this rule, there are only guidelines to help you construct useful frequency distributions. As you will see, the researcher has a fair amount of discretion in stating the categories of the frequency distribution (especially with variables measured at the interval-ratio level). We will identify the issues to consider as you make decisions about the nature of any particular frequency distribution. Ultimately, however, the guidelines we state are aids for decision making, nothing more than helpful suggestions. As always, the researcher has the final responsibility for making sensible decisions and presenting his or her data in a meaningful way.

2.4 FREQUENCY DISTRIBUTIONS FOR VARIABLES MEASURED AT THE NOMINAL AND ORDINAL LEVELS

Nominal-Level Variables. For nominal-level variables, construction of the frequency distribution is typically very straightforward. For each category of the variable being displayed, the occurrences are counted and the subtotals, along with the total number of cases (N), are reported. Table 2.6 displays a frequency distribution for the variable "sex" from the counselling centre survey. For purposes of illustration, a column for tallies has been included in this table to illustrate how the cases would be sorted into categories. (This column would not be included in the final form of the frequency distribution.) Take a moment to notice several other features of the table. Specifically, the table has a descriptive title, clearly labelled categories (male and female), and a report of

TABLE 2.6 SEX OF RESPONDENTS, COUNSELLING CENTRE SURVEY

Sex	Tallies	Frequency (f)
Male	*LHT LHT*	10
Female	*LHT LHT*	10
		$N = 20$

the total number of cases at the bottom of the frequency column. These items must be included in all tables regardless of the variable or level of measurement.

The meaning of the table is quite clear. There are 10 males and 10 females in the sample, a fact that is much easier to comprehend from the frequency distribution than from the unorganized data presented in Table 2.5.

For some nominal variables, the researcher might have to make some choices about the number of categories he or she wishes to report. For example, the distribution of the variable "marital status" could be reported using the categories listed in Table 2.5. The resultant frequency distribution is presented in Table 2.7. Although this is a perfectly fine frequency distribution, it may be too detailed for some purposes. For example, the researcher might want to focus solely on "nonmarried" as distinct from "married" students. That is, the researcher might not be concerned with the difference between single and divorced respondents but may want to treat both as simply "not married." In that case, these categories could be grouped together and treated as a single entity, as in Table 2.8. Notice that, when categories are collapsed like this, information and detail will be lost. This latter version of the table would not allow the researcher to discriminate between the two unmarried states.

Ordinal-Level Variables. Frequency distributions for ordinal-level variables are constructed following the same routines used for nominal-level variables. Table 2.9 reports the frequency distribution of the "satisfaction" variable from the counselling centre survey. Note that a column of percentages by category has been added to this table. Such columns heighten the clarity of the table (especially with larger samples) and are common adjuncts to the basic frequency distribution for variables measured at all levels.

TABLE 2.7 MARITAL STATUS OF RESPONDENTS, COUNSELLING CENTRE SURVEY

Status	Frequency (f)
Single	10
Married	7
Divorced	3
	$N = 20$

TABLE 2.8 MARITAL STATUS OF RESPONDENTS, COUNSELLING CENTRE SURVEY

Status	Frequency (f)
Married	7
Not married	13
	$N = 20$

TABLE 2.9 SATISFACTION WITH SERVICES, COUNSELLING CENTRE SURVEY

Satisfaction	Frequency (f)	Percentage (%)
(4) Very satisfied	4	20
(3) Satisfied	9	45
(2) Dissatisfied	4	20
(1) Very dissatisfied	3	15
	N = 20	100

TABLE 2.10 SATISFACTION WITH SERVICES, COUNSELLING CENTRE SURVEY

Satisfaction	Frequency (f)	Percentage (%)
Satisfied	13	65
Dissatisfied	7	35
	N = 20	100

This table reports that most students were either satisfied or very satisfied with the services of the counselling centre. The most common response (nearly half the sample) was "satisfied." If the researcher wanted to emphasize this major trend, the categories could be collapsed as in Table 2.10. Again, the price paid for this increased compactness is that some information (in this case, the exact breakdown of degrees of satisfaction and dissatisfaction) is lost. *(For practice in constructing and interpreting frequency distributions for nominal- and ordinal-level variables, see problem 2.5.)*

2.5 FREQUENCY DISTRIBUTIONS FOR VARIABLES MEASURED AT THE INTERVAL-RATIO LEVEL

Basic Considerations. In general, the construction of frequency distributions for variables measured at the interval-ratio level is more complex than for nominal and ordinal variables. Interval-ratio variables usually have a large number of possible scores (i.e., a wide range from the lowest to the highest score). The large number of scores requires some collapsing or grouping of categories to produce reasonably compact frequency distributions. To construct frequency distributions for interval-ratio-level variables, you must decide how many categories to use and how wide these categories should be.

For example, suppose you wished to report the distribution of the variable "age" for a sample drawn from a community. Unlike the university data reported in Table 2.5, a community sample would have a very broad range of ages. If you simply reported the number of times that each year of age (or score) occurred, you could easily wind up with a frequency distribution that contained 70, 80, or even more categories. Such a large frequency distribution would not present a concise picture. The scores (years) must be grouped into larger categories to heighten clarity and ease of comprehension. How large should these categories be? How many categories should be included in the table? Although there are no hard-and-fast rules for making these decisions, they always involve a trade-off between more detail (a greater number of narrow categories) or more compactness (a smaller number of wide categories).

Constructing the Frequency Distribution. To introduce the mechanics and decision-making processes involved, we will construct a frequency distribution to display the ages of the students in the counselling centre survey. Because of the narrow age range of a group of university students, we can use categories of only one year (these categories are often called **class intervals** when working with interval-ratio data). The frequency distribution is constructed by listing the ages from youngest to oldest, counting the number of times each score (year of age) occurs, and then totalling the number

---

Application 2.5

The following list shows the ages of 50 prisoners enrolled in a work-release program. Is this group young or old? A frequency distribution will provide an accurate picture of the overall age structure.

18	60	57	27	19
20	32	62	26	20
25	35	75	25	21
30	45	67	41	30
37	47	65	42	25
18	51	22	52	30
22	18	27	53	38
27	23	32	35	42
32	37	32	40	45
55	42	45	50	47

We will use about 10 intervals to display these data. By inspection we see that the youngest prisoner is 18 and the oldest is 75. The range is thus 57. Interval size will be 57/10, or 5.7, which we can round off to either 5 or 6. Let's use a six-year interval beginning at 18. The limits of the lowest interval will be 18–23. Now we must state the limits of all other intervals, count the number of cases in each interval, and display these counts in a frequency distribution. Columns may be added for percentages, cumulative percentages, and/or cumulative frequency. The complete distribution, with a column added for percentages, is

Ages	Frequency	Percentages
18–23	10	20
24–29	7	14
30–35	9	18
36–41	5	10
42–47	8	16
48–53	4	8
54–59	2	4
60–65	3	6
66–71	1	2
72–77	1	2
	$N = 50$	100

The prisoners seem to be fairly evenly spread across the age groups up to the 48–53 interval. There is a noticeable lack of prisoners in the oldest age groups and a concentration of prisoners in their 20s and 30s.

of scores for each category. Table 2.11 presents the information and reveals a concentration or clustering of scores in the 18 and 19 class intervals.

Even though the picture presented in this table is fairly clear, assume for the sake of illustration that you desire a more compact (less detailed) summary. To do this, you will have to group scores into wider class intervals. By increasing the interval width (say to two years), you can reduce the number of intervals and achieve a more compact expression. The grouping of scores in Table 2.12 clearly emphasizes the relative predominance of younger respondents. This trend in the data can be stressed even more by the addition of a column displaying the percentage of cases in each category.

Note that the class intervals in Table 2.12 have been stated with an apparent gap between them (i.e., the class intervals are separated by a distance of one unit). At first glance, these gaps may appear to violate the principle of exhaustiveness; but because age has been measured in whole numbers, the gaps actually pose no problem. Given the level of precision of the measurement (in years, as opposed to 10ths or 100ths of a year), no case could have a score falling between these class intervals. In fact, for these data, the set of class intervals contained in Table 2.12 constitutes a scale that is exhaustive and

TABLE 2.11   AGE OF RESPONDENTS, COUNSELLING CENTRE SURVEY
(interval width = one year of age)

Class Interval	Frequency (f)
18	5
19	6
20	3
21	2
22	1
23	1
24	1
25	0
26	1
	$N = 20$

TABLE 2.12   AGE OF RESPONDENTS, COUNSELLING CENTRE SURVEY
(interval width = two years of age)

Class Interval	Frequency (f)	Percentage (%)
18–19	11	55
20–21	5	25
22–23	2	10
24–25	1	5
26–27	1	5
	$N = 20$	100

mutually exclusive. Each of the 20 respondents in the sample can be sorted into one and only one age category.

However, consider the difficulties that might have been encountered if age had been measured with greater precision. If age had been measured in 10ths of a year, into which class interval in Table 2.12 would a 19.4-year-old subject be placed? You can avoid this ambiguity by always stating the limits of the class intervals at the same level of precision as the data. Thus, if age were being measured in 10ths of a year, the limits of the class intervals in Table 2.12 would be stated in 10ths of a year. For example:

17.0–18.9
19.0–20.9
21.0–22.9
23.0–24.9
25.0–26.9

To maintain mutual exclusivity between categories, do not overlap the class intervals. If you state the limits of the class intervals at the same level of precision as the data (which might be in whole numbers, tenths, hundredths, etc.) and maintain a "gap" between intervals, you will always produce a frequency distribution where each case can be assigned to one and only one category.

Midpoints.   On occasion, you will need to work with the **midpoints** of the class intervals, for example, when constructing or interpreting certain graphs. Midpoints are defined as the points exactly halfway between the upper and lower limits and can be found for any interval by dividing the sum of the upper and lower limits by two. Table 2.13 displays midpoints for two different sets of class intervals. *(For practice in finding midpoints, see problems 2.8b and 2.9b.)*

TABLE 2.13   MIDPOINTS

Class Interval Width = Three	
Class Interval	Midpoints
0–2	1
3–5	4
6–8	7
9–11	10
Class Interval Width = Six	
Class Interval	Midpoints
100–105	102.5
106–111	108.5
112–117	114.5
118–123	120.5

Real Limits.*   For certain purposes, you must eliminate the "gap" between class intervals and treat a distribution as a continuous series of categories that border each other. This is necessary, for example, in constructing some graphs, such as the histogram (see Section 2.7).

To illustrate, let's begin with Table 2.12. Note the "gap" of one year between intervals. As we saw before, the gap is only apparent: scores are measured in whole years (i.e., 19, 21 vs. 19.5 or 21.3) and cannot fall between intervals. These types of class intervals are called **stated class limits** and they organize the scores of the variable into a series of discrete, non-overlapping intervals.

To treat the variable as continuous, we must use the **real class limits.** To find the real limits of any class interval, divide the distance between the stated class intervals (the "gap") in half and add the result to all upper stated limits and subtract it from all lower stated limits. This process is illustrated below with the class intervals stated in Table 2.12. The distance between intervals is one, so the real limits can be found by adding 0.5 to all upper limits and subtracting 0.5 from all lower limits.

Stated Limits	Real Limits
18–19	17.5–19.5
20–21	19.5–21.5
22–23	21.5–23.5
24–25	23.5–25.5
26–27	25.5–27.5

Note that when conceptualized with real limits, the class intervals overlap with each other and the distribution can be seen as continuous. Table 2.14

TABLE 2.14   REAL CLASS LIMITS

Class Intervals (stated limits)	Real Class Limits
3–5	2.5–5.5
6–8	5.5–8.5
9–11	8.5–11.5

Class Intervals (stated limits)	Real Class Limits
100–105	99.5–105.5
106–111	105.5–111.5
112–117	111.5–117.5
118–123	117.5–123.5

---

*This section is optional.

presents additional illustrations of real limits for two different sets of class intervals. In both cases, the "gap" between the stated limits is one. *(For practice in finding real limits, see problem 2.7c and problem 2.8d.)*

Cumulative Frequency and Cumulative Percentage. Two commonly used adjuncts to the basic frequency distribution for interval-ratio data are the **cumulative frequency** and **cumulative percentage** columns. Their primary purpose is to allow the researcher (and his or her audience) to tell at a glance how many cases fall below a given score or class interval in the distribution.

To construct a cumulative frequency column, begin with the lowest class interval (i.e., the class interval with the lowest scores) in the distribution. The entry in the cumulative frequency columns for that interval will be the same as the number of cases in the interval. For the next higher interval, the cumulative frequency will be all cases in the interval plus all the cases in the first interval. For the third interval, the cumulative frequency will be all cases in the interval plus all cases in the first two intervals. Continue adding (or accumulating) cases until you reach the highest class interval, which will have a cumulative frequency of all the cases in the interval plus all cases in all other intervals. For the highest interval, cumulative frequency equals the total number of cases. Table 2.15 shows a cumulative frequency column added to Table 2.12.

The cumulative percentage column is quite similar to the cumulative frequency column. Begin by adding a column to the basic frequency distribution for percentages as in Table 2.12. This column shows the percentage of all cases in each class interval. To find cumulative percentages, follow the same addition pattern explained above for cumulative frequency. That is, the cumulative percentage for the lowest class interval will be the same as the percentage of cases in the interval. For the next higher interval, the cumulative percentage is the percentage of cases in the interval plus the percentage of

TABLE 2.15   AGE OF RESPONDENTS, COUNSELLING CENTRE SURVEY

Class Interval	Frequency (f)	Cumulative Frequency
18–19	11	11
20–21	5	16
22–23	2	18
24–25	1	19
26–27	1	20
	N = 20	

TABLE 2.16 AGE OF RESPONDENTS, COUNSELLING CENTRE SURVEY

Class Interval	Frequency (f)	Cumulative Frequency	Percentage (%)	Cumulative Percentage (%)
18–19	11	11	55	55
20–21	5	16	25	80
22–23	2	18	10	90
24–25	1	19	5	95
26–27	1	20	5	100
	N = 20		100%	

cases in the first interval, and so on. Table 2.16 shows the age data with a cumulative percentage column added.

These cumulative columns are quite useful in situations where the researcher wants to make a point about how cases are spread across the range of scores. For example, Tables 2.15 and 2.16 show quite clearly that most students in the counselling centre survey are less than 21 years of age. If the researcher wishes to impress this feature of the age distribution on his or her audience, then these cumulative columns are quite handy. Most realistic research situations will be concerned with many more than 20 cases and/or many more categories than our tables have. Because the cumulative percentage column is clearer and easier to interpret in such cases, it is normally preferred to the cumulative frequencies column.

Procedures for Constructing Frequency Distributions for Interval-Ratio Variables. Guidelines for dealing with interval-ratio variables with many scores (wide ranges) can now be stated:

1. Decide how many class intervals you wish to use. One reasonable convention suggests that the number of intervals should be about 10. Many research situations may require fewer than 10 intervals, and it is common to find frequency distributions with as many as 15 intervals. Only rarely will more than 15 intervals be used, as the resultant frequency distribution would not be very concise.
2. Find the size of the class interval. Once you have decided how many intervals you will use, interval size can be found by dividing the range of the scores by the number of intervals and rounding to a convenient whole number.
3. State the lowest interval so that its lower limit is equal to or below the lowest score. By the same token, your highest interval will be the one that contains the highest score. All intervals must be equal in size.
4. State the limits of the class intervals at the same level of precision as you have used to measure the data. Do not overlap intervals. You will thereby

define the class intervals so that each case can be sorted into one and only one category.

5. Count the number of cases in each class interval and report these subtotals in a column labelled "frequency." Report the total number of cases (N) at the bottom of this column. The table may also include a column for percentages, cumulative frequencies, and cumulative percentages.

6. Inspect the frequency distribution carefully. Has too much detail been lost? If so, reconstruct the table with a greater number of class intervals (or smaller interval size). Is the table too detailed? If so, reconstruct the table with fewer class intervals (or use wider intervals). Remember that the frequency distribution results from a number of decisions you make in a rather arbitrary manner. If the appearance of the table seems less than optimal given the purpose of the research, redo the table until you are satisfied that you have struck the best balance between detail and conciseness.

7. Remember to give your table a clear, concise title, and number the table if your report contains more than one. All categories and columns must also be clearly labelled. *(For practice in constructing and interpreting frequency distributions for interval-ratio-level variables, see problems 2.5 to 2.9.)*

2.6 CONSTRUCTING FREQUENCY DISTRIBUTIONS FOR INTERVAL-RATIO-LEVEL VARIABLES: A REVIEW

We covered a lot of ground in the preceding section, so let's pause and review these principles by considering a specific research situation. Below are the numbers of visits received over the past year by 90 residents of a retirement community.

0	52	21	20	21	24	1	12	16	12
16	50	40	28	36	12	47	1	20	7
9	26	46	52	27	10	3	0	24	50
24	19	22	26	26	50	23	12	22	26
23	51	18	22	17	24	17	8	28	52
20	50	25	50	18	52	46	47	27	0
32	0	24	12	0	35	48	50	27	12
28	20	30	0	16	49	42	6	28	2
16	24	33	12	15	23	18	6	16	50

Listed in this format, the data are a hopeless jumble from which no one could derive much meaning. The function of the frequency distribution is to arrange and organize these data so that their meanings will be made obvious.

First, we must decide how many class intervals to use in the frequency distribution. Following the guidelines established in the previous section, let's use about 10 intervals. By inspecting the data, we can see that the lowest score is 0 and the highest is 52. The range of these scores

READING STATISTICS 2: Frequency Distributions and Charts

You will often need to interpret and understand tables, charts, and graphs as you become more involved in the professional literature of the social sciences. These figures will be explained in the text of the article, but you should develop the habit of reading them for yourself and coming to your own conclusions. Here are some ideas to keep in mind when reading tables and charts.

First, there are many different formats for presenting results and the tables and graphs you find in the research literature will not necessarily follow the conventions used in this text. Second, because of space limitations, tables and graphs will be presented with a minimum of detail. For example, the researcher may present a frequency distribution with only a percentage column.

Begin your analysis by first reading the title, all labels (i.e., row and/or column headings), and any footnotes to the table. These will tell you exactly what information is contained in the figure or table. Inspect the body of the table or graph with the author's analysis in mind. See if you agree with the author's analysis. (You almost always will, but it never hurts to double-check and exercise your critical abilities.)

Finally, remember that most research projects analyze interrelationships among many variables. Because the tables, graphs, and charts covered in this chapter display variables one at a time, they are unlikely to be included in such research reports (or perhaps, included only as background information). Even when not reported, you can be sure that the research began with an inspection of frequency distributions or graphs for each variable. Univariate tables and graphs display a great deal of information about the variables in a compact, easily understood format and are almost universally used as descriptive devices.

Statistics in the Professional Literature

In this section, two brief excerpts from social science research are presented so that you can see how statistical information is actually interpreted and

reported. The first excerpt presents a frequency distribution and the second a line chart.

Excerpt 1 Frequencies and Rates:
Which Jurisdictions Are Most Dangerous?

In a research report titled "Five Deaths a Day: Workplace Fatalities in Canada, 1993–2005," Sharpe and Hardt provide a comprehensive examination of workplace fatalities in Canada, including the characteristics of those who died on the job and the reasons they died. The researchers also provide the frequency distribution and the rate of workplace fatalities per 100,000 workers employed in the provinces and territories. This rate was computed by dividing the number of fatalities by the number of workers and multiplying it by 100,000. Table 1 shows that workers in Ontario had the highest number of fatalities (412) in 2005, yet after taking account of the size of the workforce, workers in Nunavut, Yukon, and Northwest Territories had the highest rate of fatal accidents:

$$\text{Fatality rate} = \frac{12}{43,800} \times 100,000$$
$$= (.000274) \times 100,000 = 27.4$$

By contrast, workers in Prince Edward Island and New Brunswick had the lowest rates of fatal accidents. The fatality rates per 100,000 workers employed in these provinces in 2005 were 1.5 and 3.4 respectively.

Why does the rate vary by province? One explanation is the characteristics of the workforce. Sharpe and Hardt report that the chances of a worker dying from a workplace accident or occupational disease vary significantly by industry and occupation. The three most dangerous industries in which to work are: mining, quarrying, and oil wells (49.9 fatalities per 100,000 workers); logging and forestry (42.9 per 100,000); and fishing and trapping (35.6 per 100,000). Workplace fatalities are also concentrated in sectors unique to

(continued)

READING STATISTICS 2: *(continued)*

TABLE 1   NUMBER AND RATE OF FATAL OCCUPATIONAL INJURIES BY PROVINCE/TERRITORY

Rank	Provinces and Territories	Number of Fatalities	Employment (000s)	Fatality Rate (per 100,000 Workers)
	All Canada	1,097	16,213.5	6.8
1	Nunavut, Yukon, and Northwest Territories	12	43.8	27.4
2	Newfoundland and Labrador	25	214.1	11.7
3	British Columbia	189	2,130.5	8.9
4	Alberta	143	1,784.4	8.0
5	Ontario	412	6,397.7	6.4
6	Nova Scotia	27	443.1	6.1
7	Quebec	223	3,717.3	6.0
8	Saskatchewan	27	483.5	5.6
9	Manitoba	26	580.3	4.5
10	New Brunswick	12	350.5	3.4
11	Prince Edward Island	1	68.2	1.5

Source: Sharpe, A. and Hardt, J. 2006. "Five Deaths a day: Workplace Fatalities in Canada, 1993–2005." Centre for the Study of Living Standards.
Note: Employment data were obtained from Statistics Canada, CANSIM, Table 282-0008.

trades and transport-equipment operators (19.0 per 100,000) and processing, manufacturing, and utilities (10.2 per 100,000 workers). These industries and occupations make up a significant component of the economies and workforces of Nunavut, Yukon, and Northwest Territories, contributing to the high rate of workplace fatalities. Do you want to learn more on this issue? The citation for the report is listed below.

Source: Sharpe, A. and Hardt, J. 2006. "Five Deaths a Day: Workplace Fatalities in Canada, 1993–2005." *Centre for the Study of Living Standards. Note:* Employment data were obtained from Statistics Canada, CANSIM, Table 282-0008.

Excerpt 2 Suicide and Homicide

How do suicide and homicide rates vary by age? To investigate this issue, Pampel and Williamson gathered data from 18 "high income" nations, including Canada, for the time period 1955–1994. Among other findings, they found a stable relationship between age and both suicide and homicide rates. The graphs below show suicide and homicide rates (number of deaths from suicide or homicide per 100,000 population) for both males and females for all nations and all years in the sample.

Each graph shows the distribution of suicide rates along the left-hand vertical axis and homicide rates on the right-hand vertical axis. Age groups are arrayed across the horizontal axis. Here's what the authors have to say about the graphs:

> The suicide rate for males . . . rises steadily from its lowest value among persons age 15–24 until it peaks at the oldest ages. Female suicide rates . . . rise earlier . . . and level off at ages over 75 when the male rate continues to rise. These results . . . demonstrate across a diverse set of nations and time points a [lower suicide rate] for youth. Homicide rates exhibit the opposite pattern . . . they peak at ages 25–34, then fall until age 75 and older. . . (p. 265).

If you want to learn more about this fascinating study, the reference is given below.

Source: Pampel, Fred, and Williamson, John. 2001. "Age Patterns of Suicide and Homicide Mortality Rates in High-Income Nations." *Social Forces,* 80:251–282.

(continued)

READING STATISTICS 2: *(continued)*

FIGURE 1 MALE SUICIDE AND HOMICIDE RATES PER 100,000 POPULATION

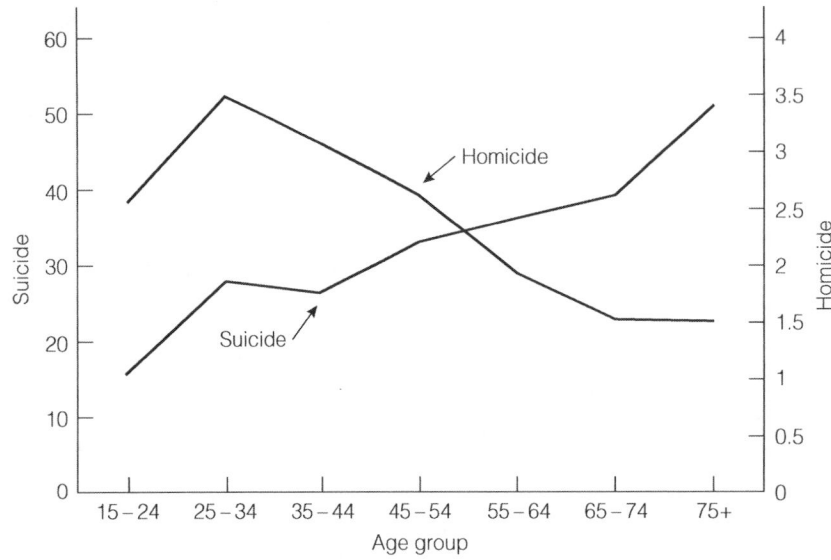

FIGURE 2 FEMALE SUICIDE AND HOMICIDE RATES PER 100,000 POPULATION

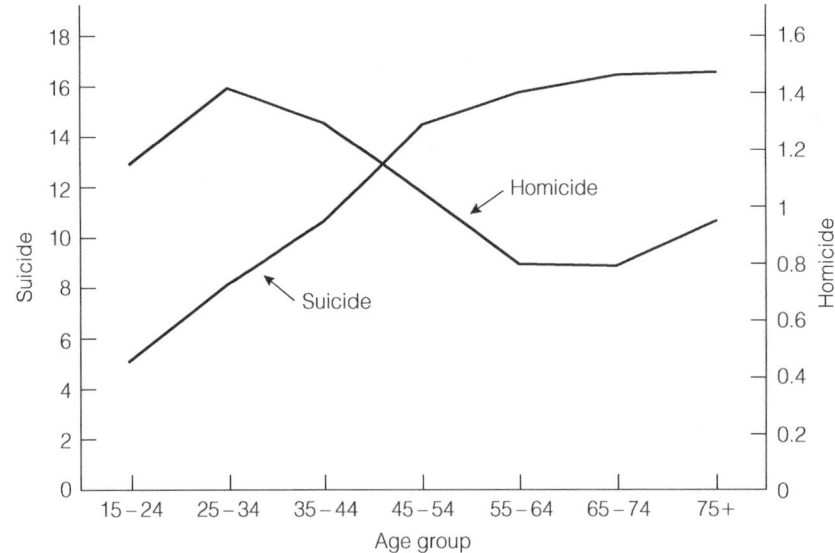

Source: Pampel, Freid and Williamson, John. 2001. "Age Patterns of Suicide and Homicide Mortality Rates in High-Income Nations." *Social Forces,* 80(1), Copyright © 2001 by the University of North Carolina Press. Used by permission of the publisher. www.uncpress.unc.edu

is 52 − 0, or 52. To find the approximate interval size, divide the range (52) by the number of intervals (10). Since 52/10 = 5.2, we can set the interval size at 5.

The lowest score is 0, so the lowest class interval will be 0–4. The highest class interval will be 50–54, which will include the high score of 52. All that remains is to state the intervals in table format, count the number of scores that fall into each interval, and report the totals in a frequency column. These steps have been taken in Table 2.17, which also includes columns for the percentages and cumulative percentages. Note that this table is the product of several relatively arbitrary decisions. The researcher should remain aware of this fact and inspect the frequency distribution carefully. If the table is unsatisfactory for any reason, it can be reconstructed with a different number of categories and interval sizes.

Now, with the aid of the frequency distribution, some patterns in the data can be discerned. There are three distinct clusterings of scores in the table. Ten residents were visited rarely, if at all (the 0–4 visits per year interval). The single largest interval, with 18 cases, is 20–24. Combined with the intervals immediately above and below, this represents quite a sizable grouping of cases (42 out of 90, or 46.66% of all cases) and suggests that the dominant visiting rate is about twice a month, or approximately 24 visits per year. The third grouping is in the 50–54 class interval with 12 cases, reflecting a visiting rate of about once a week. The cumulative percentage column indicates that the majority of the residents (58.89%) were visited 24 or fewer times a year.

TABLE 2.17 NUMBER OF VISITS PER YEAR, 90 RETIREMENT COMMUNITY RESIDENTS

Class Interval	Frequency (f)	Cumulative Frequency	Percentage (%)	Cumulative Percentage (%)
0–4	10	10	11.11	11.11
5–9	5	15	5.56	16.67
10–14	8	23	8.89	25.56
15–19	12	35	13.33	38.89
20–24	18	53	20.00	58.89
25–29	12	65	13.33	72.22
30–34	3	68	3.33	75.55
35–39	2	70	2.22	77.77
40–44	2	72	2.22	79.99
45–49	6	78	6.67	86.66
50–54	12	90	13.33	99.99
	$N = 90$		99.99%*	

*Percentage columns will occasionally fail to total to 100% because of rounding error. If the total is between 99.90% and 100.10%, ignore the discrepancy. Discrepancies greater than ± 0.10% may indicate mathematical errors, and the entire column should be computed again.

2.7 CHARTS AND GRAPHS

Researchers frequently use charts and graphs to present their data in ways that are visually more dramatic than frequency distributions. These devices are particularly useful for conveying an impression of the overall shape of a distribution and for highlighting any clustering of cases in a particular range of scores. Many graphing techniques are available, but we will examine just five. The first two, pie and bar charts, are appropriate for discrete variables at any level of measurement. The last three, histograms, stem-and-leaf plots, and line charts or frequency polygons, are used with both discrete and continuous interval-ratio variables but are particularly appropriate for the latter.

The sections that follow explain how to construct graphs and charts "by hand." These days, however, computer programs are almost always used to produce graphic displays. Graphing software is sophisticated and flexible but also relatively easy to use and, if such programs are available to you, you should familiarize yourself with them. The effort required to learn these programs will be repaid in the quality of the final product. The section on computer applications at the end of this chapter includes a demonstration of how to produce bar charts and line charts.

Pie Charts.   To construct a **pie chart,** begin by computing the percentage of all cases that fall into each category of the variable. Then divide a circle (the pie) into segments (slices) proportional to the percentage distribution. Be sure that the chart and all segments are clearly labelled.

Figure 2.1 is a pie chart that displays the distribution of "marital status" from the counselling centre survey. The frequency distribution (Table 2.7) is reproduced as Table 2.18, with a column added for the percentage distribution. Because a circle's circumference is 360°, we will apportion 180° (or 50%) for the first category, 126° (35%) for the second, and 54° (15%) for the last category. The pie chart visually reinforces the relative preponderance of single respondents and the relative absence of divorced students in the counselling centre survey.

FIGURE 2.1   SAMPLE PIE CHART: MARITAL STATUS OF RESPONDENTS ($N = 20$)

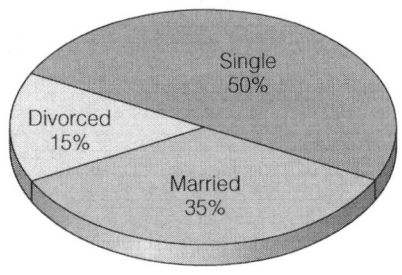

TABLE 2.18   MARITAL STATUS OF RESPONDENTS, COUNSELLING CENTRE SURVEY

Status	Frequency (f)	Percentage (%)
Single	10	50
Married	7	35
Divorced	3	15
	$N = 20$	100

Bar Charts.   Like pie charts, **bar charts** are relatively straightforward. Conventionally, the categories of the variable are arrayed along the horizontal axis (or abscissa) and frequencies, or percentages if you prefer, along the vertical axis (or ordinate). For each category of the variable, construct (or draw) a rectangle of constant width and with a height that corresponds to the number of cases in the category. The bar chart in Figure 2.2 reproduces the marital status data from Figure 2.1 and Table 2.18.

This chart would be interpreted in exactly the same way as the pie chart in Figure 2.1, and researchers are free to choose between these two methods of displaying data. However, if a variable has more than four or five categories, the bar chart would be preferred. With too many categories, the pie chart gets very crowded and loses its visual clarity. To illustrate, Figure 2.3 uses a bar chart to display the data on visiting rates for the retirement community presented in Table 2.17. A pie chart for this same data would have had 11 different "slices," a more complex or "busier" picture than that

FIGURE 2.2   SAMPLE BAR CHART: MARITAL STATUS OF RESPONDENTS, COUNSELLING CENTRE SURVEY ($N = 20$)

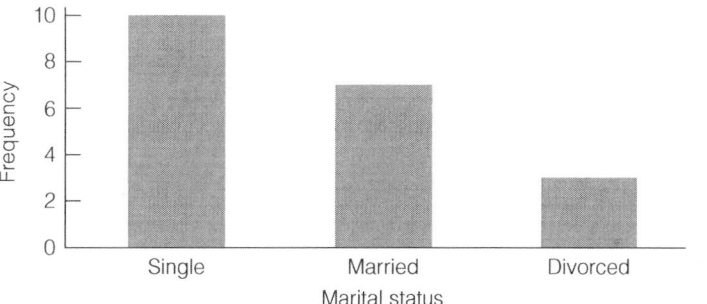

FIGURE 2.3   SAMPLE BAR CHART FOR VISITS PER YEAR, RETIREMENT COMMUNITY RESIDENTS ($N = 90$)

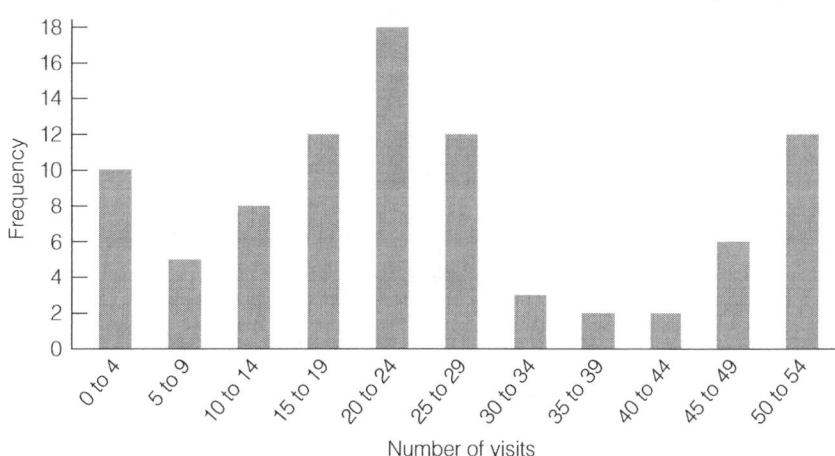

presented by the bar chart. In Figure 2.3, the clustering of scores in the "20 to 24" range (approximately two visits a month) is readily apparent, as are the groupings in the "0 to 4" and "50 to 54" ranges.

Bar charts are particularly effective ways to display the relative frequencies for two or more categories of a variable when you want to emphasize some comparisons. Suppose, for example, that you wished to compare rates of homicide for males and females in various age groups. Figure 2.4 displays the data in an easily comprehensible way. The bar chart shows that rates for males are higher than rates for females and that the rate for males peaks at 25 to 29 years of age, and then steadily declines with increasing age. *(For practice in constructing and interpreting pie and bar charts, see problems 2.5b and 2.10.)*

Histograms. **Histograms** look a lot like bar charts and, in fact, are constructed in much the same way. However, histograms use real limits rather than stated limits and the categories or scores of the variable border each other, as if they merged into each other in a continuous series. Therefore, these graphs are most appropriate for continuous interval-ratio-level variables but they are commonly used for discrete interval-ratio-level variables as well. To construct a histogram from a frequency distribution, follow these steps:

1. Array the real limits of the class intervals or scores along the horizontal axis (abscissa).
2. Array frequencies along the vertical axis (ordinate).
3. For each category in the frequency distribution, construct a bar with height corresponding to the number of cases in the category and with width corresponding to the real limits of the class intervals.
4. Label each axis of the graph.
5. Title the graph.

As an example, Figure 2.5 uses a histogram to display the age distribution for a sample of Canadians aged 0 to 84. The graph shows that the

FIGURE 2.4 HOMICIDE RATES BY AGE GROUP AND SEX, CANADA, 2005

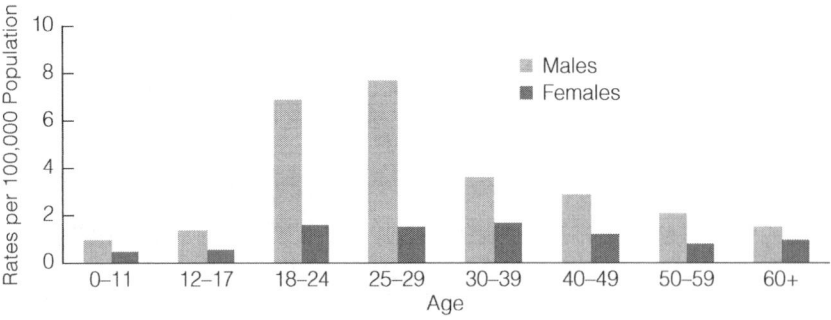

Source: Extracted from "Victim Homicide Rates by Age, Group and Sex, Canada, 2005" Juristat, Catalogue no. 85-002-XIE, 26(6), Figure 8. Statistics Canada. http://www.statcan.ca/english/freepub/85-002-XIE/85-002-XIE2006006.pdf

FIGURE 2.5   AGE DISTRIBUTION IN CANADA

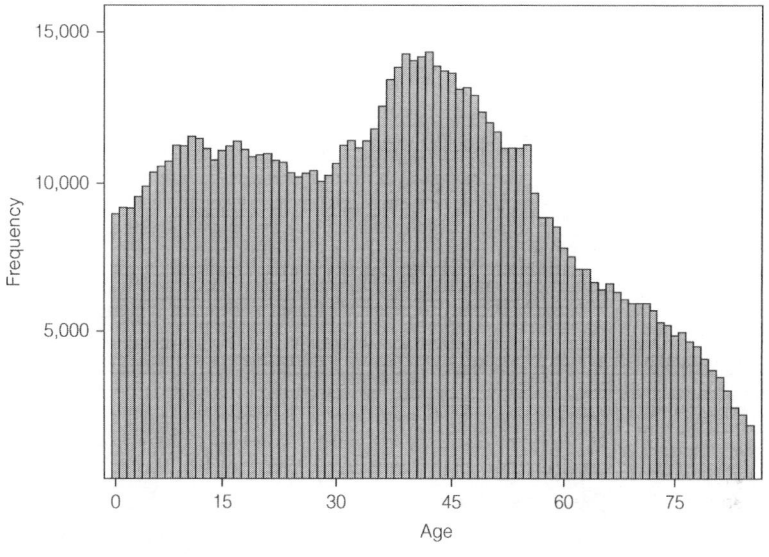

Source: Statistics Canada, 2001 Canadian Census, individual PUMF.

sample respondents are concentrated in their mid-30s to early 50s. This is the "baby-boom" generation. The number of respondents, then, declines in old age.

Stem-and-Leaf Plots.   The **stem-and-leaf plot** is a variation of the histogram; however it uses digits to represent the frequencies of each interval. Its advantage is that it retains the information about the actual data values from which it was constructed. In a stem-and-leaf plot, each of these values is divided into two pieces: a stem and a leaf. The leading digit(s) of each value forms the stem and the remaining digit(s) of the value form the leaf.

Suppose, for example, that five adults were randomly sampled and asked about their total years of education. Their responses were as follows: 12, 11, 11, 09, and 20. To construct a stem-and-leaf plot from these data, three steps are followed:

1. Order the values from lowest to highest: 09, 11, 11, 12, 20.
2. Write each leading digit (stem) in a vertical column with a line to the right of the column. For these five observations, there are three unique leading (the leftmost) digits: 0, 1, and 2:

0 |
1 |
2 |

3. For the first observation, write the last digit (the leaf) next to its first digit (the stem):

```
0 | 9 (here 0 | 9 represents the stem and leaf of the value 09 years of
1               education)
2 |
```

Then repeat Step 3 for each observation:

```
0 | 9
1 | 1 1 2 (here 1 | 1 1 2 represent the values 11, 11, and 12 respectively)
2 | 0
```

Thus, the stem-and-leaf plot is a histogram turned on its side as the length of each row (analogous to the height of a bar in a histogram) corresponds to the number of cases in the interval. However, the stem-and-leaf plot additionally provides information on the exact values that make up each interval. A histogram does not provide this information.

When a variable has just two digits there can be only one leading digit (stem) and one remaining digit (leaf). However, if a variable has more than two digits a decision must be made on how many leading digits to use for the stem. The decision is often based on what plot best summarizes the data in an interesting and meaningful way.

For example, 20 adults were randomly sampled and asked about their body weight (in pounds): 135, 139, 145, 148, 149, 150, 154, 155, 159, 159, 160, 168, 169, 179, 179, 185, 189, 200, 202, and 210. The stem for this variable can be either the first digit only or the first and second digits. If we construct the stem-and-leaf plot using only the first digit, there would be just two stems— 1 and 2—and many leaves. The single-digit stem-and-leaf plot follows:

```
1 | 35 39 45 48 49 50 54 55 59 59 60 68 69 79 79 85 89
2 | 00 02 10
```

However, using the first two digits there are many more (eight) stems— 13, 14, 15, 16, 17, 18, 20, and 21—with fewer leaves. This two-digit stem-and-leaf plot is displayed below. Note that when there are no observations in an intervening interval its stem should be included in the plot to give a clear description of how the values are distributed. In this plot there are no observations in the 190-pound interval, but the stem 19 is included:

```
13 | 5 9
14 | 5 8 9
15 | 0 4 5 9 9
16 | 0 8 9
17 | 9 9
18 | 5 9
19 |
20 | 0 2
21 | 0
```

When comparing these two plots it is obvious that the two-digit stem-and-leaf plot provides a more meaningful plot than the single-digit stem-and-leaf plot. As a general rule of thumb, when a variable has more than two digits the decision on how many leading digits to use for the stem is based on the appearance of a plot. It should strike a balance between the number of stems and leaves. It should not have a few stems with many leaves. Nor should it have too many stems with a few leaves.

Line Charts.   Construction of a **line chart** or **frequency polygon** is similar to construction of a histogram or a stem-and-leaf plot. Instead of using bars or digits to represent the frequencies, however, it uses dots at the midpoint of each interval. Straight lines then connect the dots. Because the line is continuous from highest to lowest score, these graphs are especially appropriate for continuous interval-ratio-level variables but are frequently used with discrete interval-ratio-level variables. Figure 2.6 displays a line chart for the visiting data previously displayed in the bar chart in Figure 2.3.

Line charts can also be used to display trends across time. Figure 2.7 shows both marriage and divorce rates per 1,000 Canadians from 1976 to 2003. Marriage rates decreased over this whole period, while divorce rates increased up to the mid-1980s and then decreased. Figure 2.8 provides another example of a line chart, based on a series of annual Leger Marketing polls from 1996 to 2005. It shows that the trend in the percentage of Quebeckers who support sovereignty generally decreased from 1996 to 2003 and then increased. Ten years after the 1995 Quebec

FIGURE 2.6   NUMBER OF VISITS PER YEAR, RETIREMENT COMMUNITY RESIDENTS ($N = 90$)

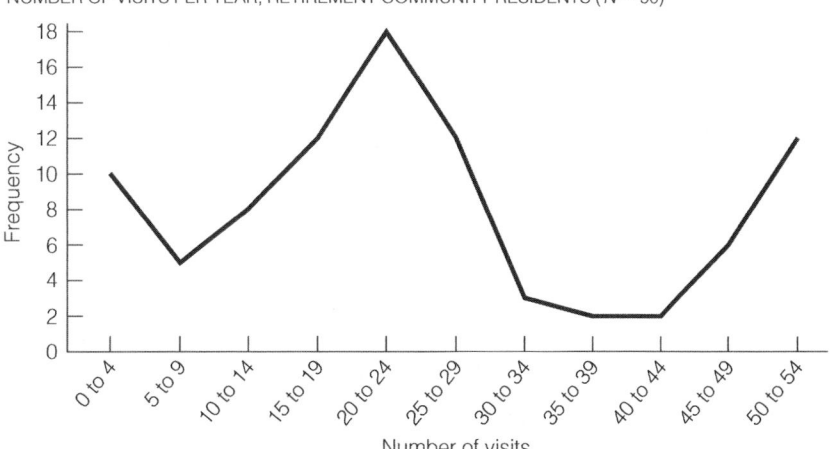

FIGURE 2.7 MARRIAGE AND DIVORCE RATES, 1976–2003, CANADA

Source: Statistics Canada, CANSIM, Tables 053-0001 and 053-0002.

FIGURE 2.8 QUEBEC SOVEREIGNTY REFERENDUM VOTING INTENTIONS, PERCENT FOR, 1996–2005*

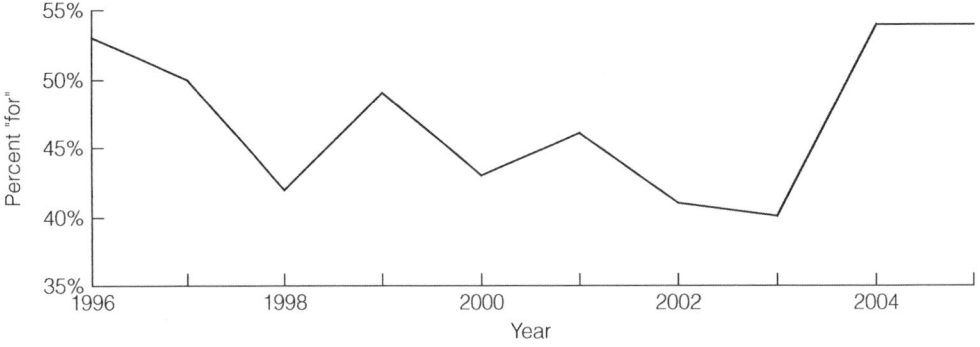

*Based on the polling question "If a referendum were held today on Quebec sovereignty, with an offer of economic and political partnership with the rest of Canada, would you vote for or against Quebec sovereignty?"
Source: Leger Marketing. 2005. *Quebec Survey.*
http://www.legermarketing.com/documents/SPCLM/050516ENG.pdf.

referendum, Quebeckers remain split in their support for sovereignty. In 2005, 54% of Quebeckers said that they would vote in favour of sovereignty in a referendum. During the actual referendum in 1995, 49.4% did vote for sovereignty.

Histograms, stem-and-leaf plots, and frequency polygons are alternative ways of displaying essentially the same message. Thus, the choice between the three techniques is left to the aesthetic pleasures of the researcher. *(For practice in constructing and interpreting histograms, stem-and-leaf plots, and line charts, see problems 2.7b, 2.8e, 2.9d, 2.11, and 2.12.)*

2.8 INTERPRETING STATISTICS: USING PERCENTAGES, FREQUENCY DISTRIBUTIONS, CHARTS, AND GRAPHS TO ANALYZE CHANGING PATTERNS OF WORK-PLACE SURVEILLANCE

A sizable volume of statistical material has been introduced in this chapter, and it will be useful to conclude by focusing on meaning and interpretation. What can you say after you have calculated percentages, built a frequency distribution, or constructed a graph or chart? Remember that statistics are tools to help us analyze information and answer questions. They never speak for themselves and they always have to be understood in the context of some research question or test of a hypothesis. This section will provide an example of interpretation by posing and answering some questions from social science research. The interpretation (words) will be explicitly linked to the statistics (numbers) so that you will be able to see how and why conclusions are developed.

Your New Job and Workplace Surveillance.   Congratulations! You have just landed a job with a major corporation based in the U.S., and you now find yourself in the middle of the lunch hour in your cubicle. Should you log on to the D&D website and briefly engage in your favourite role-playing game? Are you considering sending a chain letter via the company's e-mail system to your old university friends back in Canada or using your desk phone to make an appointment to get a haircut? Before making a decision, consider a series of reports issued by the American Management Association (AMA). These reports suggest that the chances are growing that you may be the subject of workplace surveillance and that your e-mail, telephone, and, more recently, your Internet use may be monitored by your employer.

Overall Trends.   Since 1997, the AMA has surveyed companies about workplace surveillance and monitoring of employees.* The companies in the study are among the largest U.S. businesses, and the percentages in Table 2.19 suggest a relatively high level of employee surveillance and monitoring.

TABLE 2.19   WORKPLACE MONITORING AND SURVEILLANCE, 1997–2001

Does your company engage in monitoring?	Year				
	1997	1998	1999	2000	2001
Yes	63.4	67.1	67.3	78.4	82.0
No	36.6	32.9	32.7	21.6	18.0
Total	100.0	100.0	100.0	100.0	100.0
$N =$	906	1085	1054	2133	1627

*American Management Association. 1998 Workplace Testing: Monitoring and Surveillance. 1999 Workplace Testing: Monitoring and Surveillance. 2000 AMA Research Reports: New York: AMA. 2001 AMA Survey: Workplace Monitoring and Surveillance.

Take a moment to note the components of Table 2.19: the table is numbered, titled, and completely labelled. Each column represents a specific year, and the rows represent responses (Yes or No) to the question "Does your company engage in monitoring?" The total number of companies surveyed in each year is reported across the bottom row. The table is actually five different frequency distributions (one for each year) combined into a single table. The entries in the table are percentages (not frequencies), and each column totals to 100%.

The table shows a gradual increase in monitoring and surveillance between 1997 and 1999 followed by a dramatic increase in 2000 and a more modest increase in 2001. The percentage of companies reporting that they engaged in employee oversight increased from approximately two-thirds in 1999 to over three-quarters in 2000. One possible explanation for the increase is that the AMA included Internet monitoring for the first time in the 2000 survey.

Monitoring and Surveillance in 2001. Although the computer has become an important component of the workday for more and more people, your employer may feel compelled to monitor its use. Table 2.20 reports the percentage of companies that indicated that they practised a specific form of monitoring and surveillance.

Graphs are almost always a more effective method of presenting this type of information. The variable (type of monitoring and surveillance) is nominal level (the "types" are different from each other but do not form a scale) and, with nine possible scores, a bar chart would be preferred to a pie chart. Figure 2.9 clearly shows that monitoring Internet connections was the most common form of surveillance with well over half of the companies (62.8%) practising it. Storage and review of e-mail messages (46.5%) and telephone monitoring (43.3%) were also very common. This graph clearly shows that it would be unwise to surf the net on company time, or use the phone or e-mail for personal business.

TABLE 2.20   MONITORING AND SURVEILLANCE IN 2001

Type of Monitoring and Surveillance	% Yes
Monitoring Internet connections	62.8
Storage and review of e-mail messages	46.5
Telephone use (time spent, numbers called)	43.3
Video surveillance for security purposes	37.7
Storage and review of computer files	36.1
Computer use (time logged on, keystroke counts, etc.)	18.9
Video recording of employee job performance	15.2
Recording and review of telephone conversations	11.9
Storage and review of voice mail messages	7.8

Source: Leger Marketing. 2005. *Quebec Survey*. http://www.legermarketing.com/documents/SPCLM/050516ENG.pdf.

FIGURE 2.9   MONITORING AND SURVEILLANCE IN 2001

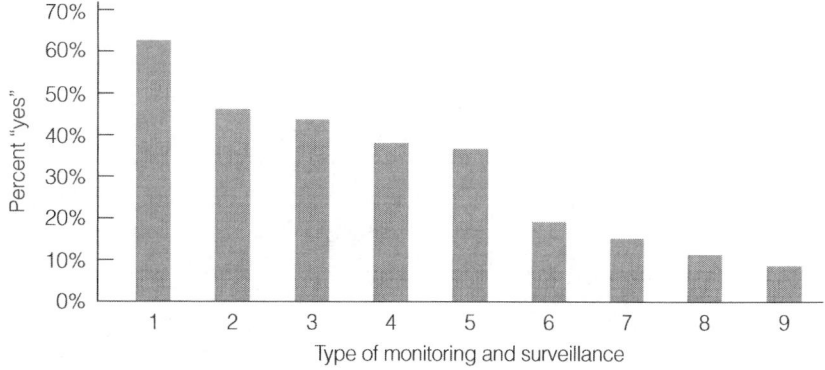

Key for types of monitoring and surveillance:

1. Monitoring Internet connections
2. Storage and review of e-mail messages
3. Telephone use (time spent, numbers called)
4. Video surveillance for security purposes
5. Storage and review of computer files
6. Computer use (time logged on, keystroke counts, etc.)
7. Video recording of employee job performance
8. Recording and review of telephone conversations
9. Storage and review of voice mail messages

Source: Leger Marketing. 2005. *Quebec Survey.* http://www.legermarketing.com/documents/SPCLM/ 050516ENG.pdf.

Monitoring and Surveillance over Time.   What changes occurred in specific workplace monitoring practices between 1997 and 2001? Table 2.21 shows that in 1997 companies engaged in monitoring telephone use and video surveillance for security purposes at comparable rates (about 34%). Many forms of workplace monitoring and surveillance occurred among 10

TABLE 2.21   MONITORING AND SURVEILLANCE, 1997–2001

Type of Monitoring and Surveillance	Percent "Yes"				
	1997	1998	1999	2000	2001
Recording and review of telephone conversations	10.4%	11.2%	10.6%	11.5%	11.9%
Storage and review of voice mail messages	5.3%	5.3%	5.8%	6.8%	7.8%
Storage and review of computer files	13.7%	19.6%	21.4%	30.8%	36.1%
Storage and review of e-mail messages	14.9%	20.2%	27.0%	38.1%	46.5%
Video recording of employee job performance	15.7%	15.6%	16.1%	14.6%	15.2%
Telephone use (time spent, numbers called)	34.4%	40.2%	38.6%	44.0%	43.3%
Computer use (time logged on, keystroke counts, etc.)	16.1%	15.9%	15.2%	19.4%	18.9%
Video surveillance for security purposes	33.7%	32.7%	32.8%	35.3%	37.7%

Source: Leger Marketing. 2005. *Quebec Survey.* http://www.legermarketing.com/documents/ SPCLM/050516ENG.pdf.

and 15% of the companies surveyed. Only 5% of the companies engaged in the storage and review of voice mail messages in 1997.

By 1998, the percentage of companies monitoring the use of their telephones had increased to 40.2%. The percentage of companies reporting that they stored and reviewed e-mail messages and computer files also increased. In 1999, four different forms of monitoring and surveillance were being used by over 20% of the companies: telephone monitoring, video surveillance, and storage and review of e-mail messages and computer files. By 2001, a higher percentage of companies were storing and reviewing e-mail messages than were videotaping for security purposes. Also noteworthy is the percentage of companies indicating that they store and review employee computer files, over one-third (36.1%) of the sample.

Once again, these trends and patterns would be more clearly presented and appreciated in the form of a graph. Since we are looking at changes in percentages over time, a line graph will be appropriate. Figure 2.10 shows the changes for the four most widely used forms of surveillance in 2001 and illustrates relative stability in the rates of some forms of surveillance (e.g., video surveillance for security purposes) and sizable increases in others (e.g., reviewing computer files). The chart also shows a steady increase in the percentage of companies that

FIGURE 2.10   FOUR COMMON TYPES OF MONITORING AND SURVEILLANCE, 1997–2001

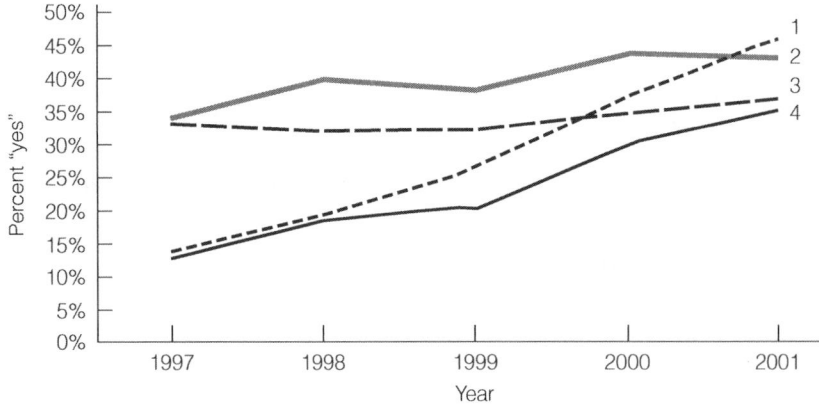

Key for types of monitoring and surveillance:
1. Storage and review of e-mail messages
2. Telephone use (time spent, numbers called)
3. Video surveillance for security purposes
4. Storage and review of computer files

Source: Leger Marketing. 2005. *Quebec Survey.* http://www.legermarketing.com/documents/SPCLM/ 050516ENG.pdf.

monitor employee e-mail messages. In 1997, only about 15% of the companies engaged in this form of monitoring and surveillance. By 2001, this percentage had tripled to 47%, the most common form of surveillance.

Computers may be ubiquitous features of employment in our information-age economy, but these data suggest that the potential for workplace monitoring and surveillance is also increasing. The computer on your desk is a double-edged sword. While it provides you with the necessary tools to do your job, employers are increasingly using the very same technology to watch you.

SUMMARY

1. We considered several different ways of summarizing the distribution of a single variable and, more generally, reporting the results of our research. Our emphasis throughout was on the need to communicate our results clearly and concisely. You will often find that, as you strive to communicate statistical information to others, the meanings of the information will become clearer to you as well.

2. Percentages and proportions, ratios, rates, and percentage change represent several different techniques for enhancing clarity by expressing our results in terms of relative frequency. Percentages and proportions report the relative occurrence of some category of a variable compared with the distribution as a whole. Ratios compare two categories with each other, and rates report the actual occurrences of some phenomenon compared with the number of possible occurrences per some unit of time. Percentage change shows the relative increase or decrease in a variable over time.

3. Frequency distributions are tables that summarize the entire distribution of some variable. It is very common to construct these tables for each variable of interest as the first step in a statistical analysis. Columns for percentages, cumulative frequency, and/or cumulative percentages often enhance the readability of frequency distributions.

4. Pie and bar charts, histograms, stem-and-leaf plots, and line charts or frequency polygons are graphic devices used to express the basic information contained in the frequency distribution in a compact and visually dramatic way.

SUMMARY OF FORMULAS

Proportions	2.1	$p = \dfrac{f}{N}$
Percentage	2.2	$\% = \left(\dfrac{f}{N}\right) \times 100$
Ratios	2.3	$\text{Ratio} = \dfrac{f_1}{f_2}$
Percentage change	2.4	$\text{Percentage change} = \left(\dfrac{f_2 - f_1}{f_1}\right) \times 100$

GLOSSARY

Bar chart. A graphic display device for discrete variables. Categories are represented by bars of equal width, the height of each corresponding to the number (or percentage) of cases in the category.

Class intervals. The categories used in the frequency distributions for interval-ratio variables.

Cumulative frequency. An optional column in a frequency distribution that displays the number of cases within an interval and all preceding intervals.

Cumulative percentage. An optional column in a frequency distribution that displays the percentage of cases within an interval and all preceding intervals.

Frequency distribution. A table that displays the number of cases in each category of a variable.

Frequency polygon. A graphic display device for interval-ratio variables. Class intervals are represented by dots placed over the midpoints, the height of each corresponding to the number (or percentage) of cases in the interval. All dots are connected by straight lines. Same as a line chart.

Histogram. A graphic display device for interval-ratio variables. Class intervals are represented by contiguous bars of equal width (equal to the class limits), the height of each corresponding to the number (or percentage) of cases in the interval.

Line chart. See **Frequency polygon.**

Midpoint. The point exactly halfway between the upper and lower limits of a class interval.

Percentage. The number of cases in a category of a variable divided by the number of cases in all categories of the variable, the entire quantity multiplied by 100.

Percentage change. A statistic that expresses the magnitude of change in a variable from time 1 to time 2.

Pie chart. A graphic display device especially for discrete variables with only a few categories. A circle (the pie) is divided into segments proportional in size to the percentage of cases in each category of the variable.

Proportion. The number of cases in one category of a variable divided by the number of cases in all categories of the variable.

Rate. The number of actual occurrences of some phenomenon or trait divided by the number of possible occurrences per some unit of time.

Ratio. The number of cases in one category divided by the number of cases in some other category.

Real class limits. The class intervals of a frequency distribution when stated as continuous categories.

Stated class limits. The class intervals of a frequency distribution when stated as discrete categories.

Stem-and-leaf plot. A graphic display device for interval-ratio variables. Class intervals are represented by rows of digits of equal width (equal to the class limits), the length of each corresponding to the number of cases in the interval.

MULTIMEDIA RESOURCES

 http://www.healeystatistics.nelson.com

Visit the companion Web site for the first Canadian edition of *Statistics: A Tool for Social Research* to access a wide range of student resources. Begin by clicking on the Student Resources section of the book's Web site to access review quizzes, flash cards, and other study tools.

PROBLEMS

2.1 SOC The tables that follow report the marital status of 20 respondents in two different apartment complexes. *(HINT: Make sure that you have the correct numbers in the numerator and denominator before solving the following problems. For example, problem 2.1a asks for "the percentage of respondents who are married in each complex," and the denominators will be 20 for these two fractions.*

Problem 2.1d, however, asks for the "percentage of the single respondents who live in Complex B," and the denominator for this fraction will be 4 + 6, or 10.

Status	Complex A	Complex B
Married	5	10
Unmarried ("living together")	8	2
Single	4	6
Separated	2	1
Widowed	0	1
Divorced	1	0
	20	20

a. What percentage of the respondents in each complex are married?

b. What is the ratio of single to married respondents at each complex?

c. What proportion of each sample are widowed?

d. What percentage of the single respondents live in Complex B?

e. What is the ratio of the "unmarried/living together" to the married at each complex?

2.2 At Algebra University, the numbers of males and females in the various major fields of study are as follows:

Major	Males	Females	Totals
Humanities	117	83	200
Social sciences	97	132	229
Natural sciences	72	20	92
Business	156	139	295
Nursing	3	35	38
Education	30	15	45
Totals	475	424	899

Read each of the following problems carefully before constructing the fraction and solving for the answer. *(HINT: Be sure you place the proper number in the denominator of the fractions. For example, some problems use the total number of males or females as the denominator but others use the total number of majors.)*

a. What percentage of social science majors are male?

b. What proportion of business majors are female?

c. For the humanities, what is the ratio of males to females?

d. What percentage of the total student body are males?

e. What is the ratio of males to females for the entire sample?

f. What proportion of the nursing majors are male?

g. What percentage of the sample are social science majors?

h. What is the ratio of humanities majors to business majors?

i. What is the ratio of female business majors to female nursing majors?

j. What proportion of the males are education majors?

2.3 [CJ] The city of Pearson, Ontario, has a population of 211,732 and experienced 47 bank robberies, 13 murders, and 23 auto thefts during the past year. Compute a rate for each type of crime per 100,000 population. *(HINT: Make sure that you set up the fraction with size of population in the denominator.)*

2.4 [CJ] The numbers of homicides in five states and five Canadian provinces for the years 1997 and 2001 are as follows:

State	1997		2001	
	Homicides	Population	Homicides	Population
New Jersey	338	8,053,000	336	8,484,431
Iowa	52	2,852,000	50	2,923,179
Alabama	426	4,139,000	379	4,464,356
Texas	1,327	19,439,000	1,332	21,325,018
California	2,579	32,268,000	2,206	34,501,130

(continued next page)

(continued)

Province	1997		2001	
	Homicides	Population	Homicides	Population
Nova Scotia	24	936,100	9	942,900
Quebec	132	7,323,600	149	7,417,700
Ontario	178	11,387,400	170	12,068,300
Manitoba	31	1,137,900	34	1,150,800
British Columbia	116	3,997,100	85	4,141,300

Source: Statistics Canada. Adapted from "Number of homicides, by province/territory, 1961 to 2005," Juristat, Catalogue 85-002-XIE, 26 (6), Table 1. http://www.statcan.ca/english/freepub/85-002-XIE/85-002-XIE 2006006.pdf and "Annual population estimates for July 1, 1971 to 2005, Canada, Provinces and Territories, Annual Demographic Statistics, 2005, Catalogue 91-213-XIB, Table 1.1. http://www.statcan.ca/english/freepub/91-213-XIB/0000591-213-XIB.pdf.

a. Calculate the homicide rate per 100,000 population for each state and each province for each year. Relatively speaking, which state and which province had the highest homicide rates in each year? Which society seems to have the higher homicide rate? Write a describing these results.

b. Using the rates you calculated in part a, calculate the percentage change between 1997 and 2001 for each state and each province. Which states and provinces had the largest increase and decrease? Which society seems to have the largest change in homicide rates? Summarize your results in a paragraph.

2.5 SOC The scores of 15 respondents on four variables are reported below. The numerical codes for the variables are as follows:

Sex	Support for Legalization of Marijuana	Level of Education	Age
1 = Male	1 = In favour	0 = Less than high school	Actual years
2 = Female	2 = Opposed	1 = High school	
		2 = Community college	
		3 = Bachelor's	
		4 = Graduate	

Case Number	Sex	Support for Legalization of Marijuana	Level of Education	Age
1	2	1	1	45
2	1	2	1	48
3	2	1	3	55
4	1	1	2	32
5	2	1	3	33
6	1	1	1	28
7	2	2	0	77
8	1	1	1	50
9	1	2	0	43
10	2	1	1	48
11	1	1	4	33
12	1	1	4	35
13	1	1	0	39
14	2	1	1	25
15	1	1	1	23

a. Construct a frequency distribution for each variable. Include a column for percentages.

b. Construct pie and bar charts to display the distributions of sex, support for legalization of marijuana and level of education.

2.6 SW A local youth service agency has begun a sex education program for teenage girls who have been referred by the youth courts. The girls were given a 20-item test for general knowledge about sex, contraception, and anatomy and physiology upon admission to the program and again after completing the program. The scores of the first 15 girls to complete the program are listed below.

Case	Pretest	Post-test	Case	Pretest	Post-test
A	8	12	I	5	7
B	7	13	J	15	12
C	10	12	K	13	20
D	15	19	L	4	5
E	10	8	M	10	15
F	10	17	N	8	11
G	3	12	O	12	20
H	10	11			

Construct frequency distributions for the pretest and post-test scores. Include a column for percentages. *(HINT: There were 20 items on the test, so the maximum range for these scores is 20. If you use 10 class intervals to display these scores, the interval size will be 2. Because there are no scores of 0 or 1 for either test, you may state the first interval as 2–3. To make comparisons easier, both frequency distributions should have the same intervals.)*

2.7 SOC Sixteen students in their final year of undergraduate studies completed a class to prepare them for the GRE (Graduate Record Examination). Their scores are reported below.

420	345	560	650
459	499	500	657
467	480	505	555
480	520	530	589

These same 16 students were given a test of math and verbal ability to measure their readiness for graduate-level work. Scores are reported below in terms of the percentage of correct answers for each test.

Math Test

67	45	68	70
72	85	90	99
50	73	77	78
52	66	89	75

Verbal Test

89	90	78	77
75	70	56	60
77	78	80	92
98	72	77	82

a. Display each of these variables in a frequency distribution with columns for percentages and cumulative percentages.
b. Construct a histogram, stem-and-leaf plot, and a frequency polygon for these data.

c. Find the upper and lower real limits for the intervals you established.*

2.8 GER Following are reported the number of times 25 residents of a community for senior citizens left their homes for any reason during the past week.

0	2	1	7	3
7	0	2	3	17
14	15	5	0	7
5	21	4	7	6
2	0	10	5	7

a. Construct a frequency distribution to display these data.
b. What are the midpoints of the class intervals?
c. Add columns to the table to display the percentage distribution, cumulative frequency, and cumulative percentages.
d. Find the real limits for the intervals you selected.*
e. Construct a histogram, stem-and-leaf plot, and a frequency polygon to display these data.
f. Write a paragraph summarizing this distribution of scores.

2.9 SOC Twenty-five students completed a questionnaire that measured their attitudes toward interpersonal violence. Respondents who scored high believed that in many situations a person could legitimately use physical force against another person. Respondents who scored low believed that in no situation (or very few situations) could the use of violence be justified.

52	47	17	8	92
53	23	28	9	90
17	63	17	17	23
19	66	10	20	47
20	66	5	25	17

a. Construct a frequency distribution to display these data.
b. What are the midpoints of the class intervals?
c. Add columns to the table to display the percentage distribution, cumulative frequency, and cumulative percentage.
d. Construct a histogram, a stem-and-leaf plot, and a frequency polygon to display these data.

---

*This problem is optional.

e. Write a paragraph summarizing this distribution of scores.

2.10 | PA/CJ | As part of an evaluation of the efficiency of your local police force, you have gathered the following data on police response time to calls for assistance during two different years. (Response times were rounded off to whole minutes.) Convert both frequency distributions into percentages and construct pie charts and bar charts to display the data. Write a paragraph comparing the changes in response time between the two years.

Response Time, 2000	f

Response Time, 2010	f

21 minutes or more	35	21 minutes or more	45
16–20 minutes	75	16–20 minutes	95
11–15 minutes	180	11–15 minutes	155
6–10 minutes	375	6–10 minutes	350
Less than 6 minutes	210	Less than 6 minutes	250
	875		895

2.11 | SOC | Figures 2.11 through 2.13 display trends in crime in Canada. Write a paragraph describing each of these graphs. What similarities and differences can you observe among the three graphs? (e.g., do crime rates always change in the same direction?) Note the differences in the vertical axes from chart to chart—for example,

FIGURE 2.11 HOMICIDE RATES, 1985–2004

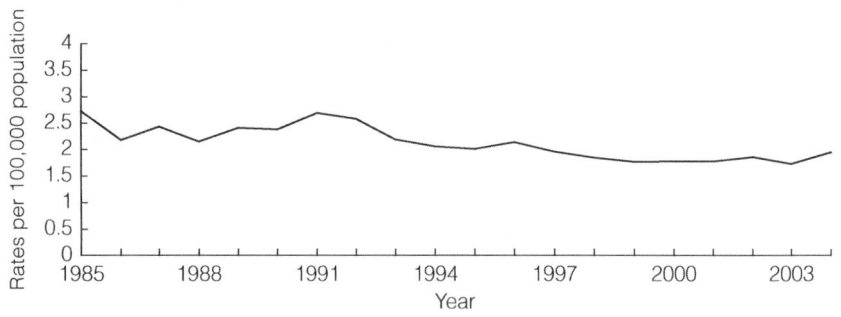

Source: Data from Statistics Canada, CANSIM, Table 252-0013.

FIGURE 2.12 ROBBERY AND SEXUAL ASSAULT RATES, 1985-2004

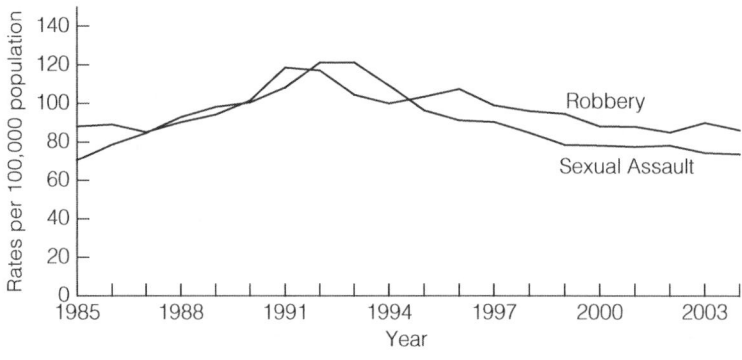

Source: Data from Statistics Canada, CANSIM, Table 252-0013.

FIGURE 2.13   BREAK-INS AND AUTO THEFT RATES, 1985–2004

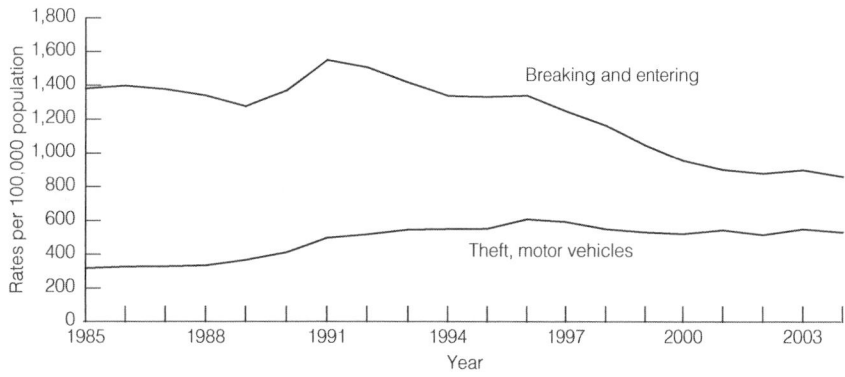

Source: Statistics Canada, CANSIM, Table 252-0013.

for homicide the axis ranges from 0 to 4, while for break-in and auto theft the range is from 0 to 1,800. The latter crimes are far more common, and a scale with larger intervals is needed to display the rates.

2.12 PA The city's engineering department has been keeping track of accidents on a particularly dangerous stretch of highway. Early in the year, the city lowered the speed limit on this highway and increased police patrols. Data on number of accidents before and after the changes are presented below. Did the changes work? Is the highway safer? Construct a line chart to display these two sets of data (use graphics software if available) and write a paragraph describing the changes.

Month	12 Months Before	12 Months After
January	23	25
February	25	21
March	20	18
April	19	12
May	15	9
June	17	10
July	24	11
August	28	15
September	23	17
October	20	14
November	21	18
December	22	20

SPSS for Windows

Using SPSS for Windows to Produce Frequency Distributions and Graphs with the 2004 GSS

The demonstrations and exercises below use the 2004 GSS data set supplied with this text. Click the SPSS icon on your monitor screen to start SPSS for Windows. Load the 2004 GSS by clicking the file name (*GSS.sav*) on the first screen, or by clicking **File, Open,** and **Data** on the **SPSS Data Editor** window. In the **Open Data** dialog box, you may have to change the drive specification to locate the 2004 GSS data. Double-click the file name (*GSS.sav*) to open the data set. You are ready to proceed when you see the message "SPSS Processor is Ready" on the status bar at the bottom of the **SPSS Data Editor** window as shown in Figure 2.14.

The **SPSS Data Editor** window can actually be viewed in one of two unique modes. The **Data View** mode (Figure 2.14), which is the default mode when you start SPSS, displays the data in the data set. Each row represents a particular case and each column a particular variable. By contrast, the **Variable View** mode (Figure 2.15) shows the variables in that data set, where each row represents a particular variable and each column a particular piece of information (e.g., name, label) about the variable. To change from one mode to the other, click the appropriate tab located at the bottom of the **SPSS Data Editor** window. Figure 2.16 describes each toolbar icon, created to provide easy access to popular SPSS functions, located at the top of the **SPSS Data Editor** window.

Before we begin our demonstrations, it is important to note that SPSS provides the user with a variety of options for displaying information about the data file and output on the screen. We highly recommend that you tell SPSS to display lists of variables by name (e.g., *acmyr*) rather than labels (e.g., main activity in past year). Lists displayed this way will be easier to read and to compare to the GSS and Census codebooks in Appendix G. To do this, click **Edit** on the main menu bar at the top of the **SPSS Data Editor** window, and then click **Options** from the drop-down submenu. A dialog box labelled **Options** will

FIGURE 2.14 SPSS DATA EDITOR WINDOW: DATA VIEW

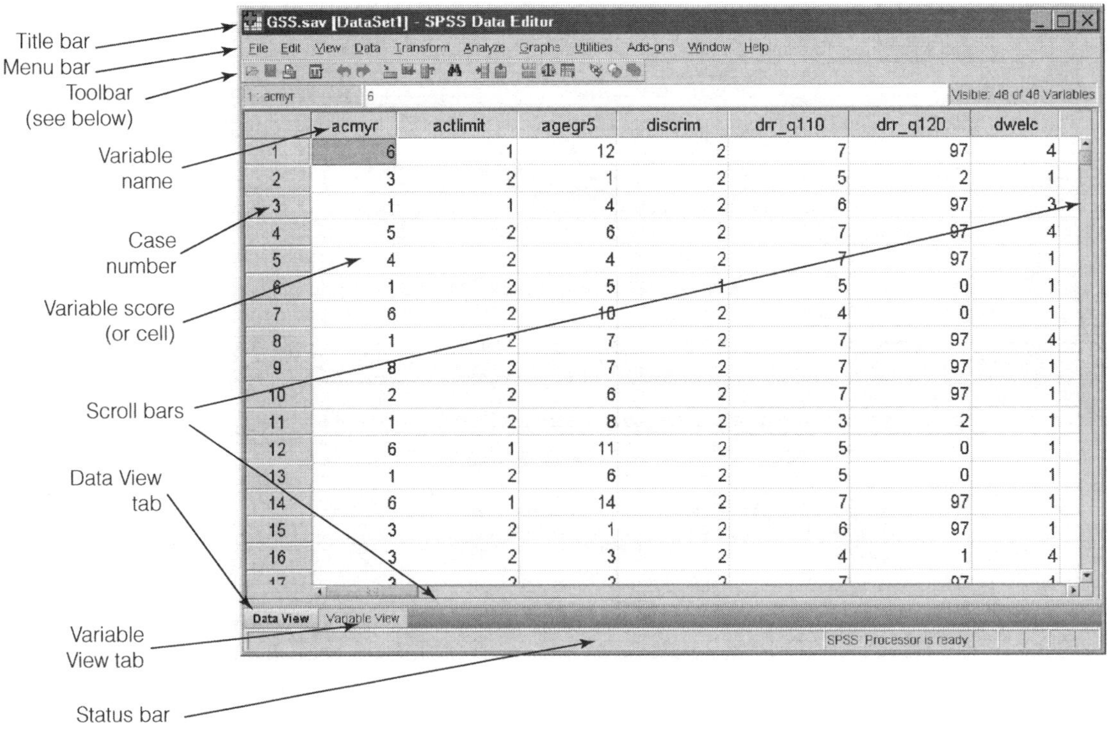

FIGURE 2.15   SPSS DATA EDITOR WINDOW: VARIABLE VIEW

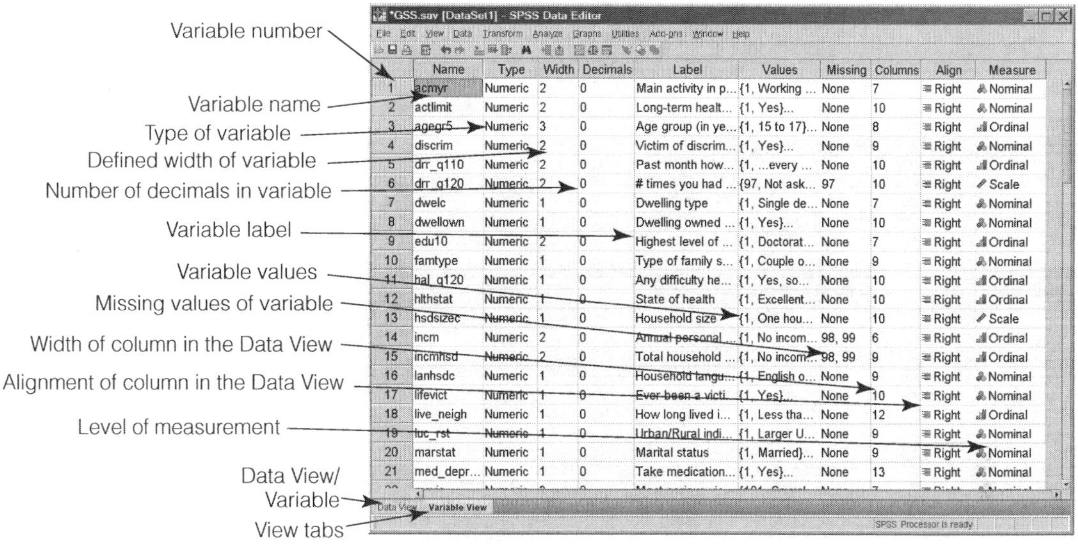

appear with a series of tabs along the top. The **General** options should be displayed but, if not, click on the **General** tab. On the **General** screen, find the box labelled **Variable Lists** and, if they are not already selected, click **Display names** and then **Alphabetical** and then click **OK**. If you make changes, a message may appear on the screen that tells you that changes will take effect the next time a data file is opened. Click **OK**.

FIGURE 2.16   TOOLBAR IN SPSS DATA EDITOR WINDOW

Icon	Action	Icon	Action
	Open a file		Find or replace data
	Save		Insert a new case (row)
	Print		Insert a new variable (column)
	Recently used commands		Split data file
	Undo last action		Weight cases
	Redo last action		Select cases
	Go to a particular case		Show variable labels in Data View
	Go to a particular variable		Use variable sets (restricts variables in Data Editor)
	Variable information		Show all variables

SPSS DEMONSTRATION 2.1 Frequency Distributions

In this demonstration, we will use the **Frequencies** procedure to produce a frequency distribution for the variable *marstat* (marital status).

From the menu bar on the **SPSS Data Editor** window, click **Analyze**. From the menu that drops down, click **Descriptive Statistics** and then **Frequencies**. The **Frequencies** dialog box appears with the variables listed in alphabetical order in the left-hand box. Find *marstat* in the left-hand box by using the slider button or the arrow keys on the right-hand border to scroll through the variable list. As an alternative, type "m," and the cursor will move to the first variable name in the list that begins with the letter "m." In this case, the variable is *marstat,* the variable in which we are interested. Once *marstat* is highlighted, click the arrow button in the centre of the screen to move the variable name to the **Variable(s)** box. The variable name *marstat* should now appear in the box. Click the **OK** button at the bottom of the dialog box, and SPSS will rush off to create the frequency distributions you requested.

The output table (frequency distribution) will be in the **SPSS Output**, or **Viewer**, window that will now be "closest" to you on the screen. As illustrated in Figure 2.17, the output table, along with other information, is in the right-hand box of the window, while the left-hand box contains an "outline" of the entire output. To change the size of the **SPSS Output** window, click on the **Maximize** button, the middle symbol (shaped like either a square or two intersecting squares) in the upper-right-hand corner of the window. The actual output can also be edited by double-clicking on any part of the table. (See Appendix F.6 for more information on editing output.)

The **SPSS Output** window, including the frequency distribution for *marstat,* will look like this:

FIGURE 2.17 SPSS VIEWER (OUTPUT) WINDOW

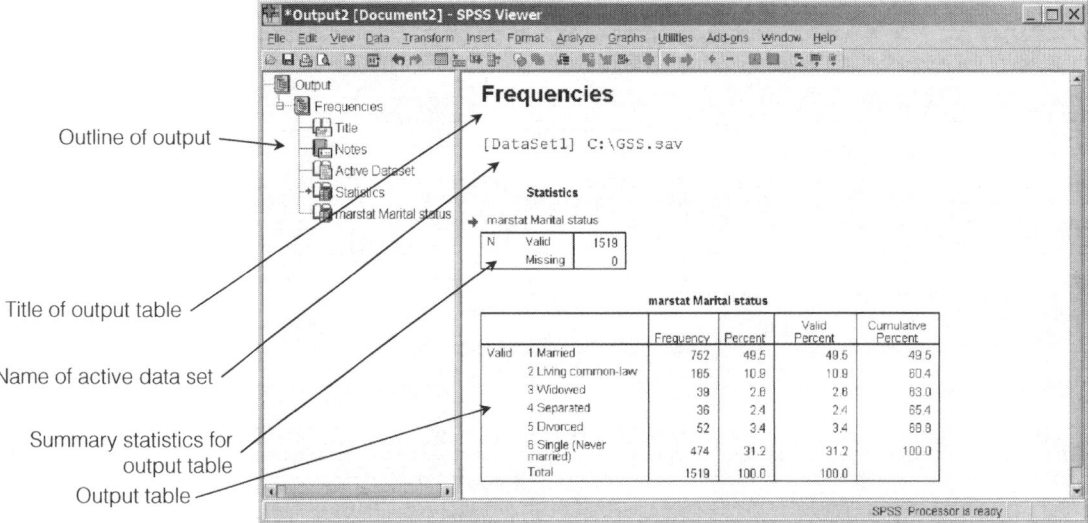

Let's briefly examine the elements of the output table. The variable description, or label, is printed at the top of the output ("Marital status"). The various categories are printed on the left. Moving one column to the right, we find the actual frequencies, or the number of times each score of the variable occurred. We see that 752 of the respondents were married, 165 had common-law status, and so forth.

Next are two columns that report percentages. The entries in the "Percent" column are based on all respondents in the sample. In this case, the denominator would include any respondents, even the ones coded as missing. The "Valid Percent" column eliminates all cases with missing values. Because we almost always ignore missing values, we will pay attention only to the "Valid Percent" column. (Note that because all respondents supplied information on marital status, there is no difference between the two columns.) The final column is a cumulative percentage column (see Table 2.16). For nominal-level variables like *marstat,* this information is not meaningful because the order in which the categories are stated is arbitrary.

The output table in the **SPSS Output** window can be printed or saved by selecting the appropriate command from the **File** menu. You can also transfer the table to a word processor document: right-click on any part of the table, choose **Copy**, right-click on the spot in the word processor document where you want to place the table, and choose **Paste**. Appendix F.7 provides more information on these topics.

As a final note, the total number of cases in the GSS data set is 1,500. This can be verified by scrolling to the bottom of the **SPSS Data Editor** window, where you will find a total of 1,500 rows. However, the "total" number of cases in the output table above is 1,519. The reason for the difference is that the GSS data set is weighted to correct for sampling bias. Like many social surveys, the GSS under- and over-samples various groups of individuals. Some individuals are therefore more likely than others to be included in the GSS sample. The weight variable included with the GSS, *wght_per,* corrects for this bias. Once you open the *GSS.sav* file, the weight variable is automatically "turned on." So, you are really analyzing 1,519, not 1,500, individuals when using this data file. (See Appendix G.4 for more information on this topic.)

SPSS DEMONSTRATION 2.2 Graphs and Charts

SPSS for Windows can produce a variety of graphs and charts, and we will use the program to produce a bar chart and a line chart (frequency polygon) in this demonstration. To conserve space, we will keep the choices as simple as possible, but you should explore the options for yourself. For any questions you might have that are not answered in this demonstration, click **Help** on the main menu bar.

To produce a bar chart, first click **Graphs** on the main menu bar and then click **Legacy Dialogs** and then **Bar**. The **Bar Charts** dialog box appears with three choices for the type of graph we want. The **Simple** option is already highlighted, and this is the one we want. Make sure that **Summaries for groups of cases** in the **Data in Chart Are** box is selected and then click **Define** at the bottom of the dialog box. The **Define Simple Bar** dialog box appears with variable names listed on the left. Choose *edu10* (highest level of education) from the variable list by moving the cursor to highlight this variable name. Click the arrow button in the middle of the screen to move *edu10* to the **Category Axis** text box.

Note the **Bars Represent** box is above the **Category Axis** box. The options in this box give you control over the vertical axis of the graph, which can be calibrated in frequencies, percentages, or cumulative frequencies or percentages. Let's choose **N of cases** (frequencies), the option that is already selected. Click **OK** in the **Define Simple Bar** dialog box, and the following bar chart will be produced. (Note, to save space only the output graph, and not the whole **SPSS Output** window, is shown. Also, this output has been slightly edited for clarity, and will not exactly match the output on your screen.)

Figure 2.18 reveals that the most common levels of education for this sample are "Bachelor's degree" and "Some secondary/high school." The least common level is "Elementary school/no schooling."

The procedures for producing a line chart are very similar to those for a bar chart. Click **Graphs**, then **Legacy Dialogs**, and then **Line**. The **Line Charts** dialog box will appear with the **Simple** option already chosen. This is the one we want, so click **Define**, and the **Define Simple Line** dialog box appears. Your choices here are the same as in the **Define Simple Bar** dialog box. Line charts are appropriate for interval-ratio data, so let's use *numevact_c* (average number of nightly activities conducted per month) for this demonstration.

FIGURE 2.18

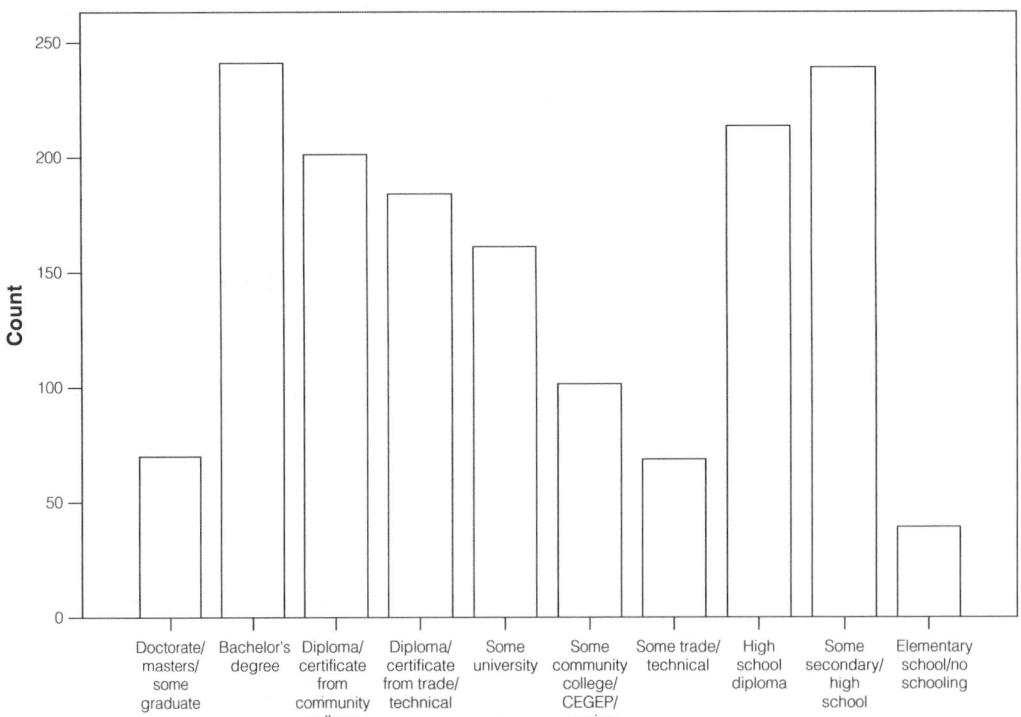

Highest level of education: 10 grps

Select *numevact_c* from the variable list on the left and click the arrow button in the middle of the screen to move *numevact_c* to the **Category Axis** box. Note that the options in the **Lines Represents** box are the same as in the **Simple Bar** dialog box. We want the line to represent **N of cases** (frequencies), the option that has been already selected. Click **OK** in the **Define Simple Line** dialog box, and the line chart shown in Figure 2.19 will be produced:

The line chart shows us that the sample is clustered between 10 and 30 evening activities per month. Because respondents engaged in 62 or more evening activities are aggregated into a single value, the line dramatically increases at the end of the chart. It is common for Statistics Canada, which produces the General Social Survey, to collapse values of variables into wider categories to protect the anonymity of individual survey respondents. This is the case for *numevact_c,* where each respondent engaged in 62, 63, 64, 65, and so on activities were placed into the single category of "62 and more." Don't forget to **Save** or **Print** the charts if you wish.

FIGURE 2.19

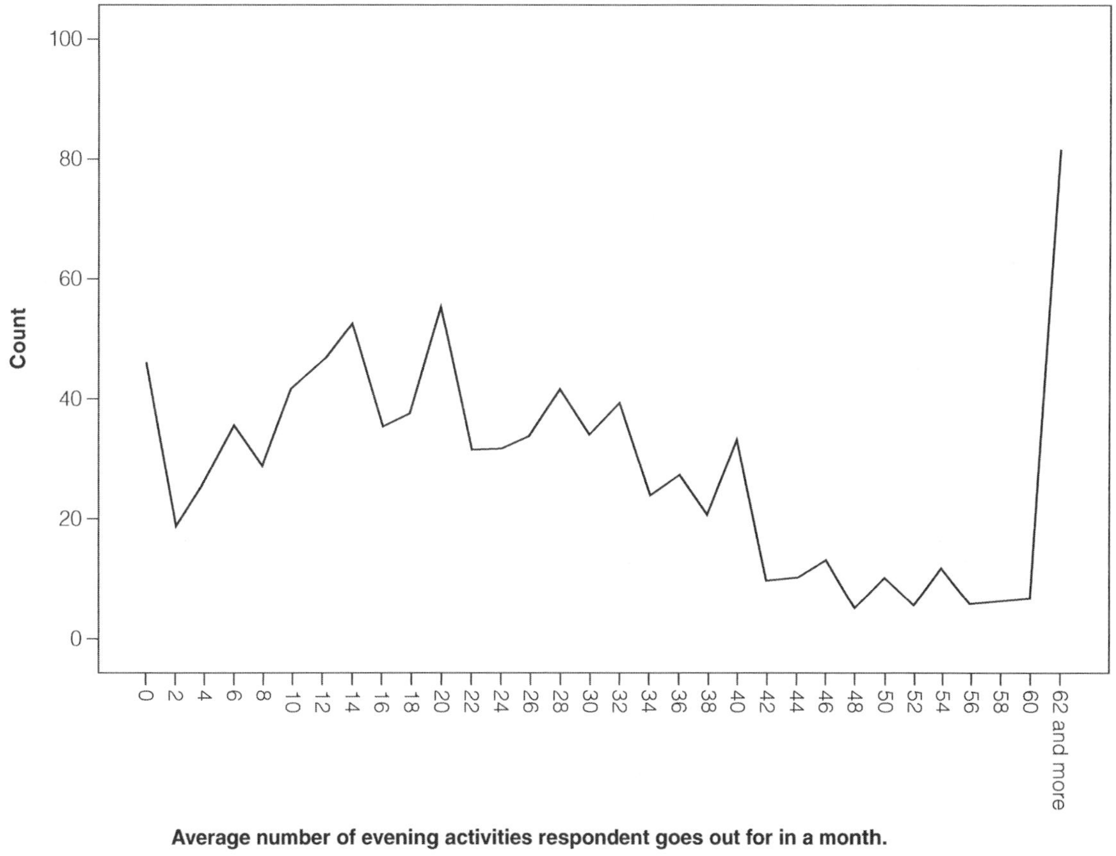

Average number of evening activities respondent goes out for in a month.

Exercises (using *GSS.sav*)

2.1 Get frequency distributions for five nominal or ordinal variables in the GSS data set. Write a sentence or two summarizing each frequency distribution. Your description should clearly identify the most and least common scores and any other noteworthy patterns you observe.

2.2 Get a bar chart for *hlthstat* (state of health of the respondent) and *hsdsizec* (household size). Write a sentence or two of interpretation for each chart.

2.3 Get a line chart for *drr_q120* (# times you had 5+ drinks past month) and *wkwehr_c* (# of hours usually worked per week). Write a sentence or two of interpretation for each chart.

3 MEASURES OF CENTRAL TENDENCY

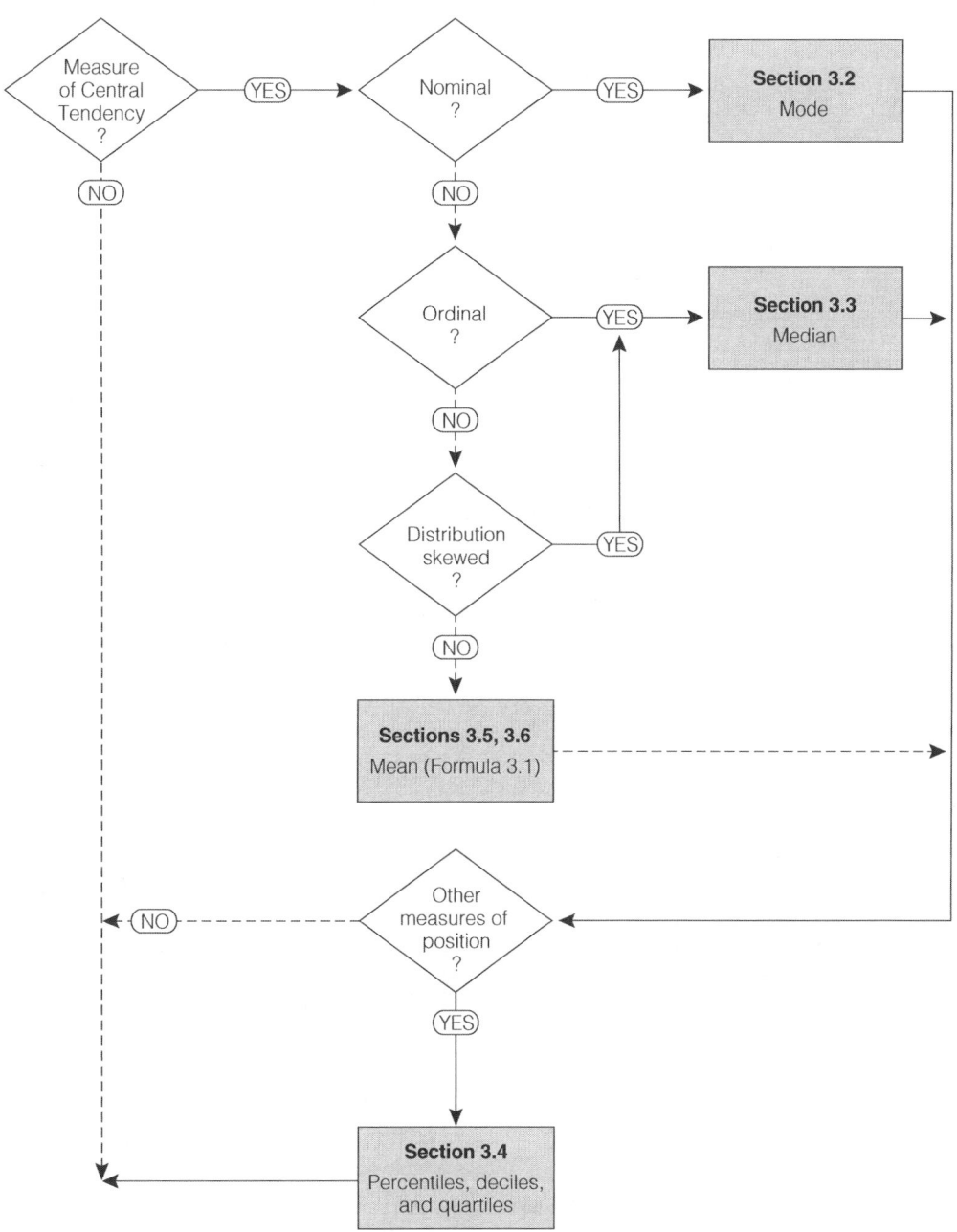

LEARNING OBJECTIVES   By the end of this chapter, you will be able to

1. Explain the purposes of measures of central tendency and interpret the information they convey.
2. Calculate, explain, and compare and contrast the mode, median, and mean.
3. Explain the mathematical characteristics of the mean.
4. Select an appropriate measure of central tendency according to level of measurement and skew.

3.1 INTRODUCTION

One clear benefit of frequency distributions, graphs, and charts is that they summarize the overall shape of a distribution of scores in a way that can be quickly comprehended. Often, however, you will need to report more detailed information about the distribution. Specifically, two additional kinds of statistics are almost always useful: some idea of the typical or average case in the distribution (e.g., "the average starting salary for social workers is $49,000 per year") and some idea of how much variety or heterogeneity there is in the distribution ("In this province, starting salaries for social workers range from $43,000 per year to $55,000 per year"). The first kind of statistic, called **measures of central tendency,** will be the subject of this chapter. The second kind of statistic, measures of dispersion, will be presented in Chapter 4.

The three commonly used measures of central tendency—the mode, median, and mean—are all probably familiar to you. All three summarize an entire distribution of scores by describing the most common score (the mode), the middle case (the median), or the typical score of the cases (the mean) of that distribution. These statistics are powerful because they can reduce huge arrays of data to a single, easily understood number. Remember that the central purpose of descriptive statistics is to summarize or "reduce" data.

Even though they share a common purpose, the three measures of central tendency are quite different from each other. In fact, they will have the same value only under specific and limited conditions. As we shall see, they vary in terms of level-of-measurement considerations and, perhaps more importantly, they also vary in terms of how they define central tendency—they will not necessarily identify the same score or case as "typical." Thus, your choice of an appropriate measure of central tendency will depend in part on the way you measure the variable and in part on the purpose of the research.

3.2 THE MODE

The **mode** of any distribution is the value that occurs most frequently. For example, in the set of scores 58, 82, 82, 90, 98, the mode is 82 because it occurs twice and the other scores occur only once.

The mode is, relatively speaking, a rather simple statistic, most useful when you want a "quick and easy" indicator of central tendency and

TABLE 3.1   RELIGIOUS AFFILIATION, CANADA, 2001

Denomination	Frequency
Catholic	12,936,905
Protestant	8,654,850
Christian Orthodox	479,620
Other Christian	780,450
Muslim	579,640
Jewish	329,995
Buddhist	300,345
Hindu	297,200
Sikh	278,410
Eastern religions	37,550
Other religions	63,975
None	4,900,090
Total population	**29,639,035**

Source: Statistics Canada. http://www40.statcan.ca/ l01/cst01/demo30b.htm.

when you are working with nominal-level variables. In fact, the mode is the only measure of central tendency that can be used with nominal-level variables. Such variables do not, of course, have numerical "scores" per se, and the mode of a nominally measured variable would be its largest category. For example, Table 3.1 reports the religious affiliations of Canadians. The mode of this distribution, the single largest category, is Catholic.

If a researcher desires to report only the most popular or common value of a distribution, or if the variable under consideration is nominal, then the mode is the appropriate measure of central tendency. However, keep in mind that the mode does have several limitations. First, some distributions have no mode at all (see Table 2.6) or so many modes that the statistic loses all meaning. Second, with ordinal and interval-ratio data, the modal score may not be central to the distribution as a whole. That is, *most common* does not necessarily mean "typical" in the sense of identifying the centre of the distribution. For example, consider the rather unusual (but not impossible) distribution of scores on an introductory sociology exam as illustrated in Table 3.2. The mode of the distribution is 93. Is this score very close to the majority of the scores? If the instructor summarized this distribution by reporting only the modal score, would he or she be conveying an accurate picture of the distribution as a whole? *(For practice in finding and interpreting the mode, see problems 3.1 to 3.7.)*

3.3 THE MEDIAN

Unlike the mode, the **median (Md)** always represents the exact centre of a distribution of scores. The median is the score of the case that is in the exact middle of a distribution: half the cases have scores higher and half the

TABLE 3.2 A DISTRIBUTION OF EXAM SCORES

Scores	Frequency
58	2
60	2
62	3
64	2
66	3
67	4
68	1
69	1
70	2
93	5
	$N = 25$

cases have scores lower than the case with the median score. Thus, if the median family income for a community is $35,000, half the families earn more than $35,000 and half earn less.

Before finding the median, the cases must be placed in order from the highest to the lowest score—or from the lowest to the highest. Once this is done, find the central or middle case. The median is the score associated with that case. If five students received grades of 93, 87, 80, 75, and 61 on a test, the median would be 80, the score that splits the distribution into two equal halves.

When the number of cases (N) is odd, the value of the median is unambiguous because there will always be a middle case. With an even number of cases, however, there will be two middle cases; in this situation, the median is defined as the score exactly halfway between the scores of the two middle cases.

To illustrate, assume that seven students were asked to indicate their level of support for the interuniversity athletic program at their universities on a scale ranging from 10 (indicating great support) to 0 (no support). After arranging their responses from high to low, you can find the median by locating the case that divides the distribution into two equal halves. With a total of seven cases, the middle case would be the fourth case, as there will be three cases above and three cases below this case. If the seven scores were 10, 10, 8, 7, 5, 4, and 2, then the median is 7, the score of the fourth case.

To summarize: when N is odd, find the middle case by adding 1 to N and then dividing that sum by 2. With an N of 7, the median is the score associated with the $(7 + 1)/2$, or fourth, case. If N had been 21, the median would be the score associated with the $(21 + 1)/2$, or 11th, case.

Now, if we make N an even number (8) by adding a student to the sample whose support for athletics was measured as a 1, we would no longer have a single middle case. The ordered distribution of scores would now be 10, 10, 8, 7, 5, 4, 2, 1; any value between 7 and 5 would technically satisfy the definition of a median (that is, would split the distribution into two equal halves of four cases each). This ambiguity is resolved by defining the median as the average of the scores of the two middle cases. In the example above, the median would be defined as $(7 + 5)/2$, or 6.

To summarize: to identify the two middle cases when N is an even number, divide N by 2 to find the first middle case and then increase that number by 1 to find the second middle case. In the example above with eight cases, the first middle case would be the fourth case ($N/2 = 4$) and the second middle case would be the $(N/2) + 1$, or fifth, case. If N had been 142, the first middle case would have been the 71st case and the second the 72nd case. Remember that the median is defined as the average of the scores associated with the two middle cases.*

The same strategy is applied to obtain the median for aggregate data in a frequency distribution. For example, Table 3.3, derived from the previous table, shows the distribution of exam scores. Cumulative frequencies are added to more easily locate the median.

Because the number of cases is odd, the median in this distribution is the score associated with the 13th case, or $(25 + 1)/2$. By adding frequencies, starting with the lowest score, we see that the 13th case is associated with the score 67. Table 3.4 summarizes the procedures for finding the median.

TABLE 3.3   COMPUTING THE MEDIAN FOR AGGREGATE DATA IN A FREQUENCY DISTRIBUTION

Score	Frequency	Cumulative Frequency
58	2	2
60	2	4
62	3	7
64	2	9
66	3	12
67	4	16
68	1	17
69	1	18
70	2	20
93	5	25
	$N = 25$	

*If the middle cases have the same score, that score is defined as the median. In the distribution 10, 10, 8, 6, 6, 4, 2, 1, the middle cases both have scores of 6 and, thus, the median would be defined as 6.

TABLE 3.4 FINDING THE MEDIAN

Situation	Location of Md	Procedure to Find Md	Examples
N is odd	The Md is the score of the middle case.	Add 1 to N and divide by 2. This is the number of the middle case. The Md is the score of this case.	If N is 13, the Md is the score of the (13 + 1)/2, or seventh, case. If N is 365, the Md would be the score of the (365 + 1)/2, or 183rd case.
N is even	The Md is halfway between the scores of the two middle cases.	Divide N by 2 to find the first middle case and then increase that number by 1 to find the second middle case. The Md is the average of the scores of the two middle cases.	If N is 14, the Md is the score halfway between the scores of the seventh and eighth cases. If N is 366, the Md is the score halfway between the scores of the 183rd and 184th cases.

Because the median requires that scores be ranked from high to low, it cannot be calculated for variables measured at the nominal level. Remember that the scores of nominal-level variables cannot be ordered or ranked: the scores are different from each other but do not form a mathematical scale of any sort. The median can be found for either ordinal or interval-ratio data but is generally more appropriate for the former. *(The median may be found for any problem at the end of this chapter.)*

3.4 OTHER MEASURES OF POSITION: PERCENTILES, DECILES, AND QUARTILES*

In addition to serving as a measure of central tendency, the median is also a member of a class of statistics that measure position or location. The median identifies the exact middle of a distribution, but it is sometimes useful to locate other points as well. We may want to know, for example, the scores that split the distribution into thirds or fourths, or the point below which a given percentage of the cases fall. A familiar application of these measures would be scores on standardized tests, which are often reported in terms of location (for example, "a score of 476 is higher than 46% of the scores").

One commonly used statistic for reporting position is the **percentile.** A percentile identifies the point below which a specific percentage of cases fall. If a score of 476 is reported as the 46th percentile, this means that 46% of the cases had scores lower than 476. To find a percentile, first arrange the scores in order. Next, multiply the number of cases (N) by the proportional

---

*This section is optional.

value of the percentile. For example, the proportional value for the 46th percentile would be 0.46. The resultant value identifies the number of the case that marks the percentile. To find the 37th percentile for a sample of 78 cases, multiply 78 by .37. The result is 28.86, and the 37th percentile would be 86/100 of the distance between the scores of the 28th and 29th cases. In most cases, we would probably round off 28.86 to 29, and call the score of the 29th case the 37th percentile. The slight inaccuracy would be worth the savings in time and calculational effort.

Note that, if we think in terms of percentiles, then the median is simply the 50th percentile and, in our example above, we would find the median by multiplying 78 by .50, finding the 39th case, and declaring the score of that case to be the 50th percentile. Notice again that we are cutting some corners here. Technically, the median would be the score halfway between the two middle cases (the 39th and 40th cases), but it is unlikely that this inaccuracy would be very significant.

Some other commonly used measures of position are **deciles** and **quartiles.** Deciles divide the distribution of scores into tenths. So, the first decile is the point below which 10% of the cases fall and is equivalent to the 10th percentile. The fifth decile is also the same as the 50th percentile, which is the same as (you guessed it) the median. Quartiles divide the distribution into quarters, and the first quartile is the same as the 25th percentile, the second quartile is the 50th percentile, and the third quartile is the 75th percentile. Any of these measures can be found by the method described above for percentiles. Remember that multiplying N by the proportional value of the percentile, decile, or quartile gives the number of the appropriate *case,* and it's the *score* of the case that actually marks the location. Also remember that this technique cuts some (probably minor) computational corners, and use it with caution. *(Quartiles, deciles, and percentiles may be found for any ordinal or interval-ratio variable in the problems at the end of this chapter.)*

3.5 THE MEAN

The **mean** ($\overline{X}$, read this as "ex-bar"),* or arithmetic average, is by far the most commonly used measure of central tendency. It reports the average score of a distribution, and its calculation is straightforward: to compute the mean, add the scores and then divide by the number of scores (N). To illustrate: a birth control clinic administered a 20-item test of general knowledge about contraception to 10 clients. The number of correct responses was 2, 10, 15, 11, 9, 16, 18, 10, 11, 7. To find the mean of this distribution, add the scores (total = 109) and divide by the number of scores (10). The result (10.9) is the average score on the test.

---

*This is the symbol for the mean of a sample. The mean of a population is symbolized with the Greek letter mu (μ—read this symbol as "mew").

The mathematical formula for the mean is

FORMULA 3.1

$$\bar{X} = \frac{\Sigma(X_i)}{N}$$

where $\bar{X}$ = the mean
$\Sigma(X_i)$ = the summation of the scores
N = the number of cases

Since this formula introduces some new symbols, let us take a moment to consider it. First, the symbol Σ (uppercase Greek letter sigma) is a mathematical operator just like the plus sign ($+$) or divide sign ($\div$). It stands for "the summation of" and directs us to add whatever quantities are stated immediately following it.* The second new symbol is X_i (**"X sub i"**), which refers to any single score—the "ith" score. If we wished to refer to a particular score in the distribution, the specific number of the score could replace the subscript. Thus, X_1 would refer to the first score, X_2 to the second, X_{26} to the 26th, and so forth. The operation of adding all the scores is symbolized as $\Sigma(X_i)$.

This combination of symbols directs us to sum the scores, beginning with the first score and ending with the last score in the distribution. Thus, Formula 3.1 states in symbols what has already been stated in words (to calculate the mean, add the scores and divide by the number of scores), but in a very succinct and precise way.

We can also readily obtain the mean for aggregate data in a frequency distribution using a slightly modified version of Formula 3.1. The formula for aggregate data is

FORMULA 3.2

$$\bar{X} = \frac{\Sigma(fX)}{N}$$

where $\bar{X}$ = the mean
$\Sigma(fX)$ = the summation of each score multiplied by its frequency
N = the number of cases

Table 3.5 demonstrates the calculation of the mean for the distribution of exam scores described in Table 3.2.

The first (X_i) and second (f) columns in the distribution show each score and its frequency respectively. The third column (fX) displays the product of multiplying these numbers together. For example, the first score 58 is multiplied by its frequency 2, which equals 116. The mean of the

---

*See Appendix H (Basic Mathematics Review) for further information on the summation sign and on summation operations.

TABLE 3.5 COMPUTING THE MEAN FOR AGGREGATE DATA IN A FREQUENCY DISTRIBUTION

Scores (X_i)	Frequency (f)	Frequency $\times$ Score (fX)
58	2	116
60	2	120
62	3	186
64	2	128
66	3	198
67	4	268
68	1	68
69	1	69
70	2	140
93	5	465
	$N = 25$	$\Sigma(fX) = 1758$

frequency distribution is the sum of each score multiplied by its frequency, labelled $\Sigma(fX)$, divided by the number of cases (N),

$$\overline{X} = \frac{\Sigma(fX)}{N} = \frac{1758}{25} = 70.32$$

Thus, these 25 students have an average exam score of 70.32.

Since computation of the mean requires addition and division, it should be used with variables measured at the interval-ratio level. However, researchers do calculate the mean for variables measured at the ordinal level, because the mean is much more flexible than the median and is a central feature of many interesting and powerful advanced statistical techniques. Thus, if the researcher plans to do any more than merely describe his or her data, the mean will probably be the preferable measure of central tendency even for ordinal-level variables. *(For practice in computing the mean, see any of the problems at the end of this chapter.)*

3.6 SOME CHARACTERISTICS OF THE MEAN

The mean is the most commonly used measure of central tendency, and we will consider its mathematical and statistical characteristics in some detail. First, the mean is always the centre of any distribution of scores in the sense that it is the point around which all of the scores cancel out. Symbolically:

$$\sum (X_i - \overline{X}) = 0$$

Or, if we take each score in a distribution, subtract the mean from it, and add all of the differences, the resultant sum will always be zero. To illustrate, consider the following set of test scores: 65, 73, 77, 85, and 90. The mean of these five scores is 390/5, or 78, and the sum of the differences is presented in Table 3.6.

TABLE 3.6 A DEMONSTRATION SHOWING THAT ALL
SCORES CANCEL OUT AROUND THE MEAN

X_i	$(X_i - \bar{X})$
65	$65 - 78 = -13$
73	$73 - 78 = -5$
77	$77 - 78 = -1$
85	$85 - 78 = 7$
90	$90 - 78 = 12$
$\Sigma(X_i) = 390$	$\Sigma(X_i - \bar{X}) = 0$

The total of the negative differences (-19) is exactly equal to the total of the positive differences ($+19$), as will always be the case. This algebraic relationship between the scores and the mean indicates that the mean is a good descriptive measure of the centrality of scores. You may think of the mean as a fulcrum that exactly balances all of the scores.

A second characteristic of the mean is called the "least squares" principle, a characteristic that is expressed in the statement:

$$\sum (X_i - \bar{X})^2 = \text{minimum}$$

or: the mean is the point in a distribution around which the variation of the scores (as indicated by the squared differences) is minimized. If the differences between the scores and the mean are squared and then added, the resultant sum will be less than the sum of the squared differences between the scores and any other point in the distribution.

To illustrate this principle, consider the distribution of five scores mentioned above: 65, 73, 77, 85, and 90. The differences between the scores and the mean have already been found. As illustrated in Table 3.7, if we square and sum these differences, we would get a total of 388. If we performed that same mathematical operation with any number other than the mean—say the value 77—the resultant sum would be greater than 388. Table 3.7 illustrates this point by showing that the sum of the squared differences around 77 is 393, a value greater than 388.

In a sense, the least-squares principle merely underlines the fact that the mean is closer to all of the scores than the other measures of central tendency. However, this characteristic of the mean is also the foundation of some of the most important techniques in statistics, including the variance and standard deviation (Chapter 4) and correlation and regression (Chapters 15 and 17).

The final important characteristic of the mean is that every score in the distribution affects it. The mode (which is only the most common score) and the median (which deals only with the score of the middle case or cases) are not so affected. This quality is both an advantage and a disadvantage. On one hand, the mean utilizes all the available information—every score

TABLE 3.7   A DEMONSTRATION SHOWING THAT THE MEAN IS THE POINT OF MINIMIZED VARIATION

X_i	$(X_i - \bar{X})$	$(X_i - \bar{X})^2$	$(X_i - 77)^2$
65	$65 - 78 = -13$	$(-13)^2 = 169$	$(65 - 77)^2 = (-12)^2 = 144$
73	$73 - 78 = -5$	$(-5)^2 = 25$	$(73 - 77)^2 = (-4)^2 = 16$
77	$77 - 78 = -1$	$(-1)^2 = 1$	$(77 - 77)^2 = (0)^2 = 0$
85	$85 - 78 = 7$	$(7)^2 = 49$	$(85 - 77)^2 = (8)^2 = 64$
90	$90 - 78 = 12$	$(12)^2 = 144$	$(90 - 77)^2 = (13)^2 = 169$
$\Sigma(X_i) = 390$	$\Sigma(X_i - \bar{X}) = 0$	$\Sigma(X_i - \bar{X})^2 = 388$	$\Sigma(X_i - 77)^2 = 393$

in the distribution affects the mean. On the other hand, when a distribution has a few very high or very low scores, the mean may become a very misleading measure of centrality.

To illustrate, consider the following set of five scores: 15, 20, 25, 30, 35. Both the mean and the median of this distribution are 25. ($\bar{X} = 125/5 = 25$. Md = score of third case = 25.) What will happen if we change the last score from 35 to 3500? This change would not affect the median at all; it would remain at exactly 25. This is because the median is based only on the score of the middle case and is not affected by changes in the scores of other cases in the distribution.

The mean, in contrast, would be very much affected because it takes *all* scores into account. The mean would become 3590/5, or 718. Clearly, the one extreme score in the data set disproportionately affects the mean. For a distribution that has a few scores much higher or lower than the other scores, the mean may present a very misleading picture of the typical or central score. *(For practice in dealing with the effects of extreme scores on means and medians, see problems 3.11, 3.13, 3.14, and 3.15.)*

The general principle to remember is that, relative to the median, the mean is always pulled in the direction of extreme scores (i.e., scores that are much higher or lower than other scores). The mean and median will have the same value when and only when a distribution is symmetrical. When a distribution has some extremely high scores (this is called a positive **skew**), the mean will always have a greater numerical value than the median. If the distribution has some very low scores (a negative skew), the mean will be lower in value than the median. Figures 3.1 to 3.3 depict three different frequency polygons that demonstrate these relationships.

These relationships between medians and means also have a practical value. For one thing, a quick comparison of the median and mean will always tell you if a distribution is skewed and the direction of the skew. If the mean is less than the median, the distribution has a negative skew. If the mean is greater than the median, the distribution has a positive skew.

FIGURE 3.1   A POSITIVELY SKEWED DISTRIBUTION (The mean is greater in value than the median.)

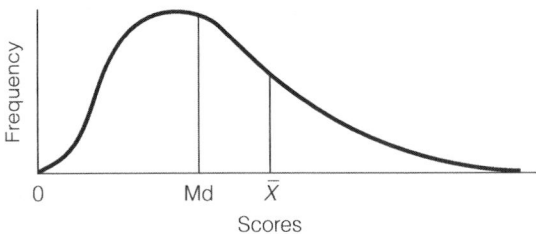

FIGURE 3.2   A NEGATIVELY SKEWED DISTRIBUTION (The mean is less than the median.)

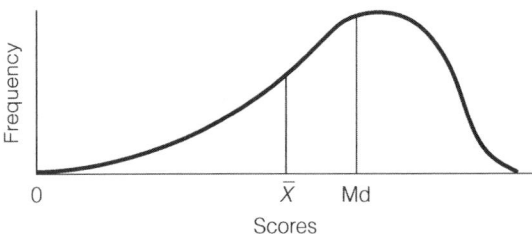

FIGURE 3.3   AN UNSKEWED, SYMMETRICAL DISTRIBUTION (The mean and median are equal.)

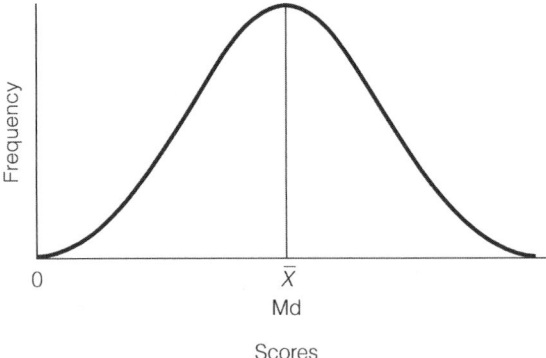

Second, these characteristics of the mean and median also provide a simple and effective way to "lie" with statistics. For example, if you want to maximize the average score of a positively skewed distribution, report the mean. Income data usually have a positive skew (there are only a few very wealthy people). If you want to impress someone with the general affluence of a mixed-income community, report the mean. If you want a lower figure, report the median.

FIGURE 3.4   SYMMETRICAL DISTRIBUTION OF HOURS SPENT SLEEPING EACH NIGHT BY ADULT CANADIANS

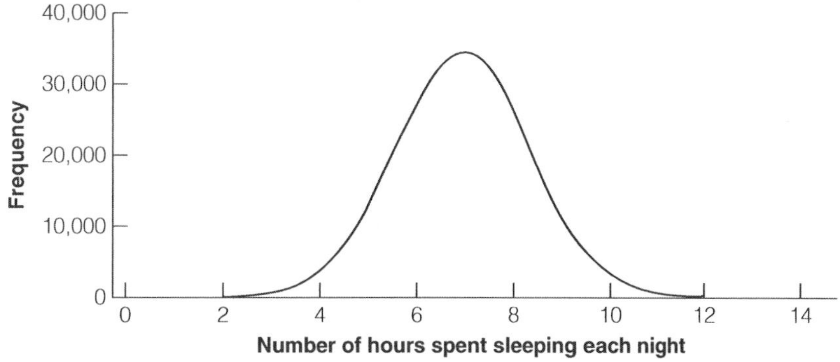

Source: Data from Statistics Canada, 2001 Canadian Community Health Survey, PUMF.

So, which measure is most appropriate for each distribution? If the distribution is skewed, this will depend on what point the researcher wishes to make but, as a rule, either both statistics or the median alone should be reported. If the distribution is unskewed, it makes no difference what measure is used. To illustrate, take a look at Figure 3.4, which shows the frequency polygon for the number of hours spent sleeping each night by adults in Canada. The data in this chart come from the 2001 Canadian Community Health Survey, Statistics Canada's main health survey used to collect information on the health status and health determinants of 122,000 Canadians. As you can see, the shape of the distribution of hours spent sleeping is symmetrical, where the mean and median both equal 7.0 hours.

3.7 CHOOSING A MEASURE OF CENTRAL TENDENCY

The selection of a measure of central tendency should, in general, be based on level-of-measurement considerations and on an evaluation of what each of the three statistics shows. Remember that the mode, median, and mean are three different statistics that will be the same value only under certain, specific conditions (i.e., for symmetrical distributions with one mode). Each of the three has its own message to report and, in many circumstances, you might want to report all three. When choosing a single measure of central tendency, the following guidelines may be helpful:

Use the mode when

1. Variables are measured at the nominal level.
2. You want a quick and easy measure for ordinal and interval-ratio variables.
3. You want to report the most common score.

The cost of a litre of gasoline in Canada is affected by costs for crude oil, refining, and retailing, as well as by government taxes. Gasoline is taxed by both federal and provincial/territorial governments. The table below shows the tax components of a litre of gasoline in cents (assuming a retail price of $1 per litre) for each province and territory. Here we will find the mode, the median, and the mean for the total federal and provincial/ territorial taxes paid on a litre of gasoline as shown in the "total tax component" column.

Tax Components of Gasoline at $1 per Litre (*in cents*)

Province/ Territory	Provincial Excise Tax	Provincial Sales Tax	Federal Excise Tax	Total GST	Total Tax Component (X_i)
Yukon	6.2	n/a	10	5.8	**22.0**
Alberta	9.0	n/a	10	6.0	**25.0**
Northwest Territories	10.7	n/a	10	6.1	**26.8**
Nunavut	10.7	n/a	10	6.1	**26.8**
Manitoba	11.5	n/a	10	6.2	**27.7**
British Columbia	14.5	n/a	10	6.4	**30.9**
Ontario	14.7	n/a	10	6.4	**31.1**
Saskatchewan	15.0	n/a	10	6.4	**31.4**
New Brunswick	14.5	7.3	10	6.4	**38.2**
Prince Edward Island	21.3	n/a	10	6.9	**38.2**
Quebec	15.2	7.4	10	6.5	**39.1**
Nova Scotia	15.5	7.4	10	6.5	**39.4**
Newfoundland and Labrador	16.5	7.5	10	6.5	**40.5**

Source: Oil and Gas prices, Taxes and Consumers, Department of Finance Canada, October 2005. Reproduced with the permission of the Minister of Public Works and Government Services Canada, 2008. http://www.fin.gc.ca/toce/2005/gas_taxre.html.

By scanning the scores, we can see that two scores, 26.8 and 38.2, occur twice, and no other score occurs more than once. This distribution has two modes, 26.8 cents and 38.2 cents.

Because the number of cases is odd, the median will be the middle case after all cases have been ranked. To find the middle case we add 1 to N and then divide that sum by 2. With an N of 13, the median is the score associated with the (13 + 1)/2, or seventh, case. Counting down from the top, we find that the score of the seventh case is 31.1. The median, the score that divides this distribution in half, is 31.1 cents.

The mean is found by first adding all the scores and then dividing by the number of scores. The sum of the scores is 417.1, so the mean is

$$\overline{X} = \frac{\Sigma(X_i)}{N} = \frac{417.1}{13} = 32.1$$

The national average of federal and provincial/ territorial taxes on a litre of gasoline is 32.1 cents. The costs for crude oil, refining, and retailing make up the remaining 67.9 cents. The Department of Finance Canada points out that, at 32.1 cents, the average tax component of gasoline prices in Canada is lower than in the other G7 countries with the exception of the United States.

Use the median when

1. Variables are measured at the ordinal level.
2. Variables measured at the interval-ratio level have highly skewed distributions.
3. You want to report the central score. The median always lies at the exact centre of a distribution.

Use the mean when

1. Variables are measured at the interval-ratio level (except for highly skewed distributions).
2. You want to report the typical score. The mean is "the fulcrum that exactly balances all of the scores."
3. You anticipate additional statistical analysis.

SUMMARY

1. The three measures of central tendency presented in this chapter share a common purpose. Each reports some information about the most typical or representative value in a distribution. Appropriate use of these statistics permits the researcher to report important information about an entire distribution of scores in a single, easily understood number.
2. The mode reports the most common score and is used most appropriately with nominally measured variables.
3. The median (Md) reports the score that is the exact centre of the distribution. It is most appropriately used with variables measured at the ordinal level and with variables measured at the interval-ratio level when the distribution is skewed.

4. The mean ($\overline{X}$), the most frequently used of the three measures, reports the most typical score. It is used most appropriately with variables measured at the interval-ratio level (except when the distribution is highly skewed).
5. The mean has a number of mathematical characteristics that are significant for statisticians. First, it is the point in a distribution of scores around which all other scores cancel out. Second, the mean is the point of minimized variation. Last, as distinct from the mode or median, the mean is affected by every score in the distribution and is therefore pulled in the direction of extreme scores.

SUMMARY OF FORMULAS

Mean 3.1 $$\overline{X} = \frac{\Sigma(X_i)}{N}$$

Mean, aggregate data 3.2 $$\overline{X} = \frac{\Sigma(fX)}{N}$$

GLOSSARY

Deciles. The points that divide a distribution of scores into 10ths.

Mean. The arithmetic average of the scores. $\overline{X}$ represents the mean of a sample, and μ, the mean of a population.

Measures of central tendency. Statistics that summarize a distribution of scores by reporting the most typical or representative value of the distribution.

Median (Md). The point in a distribution of scores above and below which exactly half of the cases fall.

Mode. The most common value in a distribution or the largest category of a variable.

Percentile. A point below which a specific percentage of the cases fall.

Quartiles. The points that divide a distribution into quarters.

Σ (uppercase Greek letter sigma). "The summation of."

Skew. The extent to which a distribution of scores has a few scores that are extremely high (positive skew) or extremely low (negative skew).

X_i ("X sub i"). Any score in a distribution.

MULTIMEDIA RESOURCES

http://www.healeystatistics.nelson.com

Visit the companion Web site for the first Canadian edition of *Statistics: A Tool for Social Research* to access a wide range of student resources. Begin by clicking on the Student Resources section of the book's Web site to access review quizzes, flash cards, and other study tools.

PROBLEMS

3.1 | SOC | A variety of information has been gathered from a sample of lower- and upper-year students living in residence at a large university, including their region of birth; the extent to which they support legalization of marijuana (measured on a scale on which 7 = strong support, 4 = neutral, and 1 = strong opposition); the amount of money they spend each week out-of-pocket for food, drinks, and entertainment; how many movies they watched in their residence rooms last week, and their opinion of cafeteria food (10 = excellent, 0 = very bad). Some results are presented below. Find the *most appropriate* measure of central tendency for each variable for lower-year students and then for upper-year students. Report both the measure you selected as well as its value for each variable (e.g., "Mode = 3" or "Median = 3.5"). *(HINT: Determine the level of measurement for each variable first. In general, this will tell you which measure of central tendency is appropriate. See Section 3.7 to review the relationship between measure of central tendency and level of measurement. Also, remember that the mode is the most common score and, especially, remember to array scores from high to low before finding the median.)*

LOWER-YEAR STUDENTS

Student	Region of Birth	Legalization	Out-of-pocket Expenses	Movies	Cafeteria Food
A	Atlantic	7	33	0	10
B	Atlantic	4	39	14	7
C	Ontario	3	45	10	2

(continued next page)

(continued)

Student	Region of Birth	Legali- zation	Out-of- pocket Expenses	Movies	Cafeteria Food
D	Prairies/West	2	47	7	1
E	Atlantic	3	62	5	8
F	Atlantic	5	48	1	6
G	Ontario	1	52	0	10
H	Ontario	4	65	14	0
I	Prairies/West	1	51	3	5
J	Quebec	2	43	4	6
		UPPER-YEAR STUDENTS			
K	Atlantic	7	65	0	1
L	Prairies/West	6	62	5	2
M	Atlantic	7	60	11	8
N	Atlantic	5	90	3	4
O	Ontario	1	62	4	3
P	Ontario	5	57	14	6
Q	Quebec	6	40	0	2
R	Quebec	7	49	7	9
S	Atlantic	3	45	5	4
T	Quebec	5	85	3	7
U	Atlantic	4	78	5	4

3.2 A variety of information has been collected for each of the nine high schools in a district. Find the most appropriate measure of central tendency for each variable and summarize this information in a paragraph. *(HINT: The level of measurement of the variable will generally tell you which measure of central tendency is appropriate. Remember to organize the scores from high to low before finding the median.)*

High School	Total Enrollment	Largest Sex Group	Percent University Bound	Most Popular Sport	Number of Varsity Sports Programs
1	1400	Male	25	Football	10
2	1223	Female	77	Hockey	7
3	876	Female	52	Football	5
4	1567	Male	29	Football	8
5	778	Female	43	Basketball	4
6	1690	Male	35	Basketball	5
7	1250	Female	66	Soccer	6
8	970	Female	54	Hockey	9
9	1109	Male	64	Soccer	3

3.3 PS You have been observing the local Liberal Party in a large city and have compiled some information about a small sample of party regulars. Find the appropriate measure of central tendency for each variable.

Respondent	Sex	Social Class	Number of Years in Party	Education	Marital Status	Number of Children
A	M	High	32	High school	Married	5
B	M	Medium	17	High school	Married	0
C	M	Low	32	High school	Single	0
D	M	Low	50	Grade 8	Widowed	7
E	M	Low	25	Grade 4	Married	4
F	M	Medium	25	High school	Divorced	3
G	F	High	12	College/University	Divorced	3
H	F	High	10	College/University	Separated	2
I	F	Medium	21	College/University	Married	1
J	F	Medium	33	College/University	Married	5
K	M	Low	37	High school	Single	0
L	F	Low	15	High school	Divorced	0
M	F	Low	31	Grade 8	Widowed	1

3.4 SOC You have compiled the information below on each of the graduates voted "most likely to succeed" by a local high school for a 10-year period. For each variable, find the appropriate measure of central tendency.

Case	Present Income	Marital Status	Owns a BMW?	Years of Education Post–High School
A	24,000	Single	No	8
B	48,000	Divorced	No	4
C	54,000	Married	Yes	4
D	45,000	Married	No	4
E	30,000	Single	No	4
F	35,000	Separated	Yes	8
G	30,000	Married	No	3
H	17,000	Married	No	1
I	33,000	Married	Yes	6
J	48,000	Single	Yes	4

3.5 SOC For 15 respondents, data have been gathered on four variables. Find and report the appropriate measure of central tendency for each variable.

Respondent	Marital Status	Sex	Age	Attitude on Legalization of Marijuana Scale*
A	Single	Female	18	10
B	Single	Male	20	9
C	Widowed	Female	21	8

(continued next column)

(continued)

Respondent	Marital Status	Sex	Age	Attitude on Legalization of Marijuana Scale*
D	Married	Female	30	10
E	Married	Male	25	7
F	Married	Female	26	7
G	Divorced	Male	19	9
H	Widowed	Female	29	6
I	Divorced	Female	31	10
J	Married	Male	55	5
K	Widowed	Male	32	4
L	Married	Male	28	3
M	Divorced	Female	23	2
N	Married	Female	24	1
O	Divorced	Male	32	9

*This scale is constructed so that a high score indicates strong opposition to legalization of marijuana.

3.6 SOC Below are four variables for 30 cases taken from a national survey. Age is reported in years. The variable "happiness" consists of answers to the question "Taken all together, would you say that you are (1) very happy, (2) pretty happy, or (3) not too happy?" Respondents were asked how many sex partners they had over the past five years. Responses were measured on the following scale: 0–4 = actual numbers; 5 = 5–10 partners; 6 = 11–20 partners; 7 = 21–100 partners; 8 = more than 100. For each variable, find the appropriate measure of central tendency and write a sentence reporting this statistical information as you would in a research report.

Respondent	Age	Happi-ness	Number of Partners	Sex
1	20	1	2	Male
2	32	1	1	Male
3	31	1	1	Female
4	34	2	5	Male
5	34	2	3	Male
6	31	3	0	Female
7	35	1	4	Male
8	42	1	3	Male
9	48	1	1	Female
10	27	2	1	Male
11	41	1	1	Male
12	42	2	0	Female
13	29	1	8	Male
14	28	1	1	Female
15	47	2	1	Male
16	69	2	2	Female
17	44	1	4	Female
18	21	3	1	Male
19	33	2	1	Male
20	56	1	2	Male
21	73	2	0	Female
22	31	1	1	Female
23	53	2	3	Male
24	78	1	0	Male
25	47	2	3	Male
26	88	3	0	Female
27	43	1	2	Male
28	24	1	1	Male
29	24	2	3	Male
30	60	1	1	Male

3.7 Find the appropriate measure of central tendency for each variable displayed in Table 2.5. Report each statistic as you would in a formal research report.

3.8 SOC The table below lists the average weekly earnings for the 10 provinces in 2000 and 2005 (fictitious data). Compute the mean and median for each year and compare the two measures of central tendency. Which measure of central tendency is greater for each year? Are the distributions skewed? In which direction?

Province	2000	2005
Newfoundland and Labrador	712	734
Prince Edward Island	667	709
Nova Scotia	570	697
New Brunswick	660	662
Quebec	648	745
Ontario	682	700
Manitoba	633	656
Saskatchewan	645	706
Alberta	617	680
British Columbia	712	741

3.9 SOC The administration is considering a total ban on student automobiles. You have conducted a poll on this issue of 20 fellow students and 20 of the neighbours who live around the campus and have calculated scores for your respondents. On the scale you used, a high score indicates strong opposition to the proposed ban. The scores are presented below for both groups. Calculate an appropriate measure of central tendency and compare the two groups in a sentence or two.

Students		Neighbours	
10	11	0	7
10	9	1	6
10	8	0	0
10	11	1	3
9	8	7	4
10	11	11	0
9	7	0	0
5	1	1	10
5	2	10	9
0	10	10	0

3.10 SW As the head of a social services agency, you believe that your staff of 20 social workers is very much overworked compared to 10 years ago. The case loads for each worker are reported below for each of the two years in question. Has the average case load increased? What measure of central tendency is most appropriate to answer this question? Why?

2000		2010	
52	55	42	82
50	49	75	50
57	50	69	52
49	52	65	50
45	59	58	55
65	60	64	65
60	65	69	60
55	68	60	60
42	60	50	60
50	42	60	60

3.11 SOC The table below lists the approximate number of cars per 100 population for eight nations. Compute the mean and median for this data. Which is greater in value? Is there a positive skew in this data? How do you know?

Nation	Number of Cars per 100 Population
United States	50
Canada	45
France	46
Germany	51
Japan	39
Mexico	10
Sweden	44
United Kingdom	37

3.12 SW For the test scores first presented in problem 2.6 and reproduced below, compute a median and mean for both the pretest and post-test. Interpret these statistics.

Case	Pretest	Post-test
A	8	12
B	7	13
C	10	12
D	15	19
E	10	8
F	10	17
G	3	12
H	10	11
I	5	7
J	15	12
K	13	20
L	4	5
M	10	15
N	8	11
O	12	20

3.13 SOC A sample of 25 first-year students at a major university wrote a test that measured their literacy skills in reading and writing (their test scores were the number of incorrect answers, so the higher the score, the poorer the skills).

a. Compute the median and mean scores for these data.

10	43	30	30	45
40	12	40	42	35
45	25	10	33	50
42	32	38	11	47
22	26	37	38	10

b. These same 25 students wrote the same test during their final year. Compute the median and mean for this second set of scores and compare them to the earlier set. What happened?

10	45	35	27	50
35	10	50	40	30
40	10	10	37	10
40	15	30	20	43
23	25	30	40	10

3.14 PA The data below represent the percentage of workers living in each city who used public transportation to commute to work in 2010 (fictitious data).

City	Percent
Abbotsford	20
Barrie	32
Calgary	26
Dawson	6
Fredericton	9
Edmonton	6
Hamilton	10
Halifax	11
Kelowna	15
Mississauga	14
Montreal	53
Quebec	25
Saskatoon	3
St. John's	4
Thunder Bay	4
Toronto	31
Vancouver	18
Winnipeg	33

a. Calculate the mean and median of this distribution.

b. Compare the mean and median. Which is the higher value? Why?

c. If you removed Montreal from this distribution and recalculated, what would happen to the mean? To the median? Why?

d. Report the mean and median as you would in a formal research report.

3.15 Professional athletes are threatening to strike because they claim that they are underpaid. The team owners have released a statement that says, in part, "the average salary for players was $1.2 million last year." The players counter by issuing their own statement that says, in part, "the average player earned only $753,000 last year." Is either side necessarily lying? If you were a sports reporter and had just read Chapter 3 of this text, what questions would you ask about these statistics?

SPSS for Windows

Using SPSS for Windows to Compute Measures of Central Tendency and Percentiles with the 2001 Census

The demonstrations and exercises below use the shortened version of the 2001 Census data set (*Census.sav*) supplied with this text. Start SPSS for Windows by clicking the SPSS icon on your monitor screen. Load the 2001 Census, and when you see the message "SPSS Processor is Ready" on the bottom of the "closest" screen, you are ready to proceed.

It is again important to note that SPSS displays information on variables by name (e.g., *acmyr*) or by label (e.g., main activity in past year). If labels are displayed, we highly recommend that you switch to variable names by clicking **Edit, Options,** and then, on the **General** tab, select **Display names** and **Alphabetical** and then click **OK.** These changes may not take effect until you load a new data set or restart SPSS.

SPSS DEMONSTRATION 3.1 Producing Measures of Central Tendency

The only procedure in SPSS that will produce all three commonly used measures of central tendency (mode, median, and mean) is **Frequencies.** We used this procedure to produce a frequency distribution in Demonstration 2.1. Here we will use **Frequencies** to calculate measures of central tendency for three variables: *religrpa* (religion group), *uphwkp* (unpaid housework/yard work/maintenance), and *agep* (age).

The three variables vary in level of measurement, and we could request only the appropriate measure of central tendency for each variable. That is, we could request the mode for *religrpa* (nominal), the median for *uphwkp* (ordinal), and the mean for *agep* (interval-ratio). While this would be reasonable, it's actually more convenient to get all three measures for each variable and ignore the irrelevant output. Statistical packages typically generate more information than necessary, and it is common to disregard some of the output.

To produce modes, medians, and means, begin by clicking **Analyze** from the menu bar and then click **Descriptive Statistics** and **Frequencies.** In the **Frequencies** dialog box, find the variable names in the list on the left and click the arrow button in the middle of the screen to move the names (*religrpa, uphwkp,* and *agep*) to the **Variable(s)** box on the right.

To request specific statistics, click the **Statistics** button in the upper-right-hand corner of the **Frequencies** dialog box, and the **Frequencies: Statistics** dialog box opens. Find the **Central Tendency** box on the right and click **Mean, Median,** and **Mode.** Click **Continue,** and you will be returned to the **Frequencies** dialog box, where you might want to click the **Display Frequency Tables** box. When this box is *not* checked, SPSS will not produce frequency distribution tables, and only the statistics we request (mode, median, and mean) will appear in the **Output** window. Click **OK,** and SPSS will produce the following output:

Statistics

		RELIGION GROUP	HOURS: UNPAID HOUSEWORK/YARD WORK/MAINTENANCE	AGE IN YEARS
N	Valid	1385	1500	1500
	Missing	115	0	0
Mean		3.68	2.08	42.80
Median		2.00	2.00	42.00
Mode		1	2	38[*]

[*]Multiple modes exist. The smallest value is shown.

Looking only at the most appropriate measures for each variable, the mode for *religrpa* (religion group) is "1" (see the bottom line of output). You can find out about the meaning or label of this value by consulting either the code book in Appendix G of the text or the online code book. To use the latter, click **Utilities** and then click **Variables** and find *religrpa* in the variable list on the left. Either way, you will find that a score of 1 indicates "Catholic." This was the most common religious affiliation in the sample and, thus, is the mode.

The median for *uphwkp* (unpaid housework/yard work/maintenance) is a value of "2.00." Again, use either Appendix G or the online code book, and you will see that the category associated with this score is "5–14 hours." This means that the middle case in this distribution of 1,500 cases has a score of 2 (or that the middle case is in the interval "5–14 hours").

The output for *agep* (age) indicates that respondents were, on the average, 42.8 years of age. Since age is an interval-ratio variable that has been measured in a defined unit (years), the value of the mean is numerically meaningful, and we do not need to consult the code book to interpret its meaning.

Note that SPSS did not hesitate to compute means for the two variables that were not interval-ratio. The program cannot distinguish between numerical codes (such as the scores for *religrpa*) and actual numbers—to SPSS, all numbers are the same. Also, SPSS cannot screen your commands to see if they are statistically appropriate. If you request nonsensical statistics (e.g., average sex or median religion), SPSS will carry out your instructions without hesitation. The blind willingness of SPSS to simply obey commands makes it easy for you, the user, to request statistics that are completely meaningless. Computers don't care about meaning; they just crunch the numbers.

In this case, it was more convenient for us to produce statistics indiscriminately and then ignore the ones that are nonsensical. This will not always be the case, and the point of all this, of course, is to caution you to use SPSS wisely. As the manager of your local computer centre will be quick to remind you, computer resources (including paper) are not unlimited.

SPSS DEMONSTRATION 3.2 The Descriptives Command

The **Descriptives** command in SPSS for Windows is designed to provide summary statistics for continuous interval-ratio-level variables. By default (i.e., unless you tell it otherwise), **Descriptives** produces the mean, the minimum and maximum scores (i.e., the lowest and highest scores), and the standard deviation (which will be discussed in Chapter 4). Unlike **Frequencies,** this procedure will not produce frequency distributions.

To illustrate the use of **Descriptives,** let's run the procedure for *agep* (age), *totincp* (total income), and *grosrtp* (monthly gross rent). Click **Analyze, Descriptive Statistics,** and **Descriptives.** The **Descriptives** dialog box will open. This dialog box looks just like the **Frequencies** dialog box and works in the same way. Find the variable names in the list on the left and, once they are highlighted, click the arrow button in the middle of the screen to transfer them to the **Variable(s)** box on the right. Click **OK,** and the following output will be produced:

Descriptive Statistics

	N	Minimum	Maximum	Mean	Std. Deviation
AGE in YEARS	1500	15	85	42.80	17.694
TOTAL INCOME $	1500	−3213	200000	26990.03	26722.556
MONTHLY GROSS RENT $	397	99	1100	656.53	259.730
VALID N (LISTWISE)	397				

On the average, the sample is 42.8 years of age (this duplicates the frequencies output in Demonstration 3.1), has a total annual income of $26,990.03, and (for the 397 tenants in the sample) pays $656.53 in monthly rent.

SPSS DEMONSTRATION 3.3 Finding Percentiles, Deciles, and Quartiles

The **Frequencies** procedure can be used to find percentiles, deciles, and quartiles for any variable (see Section 3.4). These statistics are especially useful for continuous variables with broad ranges of scores, such as *agep* (age). We will once again use this variable for our illustrations.

Click **Analyze, Descriptive Statistics,** and **Frequencies** to get the **Frequencies** dialog box. Make sure that *agep* is in the **Variable(s)** box. You can move variables into and out to the box by using the arrow button. Click the **Statistics** button to get the **Frequencies: Statistics** dialog box. For purposes of illustration, let's find quartiles, deciles, and the 23rd and 47th percentiles.

In the **Percentile Values** section, click the checkboxes next to **Quartiles** and next to **Cut points for 10 equal groups.** The latter instruction will find deciles (10 equal groups) and could be changed to split the distribution in other ways (e.g., into thirds).

To get specific percentiles, click the checkbox next to **Percentiles,** type the desired percentile values in the textbox to the right (23 and 47), and click the **Add** button after each value. Click **Continue,** and you will return to the **Frequencies** dialog box, where you might want to click the **Display Frequency Tables** box. Recall that when this box is *not* checked, SPSS will not produce frequency distribution tables. Click **OK,** and SPSS will produce the following output in the **SPSS Output** window:

Statistics

AGE IN YEARS		
N	Valid	1500.00
	Missing	.00
Mean		42.80
Median		42.00
Mode		38.00[a]
Percentiles	10	19.00
	20	26.00
	23	28.00
	25	29.00
	30	32.00
	40	37.00
	47	40.00
	50	42.00
	60	46.00
	70	52.00
	75	54.00
	80	58.00
	90	69.00

[a]Multiple modes exist. The smallest value is shown.

The output prints the deciles, quartiles, and percentiles we requested in order. Find the 10th percentile (noted as 10 in the column labelled "Percentiles"). The score associated with this percentile is 19 (noted as a value of 19.00). This indicates that 10% of the sample were younger than 19. Similarly, 20% were younger than age 26, 23% (the percentile we requested) were less than 28, 25% (the first quartile) were younger than 29, and so forth. Note that the 5th decile, 2nd quartile, and 50th percentile are all associated with the age of 42, which is also the value of the median.

Exercises (using *Census.sav*)

3.1 Use the **Frequencies** command to get the most appropriate measure of central tendency for any three nominal or ordinal variables of your own choosing.

(*Hint: Use the level of measurement of the variable as your criteria for selecting the appropriate measure of central tendency.*) Write a sentence or two reporting each measure.

3.2 Use the **Descriptives** command to get means for any two interval-ratio variables. Write a sentence or two reporting and explaining the mean of each variable.

3.3 Use the **Frequencies** command to find the quartiles and deciles for each variable in Exercise 3.2. Write a few sentences summarizing these results.

4

MEASURES OF DISPERSION

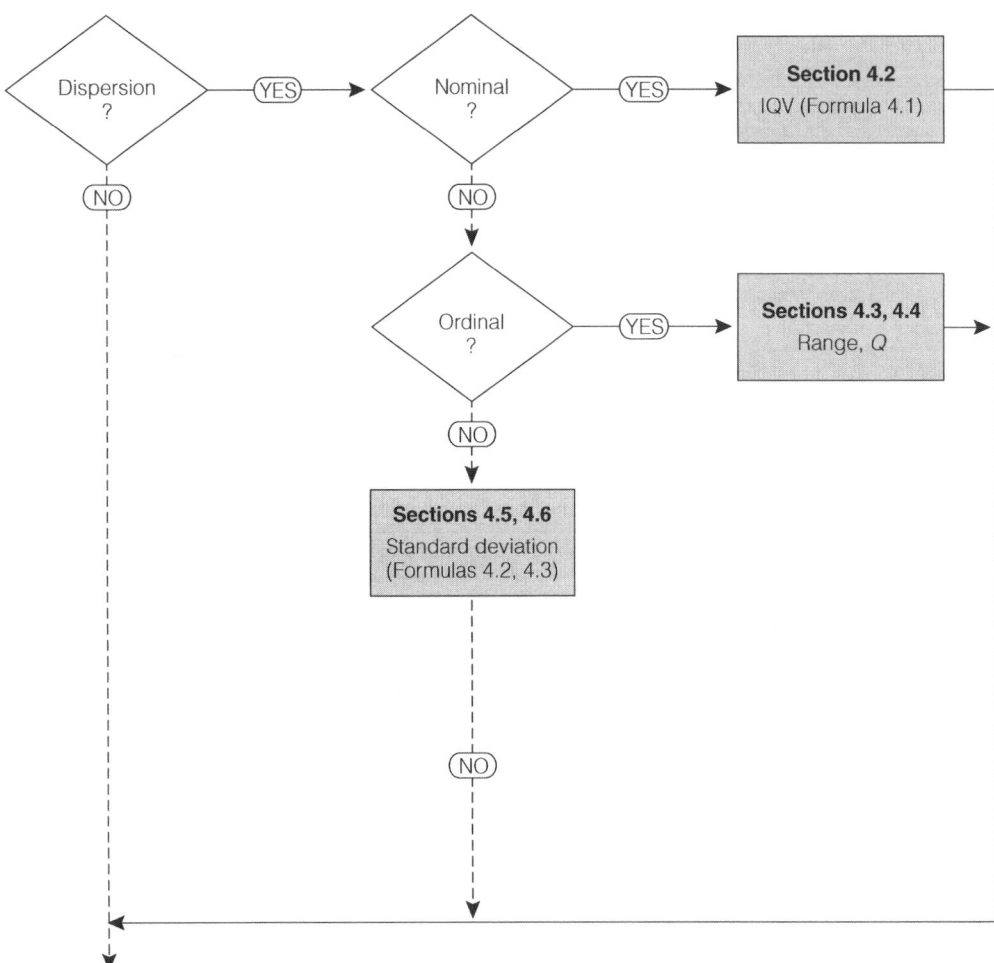

LEARNING OBJECTIVES   By the end of this chapter, you will be able to

1. Explain the purpose of measures of dispersion and the information they convey.
2. Compute and explain the index of qualitative variation (IQV), the range (R), the interquartile range (Q), the boxplot, the standard deviation (s), and the variance (s^2).
3. Select an appropriate measure of dispersion and correctly calculate and interpret the statistic.
4. Describe and explain the mathematical characteristics of the standard deviation.

4.1 INTRODUCTION

By themselves, measures of central tendency cannot summarize data completely. For a full description of a distribution of scores, measures of central tendency must be paired with **measures of dispersion.** In contrast to the mean, median, and mode—which are designed to locate the typical and/or central scores—measures of dispersion provide information about the amount of variety, diversity, or heterogeneity within a distribution of scores.

The importance of the concept of **dispersion** might be easier to grasp if we consider a brief example. Suppose that the director of public safety wants to evaluate two ambulance services that have contracted with the city to provide emergency medical aid. As a part of the investigation, she has collected data on the response time of both services to calls for assistance. Data collected for the past year show that the mean response time is 7.4 minutes for Service A and 7.6 minutes for Service B. The average response times are essentially the same and provide no basis for judging one service as more or less efficient than the other. Measures of dispersion, however, can reveal substantial differences in the underlying distributions even when the measures of central tendency are equivalent. For example, consider Figure 4.1, which displays the distribution of response times for the two services in the form of frequency polygons or line charts (see Chapter 2).

Compare the shapes of these two figures. Note that the line chart for Service B is much flatter than that for Service A. This is because the scores for Service B are more spread out or more diverse than the scores for Service A. In other words, Service B was much more variable in response time and had more scores in the high and low ranges and fewer in the middle. Service A was more consistent in its response time and its scores are more clustered or grouped around the mean. Both distributions have essentially the same *average* response time but there is considerably more *variation* or dispersion in the response times for Service B. If you were the director of public safety, would you be more likely to select an ambulance service that was always on the scene of an emergency in about the same amount of time (Service A) or one that was sometimes very slow and sometimes very quick to respond (Service B)? Note that if you had not considered dispersion, a possibly important difference in the performance of the two ambulance services might have gone unnoticed.

Keep the two shapes in Figure 4.1 in mind as visual representations of the concept of dispersion. The greater clustering of scores around the mean in the upper distribution (Service A) indicates *less* dispersion and the flatter curve of the lower distribution indicates *more* variety or dispersion. Any of the measures of dispersion discussed in this chapter will increase in value as distributions become flatter (as the scores become more dispersed) and decrease as they become more peaked (as the scores become less dispersed).

These ideas and Figure 4.1 may give you a general notion of what is meant by dispersion but the concept is not easily described in words alone. In this chapter we will introduce some of the more common

FIGURE 4.1   RESPONSE TIME FOR TWO AMBULANCE SERVICES

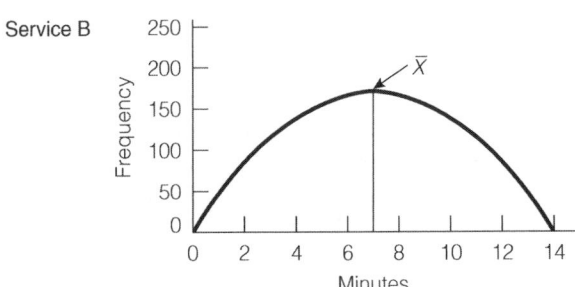

measures of dispersion, each of which provides a quantitative indication of the variety in a set of scores. We will begin with the index of qualitative variation, mention two measures—the range and the interquartile range—briefly, and devote most of our attention to the standard deviation and the variance.

4.2 THE INDEX OF QUALITATIVE VARIATION (IQV)

We begin our consideration of measures of dispersion with the **index of qualitative variation (IQV).** This statistic is the only measure of dispersion available for nominal level variables (although it can be used with any variable that has been grouped into a frequency distribution). The IQV is the ratio of the amount of variation actually observed in a distribution of scores to the maximum variation that could exist in that distribution. The index varies from 0.00 (no variation) to 1.00 (maximum variation).

To illustrate the logic of this statistic, consider the idea that Canada will grow more ethnoculturally diverse in the future. Over the past few decades Canada has experienced an increase in immigration from non-European countries. This has led to a change in the ethnocultural makeup of Canada. Will Canada continue to grow more diverse in the years to come?

TABLE 4.1   ETHNOCULTURAL GROUPS IN CANADA, 1996, 2006, 2017

	Percent of Total Population		
Group	1996	2006	2017
Visible minority	11.2	15.7	20.6
Non-visible minority	88.8	84.3	79.4
Total =	100.0	100.0	100.0

Source: Statistics Canada. 2005. *Population Projections of Visible Minority Groups, Canada, Provinces and Regions, 2001–2017.* Catalogue no. 91-541-XIE.

Table 4.1 presents some information about the relative size of visible and non-visible minority groups for 1996 and projections for 2006 and 2017.* (Note that the values in the table are percentages instead of frequencies. This will greatly simplify computations.) If there were no diversity in Canada (e.g., if everyone were a non-visible minority), the IQV would be 0.00. At the other extreme, if Canadians were distributed equally across the two groups (i.e., if each group comprised exactly 50% of the population), the IQV would achieve its maximum value (1.00).

By inspection, you can see that Canada is not close to the extreme of zero diversity (or an IQV of 0.00) in 1996, and is becoming more ethnocultural diverse over time. The population will be much closer to maximum variation (an IQV of 1.00) in 2017. Visible minorities are projected to comprise 20.6% of the population in 2017 compared to 11.2% in 1996. Let's see how the IQV substantiates these observations. The computational formula for the IQV is:

FORMULA 4.1

$$IQV = \frac{k(N^2 - \Sigma f^2)}{N^2(k-1)}$$

where k = the number of categories
N = the number of cases
Σf^2 = the sum of the squared frequencies

To use this formula, the sum of the squared frequencies must first be computed. We do this by adding a column to the frequency distribution for the squared frequencies and then by summing this column. This procedure is illustrated in Table 4.2.

*In Canada, visible minorities, defined by the Employment Equity Act, are persons, other than Aboriginal peoples, who are non-Caucasian in race or non-white in colour. The visible minority groups include Blacks, South Asians, Chinese, Koreans, Japanese, Southeast Asians, Filipinos, Arabs and West Asians, Latin Americans, and Pacific Islanders.

TABLE 4.2   FINDING THE SUM OF THE SQUARED FREQUENCIES

	1996		2006		2017	
Group	f	f^2	f	f^2	f	f^2
Visible minority	11.2	125.44	15.7	246.49	20.6	424.36
Non-visible minority	88.8	7,885.44	84.3	7,106.49	79.4	6,304.36
Σf or $N =$	100.0		100.0		100.0	
$\Sigma f^2 =$		8,010.88		7,352.98		6,728.72

For each year, the sum of the frequency column is N and the sum of the squared frequency (Σf^2) is the total of the second column. Substituting these values into Formula 4.1 for the year 1996, we have an IQV of 0.40:

$$IQV = \frac{2(10,000 - 8,010.88)}{10,000(1)} = \frac{2(1,989.12)}{10,000(1)} = \frac{3,978.24}{10,000} = 0.40$$

Because the values of k and N are the same for all three years, the IQV for the remaining years can be found by simply changing the values for Σf^2. For 2006,

$$IQV = \frac{2(10,000 - 7,352.98)}{10,000(1)} = \frac{2(2,647.02)}{10,000(1)} = \frac{5,294.04}{10,000} = 0.53$$

and similarly, for 2017,

$$IQV = \frac{2(10,000 - 6,728.72)}{10,000(1)} = \frac{2(3,271.28)}{10,000(1)} = \frac{6,542.56}{10,000} = 0.65$$

Thus, the IQV, in a quantitative and precise way, substantiates our earlier impressions.

The IQV of 0.40 for the year 1996 means that the distribution of frequencies shows about 40% of the maximum variation possible. By 2017, the variation will increase to 65% of the maximum variation possible for this distribution of ethnocultural categories. Canadian society has grown increasingly diverse, and will be quite heterogeneous by 2017. *(For practice in calculating and interpreting the IQV, see problems 4.1 and 4.2.)*

4.3 THE RANGE (R), INTERQUARTILE RANGE (Q), AND BOXPLOT

The **range (R)** is defined as the distance between the highest and lowest scores in a distribution. It is quite easy to calculate (high score minus low score) and is perhaps most useful to gain a quick and general notion of variability while scanning many distributions. Unfortunately, because it is based on only two scores (the highest and lowest scores), the range is often deceptive as a measure of dispersion. Because almost any sizable distribution will contain some atypically high and low scores, the range might be quite misleading as a measure of dispersion. Also, R yields no information about the variation of the scores between the highest and lowest scores.

The **interquartile range (Q)** is a kind of range. It avoids some of the problems associated with R by considering only the middle 50% of the cases in a distribution. To find Q, arrange the scores from highest to lowest and then divide the distribution into quarters (as distinct from halves, as in locating the median). The first quartile (Q_1) is the point below which 25% of the cases fall and above which 75% of the cases fall. The second quartile (Q_2) divides the distribution into halves (thus, Q_2 is equal in value to the median). The third quartile (Q_3) is the point below which 75% of the cases fall and above which 25% of the cases fall. Thus, if line LH represents a distribution of scores, the quartiles are located as shown:

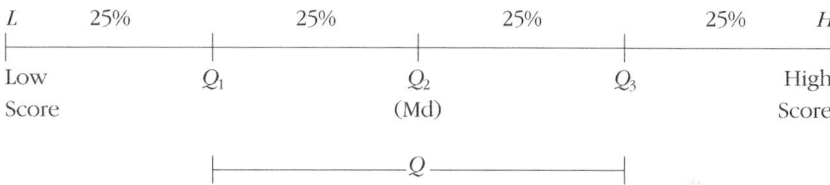

The interquartile range is defined as the distance from the third to the first quartile ($Q = Q_3 - Q_1$). Thus, Q essentially extracts the middle 50% of the distribution and, like R, is based on only two scores. While Q avoids the problem of being based on the most extreme scores, it has all the other disadvantages associated with R. Most importantly, Q also fails to yield any information about the variation of the scores other than the two upon which it is based.

The diagram of the LH line shown above is the basis for a graph called the **boxplot,** or the "box and whisker" plot. The boxplot has the advantage of conveniently displaying the centre, spread, and overall range of scores in a distribution. It is based on information from a five-number summary, consisting of the lowest score, first quartile, second quartile (the median), third quartile, and highest score in a distribution.

A box (hence the name boxplot) is drawn where the first (Q_1) and third (Q_3) quartiles mark the end of the box. (The length of the box is, therefore, the interquartile range, Q.) The second quartile (Q_2), or the median, is marked with a vertical line in the middle of the box. To show the level of dispersion in the distribution of scores, a horizontal line, a "whisker," is drawn from the first quartile to the lowest score (L), marked by a small vertical line, and from the third quartile to the highest score (H). Whisker lines may span either the full data set as in Figure 4.2, or the data set excluding extreme scores or outliers. Boxplots are particularly useful when two or more data sets are being compared, such as comparing annual income for males and females.

FIGURE 4.2 THE BOXPLOT

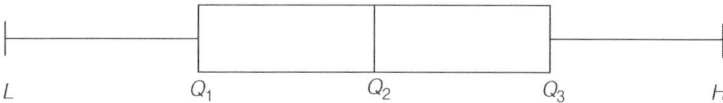

4.4 COMPUTING THE RANGE, INTERQUARTILE RANGE, AND BOXPLOT*

Table 4.3 presents per capita (per person) health expenditures in 2003 for 20 countries. What are the range and interquartile range of these data? Note that the scores have already been ordered from high to low. This makes the range easy to calculate and is necessary for finding the interquartile range. Of these 20 countries, the United States spent the most per capita on health ($5,711) and Greece spent the least ($1,997). The range is therefore $5,711 − $1,997, or $3,714 ($R = \$3,714$).

To find Q, we must locate the first and third quartiles (Q_1 and Q_3). In a manner analogous to the technique for finding the median, we can define both of these points in terms of the scores associated with certain cases. Q_1 is determined by multiplying N by (.25). Since (20) × (.25) is 5, Q_1 is the score associated with the fifth case, counting up from the lowest score. The fifth case is Austria, with a score of $2,306. So, $Q_1 = \$2,306$. The case that lies at the third quartile (Q_3) is given by multiplying N by (.75), and (20) × (.75) = 15th case. The 15th case, again counting up from the lowest score, is Germany with a score of $3,001 ($Q_3 = \$3,001$). Therefore:

$$Q = Q_3 - Q_1 = \$3,001 - \$2,306 = \$695$$

Remember that multiplying N by the proportional value of the quartile gives the number of the *approximate* case that actually marks the location (see Section 3.4). In finding Q_1, for example, we multiplied 20 by .25, which

TABLE 4.3   HEALTH EXPENDITURE PER CAPITA (IN US$), 2003

Rank	Country	Expenditure
20 (highest)	United States	$5,711
19	Norway	3,809
18	Switzerland	3,776
17	Luxembourg	3,680
16	Iceland	3,110
15	Germany	3,001
14	Canada	2,989
13	Netherlands	2,987
12	France	2,902
11	Australia	2,874
10	Belgium	2,828
9	Denmark	2,762
8	Sweden	2,704
7	Ireland	2,496
6	United Kingdom	2,389
5	Austria	2,306
4	Italy	2,266
3	Japan	2,244
2	Finland	2,108
1 (lowest)	Greece	1,997

Source: United Nations. http://hdr.undp.org/hdr2006/statistics/indicators/52.html.

*This section is optional.

equals 5. Thus using this technique, Q_1 is the score associated with the fifth case, or $2,306. However, Q_1 is *actually* the average of the scores associated with the 5th case, Austria, and 6th case, United Kingdom. In this example, Q_1 is technically defined as ($2,389 + $2,306)/2, or $2347.50. There is a slight inaccuracy produced by using the technique of multiplying N by the proportional value of the quartile, and while time and calculational effort are saved, it should be used with caution.

A boxplot can be produced to provide a graphical representation of this information. The construction of a boxplot requires a few steps. First, we calculate the first, second (the median), and third quartiles. Second, we draw a box between the first and third quartiles. (The height of the box is arbitrary, but should be reasonably proportional to the rest of the graph.) Third, we draw a line dividing the box at the median value. Fourth, we draw a horizontal line (whisker) from the lowest score, indicated by a small vertical line, to the box. Do the same for the largest score to the box.

Figure 4.3 displays a boxplot of the data provided in Table 4.3. The first quartile, $2,306, and the third quartile, $3,001, were calculated above in computing the interquartile range. The median value is calculated in a similar manner: $20 \times .50 = 10$th case, or the value associated with Belgium ($2,828). The lowest and highest scores are $1,997 (Greece) and $5,711 (United States).

At a quick glance the boxplot in Figure 4.3 shows us that the centre (the median) of the distribution of health care expenditure per capita is approximately $2,800. It also shows that the distribution is quite spread out, with an extreme score (i.e., United States) and a positive skew. The positive skew is indicated by the greater length of the upper whisker compared to the lower whisker.

In most situations, the locations of Q_1 and Q_3 will not be as obvious as they are when $N = 20$. For example, if N had been 157, then Q_1 would be (157)(.25), or the score associated with the 39.25th case, and Q_3 would be (157)(.75), or the score associated with the 117.75th case. Because fractions of cases are impossible, these numbers present some problems. The easy solution to this difficulty is to round off and take the score of the closest case to the numbers that mark the quartiles. Thus, Q_1 would be defined as the score of the 39th case and Q_3 as the score of the 118th case.

The more accurate solution would be to take the fractions of cases into account. For example, Q_1 could be defined as the score that is one-quarter of the distance between the scores of the 39th and 40th cases, and Q_3 could be defined as the score that is three-quarters of the distance between the

FIGURE 4.3   BOXPLOT OF HEALTH EXPENDITURE PER CAPITA (IN US$), 2003

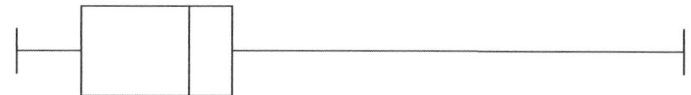

$1,900 $2,300 $2,700 $3,100 $3,500 $3,900 $4,300 $4,700 $5,100 $5,500 $5,900

Health Expenditure (in US$)

scores of the 117th and 118th cases. (This procedure could be analogous to defining the median—which is also Q_2—as halfway between the two middle scores when N is even.) In most cases, the differences in the values of Q for these two methods would be quite small. *(For practice in finding and interpreting Q, see problem 4.12b. For practice in constructing and interpreting the boxplot, see problem 4.12c. The range may be found for any of the problems at the end of this chapter except 4.1 and 4.2.)*

4.5 THE STANDARD DEVIATION

A basic limitation of both Q and R is that they are based on only two scores. They do not use all the scores in the distribution, and, in this sense, they do not capitalize on all the available information. Also, neither statistic provides any information on how far the scores are from each other or from some central point such as the mean. How can we design a measure of dispersion that would correct these faults? We can begin with some specifications: a good measure of dispersion should

1. Use all the scores in the distribution. The statistic should use all the information available.
2. Describe the average or typical deviation of the scores. The statistic should give us an idea about how far the scores are from each other or from the centre of the distribution.
3. Increase in value as the distribution of scores becomes more diverse. This would be a very handy feature because it would permit us to tell at a glance which distribution was more variable: the higher the numerical value of the statistic, the greater the dispersion.

One way to develop a statistic to meet these criteria would be to start with the distances between each score and the mean. The distances between the scores and the mean $(X_i - \overline{X})$ are called **deviations** and this quantity will increase in value as the scores increase in their variety or heterogeneity. If the scores are more clustered around the mean (remember the graph for Service A in Figure 4.1), the deviations would be small. If the scores are more spread out or more varied (like the scores for Service B in Figure 4.1), the deviations would be greater in value. How can we use the deviations of the scores around the mean to develop a useful statistic?

One course of action would be to use the sum of the deviations—$\Sigma(X_i - \overline{X})$—as the basis for a statistic, but, as we saw in Section 3.6, the sum of deviations will always be zero. To illustrate, consider a distribution of five scores: 10, 20, 30, 40, and 50. If we sum the deviations of the scores from the mean, we would always wind up with a total of zero:

Scores (X_i)	Deviations $(X_i - \overline{X})$
10	$(10 - 30) = -20$
20	$(20 - 30) = -10$
30	$(30 - 30) = 0$

$$
\begin{array}{lll}
40 & (40 - 30) = & 10 \\
\underline{50} & \underline{(50 - 30) =} & \underline{20} \\
\Sigma(X_i) = 150 & \Sigma(X_i - \overline{X}) = & 0
\end{array}
$$

$$\overline{X} = 150/5 = 30$$

Still, the sum of the deviations are a logical basis for a statistic that measures the amount of variety in a set of scores, and statisticians have developed two ways around the fact that the positive deviations always equal the negative deviations. Both solutions eliminate the negative signs. The first does so by using the absolute values or by ignoring signs when summing the deviations. This is the basis for a statistic called the **average deviation,** a measure of dispersion that is rarely used and will not be mentioned further.

The second solution squares each of the deviations. This makes all values positive because a negative number multiplied by a negative number becomes positive. For example: $(-20) \times (-20) = 400$. In the example above, the sum of the squared deviations would be $(400 + 100 + 0 + 100 + 400)$ or 1,000. Thus, a statistic based on the sum of the squared deviations will have many of the properties we want in a good measure of dispersion.

Before we finish designing our measure of dispersion, we must deal with another problem. The sum of the squared deviations will increase with sample size: the larger the *number* of scores, the greater the value of the measure. This would make it very difficult to compare the relative variability of distributions based on samples of different size. We can solve this problem by dividing the sum of the squared deviations by N (sample size) and thus standardizing for samples of different sizes.

These procedures yield a statistic known as the **variance,** which is symbolized as s^2 for a sample and σ^2 for a population. The variance is used primarily in inferential statistics, although it is a central concept in the design of some measures of association. For purposes of describing the dispersion of a distribution, a closely related statistic called the **standard deviation** (symbolized as s for a sample and σ for a population) is typically used, and this statistic will be our focus for the remainder of the chapter.

The formulas for the variance and standard deviation are

FORMULA 4.2
$$s^2 = \frac{\Sigma(X_i - \overline{X})^2}{N}$$

FORMULA 4.3
$$s = \sqrt{\frac{\Sigma(X_i - \overline{X})^2}{N}}$$

Strictly speaking, Formulas 4.2 and 4.3 are for the variance and standard deviation of a population. Slightly different formulas, with $N - 1$ instead of N in the denominator, should be used when we are working with random samples rather than entire populations. This is an important point because many of the electronic calculators and statistical software packages (including SPSS) that you might be using use "$N - 1$" in the denominator and, thus,

TABLE 4.4 COMPUTING THE STANDARD DEVIATION

Scores (X_i)	Deviations $(X_i - \bar{X})$	Deviations Squared $(X_i - \bar{X})^2$
10	$(10 - 30) = -20$	$(-20)^2 = 400$
20	$(20 - 30) = -10$	$(-10)^2 = 100$
30	$(30 - 30) = 0$	$(-0)^2 = 0$
40	$(40 - 30) = 10$	$(-10)^2 = 100$
50	$(50 - 30) = 20$	$(-20)^2 = 400$
$\Sigma(X_i) = 150$	$\Sigma(X_i - \bar{X}) = 0$	$\Sigma(X_i - \bar{X})^2 = 1000$

produce results that are at least slightly different from Formulas 4.2 and 4.3. The size of the difference will decrease as sample size increases but the problems and examples in this chapter use small samples and the differences between using N and $N - 1$ in the denominator can be considerable in such cases. Some calculators offer the choice of "$N - 1$" or "N" in the denominator. If you use the latter, the values calculated for the standard deviation should match the values in this text.

To compute the standard deviation, it is advisable to construct a table such as Table 4.4 to organize computations. The five scores used in the previous example are listed in the left-hand column, the deviations are in the middle column, and the squared deviations are in the right-hand column.

The sum of the last column in Table 4.4 is the sum of the squared deviations and can be substituted into the numerator of the formula:

$$s = \sqrt{\frac{\Sigma(X_i - \bar{X})^2}{N}}$$

$$= \sqrt{\frac{1000}{5}}$$

$$= \sqrt{200}$$

$$= 14.14$$

To finish solving the formula, divide the sum of the squared deviations by N and take the square root of the result. To find the variance, square the standard deviation. For this problem, the variance is $s^2 = (14.14)^2 = 200$.

We can also readily obtain the standard deviation for aggregate data in a frequency distribution. In this case the formula for the standard deviation (s) is:

FORMULA 4.4

$$s = \sqrt{\frac{\Sigma f(X_i - \bar{X})^2}{N}}$$

where f = the number of cases with a score
X_i = the score
$\bar{X}$ = the mean
N = the number of cases

Table 4.5 demonstrates the calculation s for the distribution of scores on a sociology exam illustrated in Table 3.5.

TABLE 4.5 COMPUTING THE STANDARD DEVIATION FOR AGGREGATE DATA IN A FREQUENCY DISTRIBUTION

Scores (X_i)	Frequency (f)	Deviations $(X_i - \overline{X})$	Deviations Squared $(X_i - \overline{X})^2$	Deviations Squared × Frequency $f(X_i - \overline{X})^2$
58	2	−12.32	151.78	303.56
60	2	−10.32	106.50	213.00
62	3	−8.32	69.22	207.66
64	2	−6.32	39.94	79.88
66	3	−4.32	18.66	55.98
67	4	−3.32	11.02	44.08
68	1	−2.32	5.38	5.38
69	1	−1.32	1.74	1.74
70	2	−.32	.10	.20
93	5	22.68	514.38	2,571.90
	$N = 25$			$\Sigma f(X_i - \overline{X})^2 = 3{,}483.40$

Recall from Table 3.5: $\overline{X} = 70.32$

The first (X_i) and second (f) columns in the distribution show each score and its frequency respectively. The third column $(X_i - \overline{X})$ contains the deviations and the fourth column $(X_i - \overline{X})^2$ contains the squared deviations. The fifth column $f(X_i - \overline{X})^2$ displays the product of multiplying the frequencies and squared deviations together. Formula 4.4 is solved by taking the square root of the sum of these products $\Sigma f(X_i - \overline{X})^2$ divided by N,

$$s = \sqrt{\frac{\Sigma f(X_i - \overline{X})^2}{N}} = \sqrt{\frac{3{,}483.40}{25}} = \sqrt{139.34} = 11.8$$

Thus, the average deviation of these 25 exam scores from the mean, 70.32, is 11.8.

4.6 COMPUTING THE STANDARD DEVIATION: AN ADDITIONAL EXAMPLE*

An additional example will help to clarify the procedures for computing and interpreting the standard deviation. Studies have found that first-time tobacco use typically occurs before the age of 20. Many youth who smoke will continue to smoke for decades. The youth who do not smoke, on the other hand, are unlikely to start smoking when they are adults.

For this reason, there is significant public effort aimed at reducing youth smoking rates. Youth smoking prevention policies and programs, such as anti-smoking campaigns in the media, schools, and communities, as well as legal limits placed on tobacco advertising and sales to youth, have been very successful. The percentage of youth who smoke in Canada has been in decline.

_____

*This section is optional.

TABLE 4.6 COMPUTING THE STANDARD DEVIATION FOR PERCENT OF POPULATION AGED 15 TO 19 WHO ARE DAILY SMOKERS, 2005

Province/Territory	Daily Smokers (X_i)	Deviations $(X_i - \bar{X})$	Deviations Squared $(X_i - \bar{X})^2$
Newfoundland and Labrador	19.1	$19.1 - 14.88 = 4.22$	17.81
Prince Edward Island	9.6	$9.6 - 14.88 = -5.28$	27.88
Nova Scotia	8.3	$8.3 - 14.88 = -6.58$	43.30
New Brunswick	10.7	$10.7 - 14.88 = -4.18$	17.47
Quebec	12.8	$12.8 - 14.88 = -2.08$	4.33
Ontario	9.0	$9.0 - 14.88 = -5.88$	34.57
Manitoba	9.1	$9.1 - 14.88 = -5.78$	33.41
Saskatchewan	12.4	$12.4 - 14.88 = -2.48$	6.15
Alberta	10.1	$10.1 - 14.88 = -4.78$	22.85
British Columbia	8.6	$8.6 - 14.88 = -6.28$	39.44
Yukon	19.1	$19.1 - 14.88 = 4.22$	17.81
Northwest Territories	19.8	$19.8 - 14.88 = 4.92$	24.21
Nunavut	44.9	$44.9 - 14.88 = 30.02$	901.20

$$\Sigma(X_i) = 193.50 \qquad \Sigma(X_i - \bar{X}) = 0 \qquad \Sigma(X_i - \bar{X})^2 = 1{,}190.43$$

$$\bar{X} = \frac{\Sigma(X_i)}{N} = \frac{193.50}{13} = 14.88$$

Source: Data from Statistics Canada, CANSIM, Table 105–0427.

By inspection of Table 4.6, however, you can see that there is diversity from place to place in Canada in the percentage of youth who smoke. The percentage of the population aged 15 to 19 who smoke daily ranges from a low of 8.3% in Nova Scotia to a high of 44.9% in Nunavut. How much diversity is there in this variable? Computing the standard deviation will answer this question.

To solve Formula 4.3, substitute the sum of the right-hand column ("Deviations Squared") in the numerator and N (13 in this case) in the denominator:

$$s = \sqrt{\frac{\Sigma(X_i - \bar{X})^2}{N}} = \sqrt{\frac{1{,}190.43}{13}}$$
$$= \sqrt{91.57} = 9.57$$

For this problem, the standard deviation is 9.57%. *(For practice in computing and interpreting the standard deviation see any of the problems at the end of this chapter except 4.1 and 4.2. Problems with smaller data sets, such as 4.3 to 4.5, are recommended for practising computations until you are comfortable with these procedures.)*

4.7 INTERPRETING THE STANDARD DEVIATION

It is very possible that the meaning of the standard deviation (i.e., why we calculate it) is not completely obvious to you at this point. You might be asking: "Once I've gone to the trouble of calculating the standard deviation, what do I have?" The meaning of this measure of dispersion can be expressed in three ways. The first and most important involves the normal curve, and we will defer this interpretation until the next chapter.

A second way of thinking about the standard deviation is as an index of variability that increases in value as the distribution becomes more variable. In other words, the standard deviation is higher for more diverse distributions and lower for less diverse distributions. The lowest value the standard deviation can have is zero, and this would occur for distributions with no dispersion (i.e., if every single case in the sample had exactly the same score). Thus, 0 is the lowest value possible for the standard deviation (although there is no upper limit).

A third way to get a feel for the meaning of the standard deviation is by comparing one distribution with another. You might do this when comparing one group against another (e.g., men vs. women) or the same variable at two different times. For example, a recent survey (2002–2003 Joint Canada/United States Survey of Health conducted by Statistics Canada and the U.S. Centers for Disease Control and Prevention) found a large difference in the body weight (in pounds) of Canadian women compared to American women, as indicated by the following summary statistics:

Canada	United States
$\bar{X} = 145$	$\bar{X} = 155$
$s = 30$	$s = 37$

Canadian women on average weigh 145 pounds. The average American woman weighs 155 pounds. Clearly, Canadian women tend to have lower body weight, and according to the standard deviation, are also less diverse in terms of weight. The lower standard deviation for Canadian women indicates a distribution of weight that is more clustered around the mean (remember the distribution for Service A in Figure 4.1), while the higher standard deviation for American women reflects a distribution that is flatter and more spread out, like the distribution for Service B in Figure 4.1. In other words, compared to women in the U.S., Canadian women are more similar to each other and more clustered in a narrower weight range. The standard deviation is extremely useful for making comparisons of this sort between distributions of scores.

4.8 INTERPRETING STATISTICS: THE CENTRAL TENDENCY AND DISPERSION OF INCOME IN CANADA

In this installment of "interpreting statistics," we will examine the changing distribution of income in Canada. We will use the latest information from Statistics Canada to answer several questions: Is average income rising or falling? Does the average Canadian receive more or less income today than in the past? Is the distribution of income becoming more unequal (i.e., are the rich getting richer)? We can answer these questions by looking at changes in measures of central tendency and dispersion.

Changes in the mean and median will tell us, respectively, about changes in the average income for all Canadians (mean income) and income for the average Canadian (median income). The standard deviation would

The percent of persons in the labour force that work part-time in five cities in Western Canada and five cities in Eastern Canada is compared using data from the 2001 Census of Canada. Part-time workers are defined in the census as persons who work mainly part-time weeks (29 hours or less per week) on the basis of all jobs held during the year in 2000. Columns for the computation of the standard deviation have already been added to the tables below. Which groups of cities vary the most in terms of this variable? Computations for both the mean and standard deviation are shown below.

PERCENT OF LABOUR FORCE WITH PART-TIME JOBS, 2000, EASTERN CITIES

City	Part-timers (X_i)	Deviations ($X_i - \bar{X}$)	Deviations Squared ($X_i - \bar{X}$)^2
Halifax	21.3	$21.3 - 20.22 = 1.08$	1.1664
Quebec	20.6	$20.6 - 20.22 = .38$	0.1444
Ottawa-Hull	20.1	$20.1 - 20.22 = -.12$	0.0144
Montreal	19.5	$19.5 - 20.22 = -.72$	0.5184
Toronto	19.6	$19.6 - 20.22 = -.62$	0.3844
	$\Sigma(X_i) = 101.1$	$\Sigma(X_i - \bar{X}) = 0$	$\Sigma(X_i - \bar{X})^2 = 2.228$

Source: Data from Statistics Canada, 2001 Canadian Census, individual PUMF.

$$\bar{X} = \frac{\Sigma(X_i)}{N} = \frac{101.1}{5} = 20.22$$

$$s = \sqrt{\frac{\Sigma(X_i - \bar{X})^2}{N}} = \sqrt{\frac{2.228}{5}}$$

$$= \sqrt{.4456} = 0.6675$$

PERCENT OF LABOUR FORCE WITH PART-TIME JOBS, 2000, WESTERN CITIES

City	Part-timers (X_i)	Deviations ($X_i - \bar{X}$)	Deviations Squared ($X_i - \bar{X}$)^2
Victoria	27.4	$27.4 - 23.96 = 3.44$	11.8336
Regina/Saskatoon	24.7	$24.7 - 23.96 = .74$	.5476
Vancouver	23.9	$23.9 - 23.96 = -.06$	.0036
Winnipeg	22.8	$22.8 - 23.96 = -1.16$	1.3456
Calgary	21.0	$21.0 - 23.96 = -2.96$	8.7616
	$\Sigma(X_i) = 119.8$	$\Sigma(X_i - \bar{X}) = 0$	$\Sigma(X_i - \bar{X})^2 = 22.492$

Source: Data from Statistics Canada, 2001 Canadian Census, individual PUMF.

$$\bar{X} = \frac{\Sigma(X_i)}{N} = \frac{119.8}{5} = 23.96$$

$$s = \sqrt{\frac{\Sigma(X_i - \bar{X})^2}{N}} = \sqrt{\frac{22.492}{5}}$$

$$= \sqrt{4.4984} = 2.1209$$

With such small groups, you can tell by simply inspecting the scores that the western cities have higher percentages of part-time workers in their labour forces. This impression is confirmed by both the median, which is 20.1 for the eastern cities (Ottawa-Hull is the middle case) and 23.9 for the western cities (Vancouver is the middle case), and the mean (20.22 for the eastern cities and 23.96 for the western cities). For both groups, the mean is very similar to the median, indicating an unskewed distribution of scores. The five western cities are also much more variable and diverse than the eastern cities. The range for the western cities is 6.4 ($R = 27.4 - 21.0 = 6.4$), much higher than the range for the eastern cities of 1.7 ($R = 21.3 - 19.6 = 1.7$). Similarly, the standard deviation for the western cities (2.12) is about three times greater in value than the standard deviation for the eastern cities (0.67). In summary, the five western cities average higher rates of part-time work and are also more variable than the five eastern cities.

be the preferred measure of dispersion for an interval-ratio level variable like income, but unfortunately, Statistics Canada does not provide this information. We will instead measure dispersion with a statistic called the Gini coefficient that is calculated by Statistics Canada.

The Gini coefficient measures the level of dispersion, or more specifically the level of inequality, in a given distribution. So, if everyone in Canada had the same income (i.e., no dispersion or inequality), the Gini coefficient would be 0; conversely, if just one individual held all income in Canada, it would be 1. Thus, the Gini coefficient ranges from 0 to 1. A decrease in the value of the Gini coefficient means a decrease in income inequality (less dispersion), and vice versa.

Before considering the data, we should keep in mind that virtually any distribution of income will be positively skewed (see Figure 3.1). That is, in any group, locality, province, or nation, the incomes of most people will be grouped around the mean or median, but some people—the wealthiest members of the group—will have incomes far higher than the average. Because the mean uses *all* the scores, it will be pulled in the direction of the extreme scores relative to the median. In a positively skewed distribution, the mean will be greater than the median.

Also, be aware that the values in Figure 4.4 are expressed in 2004 dollars. This eliminates any changes in the mean and median caused by inflation over the years. Without this adjustment, recent incomes would appear to be much higher than older incomes, not because of increased purchasing power and well-being, but rather because of the changing value of the dollar. Finally, Figure 4.4 is based on total income of Canadian households, not individual income.

FIGURE 4.4   MEAN AND MEDIAN INCOME OF HOUSEHOLDS, 1980–2004, CANADA

Source: Data from Statistics Canada, CANSIM, Table 202–0403 (Mean Income) and Table 202–0411 (Median Income).

Figure 4.4 shows that, expressed in 2004 dollars, the average Canadian household earned about $50,000 in 1980 (median = $49,700). By 2004, median income for the average Canadian household was $47,200, or $2,500 less than in 1980, indicating a marked decrease in standard of living. This trend downward has some noticeable declines in both the early 1980s and 1990s, both periods of recession. However, we also see periods of incline during the "boom economies" of the late 1980s and the late 1990s to early 2000s.

The overall pattern of the mean income is almost identical to that of the median. It rises and falls in almost exactly the same ways and at the same times. Notice, however, that the mean is always higher than the median, a reflection of the characteristic positive skew of income data. In 1980, the mean income was $55,600, almost $6,000 higher than the median. By 2004, the mean was $61,000, almost $14,000 higher. What is this telling us? This increasingly positive skew means that the households with the highest incomes are becoming even more affluent relative to the bulk of the population. In other words, the growing distance between the mean and median suggests that, in recent years, the wealthiest Canadians are growing even wealthier relative to the rest of the population.

An increasing positive skew will be reflected by increases in the value of virtually any measure of dispersion. Although it does not supply information about the standard deviation, Statistics Canada calculates the Gini coefficient, reproduced in Figure 4.5. You can see by inspecting Figure 4.5 that the Gini coefficient is increasing, which indicates that incomes are growing in dispersion or variety. (Recall that the higher the Gini coefficient, the more dispersion or inequality that exists.) In 1980, the Gini coefficient was at 0.379. It rises to 0.43 by 2004, with most of the increase occurring in the 1990s. (To put this

FIGURE 4.5 DISPERSION OF HOUSEHOLD INCOME MEASURED BY THE GINI COEFFECIENT, 1980–2004, CANADA

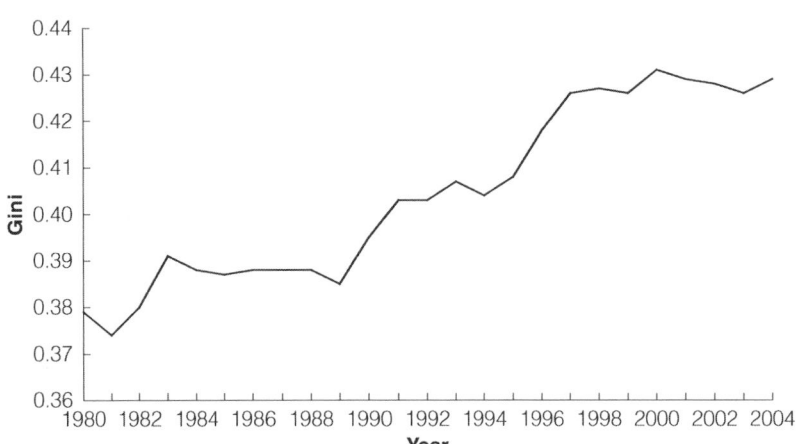

Source: Data from Statistics Canada, CANSIM, Table 202-0705.

READING STATISTICS 3: Measures of Central Tendency and Dispersion

As was the case with frequency distributions, measures of central tendency and dispersion may not be presented in research reports in the professional literature. Given the large number of variables included in a typical research project and the space limitations in journals and other media, there may not be room for the researcher to describe each variable fully. Furthermore, the great majority of research reports focus on relationships between variables rather than the distribution of single variables. In this sense, univariate descriptive statistics will be irrelevant to the main focus of the report.

This does not mean, of course, that univariate descriptive statistics are irrelevant to the research project. Nor do we mean to imply that researchers do not calculate and interpret these statistics. In fact, measures of central tendency and dispersion will be calculated and interpreted for virtually every variable, in virtually every research project. However, these statistics are less likely to be included in final research reports than the more analytical statistical techniques to be presented in the remainder of this text. Furthermore, some of these statistics (for example, the mean and standard deviation) serve a dual function. They not only are valuable descriptive statistics but also form the basis for many analytical techniques. Thus, they may be reported in the latter role if not in the former.

When included in research reports, measures of central tendency and dispersion will most often be presented in some summary form for all relevant variables—often in the form of a table. Means and standard deviations for many variables might, for example, be presented in the following table format.

Variable	$\overline{X}$	s	N
Age	33.2	1.3	1078
Number of children	2.3	.7	1078
Years married	7.8	1.5	1052
Income	55,786	1500	987
.	.	.	.
.	.	.	.
.	.	.	.
.	.	.	.

These tables describe the overall characteristics of the sample succinctly and clearly. If you inspect the table carefully, you will have a good sense of the nature of the sample on the traits relevant to the project. Note that the number of cases varies from variable to variable in the preceding table. This is normal and is caused by missing data or incomplete information on some of the cases.

Statistics in the Professional Literature

The Program for International Student Assessment, or PISA, is an international study of youth literacy skills in reading, mathematics, and science. It is sponsored by the Organization for Economic Cooperation and Development (OECD). It started in 2000 with 32 countries, including 28 OECD countries and 4 non-OECD countries, and is conducted every three years.

The PISA study involves testing 15-year-olds in their reading, mathematics, and science literacy skills. It also administers questionnaires to these students and their school administrators to collect information on family- and school-related variables relevant to the development of literacy skills. Students 15 years of age are the focus of the PISA study as they are near the end of compulsory schooling. PISA assumes that by this age, students have accumulated the necessary learning experiences that are crucial for adulthood. More than 250,000 15-year-old students participated in the 2000 PISA, representing some 17 million 15-year old students in the 32 countries.

The findings from the 2000 PISA are reported in the OECD paper *Knowledge and Skills for Life: First Results from the OECD Programme for International Student Assessment (PISA) 2000.* Below are the some of the key findings of the 2000 study: the average and standard deviation of PISA test scores for reading, mathematical, and science literacy for each of the 32 countries. The scores are reported on a scale of 0 to 1,000, with higher scores indicating higher literacy skills.

(continued)

READING STATISTICS 3: *(continued)*

To provide a convenient reference point, PISA test scores were scaled to have an overall mean of 500 and a standard deviation of 100.

The second column of Table 1, labelled "Mean," shows the average test scores in reading literacy for 15-year-olds by country, ranked from highest to lowest score. In Canada, for instance, 15-year-olds performed well above average on the PISA reading literacy scale. Only students in Finland (mean = 546) outperformed Canadian students (mean = 534). Canadian 15-year-olds also did much better than their U.S. counterparts. American 15-year-olds performed about average, with a mean score of

TABLE 1 TEST SCORES FOR READING LITERACY, BY COUNTRY

Country	Mean	SD
Finland	546	89
Canada	534	95
New Zealand	529	108
Australia	528	102
Ireland	527	94
South Korea	525	70
United Kingdom	523	100
Japan	522	86
Sweden	516	92
Austria	507	93
Belgium	507	107
Iceland	507	92
France	505	92
Norway	505	104
United States	504	105
OECD	**500**	**100**
Denmark	497	98
Switzerland	494	102
Spain	493	85
Czech Republic	492	96
Italy	487	91
Germany	484	111
Liechtenstein	483	96
Hungary	480	94
Poland	479	100
Greece	474	97
Portugal	470	97
Russia	462	92
Latvia	458	102
Luxembourg	441	100
Mexico	422	86
Brazil	396	86

Source: © OECD 2001. www.pisa.oecd.org

504, very close to the overall average of 500 for all OECD countries. To put this in context, it has been shown that a difference in PISA test scores in the range of 30 to 40 points (such as the Canada–U.S. difference, where there is a 30-point gap, or 534 to 504) is equal to about one full year of schooling.

The third column of Table 1 (labelled "SD," or standard deviation) shows the amount of variation in reading literacy test scores for 15-year-olds in each country. In Canada there is generally less variation in reading scores as the standard deviation is 95, or 5 points lower than the overall standard deviation of 100. That is, Canadian students are more alike in reading performance compared to the average OECD country. By contrast, the U.S., with a standard deviation of 105, has above-average variation.

Table 2 shows the average test score (mean) and variation (SD) in mathematical literacy. Table 3 shows the scores for scientific literacy. Overall, Canada outscores most countries in mathematics literacy and science literacy, with mean test scores of 533 and 529, respectively. These scores are also above the OECD average of 500. Further, the standards deviations for Canada tell us that both mathematical test scores (SD = 85) and science test scores (SD = 89) are less dispersed than the OECD average (SD = 100). Overall, mathematical and science performance is above average in Canada with less-than-average variation in students' performance.

Together, the mean and standard deviation provide a robust numerical description of literacy within and between countries. Canadian students perform better than average (mean scores greater than 500) with less-than-average variation (SD scores less than 100) on all three measures of literacy. Do you want to find out more? The reference is given below.

Source: OECD, 2001. *Knowledge and Skills for Life: First Results from the OECD Programme for International Student Assessment (PISA) 2000.* Paris: OECD Publications.

(continued)

READING STATISTICS 3:   *(continued)*

TABLE 2   TEST SCORES FOR MATHEMATICAL LITERACY, BY COUNTRY

Country	Mean	SD
Japan	557	87
South Korea	547	84
New Zealand	537	99
Finland	536	80
Australia	533	90
Canada	533	85
Switzerland	529	100
United Kingdom	529	92
Belgium	520	106
France	517	89
Austria	515	92
Denmark	514	87
Iceland	514	85
Liechtenstein	514	96
Sweden	510	93
Ireland	503	84
OECD	**500**	**100**
Norway	499	92
Czech Republic	498	96
United States	493	98
Germany	490	103
Hungary	488	98
Russia	478	104
Spain	476	91
Poland	470	103
Latvia	463	103
Italy	457	90
Portugal	454	91
Greece	447	108
Luxembourg	446	93
Mexico	387	83
Brazil	334	97

Source: © OECD 2001. www.pisa.oecd.org

TABLE 3   TEST SCORES FOR SCIENTIFIC LITERACY, BY COUNTRY

Country	Mean	SD
South Korea	552	81
Japan	550	90
Finland	538	86
United Kingdom	532	98
Canada	529	89
Australia	528	94
New Zealand	528	101
Austria	519	91
Ireland	513	92
Sweden	512	93
Czech Republic	511	94
France	500	102
Norway	500	96
OECD	**500**	**100**
United States	499	101
Belgium	496	111
Hungary	496	103
Iceland	496	88
Switzerland	496	100
Spain	491	95
Germany	487	102
Poland	483	97
Denmark	481	103
Italy	478	98
Liechtenstein	476	94
Greece	461	97
Latvia	460	98
Russia	460	99
Portugal	459	89
Luxembourg	443	96
Mexico	422	77
Brazil	375	90

Source: © OECD 2001. www.pisa.oecd.org

increase of 0.051, from 0.379 to 0.43, in the Gini coefficient in context, a difference of just 0.01 or more between two Gini coefficients is often considered to be meaningful and of consequence.) This trend would seem to indicate a growing income gap between less and more affluent Canadians over the time period, and is very consistent with the increasing positive skew in Figure 4.4.

In the end, the data show no increase in the income of the average Canadian (median) but an increase in the average income for all Canadians (mean). The increasing Gini coefficient indicates that incomes are growing in dispersion. Taken together, these findings would suggest that people with modest incomes continue to have modest incomes and, consistent with the ancient folk wisdom, the rich are getting richer.

SUMMARY

1. Measures of dispersion summarize information about the heterogeneity or variety in a distribution of scores. When combined with an appropriate measure of central tendency, these statistics convey a large volume of information in just a few numbers. While measures of central tendency locate the central points of the distribution, measures of dispersion indicate the amount of diversity in the distribution.

2. The index of qualitative variation (IQV) can be computed for any variable that has been organized into a frequency distribution. It is the ratio of the amount of variation observed in the distribution to the maximum variation possible in the distribution. The IQV is most appropriate for variables measured at the nominal level.

3. The range (R) is the distance from the highest to the lowest score in the distribution. The interquartile range (Q) is the distance from the third to the first quartile (the "range" of the middle 50% of the scores). These two ranges can be used with variables measured at either the ordinal or interval-ratio level.

4. The boxplot is a graph constructed from a five-number summary: the lowest score, first quartile, second quartile (the median), third quartile, and highest score in a distribution.

5. The standard deviation (s) is the most important measure of dispersion because of its central role in many more advanced statistical applications. The standard deviation has a minimum value of zero (indicating no variation in the distribution) and increases in value as the variability of the distribution increases. It is used most appropriately with variables measured at the interval-ratio level.

6. The variance (s^2) is used primarily in inferential statistics and in the design of some measures of association.

SUMMARY OF FORMULAS

Index of Qualitative Variation	4.1	$IQV = \dfrac{k(N^2 - \Sigma f^2)}{N^2(k-1)}$
Variance	4.2	$s^2 = \dfrac{\Sigma(X_i - \overline{X})^2}{N}$
Standard Deviation	4.3	$s = \sqrt{\dfrac{\Sigma(X_i - \overline{X})^2}{N}}$
Standard Deviation, aggregate data	4.4	$s = \sqrt{\dfrac{\Sigma f(X_i - \overline{X})^2}{N}}$

GLOSSARY

Average deviation. The average of the absolute deviations of the scores around the mean.

Boxplot. A graphic display device based on the median, interquartile range, and range. It is used to display the centre, dispersion, and overall range of scores in a distribution.

Deviations. The distances between the scores and the mean.

Dispersion. The amount of variety or heterogeneity in a distribution of scores.

Index of qualitative variation (IQV). A measure of dispersion for variables that have been organized into frequency distributions.

Interquartile range (Q). The distance from the third quartile to the first quartile.

Measures of dispersion. Statistics that indicate the amount of variety or heterogeneity in a distribution of scores.

Range (R). The highest score minus the lowest score.

Standard deviation. The square root of the squared deviations of the scores around the mean, divided by N. The most important and useful descriptive measure of dispersion; s represents the standard deviation of a sample; σ, the standard deviation of a population.

Variance. The squared deviations of the scores around the mean divided by N. A measure of dispersion used primarily in inferential statistics and also in correlation and regression techniques; s^2 represents the variance of a sample; σ^2, the variance of a population.

MULTIMEDIA RESOURCES

http://www.healeystatistics.nelson.com

Visit the companion Web site for the first Canadian edition of *Statistics: A Tool for Social Research* to access a wide range of student resources. Begin by clicking on the Student Resources section of the book's Web site to access review quizzes, flash cards, and other study tools.

PROBLEMS

4.1 SOC The marital status of residents of four apartment complexes is reported below. Compute the index of qualitative variation (IQV) for each neighbourhood. Which is the most heterogeneous of the four? Which is the least? *(HINT: It may be helpful to organize your computations as in Table 4.2.)*

Complex A	
Marital Status	Frequency
Single	26
Married	31
Divorced	12
Widowed	5
	$N = 74$

Complex B	
Marital Status	Frequency
Single	10
Married	12
Divorced	8
Widowed	7
	$N = 37$

Complex C	
Marital Status	Frequency
Single	20
Married	30
Divorced	2
Widowed	1
	$N = 53$

Complex D	
Marital Status	Frequency
Single	52
Married	3
Divorced	20
Widowed	10
	$N = 85$

4.2 The tables below show the program of study of university students living in two small dormitories. Compute the index of qualitative variation for each table. Which dorm is more diverse in terms of this variable?

Program	Dorm A	Dorm B
Social Sciences	20	10
Business	7	17
Engineering	3	8
Natural Sciences	10	3
Other	7	10
	47	48

4.3 Compute the range and standard deviation of the 10 scores reported below. *(HINT: It will be helpful to organize your computations as in Table 4.4.)*

10, 12, 15, 20, 25, 30, 32, 35, 40, 50

4.4 Compute the range and standard deviation of the 10 test scores below.

77, 83, 69, 72, 85, 90, 95, 75, 55, 45

4.5 SOC In problem 3.8, you computed the mean and median weekly earnings for 10 Canadian provinces in two separate years. Now compute the standard deviation and range for each year and, taking account of the two measures of central tendency and the two measures of dispersion, write a paragraph summarizing the distributions. What do the measures of dispersion add to what you already knew about central tendency? Did the provinces become more or less variable over the period? The scores are reproduced below.

Province	2000	2005
Newfoundland and Labrador	712	734
Prince Edward Island	667	709
Nova Scotia	570	697
New Brunswick	660	662
Quebec	648	745
Ontario	682	700
Manitoba	633	656
Saskatchewan	645	706
Alberta	617	680
British Columbia	712	741

4.6 SOC Data on several variables measuring overall health and well-being for 10 nations are reported below for 2000 with projections to 2010. Are these nations becoming more or less diverse on these variables? Calculate the mean, range, and standard deviation for each year for each variable. Summarize the results in a paragraph.

	Life Expectancy (years)		Infant Mortality Rate*		Fertility Rate#	
	2000	2010	2000	2010	2000	2010
Canada	80	81	5.0	4.5	1.6	1.6
United States	77	79	6.8	6.2	2.0	2.1
Mexico	72	74	25.4	18.5	2.6	2.3
Colombia	71	73	24.0	17.8	2.7	2.4
Japan	80	82	3.9	3.6	1.4	1.5
China	72	74	28.1	20.5	1.8	1.8
Sudan	57	61	68.7	55.2	5.4	4.2
Kenya	48	44	68.0	60.4	3.5	2.4
Italy	79	80	5.8	5.1	1.2	1.2
Germany	78	79	4.7	4.2	1.4	1.4

Source: U.S. Bureau of the Census. 2003. *Statistical Abstract of the United States, 2002.*
* Number of deaths of children under one year of age per 1000 live births
# Average number of children per female

4.7 SOC Labour force participation rates (percent employed), percent high school graduates, and mean income for males and females in 10 Ontario cities are reported below. Calculate a mean and a standard deviation for both groups for each variable and describe the differences. Are males and females unequal or more diverse on any of these variables? How great is the gender inequality?

	Labour Force Participation		% High School Graduates		Mean Income	
City	Male	Female	Male	Female	Male	Female
A	74	54	65	67	35,623	27,345
B	81	63	57	60	32,345	28,134
C	81	59	72	76	35,789	30,546
D	77	60	77	75	38,907	31,788
E	80	61	75	74	42,023	35,560
F	74	52	70	72	34,000	35,980
G	74	51	68	66	25,800	19,001
H	78	55	70	71	29,000	26,603
I	77	54	66	66	31,145	30,550
J	80	75	72	75	34,334	29,117

4.8 Compute the standard deviation for the pretest and post-test scores that were used in problems 2.6 and 3.12. The scores are reproduced below. Taking into account all of the information you have on these variables, write a paragraph describing how the sample changed from test to test. What does the standard deviation add to the information you already had?

Case	Pretest	Post-test
A	8	12
B	7	13
C	10	12
D	15	19
E	10	8
F	10	17
G	3	12
H	10	11
I	5	7
J	15	12
K	13	20
L	4	5
M	10	15
N	8	11
O	12	20

4.9 In problem 3.11, you computed measures of central tendency for the number of cars per 100 population for 8 nations. The scores are reproduced below. Compute the standard deviation for this variable and write a paragraph summarizing the mean, median, and standard deviation.

Nation	Number of Cars per 100 Population
United States	50
Canada	45
France	46
Germany	51
Japan	39
Mexico	10
Sweden	44
United Kingdom	37

4.10 CJ Per capita expenditures for police services for 20 Canadian cities are reported below for 1995 and 2005. Compute a mean and standard deviation for each year, and describe the differences in expenditures for the ten year period.

City	1995	2005
A	180	210
B	95	110
C	87	124
D	101	131
E	52	197
F	117	200
G	115	119
H	88	87
I	85	125
J	100	150
K	167	225
L	101	209
M	120	201
N	78	141
O	107	94
P	55	248
Q	78	140
R	92	131
S	99	152
T	103	178

4.11 Compute the range and standard deviation for the data presented in problem 3.14. The data are reproduced below. What would happen to the value of the standard deviation if you removed Montreal from this distribution and recalculated? Why?

City	Percent
Abbotsford	20
Barrie	32
Calgary	26
Dawson	6
Fredericton	9
Edmonton	6
Hamilton	10
Halifax	11
Kelowna	15
Mississauga	14
Montreal	53
Quebec	25
Saskatoon	3
St. John's	4
Thunder Bay	4
Toronto	31
Vancouver	18
Winnipeg	33

4.12 [SOC] Below are listed the rates of abortion per 100,000 women for 20 U.S. states in 1973 and 1975.

a. Describe what happened to these distributions over the two-year period. Did the average rate increase or decrease? What happened to the dispersion of this distribution? What happened between 1973 and 1975 that might explain these changes in central tendency and dispersion? *(HINT: It was a landmark decision by the U.S. Supreme Court)*

b.* Calculate Q for these states for both years.

c.* Construct a boxplot to display the distribution of data for both years.

State	1973	1975
Maine	3.5	9.5
Massachusetts	10.0	25.7
New York	53.5	40.7
Pennsylvania	12.1	18.5
Ohio	7.3	17.9
Michigan	18.7	20.3
Iowa	8.8	14.7
Nebraska	7.3	14.3
Virginia	7.8	18.0
South Carolina	3.8	10.3
Florida	15.8	30.5
Tennessee	4.2	19.2
Mississippi	0.2	0.6
Arkansas	2.9	6.3
Texas	6.8	19.1
Montana	3.1	9.9
Colorado	14.4	24.6
Arizona	6.9	15.8
California	30.8	33.6
Hawaii	26.3	31.6

Source: U.S. Bureau of the Census. 1977. *Statistical Abstracts of the United States: 1977.*

4.13 [SW] One of your goals as the new chief administrator of a large social service bureau is to equalize workloads within the various divisions of the agency. You have gathered data on caseloads per worker within each

*This problem is optional.

division. Which division comes closest to the ideal of an equalized workload? Which is farthest away?

A	B	C	D
50	60	60	75
51	59	61	80
55	58	58	74
60	55	59	70
68	56	59	69
59	61	60	82
60	62	61	85
57	63	60	83
50	60	59	65
55	59	58	60

4.14 Compute the standard deviation for both sets of data presented in problem 3.13 and reproduced below. Compare the standard deviation computed for students in their first year of study with the standard deviation computed for their final year of study. What happened? Why? Does this change relate at all to what happened to the mean over this (first to final year) period? How? What happened to the shapes of the underlying distributions?

First Year				
10	43	30	30	45
40	12	40	42	35
45	25	10	33	50
42	32	38	11	47
22	26	37	38	10

Final Year				
10	45	35	27	50
35	10	50	40	30
40	10	10	37	10
40	15	30	20	43
23	25	30	40	10

4.15 At Algebra University the math department ran some special sections of the introductory math course using a variety of innovative teaching techniques. Students were randomly assigned to either the traditional sections or the experimental sections, and all students were given the same final exam. The results of the final are summarized below. What was the effect of the experimental course?

Traditional	Experimental
$\overline{X} = 77.8$	$\overline{X} = 76.8$
$s = 12.3$	$s = 6.2$
$N = 478$	$N = 465$

4.16 You're the premier of the province and must decide which of four metropolitan police departments will win the annual award for efficiency. The performance of each department is summarized in monthly arrest statistics as reported below. Which department will win the award? Why?

Departments			
A	B	C	D
$\overline{X} = 601.30$	633.17	592.70	599.99
$s = 2.30$	27.32	40.17	60.23

Using SPSS for Windows to Produce Measures of Dispersion with the 2004 GSS

The demonstration and exercises below use the 2004 GSS data set supplied with this text. Start SPSS for Windows and open the *GSS.sav* file.

SPSS DEMONSTRATION 4.1   Producing the Range and the Standard Deviation

Most of the statistics discussed in this chapter are available from either the **Frequencies** or **Descriptives** procedures that you are already familiar with. In this demonstration, we will use the **Descriptives** command to find the range and standard deviation for *hsdsizec* (household size) and *numevact_c* (average number of evening activities respondent goes out for in a month).

From the main menu, click **Analyze, Descriptive Statistics,** and then **Descriptives.** The **Descriptives** dialog box will open. Use the cursor to find the names of the two variables in the list on the left and click the right-arrow button to transfer them to the **Variable(s)** box. Click **OK.** Under the **Descriptive** output, SPSS will produce two types of information, central tendency and dispersion. The output looks like this:

Descriptive Statistics

	N	Minimum	Maximum	Mean	Std. Deviation
HOUSEHOLD SIZE	1519	1	6	3.04	1.333
AVERAGE NUMBER OF EVENING ACTIVITIES RESPONDENT GOES OUT FOR IN A MONTH.	1519	0	62	25.97	16.659
Valid N (listwise)	1519				

We already discussed central tendency in Demonstration 3.2. In the present section, we focus on parts of the descriptive output related to dispersion of variables. The standard deviation for each variable is reported in the column labelled "Std. Deviation," and the range can be computed from the values given in the Minimum and Maximum columns. The standard deviation for *hsdsizec* is about 1.3 persons, and scores ranged from 1-person households to households of 6 (or more) persons. For *numevact_c*, the standard deviation was 16.659 with scores ranging from 0 to 62.

At this point, the range is probably easier to understand and interpret than the standard deviation. As we saw in Section 4.7, the latter is more meaningful when we have a point of comparison. For example, suppose we were interested in the variable *hsdsizec* and how household size has changed over the years. The "Descriptives" output for 2004 shows that people lived in households with an average size of 3.04 people with a standard deviation of 1.333 persons. Suppose that a sample from 1985 showed an average of 4.00 persons with a standard deviation of 0.95. You could conclude that household size had, on the average, decreased over the 19-year period but that Canadians had also become much more diverse in their living arrangements or, more precisely, in the number of persons they live with.

Exercises (using *GSS.sav*)

4.1 Use **Descriptives** to produce univariate descriptive statistics for *drr_q120* (# times you had 5+ drinks past month). Write a sentence or two summarizing these results.

4.2 Use **Descriptives** to produce univariate descriptive statistics for *incm* (respondent's annual personal income) and *incmhsd* (respondent's total household income). Compare the statistics for *incm* and *incmhsd*. Do respondents have higher or lower annual personal income than total household income? Is the sample more or less homogeneous on annual personal income than total household income?*

---

*These variables are ordinal in level of measurement, so calculation of a mean and standard deviation is not fully justified but is common practice in social science research. Make sure you review the coding scheme in Appendix G, or click Utilities and then Variables from the SPSS main menu bar, to help interpret the values.

5

THE NORMAL CURVE

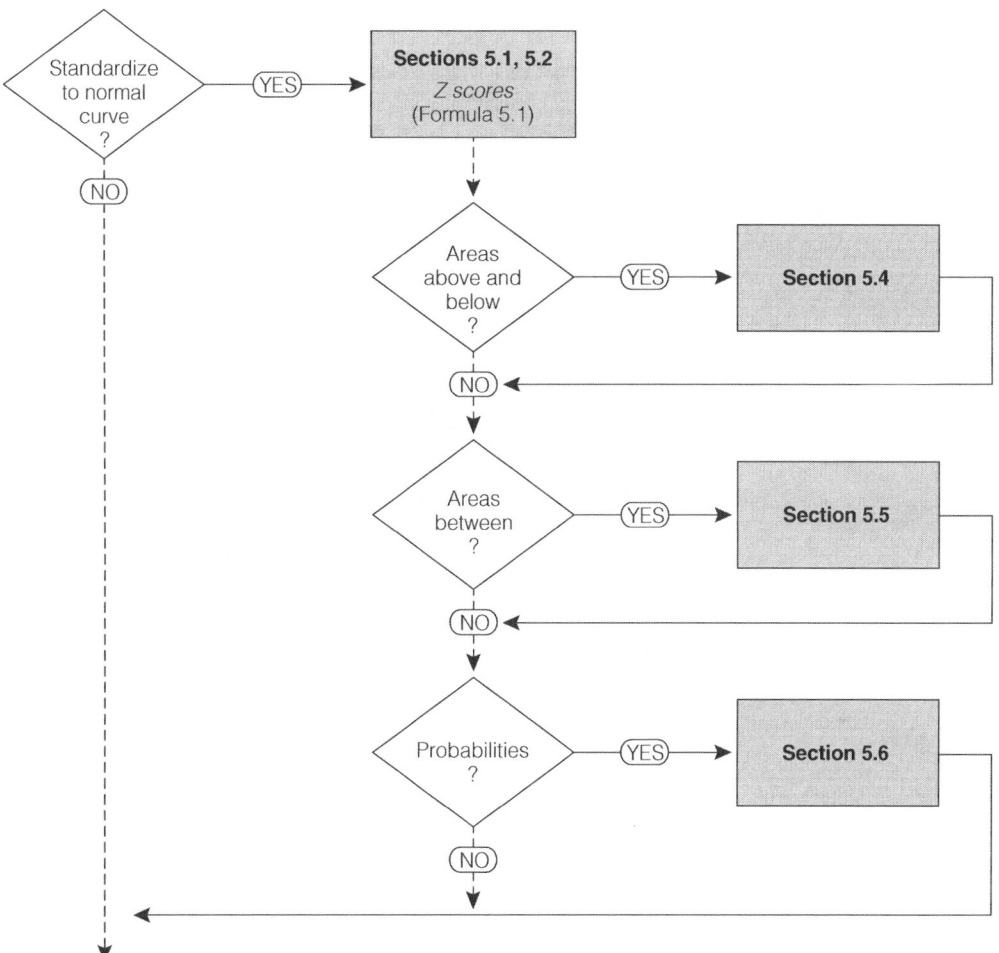

LEARNING OBJECTIVES   By the end of this chapter, you will be able to

1. Define and explain the concept of the normal curve.
2. Convert raw (original) scores to Z scores and use Z scores and the normal curve table (Appendix A) to find areas above, below, and between points on the curve.
3. Express areas under the curve in terms of probabilities.

5.1 INTRODUCTION

The **normal curve** is a concept of great importance in statistics. In combination with the mean and standard deviation, the normal curve can be used to construct precise descriptive statements about empirical distributions. In addition, as we shall see in Part II, it is also central to the theory that underlies inferential statistics. This chapter will conclude our treatment of descriptive statistics in Part I and lay important groundwork for Part II.

The normal curve is a theoretical model, a kind of frequency polygon or line chart that is unimodal (i.e., it has a single mode or peak), perfectly smooth and symmetrical (unskewed) so that its mean, median, and mode are all exactly the same value. It is bell shaped and its tails extend infinitely in both directions. Of course, no empirical distribution has a shape that perfectly matches this ideal model, but many variables (e.g., test results from large classes, standardized test scores such as the GRE, people's height and weight) are close enough to permit the assumption of normality. In turn, this assumption makes possible one of the most important uses of the normal curve—the description of empirical distributions based on our knowledge of the theoretical normal curve.

The crucial point about the normal curve is that distances along the abscissa (horizontal axis) of the distribution, when measured in standard deviations from the mean, always encompass the *same* proportion of the total area under the curve. In other words, on any normal curve, the distance from any given point to the mean (when measured in standard deviations) will cut off exactly the *same* proportion of the total area.

To illustrate, Figures 5.1 and 5.2 present two hypothetical distributions of IQ scores, one for a group of males and one for a group of females, both normally distributed (or nearly so), such that:

Males	Females
$\overline{X} = 100$	$\overline{X} = 100$
$s = 20$	$s = 10$
$N = 1,000$	$N = 1,000$

Figures 5.1 and 5.2 are drawn with two scales on the horizontal axis or abscissa of the graph. The upper scale is stated in "IQ units" and the lower scale in standard deviations from the mean. These scales are interchangeable, and we can easily shift from one to the other. For example, for the males, an IQ score of 120 is one standard deviation (remember that, for the male group, $s = 20$) above the mean and an IQ of 140 is two standard deviations above (to the right of) the mean. Scores to the left of the mean are marked as negative values because they are less than the mean. An IQ of 80 is one standard deviation below the mean, an IQ score of 60 is two standard deviations less than the mean, and so forth. Figure 5.2 is marked in a similar way except that, because its standard deviation is a different value ($s = 10$), the markings occur at different points. For the female sample, one standard deviation above the mean is an IQ of 110, one standard deviation below the mean is an IQ of 90, and so forth.

FIGURE 5.1   IQ SCORES FOR A GROUP OF MALES

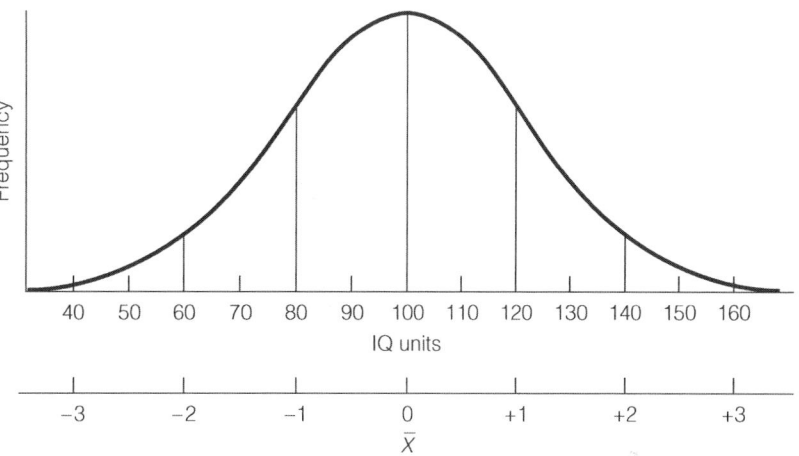

FIGURE 5.2   IQ SCORES FOR A GROUP OF FEMALES

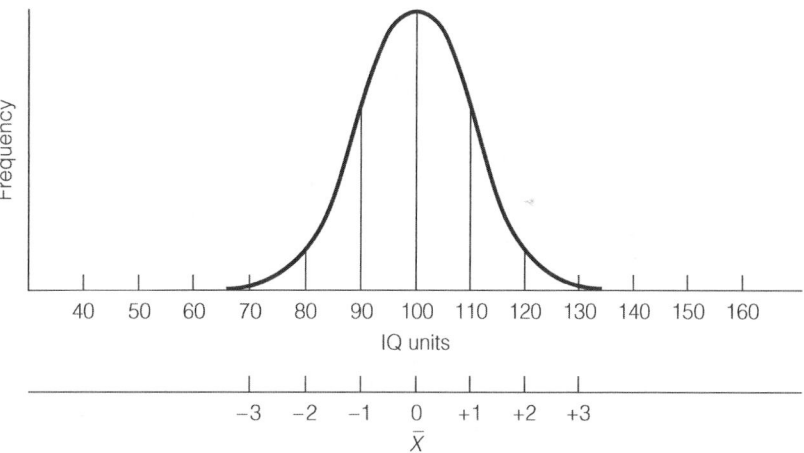

Recall that, on any normal curve, distances along the horizontal axis (or abscissa), when measured in standard deviations, always encompass exactly the same proportion of the total area under the curve. Specifically, the distance between one standard deviation above the mean and one standard deviation below the mean (or ±1 standard deviation) encompasses exactly 68.26% of the total area under the curve. This means that in Figure 5.1, 68.26% of the total area lies between the score of 80 (−1 standard deviation) and 120 (+1 standard deviation). The standard deviation for females is 10, so the same percentage of the area (68.26%) lies between the scores of 90 and 110. As long

FIGURE 5.3   AREAS UNDER THE THEORETICAL NORMAL CURVE

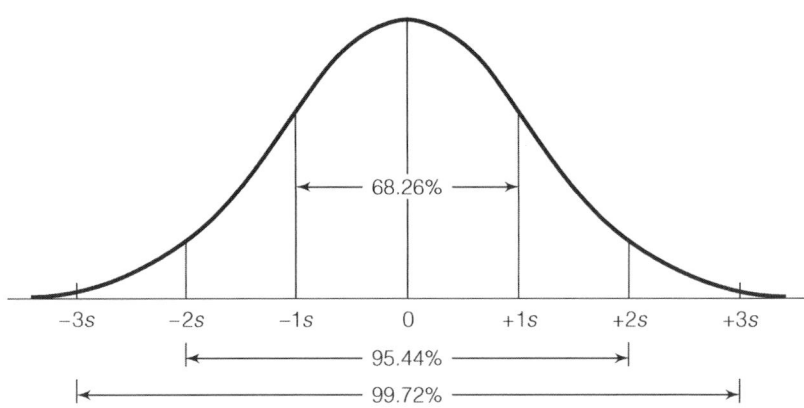

as an empirical distribution is normal, 68.26% of the total area will always be encompassed between ±1 standard deviation—regardless of the trait being measured and the number values of the mean and standard deviation.

It will be useful to familiarize yourself with the following relationships between distances from the mean and areas under the curve:

Between	Lies
±1 standard deviation	68.26% of the area
±2 standard deviations	95.44% of the area
±3 standard deviations	99.72% of the area

These relationships are displayed graphically in Figure 5.3.

The relationship between distance from the mean and area allows us to describe empirical distributions that are at least approximately normal. The position of individual scores can be described with respect to the mean, the distribution as a whole, or any other score in the distribution.

The areas between scores can also be expressed, if desired, in numbers of cases rather than percentage of total area. For example, a normal distribution of 1,000 cases will contain about 683 cases (68.26% of 1,000 cases) between ±1 standard deviation of the mean, about 954 between ±2 standard deviations, and about 997 between ±3 standard deviations. Thus, for any normal distribution, only a few cases will be farther away from the mean than ±3 standard deviations.

5.2 COMPUTING *Z* SCORES   To find the percentage of the total area (or number of cases) above, below, or between scores in an empirical distribution, the original scores must first be expressed in units of the standard deviation or converted into **Z scores.** The original scores could be in any unit of measurement (metres, IQ, dollars), but Z scores always have the same values for their mean (0) and standard deviation (1).

Think of converting the original scores into Z scores as a process of changing value scales—similar to changing from metres to yards, kilometres to miles, or gallons to litres. These units are different but equally valid ways of expressing distance, length, or volume. For example, a mile is equal to 1.61 kilometres, so two towns that are 10 miles apart are also 16.1 kilometres apart and a "5k" race covers about 3.10 miles. Although you may be more familiar with kilometres than miles, either unit works perfectly well as a way of expressing distance.

In the same way, the original (or "raw") scores and Z scores are two equally valid but different ways of measuring distances under the normal curve. In Figure 5.1, for example, we could describe a particular score in terms of IQ units ("Amal's score was 120") or standard deviations ("Amal scored one standard deviation above the mean").

When we compute Z scores, we convert the original units of measurement (IQ units, centimetres, dollars, etc.) to Z scores and, thus, "standardize" the normal curve to a distribution that has a mean of 0 and a standard deviation of 1. The mean of the empirical normal distribution will be converted to 0, its standard deviation to 1, and all values will be expressed in Z-score form. The formula for computing Z scores is

FORMULA 5.1

$$Z = \frac{X_i - \overline{X}}{s}$$

Formula 5.1 will convert any score (X_i) from an empirical distribution into the equivalent Z score. To illustrate, consider the following set of scores from Table 4.4: 10, 20, 30, 40, and 50. Their Z-score equivalent are presented in Table 5.1.

TABLE 5.1   COMPUTING Z SCORES

Score (X_i)	Z Score $= \dfrac{X_i - \overline{X}}{s}$
10	$\dfrac{10 - 30}{14.14} = -1.414$
20	$\dfrac{20 - 30}{14.14} = -.707$
30	$\dfrac{30 - 30}{14.14} = 0$
40	$\dfrac{40 - 30}{14.14} = .707$
50	$\dfrac{50 - 30}{14.14} = 1.414$

Recall from Table 4.4: $\overline{X} = 30$, $s = 14.14$

TABLE 5.2   COMPUTING THE MEAN AND STANDARD DEVIATION FOR A DISTRIBUTION OF Z SCORES

Scores (X_i)	Deviations ($X_i - \overline{X}$)	Deviations Squared ($X_i - \overline{X})^2$
−1.414	−1.414	2.0
−.707	−.707	.5
0	0	0
.707	.707	.5
1.414	1.414	2.0

$\sum(X_i) = 0$ $\sum(X_i - \overline{X})^2 = 5$

$$\overline{X} = \frac{\sum(X_i)}{N} = \frac{0}{5} = 0 \quad \text{(Formula 3.1)}$$

$$s = \sqrt{\frac{\sum\left(X_i - \overline{X}\right)^2}{N}} = \sqrt{\frac{5}{5}} = \sqrt{1} = 1 \quad \text{(Formula 4.3)}$$

A Z score of positive 1.00 indicates that the original score lies one standard deviation unit above (to the right of) the mean. A negative Z score of 1.00 would fall one standard deviation unit below (to the left of) the mean. Thus in the above example, the Z score of 1.414 indicates that the original score of 50 lies 1.414 standard deviation units above the mean, while −1.414 indicates that the original score of 10 lies 1.414 standard deviation units below the mean.

By inspection, you can see that the distribution of Z scores in Table 5.1 has a mean of 0 and a standard deviation of 1. To substantiate these observations, the mean and standard deviation of the Z distribution are computed using Formulas 3.1 and 4.3. The results are shown in Table 5.2. *(For practice in computing Z scores, see any of the problems at the end of this chapter.)*

5.3 THE NORMAL CURVE TABLE

The theoretical normal curve has been very thoroughly analyzed and described by statisticians. The areas related to any Z score have been precisely determined and organized into a table format. This **normal curve table** or Z-score table is presented as Appendix A in this text and a small portion of it is reproduced here for purposes of illustration as Table 5.3.

The normal curve table consists of three columns, with Z scores in the left-hand column "a," areas between the Z score and the mean of the curve in the middle column "b," and areas beyond the Z score in the right-hand column "c." To find the area between any Z score and the mean, go down the column labelled "Z" until you find the Z score. For example, go down column "a" either in Appendix A or in Table 5.3 until you find a Z score of +1.00. The entry in column "b" ("Area between Mean and Z") is 0.3413. The table presents all areas in the form of proportions, but we can easily translate these into percentages by multiplying them by 100 (see Chapter 2).

TABLE 5.3   AN ILLUSTRATION OF HOW TO FIND AREAS UNDER THE
NORMAL CURVE USING APPENDIX A

(a) Z	(b) Area between Mean and Z	(c) Area beyond Z
0.00	0.0000	0.5000
0.01	0.0040	0.4960
0.02	0.0080	0.4920
0.03	0.0120	0.4880
⋮	⋮	⋮
1.00	0.3413	0.1587
1.01	0.3438	0.1562
1.02	0.3461	0.1539
1.03	0.3485	0.1515
⋮	⋮	⋮
1.50	0.4332	0.0668
1.51	0.4345	0.0655
1.52	0.4357	0.0643
1.53	0.4370	0.0630
⋮	⋮	⋮

We could say either "a proportion of 0.3413 of the total area under the curve lies between a Z score of 1.00 and the mean," or "34.13% of the total area lies between a score of 1.00 and the mean."

To illustrate further, find the Z score of 1.50 either in column "a" of Appendix A or the abbreviated table presented in Table 5.3. This score is $1\frac{1}{2}$ standard deviations to the right of the mean and corresponds to an IQ of 130 for the men's IQ data. The area in column "b" for this score is 0.4332. This means that a proportion of 0.4332—or a percentage of 43.32%—of all the area under the curve lies between this score and the mean.

The third column in the table presents "Area beyond Z." These are areas above positive scores or below negative scores. This column will be used when we want to find an area above or below certain Z scores, an application that will be explained in Section 5.4.

To conserve space, the normal curve table in Appendix A includes only positive Z scores. Because the normal curve is perfectly symmetrical, however, the area between the score and the mean (column b) for a negative score will be exactly the same as those for a positive score of the same numerical value. For example, the area between a Z score of -1.00 and the mean will also be 34.13%, exactly the same as the area we found previously for a score of $+1.00$. As will be repeatedly demonstrated below, however, the sign of the Z score is extremely important and should be carefully noted.

For practice in using Appendix A to describe areas under an empirical normal curve, verify that the Z scores and areas given below are correct for the men's IQ distribution. For each IQ score, the equivalent Z score is computed using Formula 5.1, and then Appendix A is used to find areas between the score and the mean. $(\overline{X} = 100,\ s = 20$ throughout.)

IQ Score	Z Score	Area between Z and the Mean
110	+0.50	19.15%
125	+1.25	39.44%
133	+1.65	45.05%
138	+1.90	47.13%

The same procedures apply when the Z-score equivalent of an actual score happens to be a minus value (i.e. when the raw score lies below the mean).

IQ Score	Z Score	Area between Z and the Mean
93	−0.35	13.68%
85	−0.75	27.34%
67	−1.65	45.05%
62	−1.90	47.13%

Remember that the areas in Appendix A will be the same for Z scores of the same numerical value regardless of sign. The area between the score of 138 (+1.90) and the mean is the same as the area between 62 (−1.90) and the mean. *(For practice in using the normal curve table, see any of the problems at the end of this chapter.)*

5.4 FINDING TOTAL AREA ABOVE AND BELOW A SCORE

To this point, we have seen how the normal curve table can be used to find areas between a Z score and the mean. The information presented in the table can also be used to find other kinds of areas in empirical distributions that are at least approximately normal in shape. For example, suppose you need to determine the total area below the scores of two male subjects in the distribution described in Figure 5.1. The first subject has a score of 117 ($X_1 = 117$), which is equivalent to a Z score of +0.85:

$$Z_1 = \frac{X_1 - \overline{X}}{s} = \frac{117 - 100}{20} = \frac{17}{20} = +0.85$$

The plus sign of the Z score indicates that the score should be placed above (to the right of) the mean. To find the area below a positive Z score, the area between the score and the mean (given in column b) must be added to the area below the mean. As we noted earlier, the normal curve is symmetrical (unskewed) and its mean will be equal to its median. Therefore, the area below the mean (just like the median) will be 50%. Study Figure 5.4 carefully. We are interested in the shaded area.

By consulting the normal curve table, we find that the area between the score and the mean (see column b) is 30.23% of the total area. The area below a Z score of +0.85 is therefore 80.23% (50.00% + 30.23%). This subject scored higher than 80.23% of the persons tested.

FIGURE 5.4   FINDING THE AREA BELOW A POSITIVE Z SCORE

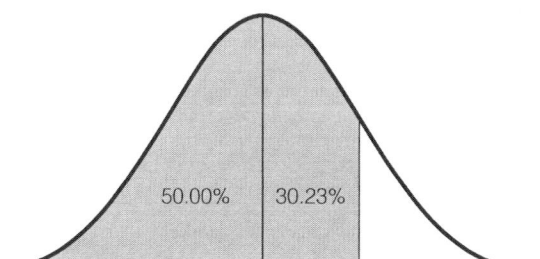

FIGURE 5.5   FINDING THE AREA BELOW A NEGATIVE Z SCORE

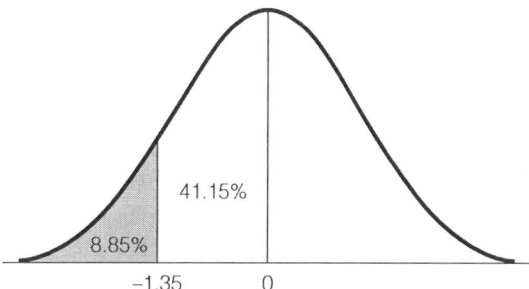

The second subject has an IQ score of 73 ($X_2 = 73$), which is equivalent to a Z score of -1.35:

$$Z_2 = \frac{X_2 - \overline{X}}{s} = \frac{73 - 100}{20} = -\frac{27}{20} = -1.35$$

To find the area below a negative score, we use the column labelled "Area beyond Z." The area of interest is depicted in Figure 5.5, and we must determine the size of the shaded area. The area beyond a score of -1.35 is given as 0.0885, which we can express as 8.85%. The second subject ($X_2 = 73$) scored higher than 8.85% of the tested group.

In the examples above, we use the techniques for finding the area below a score. Essentially the same techniques are used to find the area above a score. If we need to determine the area above an IQ score of 108, for example, we would first convert to a Z score,

$$Z = \frac{X_i - \overline{X}}{s} = \frac{108 - 100}{20} = \frac{8}{20} = +0.40$$

and then proceed to Appendix A. The shaded area in Figure 5.6 represents the area in which we are interested. The area above a positive score is found in the "Area beyond Z" column, and, in this case, the area is 0.3446, or 34.46%.

FIGURE 5.6   FINDING THE AREA ABOVE A POSITIVE Z SCORE

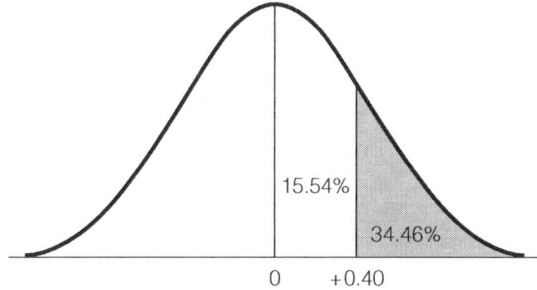

TABLE 5.4 FINDING AREAS ABOVE AND BELOW POSITIVE AND NEGATIVE *Z* SCORES

	When the *Z* Score Is	
To Find Area:	Positive	Negative
Above *Z*	Look in column c	Add column b area to .5000 or 50.00%
Below *Z*	Add column b area to .5000 or 50.00%	Look in column c

These procedures are summarized in Table 5.4. To find the total area above a positive *Z* score or below a negative *Z* score, go down the "*Z*" column of Appendix A until you find the score. The area you are seeking will be in the "Area beyond *Z*" column (column c). To find the total area below a positive *Z* score or above a negative score, locate the score and then add the area in the "Area between Mean and *Z*" (column b) to either .5000 (for proportions) or 50.00 (for percentages). These techniques might be confusing at first, and you will find it helpful to draw the curve and shade in the areas in which you are interested. *(For practice in finding areas above or below Z scores, see problems 5.1 to 5.7.)*

5.5 FINDING AREAS BETWEEN TWO SCORES

On occasion, you will need to determine the area between two scores rather than the total area above or below one score. In the case where the scores are on opposite sides of the mean, the area between the scores can be found by adding the areas between each score and the mean. Using the men's IQ data as an example, if we wished to know the area between the IQ scores of 93 and 112, we would convert both scores to *Z* scores, find the area between each score and the mean from Appendix A, and add these two areas together. The first IQ score of 93 converts to a *Z* score of −0.35:

$$Z_1 = \frac{X_1 - \overline{X}}{s} = \frac{93 - 100}{20} = -\frac{7}{20} = -0.35$$

The second IQ score (112) converts to +0.60:

$$Z_2 = \frac{X_2 - \overline{X}}{s} = \frac{112 - 100}{20} = \frac{12}{20} = 0.60$$

Both scores are placed on Figure 5.7. We are interested in the total shaded area. The total area between these two scores is 13.68% + 22.57%, or 36.25%. Therefore, 36.25% of the total area (or about 363 of the 1,000 cases) lies between the IQ scores of 93 and 112.

FIGURE 5.7   FINDING THE AREA BETWEEN TWO SCORES

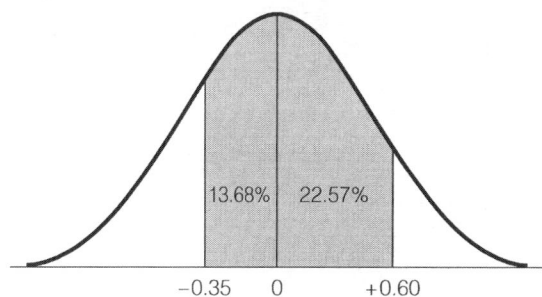

When the scores of interest are on the same side of the mean, a different procedure must be followed to determine the area between them. For example, if we were interested in the area between the scores of 113 and 121, we would begin by converting these scores into Z scores:

$$Z_1 = \frac{X_1 - \overline{X}}{s} = \frac{113 - 100}{20} = \frac{13}{20} = +0.65$$

$$Z_2 = \frac{X_2 - \overline{X}}{s} = \frac{121 - 100}{20} = \frac{21}{20} = +1.05$$

The scores are noted in Figure 5.8; we are interested in the shaded area. To find the area between two scores on the same side of the mean, find the area between each score and the mean (given in column b of Appendix A) and then subtract the smaller area from the larger. Between the Z score of $+0.65$ and the mean lies 24.22% of the total area. Between $+1.05$ and the mean lies 35.31% of the total area. Therefore, the area between these two scores is 35.31% $-$ 24.22%, or 11.09% of the total area. The same technique would be

FIGURE 5.8   FINDING THE AREA BETWEEN TWO SCORES

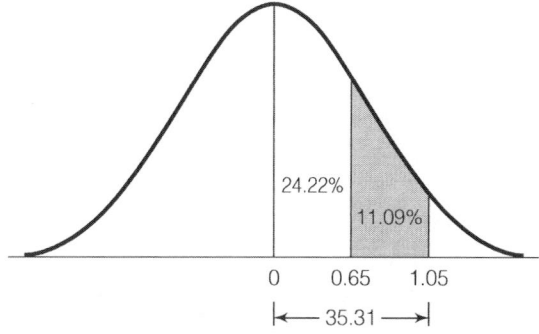

Application 5.1

There has been a sharp increase in the number of overweight and obese Canadians over the last 30 years—a trend that has been observed in several developed countries. The rise in obesity is due to a variety of factors, notably changes in the general dietary and lifestyle habits of Canadians, including increased levels of sedentary living and increased consumption of processed and "junk" food. Social scientists also have shown that present social, economic, and political factors create an environment in which it is challenging to maintain a healthy diet and weight. Sociologists, for example, contend that time and cost pressures on families have led to an increase in families' consumption of fast food, which is high in calories and fats and is readily available to consumers. Also, many children and youth spent their leisure time doing sedentary activities such as watching television and playing video games instead of participating in physical outdoor activities.

Trends in overweight and obesity are observed using the body mass index (BMI), which is a measure of body fat for men and women. BMI is a number calculated from an individual's body weight and height. The BMI is not a direct measure of body fat (e.g., it can overestimate body fatness in muscular and athletic persons, such as many professional football players), but studies show that it is correlated with direct measures of body fat (e.g., skinfold thickness) as well as several overweight- and obesity-related diseases (e.g., Type II diabetes and heart disease). BMI is also easy to calculate. The BMI formula is

in standard units: $\left(\dfrac{\text{weight in pounds}}{\text{height in inches}^2} \right) \times 703$

in metric units: $\left(\dfrac{\text{weight in kilograms}}{\text{height in metres}^2} \right)$

The BMI is interpreted using a weight classification system that is the same for adult men and women (but not for children as their body fat changes with age) as follows:

BMI Score	Weight Status
Less than 18.5	Underweight
18.5–24.9	Normal
25.0–29.9	Overweight
30.0 and over	Obese

Note that health care professionals and researchers often further divide the obese category, for example, into obese (BMI of 30.0–34.9), severely obese (BMI of 35.0–39.9), and morbidly obese (BMI of 40.0 and over).

Using this system, an adult with a height of 5'9" and weight of 200 pounds has a BMI score of 29.5 and is classified as overweight. However, how does this score compare with the distribution of all BMI scores? To answer this question we can compute a Z score and find the area below or above the score.

According to the 2005 Canadian Community Health Survey, Statistics Canada's main health survey, the distribution of BMI scores of adult Canadians is normal with a mean of 26.1 and a standard deviation of 4.9 (see the frequency polygon on the next page):

Hence, the Z-score equivalent of the original raw BMI score of 29.5 would be

$$Z = \frac{X_i - \overline{X}}{s} = \frac{29.5 - 26.1}{4.9} = \frac{3.4}{4.9} = 0.69$$

Turning to Appendix A, we find that the "Area between Mean and Z" for a Z score of +0.69 is 0.2549, which could also be expressed as 25.49%. Because this is a positive Z score, we need to add this area to 50.00% to find the total area below. A BMI score of 29.5 is higher than 75.49% (or 25.49 + 50.00) of all adult BMI scores in Canada.

(continued next page)

Application 5.1: *(continued)*

BMI SCORES OF ADULT CANADIANS, 2005

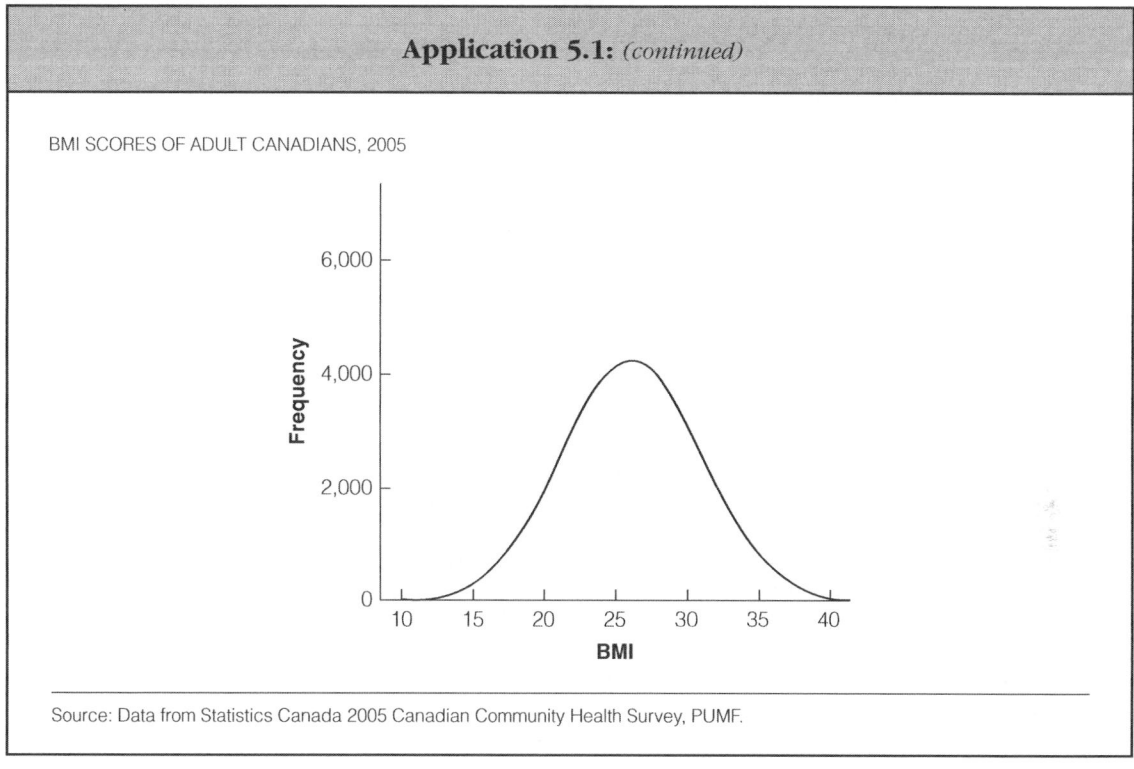

Source: Data from Statistics Canada 2005 Canadian Community Health Survey, PUMF.

TABLE 5.5   FINDING AREAS BETWEEN SCORES

Situation	Procedure
Scores are on the SAME side of the mean	Find areas between each score and the mean in column b. Subtract the smaller area from the larger area.
Scores are on OPPOSITE sides of the mean	Find areas between each score and the mean in column b. Add the two areas together.

followed if both scores had been below the mean. The procedures for finding areas between two scores are summarized in Table 5.5. *(For practice in finding areas between two scores, see problems 5.3, 5.4, and 5.6 to 5.9.)*

5.6 USING THE NORMAL CURVE TO ESTIMATE PROBABILITIES

To this point, we have thought of the theoretical normal curve as a way of describing the percentage of total area above, below, and between scores in an empirical distribution. We have also seen that these areas can be converted into the number of cases above, below, and between scores. In this section, we

Application 5.2

In Application 5.1 we used a Z score and the normal curve table to find the total area below a BMI (a measure of body fat) score of 29.5 in the distribution of BMI scores. In this application we will determine the area between two BMI scores rather than the total area below one BMI score. We should recall that according to the Canadian Community Health Survey, BMI scores among adults in Canada are distributed normally with a mean of 26.1 and a standard deviation of 4.9.

What percentage of adults in Canada is normal weight and what percentage is overweight? That is, what percentage has a BMI score between 18.5 and 24.9 (normal) and what percentage has a score between 25.0 and 29.9 (overweight)?

The first two scores are both below the mean. Using Table 5.5 as a guide, we must first compute Z scores, find areas between each score and the mean, and then subtract the smaller area from the larger.

$$Z_1 = \frac{X_1 - \overline{X}}{s} = \frac{18.5 - 26.1}{4.9} = -\frac{7.6}{4.9} = -1.55$$

$$Z_2 = \frac{X_2 - \overline{X}}{s} = \frac{24.9 - 26.1}{4.9} = -\frac{1.2}{4.9} = -0.25$$

Using column b, we see that the area between $Z = -1.55$ and the mean is 0.4394 and the area between $Z = -0.25$ and the mean is 0.0987. Subtracting the smaller from the larger (0.4394 − 0.0987) gives 0.3407. Changing to percentage format, we can say that 34.07% of adults in Canada have normal body weight.

To find the percentage of Canadians who are overweight, we must add column b areas together since the scores (25.0 and 29.9) are on opposite sides of the mean (see Table 5.5).

$$Z_1 = \frac{X_1 - \overline{X}}{s} = \frac{25.0 - 26.1}{4.9} = -\frac{1.1}{4.9} = -0.23$$

$$Z_2 = \frac{X_2 - \overline{X}}{s} = \frac{29.9 - 26.1}{4.9} = \frac{3.8}{4.9} = 0.78$$

Using column b, we see that the area between $Z-0.23$ and the mean is 0.0910 and the area between $Z+0.78$ and the mean is 0.2823. Therefore, the total area between these two scores is (0.0910 + 0.2823) or 0.3733. Translating to percentages again, we can say that 37.33% of Canadian adults are overweight. In fact, more adults in Canada are overweight than normal weight: 37.33% vs. 34.07%.

introduce the idea that the theoretical normal curve may also be thought of as a distribution of probabilities. Specifically, we may use the properties of the theoretical normal curve (Appendix A) to estimate the probability that a case randomly selected from an empirical normal distribution will have a score that falls in a certain range. In terms of techniques, these probabilities will be found in exactly the same way as areas were found. Before we consider these mechanics, however, let us examine what is meant by the concept of probability.

Although we are rarely systematic or rigorous about it, we all attempt to deal with probabilities every day and, indeed, we base our behaviour on our estimates of the likelihood that certain events will occur. We constantly ask (and answer) questions such as: What is the probability of rain? Of drawing to an inside straight in poker? Of the worn-out tires on my car going flat? Of passing a test if I don't study?

To estimate the probability of an event, we must first be able to define what would constitute a "success." The examples above contain several

Application 5.3

We know that the BMI scores of adult Canadians are normally distributed with a mean of 26.1 and a standard deviation of 4.9 (see Applications 5.1 and 5.2). What is the probability that a Canadian adult selected at random will have a BMI score of less than 20.0? More than 31? Less than 40? To answer these questions, we must first calculate Z scores and then consult Appendix A. We are looking for probabilities, so we will leave the areas in proportion form. The Z score for a score of 20 is

$$Z = \frac{X_i - \overline{X}}{s} = \frac{20.0 - 26.1}{4.9} = -\frac{6.1}{4.9} = -1.25$$

This score is a negative value (below or to the left of the mean) and we are looking for the area below. Using Table 5.4 as a guide, we see that we must use column c to find the area below a negative score. This area is 0.1056. Rounding off, we can say that the odds of selecting a Canadian adult with a BMI score of less than 20 are only 1 out of 10. This low value tells us that this would be an unlikely event.

The Z score for the score of 31 is

$$Z = \frac{X_i - \overline{X}}{s} = \frac{31.0 - 26.1}{4.9} = \frac{4.9}{4.9} = 1.00$$

The Z score is positive and to find the area above (greater than) 31, we look in column c (see Table 5.4). This value is 0.1587. The odds of selecting a Canadian with a BMI score of greater than 31 is roughly 16 out of 100, slightly more likely than selecting a Canadian with a BMI score of less than 20.

The Z score for the score of 40 is

$$Z = \frac{X_i - \overline{X}}{s} = \frac{40.0 - 26.1}{4.9} = \frac{13.9}{4.9} = 2.84$$

To find the area below a positive Z score, we add the area between the score and the mean (column b) to 0.5000 (see Table 5.4). This value is (0.4977 + 0.5000) or 0.9977. It is extremely likely that a randomly selected Canadian adult will have a BMI score of less than 40.

different definitions of a success (i.e. rain, drawing a certain card, flat tires, and passing grades). To determine a probability, a fraction must be established, with the numerator equalling the number of events that would constitute a success and the denominator equalling the total number of possible events where a success could theoretically occur:

$$\text{Probability} = \frac{\text{\# successes}}{\text{\# events}}$$

To illustrate, assume that we wish to know the probability of selecting a specific card—say, the king of hearts—in one draw from a well-shuffled deck of cards. Our definition of a success is quite specific (drawing the king of hearts); and with the information given, we can establish a fraction. Only one card satisfies our definition of success, so the number of events that would constitute a success is 1; this value will be the numerator of the fraction. There are 52 possible events (i.e. 52 cards in the deck), so the denominator will be 52. The fraction is thus 1/52, which represents the probability of selecting the king of hearts on one draw from a well-shuffled deck of cards. Our probability of success is 1 out of 52.

We can leave the fraction established above as it is, or we can express it in several other ways. For example, we can express it as an odds ratio by inverting the fraction, showing that the odds of selecting the king of hearts on a single draw are 52:1 (or fifty-two to one). We can express the fraction as a proportion by dividing the numerator by the denominator. For our example above, the corresponding proportion is .0192, which is the proportion of all possible events that would satisfy our definition of a success. In the social sciences, probabilities are usually expressed as proportions, and we will follow this convention throughout the remainder of this section. Using p to represent "probability," the probability of drawing the king of hearts (or any specific card) can be expressed as

$$p \text{ (king of hearts)} = \frac{\text{\# successes}}{\text{\# events}} = \frac{1}{52} = .0192$$

As conceptualized here, probabilities have an exact meaning: over the long run, the events that we define as successes will bear a certain proportional relationship to the total number of events. The probability of .0192 for selecting the king of hearts in a single draw really means that, over an infinite number of draws of one card at a time from a full deck of 52 cards, the proportion of successful draws would be .0192. Or, for every 10,000 draws, 192 would be the king of hearts, and the remaining 9,808 selections would be other cards. Thus, when we say that the probability of drawing the king of hearts in one draw is .0192, we are essentially applying our knowledge of what would happen over an infinite number of draws to a single draw.

Like proportions, probabilities range from 0.00 (meaning that the event has absolutely no chance of occurrence) to 1.00 (a certainty). As the value of the probability increases, the likelihood that the defined event will occur also increases. A probability of .0192 is close to zero, and this means that the event (drawing the king of hearts) is unlikely or improbable.

These techniques can be used to establish simple probabilities in any situation in which we can specify the number of successes and the total number of events. For example, a single die has six sides or faces, each with a different value ranging from 1 to 6. The probability of getting any specific number (say, a 4) in a single roll of a die is therefore

$$p \text{ (rolling a four)} = \frac{1}{6} = .1667$$

Combining this way of thinking about probability with our knowledge of the theoretical normal curve allows us to estimate the likelihood of selecting a case that has a score within a certain range. For example, suppose we wished to estimate the probability that a randomly chosen subject from the distribution of men's IQ scores would have an IQ score between 95 and the mean score of 100. Our definition of a success here would be the selection of any subject with a score in the specified range. Normally, we would next establish a fraction with the numerator equal to the number of subjects with scores in the defined range and the denominator equal to the total number of subjects. However, if the empirical distribution is normal in form, we can skip this step since the probabilities, in proportion form, are already stated in Appendix A. That is, the areas in Appendix A can be interpreted as probabilities.

To determine the probability that a randomly selected case will have a score between 95 and the mean, we would convert the original score to a Z score:

$$Z = \frac{X_i - \overline{X}}{s} = \frac{95 - 100}{20} = -\frac{5}{20} = -0.25$$

Using Appendix A, we see that the area between this score and the mean is 0.0987. This is the probability we are seeking. The probability that a randomly selected case will have a score between 95 and 100 is 0.0987 (or, rounded off, 0.1, or one out of 10). In the same fashion, the probability of selecting a subject from any range of scores can be estimated. Note that the techniques for estimating probabilities are exactly the same as those for finding areas. The only new information introduced in this section is the idea that the areas in the normal curve table can also be thought of as probabilities.

To consider an additional example, what is the probability that a randomly selected male will have an IQ less than 123? We will find probabilities in exactly the same way we found areas. The score (X_i) is above the mean and, following the directions in Table 5.4, we will find the probability we are seeking by adding the area in column b to 0.5000. First, we find the Z score:

$$Z = \frac{X_i - \overline{X}}{s} = \frac{123 - 100}{20} = \frac{23}{20} = +1.15$$

Next, look in column b of Appendix A to find the area between this score and the mean. Then, add the area (0.3749) to 0.5000. The probability of selecting a male with an IQ of less than 123 is 0.3749 + 0.5000 or 0.8749. Rounding this value to .88, we can say that the odds are .88 (very high) that we will select a male with an IQ score in this range. Technically, remember that this probability expresses what would happen over the long run: for every 100 males selected from this group over an infinite number of trials, 88 would have IQ scores less than 123 and 12 would not.

Let us close by stressing a very important point about probabilities and the normal curve. The probability is very high that any case randomly selected from a normal distribution will have a score close in value to that of the mean. The shape of the normal curve is such that most cases are clustered around the mean and decline in frequency as we move farther away— either to the right or to the left—from the mean value. In fact, given what we know about the normal curve, the probability that a randomly selected case will have a score within ±1 standard deviation of the mean is 0.6826.

Rounding off, we can say that 68 out of 100 cases—or about two-thirds of all cases—selected over the long run will have a score between ±1 standard deviation or Z score of the mean. The probabilities are that any randomly selected case will have a score close in value to the mean.

In contrast, the probability of the case having a score beyond 3 standard deviations from the mean is very small. Look in column c ("Area beyond Z") for a Z score of 3.00 and you will find the value .0014. Adding the areas in the upper tail (beyond +3.00) to the area in the lower tail (beyond −3.00), gives us .0014 + .0014 for a total of .0028. The probability of selecting a case with a very high score or a very low score is .0028. If we randomly select cases from a normally distributed variable, we would select cases with Z scores beyond ±3.00 only 28 times out of every 10,000 trials.

The general point to remember is that cases with scores close to the mean are common and cases with scores far above or below the mean are rare. This relationship is central for an understanding of inferential statistics in Part II. As a final note, a supplement containing a more detailed and methodical discussion of probability has been added to our website. The supplement should be read in conjunction with Section 5.6, and not as a replacement for it. *(For practice in using the normal curve table to find probabilities, see problems 5.8 to 5.10 and 5.13.)*

SUMMARY

1. The normal curve, in combination with the mean and standard deviation, can be used to construct precise descriptive statements about empirical distributions that are normally distributed. This chapter also lays some important groundwork for Part II.

2. To work with the theoretical normal curve, raw scores must be transformed into their equivalent Z scores. Z scores allow us to find areas under the theoretical normal curve (Appendix A).

3. We considered three uses of the theoretical normal curve: finding total areas above and below a score, finding areas between two scores, and expressing these areas as probabilities. This last use of the normal curve is especially germane because inferential statistics are centrally concerned with estimating the probabilities of defined events in a fashion very similar to the process introduced in Section 5.6.

SUMMARY OF FORMULAS

Z scores	5.1	$Z = \dfrac{X_i - \overline{X}}{s}$

GLOSSARY

Normal curve. A theoretical distribution of scores that is symmetrical, unimodal, and bell shaped. The standard normal curve always has a mean of 0 and a standard deviation of 1.

Normal curve table. Appendix A; a detailed description of the area between a Z score and the mean of any standardized normal distribution.

Z scores. Standard scores; the way scores are expressed after they have been standardized to the theoretical normal curve.

MULTIMEDIA RESOURCES

   http://www.healeystatistics.nelson.com

Visit the companion Web site for the first Canadian edition of *Statistics: A Tool for Social Research* to access a wide range of student resources. Begin by clicking on the Student Resources section of the book's Web site to access review quizzes, flash cards, and other study tools.

PROBLEMS

5.1 Scores on a quiz were normally distributed and had a mean of 10 and a standard deviation of 3. For each score below, find the Z score and the percentage of area above and below the score.

X_i	Z Score	% Area Above	% Area Below
5			
6			
7			
8			
9			
11			
12			
14			
15			
16			
18			

5.2 Assume that the distribution of a graduate-school entrance exam is normal with a mean of 500 and a standard deviation of 100. For each score below, find the equivalent Z score, the percentage of the area above the score, and the percentage of the area below the score.

X_i	Z Score	% Area Above	% Area Below
650			
400			
375			
586			
437			
526			
621			
498			
517			
398			

5.3 A class of final-year students at a small university has been given a comprehensive examination to assess their educational experience. The mean on the test was 74 and the standard deviation was 10. What percentage of the students had scores

a. between 75 and 85? _____
b. between 80 and 85? _____
c. above 80? _____
d. above 83? _____
e. between 80 and 70? _____
f. between 75 and 70? _____
g. below 75? _____

h. below 77? _____
i. below 80? _____
j. below 85? _____

5.4 For a normal distribution where the mean is 50 and the standard deviation is 10, what percentage of the area is
    a. between the scores of 40 and 47? _____
    b. above a score of 47? _____
    c. below a score of 53? _____
    d. between the scores of 35 and 65? _____
    e. above a score of 72? _____
    f. below a score of 31 and above a score of 69? _____
    g. between the scores of 55 and 62? _____
    h. between the scores of 32 and 47? _____

5.5 At Algebra University the 200 students enrolled in Introductory Biology took a final exam on which their mean score was 72 and their standard deviation was 6. The table below presents the grades of 10 students. Convert each into a Z score and determine the *number of people* who scored higher or lower than each of the 10 students. *(HINT: Multiply the appropriate proportion by N and round the result.)*

X_i	Z Score	Number of Students Above	Number of Students Below
60			
57			
55			
67			
70			
72			
78			
82			
90			
95			

5.6 If a distribution of test scores is normal with a mean of 78 and a standard deviation of 11, what percentage of the area lies
    a. below 60? _____
    b. below 70? _____
    c. below 80? _____
    d. below 90? _____
    e. between 60 and 65? _____
    f. between 65 and 79? _____
    g. between 70 and 95? _____
    h. between 80 and 90? _____

i. above 99? _____
j. above 89? _____
k. above 75? _____
l. above 65? _____

5.7 A scale measuring ageism (age discrimination) has been administered to a large sample of human resources managers at major corporations. The distribution of scores is approximately normal with a mean of 31 and a standard deviation of 5. What percentage of the sample had scores
    a. below 20? _____
    b. below 40? _____
    c. between 30 and 40? _____
    d. between 35 and 45? _____
    e. above 25? _____
    f. above 35? _____

5.8 The average burglary rate for a jurisdiction has been 311 per year with a standard deviation of 50. What is the probability that next year the number of burglaries will be
    a. less than 250? _____
    b. less than 300? _____
    c. more than 350? _____
    d. more than 400? _____
    e. between 250 and 350? _____
    f. between 300 and 350? _____
    g. between 350 and 375? _____

5.9 For a math test on which the mean was 59 and the standard deviation was 4, what is the probability that a student randomly selected from this class will have a score
    a. between 55 and 65? _____
    b. between 60 and 65? _____
    c. above 65? _____
    d. between 60 and 50? _____
    e. between 55 and 50? _____
    f. below 55? _____

5.10 SOC On the scale mentioned in problem 5.7, if a score of 40 or more is considered "highly discriminatory" what is the probability that a human resources manager selected at random will have a score in that range?

5.11 The local police force gives all applicants an entrance exam and accepts only those applicants who score in the top 15% on this test. If the mean score this year is 87 and the standard deviation is 8, would an individual with a score of 110 be accepted?

5.12 After taking a city's merit examinations for the positions of social worker and employment counsellor you receive the following information on the tests and on your performance. On which of the tests did you do better?

Social Worker	Employment Counsellor
$\overline{X} = 118$	$\overline{X} = 27$
$s = 17$	$s = 3$
Your score = 127	Your score = 29

5.13 In a distribution of scores with a mean of 35 and a standard deviation of 4, which event is more likely: that a randomly selected score will be between 29 and 31 or that a randomly selected score will be between 40 and 42?

5.14 To be accepted into a university's co-op education program students must have GPAs in the top 10% of the school. If the mean GPA is 2.78 and the standard deviation is .33, which of the following GPAs would qualify?
3.20, 3.21, 3.25, 3.30, 3.35

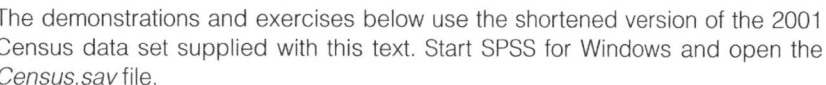

SPSS for Windows

Using SPSS for Windows to Produce Histograms and Compute *Z* Scores with the 2001 Census

The demonstrations and exercises below use the shortened version of the 2001 Census data set supplied with this text. Start SPSS for Windows and open the *Census.sav* file.

SPSS DEMONSTRATION 5.1 The Histogram

Before we can compute *Z* scores, we need to find out if a variable has a normal, bell-shaped curve. The histogram, discussed in Chapter 2, provides a convenient method to display the distribution of a variable. Here we will use the **Histogram** command to show the distribution of *agep* (age in years).

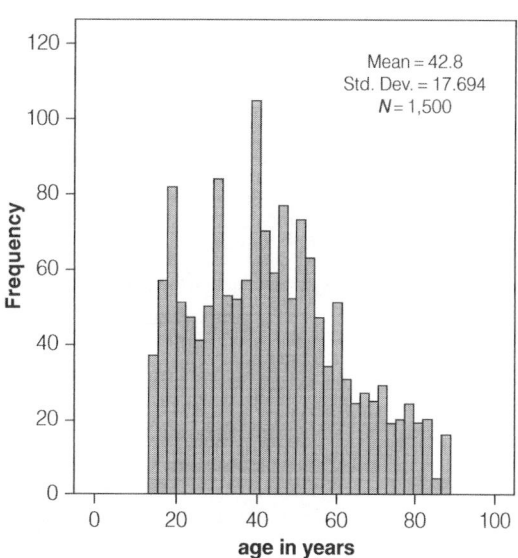

The SPSS procedure for producing a histogram is very similar to that of the bar and line chart illustrated in Demonstration 2.3. Click **Graphs, Legacy Dialogs,** and then **Histogram.** The **Histogram** dialog box will appear. Select *agep* from the variable list on the left and click the arrow button at the top of the screen to move *agep* to the **Variable** box. Click **OK** in the **Histogram** dialog box, and the histogram for *agep* will be produced.

The distribution of *agep* is approximately normal in shape. No empirical distribution is perfectly normal, but *agep* is close enough to permit the assumption of normality. We can proceed to use the normal curve to convert the original scores of *agep* into *Z* scores.

SPSS DEMONSTRATION 5.2 Computing *Z* Scores

The **Descriptives** program introduced in Demonstration 3.2 can also be used to compute *Z* scores for any variable. These *Z* scores are then available for further operations and may be used in other tasks. SPSS will create a new variable consisting of the transformed scores of the original variable. The program uses the letter *Z* with the letters of the variable name to designate the normalized scores of a variable.

In this demonstration, we will have SPSS compute *Z* scores for *agep.* First, click **Analyze, Descriptive Statistics,** and **Descriptives.** Find *agep* in the variable list and click the arrow to move the variable to the **Variable(s)** box. Find the "**Save standardized values as variables**" option below the variable list and click the checkbox next to it. With this option selected for **Descriptives,** SPSS will compute *Z* scores for all variables listed in the **Variable(s)** box. Click **OK,** and SPSS will produce the usual set of descriptive statistics for *agep.* It will also add the new variable (called *Zagep*), which contains the standardized scores for *agep,* to the data set. To verify this, run the **Descriptives** command again, and you will find *Zagep* in the variable list. Transfer *Zagep* to the **Variable(s)** box with *agep,* then unclick the checkbox next to "**Save standardized values as variables**" and finally click **OK.** The following output will be produced:

Descriptive Statistics

	N	Minimum	Maximum	Mean	Std. Deviation
Age in years	1500	15	85	42.80	17.694
Z Score: Age in years	1500	-1.57105	2.38512	.0000000	1.0000000
Valid N (listwise)	1500				

Like any set of *Z* scores, *Zagep* has a mean of 0 and a standard deviation of 1. The new variable *Zagep* can be treated just like any other variable and used in any SPSS procedure.

If you would like to inspect the scores of *Zagep,* use the **Case Summaries** procedure. Click **Analyze, Reports,** and then **Case Summaries.** Move both *agep* and *Zagep* to the **Variable(s)** box. Be sure that "**Display cases**" checkbox at the bottom of the window is selected. Find the "**Limit cases to first**" option. This option can be used to set the number of cases included in the output. By default, the system lists only the first 100 cases in your file. You can raise or lower the value for

"Limit cases to first" *n* cases in your file or deselect this option to list all cases. For this exercise, let's set a limit of 10 cases. Make sure the checkbox to the left of the option is checked and type 10 in the textbox to the right. Click **OK,** and the following output will be produced:

Case Summaries*

	AGE IN YEARS	Z score: AGE IN YEARS
1	48	.29400
2	41	-.10162
3	27	.89285
4	60	.97220
5	46	.18097
6	16	-1.51454
7	25	-1.00589
8	58	.85917
9	53	.57658
10	55	.68692
Total *N*	10	10

*Limited to first 10 cases.

Scan the list of scores and note that the scores that are close in value to the mean of *agep* (42.80), are very close to the mean of *Zagep* (0.00), and the further away the score is from 42.80, the greater the numerical value of the *Z* score. Also note that, of course, scores below the mean (less than 42.80) have negative signs and scores above the mean (greater than 42.80) have positive signs.

Exercises (using *Census.sav*)

5.1 Use the **Histogram** command to get a histogram of *unitsp* and *grosrtp*. How close are these charts to smooth, bell-shaped normal curves? Write a sentence or two of interpretation for each graph.

5.2 Using Demonstration 5.2 as a guide, compute *Z* scores for *unitsp* and *grosrtp*. Use the **Case Summaries** procedure to display the normalized and raw scores for each variable for 10 cases. Write a sentence or two summarizing these results.

1. To what extent do people apply religion to the problems of everyday living? Fifteen people have responded to a series of questions including the following:

   1. What is your religious preference?
      1. Protestant
      2. Catholic
      3. Jewish
      4. Muslim
      5. Other
      6. None
   2. On a scale of 1 to 10 (with 10 being the highest), how strong would you say your faith is?
   3. How many times a day do you pray?
   4. When things aren't going well, my religion is my major source of comfort.
      1. Strongly agree
      2. Slightly agree
      3. Neither agree nor disagree
      4. Slightly disagree
      5. Strongly disagree
   5. How old are you?

Case	Religion	Strength	Pray	Comfort	Age
1	1	2	0	2	30
2	4	8	1	1	67
3	1	8	3	1	45
4	5	6	0	1	43
5	3	9	3	1	32
6	3	3	0	3	18
7	6	0	0	5	52
8	5	9	6	1	37
9	1	5	0	2	54
10	2	8	2	1	55
11	2	3	0	5	33
12	1	6	1	3	45
13	1	8	2	2	37
14	4	7	2	1	50
15	5	9	1	1	25

   For each variable, construct a frequency distribution and calculate appropriate measures of central tendency and dispersion. Write a sentence summarizing each variable.

2. A survey measuring attitudes toward same-sex marriage was administered to 1,000 people. The survey asked the following questions:

   1. What is your age?
   2. What is your sex?
      1. Male
      2. Female

3. Marriages between people of the same sex do not work out and should be banned by law.
   1. Strongly agree
   2. Agree
   3. Undecided
   4. Disagree
   5. Strongly disagree
4. How many years of schooling have you completed?
5. Which category below best describes the place where you grew up?
   1. Large city
   2. Medium-size city
   3. Suburbs of a city
   4. Small town
   5. Rural area
6. What is your marital status?
   1. Married
   2. Separated or divorced
   3. Widowed
   4. Never married

The scores of 20 respondents are reproduced below.

Case	Age	Sex	Attitude on Same-sex Marriage	Years of School	Area	Marital Status
1	17	1	5	12	1	4
2	25	2	3	12	2	1
3	55	2	3	14	2	1
4	45	1	1	12	3	1
5	38	2	1	10	3	1
6	21	1	1	16	5	1
7	29	2	2	16	2	2
8	30	2	1	12	4	1
9	37	1	1	12	2	1
10	42	2	3	18	5	4
11	57	2	4	12	2	3
12	24	2	2	12	4	1
13	27	1	2	18	3	2
14	44	1	1	15	1	1
15	37	1	1	10	5	4
16	35	1	1	12	4	1
17	41	2	2	15	3	1
18	42	2	1	10	2	4
19	20	2	1	16	1	4
20	21	2	1	16	1	4

a. For each variable, construct a frequency distribution and select and calculate an appropriate measure of central tendency and a measure of dispersion. Summarize each variable in a sentence.

b. For all 1,000 respondents, the mean age was 34.70 with a standard deviation of 3.4 years. Assuming the distribution of age is approximately normal, compute Z scores for each of the first 10 respondents above and determine the percentage of the area below (younger than) each respondent.

3. The data from 25 respondents shown below are taken from a social survey administered to adults. Abbreviated versions of the survey questions, along with the meanings of the codes, are also presented. For each variable, construct a frequency distribution and select and calculate an appropriate measure of central tendency and a measure of dispersion. Summarize each variable in a sentence.

1. How many children have you ever had? (Values are actual numbers.)
2. Respondent's educational level:
    0. Less than high school
    1. High school diploma
    2. Diploma/certificate from community college or trade school
    3. Bachelor's degree
    4. Graduate degree
3. Sex
    1. Male
    2. Female
4. It is sometimes necessary to discipline a child with a good, hard spanking.
    1. Strongly agree
    2. Agree
    3. Disagree
    4. Strongly disagree
5. Number of hours of TV watched per day. (Values are actual numbers of hours.)
6. What is your age?
    1. Less than 35 years
    2. 35 to 54 years
    3. 55 or more years

Case	Number of Children	Years of School	Sex	Attitude on Spanking	TV Hours	Age
1	3	1	1	3	3	1
2	2	0	1	4	1	1
3	4	2	1	2	3	1
4	0	3	1	1	2	1
5	5	1	1	3	2	1
6	1	1	1	3	3	1
7	9	0	1	1	6	1
8	6	1	2	3	4	1
9	4	3	1	1	2	3
10	2	1	2	1	1	1
11	2	0	1	2	4	1
12	4	1	2	1	5	2
13	0	1	1	3	2	2

(continued next page)

(continued)

Case	Number of Children	Years of School	Sex	Attitude on Spanking	TV Hours	Age
14	2	1	1	4	2	1
15	3	1	2	3	4	1
16	2	0	1	2	2	1
17	2	1	1	2	2	1
18	0	3	1	3	2	1
19	3	0	1	3	5	2
20	2	1	2	1	10	1
21	2	1	1	3	4	1
22	1	0	1	3	5	1
23	0	2	1	1	2	2
24	0	1	1	2	0	3
25	2	4	1	1	1	2

Part II Inferential Statistics

The six chapters in this part cover the techniques and concepts of inferential or inductive statistics. Generally speaking, these applications allow us to learn about large groups (populations) from small, carefully selected subgroups (samples). These statistical techniques are powerful and extremely useful. They are used to poll public opinion, research the potential market for new products, project the winners of elections, test the effects of new drugs, and in hundreds of other ways both inside and outside of the social sciences.

Chapter 6 includes a brief description of the sampling technology used to select subgroups so as to justify making inferences to populations. This section is intended to give you a general overview of the process, not as a comprehensive or detailed treatment of the subject. The most important part of this chapter, however, concerns the sampling distribution, the single most important concept in inferential statistics. The sampling distribution is normal in shape and is the key link between populations and samples.

There are two main applications in inferential statistics and Chapter 7 covers the first: using statistical information from a sample (e.g., a mean or a proportion) to estimate the characteristics of a population. The technique is called *estimation,* and it is most commonly used in public-opinion polling and election projection.

Chapters 8 through 11 cover the second application of inferential statistics: hypothesis testing. Most of the relevant concepts for this material are introduced in Chapter 8, and each chapter covers a different situation in which hypothesis testing is done. For example, Chapter 9 presents the techniques that are used when we are comparing information from two different samples or groups (e.g., men vs. women), while Chapter 10 covers applications involving more than two groups or samples (e.g., Daily Smoker, Occasional Smoker, Nonsmoker).

Because hypothesis testing is one of the more challenging aspects of statistics for beginning students, we have included an abundance of learning aids to ease the chore of assimilating this material. Hypothesis testing is also one of the most common and important statistical applications to be found in social science research, and mastery of this material is essential for developing the ability to read the professional literature.

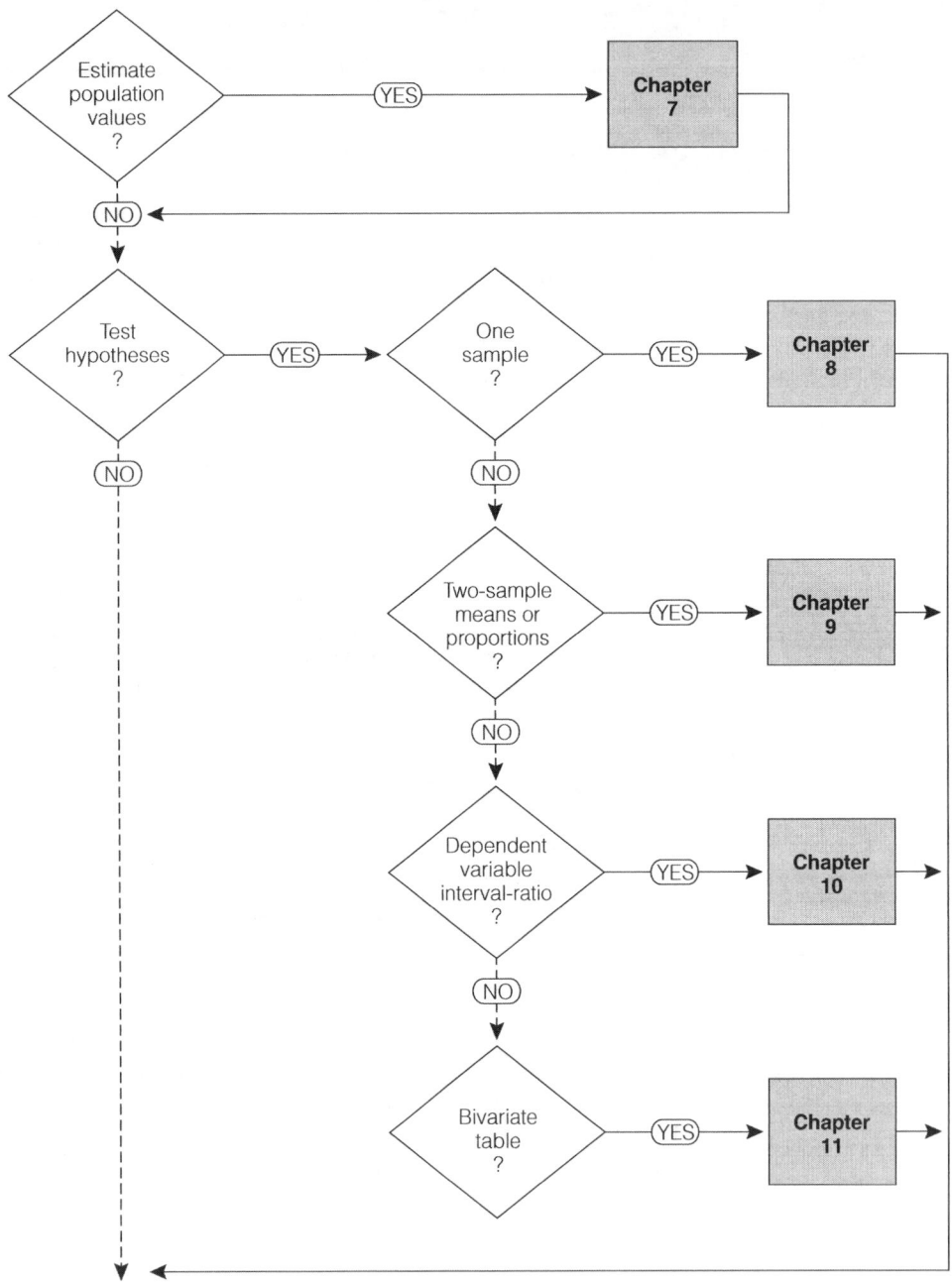

6

INTRODUCTION TO INFERENTIAL STATISTICS
SAMPLING AND THE SAMPLING DISTRIBUTION

LEARNING OBJECTIVES

By the end of this chapter, you will be able to

1. Explain the purpose of inferential statistics in terms of generalizing from a sample to a population.
2. Define and explain the basic techniques of random sampling.
3. Explain and define these key terms: population, sample, parameter, statistic, representative, EPSEM.
4. Differentiate between the sampling distribution, the sample, and the population.
5. Explain the two theorems presented.

6.1 INTRODUCTION

One of the goals of social science research is to test our theories and hypotheses using many different populations of people, groups, societies, and historical eras. Obviously, we can have the greatest confidence in theories that have stood up to testing against the greatest variety of populations and social settings. A major problem we often face in social science research, however, is that the populations in which we are interested are too large to test. For example, a theory concerning political party preference among Canadian voters would be most suitably tested using the entire electorate, but it is impossible to interview every member of this group (about 23 million people). Indeed, even for theories that could be reasonably tested with smaller populations—such as a local community or the student body at a university—the logistics of gathering data from every single case (entire populations) are staggering to contemplate.

If it is too difficult or expensive to do research with entire populations, how can we reasonably test our theories? To deal with this problem, social scientists select samples, or subsets of cases, from the populations of interest. Our goal in inferential statistics is to learn about the characteristics of a population (often called **parameters**), based on what we can learn from our samples. Two applications of inferential statistics are covered in this text. In estimation procedures, covered in Chapter 7, a "guess" of the population parameter is made, based on what is known about the sample. In hypothesis testing, covered in Chapters 8 through 11, the validity of a hypothesis about the population is tested against sample outcomes. In this chapter, we will look briefly at sampling (the techniques for selecting cases for a sample) and then introduce a key concept in inferential statistics: the sampling distribution.

6.2 TECHNIQUES FOR PROBABILITY SAMPLING

Social scientists have developed a variety of techniques for selecting samples from populations. In this chapter, we will review the basic procedures for selecting probability samples, the only type of sample that fully supports the use of inferential statistical techniques to generalize to populations. These types of samples are often described as "random," and you may be more familiar with this terminology. Because of its greater familiarity, we will often use the phrase "random sample" in the following chapters. The term "probability sample" is preferred, however, because, in everyday language, "random" is often used to mean "by coincidence" or to give a connotation of unpredictability. As you will see, probability samples are selected by techniques that are careful and methodical and leave no room for haphazardness. Interviewing the people you happen to meet in a mall one afternoon may be "random" in some sense, but this technique will not result in a sample that could support inferential statistics.

Before considering probability sampling, let us point out that social scientists often use nonprobability samples. For example, social scientists studying small group dynamics or the structure of attitudes or personal values might use the students enrolled in their classes as subjects. Such "convenience" samples are very useful for a number of purposes (e.g., exploring ideas or pretesting survey forms before embarking on a more ambitious project) and are typically less costly and easier to assemble. The major limitation of these samples is that results cannot be generalized beyond the group being tested. If a theory of ageism (prejudice, discrimination, and stereotyping of older people and old age), for example, has been tested only on the students who happen to have been enrolled in a particular section of Introductory Gerontology at a particular university, we cannot conclude that the theory would be true for other types of people. Therefore, even when the evidence is very strong, we cannot place a lot of confidence in theories tested on nonprobability samples only.

When constructing a probability sample, our goal is to select cases so that the final sample is **representative** of the population from which it was drawn. A sample is representative if it reproduces the important characteristics of the population. For example, if the population consists of 60% females and 40% males, the sample should contain essentially the same proportions. In other words, a representative sample is very much like the population—only smaller. It is crucial for inferential statistics that samples be representative; if they are not, generalizing to the population becomes, at best, extremely hazardous.

How can we assure ourselves that our samples are representative? Unfortunately, it is not possible to guarantee that our samples will meet this crucial criterion. However, we can maximize the chances of a representative sample by following the principle of **EPSEM** (the "**E**qual **P**robability of **SE**lection **M**ethod"), the fundamental principle of probability sampling. To follow the EPSEM principle, we select the sample so that every element or case in the population has an equal probability of being selected. Our goal is to select a representative sample, and the technique we use to achieve that goal is to follow the rule of EPSEM.

Remember that the EPSEM selection technique and the representativeness of the final sample are two different things. In other words, the fact that a sample is selected according to EPSEM does not guarantee that it will be an exact representation or microcosm of the population. The probability is very high that an EPSEM sample will be representative but, just as a perfectly honest coin will sometimes show 10 heads in a row when flipped, an EPSEM sample will occasionally present an inaccurate picture of the population. One of the great strengths of inferential statistics is that they allow the researcher to estimate the probability of this type of error and interpret results accordingly.

6.3 EPSEM SAMPLING TECHNIQUES

The most basic EPSEM sampling technique produces a **simple random sample.** To use this technique, we need a list of all elements or cases in the population and a system for selecting cases from the list that will guarantee that every case has an equal chance of being selected for the sample. The selection process could be based on a number of different kinds of operations (e.g., drawing cards from a well-shuffled deck, flipping coins, throwing dice, drawing numbers from a hat, etc.). Cases are often selected by using tables of random numbers. These tables are lists of numbers that have no pattern to them (i.e., they are random), and an example of such a table is available at the website for this text.

To use the table of random numbers, first assign each case on the population list a unique identification number. Then, select cases for the sample when their identification number corresponds to the number chosen from the table. This procedure will produce an EPSEM sample because the numbers in the table are in random order and any number is just as likely as any other number. Stop selecting cases when you have reached your desired sample size and, if an identification number is selected more than once, ignore the repeats.*

Rigidly following the procedures above will produce random samples as long as you select from a complete list of the population. However, these procedures can be very cumbersome when there is a long list of cases. Consider the situation when your population numbers 10,000 cases. It is perfectly possible that the first case you select will come from the front of the list, the second from the back, the third from the front again, and so on—leading to a great deal of paper shuffling and a fair amount of confusion. To save time and money in such a situation, researchers often use a technique called

---

*Ignoring identification numbers when they are repeated is called "sampling without replacement." Technically, this practice compromises the randomness of the selection process. However, if the sample is a small fraction of the total population, we will be unlikely to select the same case twice and ignoring repeats will not bias our conclusions.

systematic sampling, where only the first case is randomly selected. Thereafter, every *k*th case is selected. For example, if you are drawing from a list of 10,000 and desire a sample of 200, select the first case randomly and every 10,000/200th, or 50th, case thereafter. If you randomly start with case #13, then your second case will be #63, your third #113, and so on, until you reach the end of the list.

Note that systematic sampling does not strictly conform to the criterion of EPSEM. That is, once the first case has been selected, the other cases no longer have an equal probability of being chosen. In our example above, cases other than the 13th, the 63rd, the 113th, and so on will not be selected for the sample. In general, this increased probability of error is very slight as long as the list from which cases are chosen is random, or at least non-cyclical with respect to the traits you wish to measure. For example, if you are concerned with ethnicity and are drawing your sample from an alphabetical list, you might encounter difficulties because there is a tendency for certain ethnic names to begin with the same letter (e.g., the Irish prefix *O*). Therefore, when using systematic sampling, pay careful attention to the nature of the population list as well as your sampling technique.

A third type of EPSEM sampling produces the **stratified sample.** This technique is very desirable because it guarantees that the sample will be representative on the selected traits. To apply this technique, you first stratify (or divide) the population list into sublists according to some relevant trait and then sample from the sublists. If you select a number of cases from each sublist proportional to the numbers for that characteristic in the population, the sample will be representative of the population.

For example, suppose that you are drawing a sample of 300 of your classmates and you wish to have proportional representation from every major field on campus. If only 10% of the student body is majoring in zoology, the first two sampling techniques we discussed could result in a sample with very few (or even no) zoologists. If, however, you first divide the population into sublists by major, you can use EPSEM to select exactly 30 zoologists from the appropriate sublist. Following the same procedure with other majors will create a sample that is, by definition, representative of the population on this characteristic. Thus, stratified samples are guaranteed to meet the all-important criterion of representativeness (at least for the traits that are used to stratify the samples).

The major limitation of stratified random sampling is that the exact composition of the population is often unknown. If we have no information about the population, we will be unable to establish a scheme for stratification and determine how many cases should be taken from each sublist.

To this point, sampling techniques have been presented as straightforward processes of randomly selecting cases from a list or sublists of the population. However, sampling is rarely so uncomplicated, and the major difficulty almost always centres on what might appear, at first glance, to be the easiest part: establishing the list of the population. For many of the populations of interest to the social sciences, there are no complete, up-to-date lists. There is no list of Canadian citizens, no list of the residents of any given province, and no complete, up-to-date list of residents of your local community. Devices such as telephone books or city directories might appear to contain complete lists of local residents. However, the former will omit unlisted numbers and the latter is very likely to be outdated.

Social scientists have devised several ways of dealing with the limitations imposed by the scarcity of lists. Probably the most significant of these is **cluster sampling,** which involves selecting groups of cases (clusters) rather than single cases. The clusters are often based on geography, and the selection of clusters often proceeds in stages. For example, you might draw a cluster sample of your city by first numbering all of the census tract areas within the city limits (census tracts divide cities into small geographic communities with populations of about 4,000). Next, you would use an EPSEM technique to select a sample of census tracts. The second stage of selection would involve numbering the street blocks within each of the selected census tracts and, following EPSEM, selecting a sample of blocks. A third stage might involve the selection of households within each selected block. When these stages are completed, you would have a sample that had a very high probability of being representative of the entire city without ever using a list of city residents.

Unfortunately, a cluster sample is somewhat less likely to be representative of the population than a simple random sample of comparable size. In part, this lower accuracy is a result of the multiple selection stages described above. With a simple random sample, the sample is drawn in one selection from the list of the population. In a multistage cluster sample, each stage in the selection process (e.g., first the census tracts, then the blocks, and then the households) has a probability of error. That is, each time we sample, we run the risk of selecting an unrepresentative sample. In simple random sampling, we run this risk once; with cluster sampling we will run the risk anew at each stage.

Although we have to treat inferences to populations based on cluster samples with some additional caution, we usually have no alternative method of sampling. While it may be extremely difficult (or even impossible) to construct an accurate list of an entire city population, all you need to compile a cluster sample is a map (or a list of census tracts, electoral districts, postal codes, and so forth).

By way of summary, let's return to a major point. The purpose of inferential statistics is to acquire knowledge about populations, based on the information derived from samples of that population. Each of the statistics to be presented in the following chapters requires that samples be selected according to EPSEM. While even the most painstaking and sophisticated sampling techniques will not guarantee representativeness, the probability is high that EPSEM samples will be representative of the populations from which they are selected.

6.4 THE SAMPLING DISTRIBUTION

Once we have selected a probability sample according to some EPSEM procedure, what do we know? On one hand, we can gather a great deal of information from the cases in the sample. On the other hand, we know nothing about the population. Indeed, if we had information about the population, we probably wouldn't need the sample. Remember that we use inferential statistics to learn more about populations, and information from the sample is important primarily insofar as it allows us to generalize to the population.

When we use inferential statistics, we generally measure some variable (e.g., age, political party preference, or opinions about global warming) in the sample and then use the information from the sample to learn more about that variable in the population. In Part I of this text, you learned that three types of information are generally necessary to adequately characterize a variable: (1) the shape of its distribution, (2) some measure of central tendency, and (3) some measure of dispersion. Clearly, all three kinds of information can be gathered (or computed) on a variable from the cases in the sample. Just as clearly, none of the information is available for the population. Except in rare situations (e.g., IQ and height are thought to be approximately normal in distribution), nothing can be known about the exact shape of the distribution of a variable in the population. The means and standard deviations of variables in the population are also unknown. Let us remind you that if we had this information for the population, inferential statistics would be unnecessary.

In statistics, we link information from the sample to the population with a device known as the **sampling distribution,** the theoretical, probabilistic distribution of a statistic for all possible samples of a certain sample size (N). That is, the sampling distribution includes statistics that represent every conceivable combination of cases (i.e., every possible sample) from the population. A crucial point about the sampling distribution is that its characteristics are based on the laws of probability, not on empirical information, and are very well known. In fact, the sampling distribution is the central concept in inferential statistics, and a prolonged examination of its characteristics is certainly in order.

As illustrated by Figure 6.1, the general strategy of all applications of inferential statistics is to move between the sample and the population via the sampling distribution. Thus, three separate and distinct distributions are involved in every application of inferential statistics:

FIGURE 6.1 THE RELATIONSHIPS BETWEEN THE SAMPLE, SAMPLING DISTRIBUTION, AND POPULATION

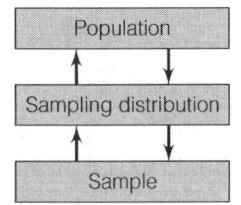

1. The sample distribution, which is empirical (i.e., it exists in reality) and known in the sense that the shape, central tendency, and dispersion of any variable can be ascertained for the sample. Remember that the information from the sample is important primarily insofar as it allows the researcher to learn about the population.
2. The population distribution, which, while empirical, is unknown. Amassing information about or making inferences to the population is the sole purpose of inferential statistics.

3. The sampling distribution, which is nonempirical or theoretical. Because of the laws of probability, a great deal is known about this distribution. Specifically, the shape, central tendency, and dispersion of the distribution can be deduced and, therefore, the distribution can be adequately characterized.

The utility of the sampling distribution is implied by its definition. Because it encompasses all possible sample outcomes, the sampling distribution enables us to estimate the probability of any particular sample outcome, a process that will occupy our attention for the next five chapters.

The sampling distribution is theoretical, which means that it is obtained hypothetically, but not in practice. However, to understand better the structure and function of the distribution, let's consider an example of how one might be constructed. Suppose that we wanted to gather some information about the age of a particular community of 10,000 individuals. We draw an EPSEM sample of 100 residents, ask all 100 respondents their age, and use those individual scores to compute a mean age of 27. This score is noted on the graph in Figure 6.2. Note that this sample is one of countless possible combinations of 100 people taken from this population of 10,000, and the mean of 27 is one of millions of possible sample outcomes.

Now, replace the 100 respondents in the first sample and draw another sample of the same size ($N = 100$) and again compute the average age. Assume that the mean for the second sample is 30 and note this sample outcome on Figure 6.2. This second sample is another of the countless possible combinations of 100 people taken from this population of 10,000, and the sample mean of 30 is another of the millions of possible sample outcomes. Replace the respondents from the second sample and draw still another sample, calculate and note the mean, replace this third sample, and draw a fourth sample, continuing these operations an infinite number of times, calculating and noting the mean of each sample. Now, try to imagine what Figure 6.2 would look like after tens of thousands of individual samples had been collected and the mean had been computed for each sample. What shape, mean, and standard deviation would this distribution of sample means have after we had collected all possible combinations of 100 respondents from the population of 10,000?

For one thing, we know that each sample will be at least slightly different from every other sample, as it is very unlikely that we will sample exactly the same 100 people twice. Because each sample will almost certainly be a

FIGURE 6.2 CONSTRUCTING A SAMPLING DISTRIBUTION

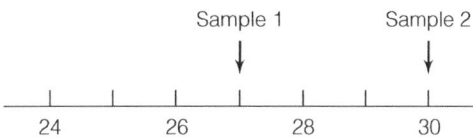

unique combination of individuals, each sample mean will be at least slightly different in value. We also know that even though the samples are chosen according to EPSEM, they will not be representative of the population in every single case. For example, if we continue taking samples of 100 people long enough, we will eventually choose a sample that includes only the very youngest residents. Such a sample would have a mean much lower than the true population mean. Likewise, some of our samples will include only senior citizens and will have means that are much higher than the population mean. Common sense suggests, however, that such non-representative samples will be rare and that most sample means will cluster around the true population value.

To illustrate further, assume that we somehow come to know that the true mean age of the population is 30. As we have seen above, most of the sample means will also be approximately 30 and the sampling distribution of these sample means should peak at 30. Some of the sample means will "miss the mark," but the frequency of such misses should decline as we get farther away from 30. That is, the distribution should slope to the base as we get farther away from the population value—sample means of 29 or 31 should be common; means of 20 or 40 should be rare. Because the samples are random, the means should miss an equal number of times on either side of the population value, and the distribution itself should therefore be roughly symmetrical. In other words, the sampling distribution of all possible sample means should be approximately normal and will resemble the distribution presented in Figure 6.3. Recall from Chapter 5 that, on any normal curve, cases close to the mean (say, within ±1 standard deviation) are common and cases far away from the mean (say, beyond ±3 standard deviations) are rare.

These common-sense notions about the shape of the sampling distribution and other very important information about central tendency and dispersion are stated in two theorems. The first of these theorems states that

If repeated random samples of size N are drawn from a normal population with mean μ and standard deviation σ, then the sampling distribution of sample means will be normal with a mean μ and a standard deviation of $\sigma/\sqrt{N}$.

FIGURE 6.3 A SAMPLING DISTRIBUTION OF SAMPLE MEANS

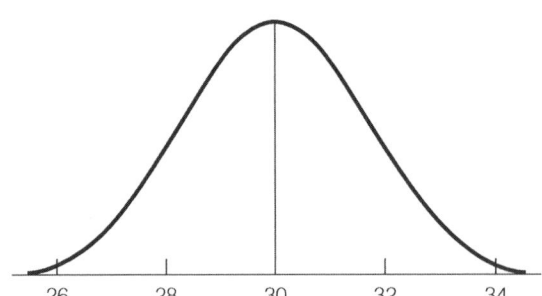

| 26 | 28 | 30 | 32 | 34 |

To translate: if we begin with a trait that is normally distributed across a population (IQ, height, or weight, for example) and take an infinite number of equally sized random samples from that population, then the sampling distribution of sample means will be normal. If it is known that the variable is distributed normally in the population, it can be assumed that the sampling distribution will be normal.

The theorem tells us more than the shape of the sampling distribution of all possible sample means, however. It also defines its mean and standard deviation. In fact, it says that the mean of the sampling distribution will be exactly the same value as the mean of the population. That is, if we know that the mean IQ of the entire population is 100, then we know that the mean of any sampling distribution of sample mean IQs will also be 100. Exactly why this should be so is explained and demonstrated in Section 6.5. Recall for now, however, that most sample means will cluster around the population value over the long run. Thus, the fact that these two values are equal should have intuitive appeal. As for dispersion, the theorem says that the standard deviation of the sampling distribution, also called the **standard error of the mean,** will be equal to the standard deviation of the population divided by the square root of N (symbolically: $\sigma/\sqrt{N}$).

If the mean and standard deviation of a normally distributed population are known, the theorem allows us to compute the mean and standard deviation of the sampling distribution.* Thus, we will know exactly as much about the sampling distribution (shape, central tendency, and dispersion) as we ever knew about any empirical distribution.

The first theorem requires a normal population distribution. What happens when the distribution of the variable in question is unknown or is known to not be normal in shape (like income, which always has a positive skew)? These eventualities (very common, in fact) are covered by a second theorem, called the **Central Limit Theorem:**

> If repeated random samples of size N are drawn from any population, with mean μ and standard deviation σ, then, as N becomes large, the sampling distribution of sample means will approach normality, with mean μ and standard deviation $\sigma/\sqrt{N}$.

To translate: for *any* trait or variable, even those that are not normally distributed in the population, as sample size grows larger, the sampling distribution of sample means will become normal in shape. When N is large, the mean of the sampling distribution will equal the population mean and its standard deviation (or the standard error of the mean) will be equal to $\sigma/\sqrt{N}$.

The importance of the Central Limit Theorem is that it removes the constraint of normality in the population. Whenever sample size is large, we can

---

*In the typical research situation, the values of the population mean and standard deviation are, of course, unknown. However, these values can be estimated from sample statistics, as we shall see in the chapters that follow.

assume that the sampling distribution is normal, with a mean equal to the population mean and a standard deviation equal to $\sigma/\sqrt{N}$ regardless of the shape of the variable in the population. Thus, even if we are working with a variable that is known to have a skewed distribution (like income), we can still assume a normal sampling distribution.

The issue remaining, of course, is to define what is meant by a large sample. A good rule of thumb is that if sample size (N) is 100 or more, the Central Limit Theorem applies, and you can assume that the sampling distribution is normal in shape. When N is less than 100, you must have good evidence of a normal population distribution before you can assume that the sampling distribution is normal. Thus, a normal sampling distribution can be ensured by the expedient of using fairly large samples.

6.5 CONSTRUCTING THE SAMPLING DISTRIBUTION

Developing an understanding of the sampling distribution—what it is and why it's important—is often one of the more challenging tasks for beginning students of statistics. It may be helpful to briefly list the most important points about the sampling distribution:

1. Its definition: *the sampling distribution is the distribution of a statistic (like means or proportions) for all possible sample outcomes of a certain size.*
2. Its shape: *normal* (see Appendix A).
3. Its central tendency and dispersion: *the mean of the sampling distribution is the same value as the mean of the population. The standard deviation of the sampling distribution—or the standard error—is equal to the population standard deviation divided by the square root of N.* (See the theorems.)

To reinforce these points, we will construct a sampling distribution from hypothetical data. Suppose we have a population of four people and are interested in the amount of money each person has in his/her possession. (The number of cases in this problem is kept very small to simplify the computations.) We find that the first person in our population has \$2, the second person has \$4, the third person has \$6, and the fourth person has \$8. So this population has a mean, μ, of \$5 and a standard deviation, σ, of \$2.236, as calculated in Table 6.1.

Recall that the sampling distribution of sample means is the theoretical distribution of the mean for all possible samples of a certain sample size (N), with a mean, μ, and a standard deviation of $\sigma/\sqrt{N}$. So let us derive the sampling distribution of sample means for $N = 2$; that is, draw every conceivable combination (every possible sample) of two people from our population of four people. In order to draw every possible sample, sampling

TABLE 6.1   CALCULATING THE MEAN AND STANDARD DEVIATION OF THE POPULATION

Case	(X_i)	Deviations $(X_i - \mu)$	Deviations Squared $(X_i - \mu)^2$
1	2	$2 - 5 = -3.0$	9
2	4	$4 - 5 = -1.0$	1
3	6	$6 - 5 = 1.0$	1
4	8	$8 - 5 = 3.0$	9
	$\Sigma(X_i) = 20$	$\Sigma(X_i - \mu) = 0$	$\Sigma(X_i - \mu)^2 = 20$

$$\mu = \frac{\Sigma(X_i)}{N} = \frac{20}{4} = 5 \text{ (Formula 3.1)}$$

$$\sigma = \sqrt{\frac{\Sigma(X_i - \mu)^2}{N}} = \sqrt{\frac{20}{4}} = \sqrt{5} = 2.236 \text{ (Formula 4.3)}$$

with replacement must be used; we randomly select a person from the population, replace that person back in the population, and then again randomly select a person from the population. Hence, we end up drawing several "odd" looking samples as the same person can be selected twice into the same sample.

In a population of four people, there will be 16 theoretical samples of two people (i.e., when $N = 2$). With 16 samples, there will be 16 sample means. Table 6.2 presents every possible sample of two people from our population of four people.

TABLE 6.2   CALCULATING THE SAMPLING DISTRIBUTION OF SAMPLE MEANS

	Sample Scores	Sample Mean
1	($2, $2)	$2
2	($2, $4)	$3
3	($2, $6)	$4
4	($2, $8)	$5
5	($4, $2)	$3
6	($4, $4)	$4
7	($4, $6)	$5
8	($4, $8)	$6
9	($6, $2)	$4
10	($6, $4)	$5
11	($6, $6)	$6
12	($6, $8)	$7
13	($8, $2)	$5
14	($8, $4)	$6
15	($8, $6)	$7
16	($8, $8)	$8

In the first sample, the person in our population with $2 in his/her possession was randomly selected twice—this is one of those "odd" looking samples. The mean for this sample is $2, or $(2 + 2)/2 = 2$. In the second theoretical sample, the first person randomly selected from the population was again the person with $2. This person was replaced back in the population. Next a second person was then randomly selected from the population, which was the person with $4. The mean for this sample is $3, or $(2 + 4)/2 = 3$. This process continues until every possible sample of two people from our population of four people has been drawn, as shown in Table 6.2.

With all possible combinations of samples in hand (16 in total), we can build the sampling distribution of sample means. The histogram in Figure 6.4 displays this information. The histogram shows that the sample mean of 5 occurs four times, more than any other mean. We can confirm this by counting the number of times the mean of 5 occurs in Table 6.2. The means of 4 and 6 occur three times each, while the means of 3 and 7 occur twice, and the means of 2 and 8 occur once each. Our sampling distribution of means is perfectly symmetrical, and is approximately similar in shape to the normal distribution presented in Figure 6.3.

The theorems in Section 6.4 tell us that the sampling distribution of all possible sample means becomes increasingly normal in shape as N increases. Indeed, if we repeated this exercise using $N = 3$, instead $N = 2$, the sampling distribution of means would be even more normal. The theorems tell that when either sample size is large ($N = 100$ or more) or population scores are normally distributed, the sampling distribution will reach normality. Yet, we find that these theorems still apply with our very modest example of $N = 2$ and a population of just four people.

The theorems also tell us that the mean of the sampling distribution will be exactly the same value as the mean of the population and that the

FIGURE 6.4   SAMPLING DISTRIBUTION OF SAMPLE MEANS (*BASED ON TABLE 6.2*)

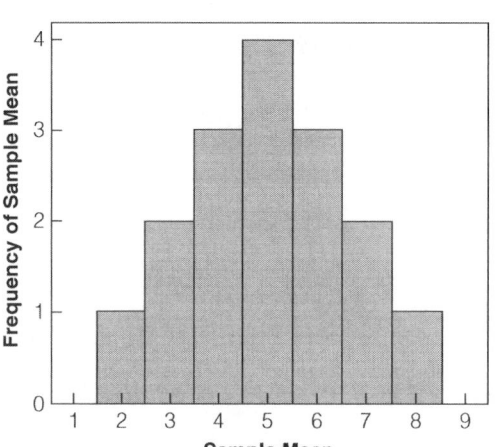

TABLE 6.3   CALCULATING THE MEAN AND STANDARD DEVIATION OF THE SAMPLING DISTRIBUTION OF SAMPLE MEANS

	Sample Mean (X_i)	Deviations ($X_i - \mu$)	Deviations Squared ($X_i - \mu$)^2
1	2	2 − 5 = −3.0	9
2	3	3 − 5 = −2.0	4
3	4	4 − 5 = −1.0	1
4	5	5 − 5 = 0.0	0
5	3	3 − 5 = −2.0	4
6	4	4 − 5 = −1.0	1
7	5	5 − 5 = 0.0	0
8	6	6 − 5 = 1.0	1
9	4	4 − 5 = −1.0	1
10	5	5 − 5 = 0.0	0
11	6	6 − 5 = 1.0	1
12	7	7 − 5 = 2.0	4
13	5	5 − 5 = 0.0	0
14	6	6 − 5 = 1.0	1
15	7	7 − 5 = 2.0	4
16	8	8 − 5 = 3.0	9
	$\Sigma(X_i) = 80$	$\Sigma(X_i - \mu) = 0$	$\Sigma(X_i - \mu)^2 = 40$

$$\mu = \frac{\Sigma(X_i)}{N} = \frac{80}{16} = 5 \text{ (Formula 3.1)}$$

$$\sigma = \sqrt{\frac{\Sigma(X_i - \mu)^2}{N}} = \sqrt{\frac{40}{16}} = \sqrt{2.5} = 1.581 \text{ (Formula 4.3)}$$

standard deviation of the sampling distribution will be equal to the standard deviation of the population divided by the square root of N (symbolically: $\sigma/\sqrt{N}$). This is proved in Table 6.3.

Comparing Table 6.3 and Table 6.1 we see that the mean of the sampling distribution, 5, is exactly the same as the mean of the population, 5. We also see that the standard deviation of the sampling distribution, 1.581, is equal to the standard deviation of the population divided by the square root of N. That is, the population standard deviation, 2.236, divided by the square root of 2, or 2.236/$\sqrt{2}$, is 1.581, which is identical to standard deviation of the sampling distribution.

In conclusion, we have confirmed the three fundamental components of the theorems in Section 6.4. First, the sampling distribution is normal if either the sample size is large ($N = 100$ or more) or the shape of the distribution of the variable in the population is normal. We have seen that a sampling distribution will be approximately normal in shape even with a small sample size of $N = 2$ and a population of just four cases. Second, the sampling distribution has a mean, $\mu = 5$, which is identical to the mean of the population. Third, the standard deviation of the sampling distribution of sample means, σ, is equal to the standard deviation of the population divided by the square root of N.

6.6 LINKING THE POPULATION, SAMPLING DISTRIBUTION, AND SAMPLE

The role of the sampling distribution in inferential statistics is to link the sample with the population. In this section we look at how the sampling distribution works together with the sample and the population using the General Social Survey (GSS), the database used for SPSS exercises in this text.

We will start with the *population,* or the group we are actually interested in and want to learn more about. In the case of the GSS, the population consists of all Canadians (aged 15 and older) living in private households in the 10 provinces. This includes about 27 million people. Clearly, we can never interview all of these people and learn what they are like or what they think about gun control, the numbers of children they want to have, their plans for retirement, their access to and use of information technologies, or any other issues.

What can be done to learn more about this huge population? This brings us to the concepts of *sample,* a carefully chosen subset of the population. The GSS is administered to about 25,000 people, each of whom is chosen by a sophisticated technique that is ultimately based on the principle of EPSEM. The respondents are contacted at home and asked for background information (e.g., age, gender, years of education) as well as their opinions and attitudes. When all of this information is collated, the GSS database includes information (shape, central tendency, dispersion) on hundreds of variables (e.g., volunteering, voting, and other social/political activities) for the people in the sample.

So we have a lot of information about the variables for the sample (the 25,000 or so people who actually respond to the survey), but no information about these variables for the population (the 27 million Canadians aged 15 and older). How do we go from the known characteristics of the sample to the unknown population?

This is the central question of inferential statistics, and the answer is "by using the *sampling distribution.*" Remember that, unlike the sample and the population, the sampling distribution is a theoretical device. However, we can work with the sampling distribution because its shape, central tendency, and dispersion are defined by the theorems presented earlier in this chapter. First, for any variable from the GSS, we know that the sampling distribution will be normal in shape because the sample is "large" (N is much greater than 100). Second, the theorems tell us that the mean of the sampling distribution will be the same value as the mean of the population. If all Canadians aged 15 and older spend on average 7.5 hours using the Internet at home per week ($\mu = 7.5$), the mean of the sampling distribution will also be 7.5. Third, the theorems tell us that the standard deviation (or standard error) of the sampling distribution is equal to the population standard deviation (σ) divided by the square root of N. Therefore, the theorems tell us the statistical characteristics of this distribution (shape, central tendency, and dispersion), and this information allows us to link the sample to the population.

How does the sampling distribution link the sample to the population? It is crucial to know that the sampling distribution will be normal when N is large. This means that more than two-thirds (68%) of all samples will be within $\pm 1Z$ score of the mean (which is the same value as the population parameter), about 95% are within $\pm 2Z$ scores, and so forth. We do not (and cannot) know the actual value of the mean of the sampling distribution because it is impractical to draw every conceivable combination (i.e., every possible sample) of 25,000 Canadians from the population of 27 million Canadians. However, there is no need to draw all possible samples because the theorems give us crucial information about the mean and standard error of the sampling distribution that we can use to link the sample to the population. In practice, as you will see in the following chapters, we draw just one sample and use this information (i.e., the sampling distribution of all possible sample means will be normal with a mean equal to the population mean and a standard deviation equal to the population standard deviation divided by the square root of N) to link the sample to the population.

To summarize, we have focused on the GSS to see the roles played by the population, sample, and sampling distribution. Our goal is to infer information about the population (all Canadians aged 15 and older). When populations are too large to test (and contacting 27 million Canadians is far beyond the capacity of even the most energetic pollster), we use information from carefully drawn probability samples to estimate the characteristics of the population—the full sample of the GSS consists of about 25,000 Canadians aged 15 and older. The sampling distribution, the theoretical distribution whose characteristics are defined by the theorems, links the known sample to the unknown population.

6.7 SYMBOLS AND TERMINOLOGY

In the following chapters, we will be working with three entirely different distributions. The purpose of inferential statistics is to acquire knowledge of the population from information gathered from a sample by means of the sampling distribution. Further, while we have focused on the sampling distribution of sample means, other statistics like the sample proportion, which the Central Limit Theorem applies to, have a sampling distribution.

To distinguish clearly among these various distributions, we will often use symbols. The symbols used for the means and standard deviations of samples and populations have already been introduced in Chapters 3 and 4. In this chapter, we also used for convenience these population symbols for the sampling distribution. However, Table 6.4 provides new symbols for this distribution, denoted with Greek letter symbols that are subscripted according to the sample statistic of interest.

To read this table, note that the mean and standard deviation of a sample are denoted with English letters ($\overline{X}$ and s) while the mean and standard deviation of a population are denoted with the Greek letter equivalents (μ and σ). Proportions calculated on samples are symbolized as P-sub-s (s for sample) while population proportions are denoted as P-sub-u

TABLE 6.4   SYMBOLS FOR MEANS AND STANDARD DEVIATIONS OF THREE DISTRIBUTIONS

	Mean	Standard Deviation	Proportion
1. Samples	$\overline{X}$	s	P_s
2. Populations	μ	σ	P_u
3. Sampling distributions			
of means	μ_X	σ_X	
of proportions	μ_p	σ_p	

(u for "universe" or population). The symbols for the sampling distribution are Greek letters with English letter subscripts. The mean and standard deviation of a sampling distribution of sample means are "mu-sub-x-bar" and "sigma-sub-x-bar." The mean and standard deviation of a sampling distribution of sample proportions are "mu-sub-p" and "sigma-sub-p."

SUMMARY

1. Because populations are almost always too large to test, a fundamental strategy of social science research is to select a sample from the defined population and then use information from the sample to generalize to the population. This is done either by estimation or by hypothesis testing.

2. Several techniques are commonly used for selecting random samples. Each of these techniques involves selecting cases for the sample according to EPSEM. Even the most rigorous technique, however, cannot guarantee representativeness. One of the great strengths of inferential statistics is that the probability of this kind of error (nonrepresentativeness) can be estimated.

3. The sampling distribution, the central concept in inferential statistics, is a theoretical distribution of all possible sample outcomes. Because its overall shape, mean, and standard deviation are known

(under the conditions specified in the two theorems), the sampling distribution can be adequately characterized and utilized by researchers.

4. The two theorems that were introduced in this chapter state that when the variable of interest is normally distributed in the population or when sample size is large, the sampling distribution will be normal in shape, its mean will be equal to the population mean, and its standard deviation (or standard error) will be equal to the population standard deviation divided by the square root of N.

5. All applications of inferential statistics involve generalizing from the sample to the population by means of the sampling distribution. Both estimation procedures and hypothesis testing incorporate the three distributions, and it is crucial that you develop a clear understanding of each distribution and its role in inferential statistics.

GLOSSARY

Central Limit Theorem. A theorem that specifies the mean, standard deviation, and shape of the sampling distribution, given that the sample is large.

Cluster sampling. A method of sampling by which geographical units are randomly selected and all cases within each selected unit are tested.

EPSEM. The **E**qual **P**robability of **SE**lection **M**ethod for selecting samples. Every element or case in the population must have an equal probability of selection for the sample.

μ. The mean of a population.

$\boldsymbol{\mu_{\overline{X}}}.$ The mean of a sampling distribution of sample means.

$\boldsymbol{\mu_p}.$ The mean of a sampling distribution of sample proportions.

Parameter. A characteristic of a population.

$\boldsymbol{P_s}$ **(P-sub-s).** Any sample proportion.

$\boldsymbol{P_u}$ **(P-sub-u).** Any population proportion.

Representative. The quality a sample is said to have if it reproduces the major characteristics of the population from which it was drawn.

Sampling distribution. The distribution of a statistic for all possible sample outcomes of a certain size. Under conditions specified in two theorems, the sampling distribution will be normal in shape with a mean equal to the population value and a standard deviation equal to the population standard deviation divided by the square root of N.

Simple random sample. A method for choosing cases from a population by which every case and every combination of cases has an equal chance of being included.

Standard error of the mean. The standard deviation of a sampling distribution of sample means.

Stratified sample. A method of sampling by which cases are selected from sublists of the population.

Systematic sampling. A method of sampling by which the first case from a list of the population is randomly selected. Thereafter, every kth case is selected.

MULTIMEDIA RESOURCES

 http://www.healeystatistics.nelson.com

Visit the companion Web site for the first Canadian edition of *Statistics: A Tool for Social Research* to access a wide range of student resources. Begin by clicking on the Student Resources section of the book's Web site to access review quizzes, flash cards, and other study tools.

PROBLEMS

6.1 Imagine that you had to gather a random sample ($N = 300$) of the student body at your university. How would you acquire a list of the population? Would the list be complete and accurate? What procedure would you follow in selecting cases (i.e., simple or systematic random sampling)? Would cluster sampling be an appropriate technique (assuming that no list was available)? Describe in detail how you would construct a cluster sample.

6.2 This exercise is extremely tedious and hardly ever works out the way it ought to (mostly because not many people have the patience to draw an "infinite" number of even very small samples). However, if you want a more concrete and tangible understanding of sampling distributions and the two theorems presented in this chapter, then this exercise may have a significant payoff. Below are listed the ages of a population of university students ($N = 50$). By a random method (such as a table of random numbers), draw at least 50 samples of size 2 (i.e., 50 pairs of cases), compute a mean for each sample, and plot the means on a frequency polygon. (Incidentally, this exercise will work better if you draw 100 or 200 samples and/or use larger samples than $N = 2$.)

a. The curve you've just produced is a sampling distribution. Observe its shape; after 50 samples, it should be approaching normality. What is your estimate of the population mean (μ) based on the shape of the curve?

b. Calculate the mean of the sampling distribution ($\mu_{\overline{X}}$). Be careful to do this by summing the sample means (not the scores) and dividing by the number of samples you've drawn. Now compute the population mean (μ).

These two means should be very close in value because $\mu_{\bar{X}} = \mu$ by the Central Limit Theorem.

c. Calculate the standard deviation of the sampling distribution (use the means as scores) and the standard deviation of the population. Compare these two values. You should find that $\sigma_{\bar{X}} = \sigma/\sqrt{N}$.

d. If none of the above exercises turned out as they should have, it is for one or more of the following reasons:

1. You didn't take enough samples. You may need as many as 100 or 200 (or more) samples to see the curve begin to look "normal."

2. Sample size (2) is too small. An N of 5 or 10 would work much better.

3. Your sampling method is not truly random and/or the population is not arranged in random fashion.

17	20	20	19	20
18	21	19	20	19
19	22	19	23	19
20	23	18	20	20
22	19	19	20	20
23	17	18	21	20
20	18	20	19	20
22	17	21	21	21
21	20	20	20	22
18	21	20	22	21

SPSS for Windows

Using SPSS for Windows to Draw Random Samples with the 2001 Census

The demonstration and exercise below use the shortened version of the 2001 Census data. Start SPSS for Windows and open the *Census.sav* file.

SPSS DEMONSTRATION 6.1 Estimating Average Age

SPSS for Windows includes a procedure for drawing random samples from a database. We can use this procedure to illustrate some points about sampling and to convince the skeptics in the crowd that properly selected samples will produce statistics that are close approximations of the corresponding population values or parameters. For purposes of this demonstration, the Census sample will be treated as a population and its characteristics will be treated as parameters.

The instructions below will calculate a mean for *agep* for three random samples of different sizes drawn from the Census sample. The actual average age of the sample (which will be the parameter or μ) is 42.80 (see Demonstration 5.2). The samples are roughly 10%, 25%, and 50% of the population size, and the program selects them by a process that is quite similar to a table of random numbers. Therefore, these samples may be considered "simple random samples."

As a part of this procedure we also request the "standard error of the mean" or S.E. MEAN. This is the standard deviation of the sampling distribution ($\sigma_{\bar{X}}$) for a sample of this size. This statistic will be of interest because we can expect our sample means to be within this distance of the population value or parameter.

With the *Census.sav* file loaded, click **Data** from the menu bar of the **Data Editor** window and then click **Select Cases.** The **Select Cases** window appears and presents a number of different options. To select random samples, check the circle next to "**Random sample of cases**" and then click on the **Sample** button. The **Select Cases: Random Sample** dialog box will open. We can specify the size of the sample in two different ways. If we use the first option, we can specify that the sample will include a certain percentage of cases in the database. The second option allows us to specify the exact number of cases in the sample. Let's use the first option and request a 10% sample by typing 10 into the box on the first line. Click **Continue,** and then click **OK** on the **Select Cases** window. The sample will be selected and can now be processed.

To find the mean age for the 10% sample, click **Analyze, Descriptive Statistics,** and then **Descriptives.** The **Descriptives** dialog box will be open. Find *agep* in the variable list and transfer it to the **Variable(s)** box. On the **Descriptives** dialog box, click the **Options** button and select **S.E. mean** in addition to the usual statistics. Click **Continue** and then **OK,** and the requested statistics will appear in the output window.

Now, to produce a 25% sample, return to the **Select Cases** window by clicking **Data** and **Select Cases.** Click the **Reset** button at the bottom of the window and then click **OK** and the full data set ($N = 1500$) will be restored. Repeat the procedure we followed for selecting the 10% sample. Click the button next to "**Random sample of cases**" and then click on the **Sample** button. The **Select Cases: Random Sample** window will open. Request a 25% sample by typing 25 in the box, click **Continue** and **OK,** and the new sample will be selected.

Run the **Descriptives** procedure for the 25% sample (don't forget **S.E. mean**) and note the results. Finally, repeat these steps for a 50% sample. Results are summarized below:

Sample %	Sample Size	Sample Mean	Standard Error	Sample Mean ± Standard Error
10%	155	43.31	1.35	41.96 – 44.66
25%	340	41.87	.94	40.93 – 42.81
50%	747	42.44	.66	41.78 – 43.10

Notice that standard error (or the standard deviation of the sampling distribution) decreases as sample size increases. This should reinforce the common-sense notion that larger samples will provide more accurate estimates of population values. All three samples produced estimates (sample means) that are quite close in value to the population value of 42.80. All three sample means are within a standard error of the population mean. Furthermore, the largest sample is the most accurate or closest to the true population value of 42.80, only .36 of a year too low.

This demonstration should reinforce one of the main points of this chapter: statistics calculated on samples that have been selected according to the principle of EPSEM will (almost always) be reasonable approximations of their population counterparts.

Exercise (using *Census.sav*)

6.1 Following the procedures in Demonstration 6.1, select three samples from the 2001 Census database (*Census.sav*): 15%, 30%, and 60%. Get descriptive statistics for *agep* (don't forget to get the standard error), and use the results to complete the following table:

Sample %	Sample Size	Sample Mean	Standard Error	Sample Mean ± Standard Error
15%	___	___	___	_____
30%	___	___	___	_____
60%	___	___	___	_____

Summarize these results. What happens to standard error as sample size increases? Why? How accurate are the estimates (sample means)? Are all sample means within a standard error of 42.80? How does the accuracy of the estimates change as sample size changes?

7

ESTIMATION PROCEDURES

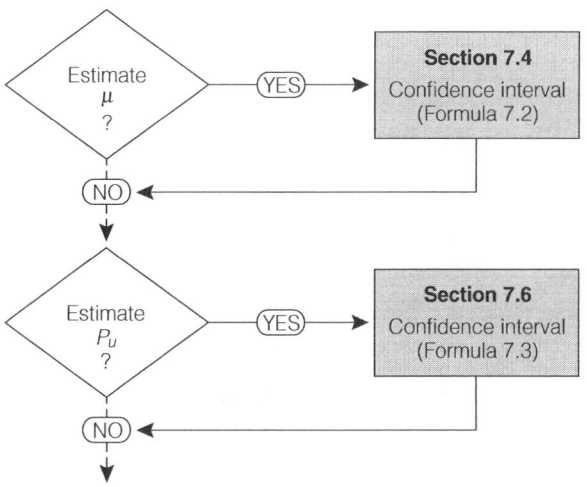

LEARNING OBJECTIVES

By the end of this chapter, you will be able to

1. Explain the logic of estimation and the role of the sample, sampling distribution, and population.
2. Define and explain the concepts of bias and efficiency.
3. Construct and interpret confidence intervals for sample means and sample proportions.
4. Use the error bar to graph a confidence interval.
5. Explain the relationships between confidence level, sample size, and the width of the confidence interval.
6. Determine the number of people needed in a sample to get a desired confidence interval.

7.1 INTRODUCTION

The object of this branch of inferential statistics is to estimate population values or parameters from statistics computed from samples. Although the techniques presented in this chapter may be new to you, you are certainly familiar with their most common applications: public-opinion polls and election projections. Polls and surveys on every conceivable issue—from the sublime to the trivial—have become a staple of the mass media and popular culture. The techniques you will learn in this chapter are essentially the same as those used by the most reputable, sophisticated, and scientific pollsters.

There are two kinds of estimation procedures. First, a **point estimate** is a sample statistic that is used to estimate a population value. For example, a newspaper story that reports that 50% of a sample of randomly selected Canadians support the use of Canada's troops for security and combat efforts in Afghanistan is reporting a point estimate. The second kind of estimation procedure involves **confidence intervals,** which consist of a range of values (an interval) instead of a single point. Rather than estimating a specific figure as in a point estimate, an interval estimate might be phrased as "between 47% and 53% of Canadians support the use of troops in Afghanistan." In this latter estimate, we are estimating that the population value falls between 47% and 53%, but we do not specify its exact value. The size of the confidence interval, which in this example is 6%, or the percentage-point difference between 47% and 53%, is called the **margin of error,** or sampling error.

7.2 BIAS AND EFFICIENCY

Both point and interval estimation procedures are based on sample statistics. Which of the many available sample statistics should be used? Estimators can be selected according to two criteria: **bias** and **efficiency.** Estimates should be based on sample statistics that are unbiased and relatively efficient. We cover each of these criteria separately.

Bias. An estimator is unbiased if and only if the mean of its sampling distribution is equal to the population value of interest. We know from the theorems presented in Chapter 6 that sample means conform to this criterion. The mean of the sampling distribution of sample means (which we will note symbolically as $\mu_{\bar{x}}$) is the same as the population mean (μ).

Sample proportions (P_s) are also unbiased. That is, if we calculate sample proportions from repeated random samples of size N and then array them in a line chart, the sampling distribution of sample proportions will have a mean (μ_p) equal to the population proportion (P_u). Thus, if we are concerned with coin flips and sample honest coins 10 at a time ($N = 10$), the sampling distribution will have a mean equal to 0.5, which is the probability that an honest coin will be heads (or tails) when flipped. All statistics other than sample means and sample proportions are biased (i.e., have sampling distributions with means not equal to the population value).*

Knowing that sample means and proportions are unbiased allows us to determine the probability that they lie within a given distance of the population values we are trying to estimate. To illustrate, consider a specific problem. Assume that we wish to estimate the average income of a community. A random sample of 500 households is taken ($N = 500$), and a sample mean of $35,000 is computed. In this example, the population mean is the average

---

*In particular, the sample standard deviation (s) is a biased estimator of the population standard deviation (σ). As you might expect, there is less dispersion in a sample than in a population and, as a consequence, s will underestimate σ. As we shall see, however, sample standard deviation can be corrected for this bias and still serve as an estimate of the population standard deviation for large samples.

FIGURE 7.1   AREAS UNDER THE SAMPLING DISTRIBUTION OF SAMPLE MEANS

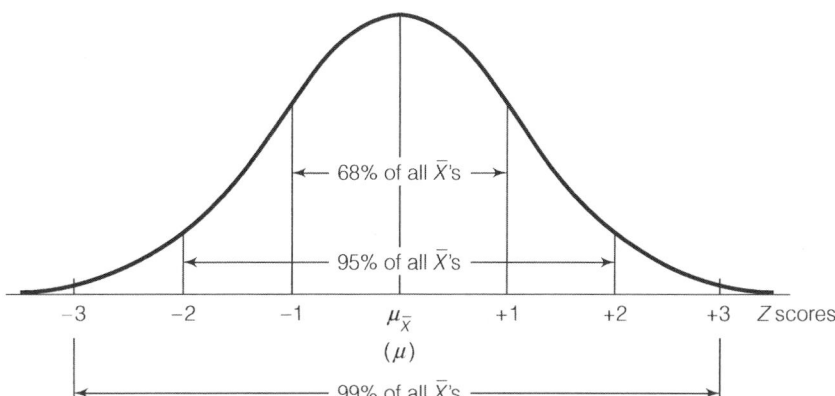

income of *all* households in the community and the sample mean is the average income for the 500 households that happened to be selected for our sample. Note that we do not know the value of the population mean (μ)—if we did, we wouldn't need the sample—but it is μ that we are interested in. The sample mean of $35,000 is important and interesting primarily insofar as it can give us information about the population mean.

The two theorems presented in Chapter 6 give us a great deal of information about the sampling distribution of all possible sample means. Because N is large, we know that the sampling distribution is normal and that its mean is equal to the population mean. We also know that all normal curves contain about 68% of the cases (the cases here are sample means) within $\pm 1Z$, 95% of the cases within $\pm 2Z$'s, and more than 99% of the cases within $\pm 3Z$'s of the mean. Remember that we are discussing the sampling distribution here—the distribution of all possible sample outcomes or, in this instance, sample means. Thus, the probabilities are very good (approximately 68 out of 100 chances) that our sample mean of $35,000 is within $\pm 1Z$, excellent (95 out of 100) that it is within $\pm 2Z$'s, and overwhelming (99 out of 100) that it is within $\pm 3Z$'s of the mean of the sampling distribution (which is the same value as the population mean). These relationships are graphically depicted in Figure 7.1.

If an estimator is unbiased, it is probably an accurate estimate of the population parameter (μ in this case). However, in less than 1% of the cases, a sample mean will be more than $\pm 3Z$'s away from the mean of the sampling distribution (very inaccurate) by random chance alone. We literally have no idea if our particular sample mean of $35,000 is in this small minority. We do know, however, that the odds are high that our sample mean is considerably closer than $\pm 3Z$'s to the mean of the sampling distribution and, thus, to the population mean.

Efficiency.   The second desirable characteristic of an estimator is efficiency, which is the extent to which the sampling distribution is clustered about its mean. Efficiency or clustering is essentially a matter of dispersion, as we saw

FIGURE 7.2 A SAMPLING DISTRIBUTION WITH $N = 100$ AND $\sigma_{\bar{x}} = \$50.00$

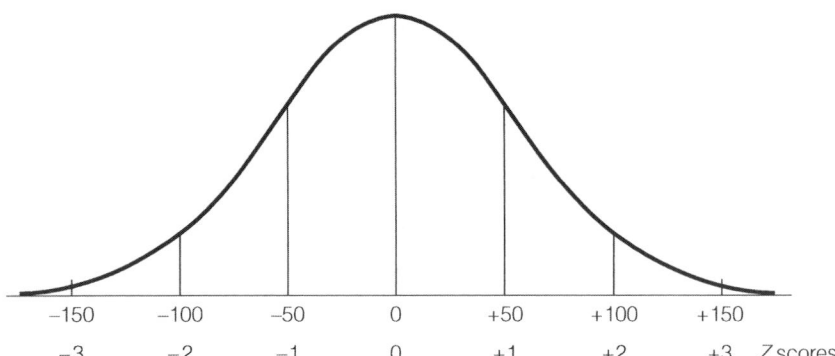

	−150	−100	−50	0	+50	+100	+150	
	−3	−2	−1	0	+1	+2	+3	Z scores

in Chapter 4 (see Figure 4.1). The smaller the standard deviation of a sampling distribution, the greater the clustering and the higher the efficiency. Remember that the standard deviation of the sampling distribution of sample means, or the standard error of the mean, is equal to the population standard deviation divided by the square root of N. Therefore, the standard deviation of the sampling distribution is an inverse function of N ($\sigma_{\bar{x}} =$ $\sigma/\sqrt{N}$). As sample size increases, $\sigma_{\bar{x}}$ will decrease. We can improve the efficiency (or decrease the standard deviation of the sampling distribution) for any estimator by increasing sample size.

An example should make this clearer. Consider two samples of different sizes:

Sample 1	Sample 2
$\overline{X}_1 = \$35,000$	$\overline{X}_2 = \$35,000$
$N_1 = 100$	$N_2 = 1,000$

Both sample means are unbiased, but which is the more efficient estimator? Consider sample 1 and assume, for the sake of illustration, that the population standard deviation (σ) is \$500.* In this case, the standard deviation of the sampling distribution of all possible sample means with an N of 100 would be or $\sigma/\sqrt{N}$ or $500/\sqrt{100}$ or \$50.00. For sample 2, the standard deviation of all possible sample means with an N of 1,000 would be much smaller. Specifically, it would be equal to $500/\sqrt{1,000}$ or \$15.81.

Sampling distribution 2 is much more clustered than sampling distribution 1. In fact, distribution 2 contains 68% of all possible sample means within ±15.81 of μ while distribution 1 requires a much broader interval of ±50.00 to do the same. The estimate based on a sample with 1,000 cases is much more likely to be close in value to the population parameter than is

---

*In reality, of course, the value of σ would be unknown.

FIGURE 7.3   A SAMPLING DISTRIBUTION WITH $N = 1{,}000$ AND $\sigma_{\bar{x}} = \$15.81$

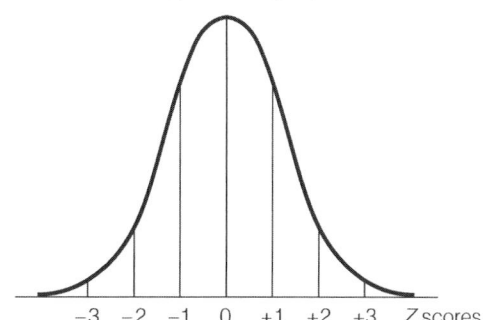

an estimate based on a sample of 100 cases. Figures 7.2 and 7.3 illustrate these relationships graphically.

To summarize: the standard deviation of all sampling distributions is an inverse function of N. Therefore, the larger the sample, the greater the clustering and the higher the efficiency. In part, these relationships between sample size and the standard deviation of the sampling distribution do nothing more than underscore our common-sense notion that much more confidence can be placed in large samples than in small (as long as both have been randomly selected).

7.3 ESTIMATION PROCEDURES: INTRODUCTION

The procedure for constructing a point estimate is straightforward. Draw an EPSEM sample, calculate either a proportion or a mean, and estimate that the population parameter is the same as the sample statistic. Remember that the larger the sample, the greater the efficiency and the more likely that the estimator is approximately the same as the population value. Also remember that, no matter how rigid the sampling procedure or how large the sample, there is always some chance that the estimator is very inaccurate.

Compared to point estimates, interval estimates are more complicated but safer because when we guess a range of values, we are more likely to include the population parameter. The first step in constructing an interval estimate is to decide on the risk that you are willing to take of being wrong. An interval estimate is wrong if it does not include the population parameter. This probability of error is called **alpha** (symbolized α). The exact value of alpha will depend on the nature of the research situation, but a 0.05 probability is commonly used. Setting alpha equal to 0.05, also called using the 95% **confidence level,** means that over the long run the researcher is willing to be wrong only 5% of the time. Or, to put it another way, if an infinite number of intervals were constructed at this alpha level (and with all other things being equal), 95% of them would contain the population value and 5% would not. In reality, of course, only one interval is constructed and, by setting the probability of error very low, we are setting the odds in our favour that the interval will include the population value.

FIGURE 7.4 THE SAMPLING DISTRIBUTION WITH ALPHA (α) EQUAL TO 0.05

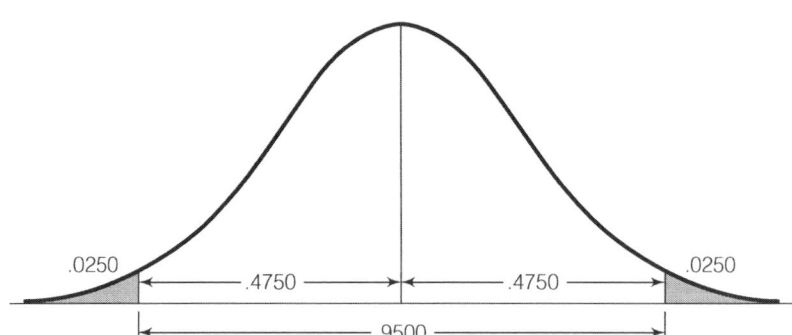

The second step is to picture the sampling distribution, divide the probability of error equally into the upper and lower tails of the distribution, and then find the corresponding *Z* score. For example, if we decided to set alpha equal to 0.05, we would place half (0.025) of this probability in the lower tail and half in the upper tail of the distribution. The sampling distribution would thus be divided as illustrated in Figure 7.4.

We need to find the *Z* score that marks the beginnings of the shaded areas. In Chapter 5, we learned how to calculate *Z* scores and find areas under the normal curve. Here, we will reverse that process. We need to find the *Z* score beyond which lies a proportion of .0250 of the total area. To do this, go down column c of Appendix A until you find this proportion (.0250). The associated *Z* score is 1.96. Because the curve is symmetrical and we are interested in both the upper and lower tails, we designate the *Z* score that corresponds to an alpha of .05 as ±1.96 (see Figure 7.5).

We now know that 95% of all possible sample outcomes fall within ±1.96 *Z*-score units of the population value. In reality, of course, there is only one sample outcome but, if we construct an interval estimate based on ±1.96*Z*'s, the probabilities are that 95% of all such intervals will trap the population value. Thus, we can be 95% confident that our interval contains the population value.

FIGURE 7.5 FINDING THE *Z* SCORE THAT CORRESPONDS TO AN ALPHA (α) OF 0.05

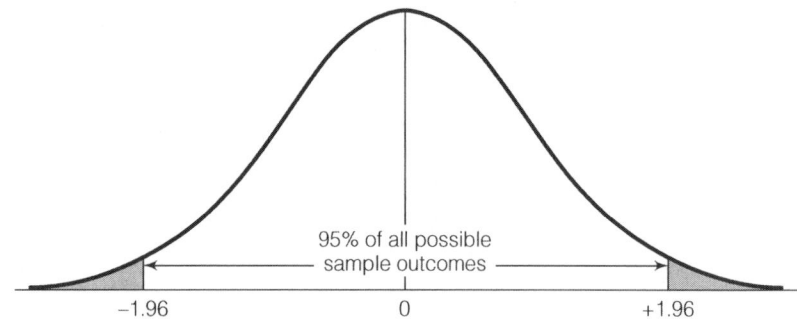

TABLE 7.1 Z SCORES FOR VARIOUS LEVELS OF ALPHA (α)

Confidence Level	Alpha	$\alpha/2$	Z Score
90%	.10	.0500	±1.65
95%	.05	.0250	±1.96
99%	.01	.0050	±2.58
99.9%	.001	.0005	±3.29

Besides the 95% level, there are three other commonly used confidence levels: the 90% level ($\alpha = .10$), the 99% level ($\alpha = 0.01$), and the 99.9% level ($\alpha = .001$). To find the corresponding Z scores for these levels, follow the procedures outlined above for an alpha of 0.05. Table 7.1 summarizes all the information you will need.

You should turn to Appendix A and confirm for yourself that the Z scores in Table 7.1 do indeed correspond to these alpha levels. As you do, note that, in the cases where alpha is set at 0.10 and 0.01, the precise areas we seek do not appear in the table. For example, with an alpha of 0.10, we would look in column c ("Area beyond") for the area .0500. Instead we find an area of .0505 ($Z = \pm1.64$) and an area of .0495 ($Z = \pm1.65$). The Z score we are seeking is somewhere between these two other scores. When this condition occurs, take the larger of the two scores as Z. This will make the interval as wide as possible under the circumstances and is thus the most conservative course of action. In the case of an alpha of 0.01, we encounter the same problem (the exact area .0050 is not in the table), resolve it the same way, and take the larger score as Z. Finally, note that in the case where alpha is set at .001, we can choose from several Z scores. Although our table is not detailed enough to show it, the closest Z score to the exact area we want is ±3.291, which we can round off to ±3.29. *(For practice in finding Z scores for various levels of confidence, see problem 7.3.)*

The third step is to actually construct the confidence interval. In the following section, we illustrate how to construct an interval estimate with sample means; in Section 7.6, we show how to construct an interval estimate with sample proportions.

7.4 INTERVAL ESTIMATION PROCEDURES FOR SAMPLE MEANS (LARGE SAMPLES)

The formula for constructing a confidence interval based on sample means is given in Formula 7.1:

FORMULA 7.1

$$\text{c.i.} = \overline{X} \pm Z\left(\frac{\sigma}{\sqrt{N}}\right)$$

where c.i. = confidence interval
$\overline{X}$ = the sample mean
Z = the Z score as determined by the alpha level
$\dfrac{\sigma}{\sqrt{N}}$ = the standard deviation of the sampling distribution or the standard error of the mean

As an example, suppose you wanted to estimate the average IQ of a community and had randomly selected a sample of 200 residents, with a sample mean IQ of 105. Assume that the population standard deviation for IQ scores is about 15, so we can set σ equal to 15. If we are willing to run a 5% chance of being wrong and set alpha at 0.05, the corresponding Z score will be 1.96. These values can be directly substituted into Formula 7.1, and an interval can be constructed

$$\text{c.i.} = \overline{X} \pm Z\left(\frac{\sigma}{\sqrt{N}}\right)$$

$$\text{c.i.} = 105 \pm 1.96\left(\frac{15}{\sqrt{200}}\right)$$

$$\text{c.i.} = 105 \pm 1.96\left(\frac{15}{14.14}\right)$$

$$\text{c.i.} = 105 \pm (1.96)(1.06)$$

$$\text{c.i.} = 105 \pm 2.08$$

That is, our estimate is that the average IQ for the population in question is somewhere between 102.92 ($105 - 2.08$) and 107.08 ($105 + 2.08$). Since 95% of all possible sample means are within $\pm 1.96Z$'s (or 2.08 IQ units in this case) of the mean of the sampling distribution, the odds are very high that our interval will contain the population mean. In fact, even if the sample mean is as far off as $\pm 1.96Z$'s (which is unlikely), our interval will still contain $\mu_{\overline{X}}$ and, thus, μ. Only if our sample mean is one of the few that is more than $\pm 1.96Z$'s from the mean of the sampling distribution will we have failed to include the population mean.

Note that in the example above, the value of the population standard deviation was supplied. Needless to say, it is unusual to have such information about a population. In the great majority of cases, we will have no knowledge of σ. In such cases, however, we can estimate σ with s, the sample standard deviation. Unfortunately, s is a biased estimator of σ, and the formula must be changed slightly to correct for the bias. For larger samples, the bias of s will not affect the interval very much. The revised formula for cases in which σ is unknown is

FORMULA 7.2

$$\text{c.i.} = \overline{X} \pm Z\left(\frac{s}{\sqrt{N-1}}\right)$$

In comparing this formula with Formula 7.1, note that there are two changes. First, σ is replaced by s, and, second, the denominator of the last term is the square root of $N - 1$ rather than the square root of N. The latter change is the correction for the fact that s is biased.

It is important to stress here that the substitution of s for σ is permitted only for large samples (i.e., samples with 100 or more cases). For smaller samples, when the value of the population standard deviation is unknown, the standardized normal distribution summarized in Appendix A cannot be

Application 7.1

Based on a random sample of 15,222 households, the Survey of Household Spending (SHS; a survey conducted by Statistics Canada to collect detailed information on the spending patterns of Canadian households) reveals that the average Canadian household spends a total of $65,535 annually. Total expenditure includes consumption of food, shelter, clothing, transportation, recreation, education, tobacco and alcohol products, and so on, as well as personal taxes, personal insurance payments, and pension and other contributions. Given the SHS sample reported a mean annual expenditure of $65,535, what is the estimate of the population mean? The information from the sample is

$$\overline{X} = 65,535$$
$$s = 51,246$$
$$N = 15,222$$

If we set alpha at 0.05, the corresponding Z score will be ± 1.96, and the 95% confidence interval will be

$$\text{c.i.} = \overline{X} \pm Z\left(\frac{s}{\sqrt{N-1}}\right)$$

$$\text{c.i.} = 65,535 \pm 1.96\left(\frac{51,246}{\sqrt{15,222-1}}\right)$$
$$\text{c.i.} = 65,535 \pm 1.96\left(\frac{51,246}{123}\right)$$
$$\text{c.i.} = 65,535 \pm (1.96)(417)$$
$$\text{c.i.} = 65,535 \pm 817$$

Based on this result, we would population spends an average of $65,535 ± $817 per year. The lower limit of our interval estimate (65,535 − 817) is 64,718, and the upper limit (65,535 + 817) is 66,352. Thus, another way to state the interval would be

$$64,718 \leq \mu \leq 66,352$$

The population mean is greater than or equal to $64,718 and less than or equal to $66,352. Because alpha was set at the .05 level, this estimate has a 5% chance of being wrong (i.e., of not containing the population mean).

Source: Data from Statistics Canada *Survey of Household Spending*, 2005, PUMF.

used in the estimation process. To construct confidence intervals from sample means with samples smaller the 100, we must use a different theoretical distribution, called the Student's *t* distribution, to find areas under the sampling distribution. We will defer the presentation of the *t* distribution until Chapter 8 and confine our attention here to estimation procedures for large samples only.

Let us close this section by working through a sample problem with Formula 7.2. Average income for a random sample of a particular community is $35,000, with a standard deviation of $200. What is the 95% interval estimate of the population mean, μ?

Given that

$$\overline{X} = \$35,000$$
$$s = \$200$$
$$N = 500$$

and using an alpha of 0.05, the interval can be constructed:

$$\text{c.i.} = \overline{X} \pm Z\left(\frac{s}{\sqrt{N-1}}\right)$$

$$\text{c.i.} = 35{,}000 \pm 1.96\left(\frac{200}{\sqrt{499}}\right)$$

$$\text{c.i.} = 35{,}000 \pm 17.55$$

The average income for the community as a whole is between \$34,982.45 (35,000 − 17.55) and \$35,017.55 (35,000 + 17.55). Remember that this interval has only a 5% chance of being wrong (i.e., of not containing the population mean). *(For practice with confidence intervals for sample means, see problems 7.1, 7.4–7.7, 7.18, and 7.19a–7.19c.)*

7.5 GRAPHING A CONFIDENCE INTERVAL OF A SAMPLE MEAN

A confidence interval of a sample mean can be depicted using a graph called the **error bar.** The error bar graph is based on the lower and upper limits of the confidence interval of a sample mean. The construction of an error bar requires a couple of steps. First, the sample mean is plotted with a symbol, such as a dot, at the centre of a graph. Second, a vertical line or "error bar" is drawn from the sample mean to the lower limit of its confidence interval, marked by a small horizontal line. The same is done between the sample mean and the upper limit of the confidence interval. The area bounded by the two error bars is equal to the width of the confidence interval of the sample mean.

Figure 7.6 displays the error bar graph for the 95% confidence interval of the mean income of the community described in Section 7.4. Recall

FIGURE 7.6   ERROR BAR GRAPH FOR THE 95% CONFIDENCE INTERVAL OF THE MEAN INCOME OF A COMMUNITY

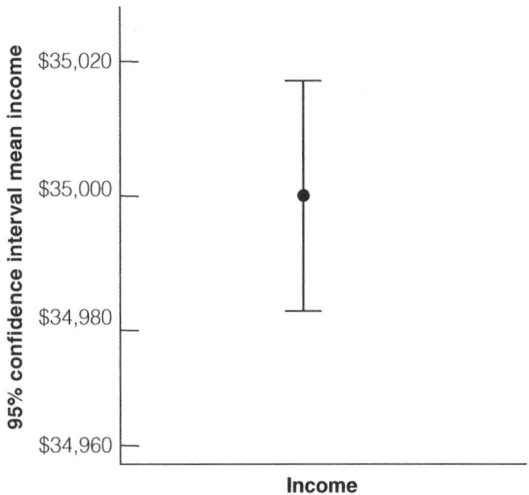

that the average income for the random sample of 500 households in that community is \$35,000, with a standard deviation of \$200. At the 95% confidence level, the average income for the community as a whole is between \$34,982.45 (35,000 − 17.55) and \$35,017.55 (35,000 + 17.55). Graphically, the dot in the middle of the error bar graph represents the sample mean and the vertical line above and below the sample mean represents the upper and lower limits of the confidence interval. *(For practice in constructing and interpreting error bars, see problems 7.4 and 7.6.)*

7.6 INTERVAL ESTIMATION PROCEDURES FOR SAMPLE PROPORTIONS (LARGE SAMPLES)

Estimation procedures for sample proportions are essentially the same as those for sample means. The major difference is that, because proportions are different statistics, we must use a different sampling distribution. In fact, again based on the Central Limit Theorem, we know that sample proportions have sampling distributions that are normal in shape with means (μ_p) equal to the population value (P_u) and standard deviations (σ_p) equal to $\sqrt{P_u(1 - P_u)/N}$. The formula for constructing confidence intervals based on sample proportions is

FORMULA 7.3

$$\text{c.i.} = P_s \pm Z\sqrt{\frac{P_u(1 - P_u)}{N}}$$

The values for P_s and N come directly from the sample, and the value of Z is determined by the confidence level, as was the case with sample means. This leaves one unknown in the formula, P_u—the same value we are trying to estimate. This dilemma can be resolved by setting the value of P_u at 0.5. Because the second term in the numerator under the radical $(1 - P_u)$ is the reciprocal of P_u, the entire expression will always have a value of 0.5 × 0.5, or 0.25, which is the maximum value this expression can attain. That is, if we set P_u at any value other than 0.5, the expression $P_u(1 - P_u)$ will decrease in value. If we set P_u at 0.4, for example, the second term $(1 - P_u)$ would be 0.6, and the value of the entire expression would decrease to 0.24. Setting P_u at 0.5 ensures that the expression $P_u(1 - P_u)$ will be at its maximum possible value and, consequently, the interval will be at maximum width. This is the most conservative solution possible to the dilemma posed by having to assign a value to P_u in the estimation equation.

To illustrate these procedures, assume that you wish to estimate the proportion of students at your university who missed at least one day of classes because of illness last semester. Out of a random sample of 200 students, 60 reported that they had been sick enough to miss classes at least once during the previous semester. The sample proportion upon which we

---

Application 7.2

Canadians overwhelmingly believe that global warming, produced by greenhouse gases, is a real and major threat to future generations. According to a Leger Marketing survey, 81% of a random sample of 1,500 Canadians said "yes" to the question, "In your view, should the Government of Canada be tougher on Canadian citizens and corporations to ensure that collectively Canadians reduce greenhouse gas emissions?" Based on this finding, what is the estimate of the population value? The sample information is

$$P_s = 0.81$$
$$N = 1,500$$

Note that the percentage of those who said "yes" to the question has been stated as a proportion. If we set alpha at 0.05, the corresponding Z score will be ±1.96, and the interval estimate of the population proportion will be

$$\text{c.i.} = P_s \pm Z\sqrt{\frac{P_u(1 - P_u)}{N}}$$

$$\text{c.i.} = 0.81 \pm 1.96\sqrt{\frac{(0.5)(0.5)}{1,500}}$$
$$\text{c.i.} = 0.81 \pm 1.96\sqrt{0.00017}$$
$$\text{c.i.} = 0.81 \pm (1.96)(0.013)$$
$$\text{c.i.} = 0.81 \pm 0.03$$

We can now estimate that the proportion of the population that believes the federal government needs to get tough on citizens and corporations to reduce greenhouse gas emissions is between 0.78 and 0.84. That is, the lower limit of the interval estimate is (0.81−0.03) or 0.78, and the upper limit is (0.81 + 0.03) or 0.84. We may also express this result in percentages and say that between 78% and 84% of the population is of the opinion that the government should be tougher on citizens and corporations in order to reduce greenhouse gas emissions. This interval has a 5% chance of not containing the population value.

Source: Leger Marketing. *Canadians and the Environmental Policies of Canada*. 2005.

---

will base our estimate is thus 60/200, or 0.30. At the 95% level, the interval estimate will be

$$\text{c.i.} = P_s \pm Z\sqrt{\frac{P_u(1 - P_u)}{N}}$$

$$\text{c.i.} = 0.30 \pm 1.96\sqrt{\frac{(0.5)(0.5)}{200}}$$

$$\text{c.i.} = 0.30 \pm 1.96\sqrt{\frac{0.25}{200}}$$

$$\text{c.i.} = 0.30 \pm (1.96)(0.035)$$
$$\text{c.i.} = 0.30 \pm 0.07$$

Based on this sample proportion of 0.30, you would estimate that the proportion of students who missed at least one day of classes because of illness was between 0.23 and 0.37. The estimate could, of course, also be phrased in percentages by reporting that between 23% and 37% of the student body was affected by illness at least once during the past semester. Additionally, as with the sample mean, the error bar can be used to graph the confidence interval of a sample proportion. *(For practice with confidence intervals for sample proportions, see problems 7.2, 7.8–7.12, 7.14–7.17, and 7.19d–7.19g.)*

TABLE 7.2 CHOOSING FORMULAS FOR CONFIDENCE INTERVALS

If the sample statistic is a	and	Use formula
mean	the population standard deviation is known	7.1 c.i. $= \bar{X} \pm Z\left(\dfrac{\sigma}{\sqrt{N}}\right)$
mean	the population standard deviation is unknown	7.2 c.i. $= \bar{X} \pm Z\left(\dfrac{s}{\sqrt{N-1}}\right)$
proportion		7.3 c.i. $= P_s \pm Z\sqrt{\dfrac{P_u(1-P_u)}{N}}$

7.7 A SUMMARY OF THE COMPUTATION OF CONFIDENCE INTERVALS

To this point, we have covered the construction of confidence intervals for sample means and sample proportions. In both cases, the procedures assume large samples (*N* greater than 100). The procedures for constructing confidence intervals for small samples are not covered in this text. Table 7.2 presents the three formulas for confidence intervals organized by the situations in which they are used. For sample means, when the population standard deviation is known, use Formula 7.1. When the population standard deviation is unknown (which is the usual case), use Formula 7.2. For sample proportions, always use Formula 7.3.

7.8 CONTROLLING THE WIDTH OF INTERVAL ESTIMATES

The width of a confidence interval for either sample means or sample proportions can be partly controlled by manipulating two terms in the equation. First, the confidence level can be raised or lowered and, second, the interval can be widened or narrowed by gathering samples of different size. The researcher alone determines the risk he or she is willing to take of being wrong (i.e., of not including the population value in the interval estimate). The exact confidence level (or alpha level) will depend, in part, on the purpose of the research. For example, if potentially harmful drugs were being tested, the researcher would naturally demand very high levels of confidence (99.99% or even 99.999%). On the other hand, if intervals are being constructed only for loose "guesstimates," then much lower confidence levels can be tolerated (such as 90%).

The relationship between interval size and confidence level is that intervals widen as confidence levels increase. This should make intuitive sense. Wider intervals are more likely to trap the population value; hence, more confidence can be placed in them.

To illustrate this relationship, let us return to the example where we estimated the average income for a community. In this problem, we were working with a sample of 500 residents, and the average income for this sample was $35,000, with a standard deviation of $200. We constructed the 95% confidence interval and found that it extended 17.55 around the sample mean (i.e., the interval was $35,000 ± $17.55).

Application 7.3

A total of 1,507 adult Canadians were randomly selected to participate in a Leger Marketing study of attitudes toward homosexuality and same-sex marriages. Some results are reported below. What is the level of support in the population? The sample information, expressed in terms of the proportion agreeing, is

"Homosexuals should have the same rights as heterosexuals."

$$P_s = 0.76$$
$$N = 1,507$$

"Homosexuals should be given access to same-sex marriages."

$$P_s = 0.65$$
$$N = 1,507$$

For the first item, the confidence interval estimate to the population at the 95% confidence level is

$$\text{c.i.} = P_s \pm Z\sqrt{\frac{P_u(1 - P_u)}{N}}$$
$$\text{c.i.} = 0.76 \pm 1.96\sqrt{\frac{(0.5)(0.5)}{1,507}}$$
$$\text{c.i.} = 0.76 \pm 1.96\sqrt{0.00017}$$

$$\text{c.i.} = 0.76 \pm (1.96)(0.013)$$
$$\text{c.i.} = 0.76 \pm 0.03$$

Expressing these results in terms of percentages, we can conclude that, at the 95% confidence level, between 73% and 79% of adult Canadians support equal rights for gays and lesbians.

For the second survey item, the confidence interval estimate to the population at the 95% confidence level is

$$\text{c.i.} = P_s \pm Z\sqrt{\frac{P_u(1 - P_u)}{N}}$$
$$\text{c.i.} = 0.65 \pm 1.96\sqrt{\frac{(0.5)(0.5)}{1,507}}$$
$$\text{c.i.} = 0.65 \pm 1.96\sqrt{0.00017}$$
$$\text{c.i.} = 0.65 \pm (1.96)(0.013)$$
$$\text{c.i.} = 0.65 \pm 0.03$$

Again expressing results in terms of percentages, we can conclude that, at the 95% confidence level, between 62% and 68% of adult Canadians support same-sex marriages. (Note that the width of the second confidence interval is exactly the same as the first. This is because we are using the same values for Z score and sample size in both estimates.)

Source: Leger Marketing. *Canadian Perceptions of Homosexuality.* 2001.

If we had constructed the 90% confidence interval for these sample data (a lower confidence level), the Z score in the formula would have decreased to ±1.65, and the interval would have been narrower:

$$\text{c.i.} = \overline{X} \pm Z\left(\frac{s}{\sqrt{N - 1}}\right)$$
$$\text{c.i.} = 35,000 \pm 1.65\left(\frac{200}{\sqrt{499}}\right)$$
$$\text{c.i.} = 35,000 \pm (1.65)(8.95)$$
$$\text{c.i.} = 35,000 \pm 14.77$$

On the other hand, if we had constructed the 99% confidence interval, the Z score would have increased to ± 2.58, and the interval would have been wider:

$$\text{c.i.} = \overline{X} \pm Z\left(\frac{s}{\sqrt{N-1}}\right)$$

$$\text{c.i.} = 35{,}000 \pm 2.58\left(\frac{200}{\sqrt{499}}\right)$$

$$\text{c.i.} = 35{,}000 \pm (2.58)(8.95)$$

$$\text{c.i.} = 35{,}000 \pm 23.09$$

At the 99.9% confidence level, the Z score would be ± 3.29, and the interval would be wider still:

$$\text{c.i.} = \overline{X} \pm Z\left(\frac{s}{\sqrt{N-1}}\right)$$

$$\text{c.i.} = 35{,}000 \pm 3.29\left(\frac{200}{\sqrt{499}}\right)$$

$$\text{c.i.} = 35{,}000 \pm (3.29)(8.95)$$

$$\text{c.i.} = 35{,}000 \pm 29.45$$

These four intervals are grouped together in Table 7.3, and the increase in interval size can be readily observed. Although sample means have been used to illustrate the relationship between interval width and confidence level, exactly the same relationships apply to sample proportions. *(To further explore the relationship between alpha and interval width, see problem 7.13.)*

Sample size bears the opposite relationship to interval width. As sample size increases, interval width decreases. Larger samples give more precise (narrower) estimates. Again, an example should make this clearer. In Table 7.4, confidence intervals for four samples of various sizes are constructed and then grouped together for purposes of comparison. The sample data are the same as in Table 7.3, and the confidence level is 95% throughout. The relationships illustrated in Table 7.4 also hold true, of course, for sample proportions. *(To further explore the relationship between sample size and interval width, see problem 7.14.)*

Notice that the decrease in interval width (or, increase in precision) does not bear a constant or linear relationship with sample size. With sample 2 as compared to sample 1, the sample size was increased by a factor of 5, but the interval is not five times as narrow. This is an important relationship

TABLE 7.3   INTERVAL ESTIMATES FOR FOUR CONFIDENCE LEVELS ($\overline{x}$ = $35,000, s = $200, N = 500 throughout)

Alpha	Confidence Level	Interval	Interval Width
.10	90%	$35,000 ± 14.77	$29.54
.05	95%	$35,000 ± 17.55	$35.10
.01	99%	$35,000 ± 23.09	$46.18
.001	99.9%	$35,000 ± 29.45	$58.90

TABLE 7.4   INTERVAL ESTIMATES FOR FOUR DIFFERENT SAMPLES
($\bar{x}$ = \$35,000, s = \$200, alpha = 0.05 throughout)

Sample 1 (N = 100)	Sample 2 (N = 500)
c.i. = \$35,000 ± 1.96(200/$\sqrt{99}$)	c.i. = \$35,000 ± 1.96(200/$\sqrt{499}$)
c.i. = \$35,000 ± 39.40	c.i. = \$35,000 ± 17.55

Sample 3 (N = 1,000)	Sample 4 (N = 10,000)
c.i. = \$35,000 ± 1.96(200/$\sqrt{999}$)	c.i. = \$35,000 ± 1.96(200/$\sqrt{9,999}$)
c.i. = \$35,000 ± 12.40	c.i. = \$35,000 ± 3.92

Sample	N	Interval Width
1	100	\$78.80
2	500	\$35.10
3	1,000	\$24.80
4	10,000	\$ 7.84

because it means that N might have to be increased many times to appreciably improve the accuracy of an estimate. Because the cost of a research project is a direct function of sample size, this relationship implies a point of diminishing returns in estimation procedures. A sample of 10,000 will cost about twice as much as a sample of 5,000, but estimates based on the larger sample will not be twice as precise.

7.9 DETERMINING SAMPLE SIZE

It is often useful prior to conducting a survey to determine how many people are needed in a random sample to obtain a desired confidence interval. For instance, a gerontologist wants to estimate the mean income of senior citizens in Canada. How many seniors would she have to sample to be 99% confident that the sample mean is within plus or minus \$1,000 (margin of error) of the population mean, where previous research showed that the population standard deviation is \$5,000 (lacking knowledge of σ, she can replace it with s, the sample standard deviation, if available). Or, what sample size would a public-opinion pollster need if she wanted to know what proportion of Canadians approve of Canada's military mission to Afghanistan within plus or minus 3% with a 95% certainty? We can solve these problems by simply rearranging the formulas for constructing a confidence interval.

For the mean, Formula 7.4 finds the minimum sample size needed in a simple random sample to get results with the desired level of precision:

FORMULA 7.4

$$N = \frac{Z^2 \times \sigma^2}{ME^2}$$

where N = required sample size
Z = Z score as determined by the alpha level
σ = population standard deviation
ME = margin of error

Using this formula the gerontologist can calculate the N she needs for a 99% confidence interval, where Z equals 2.58 and the margin of error is 1,000:

$$N = \frac{Z^2 \times \sigma^2}{ME^2}$$

$$N = \frac{2.58^2 \times 5,000^2}{1,000^2}$$

$$N = \frac{6.6564 \times 25,000,000}{1,000,000}$$

$$N = \frac{166,410,000}{1,000,000}$$

$$N = 166.41$$

The gerontologist needs to randomly sample, rounding up, at least 167 senior citizens to be 99% confident that the sample mean will be within plus or minus $1,000 of the population mean, that is, the mean income of all senior citizens in Canada.

For the proportion, Formula 7.5 finds the smallest sample size required to get the desired results in a simple random sample:

FORMULA 7.5

$$N = \frac{\left(Z^2 \times P_u \times (1 - P_u) \right) + ME^2}{ME^2}$$

where N = required sample size
Z = Z score as determined by the alpha level
P_u = population proportion
ME = margin of error

With this formula, the public opinion pollster can calculate the N she needs for a 95% confidence interval, where Z equals 1.96 and (expressed as proportions) a margin of error of 0.03 and P_u set to 0.5:

$$N = \frac{\left(Z^2 \times P_u \times (1 - P_u) \right) + ME^2}{ME^2}$$

$$N = \frac{\left(1.96^2 \times 0.5 \times (0.5) \right) + 0.03^2}{0.03^2}$$

$$N = \frac{0.9604 + 0.0009}{0.0009}$$

$$N = \frac{0.9613}{0.0009}$$

$$N = 1,068.11$$

So, at least 1,069 Canadians need to be randomly sampled for the pollster to be 95% confident that the sample proportion will be within plus or minus 0.03 of the population proportion.

The information in this example might sound familiar. Pollsters typically report their findings to the media with this information in a footnote, telling us that their estimate is "accurate within ±3%, 19 times out of 20" or that the "margin of error for a sample of 1,069 is ±3%, 19 times out of 20."

This example also reveals why political polls tend to randomly sample only 1,000 or so people—it is not necessary to have a sample much larger than around 1,000 because we are already 95% confident that our sample results will have a high level of precision, with a margin of error of just plus or minus 3%. Further, and as noted in the previous section, the relationship between sample size and level of precision is not linear. That is to say that doubling the sample size, for instance, will not cut in half the margin of error. Doubling the sample size from 1,069 to 2,138 cuts the margin of error from ±3% to just ±2.1%. A relatively small increase in precision may not justify the cost associated with doubling sample size.

As a final note, Formulas 7.4 and 7.5 are used to determine sample size of a simple random sample when the population of interest is very large, typically a population size of 100,000 or more. Otherwise these formulas need to be slightly modified to correct for sampling design (when simple random sample is not used) and/or population size (when population size is less than 100,000).

7.10 INTERPRETING STATISTICS: PREDICTING THE ELECTION OF THE GOVERNMENT OF CANADA AND JUDGING ITS PERFORMANCE

The statistical techniques covered in this chapter have become a part of everyday life in Canada and elsewhere. In politics, for example, estimation techniques are used to track public sentiment, measure how citizens perceive the performance of political leaders, and project the likely winners of upcoming elections. We should acknowledge, nonetheless, that these applications of estimation techniques are also controversial. Many wonder if the easy availability of polls makes politicians overly sensitive to the whims of public sentiment. Others are concerned that election projections might work against people's readiness to participate fully in the democratic process and, in particular, cast their votes on election day. These are serious concerns but, in this text, we can do little more than acknowledge them and hope that you have the opportunity to pursue them in other, more appropriate settings.

In this installment of Interpreting Statistics, we will examine the role of statistical estimation of voting intentions in the 2006 campaign for the federal election (election projections) that culminated in the election of Stephen Harper and the Conservative Party. We will also examine trends in post-election polls on political party support. Both kinds of polls use the same formulas introduced in this chapter to construct confidence intervals (although the random samples were assembled according to a more complex technique that is beyond the scope of this text).

A Shift in Popularity.   The federal election of 2006 among Liberals, Conservatives, New Democratic Party (NDP), Bloc Québécois (BQ), and the Green Party was one of the most interesting elections in recent Canadian history. Although the next election was not legally required until 2009, the dissolution of Parliament and a motion of "no confidence" passed by the opposition in the House of Commons in November 2005 contributed to the early election. In this section we will use our newly acquired knowledge of confidence intervals to explore how the popularity of the parties changed before and during the election campaign.

Table 7.5 presents the results of the last eight surveys conducted before the 2006 federal election by Nanos Research (formerly SES Research), a Canadian public-opinion research firm. The two left-hand columns show the dates of the polls and the sample size (N) for each poll. The five right-hand columns list the percentage of the sample that said, at the time the poll was conducted, that they intended to vote for each party. These are point estimates of the population parameters (which would be the actual percentage of the entire national electorate that would vote for the Liberals, Conservatives, NDP, BQ, or Green Party at that specific time). Table 7.5 expresses results in percentages for ease of communication, but actual estimates would be computed using sample proportions.

It can be seen from Table 7.5 that the Liberal Party had the lead for the first part of the campaign, up to the end of December 2005. Electoral support shifted to the Conservative Party, however, in the last few weeks of the campaign.

Let us assume that one wanted to predict the election results based on the January 8, 2006, poll, when the Conservative Party has a lead of about 3 percentage points over the Liberal Party. Does this mean that the Conservatives were actually ahead of the Liberals in the popular vote? The percentages in Table 7.5 are point estimates, and these types of estimates are unlikely to match their respective parameters exactly. In other

TABLE 7.5   NANOS RESEARCH POLLING RESULTS, OCTOBER 2005 TO JANUARY 2006

| Poll Date | Sample Size | Percentage of Sample for | | | | |
		Liberal	Conservative	NDP	BQ	Green
Oct. 27, 2005	854	40	28	15	12	4
Nov. 13, 2005	865	34	28	20	14	4
Dec. 1, 2005	1,008	37	29	15	14	5
Dec. 15, 2005	1,012	39	33	12	12	5
Dec. 30, 2005	1,028	35	35	14	13	4
Jan. 8, 2006	987	31	34	17	11	6
Jan. 15, 2006	1,038	29	37	18	11	5
Jan. 22, 2006	1,051	30	36	17	11	6

Source: Nanos Research.

READING STATISTICS 4: Public-Opinion Polls

You are most likely to encounter the estimation techniques covered in this chapter in the mass media in the form of public-opinion polls, election projections, and the like. Professional polling firms use interval estimates, and responsible reporting by the media will usually emphasize the estimate itself (for example, "In a survey of the Canadian public, 57% of the respondents said that they approve of the prime minister's performance") but also will report the width of the interval ("This estimate is accurate to within ±3%," or "Figures from this poll are subject to a margin of error of ±3%"), the alpha level (usually as the confidence level of 95%), and the size of the sample ("1,458 households were surveyed").

Election projections and voter analyses have been common since the middle of the 20th century and are discussed further in Section 7.10. More recently, public-opinion polling has been increasingly used to gauge reactions to everything from the newest movies to the hottest gossip to the prime minister's conduct during the latest crisis. Newsmagazines routinely report poll results as an adjunct to news stories, and similar stories are regular features of TV news and newspapers. We would include an example or two of these applications here, but polls have become so pervasive that you can choose your own example. Just pick up a newsmagazine or newspaper, leaf through it casually, and we bet that you'll find at least one poll. Read the story and try and identify the population, the confidence interval width, the sample

size, and the confidence level. Bring the news item to class and dazzle your instructor.

As a citizen, as well as a social scientist, you should be extremely suspicious of polls that do not include such vital information as sample size or interval width. You should also check to find out how the sample was assembled. Samples selected in a non-random fashion cannot be regarded as representative of the Canadian public or, for that matter, of any population larger than the sample itself. Such non-scientific polls can be found when local TV news or sports programs ask viewers to call in and register their opinions about some current controversy. These polls are for entertainment only and must not be taken seriously. You should, of course, read all polls and surveys critically and analytically, but you should place confidence only in polls that are based on samples selected according to the rule of EPSEM (see Chapter 6) from some defined population.

In addition, ads, commercials, and reports published by partisan groups sometimes report statistics that seem to be estimates to the population. Often, such estimates are based on woefully inadequate sampling sizes and biased sampling procedures, and the data are collected under circumstances that evoke a desired response. "Person in the street" (or shopper in the grocery store) interviews have a certain folksy appeal but must not be accorded the same credibility as surveys conducted by reputable polling firms.

(continued)

words, it is unlikely that the sample values in the table were exactly equal to the percentage of the electorate who were going to vote for each of the parties on that particular date. On the other hand, confidence intervals would be safer to utilize as they use ranges of values, not single points, to estimate population values.

Table 7.6 displays the 95% confidence intervals for each party for these eight polls, with the results again expressed as percentages rather than proportions. The dates and sample size of each poll are displayed in

READING STATISTICS 4: *(continued)*

The social research industry in Canada, however, is regulated to some extent. By and large, the industry is self-regulated. The Marketing Research and Intelligence Association, representing most of the industry, has adopted codes of ethics and established standards for reporting and interpreting survey research results. Further, the reporting of election survey results during federal election campaigns is formally regulated by Canada's *Elections Act.* Federal electoral legislation requires that published election-period poll results contain basic methodological information such as margin of error and date on which the poll was conducted. The *Canada Elections Act* also places restrictions on the reporting of new election polls in the period immediately before election day and on the reporting of "exit polls" prior to the close of polls and of election results from one time zone (e.g., in Eastern Canada) to those in another time zone (e.g., in Western Canada) where polls have yet to close in order to take into account Canada's many time zones.

Public-Opinion Surveys in the Professional Literature

Thousands of political, social, and market research polls are conducted each year in Canada. For the social sciences, probably the single most important consequence of the growth in opinion polling is that many nationally representative databases are now available for research purposes. These high-quality databases are often available for free

or a nominal fee and they make it possible to conduct "state-of-the-art" research without the expense and difficulty of collecting data yourself. This is an important development because we can now easily test our theories against very high-quality data, and our conclusions will thus have a stronger empirical basis. Our research efforts will have greater credibility with our colleagues, with policy-makers, and with the public at large.

One of the more important and widely used databases of this sort is the General Social Survey (GSS). Since 1985, Statistics Canada has annually questioned a nationally representative sample of Canadians about a wide variety of issues and concerns. Because many of the questions are asked every five years or so the GSS offers a longitudinal record of Canadian sentiment and opinion about a large variety of topics (for example, see Reading Statistics 5). Each year, new topics of current concern are added and explored, and the variety of information available thus continues to expand. Like other nationally representative samples, the GSS sample is chosen by a complex probability design that resembles stratified and cluster sampling (see Chapter 6). With a sample size of about 25,000, GSS estimates will be highly precise (see Table 7.4 and Section 7.8 for the discussion on the relationship between sample size and precision of estimates). The computer exercises in this text are based on the 2004 GSS, and this database is described more fully in Appendix G.

the left-most columns, followed by the 95% confidence intervals for each estimate and the width of the interval estimates. (Note that Table 7.6 underscores a very important point about estimation: As sample size increases, the width of the interval becomes narrower. The first two polls were based on smaller samples, 854 and 865, and were each 6.8 percentage points wide, while the polls taken in December and January were based on larger samples and, as a result, the intervals are narrower, at 6.2% wide.)

The most important information in Table 7.6 is, of course, the intervals themselves, and it is the overlap in some of these intervals that

TABLE 7.6 SAMPLE SIZE, CONFIDENCE INTERVALS, AND LIKELY WINNERS

Poll Date	Sample Size	95% Confidence Interval					Interval Width
		Liberal	Conservative	NDP	BQ	Green	
Oct. 27, 2005	854	40 ± 3.4	28 ± 3.4	15 ± 3.4	12 ± 3.4	4 ± 3.4	6.8
Nov. 13, 2005	865	34 ± 3.4	28 ± 3.4	20 ± 3.4	14 ± 3.4	4 ± 3.4	6.8
Dec. 1, 2005	1,008	37 ± 3.1	29 ± 3.1	15 ± 3.1	14 ± 3.1	5 ± 3.1	6.2
Dec. 15, 2005	1,012	39 ± 3.1	33 ± 3.1	12 ± 3.1	12 ± 3.1	5 ± 3.1	6.2
Dec. 30, 2005	1,028	35 ± 3.1	35 ± 3.1	14 ± 3.1	13 ± 3.1	4 ± 3.1	6.2
Jan. 8, 2006	987	31 ± 3.1	34 ± 3.1	17 ± 3.1	11 ± 3.1	6 ± 3.1	6.2
Jan. 15, 2006	1,038	29 ± 3.1	37 ± 3.1	18 ± 3.1	11 ± 3.1	5 ± 3.1	6.2
Jan. 22, 2006	1,051	30 ± 3.1	36 ± 3.1	17 ± 3.1	11 ± 3.1	6 ± 3.1	6.2

Source: Nanos Research.

caused the pollsters to declare the race "too close to call." So for example, the poll on January 8, 2006, showed that support for the Liberal Party was between 27.9% (31% − 3.1%) and 34.1% (31% + 3.1%), a width of 6.2 percentage points. Support for the Conservative Party in this poll was between 30.9% and 37.1%, again a width of 6.2 percentage points. (Note that the confidence intervals for each date have the same width because they are computed using the same sample size, or N, and the same confidence level, or 95%.)

Remember that while we can be 95% sure that the parameter is in the interval, it may be *anywhere* between the upper and lower limits. Thus, this poll tells us that it was just as likely that the Liberals would win (e.g., support for the Liberals could have been as high as 34.1%, and support for the Conservatives could have been as low as 30.9%) as it is that the Conservatives would be the victor (e.g., support for the Liberals could have been as low as 27.9%, and support for the Conservatives could have been as high as 37.1%). If the confidence intervals overlap, it is possible that the apparent losing party is actually ahead. In the end, when the intervals overlap—when the race is so close—the polls cannot identify a winner.

This was not the case, however, for the poll conducted on January 15, 2006. It predicted that the Conservative Party would win the federal election with 95% confidence. Indeed when the ballots were finally counted in the 2006 federal election, the parties wound up with similar percentages to the January 15 and January 22 polls. Table 7.7 provides a comparison of the last Nanos poll (January 22) prior to the election and the actual election results on January 23. Percentages are shown to the first decimal place to illustrate the accuracy of sample polls.

Liberals and Conservatives received 30.2% and 36.3% of the popular vote respectively, very close to the point estimates of 30.1% and 36.4% made in the January 22 poll. The difference between the poll and actual election results

TABLE 7.7   COMPARISON OF THE LAST NANOS RESEARCH POLL (JANUARY 22) PRIOR TO THE FEDERAL ELECTION AND THE FEDERAL ELECTION RESULTS (JANUARY 23)

Party	Last Poll Prior to Federal Election (Jan. 22, 2006; sample size 1,051)	Federal Election (Jan. 23, 2006)	Difference from Nanos Research Poll
Liberal	30.1	30.2	0.1
Conservative	36.4	36.3	0.1
NDP	17.4	17.5	0.1
BQ	10.6	10.5	0.1
Green	5.6	4.5	1.1
Other	-	1.0	1.0

Source: Nanos Research.

for both the Liberals and Conservatives was just 0.1%. The NDP, Bloc Québécois, and Green Party garnered 17.5%, 10.5%, and 4.5% of the vote, parameters that were within the range of the interval estimates for the last poll.

Stability in Popular Support. Once elected, a political party is not free of polls and confidence intervals. Since the federal election in January 2006, pollsters have tracked the parties' popularity by asking randomly selected samples of adult Canadians to choose their voting preferences, as illustrated in Figure 7.7. For purposes of clarity, only point estimates are shown, but

FIGURE 7.7   2006 CANADIAN FEDERAL ELECTION RESULTS AND NANOS RESEARCH POLLING DATA AFTER THE ELECTION

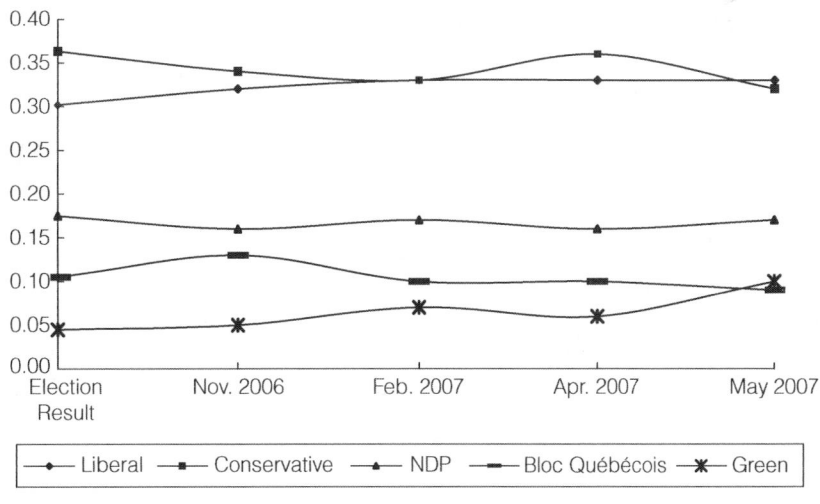

Source: Nanos Research.

READING STATISTICS 5: Using Representative Samples to Track National Trends

Among other uses, the GSS can be used to track national trends and shifts in public opinion over time because many of the questions are asked every few years. We demonstrate here how to assess trends in the nature and extent of criminal victimization using the 1993 and 2004 General Social Surveys (GSS).

We considered three questions that measure perception and experience of crime. Each question, asked in both the 1993 and the 2004 GSS, is as follows:

Q1. Compared to other areas in Canada, do you think your neighbourhood has a higher amount of crime, about the same, or a lower amount of crime?

Q2. Do you feel very safe, reasonably safe, somewhat unsafe, or very unsafe from crime walking alone in your area after dark?

Q3. During the past 12 months, did you come into contact with the police as a victim of a crime?

Over this period, respondents were less likely to say that their neighbourhood had above-average crime, to feel unsafe from crime after dark, and to be an actual victim of crime. Figure 1 shows that the point estimate for the proportion of those who think their neighbourhood has higher-than-average crime fell from 0.116 (or 11.6%) in 1993 to 0.085 (8.5%) in 2004, as did the proportion who felt unsafe from crime while walking after dark: 0.273 in 1993 to 0.16 in 2004. It is not surprising to find that the proportion of those who had contact with the police as a victim of a crime also decreased, from 0.119 to 0.073, over these years.

To estimate the population parameters or the proportions for all Canadians, interval estimates were calculated using Formula 7.3. The results,

FIGURE 1   PROPORTION OF RESPONDENTS WHO SAID THEIR NEIGHBOURHOOD HAS HIGHER CRIME, THEY FEEL UNSAFE WALKING AFTER DARK, AND THEY HAD CONTACT WITH POLICE AS A VICTIM, 1993 AND 2004

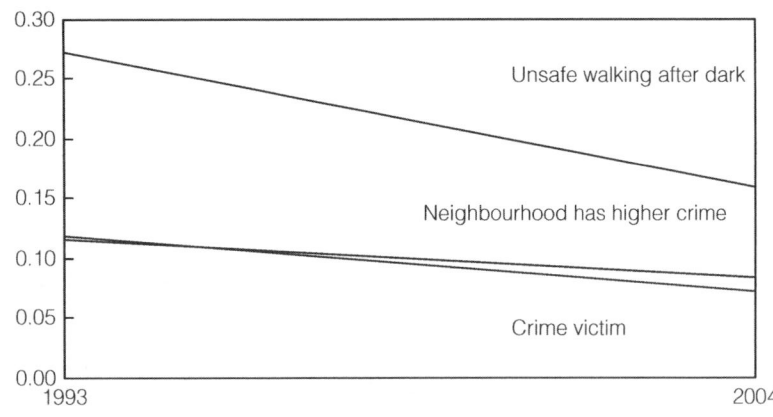

Source: Statistics Canada, 1993 and 2004 General Social Surveys, PUMFs.

(continued)

READING STATISTICS 5: *(continued)*

expressed this time in percentages, are shown in Table 1. For example, we can conclude that at the 95% confidence level, between 6.7% and 7.9% (7.3 ± 0.6) of Canadians were victims of a crime in 2004.

One last note, while these analyses of GSS data suggest that crime and victimization have declined

in recent years, we cannot be certain that this is actually the case. It is possible, for instance, that the observed decline in criminal victimization is a reflection of an increase in the reluctance of victims to report a crime to police. The trends in the data, however, suggest that crime and victimization in general have declined in Canada.

TABLE 1   95% CONFIDENCE INTERVAL OF PERCENTAGE WHO SAID NEIGHBOURHOOD HAS HIGHER CRIME, THEY FEEL UNSAFE WALKING AFTER DARK, AND THEY HAD CONTACT WITH POLICE AS A VICTIM, 1993 AND 2004

Year	Sample Size	Neighbourhood Has Higher Crime	Unsafe Walking after Dark	Victim of Crime
1993	11,960	11.6 ± 0.9	27.3 ± 0.9	11.9 ± 0.9
2004	23,766	8.5 ± 0.6	16.0 ± 0.6	7.3 ± 0.6

Source: Statistics Canada, 1993 and 2004 General Social Surveys, PUMFs.

you should remember that confidence interval estimates around these points would range about ±3% at the 95% confidence level (see Table 7.6).

As observed by Nanos Research, public opinion was rather stable after the 2006 federal election (Figure 7.7). There were minor shifts in point estimates over the four polling dates, such as a decrease in popularity of the Conservative Party and an increase for the Liberal Party. However, if the 95% confidence intervals around the point estimates were considered, we would see an overlap in the intervals for the Conservative and Liberal Parties at each of the polling dates. Thus, statistically speaking, there would have been no significant shift in popular support for the two leading parties from November 2006 to May 2007.

Returning to the many controversies surrounding public-opinion polls, critics would argue that it is not a good thing to judge the government and its leader so continuously. To some extent, these approval ratings expose the prime minister and the governing party (and other political parties and leaders whose performance is similarly measured) to the whims of public sentiment and, at some level, could pressure them to cater to popular opinion and shape ("spin") their image to maintain support. However, information like that presented in Figure 7.7 supplies some interesting insights into the affairs not only of political institutions but also of society as a whole.

SUMMARY

1. Population values can be estimated with sample values. With point estimates, a single sample statistic is used to estimate the corresponding population value. With confidence intervals, we estimate that the population value falls within a certain range of values.

2. Estimates based on sample statistics must be unbiased and relatively efficient. Of all the sample statistics, only means and proportions are unbiased. The means of the sampling distributions of these statistics are equal to the respective population values. Efficiency is largely a matter of sample size. The greater the sample size, the lower the value of the standard deviation of the sampling distribution, the more tightly clustered the sample outcomes will be around the mean of the sampling distribution, and the more efficient the estimate.

3. With point estimates, we estimate that the population value is the same as the sample statistic (either a mean or a proportion). With interval estimates, we construct a confidence interval, a range of values into which we estimate that the population value falls. The width of the interval is a function of the risk we are willing to take of being wrong (the alpha level) and the sample size. The interval widens as our probability of being wrong decreases and as sample size decreases.

4. A confidence interval can be depicted using an error bar graph. The middle of an error bar graph represents the sample statistic, and a vertical line above and below the sample statistic represents the upper and lower limits of the confidence interval.

5. The sample size needed to obtain a desired confidence interval can be determined prior to conducting a study. Sample size is determined by "rearranging" the formulas for confidence intervals.

SUMMARY OF FORMULAS

Confidence interval for a sample mean, large samples, population standard deviation known:	7.1	$\text{c.i.} = \overline{X} \pm Z\left(\dfrac{\sigma}{\sqrt{N}}\right)$
Confidence interval for a sample mean, large samples, population standard deviation unknown:	7.2	$\text{c.i.} = \overline{X} \pm Z\left(\dfrac{s}{\sqrt{N-1}}\right)$
Confidence interval for a sample proportion, large samples:	7.3	$\text{c.i.} = P_s \pm Z\sqrt{\dfrac{P_u(1 - P_u)}{N}}$

Required sample size, for a mean

$$7.4 \quad N = \frac{Z^2 \times \sigma^2}{ME^2}$$

Required sample size, for a proportion

$$7.5 \quad N = \frac{\left(Z^2 \times P_u \times (1 - P_u)\right) + ME^2}{ME^2}$$

GLOSSARY

Alpha (α). The probability of error or the probability that a confidence interval does not contain the population value. Alpha levels are usually set at 0.10, 0.05, 0.01, or 0.001.

Bias. A criterion used to select sample statistics as estimators. A statistic is unbiased if the mean of its sampling distribution is equal to the population value of interest.

Confidence interval. An estimate of a population value in which a range of values is specified.

Confidence level. A frequently used alternate way of expressing alpha, the probability that an interval estimate will not contain the population value. Confidence levels of 90%, 95%, 99%, and 99.9% correspond to alphas of 0.10, 0.05, 0.01, and 0.001, respectively.

Efficiency. The extent to which the sample outcomes are clustered around the mean of the sampling distribution.

Error bar. A graphic display device used to illustrate the confidence interval of a sample statistic.

Margin of error. The size of a confidence interval for a sample mean or sample proportion. It is also called the margin of sampling error, or just sampling error.

Point estimate. An estimate of a population value where a single value is specified.

MULTIMEDIA RESOURCES

 http://www.healeystatistics.nelson.com

Visit the companion Web site for the first Canadian edition of *Statistics: A Tool for Social Research* to access a wide range of student resources. Begin by clicking on the Student Resources section of the book's Web site to access review quizzes, flash cards, and other study tools.

PROBLEMS

7.1 For each set of sample outcomes below, construct the 95% confidence interval for estimating μ, the population mean.

a. $\overline{X} = 5.2$ **b.** $\overline{X} = 100$ **c.** $\overline{X} = 20$
$s = .7$ $s = 9$ $s = 3$
$N = 157$ $N = 620$ $N = 220$
d. $\overline{X} = 1020$ **e.** $\overline{X} = 7.3$ **f.** $\overline{X} = 33$
$s = 50$ $s = 1.2$ $s = 6$
$N = 329$ $N = 105$ $N = 220$

7.2 For each set of sample outcomes below, construct the 99% confidence interval for estimating P_u.

a. $P_s = .14$ **b.** $P_s = .37$ **c.** $P_s = .79$
$N = 100$ $N = 522$ $N = 121$
d. $P_s = .43$ **e.** $P_s = .40$ **f.** $P_s = .63$
$N = 1049$ $N = 548$ $N = 300$

7.3 For each confidence level below, determine the corresponding Z score.

Confidence Level	Alpha	Area beyond Z	Z score
95%	.05	.0250	±1.96
94%			
92%			
97%			
98%			
99.9%			

7.4 $\boxed{\text{SW}}$ You have developed a series of questions to measure "burnout" in social workers. A random sample of 100 social workers working in the greater metropolitan area of Pearson, Ontario, has an average score of 10.3, with a standard deviation of 2.7. At the 95% level, what is your estimate of the average burnout score for the population as a whole? Construct an error bar to display your results.

7.5 SOC A researcher has gathered information from a random sample of 178 households. For each variable below, construct confidence intervals to estimate the population mean. Use the 90% level.
 a. An average of 2.3 people resides in each household. Standard deviation is .35.
 b. There was an average of 2.1 television sets ($s = .10$) and .78 telephones ($s = .55$) per household.
 c. The households averaged 6.0 hours of television viewing per day ($s = 3.0$).

7.6 SOC A random sample of 100 television programs contained an average of 2.37 acts of physical violence per program. At the 99% level, what is your estimate of the population value? Construct an error bar to display your results.

$$\overline{X} = 2.37$$
$$s = 0.30$$
$$N = 100$$

7.7 SOC A random sample of 429 university students was interviewed about a number of matters.
 a. They reported that they had spent an average of $178.23 on textbooks during the previous semester. If the sample standard deviation for these data is $15.78, construct an estimate of the population mean at the 99% level.
 b. They also reported that they had visited the health services clinic an average of 1.5 times a semester. If the sample standard deviation is 0.3, construct an estimate of the population mean at the 99% level.
 c. On the average, the sample had missed 2.8 days of classes per semester because of illness. If the sample standard deviation is 1.0, construct an estimate of the population mean at the 99% level.
 d. On the average, the sample had missed 3.5 days of classes per semester for reasons other than illness. If the sample standard deviation is 1.5, construct an estimate of the population mean at the 99% level.

7.8 CJ A random sample of 500 residents of Pearson, Ontario, shows that exactly 50 of the respondents had been the victims of violent crime over the past year. Estimate the proportion of victims for the population as a whole, using the 90% confidence level. (*HINT: Calculate the sample proportion P_s before using Formula 7.3. Remember that proportions are equal to frequency divided by N.*)

7.9 SOC The survey mentioned in problem 7.5 found that 25 of the 178 households consisted of unmarried couples who were living together. What is your estimate of the population proportion? Use the 95% level.

7.10 PA A random sample of 324 residents of a community revealed that 30% were very satisfied with the quality of trash collection. At the 99% level, what is your estimate of the population value?

7.11 SOC A random sample of 1,496 respondents of a major metropolitan area was questioned about a number of issues. Construct estimates to the population at the 90% level for each of the results reported below. Express the final confidence interval in percentages (e.g. "between 40 and 45% agreed that premarital sex was always wrong").
 a. When asked to agree or disagree with the statement "Explicit sexual books and magazines lead to rape and other sex crimes," 823 agreed.
 b. When asked to agree or disagree with the statement "Guns should be outlawed," 650 agreed.
 c. 375 of the sample agreed that marijuana should be legalized.
 d. 1,023 of the sample said that they had attended a religious service at least once within the past month.
 e. 800 agreed that public elementary schools should have sex education programs starting in grade 5.

7.12 SW A random sample of 100 patients treated in a program for alcoholism and drug dependency over the past 10 years was selected. It was determined that 53 of the patients had been readmitted to the program at least once. At the 95% level, construct an estimate to the population proportion.

7.13 For the sample data below, construct four different interval estimates of the population mean, one each for the 90%, 95%, 99%, and 99.9% level. What happens to the interval width as confidence level increases? Why?

$$\overline{X} = 100$$
$$s = 10$$
$$N = 500$$

7.14 For each of the three sample sizes below, construct the 95% confidence interval. Use a sample proportion of 0.40 throughout. What happens to interval width as sample size increases? Why?

$$P_s = 0.40$$
$$\text{Sample A: } N = 100$$
$$\text{Sample B: } N = 1{,}000$$
$$\text{Sample C: } N = 10{,}000$$

7.15 [PS] Two individuals are running for mayor of Pearson, Ontario. You conduct an election survey a week before the election and find that 51% of the respondents prefer candidate A. Can you predict a winner? Use the 99% level. *(HINT: In a two-candidate race, what percentage of the vote would the winner need? Does the confidence interval indicate that candidate A has a sure margin of victory? Remember that while the population parameter is probably ($\alpha = .01$) in the confidence interval, it may be anywhere in the interval.)*

$$P_s = 0.51$$
$$N = 578$$

7.16 [SOC] The World Values Survey is administered periodically to random samples from societies around the globe. Below are listed the number of respondents in each nation who said that they are "very happy." Compute sample proportions and construct confidence interval estimates for each nation at the 95% level.

Nation	Number "very happy"	Sample Size	Confidence Interval
Great Britain	496	1,495	
Japan	505	1,476	
Brazil	329	1,492	
Nigeria	695	1,471	
China	338	1,493	

Source: World Values Survey.

7.17 [SOC] The fraternities and sororities at Algebra University have been plagued by declining membership over the past several years and want to know if the incoming first-year students will be a fertile recruiting ground. Not having enough money to survey all 1,600 first-year students they commission you to survey the interests of a random sample. You find that 35 of your 150 respondents are "extremely" interested in social clubs. At the 95% level, what is your estimate of the number of first-year students who would be extremely interested? *(HINT: The high and low values of your final confidence interval are proportions. How can proportions also be expressed as numbers?)*

7.18 [SOC] You are the consumer-affairs reporter for a daily newspaper. Part of your job is to investigate the claims of manufacturers, and you are particularly suspicious of a new economy car that the manufacturer claims will get 3.0 L/100 km. After checking the mileage figures for a random sample of 120 owners of this car, you find an average L/100 km of 3.1 with a standard deviation of 3.7. At the 99% level, do your results tend to confirm or refute the manufacturer's claims?

7.19 [SOC] The results listed below are from a survey given to a random sample of the Canadian public. For each sample statistic, construct a confidence interval estimate of the population parameter at the 95% confidence level. Sample size (N) is 2,987 throughout.

a. The average occupational prestige score was 43.87, with a standard deviation of 13.52.

b. The respondents reported watching an average of 2.86 hours of TV per day with a standard deviation of 2.20.

c. The average number of children was 1.81, with a standard deviation of 1.67.

d. Of the 2,987 respondents, 876 identified themselves as Catholic.

e. Five hundred thirty-five of the respondents said that they had never married.

f. The proportion of respondents who said they voted for the Conservative Party of Canada in the 2006 federal election was 0.36.

g. When asked about capital punishment, 2,425 of the respondents said that they opposed the death penalty for murder.

Using SPSS for Windows to Produce Confidence Intervals with the 2001 Census

The demonstrations and exercises below use the shortened version of the 2001 Census data. Start SPSS for Windows and open the *Census.sav* file.

SPSS DEMONSTRATION 7.1 Using the Explore Command for Constructing Confidence Intervals for Sample Means

The **Explore** procedure can be used to construct confidence intervals for the sample mean. The **Explore** command produces many of the same summary statistics and graphical displays produced by the **Frequencies** and **Descriptives** procedures, but offers additional features. Here we will use **Explore** to compute the confidence interval for the mean of *totincp* (total income).

From the main menu, click **Analyze, Descriptive Statistics,** and **Explore.** The **Explore** dialog box will open. Use the cursor to find *totincp* in the list on the left and click the right-arrow button to transfer the variable to the **Dependent List** box.

SPSS by default uses the 95% confidence level, which in fact we want to use for this demonstration. To request another level, you can click on the **Statistics** button at the top of the **Explore** dialog box, and the **Explore: Statistics** dialog box will open. Type the desired level (e.g., 90, 95, or 99%) in the textbox next to "**Confidence Interval for Mean,**" and click **Continue.** You will return to the **Explore** dialog box, where you might want to click the **Statistics** radio button within the **Display** section. Otherwise, SPSS will produce both summary statistics and plots (i.e., graphical displays).

Finally, click **OK,** and the output below will be produced:

Descriptives

			Statistic	Std. Error
Total Income $	Mean		26990.03	689.973
	95% Confidence	Lower Bound	25636.61	
	Interval for Mean	Upper Bound	28343.45	
	5% Trimmed Mean		24114.16	
	Median		20231.00	
	Variance		7.141E8	
	Std. Deviation		26722.556	
	Minimum		−3213	
	Maximum		200000	
	Range		203213	
	Interquartile Range		31047	
	Skewness		2.096	.063
	Kurtosis		7.419	.126

The "Descriptives" output table contains a variety of statistics used to measure central tendency and dispersion. Some of these statistics are not covered in this text. If you wish to explore them, please use SPSS's online Help facility. In the present section, we focus on parts of the table related to confidence intervals for the sample mean: the values for the "Lower Bound" and "Upper Bound" of the "95% Confidence Interval for Mean." The lower limit of our interval estimate is 25,636.61 and the upper limit is 28,343.45. Another way to state the interval would be

$$25{,}636.61 \leq \mu \leq 28{,}343.45$$

We estimate that Canadians, on average, have a total income between $25,636.61 and $28,343.45. Because alpha was set at the .05 level, this estimate has a 5% chance of being wrong (i.e., of not containing the population mean for total income).

We should point out that the values in your output may contain numbers with the letter "E" (sometimes expressed as lower case "e"). This stands for "exponent," or the number of tens you multiply a number by. SPSS will use the exponent to represent a number with too many digits to show in the output.

For example, the value 26,990.03 can be written in exponent form as 2.7E4. In other words, 2.7 multiplied by 10 four times (or 10 raised to the fourth power) is 27,000. The exact value of 26,990.03 is not returned because the exponent is rounded off to one decimal place (i.e., 2.7). A convenient way to do this calculation is to just move the decimal point to the right four places (2.7 to the right four places equals 27,000). A negative exponent means you have to move the decimal point to the left (e.g., 2.7-E4 means 2.7 to the left four places or 0.00027).

If the exponent is shown in your output, and you wish to instead view the regular value (e.g., 26,990.03), right-click on any part of the table in the **Output** window, and click **Edit Content.** There are two options: editing **"In Viewer"** (**Output** window) and **"In Separate Window"** (SPSS **Chart Editor** window). Let's select **In Separate Window** option; the SPSS **Chart Editor** window, titled **SPSS Pivot Table Descriptives,** will appear. This window gives you a wide array of options for the final appearance of the table. Next, use your mouse to increase the width of the **Statistics** column by dragging the table line that separates the **Statistics** and **Std. Error** columns to the right, until to exponent (e.g., 2.7E4) changes to regular form (26,990.03). After you finish editing, close the **SPSS Pivot Table Descriptives** window to return to the **Output** window, where you can see the changes.

SPSS DEMONSTRATION 7.2 The Error Bar Graph

Here we'll produce an error bar graph for the confidence interval for the mean of total income (*totincp*). Click **Graphs, Legacy Dialogs,** and then

Error Bar. The **Error Bars** dialog box appears with two choices for the type of graph we want. The **Simple** option is already highlighted, and this is the one we want. At the bottom of the **Error Bars** dialog box, click the "**Summaries of separate variables**" radio button within the **Data in Chart Are** box, and then click **Define.**

The **Define Simple Error Bar** dialog box appears with variable names listed on the left. Use the cursor to find *totincp* in the list on the left and click the right-arrow button to transfer the variable to the **Error Bars** box. In the **Bars Represent** box, you have the option to select whether the error bar represents the confidence interval of the mean, the standard error of mean, or the standard deviation. Let's choose "**Confidence interval for mean,**" the option that is already selected. You can also enter the desired confidence level into the **Level** box. We'll use 95% level, which is the default setting. Click **OK,** and the following error bar graph will be produced:

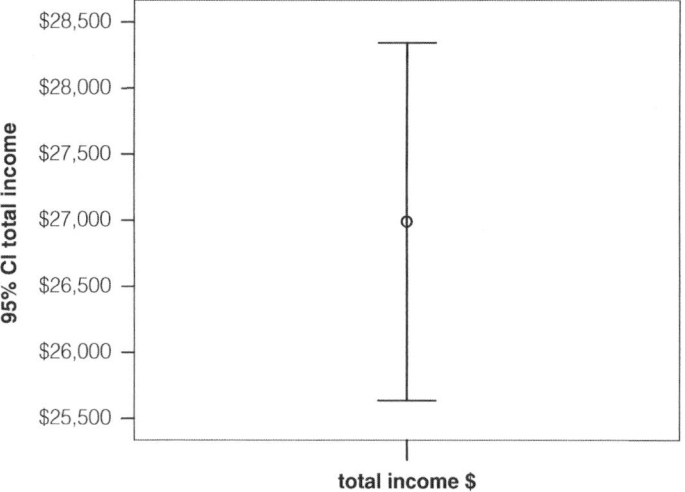

The error bar provides an illustration of the exact information given in the "Descriptives" output in Demonstration 7.1. The mean income of sample respondents is about $27,000 (marked by the small circle on the bar), and we estimate, at the 95% level of confidence (indicated by the length of the bar), that the mean income of all Canadians is somewhere between approximately $25,600 (the small horizontal line at the bottom of the bar) and $28,300 (the small horizontal line at the top of the bar).

DEMONSTRATION 7.3 Generating Statistical Information for Use in Constructing Confidence Intervals for Sample Proportions

Unlike the **Explore** procedure for construction confidence intervals for the sample mean, SPSS does not provide a program specifically for constructing intervals for the sample proportion. However, we can use SPSS to calculate the sample statistics, namely proportions, on which the interval estimates are based. Once you know these sample statistics, the confidence interval for the sample proportion is easily computed.

To illustrate this process we'll construct a confidence interval for *marsthp* (marital status). While we can estimate the population parameter for any or all of the categories of this variable, let's estimate the proportion of the population that is married (including persons living in common-law unions.)

First, calculate the sample proportion using the **Frequencies** command. From the menu bar, click **Analyze, Descriptive Statistics,** and **Frequencies.** Find *marsthp* in the left-hand box and move it to **Variable(s)** box. Click **OK.** The output for *marsthp* will look like this:

Marital Status

		Frequency	Percent	Valid Percent	Cumulative Percent
VALID	DIVORCED	82	5.5	5.5	5.5
	MARRIED-INC CL	872	58.1	58.1	63.6
	SEPARATED	53	3.5	3.5	67.1
	SINGLE	417	27.8	27.8	94.9
	WIDOWED	76	5.1	5.1	100.0
	TOTAL	1500	100.0	100.0	

Second, substitute the values into Formula 7.3, not forgetting to change the percentages to proportions. Thus, using the 95% confidence level, we would have:

$$\text{c.i.} = P_s \pm Z\sqrt{\frac{P_u(1 - P_u)}{N}}$$
$$\text{c.i.} = 0.58 \pm 1.96\sqrt{\frac{(0.5)(.05)}{1,500}}$$
$$\text{c.i.} = 0.58 \pm (1.96)(0.013)$$
$$\text{c.i.} = 0.58 \pm 0.03$$

Changing back to percentages, we can estimate that between 55% (58% − 3%) and 61% (58% + 3%) of Canadians are married or living in common-law unions.

Exercises (using *Census.sav*)

7.1 Use the **Explore** command to get the 95% confidence interval for *hrswkp* and *wkswkp*. Express the confidence intervals in words, as if you were reporting results in a newspaper story.

7.2 Use the **Error Bar** command to get an error bar graph for each variable in Exercise 7.1. Write a sentence or two of interpretation for each graph.

7.3 Use the **Frequencies** command to get sample proportions (convert the percentages in the frequency distributions) to estimate the population parameter for each of the following: proportion that is "1st generation" immigrant (*genstpob*) as well as proportion with a "University BA" (*hlosp*). Use the 95% confidence level. Express the confidence intervals in words, as if you were reporting results in a newspaper story.

8

HYPOTHESIS TESTING I
THE ONE-SAMPLE CASE

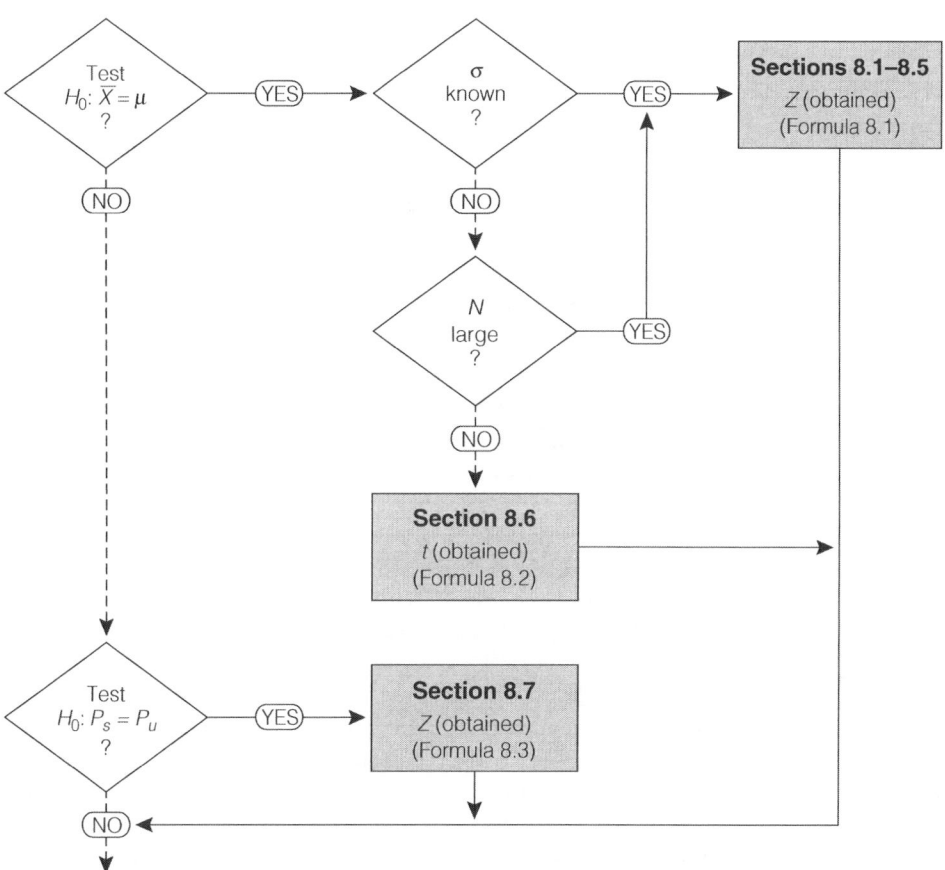

LEARNING OBJECTIVES   By the end of this chapter, you will be able to

1. Explain the logic of hypothesis testing.
2. Define and explain the conceptual elements involved in hypothesis testing, especially the null hypothesis, the sampling distribution, the alpha level, and the test statistic.
3. Explain what it means to "reject the null hypothesis" or "fail to reject the null hypothesis."
4. Identify and cite examples of situations in which one-sample tests of hypotheses are appropriate.

5. Test the significance of single-sample means and proportions using the five-step model and correctly interpret the results.

6. Explain the difference between one- and two-tailed tests and specify when each is appropriate.

7. Define and explain Type I and Type II errors and relate each to the selection of an alpha level.

8. Conduct a single-sample hypothesis test using a confidence interval.

8.1 INTRODUCTION

Chapter 7 introduced the techniques for estimating population parameters from sample statistics. In Chapters 8 through 11, we will investigate a second application of inferential statistics called **hypothesis testing** or **significance testing.** In this chapter, the techniques for hypothesis testing in the one-sample case will be introduced. These procedures could be used in situations such as the following:

1. A researcher has selected a sample of 789 senior citizens who live in a particular province and also has information on the percentage of the entire population of the province that was victimized by crime during the past year. Are older citizens, as represented by this sample, more or less likely to be victimized than the population in general?

2. Are the GPAs of university varsity athletes different from the GPAs of the student body as a whole? To investigate, the academic records of a random sample of 105 student athletes from a large university are compared with the overall GPA of all students.

3. The Law School Admission Test (LSAT) is a standardized test required for admission to most Canadian and U.S. law schools. The LSAT assesses reading and verbal reasoning skills and, along with GPA, is considered a critical factor in determining admission to law school. Companies offer an LSAT preparation (i.e., training) course, for a fee, with the claim that graduates of their course on average obtain higher scores on the LSAT than the general population of LSAT test takers. To test this claim, you randomly sample 127 graduates of the LSAT training course and find that, on average, those in the sample have higher LSAT scores than the population of LSAT writers as a whole. Do training-course graduates score higher than LSAT writers in general?

In each of these situations, we have randomly selected samples (of senior citizens, athletes, or graduates of the LSAT training course) that we want to compare to a population (the entire province, student body, or community of LSAT writers). Note that we are not interested in the sample per se but in the larger group from which it was selected (*all* senior citizens in the province, *all* athletes on this campus, or *all* graduates of the LSAT training course). Specifically, we want to know if the groups represented by the samples are different from the populations on a specific trait or variable (victimization rates, GPAs, or LSAT scores).

Of course, it would be better if we could include all senior citizens, athletes, or graduates of the LSAT training course rather than these smaller samples. However, as we have seen, researchers usually do not have the resources necessary to test everyone in a large group and must use random samples instead. In these situations, conclusions will be based on a comparison of the sample (which substitutes for the larger group) and the population. For example, if we found that the rate of victimization for the *sample* of senior citizens was higher than the provincial rate, we might conclude that *all* senior citizens are significantly more likely to be crime victims than the general population. The word "significantly" is a key word: It means that the difference between the sample's rate of victimization and the population's rate is very unlikely to be caused by random chance alone. In other words, if this difference is "significant," *all* senior citizens (not just the 789 people in the sample) have a higher victimization rate than the province as a whole. Alternatively, if we found little difference between the victimization rates of the sample and the population, we would conclude that senior citizens (*all* senior citizens) are essentially the same as other citizens in terms of their vulnerability to crime.

Thus, we can use samples to represent larger groups (senior citizens, athletes, or graduates of the LSAT training course) and compare and contrast the characteristics of the sample with the population and be extremely confident in our conclusions. Remember, however, that the EPSEM procedure for drawing random samples does not guarantee representativeness and, thus, there will always be a small amount of uncertainty in our conclusions. One of the great advantages of inferential statistics, however, is that we will be able to estimate the probability of error and evaluate our decisions accordingly.

8.2 AN OVERVIEW OF HYPOTHESIS TESTING

We will begin with a general overview of hypothesis testing, using our third research situation above as an example. Then, we will introduce more technical considerations and proper terminology throughout the remainder of the chapter. Let us examine this situation in detail. The main question here is, "Do graduates of the LSAT preparation course in Canada have an average LSAT score that is higher than other Canadians who write the LSAT?" In other words, the researcher wants to compare the LSAT scores of *all* graduates (the Canadian graduates of the LSAT training course) with the LSAT scores of all test takers (the entire Canadian population of LSAT test takers). If she had complete information for both of these groups (all graduates of the LSAT preparation course and all LSAT writers), she could answer the question easily and completely.

The problem is that the researcher does not have the time and/or money to gather information on the thousands of people who have graduated from the LSAT preparation course in Canada. Instead, she has drawn a random sample, following the rule of EPSEM, of 127 graduates from records provided by the companies offering the LSAT training course in Canada. Information on LSAT scores for the sample of LSAT preparation-course graduates and the entire population of LSAT test takers is as follows:

Entire Canadian population of LSAT test takers*	Sample of Canadian graduates from LSAT preparation course
$\mu = 151$	$\overline{X} = 154$
$\sigma = 9$	$N = 127$

* Source: Law School Admission Council.

Information from the Law School Admission Council, the organization that administers the LSAT, shows that the population of test takers in Canada has a mean LSAT score of 151. At 154, the average LSAT score for the sample is higher than the average score for the entire population. (To put this information in context, there are 101 multiple-choice questions on the LSAT. One point is given for each question answered correctly. Total test scores, ranging from 0 to 101, are converted into an LSAT score ranging from 120, the lowest possible score, to 180, the highest possible score). Although it is tempting, we cannot make any conclusions yet because we are working with a random sample of the population in which we are interested, not the population itself (all graduates of the LSAT preparation course).

Figure 8.1 should clarify these relationships. The entire Canadian population of LSAT test takers is symbolized by the largest circle because it is the largest group. The Canadian population of graduates of the LSAT training course is also symbolized by a large circle because it is a sizable group, although only a fraction of the population of LSAT writers as a whole. The

FIGURE 8.1   A TEST OF HYPOTHESIS FOR SINGLE SAMPLE MEANS

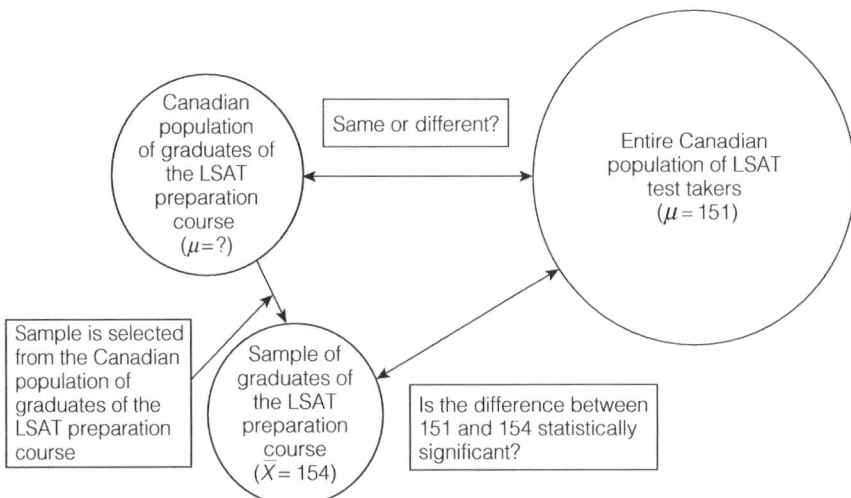

random sample of 127 Canadian graduates of the LSAT training course, the smallest of the three groups, is symbolized by the smallest circle.

The arrows between the circles show how they are connected in this research situation. The researcher wants to know if the average LSAT score of all graduates of the preparation course is the "same or different" from that of the entire population of LSAT writers. Instead of comparing all graduates (a group that is too large to gather information on) with the entire population of LSAT writers, the researcher compares the LSAT scores of a random sample of graduates with the entire population.

We observe that the mean of the sample is higher than the mean of the population (154 vs. 151). This suggests that graduates of the preparation course do better in the LSAT. However, the graduates are represented by a random sample and we know that even the most carefully chosen sample may, on rare occasion, be unrepresentative. Does the difference between the *sample mean* and the *population mean* reflect a real difference between *all* graduates of the preparation course and the entire population of LSAT writers? Or was this difference caused by mere random chance? This is the question that a test of hypothesis is designed to answer. In other words, there are two possible explanations for the difference, and we will consider them one at a time.

The first explanation, which we will label explanation A, is that the difference between the population mean of 151 and the sample mean of 154 reflects a real difference in LSAT scores between all graduates and the entire population. The difference is "statistically significant" in the sense that it is very unlikely to have occurred by random chance alone. If explanation A is true, the population of all graduates of the preparation course is different from the entire population of LSAT writers and the sample did *not* come from a population with a mean LSAT score of 151.

The second explanation, or explanation B, is that the observed difference between sample and population means was caused by mere random chance. There is no important difference between graduates and the population of LSAT writers as a whole and the difference between the sample mean of 154 and the population mean of 151 is trivial and due to random chance. If explanation B is true, the population of LSAT preparation-course graduates is just like everyone else and has a mean LSAT score of 151.

Which explanation is correct? As long as we are working with a sample rather than the entire group, we cannot know the answer to this question for sure. However, we can set up a decision-making procedure so conservative that one of the two explanations can be chosen, with the knowledge that the probability of choosing the incorrect explanation is very low.

This decision-making process, in broad outline, begins with the assumption that explanation B is correct. Symbolically, the assumption that the mean LSAT score for all graduates of the preparation course is the same as the mean LSAT score for the population of LSAT writers as a whole can be stated as

$$\mu = 151$$

Remember that this μ refers to the mean for all LSAT preparation-course graduates, not just the 127 in the sample. This assumption, $\mu = 151$, can be tested statistically.

If explanation B (the population of graduates of the preparation course is not different from the population of LSAT writers as a whole and has a μ of 151) is true, then the probability of getting the observed sample outcome ($\overline{X} = 154$) can be found. Let us add an objective decision rule in advance. If the odds of getting the observed difference are less than .05 (5 out of 100, or 1 in 20), we will reject explanation B. If this explanation were true, a difference of this size (151 vs. 154) would be a very rare event, and in hypothesis testing, we always bet against rare events.

How can we estimate the probability of the observed sample outcome ($\overline{X} = 154$) if explanation B is correct? This value can be determined by using our knowledge of the sampling distribution of all possible sample outcomes. Looking back at the information we have and applying the Central Limit Theorem (see Chapter 6), we can assume that the sampling distribution is normal in shape, has a mean of 151 (because $\mu_{\overline{x}} = \mu$), and has a standard deviation of $9/\sqrt{127}$ because $\sigma_{\overline{x}} = \sigma/\sqrt{N}$. We also know that the standard normal distribution can be interpreted as a distribution of probabilities (see Chapter 5) and that the particular sample outcome noted above ($\overline{X} = 154$) is one of thousands of possible sample outcomes. The sampling distribution, with the sample outcome noted, is depicted in Figure 8.2.

Using our knowledge of the standardized normal distribution, we can add further useful information to this sampling distribution of sample means. Specifically, with Z scores, we can depict the decision rule stated previously: any sample outcome with probability less than 0.05 (assuming

FIGURE 8.2   THE SAMPLING DISTRIBUTION OF ALL POSSIBLE SAMPLE MEANS

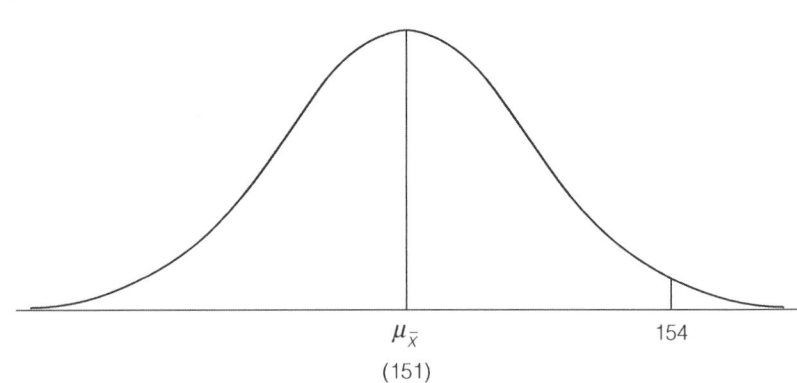

$$\mu_{\overline{X}}$$
$$(151)$$

154

FIGURE 8.3 THE SAMPLING DISTRIBUTION OF ALL POSSIBLE SAMPLE MEANS, WITH REJECTION AREAS IN SHADE

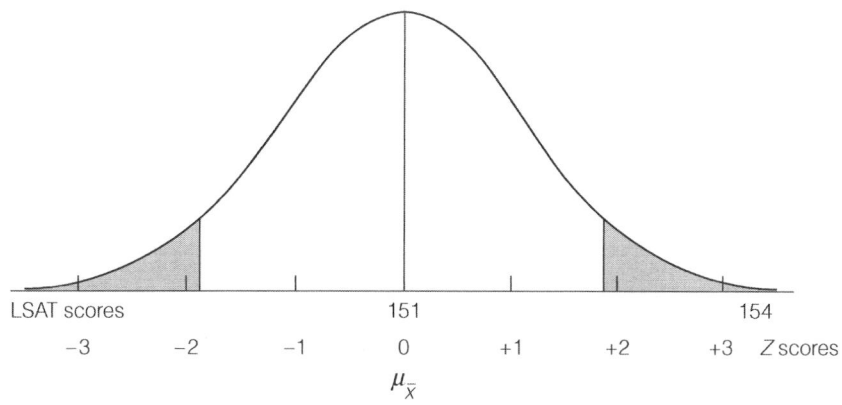

LSAT scores   151   154

−3   −2   −1   0   +1   +2   +3 Z scores

$\mu_{\overline{X}}$

that explanation B is true) will cause us to reject explanation B. The probability of 0.05 can be translated into an area and divided equally into the upper and lower tails of the sampling distribution. Using Appendix A, we find that the Z-score equivalent of this area is ± 1.96. The areas and Z scores are depicted in Figure 8.3.

The decision rule can now be rephrased. Any sample outcome falling in the shaded areas depicted in Figure 8.3 by definition has a probability of occurrence of less than 0.05. Such an outcome would be a rare event and would cause us to reject explanation B.

All that remains is to translate our sample outcome into a Z score so that we can see where it falls on the curve. To do this, we use the standard formula for locating any particular raw score under a normal distribution. When we use known or empirical distributions, this formula is expressed as

$$Z = \frac{X_i - \overline{X}}{s}$$

Or, to find the equivalent Z score for any raw score, subtract the mean of the distribution from the raw score and divide by the standard deviation of the distribution. Because we are now concerned with the sampling distribution of all sample means rather than an empirical distribution, the symbols in the formula will change, but the form remains exactly the same:

FORMULA 8.1
$$Z = \frac{\overline{X} - \mu}{\sigma / \sqrt{N}}$$

Or, to find the equivalent Z score for any sample mean, subtract the mean of the sampling distribution, which is equal to the population mean or μ, from the sample mean and divide by the standard deviation of the sampling distribution.

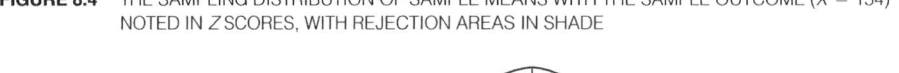

FIGURE 8.4   THE SAMPLING DISTRIBUTION OF SAMPLE MEANS WITH THE SAMPLE OUTCOME ($\bar{X}$ = 154) NOTED IN Z SCORES, WITH REJECTION AREAS IN SHADE

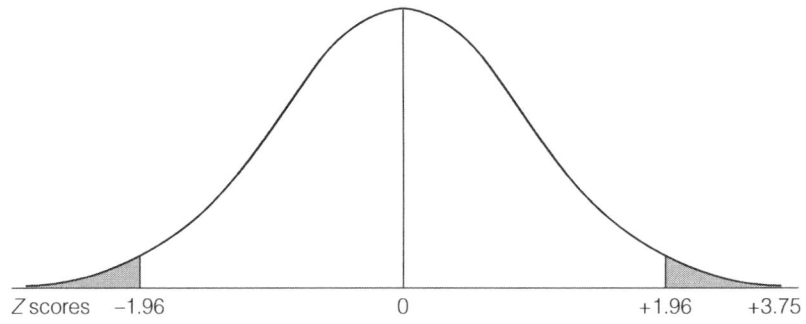

Z scores   −1.96   0   +1.96   +3.75

Recalling the data given on this problem, we can now find the Z-score equivalent of the sample mean.

$$Z = \frac{154 - 151}{9/\sqrt{127}}$$

$$Z = \frac{3}{0.80}$$

$$Z = +3.75$$

In Figure 8.4, this Z score of +3.75 is noted on the distribution of all possible sample means and we see that the sample outcome does fall in the shaded area. If explanation B is true, this particular sample outcome has a probability of occurrence of less than 0.05. The sample outcome ($\bar{X}$ = 154 or Z = +3.75) would therefore be rare if explanation B was true, and the researcher may reject explanation B. If explanation B were true, this sample outcome would be extremely unlikely. The sample of 127 graduates of the LSAT preparation course comes from a population that is significantly different from the population of LSAT writers as a whole on LSAT scoring. Or, to put it another way, the sample does not come from a population that has a mean LSAT score of 151.

Keep in mind that our decisions in significance testing are based on information gathered from random samples. On rare occasions, a sample may not be representative of the population from which it was selected. The decision-making process outlined above has a very high probability of resulting in correct decisions, but, as long as we must work with samples rather than populations, we face an element of risk. That is, the decision to reject explanation B might be incorrect if this sample happens to be one of the few that is unrepresentative of the population of graduates of the LSAT training course. One important strength of hypothesis testing is that the probability of making an incorrect decision can be estimated. In the example at hand, explanation B was rejected and the probability of this decision being incorrect is 0.05—the decision rule established at the beginning of the process. To say that the probability of rejecting explanation B incorrectly is 0.05 means that, if we repeated this same test an infinite number of times, we would incorrectly reject explanation B only 5 times out of every 100.

8.3 THE FIVE-STEP MODEL FOR HYPOTHESIS TESTING

All the formal elements and concepts used in hypothesis testing were surreptitiously sneaked into the preceding discussion. This section presents their proper names and introduces a **five-step model** for organizing all hypothesis testing:

Step 1. Making assumptions and meeting test requirements

Step 2. Stating the null hypothesis

Step 3. Selecting the sampling distribution and establishing the critical region

Step 4. Computing the test statistic

Step 5. Making a decision and interpreting the results of the test

We will look at each step individually, using the LSAT problem from Section 8.2 as an example throughout.

Step 1. Making Assumptions and Meeting Test Requirements. Any application of statistics requires that certain assumptions be made, and all tests of hypotheses have certain requirements that must be met. Specifically, three criteria have to be satisfied when conducting a test of hypothesis with a single sample mean. First, all tests of hypothesis must be based on a random sample that has been selected according to the rules of EPSEM (see Chapter 6). Second, to justify computation of a mean, the variable being tested must be interval-ratio in level of measurement. Finally, we must assume that the sampling distribution of all possible sample means is normal in shape so that we may use the standardized normal distribution to find areas under the sampling distribution. We can be sure that this assumption is satisfied by using large samples (see the Central Limit Theorem in Chapter 6).

Usually, we will summarize these deliberations in abbreviated form as a mathematical model for the test. For example:

> Model: Random sampling
> Level of measurement is interval-ratio
> Sampling distribution is normal

Step 2. Stating the Null Hypothesis (H_0). The **null hypothesis** is the formal name for explanation B and is always a statement of "no difference." The exact form of the null hypothesis will vary depending on the test being conducted. In the single-sample case, the null hypothesis states that the sample comes from a population with a certain characteristic. In our example, the null hypothesis is that the population of LSAT preparation-course graduates is "no different" from the population of LSAT writers as a whole, that their average LSAT score is also 151, and that the difference between 151 and the sample mean of 154 is caused by random chance. Symbolically, the null hypothesis would be stated as

$$H_0: \mu = 151$$

where μ refers to the mean of the population of graduates of the LSAT preparation course. The null hypothesis is the central element in any test of hypothesis because the entire process is aimed at rejecting or failing to reject the H_0.

Usually, the researcher believes that the difference is significant and wants to reject the null hypothesis. At this point in the five-step model, the researcher's belief is stated in a **research hypothesis (H_1),** a statement that directly contradicts the null hypothesis. Thus, the researcher's goal in hypothesis testing is often to gather evidence for the research hypothesis by rejecting the null hypothesis.

The research hypothesis can be stated in several ways. One form would simply assert that the population from which the sample was selected did not have a certain characteristic or, in terms of our example, had a mean that was not equal to a specific value

$$(H_1: \mu \neq 151)$$

where $\neq$ means "not equal to"

Symbolically, this statement asserts that the sample does not come from a population with a mean of 151, or that the population of graduates of the LSAT preparation course is different from the population of LSAT writers as a whole. The research hypothesis is enclosed in parentheses to emphasize that it has no formal standing or role in the hypothesis-testing process (except, as we shall see in the next section, in choosing between one-tailed and two-tailed tests). It serves as a reminder of what the researcher believes to be the truth.

Step 3. Selecting the Sampling Distribution and Establishing the Critical Region. The sampling distribution is the probabilistic yardstick against which a particular sample outcome is measured. By assuming that the null hypothesis is true (and *only* by this assumption), we can attach values to the mean and standard deviation of the sampling distribution and thus measure the probability of any specific sample outcome. There are several different sampling distributions, but for now we will confine our attention to the sampling distribution described by the standard normal curve as summarized in Appendix A.

The **critical region** consists of the areas under the sampling distribution that include unlikely sample outcomes. Prior to the test of hypothesis, we must define what we mean by *unlikely*. That is, we must specify in advance those sample outcomes so unlikely that they will lead us to reject the H_0. This decision rule will establish the critical region or **region of rejection.** The word *region* is used because, essentially, we are describing those areas under the sampling distribution that contain unlikely sample outcomes. In the example above, this area corresponded to a Z score of ± 1.96, called **Z(critical),** which was graphically displayed in Figure 8.4. The shaded area is the critical region. Any sample outcome for which the Z-score equivalent fell in this area (i.e., below -1.96 or above $+1.96$) would have caused us to reject the null hypothesis.

By convention, the size of the critical region is reported as alpha (α), the proportion of all of the area included in the critical region. In the example above, our **alpha level** was 0.05. Other commonly used alphas are 0.10, 0.01, and 0.001.

In abbreviated form, all the decisions made in this step are noted below. The critical region is noted by the Z scores that mark its beginnings.

$$\text{Sampling distribution} = Z \text{ distribution}$$
$$\alpha = 0.05$$
$$Z(\text{critical}) = \pm 1.96$$

(For practice in finding Z(critical) scores, see problem 8.1a.)

Step 4. **Computing the Test Statistic.** To evaluate the probability of any given sample outcome, the sample value must be converted into a Z score. Solving the equation for Z-score equivalents is called computing the **test statistic,** and the resultant value will be referred to as **Z(obtained)** in order to differentiate the test statistic from the critical region. In our example above, we found a $Z(\text{obtained})$ of $+3.75$. *(For practice in computing obtained Z scores for means, see problems 8.1c, 8.2 to 8.7, and 8.15e and f.)*

Step 5. **Making a Decision and Interpreting the Results of the Test.** As the last step in the hypothesis-testing process, the test statistic is compared with the critical region. If the test statistic falls into the critical region, our decision will be to reject the null hypothesis. If the test statistic does not fall into the critical region, we fail to reject the null hypothesis. In our example, the two values were

$$Z(\text{critical}) = \pm 1.96$$
$$Z(\text{obtained}) = +3.75$$

and we saw that the $Z(\text{obtained})$ fell in the critical region (see Figure 8.4). Our decision was to reject the null hypothesis which stated that graduates of the LSAT preparation course have a mean LSAT score of 151 or that there is

Application 8.1

Despite many characteristics favourable to labour-market success, such as better than average education and health, studies show that recent immigrants to Canada (those who have been in Canada for less than 10 years) face many obstacles and challenges in the labour market. We know that, based on the 2001 Census, the mean income of the Canadian population of full-time workers (30 hours or more per week) was $38,728. A random sample of 336 recent immigrants employed full-time, from the Survey of Labour and Income Dynamics (a Statistics Canada–administered survey on labour-market activity and income), reveals an average income of $28,096 with a standard deviation of $18,410 in 2001. Are these earnings of recent immigrants significantly different from the population of full-time workers as a whole? We will use the five-step model to organize the decision-making process.

Step 1. Making Assumptions and Meeting Test Requirements.

Model: Random sampling
       Level of measurement is interval-ratio
       Sampling distribution is normal

From the information given (this is a large sample with $N > 100$ and income is an interval-ratio variable), we can conclude that the model assumptions and test requirements are satisfied.

Step 2. Stating the Null Hypothesis (H_0). The null hypothesis says that the average income of *all* recent immigrants to Canada is equal to the national average. In symbols:

$$H_0: \mu = 38,728$$

The question does not specify a direction: it only asks if the incomes of recent immigrants are "different from" (not higher or lower than) the national average. This suggests a two-tailed test:

$$(H_1: \mu \neq 38,728)$$

Step 3. Selecting the Sampling Distribution and Establishing the Critical Region.

$$\text{Sampling distribution} = Z \text{ distribution}$$
$$\alpha = 0.05$$
$$Z(\text{critical}) = \pm 1.96$$

Step 4. Computing the Test Statistic. The necessary information for conducting a test of the null hypothesis is

Recent Immigrants	Nation
$\bar{X} = 28{,}096$	$\mu = 38{,}728$
$s = 18{,}410$	
$N = 336$	

The test statistic, $Z(\text{obtained})$, would be

$$Z(\text{obtained}) = \frac{\bar{X} - \mu}{s/\sqrt{N - 1}}$$

$$Z(\text{obtained}) = \frac{28,096 - 38,728}{18,410/\sqrt{336 - 1}}$$

$$Z(\text{obtained}) = \frac{-10,632}{18,410/\sqrt{335}}$$

$$Z(\text{obtained}) = \frac{-10.632}{1,006}$$

$$Z(\text{obtained}) = -10.57$$

Step 5. Making a Decision and Interpreting the Results of the Test. With alpha set at 0.05, the critical region would begin at $Z(\text{critical}) = \pm 1.96$. With an obtained Z score of -10.57, the null would be rejected. This means that the difference between the incomes of recent immigrants to Canada and the incomes of Canadians as a whole is statistically significant. The difference is so large that we may conclude that it did not occur by random chance. The decision to reject the null hypothesis has a 0.05 probability of being wrong.

Source: Statistics Canada, 2001 Canadian Census, individual PUMF, and 2001 Survey of Labour and Income Dynamics, individual PUMF.

no difference between LSAT preparation-course graduates and LSAT writers as a whole. When we reject this null hypothesis, we are saying that graduates do *not* have a mean LSAT score of 151 and that there *is* a difference between them and the population of LSAT writers as a whole. The difference between the sample mean of 154 and the mean of 151 for the entire population of LSAT writers is statistically significant or unlikely to be caused by random chance alone. In terms of LSAT score, graduates of the LSAT preparation course are different from the population of LSAT writers as a whole.

Note that there are two parts to step 5. First you make a decision about the null hypothesis: If the test statistics falls in the critical region, reject H_0. If the test statistic does not fall in the critical region, we fail to reject the H_0. Second, and just as importantly, you need to interpret the results of the test and say what your decision means. In this case, the null hypothesis was rejected: there is a significant difference between the sample mean and the mean for the entire population of LSAT writers and, therefore, graduates of the LSAT preparation course are different from the population of LSAT writers as a whole.

This five-step model will serve us as a framework for decision making throughout the hypothesis-testing chapters. The exact nature and method of expression for our decisions will be different for different situations. However, familiarity with the five-step model will assist you in mastering this material by providing a common frame of reference for all significance testing.

8.4 ONE-TAILED AND TWO-TAILED TESTS OF HYPOTHESIS

The five-step model for hypothesis testing is fairly rigid, and the researcher has little room for making choices. Nonetheless, the researcher must still make two crucial decisions. First, he or she must decide between a one-tailed and a two-tailed test. Second, an alpha level must be selected. In this section, we will discuss the former decision and, in Section 8.5, the latter.

The choice between a one- and two-tailed test is based on the researcher's expectations about the population from which the sample was selected. These expectations are reflected in the research hypothesis (H_1), which is contradictory to the null hypothesis and usually states what the researcher believes to be "the truth." In most situations, the researcher will wish to support the research hypothesis by rejecting the null hypothesis.

The format for the research hypothesis may take either of two forms, depending on the relationship between what the null hypothesis states and what the researcher believes to be the truth. The null hypothesis states that the population has a specific characteristic. In the example that has served us throughout this chapter, the null hypothesis stated that the "population of graduates of the LSAT preparation course have the *same* mean LSAT score (151) as the entire population of LSAT writers." The researcher might believe that the population of graduates actually scores *lower* on the LSAT (their population mean is *lower than* the value stated in the null hypothesis), *higher* on the LSAT (their population mean is *greater than* the value stated in the null hypothesis), or he or she might be unsure about the direction of the difference.

If the researcher is unsure about the direction, the research hypothesis states only that the population mean is "not equal" to the value stated in the null hypothesis. The research hypothesis stated in Section 8.3 ($\mu \neq 151$) was in this format. This is called a **two-tailed test** of significance because it means that the researcher will be equally concerned with the possibility that the true population value is greater than the value specified in the null hypothesis and the possibility that the true population value is less than the value specified in the null hypothesis.

In other situations, the researcher might be concerned only with differences in a specific direction. If the direction of the difference can be predicted, or if the researcher is concerned only with differences in one direction, a **one-tailed test** can be used. A one-tailed test may take one of two forms, depending on the researcher's expectations about the direction of the difference. If the researcher believes that the true population value is greater than the value specified in the null, the research hypothesis would reflect that belief. In our example, if we had predicted that graduates of the LSAT preparation course had *higher* LSAT scores than the entire population of LSAT writers (or, an average LSAT score *greater than* 151) our research hypothesis would have been

$$(H_1: \mu > 151)$$

where > signifies "greater than"

If we predicted that graduates had *lower* LSAT scores than the entire population of LSAT writers (or, an average LSAT score *less than* 151), our research hypothesis would have been

$$(H_1: \mu < 151)$$

where < signifies "less than"

One-tailed tests are often appropriate when programs designed to solve a problem or improve a situation are being evaluated. If the LSAT training course resulted in lower LSAT scoring, for example, the course would be considered a failure. In a situation like this, the researcher may well focus only on outcomes that would indicate that the program is a success (i.e., when graduates of the LSAT preparation course have higher LSAT scores) and conduct a one-tailed test with a research hypothesis in the form: $H_1: \mu > 151$.

As another example, consider the evaluation of a program designed to increase youth employment. The evaluators would be concerned only with outcomes that show an increase in the youth employment rate. If the rate shows no change or if youth employment decreases, the program is a failure. Thus, the evaluators could legitimately use a one-tailed test that stated that youth employment rates for graduates of the program would be greater than (>) rates of employment among all youth.

In terms of the five-step model, the choice of a one-tailed or two-tailed test determines what we do with the critical region under the sampling distribution in step 3. In a two-tailed test, we split the critical region equally into the upper and lower tails of the sampling distribution. In a one-tailed test, we place the entire critical region in one tail of the sampling distribution. If we believe that the population characteristic is greater than the value stated in the null hypothesis (if the H_1 includes the $>$ symbol), we place the entire critical region in the upper tail. If we believe that the characteristic is less than the value stated in the null hypothesis (if the H_1 includes the $<$ symbol), the entire critical region goes in the lower tail.

For example, in a two-tailed test with alpha equal to 0.05, the critical region begins at Z(critical) $= \pm 1.96$. In a one-tailed test at the same alpha level, the Z(critical) is $+1.65$ if the upper tail is specified and -1.65 if the lower tail is specified. Table 8.1 summarizes the procedures to follow in terms of the nature of the research hypothesis. The difference in placing the critical region is graphically summarized in Figure 8.5, and the critical Z scores for the most common alpha levels are given in Table 8.2 for both one- and two-tailed tests.

Note that the critical Z values for one-tailed tests are always closer to the mean of the sampling distribution. Thus, a one-tailed test is more likely to reject the H_0 without changing the alpha level (assuming that we have specified the correct tail). One-tailed tests are a way of statistically both having and eating your cake and should be used whenever (1) the direction of the difference can be confidently predicted, or (2) the researcher is concerned only with differences in one tail of the sampling distribution.

An example will clarify how the one-tailed test is used. After many years of work, a sociologist has noted that sociology majors seem more sophisticated, charming, and cosmopolitan than the rest of the student body. A "Sophistication Scale" test has been administered to the entire student body and to a random sample of 100 sociology majors, and these results have been obtained

Student Body	Sociology Majors
$\mu = 17.3$	$\bar{X} = 19.2$
$\sigma = 7.4$	$N = 100$

We will use the five-step model to test the H_0 of no difference between sociology majors and the general student body.

TABLE 8.1 ONE- VS. TWO-TAILED TESTS, $\alpha = .05$

If the Research Hypothesis Uses	The Test Is	And Concern Is with	Z(critical) =
$\neq$	Two-tailed	Both tails	± 1.96
$>$	One-tailed	Upper tail	$+1.65$
$<$	One-tailed	Lower tail	-1.65

FIGURE 8.5 ESTABLISHING THE CRITICAL REGION, ONE-TAILED TESTS VERSUS TWO-TAILED TESTS, WITH REJECTION REGION FOR ALPHA = 0.05 IN SHADE

A. The two-tailed test, Z (critical) = ±1.96

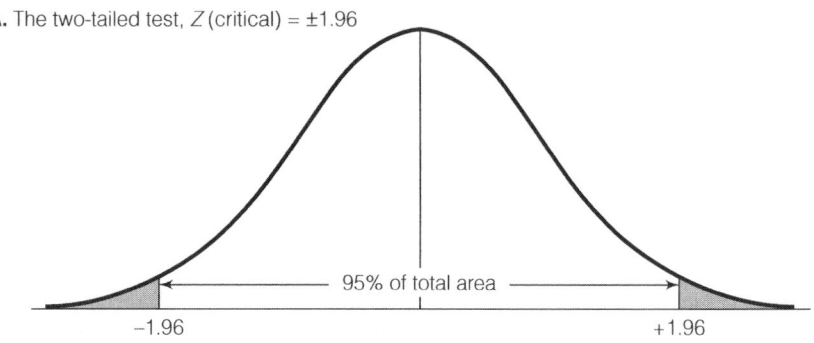

95% of total area

−1.96   +1.96

B. The one-tailed test for upper tail, Z (critical) = +1.65

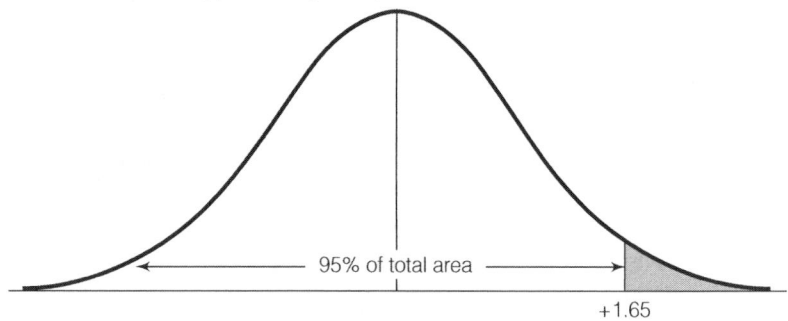

95% of total area

+1.65

C. The one-tailed test for lower tail, Z (critical) = −1.65

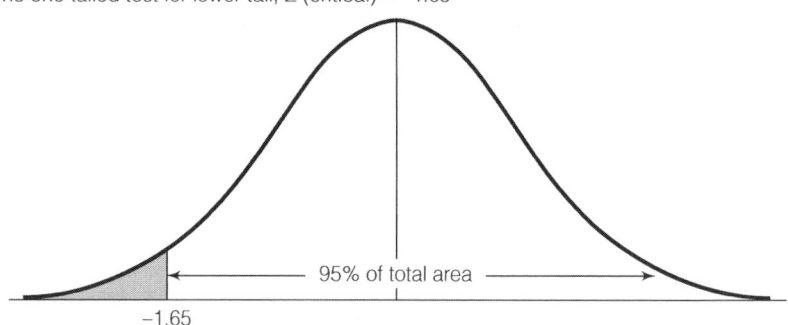

95% of total area

−1.65

TABLE 8.2   FINDING CRITICAL Z SCORES FOR ONE-TAILED TESTS
(Single Sample Means)

Alpha	Two-Tailed Value	One-Tailed Value	
		Upper Tail	Lower Tail
.10	±1.65	+1.29	−1.29
.05	±1.96	+1.65	−1.65
.01	±2.58	+2.33	−2.33
.001	±3.29	+3.10	−3.10

Step 1. Making Assumptions and Meeting Test Requirements. Because we are using a mean to summarize the sample outcome, we must assume that the Sophistication Scale generates interval-ratio-level data. With a sample size of 100, the Central Limit Theorem applies, and we can assume that the sampling distribution is normal in shape.

$$\text{Model: Random sampling}$$
$$\text{Level of measurement is interval-ratio}$$
$$\text{Sampling distribution is normal}$$

Step 2. Stating the Null Hypothesis (H_0). The null hypothesis states that there is no difference between sociology majors and the general student body. The research hypothesis (H_1) will also be stated at this point. The researcher has predicted a direction for the difference ("Sociology majors are *more* sophisticated"), so a one-tailed test is justified. The two hypotheses may be stated as

$$H_0: \mu = 17.3$$
$$(H_1: \mu > 17.3)$$

Step 3. Selecting the Sampling Distribution and Establishing the Critical Region. We will use the standardized normal distribution (Appendix A) to find areas under the sampling distribution. If alpha is set at 0.05, the critical region will begin at the Z score +1.65. That is, the researcher has predicted that sociology majors are *more* sophisticated and that this sample comes from a population that has a mean *greater than* 17.3, so he will be concerned only with sample outcomes in the upper tail of the sampling distribution. If sociology majors are *the same as* other students in terms of sophistication (if the H_0 is true), or if they are *less* sophisticated (and come from a population with a mean less than 17.3), the theory is disproved. These decisions may be summarized as

$$\text{Sampling distribution} = Z \text{ distribution}$$
$$\alpha = 0.05$$
$$Z(\text{critical}) = +1.65$$

FIGURE 8.6 *Z*(OBTAINED) VERSUS *Z*(CRITICAL) FOR THE ONE-TAILED TEST, WITH REJECTION REGION FOR ALPHA = 0.05 IN SHADE

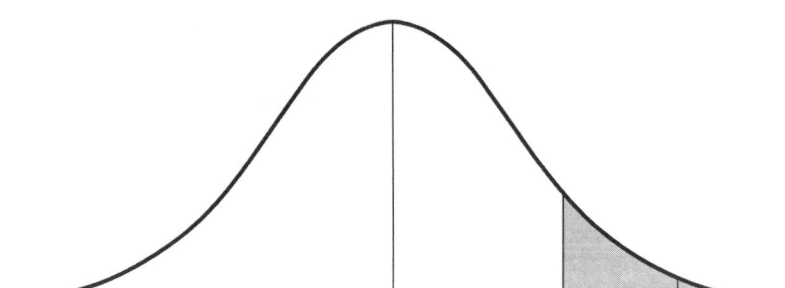

Step 4. Computing the Test Statistic.

$$Z(\text{obtained}) = \frac{\overline{X} - \mu}{\sigma/\sqrt{N}}$$

$$Z(\text{obtained}) = \frac{19.2 - 17.3}{7.4/\sqrt{100}}$$

$$Z(\text{obtained}) = +2.57$$

Step 5. Making a Decision and Interpreting the Results of the Test. Comparing the *Z*(obtained) with the *Z*(critical):

$$Z(\text{critical}) = +1.65$$
$$Z(\text{obtained}) = +2.57$$

We see that the test statistic falls into the critical region. This outcome is depicted graphically in Figure 8.6. We will reject the null hypothesis because, if the H_0 were true, a difference of this size would be very unlikely. There is a significant difference between sociology majors and the general student body in terms of sophistication. Because the null hypothesis has been rejected, the research hypothesis (sociology majors are more sophisticated) is supported. *(For practice in dealing with tests of significance for means that may call for one-tailed tests, see problems 8.2b, 8.3, 8.6, 8.8, and 8.17.)*

8.5 SELECTING AN ALPHA LEVEL

In addition to deciding between one-tailed and two-tailed tests, the researcher must also select an alpha level. We have seen that the alpha level plays a crucial role in hypothesis testing. When we assign a value to alpha, we define what we mean by an "unlikely" sample outcome. If the probability of the observed sample outcome is lower than the alpha level (if the test statistic falls into the critical region), we reject the null hypothesis as untrue. Thus, the alpha level will have important consequences for our decision in step 5.

How can reasonable decisions be made with respect to the value of alpha? Recall that, in addition to defining what will be meant by *unlikely,* the alpha level is also the probability that the decision to reject the null hypothesis, if the test statistic falls into the critical region, will be incorrect. In hypothesis testing, the error of incorrectly rejecting the null hypothesis or rejecting a null hypothesis that is actually true is called **Type I error,** or **alpha error.** Type I error can be thought of as a "false positive" outcome of a criminal trial, such that a jury finds the accused *guilty* of the crime despite really being *not guilty.* The null hypothesis in this example is that the person is not guilty, and the research hypothesis is that the person is guilty. To minimize Type I error, use very small values for alpha.

To elaborate, when an alpha level is specified, the sampling distribution is divided into two sets of possible sample outcomes. The critical region includes all unlikely or rare sample outcomes. Outcomes in this region will cause us to reject the null hypothesis. The remainder of the area consists of all sample outcomes that are "nonrare." The lower the level of alpha, the smaller the critical region and the greater the distance between the mean of the sampling distribution and the beginnings of the critical region. Compare, for the sake of illustration, the following alpha levels and values for Z(critical) for two-tailed tests. As you may recall, this information was also presented in Table 7.1.

If Alpha Equals	The Two-Tailed Critical Region Will Begin at Z(critical) Equal to
0.10	± 1.65
0.05	± 1.96
0.01	± 2.58
0.001	± 3.29

As alpha goes down, the critical region becomes smaller and moves farther away from the mean of the sampling distribution. The lower the alpha level, the harder it will be to reject the null hypothesis and, because a Type I error can be made only if our decision in step 5 is to reject, the lower the probability of Type I error. To minimize the probability of rejecting a null hypothesis that is in fact true, use very low alpha levels. For instance, with an obtained Z score of $+2.57$ for the "sophistication" example in Section 8.4, we rejected the null hypothesis that there is no difference between sociology majors and the general student body in a one-tailed test at the 0.05 alpha level, where the critical region begins at $+1.65$. However, we would fail to reject the null hypothesis at the 0.001 level with a critical region of $+3.10$.

However, there is a complication. As the critical region decreases in size (as alpha levels decrease), the noncritical region—the area between the two Z(critical) scores in a two-tailed test—must become larger. All other things being equal, the lower the alpha level, the less likely that the sample outcome will fall into the critical region. This raises the possibility of a second type of incorrect decision, called **Type II error,** or **beta (β) error:** failing to reject a null hypothesis that is, in fact, false. Type II error is thus analogous to a "false negative" outcome of a criminal trial such that a jury finds a person *not guilty* of the crime despite actually being *guilty*.

In sum, the probability of Type I error decreases as the alpha level decreases, but the probability of Type II error increases. While the two types of error are inversely related, it is not possible to minimize both in the same test. That is, in conducting a hypothesis test we calculate the probability of committing Type I error, which we control by adjusting the alpha level, but not the probability of committing Type II error—Type II error remains unknown. Through additional computation, however, we can calculate the probability of not committing Type II error; in other words, the probability of correctly rejecting the null hypothesis, or making the right decision! This is referred to as the "power" of a hypothesis test. The routines for computing the power of a hypothesis test will not be considered in this text.

We must also be aware that there are different consequences associated with making each type of error. For example, in determining guilt during a criminal trial, sending an innocent person to jail (Type I error) has far different consequences than those that result from setting a guilty person free (Type II error). Which of these errors is more serious depends on the social costs related to them. Canadians tend to be distressed when Type II errors occur in the justice system, but outraged by Type I errors. The Canadian justice system, therefore, places great importance on decreasing Type I errors (sending innocent people to jail) at the expense of increasing Type II errors (letting guilty people go free).

It may be helpful to clarify the relationships between decision making and errors in table format. Table 8.3 lists the two decisions we can make in step 5 of the five-step model: we either reject or fail to reject the null hypothesis. The other dimension of Table 8.3 lists the two possible conditions of the null hypothesis: it is either actually true or actually false. The table combines these possibilities into a total of four possible combinations, two of which are desirable ("OK") and two of which are errors.

TABLE 8.3   DECISION MAKING AND THE NULL HYPOTHESIS

The H_0 Is Actually:	Decision	
	Reject	Fail to Reject
True	Type I or α error	OK
False	OK	Type II or β error

The two desirable outcomes are rejecting null hypotheses that are actually false and failing to reject null hypotheses that are actually true. The goal of any scientific investigation is to verify true statements and reject false statements.

The remaining two combinations are errors or situations that, naturally, we wish to avoid. If we reject a null hypothesis that is in fact true, we are saying that a true statement is false. Likewise, if we fail to reject a null hypothesis that is in fact false, we are saying that a false statement is true. We want to wind up in one of the boxes labelled "OK" in Table 8.3—to always reject false statements and accept the truth when we find it. Remember, however, that hypothesis testing always carries an element of risk and that it is not possible to minimize the chances of both Type I and Type II error simultaneously.

What all of this means, finally, is that you must think of selecting an alpha level as an attempt to balance the two types of error. Higher alpha levels will minimize the probability of Type II error (saying that false statements are true), and lower alpha levels will minimize the probability of Type I error (saying that true statements are false). Normally, in social science research, we will want to minimize Type I error, and lower alpha levels (.05, .01, .001 or lower) will be used. The 0.05 level in particular has emerged as a generally recognized indicator of a significant result. However, the widespread use of the 0.05 level is simply a convention, and there is no reason that alpha cannot be set at virtually any sensible level (such as 0.04, 0.027, 0.083). The researcher has the responsibility of selecting the alpha level that seems most reasonable in terms of the goals of the research project.

8.6 THE STUDENT'S *t* DISTRIBUTION

To this point, we have considered only one type of hypothesis test. Specifically, we have focused on situations involving single sample means where the value of the population standard deviation (σ) was known. Needless to say, the value of σ will not be known in most research situations. However, a value for σ is required in order to compute the standard error of the mean ($\sigma/\sqrt{N}$), convert our sample outcome into a Z score, and place the Z(obtained) on the sampling distribution (step 4). How can a value for the population standard deviation reasonably be obtained?

It might seem sensible to estimate σ with s, the sample standard deviation. As we noted in Chapter 7, s is a biased estimator of σ, but the degree of bias decreases as sample size increases. For large samples (i.e., samples with 100 or more cases), the sample standard deviation yields an adequate estimate of σ. Thus, for large samples, we simply substitute s for σ in the formula for Z(obtained) in step 4 and continue to use the standard normal curve to find areas under the sampling distribution.

For smaller samples, however, when σ is unknown, an alternative distribution called the **Student's *t* distribution** must be used to find areas

FIGURE 8.7   THE *Z* DISTRIBUTION AND THE *t* DISTRIBUTION FOR SELECTED DEGREES OF FREEDOM (df)

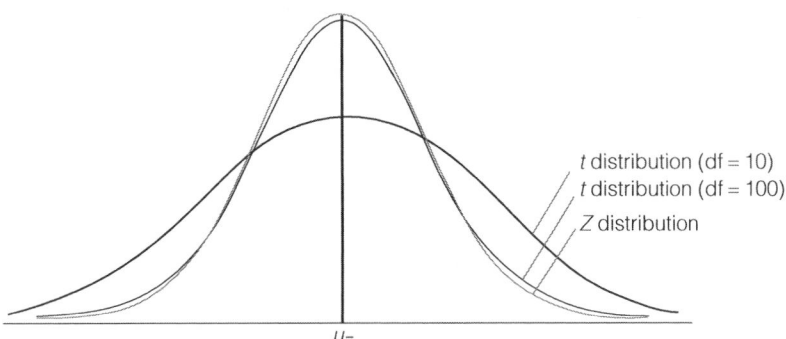

t distribution (df = 10)
t distribution (df = 100)
Z distribution

$u_{\bar{x}}$

under the sampling distribution and establish the critical region. The shape of the *t* distribution varies as a function of sample size, or more specifically as a function of degrees of freedom (symbolized as *df*).* Degrees of freedom are equal to $N - 1$ in the case of a single-sample mean. Thus, there is a "family" of *t* sampling distributions, and the value of df defines a specific "member" of this family (i.e., it defines the shape of the *t* distribution).

The relative shapes of the *Z* distribution (in grey) and two specific *t* distributions (in black) are depicted in Figure 8.7. For the smaller sample (df = 10), the *t* distribution is flatter than the *Z* distribution, but, as sample size increases (df = 100), the *t* distribution comes to resemble the *Z* distribution more and more. The *Z* and *t* distributions are essentially identical when sample size is greater than 120. As *N* increases, the sample standard deviation (*s*) becomes a more and more adequate estimator of the population standard deviation (σ), and the *t* distribution becomes more and more like the *Z* distribution.

The *t* distribution is summarized in Appendix B. The *t* table differs from the *Z* table in several ways. First, there is a column at the left of the table labelled Degrees of Freedom (df). As mentioned above, the exact shape of the *t* distribution—and thus the exact location of the critical region for any alpha level—varies as a function of sample size (degrees of freedom). Degrees of freedom must first be computed before the critical region for any alpha can be located. Second, alpha levels are arrayed across the top of Appendix B in two rows, one row for one-tailed tests and one for two-tailed tests. To use the table, we should begin by locating the selected alpha level in the appropriate row.

---

*Degrees of freedom are the number of values in a distribution that are free to vary. For a sample mean, a distribution has $N - 1$ degrees of freedom. This means that for a specific value of the mean, $N - 1$ scores are free to vary. For example, if the mean is 3 for a group of five scores, the distribution has $5 - 1$, or 4 degrees of freedom. When four of the scores are known, the fifth is fixed. If the four scores are 1, 2, 3, and 4, the fifth must be 5 and no other value.

The third difference is that the entries in the table are the actual scores, called **t(critical),** that mark the beginnings of the critical regions and not areas under the sampling distribution. To illustrate the use of this table with single-sample means, find the critical region for alpha equal to 0.05, two-tailed test, for $N = 30$. The degrees of freedom will be $N - 1$, or 29; reading down the proper column, you should find a value of 2.045. Thus, the critical region for this test will begin at $t(\text{critical}) = \pm 2.045$.

Take a moment to notice some additional features of the t distribution. First, note that the $t(\text{critical})$ we found above is larger in value than the comparable $Z(\text{critical})$, which for a two-tailed test at an alpha of 0.05 would be ± 1.96. This relationship reflects the fact that the t distribution is flatter than the Z distribution (see Figure 8.7). When you use the t distribution, the critical regions will begin farther away from the mean of the sampling distribution and, therefore, the null hypothesis will be harder to reject. Furthermore, the smaller the sample size (the lower the degrees of freedom), the larger the value of $t(\text{obtained})$ necessary for a rejection of the H_0.

Second, scan the column for an alpha of 0.05, two-tailed test. Note that, for one degree of freedom, the $t(\text{critical})$ is ± 12.706 and that the value of $t(\text{critical})$ decreases as degrees of freedom increase. For degrees of freedom greater than 120, the value of $t(\text{critical})$ is the same as the comparable value of $Z(\text{critical})$, or ± 1.96. As sample size increases, the t distribution comes to resemble the Z distribution more and more until, with sample sizes greater than 120, the two distributions are essentially identical (again see Figure 8.7).*

To demonstrate the uses of the t distribution in more detail, we will work through an example problem. Note that, in terms of the five-step model, the changes required by using t scores occur mostly in steps 3 and 4. In step 3, the sampling distribution will be the t distribution, and degrees of freedom must be computed before locating the critical region as marked by $t(\text{critical})$. In step 4, a slightly different formula for computing the test statistic, **t(obtained),** will be used. As compared with the formula for $Z(\text{obtained})$, s will replace σ and $N - 1$ will replace N.

Specifically,

FORMULA 8.2
$$t(\text{obtained}) = \frac{\overline{X} - \mu}{s/\sqrt{N - 1}}$$

A researcher wonders if sociology students are different from the general student body in terms of academic achievement. She has gathered a random sample of 30 sociology students and has learned from the registrar that the

---

*Appendix B abbreviates the t distribution by presenting a limited number of critical t scores for degrees of freedom between 31 and 120. If the degrees of freedom for a specific problem equal 77 and alpha equals 0.05, two-tailed, we have a choice between a $t(\text{critical})$ of ± 2.000 (df = 60) and a $t(\text{critical})$ of ± 1.980 (df = 120). In situations such as these, take the larger table value as $t(\text{critical})$. This will make rejection of the H_0 less likely and is therefore the more conservative course of action.

mean grade-point average for all students is 2.50 ($\mu = 2.50$), but the standard deviation of the population (σ) has never been computed. Sample data are reported below. Is the sample from a population that has a mean of 2.50?

Student Body	Sociology Students
$\mu = 2.50 \, (= \mu_{\bar{x}})$	$\bar{X} = 2.78$
$\sigma = ?$	$s = 1.23$
	$N = 30$

Step 1. Making Assumptions and Meeting Test Requirements.

> Model: Random sampling
> Level of measurement is interval-ratio
> Sampling distribution is normal

Step 2. Stating the Null Hypothesis.

$$H_0: \mu = 2.50$$
$$(H_1: \mu \neq 2.50)$$

You can see from the research hypothesis that the researcher has not predicted a direction for the difference. This will be a two-tailed test.

Step 3. Selecting the Sampling Distribution and Establishing the Critical Region. Because σ is unknown and sample size is small, the t distribution will be used to find the critical region. Alpha will be set at 0.01.

> Sampling distribution = t distribution
> $\alpha = 0.01$, two-tailed test
> df $= (N - 1) = 29$
> t(critical) $= \pm 2.756$

Step 4. Computing the Test Statistic.

$$t\text{(obtained)} = \frac{\bar{X} - \mu}{s/\sqrt{N - 1}}$$

$$t\text{(obtained)} = \frac{2.78 - 2.50}{1.23/\sqrt{29}}$$

$$t\text{(obtained)} = \frac{.28}{.23}$$

$$t\text{(obtained)} = +1.22$$

Step 5. Making a Decision and Interpreting the Results of the Test. The test statistic does not fall into the critical region. Therefore, the researcher fails to reject the H_0. The difference between the sample mean (2.78) and the

FIGURE 8.8   SAMPLING DISTRIBUTION SHOWING t (OBTAINED) VERSUS t (CRITICAL) FOR THE TWO-TAILED TEST, WITH REJECTION REGION FOR ALPHA = 0.05 (df = 29) IN SHADE

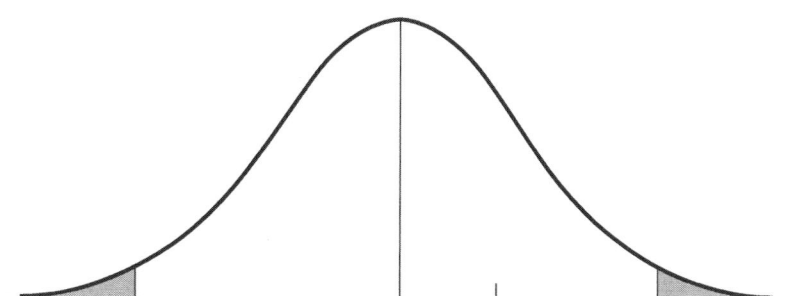

population mean (2.50) is no greater than what would be expected if only random chance were operating. The test statistic and critical regions are displayed in Figure 8.8.

To summarize, when testing single-sample means we must make a choice regarding the theoretical distribution we will use to establish the critical region. The choice is straightforward. If the population standard deviation (σ) is known or sample size is large, the Z distribution (summarized in Appendix A) will be used. If σ is unknown and the sample is small, the t distribution (summarized in Appendix B) will be used. *(For practice in using the t distribution in a test of hypothesis, see problems 8.8 to 8.10 and 8.17.)*

8.7 TESTS OF HYPOTHESES FOR SINGLE-SAMPLE PROPORTIONS (LARGE SAMPLES)

In many cases, the sample variables we are interested in will not be measured in a way that justifies the assumption of interval-ratio level of measurement. One alternative in this situation would be to use a sample proportion (P_s) rather than a sample mean as the test statistic. As we shall see, the overall procedures for testing single-sample proportions are the same as those for testing means. The central question is still "Does the population from which the sample was drawn have a certain characteristic?" We still conduct the test based on the assumption that the null hypothesis is true, and we still evaluate the probability of the obtained sample outcome against a sampling distribution of all possible sample outcomes. Our decision at the end of the test is also the same. If the obtained test statistic falls into the critical region (is unlikely, given the assumption that the H_0 is true), we reject the H_0.

Having stressed the continuity in procedures and logic, we must hastily point out the important differences as well. These differences are best related in terms of the five-step model for hypothesis testing. In step 1, when working with sample proportions, we assume that the variable is measured at the nominal level of measurement. In step 2, the symbols used to state the null hypothesis are different even though the null is still a statement of "no difference."

In step 3, we will use only the standardized normal curve (the Z distribution) to find areas under the sampling distribution and locate the critical region. This will be appropriate as long as sample size is large. We will not consider small-sample tests of hypothesis for proportions in this text.

In step 4, computing the test statistic, the form of the formula remains the same. That is, the test statistic, Z(obtained), equals the sample statistic minus the mean of the sampling distribution, divided by the standard deviation of the sampling distribution. However, the symbols will change because we are basing the tests on sample proportions. The formula can be stated as

FORMULA 8.3
$$Z(\text{obtained}) = \frac{P_s - P_u}{\sqrt{P_u(1 - P_u)/N}}$$

Step 5 is exactly the same as before. If the test statistic, Z(obtained), falls into the critical region, as marked by Z(critical), reject the H_0.

An example should clarify these procedures. A random sample of 122 households in a low-income neighbourhood revealed that 53 (or a proportion of 0.43) of the households were headed by females. In the city as a whole, the proportion of female-headed households is .39. Are households in the low-income neighbourhood significantly different from the city as a whole in terms of this characteristic?

Step 1. **Making Assumptions and Meeting Test Requirements**.

> Model: Random sampling
> Level of measurement is nominal
> Sampling distribution is normal in shape

Step 2. **Stating the Null Hypothesis.** The research question, as stated above, asks only if the sample proportion is different from the population proportion. Because no direction is predicted for the difference, a two-tailed test will be used.

$$H_0: P_u = 0.39$$
$$(H_1: P_u \neq 0.39)$$

Step 3. **Selecting the Sampling Distribution and Establishing the Critical Region**.

> Sampling distribution = Z distribution
> $\alpha = 0.10$, two-tailed test
> $Z(\text{critical}) = \pm 1.65$

Application 8.2

It was pointed out in Application 8.1 that immigrants arriving in Canada in recent years tend to be well educated. In a random sample from Statistics Canada's Survey of Labour and Income Dynamics, 22% of 645 recent immigrants (those who have been in Canada for less than 10 years) had a university degree in 2001. Census figures from that same year show that 18% of the Canadian population had a university degree. Are recent immigrants significantly more likely to have a university education than the population as a whole?

Step 1. Making Assumptions and Meeting Test Requirements.

> Model: Random sampling
> Level of measurement is nominal
> Sampling distribution is normal

This is a large sample, so we may assume a normal sampling distribution. The variable, percent with a university degree, is nominal in level of measurement.

Step 2. Stating the Null Hypothesis (H_0). The null hypothesis says that recent immigrants are not different from the nation as a whole.

$$H_0: P_u = 0.18$$

The original question ("are recent immigrants *more* likely to have a university education") suggests a one-tailed research hypothesis:

$$(H_1: P_u > .18)$$

The research hypothesis says that we will be concerned only with outcomes in which recent immigrants are more likely to hold a degree or with sample outcomes in the upper tail of the sampling distribution.

Step 3. Selecting the Sampling Distribution and Establishing the Critical Region.

$$\text{Sampling distribution} = Z \text{ distribution}$$
$$\alpha = 0.05$$
$$Z(\text{critical}) = +1.65$$

Step 4. Computing the Test Statistic. The information necessary for a test of the null hypothesis, expressed in the form of proportions, is

Recent Immigrants	Nation
$P_s = 0.22$	$P_u = 0.18$
$N = 645$	

The test statistic, $Z(\text{obtained})$, would be

$$Z(\text{obtained}) = \frac{P_s - P_u}{\sqrt{P_u(1 - P_u)/N}}$$

$$Z(\text{obtained}) = \frac{0.22 - 0.18}{\sqrt{(0.18)(1 - 0.18)/645}}$$

$$Z(\text{obtained}) = \frac{0.04}{\sqrt{(0.1476)/645}}$$

$$Z(\text{obtained}) = \frac{0.04}{0.015}$$

$$Z(\text{obtained}) = +2.67$$

Step 5. Making a Decision and Interpreting the Results of the Test. With alpha set at 0.05, one-tailed, the critical region would begin at $Z(\text{critical}) = +1.65$. With an obtained Z score of $+2.67$, the null hypothesis is rejected. The difference between recent immigrants and Canadians as a whole is statistically significant and in the predicted direction. Recent immigrants to Canada are significantly more likely to have a university degree.

Source: Statistics Canada, 2001 Canadian Census, individual PUMF, and 2001 Survey of Labour and Income Dynamics, individual PUMF.

FIGURE 8.9   SAMPLING DISTRIBUTION SHOWING Z(OBTAINED) VERSUS Z(CRITICAL) FOR THE TWO-TAILED TEST, WITH REJECT REGION FOR ALPHA = 0.10 IN SHADE

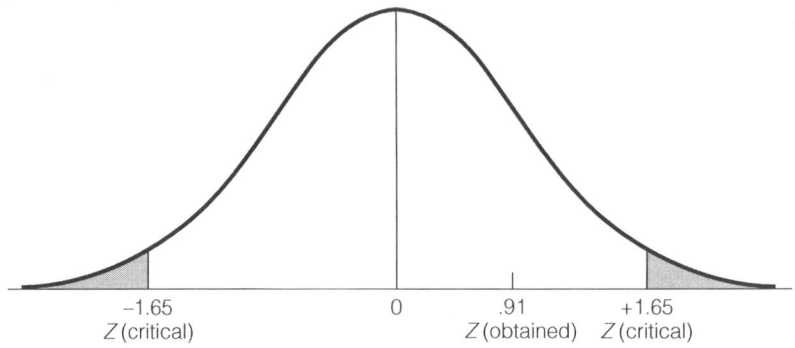

| −1.65 | 0 | .91 | +1.65 |
| Z(critical) | | Z(obtained) | Z(critical) |

Step 4. Computing the Test Statistic.

$$Z(\text{obtained}) = \frac{P_s - P_u}{\sqrt{P_u(1 - P_u)/N}}$$

$$Z(\text{obtained}) = \frac{0.43 - 0.39}{\sqrt{0.39(0.61)/122}}$$

$$Z(\text{obtained}) = +0.91$$

Step 5. **Making a Decision and Interpreting the Results of the Test.** The test statistic, Z(obtained), does not fall into the critical region. Therefore, we fail to reject the H_0. There is no statistically significant difference between the low-income community and the city as a whole in terms of the proportion of households headed by females. Figure 8.9 displays the sampling distribution, the critical region, and the Z(obtained). *(For practice in tests of significance using sample proportions, see problems 8.1c, 8.11 to 8.14, 8.15 a to d, and 8.16.)*

8.8 HYPOTHESIS TESTING USING CONFIDENCE INTERVALS

Hypothesis testing and interval estimation (see Chapter 7) are the two main applications of inferential statistics. While the objective of each technique is different, *testing* a claim about a population parameter versus *estimating* a population parameter respectively, they are in reality just different ways of expressing the same information.

If an interval estimate (i.e., confidence interval) does not contain the value of the parameter specified by the null hypothesis, then a hypothesis test will reject the null hypothesis, and vice versa. That is, if the value of H_0 *is* contained within the confidence interval at a given alpha level, then H_0 *is not* rejected at that level. On the other hand, if the value of H_0 *is not* contained within the confidence interval at a given alpha level, then H_0 *is* rejected at that level. So, if a 99% confidence interval does not contain the value of the parameter given by the null hypothesis, then the null hypothesis is rejected at the 0.01 level; if a 95% confidence interval does not contain it, then the null is rejected at the 0.05 level; and so on. The ability to use confidence intervals to test hypotheses applies to all situations, including means and proportions and the one-sample case covered in this chapter and the two-sample case to be discussed in Chapter 9.

To see how the confidence interval for the sample mean corresponds to the hypothesis test for the sample mean, let us take another look at the LSAT example in Section 8.3. Recall that the null hypothesis stated that the population of graduates of the LSAT preparation course is just like everyone else and has a mean LSAT score of 151; that is, there is no difference in LSAT scoring between the graduates and LSAT writers as a whole, or

$$H_0: \mu = 151$$
$$(H_1: \mu \neq 151)$$

For a two-tailed test (the research hypothesis does not predict a direction for the difference) with alpha set at 0.05, the critical region begins at Z (critical) ± 1.96, or

$$\text{Sampling distribution} = Z \text{ distribution}$$
$$\alpha = 0.05, \text{ two-tailed test}$$
$$Z \text{ (critical)} = \pm 1.96$$

We obtained a Z score of $+3.75$, or

$$Z = \frac{\overline{X} - \mu}{\sigma/\sqrt{N}}$$
$$Z = \frac{154 - 151}{9/\sqrt{127}}$$
$$Z = +3.75$$

Then, we reject the null hypothesis, H_0, because the test statistic, Z (obtained), falls into the critical region, as marked by Z(critical).

Next, let us construct a 95% confidence interval for the sample mean using Formula 7.1 (Chapter 7):

$$\text{c.i.} = \overline{X} \pm Z\left(\frac{\sigma}{\sqrt{N}}\right)$$
$$\text{c.i.} = 154 \pm 1.96\left(\frac{9}{\sqrt{127}}\right)$$
$$\text{c.i.} = 154 \pm (1.96)(0.80)$$
$$\text{c.i.} = 154 \pm 1.57$$

Based on this result, we estimate that the population mean is greater than or equal to 152.43 and less than or equal to 155.57 at the 95% level of confidence.

The relationship between the confidence interval and hypothesis test can now been seen. Because this interval does not include the value of the parameter specified by the null hypothesis, 151, we would reject the null. The difference between graduates of the LSAT training course and the entire population of LSAT writers is statistically significant at the .05 level. This is precisely the decision we made above using the formal hypothesis testing approach. In sum, it will always be true that if the confidence interval contains the value of the parameter specified by the null hypothesis, then the null hypothesis cannot be rejected at the stated alpha level. If it does not, then the null hypothesis can be rejected.

SUMMARY

1. All the basic concepts and techniques for testing hypotheses were presented in this chapter. We saw how to test the null hypothesis of "no difference" for single sample means and proportions. In both cases, the central question is whether the population represented by the sample has a certain characteristic.

2. All tests of a hypothesis involve finding the probability of the observed sample outcome, given that the null hypothesis is true. If the outcome has a low probability, we reject the null hypothesis. In the usual research situation, we will wish to reject the null hypothesis and thereby support the research hypothesis.

3. The five-step model will be our framework for decision making throughout the hypothesis-testing chapters. What we do during each step, however, will vary, depending on the specific test being conducted.

4. If we can predict a direction for the difference in stating the research hypothesis, a one-tailed test is called for. If no direction can be predicted, a two-tailed test is appropriate. There are two kinds of errors in hypothesis testing. Type I, or alpha, error is rejecting a true null; Type II, or beta, error is failing to reject a false null. The probabilities of committing these two types of error are inversely related and cannot be simultaneously minimized in the same test. By selecting an alpha level, we try to balance the probability of these two kinds of error.

5. When testing sample means, the t distribution must be used to find the critical region when the population standard deviation is unknown and sample size is small.

6. Sample proportions can also be tested for significance. Tests are conducted using the five-step model. Compared to the test for the sample mean, the major differences lie in the level-of-measurement assumption (step 1), the statement of the null (step 2), and the computation of the test statistic (step 4).

7. Hypothesis testing and interval estimation (Chapter 7) are just different ways of expressing the same information. If the confidence interval contains the value of the parameter specified by the null hypothesis in a one-sample test, then the null hypothesis is not rejected at the stated alpha level. Alternatively, the null hypothesis is rejected if the confidence interval does not contain the value.

8. If you are still confused about the uses of inferential statistics described in this chapter, don't be alarmed or discouraged. A sizable volume of rather complex material has been presented and only rarely will a beginning student fully comprehend the unique logic of hypothesis testing on the first exposure. After all, it is not every day that you learn how to test a statement you don't believe (the null hypothesis) against a distribution that doesn't exist (the sampling distribution)!

SUMMARY OF FORMULAS

Single-sample means, large samples:

8.1 $$Z(\text{obtained}) = \frac{\overline{X} - \mu}{\sigma/\sqrt{N}}$$

Single-sample means when samples are small and population standard deviation is unknown:

8.2 $$t(\text{obtained}) = \frac{\overline{X} - \mu}{s/\sqrt{N-1}}$$

Single-sample proportions, large samples:

8.3 $$Z(\text{obtained}) = \frac{P_s - P_u}{\sqrt{P_u(1 - P_u)/N}}$$

GLOSSARY

Alpha level (α). The proportion of area under the sampling distribution that contains unlikely sample outcomes, given that the null hypothesis is true. Also, the probability of Type I error.

Critical region (region of rejection). The area under the sampling distribution that, in advance of the test itself, is defined as including unlikely sample outcomes, given that the null hypothesis is true.

Five-step model. A step-by-step guideline for conducting tests of hypotheses. A framework that organizes decisions and computations for all tests of significance.

Hypothesis testing. Statistical tests that estimate the probability of sample outcomes if assumptions about the population (the null hypothesis) are true.

Null hypothesis (H_0). A statement of "no difference." In the context of single-sample tests of significance, the population from which the sample was drawn is assumed to have a certain characteristic or value.

One-tailed test. A type of hypothesis test used when (1) the direction of the difference can be predicted or (2) concern focuses on outcomes in only one tail of the sampling distribution.

Research hypothesis (H_1). A statement that contradicts the null hypothesis. In the context of single-sample tests of significance, the research hypothesis says that the population from which the sample was drawn does not have a certain characteristic or value.

Significance testing. See Hypothesis testing.

Student's t distribution. A distribution used to find the critical region for tests of sample means when σ is unknown and sample size is small.

t(critical). The t score that marks the beginning of the critical region of a t distribution.

t(obtained). The test statistic computed in step 4 of the five-step model. The sample outcome expressed as a t score.

Test statistic. The value computed in step 4 of the five-step model that converts the sample outcome into either a t score or a Z score.

Two-tailed test. A type of hypothesis test used when (1) the direction of the difference cannot be predicted or (2) concern focuses on outcomes in both tails of the sampling distribution.

Type I error (alpha error). The probability of rejecting a null hypothesis that is, in fact, true.

Type II error (beta error). The probability of failing to reject a null hypothesis that is, in fact, false.

Z(critical). The Z score that marks the beginnings of the critical region on a Z distribution.

Z(obtained). The test statistic computed in step 4 of the five-step model. The sample outcomes expressed as a Z score.

MULTIMEDIA RESOURCES

 http://www.healeystatistics.nelson.com

Visit the companion Web site for the first Canadian edition of *Statistics: A Tool for Social Research* to access a wide range of student resources. Begin by clicking on the Student Resources section of the book's Web site to access review quizzes, flash cards, and other study tools.

PROBLEMS

8.1 a. For each situation, find Z(critical).

Alpha	Form	Z(Critical)
.05	One-tailed	
.10	Two-tailed	
.06	Two-tailed	
.01	One-tailed	
.02	Two-tailed	

b. For each situation, find the critical t score.

Alpha	Form	N	t(Critical)
.10	Two-tailed	31	
.02	Two-tailed	24	
.01	Two-tailed	121	
.01	One-tailed	31	
.05	One-tailed	61	

c. Compute the appropriate test statistic (Z or t) for each situation:

1. $\mu = 2.40$ $\overline{X} = 2.20$
     $\sigma = 0.75$ $N = 200$

2. $\mu = 17.1$ $\overline{X} = 16.8$
          $s = 0.9$
          $N = 45$

3. $\mu = 10.2$ $\overline{X} = 9.4$
          $s = 1.7$
          $N = 150$

4. $P_u = .57$ $P_s = 0.60$
          $N = 117$

5. $P_u = 0.32$ $P_s = 0.30$
          $N = 322$

8.2 SOC **a.** The student body at Algebra University attends an average of 3.3 parties per month. A random sample of 117 sociology majors averages 3.8 parties per month with a standard deviation of 0.53. Are sociology majors significantly different from the student body as a whole? *(HINT: The wording of the research question suggests a two-tailed test. This means that the alternative or research hypothesis in step 2 will be stated as H_1: $\mu \neq 3.3$ and that the critical region will be split between the upper and lower tails of the sampling distribution. See Table 8.2 for values of Z(critical) for various alpha levels.)*

b. What if the research question were changed to "Do sociology majors attend a significantly *greater* number of parties"? How would the test conducted in 8.2a change? *(HINT: This wording implies a one-tailed test of significance. How would the research hypothesis change? For the alpha you used in problem 8.2a, what would the value of Z(critical) be?)*

8.3 SW **a.** Nationally, social workers average 10.2 years of experience. In a random sample, 203 social workers in the greater metropolitan area of Pearson, Ontario, average only 8.7 years with a standard deviation of 0.52. Are social workers in Pearson, Ontario, significantly less experienced? *(Note the wording of the research hypothesis. This situation may justify a one-tailed test of significance. If you chose a one-tailed test, what form would the research hypothesis take, and where would the critical region begin?)*

b. The same sample of social workers reports an average annual salary of $35,782 with a standard deviation of $622. Is this figure significantly higher than the national average of $34,509? *(The wording of the research hypothesis suggests a one-tailed test. What form would the research hypothesis take, and where would the critical region begin?)*

8.4 SOC Nationally, the average score on the GRE (Graduate Record Examinations) verbal test is 453 with a standard deviation of 95. A random sample of 152 first-year graduate students entering Algebra University shows a mean score of 502. Is there a significant difference?

8.5 SOC A random sample of 423 Albertans has finished an average of 12.7 years of formal education with a standard deviation of 1.7. Is this significantly different from the national average of 12.2 years?

8.6 SOC A sample of 105 workers in the Overkill Division of the Machismo Toy Factory earns an average of $24,375 per year. The average salary for all workers is $24,230 with a standard deviation of $523. Are workers in the Overkill Division overpaid? Conduct both one- and two-tailed tests.

8.7 GER **a.** Nationally, the population as a whole watches 6.2 hours of TV per day. A random sample of 1,017 senior citizens report watching an average of 5.9 hours per day with a standard deviation of .7. Is the difference significant?

b. The same sample of senior citizens reports that they belong to an average of 2.1 voluntary organizations and clubs with a standard deviation of .5. Nationally, the average is 1.7. Is the difference significant?

8.8 SOC A school system has assigned several hundred "chronic and severe underachievers" to an alternative educational experience. To assess the program, a random sample of 35 has been selected for comparison with all students in the system.

a. In terms of GPA, did the program work?

Systemwide GPA	Program GPA
$\mu = 2.47$	$\bar{X} = 2.55$
	$s = 0.70$
	$N = 35$

b. In terms of absenteeism (number of days missed per year), what can be said about the success of the program?

Systemwide	Program
$\mu = 6.13$	$\bar{X} = 4.78$
	$s = 1.11$
	$N = 35$

c. In terms of standardized test scores in math and reading, was the program a success?

Math Test Systemwide	Math Test Program
$\mu = 103$	$\bar{X} = 106$
	$s = 2.0$
	$N = 35$

Reading Test Systemwide	Reading Test Program
$\mu = 110$	$\bar{X} = 113$
	$s = 2.0$
	$N = 35$

(HINT: Note the wording of the research questions. Is a one-tailed test justified? Is the program a success if the students in the program are no different from students systemwide? What if the program students were performing at lower levels? If a one-tailed test is used, what form should the research hypothesis take? Where will the critical region begin?)

8.9 SOC A random sample of 26 sociology graduates in BC scored an average of 458 on the GRE advanced sociology test with a standard deviation of 20. Is this significantly different from the national average ($\mu = 440$)?

8.10 PA Nationally, the per capita property tax is $130 per month. A random sample of 36 western cities average $98 per month with a standard deviation of $5. Is the difference significant? Summarize your conclusions in a sentence or two.

8.11 GER/CJ A survey shows that 10% of the population is victimized by property crime each year. A random sample of 527 older citizens (65 years or more of age) shows a victimization rate of 14%. Are older people more likely to be victimized? Conduct both one- and two-tailed tests of significance.

8.12 CJ A random sample of 113 convicted sex offenders in a provincial prison system completed a program designed to change their attitudes toward women, sex, and violence before being released on parole. Fifty-eight eventually became repeat sex offenders. Is this recidivism rate significantly different from the rate for all offenders (57%) in that province? Summarize your conclusions in a sentence or two. *(HINT: You must use the information given in the problem to compute a sample proportion. Remember to convert the population percentage to a proportion).*

8.13 PS In a recent provincial election, 55% of the voters rejected a proposal to institute a new provincial lottery. In a random sample of 150 voters from rural communities, 49% rejected the proposal. Is the difference significant? Summarize your conclusions in a sentence or two.

8.14 CJ Provincially, the police clear by arrest 35% of the robberies and 42% of the aggravated assaults reported to them. A researcher takes a random sample of all the robberies ($N = 207$) and aggravated assaults ($N = 178$) reported to a metropolitan police department in one year and finds that 83 of the robberies and 80 of the assaults were cleared by arrest. Are the local arrest rates significantly different from the provincial rate? Write a sentence or two interpreting your decision.

8.15 SOC/SW A researcher has compiled a file of information on a random sample of 317 families

in a city that has chronic, long-term patterns of child abuse. Below are reported some of the characteristics of the sample along with values for the city as a whole. For each trait, test the null hypothesis of "no difference" and summarize your findings.

a. Mothers' educational level (proportion completing high school):

City	Sample
$P_u = 0.63$	$P_s = 0.61$

b. Family size (proportion of families with four or more children):

City	Sample
$P_u = 0.21$	$P_s = 0.26$

c. Mothers' work status (proportion of mothers with jobs outside the home):

City	Sample
$P_u = 0.51$	$P_s = 0.27$

d. Relations with kin (proportion of families that have contact with kin at least once a week):

City	Sample
$P_u = 0.82$	$P_s = 0.43$

e. Fathers' educational achievement (average years of formal schooling):

City	Sample
$\mu = 12.3$	$\overline{X} = 12.5$
	$s = 1.7$

f. Fathers' occupational stability (average years in present job):

City	Sample
$\mu = 5.2$	$\overline{X} = 3.7$
	$s = 0.5$

8.16 SW You are the head of an agency seeking funding for a program to reduce unemployment among teenage males. Nationally, the unemployment rate for this group is 18%. A random sample of 323 teen-age males in your area reveals an unemployment rate of 21.7%. Is the difference significant? Can you demonstrate a need for the program? Should you use a one-tailed test in this situation? Why? Explain the result of your test of significance as you would to a funding agency.

8.17 | PA | The city manager of Pearson, Ontario, has received a complaint from the local union of firefighters to the effect that they are underpaid. Not having much time, the city manager gathers the records of a random sample of 27 firefighters and finds that their average salary is $38,073 with a standard deviation of $575. If she knows that the average salary nationally is $38,202, how can she respond to the complaint? Should she use a one-tailed test in this situation? Why? What would she say in a memo to the union that would respond to the complaint?

8.18 The following essay questions review the basic principles and concepts of inferential statistics.

The order of the questions roughly follows the five-step model.

a. Hypothesis testing or significance testing can be conducted only with a random sample. Why?

b. Under what specific conditions can it be assumed that the sampling distribution is normal in shape?

c. Explain the role of the sampling distribution in a test of hypothesis.

d. The null hypothesis is an assumption about reality that makes it possible to test sample outcomes for their significance. Explain.

e. What is the critical region? How is the size of the critical region determined?

f. Describe a research situation in which a one-tailed test of hypothesis would be appropriate.

g. Thinking about the shape of the sampling distribution, why does use of the t distribution (as opposed to the Z distribution) make it more difficult to reject the null hypothesis?

h. What exactly can be concluded in the one-sample case when the test statistic falls into the critical region?

SPSS for Windows

Using SPSS for Windows to Conduct a One-Sample Test with the 2001 Census

The demonstration and exercise below use the shortened version of the 2001 Census data. Start SPSS for Windows and open the *Census.sav* file.

SPSS DEMONSTRATION 8.1 Using the Select Cases Command to Conduct a One-Sample Test

In this demonstration, we'll use conduct a one-sample test to compare the income of a sample of social science majors to the income of all Canadians, which according to Statistics Canada was $27,103 in 2001.* We predict that social science majors, with their post-secondary education, skills, and training, will have a higher income than the general population. If we find that the average income for the sample of social science majors is significantly different than that of the general population, we can conclude that social science majors in Canada tend to have better incomes than the population as a whole.

---

*Source: Statistics Canada, 2003, Cat. No. 97F0020XCB2001008.

First, we need to use the **Select Cases** command to select social science majors for the analysis. Click **Data** from the menu bar of the **Data Editor** window and then click **Select Cases**. The **Select Cases** window appears and presents a number of different options. Click the button next to "If condition is satisfied" and then click on the **If** button. The **Select Cases: If** dialog box will open, where you specify the cases to be included in the analysis. Find and highlight *dgmfsp* (major field of study) from the variable list on the left side of the dialog box, and then click the arrow to move *dgmfsp* into the text box. In this text box, type = **4** immediately to the right of the variable name *dgmfsp*. A value 4 on *dgmfsp* indicates a social science major. The expression ***dgmfsp* = 4** should appear in the text box. Click **Continue,** and then **OK.**

The **Select Cases** command confines all subsequent analysis to this subset of cases, social science majors. This is easily verified, as the status bar at the bottom of the SPSS window displays the message "Filter On." It is important to note that the unselected cases in the data file, while not included in the analysis, do remain in the dataset.

Because the sample of social science majors is small—with fewer than 100 cases—and the population standard deviation is unknown, we'll use the **One-Sample T Test** procedure, covered in Section 8.6, to test if the mean income of a social science majors differs from the mean income of all Canadians. From the main menu bar, click **Analyze, Compare Means,** and then **One-Sample T Test.** The **One-Sample T Test** dialog box will open with the usual list of variables on the left. Find and move the cursor over *totincp* (total income) and click the top arrow in the middle of the window to move *totincp* to the T̲est Variable(s) box. Next, click the **Test Value** box and type 27103. Click **OK** and the following output will be produced. Do not forget to turn filtering off after finishing the **One-Sample T Test** procedure. To do this, return to the **Select Cases** dialog box, select the "**All cases**" button, and then click **OK.**

One-Sample Statistics

	N	Mean	Std. Deviation	Std. Error Mean
Totincp total income $	59	31962.39	20042.041	2609.251

One-Sample Test

	Test Value = 27103					
					95% Confidence Interval of the Difference	
	t	df	Sig. (2-tailed)	Mean Difference	Lower	Upper
Totincp total income $	1.862	58	.068	4859.390	−363.59	10082.37

In the first block of output ("One-Sample Statistics") are some descriptive statistics. There are 59 social science majors with a mean income of $31,962, which is different from the mean income of $27,103 for the general population.

Is the difference in means significant? The results of the test for significance are reported in the next block ("One-Sample Test") of output.

In the second output block, "One-Sample Test," we are given the values of t (obtained) (1.862) and degrees of freedom (58) needed to test if the difference between the sample mean of $31,962 and the population mean of $27,103 is statistically significant. To test for significance, we look up the t (critical) in the t table in Appendix B, and then compare the t (obtained) value to the t (critical) value as practised throughout this chapter.

Because we predicted a direction for this difference (social science majors have higher income than the general population), a one-tailed test in the upper tail of the sampling distribution is justified. With alpha equal to 0.05, our usual indicator of significance, and 58 degrees of freedom, we find the t (critical) is +1.684. (The t table does not include a value for 58 degrees of freedom, so we used the value for 40 degrees of freedom.)

The test statistic, t (obtained), of 1.862 falls into the critical region (i.e., 1.862 is greater than 1.684). We reject the null hypothesis. The difference is statistically significant, and that the research hypothesis social science majors have higher income than the general population is supported.

However, we could have more conveniently used the "Sig. (2-tailed)" value (.068) in the "One-Sample Test" output to test for significance. The value of .068 is an alpha level, except that it is the *exact* probability of getting the observed difference between the sample mean of $31,962 and the population mean of $27,103 if only chance is operating. This value is a two-tailed test of significance. Because we want the value for a one-tailed test, which SPSS does not provide, we simply divide the value by two, or $.068/2 = .034$. This value, 034, is the significance for a one-tailed test. With the exact probability of a one-tailed test now in hand, there is no need to look up the test statistic in the t table. This value, .034, is less than .05 so we reject the null hypothesis.

The critical values for one-tailed tests are always closer to the mean of the sampling distribution, so a one-tailed test is more likely to reject the null hypothesis than a two-tailed test at a set alpha level. In fact, in a two-tailed test, we would fail to reject the null hypothesis that the population of social science majors has an average income that is no different from the average income of the general population since the value for the two-tailed test, .068, is greater than .05.

Exercise (using *Census.sav*)

8.1 Statistics Canada reports that the average age of an adult was 43.9 years in 2001. Are Albertans different from Canadians in general in terms of this characteristic (i.e., are adults in Alberta younger or older than the national average)? Using Demonstration 8.1 as a guide, test for a significant difference between the mean age (*agep*) of the sample of Albertans and the mean age of 43.9 years for the Canadian population. Write a sentence or two summarizing the results of this test. (Make sure to use the **Select Cases** procedure to include only Albertans in the **One-Sample T Test** analysis, and use the two-tailed test.)

9

HYPOTHESIS TESTING II
THE TWO-SAMPLE CASE

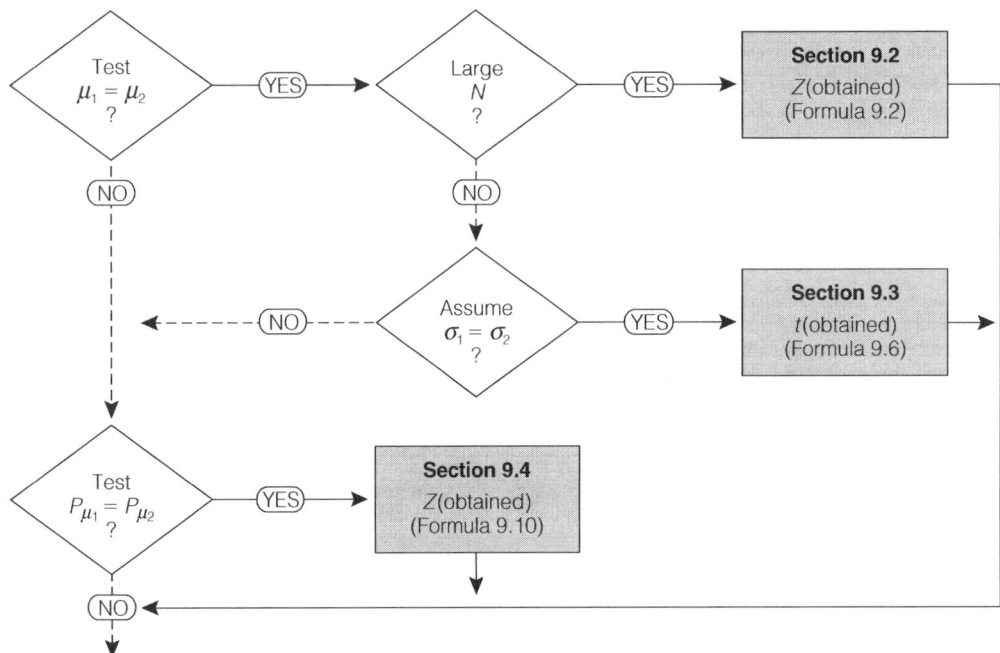

LEARNING OBJECTIVES

By the end of this chapter, you will be able to

1. Identify and cite examples of situations in which the two-sample test of hypothesis is appropriate.
2. Explain the logic of hypothesis testing as applied to the two-sample case.
3. Explain what an independent random sample is.
4. Perform a test of hypothesis for two-sample means or two-sample proportions following the five-step model and correctly interpret the results.
5. Conduct a two-sample hypothesis test using confidence intervals.
6. List and explain each of the factors (especially sample size) that affect the probability of rejecting the null hypothesis and explain the differences between statistical significance and importance.

9.1 INTRODUCTION

In Chapter 8, we dealt with hypothesis testing in the one-sample case. In that situation, our concern was with the significance of the difference between a sample value and a population value. In this chapter, we will consider research situations where we will be concerned with the significance of the difference between two separate populations. For example, in light of recent high-profile incidents of violence involving guns and controversies about the gun registry in Canada, we may ask, do men and women vary in their support for gun control? Obviously, we cannot ask every male and female for their opinions on gun control. Instead, we must draw random samples of both groups and use the information gathered from these samples to infer population patterns.

The central question asked in hypothesis testing in the two-sample case is "Is the difference between the samples large enough to allow us to conclude (with a known probability of error) that the populations represented by the samples are different?" Thus, if we find a large enough difference in support for gun control between random samples of men and women, we can argue that the difference between the samples did not occur by simple random chance but, rather, represents a real difference between men and women in the population.

In this chapter, we will consider tests for the significance of the difference between sample means and sample proportions. In both tests, the five-step model will serve as a framework for organizing our decision-making. The general flow of the hypothesis-testing process is very similar to the one followed in the one-sample case but we will also need to consider some important differences.

9.2 HYPOTHESIS TESTING WITH SAMPLE MEANS (LARGE SAMPLES)

One major difference between the one- and two-sample situations occurs in step 1 of the five-step model. The one-sample case (Chapter 8) requires that the sample be selected following the principle of EPSEM (each case in the population must have an equal chance of being selected for the sample). The two-sample situation requires that the samples be selected independently as well as randomly. This requirement is met when the selection of a case for one sample has no effect on the probability that any particular case will be included in the other sample. In our example concerning gender differences in support of gun control, this would mean that the selection of a specific male for the sample would have no effect on the probability of selecting any particular female. This new requirement will be stated as **independent random sampling** in step 1.

The requirement of independent random sampling can be satisfied by drawing EPSEM samples from separate lists (e.g., one for females and one for males). It is usually more convenient, however, to draw a single EPSEM sample from a single list of the population and then subdivide the cases into separate groups (males and females, for example). As long as the original sample is selected randomly, any subsamples created by the researcher will meet the assumption of independent random samples.

The second important difference in the five-step model for the two-sample case is in the form of the null hypothesis. The null is still a statement of "no difference." Now, however, instead of saying that the population from which the sample is drawn has a certain characteristic, it will say that the two populations are no different. ("There is no significant difference between men and women in their support of gun control.") If the test statistic falls in the critical region, the null hypothesis of no difference between the populations can be rejected, and the argument that the populations are different on the trait of interest will be supported.

A third important new element concerns the sampling distribution: the distribution of all possible sample outcomes. In Chapter 8, the sample outcome was either a mean or a proportion. Now, we are dealing with two samples (e.g., samples of men and women) and the sample outcome is the *difference between* the sample statistics. In terms of our example, the sampling distribution would include all possible differences in sample means for support of gun control between men and women. If the null hypothesis is true and men and women do *not* have different views about gun control, the difference between the population means would be zero, the mean of the sampling distribution will be zero, and the huge majority of differences between sample means would be zero (or, at any rate, very small in value). The greater the differences between the sample means, the further the sample outcome (the *difference* between the two sample means) will be from the mean of the sampling distribution (zero), and the more likely that the difference reflects a real difference between the populations represented by the samples.

To illustrate the procedure for testing sample means we will examine differences of opinion on gun control between men and women using actual data from the 2006 Canadian Election Study, an interuniversity project that regularly conducts a survey of a representative sample of Canadian voters on a variety of political issues. We divided the Canadian Election Study sample by sex, and then computed sample statistics for support of gun control for males and females. A scale was used to measure a person's overall attitude toward gun control, where higher scores indicated greater support of gun control in Canada. Assuming that the scale yields interval-ratio-level data, a test for the significance of the difference in sample means can be conducted.

As long as sample size is large (i.e., as long as the combined number of cases in the two samples exceeds 100), the sampling distribution of the differences in sample means will be normal, and the normal curve (Appendix A) can be used to establish the critical regions. The test statistic, Z(obtained), will be computed by the usual formula: sample outcome (the difference between the sample means) minus the mean of the sampling distribution, divided by the standard deviation of the sampling distribution. The formula is presented as Formula 9.1. Note that numerical subscripts are used to identify the samples and the two populations they represent. The subscript attached to $\sigma(\sigma_{\bar{x}-\bar{x}})$ indicates that we are dealing with the sampling distribution of the *differences* in sample means.

FORMULA 9.1

$$Z(\text{obtained}) = \frac{(\bar{X}_1 - \bar{X}_2) - (\mu_1 - \mu_2)}{\sigma_{\bar{x}-\bar{x}}}$$

where $(\bar{X}_1 - \bar{X}_2)$ = the difference in the sample means
$(\mu_1 - \mu_2)$ = the difference in the population means
$\sigma_{\bar{x}-\bar{x}}$ = the standard deviation of the sampling distribution
of the differences in sample means

The second term in the numerator $(\mu_1 - \mu_2)$, reduces to zero because we assume that the null hypothesis (which will be stated as $H_0: \mu_1 = \mu_2$) is true. Recall that tests of significance are always based on the assumption that the null hypothesis is true. If the means of the two populations are equal, then the term $(\mu_1 - \mu_2)$ will be zero and can be dropped from the equation. In effect, then, the formula we will actually use to compute the test statistic in step 4 will be

FORMULA 9.2

$$Z(\text{obtained}) = \frac{(\bar{X}_1 - \bar{X}_2)}{\sigma_{\bar{x}-\bar{x}}}$$

For large samples, the standard deviation of the sampling distribution of the difference in sample means is defined as

FORMULA 9.3

$$\sigma_{\bar{x}-\bar{x}} = \sqrt{\frac{\sigma_1^2}{N_1} + \frac{\sigma_2^2}{N_2}}$$

Because we will rarely, if ever, be in a position to know the values of the population standard deviations (σ_1 and σ_2), we must use the sample standard deviations, suitably corrected for bias, to estimate them. Formula 9.4 displays the equation used to estimate the standard deviation of the sampling distribution in this situation. This is called a **pooled estimate** because it combines information from both samples.

FORMULA 9.4

$$\sigma_{\bar{x}-\bar{x}} = \sqrt{\frac{s_1^2}{N_1 - 1} + \frac{s_2^2}{N_2 - 1}}$$

The sample outcomes for support of gun control are reported below, and a test for the significance of the difference can now be conducted.

Sample 1 (Men)	Sample 2 (Women)
$\bar{X}_1 = 6.9$	$\bar{X}_2 = 8.2$
$s_1 = 3.8$	$s_2 = 3.6$
$N_1 = 1{,}880$	$N_2 = 2{,}116$

Source: 2006 Canadian Election Study.

We see from the sample statistics that men have a lower average score on the support for gun control scale and are thus less supportive of gun control.

The test of hypothesis will tell us if this difference is large enough to justify the conclusion that it did not occur by random chance alone but rather reflects an actual difference between the populations of men and women on this issue.

Step 1. Making Assumptions and Meeting Test Requirements. Note that, although we now assume that the random samples are independent, the rest of the model is the same as in the one-sample case.

> Model: Independent random samples
> Level of measurement is interval-ratio
> Sampling distribution is normal

Step 2. Stating the Null Hypothesis. The null hypothesis states that the *populations* represented by the samples are not different on this variable. No direction for the difference has been predicted, so a two-tailed test is called for, as reflected in the research hypothesis.

$$H_0: \mu_1 = \mu_2$$
$$(H_1: \mu_1 \neq \mu_2)$$

Step 3. Selecting the Sampling Distribution and Establishing the Critical Region. For large samples, the Z distribution can be used to find areas under the sampling distribution and establish the critical region. Alpha will be set at 0.05.

$$\text{Sampling distribution} = Z \text{ distribution}$$
$$\text{Alpha} = 0.05$$
$$Z(\text{critical}) = \pm 1.96$$

Step 4. Computing the Test Statistic. Because the population standard deviations are unknown, Formula 9.4 will be used to estimate the standard deviation of the sampling distribution. This value will then be substituted into Formula 9.2 and Z(obtained) will be computed.

$$\sigma_{\bar{x}-\bar{x}} = \sqrt{\frac{s_1^2}{N_1 - 1} + \frac{s_2^2}{N_2 - 1}}$$

$$\sigma_{\bar{x}-\bar{x}} = \sqrt{\frac{(3.8)^2}{1,880 - 1} + \frac{(3.6)^2}{2,116 - 1}}$$

$$\sigma_{\bar{x}-\bar{x}} = \sqrt{(0.0077) + (0.0061)}$$

$$\sigma_{\bar{x}-\bar{x}} = \sqrt{0.0138}$$

$$\sigma_{\bar{x}-\bar{x}} = 0.117$$

$$Z(\text{obtained}) = \frac{(\bar{X}_1 - \bar{X}_2)}{\sigma_{\bar{x}-\bar{x}}}$$

$$Z(\text{obtained}) = \frac{6.9 - 8.2}{0.117}$$

$$Z(\text{obtained}) = \frac{-1.3}{0.117}$$

$$Z(\text{obtained}) = -11.11$$

Application 9.1

Most adult smokers started smoking in their teens. Here we will examine if there is a significant difference in the age that Canadians and Americans start smoking. We use real data from the 2002–2003 Joint Canada/United States Survey of Health, conducted by Statistics Canada and the U.S. Centers for Disease Control and Prevention, to compute the mean and standard deviation of age people start smoking ("How old were you when you first started to smoke every day?") for random samples of Canadian and American daily smokers. The sample information is:

Sample 1 (United States)	Sample 2 (Canada)
$\overline{X}_1 = 18.1$	$\overline{X}_2 = 17.4$
$s_1 = 5.0$	$s_2 = 4.7$
$N_1 = 812$	$N_2 = 682$

We can see from the sample results that Americans initiate smoking at a later age. The significance of this difference will be tested following the five-step model.

Step 1. Making Assumptions and Meeting Test Requirements.

Model: Independent random samples
Level of measurement is interval-ratio
Sampling distribution is normal

Step 2. Stating the Null Hypothesis.

$$H_0: \mu_1 = \mu_2$$
$$(H_1: \mu_1 \neq \mu_2)$$

Step 3. Selecting the Sampling Distribution and Establishing the Critical Region.

Sampling distribution = Z distribution
Alpha = 0.05, two-tailed
Z(critical) = ± 1.96

Step 4. Computing the Test Statistic.

$$\sigma_{\overline{x}-\overline{x}} = \sqrt{\frac{s_1^2}{N_1 - 1} + \frac{s_2^2}{N_2 - 1}}$$

$$\sigma_{\overline{x}-\overline{x}} = \sqrt{\frac{(5.0)^2}{812 - 1} + \frac{(4.7)^2}{682 - 1}}$$

$$\sigma_{\overline{x}-\overline{x}} = \sqrt{0.063}$$
$$\sigma_{\overline{x}-\overline{x}} = 0.25$$

$$Z(\text{obtained}) = \frac{(\overline{X}_1 - \overline{X}_2)}{\sigma_{\overline{x}-\overline{x}}}$$

$$Z(\text{obtained}) = \frac{18.1 - 17.4}{0.25}$$

$$Z(\text{obtained}) = \frac{0.70}{0.25}$$
$$Z(\text{obtained}) = 2.8$$

Step 5. Making a Decision and Interpreting the Results of the Test. Comparing the test statistic with the critical region,

$$Z(\text{obtained}) = 2.8$$
$$Z(\text{critical}) = \pm 1.96$$

we would reject the null hypothesis. This test supports the conclusion that Americans and Canadians are different with respect to age at which smoking is initiated. Given the direction of the difference, we also note that Americans are significantly older at smoking initiation.

Source: Statistics Canada, 2002–2003 Joint Canada/United States Survey of Health.

Step 5. Making a Decision and Interpreting the Results of the Test. Comparing the test statistic with the critical region:

$$Z(\text{obtained}) = -11.11$$
$$Z(\text{critical}) = \pm 1.96$$

We see that the Z score clearly falls into the critical region. This outcome indicates that a difference as large as -1.3 ($6.9 - 8.2$) between the sample means is unlikely if the null hypothesis is true. The null hypothesis of no difference can be rejected, and the notion that Canadian men and women are different in terms of their support of gun control is supported. The decision to reject the null hypothesis has only a 0.05 probability (the alpha level) of being incorrect.

Note that the value for Z (obtained) is negative, indicating that men have significantly lower scores than women for support for gun control. The sign of the test statistics reflects our arbitrary decision to label men sample 1 and women sample 2. If we had reversed the labels and called women sample 1 and men sample 2, the sign of the Z (obtained) would have been positive, but its value (11.11) would have been exactly the same, as would our decision in step 5. *(For practice in testing the significance of the difference between sample means for large samples, see problems 9.1 to 9.6, 9.9, and 9.15d to f.)*

9.3 HYPOTHESIS TESTING WITH SAMPLE MEANS (SMALL SAMPLES)

As with single-sample means, when the population standard deviation is unknown and sample size is small (combined N's of less than 100), the Z distribution can no longer be used to find areas under the sampling distribution. Instead, we will use the t distribution to find the critical region and thus to identify unlikely sample outcomes. To utilize the t distribution for testing two sample means, we need to perform one additional calculation and make one additional assumption. The calculation is for degrees of freedom, a quantity required for proper use of the t table (Appendix B). In the two-sample case, degrees of freedom are equal to $N_1 + N_2 - 2$.

The additional assumption is a more complex matter. When samples are small, we must assume that the variances of the populations of interest are equal in order to justify the assumption of a normal sampling distribution and to form a pooled estimate of the standard deviation of the sampling distribution. The assumption of equal variance in the population can be tested by an inferential statistical technique known as the analysis of variance or ANOVA (see Chapter 10). For our purposes here, however, we will simply assume equal population variances without formal testing. This assumption is safe as long as sample sizes are approximately equal.

To illustrate this procedure we will again use real data. Sponsored by the Canada Millennium Scholarship Foundation, the Student Financial Survey is one of the most comprehensive studies to date on the financial circumstances of Canadian post-secondary students. The survey collected information, via the Internet and telephone, from a random sample of 1,500 post-secondary students from across Canada during the 2001–2002 academic year. Here we will use these data to test for a significant difference in GPA (grade point average) between men and women enrolled in graduate programs at the master's level at Canadian universities. The sample statistics computed for random samples of male and female master's students are reported below.

Sample 1 (Men)	Sample 2 (Women)
$\overline{X}_1 = 83.74$	$\overline{X}_2 = 82.16$
$s_1 = 6.59$	$s_2 = 9.35$
$N_1 = 39$	$N_2 = 42$

Source: Canada Millennium Scholarship Foundation, 2001–2002 Student Financial Survey.

With this information, and following the five-step model, a test for the significance of the difference in GPA can now be conducted.

Step 1. Making Assumptions and Meeting Test Requirements. Sample size is small, and the population standard deviation is unknown. Hence, we must assume equal population variances in the model.

> Model: Independent random samples
> Level of measurement is interval-ratio
> Population variances are equal $(\sigma_1^2 = \sigma_2^2)$
> Sampling distribution is normal

Step 2. Stating the Null Hypothesis. Because no direction for the difference has been predicted, a two-tailed test will be used as reflected in the research hypothesis.

$$H_0: \mu_1 = \mu_2$$
$$(H_1: \mu_1 \neq \mu_2)$$

Step 3. Selecting the Sampling Distribution and Establishing the Critical Region. With small samples, the t distribution is used to establish the critical region. Alpha will be set at 0.05, and a two-tailed test will be used.

> Sampling distribution = t distribution
> Alpha = 0.05, two-tailed
> Degrees of freedom = $N_1 + N_2 - 2 = 39 + 42 - 2 = 79$
> t (critical) = ±2.000

Step 4. Computing the Test Statistic. With small samples, a different formula (Formula 9.5) is used for the pooled estimate of the standard deviation of the sampling distribution. This value is then substituted directly into the denominator of the formula for t (obtained) given in Formula 9.6.

FORMULA 9.5

$$\sigma_{\overline{x} - \overline{x}} = \sqrt{\frac{N_1 s_1^2 + N_2 s_2^2}{N_1 + N_2 - 2}} \sqrt{\frac{N_1 + N_2}{N_1 N_2}}$$

$$\sigma_{\overline{x} - \overline{x}} = \sqrt{\frac{(39)(6.59)^2 + (42)(9.35)^2}{39 + 42 - 2}} \sqrt{\frac{39 + 42}{(39)(42)}}$$

$$\sigma_{\bar{x}-\bar{x}} = \sqrt{\frac{5{,}365}{79}} \sqrt{\frac{81}{1{,}638}}$$

$$\sigma_{\bar{x}-\bar{x}} = (8.24)(.22)$$

$$\sigma_{\bar{x}-\bar{x}} = 1.81$$

FORMULA 9.6

$$t(\text{obtained}) = \frac{(\bar{X}_1 - \bar{X}_2)}{\sigma_{\bar{x}-\bar{x}}}$$

$$t(\text{obtained}) = \frac{83.74 - 82.16}{1.81}$$

$$t(\text{obtained}) = \frac{1.58}{1.81}$$

$$t(\text{obtained}) = 0.87$$

Step 5. **Making a Decision and Interpreting the Results of the Test.** Comparing the test statistic with the critical region,

$$t(\text{obtained}) = 0.87$$
$$t(\text{critical}) = \pm 2.00$$

we can see that the test statistic t (obtained) = 0.87 does not fall into the critical region as marked by the t (critical) of ± 2.00. Thus, we fail to reject the null hypothesis. The difference between the sample means is trivial and no greater than what would be expected if the null hypothesis were true and only random chance were operating. Male and female master's students are not significantly different in GPA. The test statistic and sampling distribution are depicted in Figure 9.1. *(For practice in testing the significance of the difference between sample means for small samples, see problems 9.7 and 9.8.)*

FIGURE 9.1   THE SAMPLING DISTRIBUTION WITH CRITICAL REGION AND TEST STATISTIC DISPLAYED

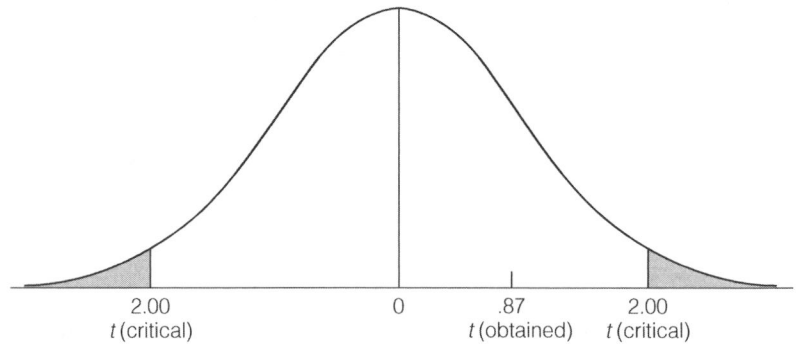

9.4 HYPOTHESIS TESTING WITH SAMPLE PROPORTIONS (LARGE SAMPLES)

Testing for the significance of the difference between two sample proportions is analogous to testing sample means. The null hypothesis states that no difference exists between the populations from which the samples are drawn on the trait being tested. The sample proportions form the basis of the test statistic computed in step 4, which is then compared with the critical region. When sample sizes are large (combined N's of more than 100), the Z distribution may be used to find the critical region. We will not consider tests of significance for proportions based on small samples in this text.

In order to find the value of the test statistics, several preliminary equations must be solved. Formula 9.7 uses the values of the two sample proportions (P_s) to give us an estimate of the population proportion (P_u), the proportion of cases in the population that have the trait under consideration assuming the null hypothesis is true.

FORMULA 9.7
$$P_u = \frac{N_1 P_{s1} + N_2 P_{s2}}{N_1 + N_2}$$

The estimated value of P_u is then used to determine a value for the standard deviation of the sampling distribution of the difference in sample proportions in Formula 9.8:

FORMULA 9.8
$$\sigma_{p-p} = \sqrt{P_u(1 - P_u)} \sqrt{\frac{(N_1 + N_2)}{N_1 N_2}}$$

This value is then substituted into the formula for computing the test statistic, presented as Formula 9.9:

FORMULA 9.9
$$Z\,(\text{obtained}) = \frac{(P_{s1} - P_{s2}) - (P_{u1} - P_{u2})}{\sigma_{p-p}}$$

where $(P_{s1} - P_{s2})$ = the difference between the sample proportions
$(P_{u1} - P_{u2})$ = the difference between the population proportions
σ_{p-p} = the standard deviation of the sampling distribution of the difference between sample proportions

As was the case with sample means, the second term in the numerator is assumed to be zero by the null hypothesis. Therefore, the formula reduces to

FORMULA 9.10
$$Z(\text{obtained}) = \frac{(P_{s1} - P_{s2})}{\sigma_{p-p}}$$

Remember to solve these equations in order, starting with Formula 9.7 (and skipping Formula 9.9).

An example, with actual data, will make these procedures clearer. The prevalence of unmet health care needs is about the same in Canada and the United States: About one in ten adults in each country reports having a recent health care need that went unmet. We speculate, however, that the *reasons* for unmet health care needs are different in each country, and predict that Canadians are significantly more likely than Americans to have an unmet need due to long waiting times for care (waiting times to see a medical specialist or to have a diagnostic test, elective surgery, etc.). Using random samples from the 2002–2003 Joint Canada/United States Survey of Health (a Statistics Canada health survey conducted in partnership with the U.S. Centers for Disease Control and Prevention), the proportion of persons with an unmet health care need due to a waiting time problem in each country is reported below.

Sample 1 (United States)	Sample 2 (Canada)
$P_{s1} = 0.06$	$P_{s2} = 0.31$
$N_1 = 643$	$N_2 = 390$

The sample data reveal a difference in the predicted direction. Of the 643 Americans with unmet health care needs, just 40 (or a proportion of 0.06) reported long waiting times as the reason for their unmet needs. For the 390 Canadians with unmet health care needs, the proportion is 0.31. The significance of this observed difference can be tested with the five-step model.

Step 1. Making Assumptions and Meeting Test Requirements.

Model: Independent random samples
Level of measurement is nominal
Sampling distribution is normal

Step 2. Stating the Null Hypothesis. Because a direction has been predicted (Canadians are more likely to have their needs unmet because of waiting times), a one-tailed test will be used, and the research hypothesis is stated in accordance with this decision.

$$H_0: P_{u1} = P_{u2}$$

$$(H_1: P_{u1} < P_{u2})$$

Step 3. Selecting the Sampling Distribution and Establishing the Critical Region. Because sample size is large, the Z distribution will be used to establish the critical region. Alpha will be set at 0.05 for a one-tailed test.

Sampling distribution = Z distribution
Alpha = 0.05, one-tailed
Z (critical) = -1.65

Step 4. Computing the Test Statistic. Begin with the formula for estimating P_u (Formula 9.7), substitute the resultant value into Formula 9.8, and then solve for Z (obtained) with Formula 9.10.

$$P_u = \frac{N_1 P_{s1} + N_2 P_{s2}}{N_1 + N_2}$$

$$P_u = \frac{(643)(0.06) + (390)(0.31)}{643 + 390}$$

$$P_u = 0.15$$

$$\sigma_{p-p} = \sqrt{P_u(1 - P_u)} \sqrt{\frac{N_1 + N_2}{N_1 N_2}}$$

$$\sigma_{p-p} = \sqrt{(0.15)(0.85)} \sqrt{\frac{643 + 390}{(643)(390)}}$$

$$\sigma_{p-p} = (0.36)(0.06)$$

$$\sigma_{p-p} = 0.02$$

$$Z(\text{obtained}) = \frac{(P_{s1} - P_{s2})}{\sigma_{p-p}}$$

$$Z(\text{obtained}) = \frac{0.06 - 0.31}{0.02}$$

$$Z(\text{obtained}) = -12.5$$

Step 5. **Making a Decision and Interpreting the Results of the Test.** Comparing the test statistic with the critical region,

$$Z(\text{obtained}) = -12.5$$
$$Z(\text{critical}) = -1.65$$

we clearly see that the test statistic falls into the critical region. If the null $(P_{u1} = P_{u2})$ were true, this would be a very unlikely outcome, so the null can be rejected. There is a statistically significant difference between Americans and Canadians (a difference so large that it is unlikely to be due to random chance) in the proportion of those with an unmet health care need due to long waiting times. Specifically, Canadians are significantly more likely than Americans to report this problem. *(For practice in testing the significance of the difference between sample proportions, see problems 9.10 to 9.14 and 9.15a to c.)*

9.5 HYPOTHESIS TESTING USING INDIVIDUAL CONFIDENCE INTERVALS

In Chapter 8 we discussed the direct relationship between the confidence interval and hypothesis testing in the one-sample case. While the objective of each technique is different, they are indeed just different ways of expressing the same information about a single sample. For this reason, a confidence interval can be used as a convenient substitute for hypothesis testing.

In the two-sample case, there is a close, but not direct, relationship between the techniques. We can assess if the difference between two means (or proportions) is statistically significant by examining the overlap of the confidence interval for each mean (or proportion). However, confidence interval overlap is only an approximation of the formal hypothesis testing method discussed in Sections 9.2 through 9.4, and it is not equal to one.

For example, when the 95% confidence intervals for two means *do not overlap,* then the two means *will be* significantly different from one another at the 0.05 level. If the 95% confidence intervals *overlap,* then the difference between the means *will not be* statistically significant at the 0.05 level, most of the time! In other words, the confidence intervals for two means can overlap and yet the two means can be significantly different. The reason you can have an overlap in the individual confidence intervals, yet still find a statistically significant difference, is because each confidence interval takes into account just one sample size and one measure of variability, the single standard deviation, while the formal hypothesis test for the difference between two samples takes into consideration the larger (pooled) variance and sample size of the two samples together. Thus, in the case of an overlap we cannot rely on this method, and instead we must conduct a formal hypothesis test.

As an example of how to assess quickly the significance of the difference between sample means using the overlap of confidence intervals, let us take another look at the gun control example of Section 9.2. Recall that actual data from the Canadian Election Study was used to compute sample statistics for attitudes toward gun control for males and females, where higher scores indicate greater support of gun control, as follows:

Males	Females
$\overline{X}_1 = 6.9$	$\overline{X}_2 = 8.2$
$s_1 = 3.8$	$s_2 = 3.6$
$N_1 = 1,880$	$N_2 = 2,116$

Source: 2006 Canadian Election Study.

Also recall that the decision was to reject the null hypothesis of no difference: Men and women are different in terms of their support of gun control.

Now, let us construct a 95% confidence interval for each sample mean using Formula 7.2 (Chapter 7) as follows.

For males:

$$\text{c.i.} = \overline{X} \pm Z\left(\frac{s}{\sqrt{N-1}}\right)$$

$$\text{c.i.} = 6.9 \pm 1.96\left(\frac{3.8}{\sqrt{1,879}}\right)$$

$$\text{c.i.} = 6.9 \pm (1.96)(0.088)$$

$$\text{c.i.} = 6.9 \pm 0.17$$

For females:

$$\text{c.i.} = \overline{X} \pm Z\left(\frac{s}{\sqrt{N-1}}\right)$$

$$\text{c.i.} = 8.2 \pm 1.96\left(\frac{3.6}{\sqrt{2{,}115}}\right)$$

$$\text{c.i.} = 8.2 \pm (1.96)(0.078)$$

$$\text{c.i.} = 8.2 \pm 0.15$$

Based on these results, we estimate, at the 95% level of confidence, that the population mean for males is greater than or equal to 6.73 and less than or equal to 7.07, and for females is greater than or equal to 8.05 and less than or equal to 8.35. Because the 95% confidence intervals for two means do not overlap, we can reject the null hypothesis of no difference at the 0.05 level. The two means are significantly different from one another—precisely the decision we made above using formal hypothesis testing.

In summary, when confidence intervals do not overlap, the "confidence interval" and the formal hypothesis testing method always lead to the same decision, so either approach can be used as a test for the significance of the difference between sample means or sample proportions. By contrast, when confidence intervals overlap, then the difference between the sample means or sample proportions is most likely (most of the time) not statistically significant. In the case of an overlap we cannot rely on confidence interval overlap to determine statistical significance, and instead must use formal hypothesis testing. To put it briefly, the overlap of confidence intervals should be used only to "eyeball," or roughly estimate, the significance of the difference between sample means or proportions.

9.6 THE LIMITATIONS OF HYPOTHESIS TESTING: SIGNIFICANCE VERSUS IMPORTANCE

Given that we are usually interested in rejecting the null hypothesis, we should take a moment to consider systematically the factors that affect our decision in step 5. Generally speaking, the probability of rejecting the null hypothesis is a function of four independent factors:

1. The size of the observed difference(s)
2. The alpha level
3. The use of one- or two-tailed tests
4. The size of the sample

Only the first of these four is not under the direct control of the researcher. The size of the difference (either between the sample outcome and the population value or between two sample outcomes) is partly a function of the testing procedures (i.e., how variables are measured) but should generally reflect the underlying realities we are trying to probe.

The relationship between alpha level and the probability of rejection is straightforward. The higher the alpha level, the larger the critical region, the

Application 9.2

Over the past two decades, there has been a dramatic increase in obesity throughout the world. In this application we ask whether obesity rates differ between Canada and the United States? Once again, we will use data from the 2002–2003 Joint Canada/United States Survey of Health to compute the proportion of obese persons for each country.

United States	Canada
$P_{s1} = 0.21$	$P_{s2} = 0.15$
$N_1 = 4,971$	$N_2 = 3,369$

This is all the information we will need to conduct a test of the null hypothesis following the familiar five-step model with alpha set at .05, two-tailed test.

Step 1. Making Assumptions and Meeting Test Requirements.

Model: Independent random samples
Level of measurement is nominal
Sampling distribution is normal

Step 2. Stating the Null Hypothesis.

$$H_0: P_{u1} = P_{u2}$$
$$(H_1: P_{u1} \neq P_{u2})$$

Step 3. Selecting the Sampling Distribution and Establishing the Critical Region.

Sampling distribution = Z distribution
Alpha = 0.05, two-tailed
$Z(\text{critical}) = \pm 1.96$

Step 4. Computing the Test Statistic. Remember to start with Formula 9.7, substitute the value for P_u into Formula 9.8, and then substitute that value into Formula 9.10 to solve for Z(obtained).

$$P_u = \frac{N_1 P_{s1} + N_2 P_{s2}}{N_1 + N_2}$$

$$P_u = \frac{(4,971)(0.21) + (3,369)(0.15)}{4,971 + 3,369}$$

$$P_u = \frac{1,549.26}{8,340}$$

$$P_u = 0.19$$

$$\sigma_{p-p} = \sqrt{P_u(1 - P_u)} \sqrt{\frac{N_1 + N_2}{N_1 N_2}}$$

$$\sigma_{p-p} = \sqrt{(0.19)(0.81)} \sqrt{\frac{4,971 + 3,369}{(4,971)(3,369)}}$$

$$\sigma_{p-p} = \sqrt{0.1539} \sqrt{\frac{8,340}{16,747,299}}$$

$$\sigma_{p-p} = \sqrt{0.1539} \sqrt{0.0005}$$

$$\sigma_{p-p} = (0.39)(0.022)$$

$$\sigma_{p-p} = 0.009$$

$$Z(\text{obtained}) = \frac{(P_{s1} - P_{s2})}{\sigma_{p-p}}$$

$$Z(\text{obtained}) = \frac{0.21 - 0.15}{0.009}$$

$$Z(\text{obtained}) = \frac{0.06}{0.009}$$

$$Z(\text{obtained}) = 6.67$$

Step 5. Making a Decision and Interpreting the Results of the Test. With an obtained Z score of 6.67, we would reject the null hypothesis. There is a statistically significant difference between the United States and Canada in their obesity rates.

Source: Statistics Canada, 2002–2003 Joint Canada/United States Survey of Health.

higher the percentage of all possible sample outcomes that fall in the critical region, and the greater the probability of rejection. Thus, it is easier to reject the H_0 at the 0.05 level than at the 0.01 level, and easier still at the 0.10 level. The danger here, of course, is that higher alpha levels will lead to more frequent Type I errors, and we might find ourselves declaring small differences to be statistically significant. In similar fashion, using a one-tailed test will increase the probability of rejection (assuming that the proper direction has been predicted).

The final factor is sample size: With all other factors constant, the probability of rejecting H_0 increases with sample size. In other words, the larger the sample, the more likely we are to reject the null hypothesis and, with very large samples (say samples with thousands of cases), we may declare small, unimportant differences to be statistically significant.

This relationship may appear to be surprising but the reasons for it can be appreciated with a brief consideration of the formulas used to compute test statistics in step 4. In all these formulas, for all tests of significance, sample size (N) is in the "denominator of the denominator." Algebraically, this is equivalent to being in the numerator of the formula and means that the value of the test statistic is directly proportional to N and that the two will increase together. To illustrate, consider Table 9.1, which shows the value of the test statistic for single sample means from samples of various sizes. The value of the test statistic, Z(obtained), increases as N increases even though none of the other terms in the formula changes. This pattern of higher probabilities for rejecting H_0 with larger samples holds for all tests of significance.

On one hand, the relationship between sample size and the probability of rejecting the null should not alarm us unduly. Larger samples are, after all, better approximations of the populations they represent. Thus, decisions based on larger samples can be trusted more than decisions based on small samples.

On the other hand, this relationship clearly underlines what is perhaps the most significant limitation of hypothesis testing. Simply because a difference is statistically significant does not guarantee that it is important in any other sense. Particularly with very large samples, relatively small differences may be statistically significant. Even with small samples, of course, differences that are otherwise trivial or uninteresting may be statistically significant. The crucial point is that statistical significance and theoretical or practical importance can be two very different things. Statistical significance is a necessary but not sufficient condition for theoretical or practical importance. A difference that is not statistically significant is almost certainly unimportant. However, significance by itself does not guarantee importance. Even when it is clear that the research results were not produced by random chance, the researcher must still assess their importance. Do they firmly support a theory or hypothesis? Are they clearly consistent with a prediction or analysis? Do they strongly indicate a line of action in solving some problem? These are the kinds of questions a researcher must ask when assessing the importance of the results of a statistical test.

Also, we should note that researchers have access to some very powerful ways of analyzing the importance (vs. the statistical significance) of research results. These statistics, including bivariate measures of association and multivariate statistical techniques, will be introduced in Parts III and IV of this text.

TABLE 9.1 TEST STATISTICS FOR SINGLE-SAMPLE MEANS COMPUTED FROM SAMPLES OF VARIOUS SIZES ($\bar{X} = 80$, $\mu = 79$, $s = 5$ throughout)

Sample Size	Test Statistic, Z(Obtained)
100	1.99
200	2.82
500	4.47

9.7 INTERPRETING STATISTICS: ARE THERE SIGNIFICANT DIFFERENCES IN INCOME BETWEEN MEN AND WOMEN?

In Canada, as in many other nations around the globe, concerted efforts have been made to equalize working conditions for men and women. How successful have these efforts been? Do significant differences in the income of men and women persist? Is there a "gender gap" in income?

We will investigate the relationship between gender and personal income using randomly selected samples of men and women from the full 2001 Census of Canada database provided with this text. If the difference between the samples of men and women is large enough, we can infer that there is a difference in average income between men and women in the population.

Before conducting the test, we need to deal with an important issue. We should not compare the personal incomes of all men and all women because some difference could be caused by the fact that women are less likely to be in the paid labour market (i.e., they may be occupied as wives and mothers) and, thus, less likely to have an income. We will deal with this by restricting the comparison to respondents who work full-time.

To test for the significance of the difference in personal income, the following sample information was calculated:

Males	Females
$\overline{X}_1 = 43,681$	$\overline{X}_2 = 31,875$
$s_1 = 33,038$	$s_2 = 20,952$
$N_1 = 200,706$	$N_2 = 145,108$

Source: Statistics Canada, 2001 Census of Canada, individual PUMF.

It appears that there is a gender gap and that, on the average, males earn more than females. Is this difference in sample means between males and females significant? Could it have occurred by random chance?

Because we are dealing with large samples, we use the test of significance described in Section 9.2. The null hypothesis is that males and females have the same average income in the population ($\mu_1 = \mu_2$). We will skip the customary trip through the five-step model and simply report that the Z(obtained) calculated with Formula 9.2 (step 4) is 119.81, much greater than the customary Z(critical) score of ± 1.96 associated with an alpha level of 0.05. The difference in sample means is so large that we must reject the null hypothesis and conclude (with a probability of error of 0.05) that the population means are different: Males earn significantly more than females.

The large obtained Z score reflects in part the large sample size of the 2001 Census. We explained in the previous section that the probability of rejecting the null hypothesis increases with sample size. The obtained Z score and probability of rejecting the null hypothesis are further influenced by the size of the observed difference in means, and the census data show that men earn much more on average than women. We can conclude, then, the results are significant, and that they are likely to be important given that males earn on the average almost $12,000 a year more than females.

Why does a significant gender gap in income exist? Is it the result of differences in levels of education? If females were significantly less educated than males, this would account for at least some of the difference in income. We will again use the 2001 Census of Canada to get information on years of education for random samples of males and females.

The census measures education with a series of categories rather than in actual years. Respondents were asked to choose from a list of education ranges, for example, less than grade 5, 5 to 8 years, and so forth. (See the "totschp" variable in Appendix G for the complete scale.) Education is measured at the ordinal level, and we need an interval-ratio dependent variable to test for the significance of the difference between sample means.

One way to deal with this problem is simply to treat the ordinal variable as an interval-ratio variable. Another approach, the one used here, is to convert the variable to a form that more closely approximates interval-ratio data by substituting the midpoints for each interval of the variable. Instead of working with the interval "less than grade 5," we let the midpoint (i.e., 2 years) stand for the interval. The midpoint 6.5 is used for the "5 to 8 years" interval, and so on.

While this technique makes education a more numerical variable, it creates possible inaccuracies. Estimates of the population parameters from this modified variable should be treated only as gross approximations. Because we are concerned with difference in education rather than actual education itself, we should nonetheless be able to develop some conclusions:

Males	Females
$\overline{X}_1 = 13.67$	$\overline{X}_2 = 14.05$
$s_1 = 3.54$	$s_2 = 3.28$
$N_1 = 200,706$	$N_2 = 145,108$

Source: Statistics Canada, 2001 Census of Canada, individual PUMF.

We can see that both males and females average more than 13 years of schooling (one-and-a-half to two years more than a high school education) and that the average for females is actually higher than the average for males. The test statistic computed in step 4 is a Z(obtained) of -59.9. The test statistic is in the critical region, as marked by a Z(critical) score of ± 1.96 at the 0.05 level, so we reject the null hypothesis of no difference. Males and females differ in levels of schooling in the population: Females are significantly better educated than males. These results suggest that females are getting a lower return in income for their education, and that education is unlikely to account for the difference in income.

If not education, what else might explain the significant income gap between males and females? To answer this question entirely is far beyond the bounds of this statistics text. We can suggest that one important part of the answer lies in the fact that men and women pursue different kinds of careers and jobs. Men tend to dominate the more lucrative, higher-prestige occupations while women are concentrated in jobs that have lower levels of remuneration. According to the 2001 Census of Canada, over half of all women in the paid labour force work in either clerical or unskilled sales and service jobs, which tend to provide low wages. Just over 20% of all men work in these occupations.

READING STATISTICS 6: Hypothesis Testing

Professional researchers use a vocabulary that is much terser than ours when presenting the results of tests of significance. This is partly because of space limitations in scientific journals and partly because professional researchers can assume a certain level of statistical literacy in their audiences. Thus, they omit many of the elements—such as the null hypothesis or the critical region—that we have been so careful to state.

Instead, researchers report only the sample values (for example, means or proportion), the value of the test statistic (for example, a Z or t score), the alpha level, the degrees of freedom (if applicable), and sample size. The results of a study on number of children in suburban vs centre-city families might be reported as "the difference between the sample means of 2.37 (suburban families) and 2.78 (centre-city families) was tested and found to be significant ($t = -2.16$, df $= 77$, $p < 0.05$)." Note that the alpha level is reported as "$p < 0.05$." This is shorthand for "the probability of a difference of this magnitude occurring by chance alone, if the null hypothesis of no difference is true, is less than 0.05" and is a good illustration of how researchers can convey a great deal of information in just a few symbols. In a similar fashion, our somewhat long-winded phrase "the test statistic falls in the critical region and, therefore, the null hypothesis is rejected" is rendered tersely and simply: "the difference . . . was . . . found to be significant."

When researchers need to report the results of many tests of significance, they will often use a summary table to report the sample information and whether the difference is significant at a certain alpha level. If you read the researcher's description and analysis of such tables, you should have little difficulty interpreting and understanding them. As a final note, these comments about how significance tests are reported in the literature apply to all of the tests of hypotheses covered in Part II of this text.

Statistics in the Professional Literature

Canadian education researcher J. Douglas Willms examined reading performances of youth in Canada and the United States using data from PISA (Programme for International Student Assessment). PISA is an international study of literacy skills of 15-year-old students. Students are selected following the principles of EPSEM. For more information on PISA, see Chapter 4.

Table 1 shows that Canadian youth outperform their American counterparts. The average PISA test score in overall reading literacy is 534 for Canadian students compared to 504 for U.S. students. Willms reports that the difference is statistically significant at $p < 0.05$.

Willms points out that the difference is also meaningful and important. A mean difference in reading scores of 30 points between Canadian and U.S. youth (534 versus 504) is equivalent to almost one full year of schooling. Canadian 15-year-olds are a full year ahead of American 15-year-olds in reading literacy skills.

TABLE 1 TEST SCORES FOR READING LITERACY, BY COUNTRY

Canada	United States
$\bar{X}_1 = 534^*$	$\bar{X}_2 = 504^*$
$s_1 = 95$	$s_2 = 105$
$N_1 = 29{,}461$	$N_2 = 3{,}700$

$^*p < 0.05$

Source: Willms, J. D. 2004. *Reading Achievement in Canada and the United States: Findings from the OECD Programme for International Student Assessment.* Human Resources Skills and Development Canada. Catalogue no. HS28-3/2004E.

SUMMARY

1. A common research situation is to test for the significance of the difference between two populations. Sample statistics are calculated for random samples of each population, and then we test for the significance of the difference between the samples as a way of inferring differences between the specified populations.

2. When sample information is summarized in the form of sample means, and N is large, the Z distribution is used to find the critical region. When N is small, the t distribution is used to establish the critical region. In the latter circumstance, we must also assume equal population variances before forming a pooled estimate of the standard deviation of the sampling distribution.

3. Differences in sample proportions may also be tested for significance. For large samples, the Z distribution is used to find the critical region.

4. A two-sample hypothesis test can be approximated using confidence intervals. When the confidence intervals for two samples do not overlap, then the null hypothesis of no difference between the populations will be rejected at the stated alpha level. If the confidence intervals overlap, then the difference will not be statistically significant most of the time. Hence, in the case of an overlap, we must further conduct the two-sample hypothesis test described in this chapter.

5. In all tests of hypothesis, a number of factors affect the probability of rejecting the null: the size of the difference, the alpha level, the use of one-versus two-tailed tests, and sample size. Statistical significance is not the same thing as theoretical or practical importance. Even after a difference is found to be statistically significant, the researcher must still demonstrate the relevance or importance of his or her findings. The statistics presented in Parts III and IV of this text will give us the tools we need to deal directly with issues beyond statistical significance.

SUMMARY OF FORMULAS

Test statistic for two sample means, large samples:

$$9.1 \qquad Z(\text{obtained}) = \frac{(\bar{X}_1 - \bar{X}_2) - (\mu_1 - \mu_2)}{\sigma_{\bar{x} - \bar{x}}}$$

Test statistic for two sample means, large samples (simplified formula):

$$9.2 \qquad Z(\text{obtained}) = \frac{(\bar{X}_1 - \bar{X}_2)}{\sigma_{\bar{x} - \bar{x}}}$$

Standard deviation of the sampling distribution of the difference in sample means, large samples:

$$9.3 \qquad \sigma_{\bar{x} - \bar{x}} = \sqrt{\frac{\sigma_1^2}{N_1} + \frac{\sigma_2^2}{N_2}}$$

Pooled estimate of the standard deviation of the sampling distribution of the difference in sample means, large samples:

$$9.4 \qquad \sigma_{\bar{x} - \bar{x}} = \sqrt{\frac{s_1^2}{N_1 - 1} + \frac{s_2^2}{N_2 - 1}}$$

Pooled estimate of the standard deviation of the sampling distribution of the difference in sample means, small samples:

$$9.5 \qquad \sigma_{\bar{x} - \bar{x}} = \sqrt{\frac{N_1 s_1^2 + N_2 s_2^2}{N_1 + N_2 - 2}} \sqrt{\frac{N_1 + N_2}{N_1 N_2}}$$

Test statistic for two sample means, small samples:

$$9.6 \qquad t(\text{obtained}) = \frac{(\bar{X}_1 - \bar{X}_2)}{\sigma_{\bar{x} - \bar{x}}}$$

Pooled estimate of population proportion, large samples:

$$9.7 \qquad P_u = \frac{N_1 P_{s1} + N_2 P_{s2}}{N_1 + N_2}$$

Standard deviation of the sampling distribution of the difference in sample proportions, large samples:

$$9.8 \qquad \sigma_{p - p} = \sqrt{P_u(1 - P_u)} \sqrt{\frac{N_1 + N_2}{N_1 N_2}}$$

Test statistic for two sample proportions, large samples:

9.9 $\qquad Z\,(\text{obtained}) = \dfrac{(P_{s1} - P_{s2}) - (P_{u1} - P_{u2})}{\sigma_{p-p}}$

Test statistic for two sample proportions, large samples (simplified formula):

9.10 $\qquad Z\,(\text{obtained}) = \dfrac{(P_{s1} - P_{s2})}{\sigma_{p-p}}$

GLOSSARY

Independent random samples. Random samples gathered in such a way that the selection of a particular case for one sample has no effect on the probability that any particular case will be selected for the other samples.

Pooled estimate. An estimate of the standard deviation of the sampling distribution of the difference

in sample means based on the standard deviations of both samples.

σ_{p-p}. Symbol for the standard deviation of the sampling distribution of the differences in sample proportions.

$\sigma_{\bar{x}-\bar{x}}$. Symbol for the standard deviation of the sampling distribution of the differences in sample means.

MULTIMEDIA RESOURCES

http://www.healeystatistics.nelson.com

Visit the companion Web site for the first Canadian edition of *Statistics: A Tool for Social Research* to access a wide range of student resources. Begin by clicking on the Student Resources section of the book's Web site to access review quizzes, flash cards, and other study tools.

PROBLEMS

9.1 For each problem below, test for the significance of the difference in sample statistics using the five-step model. *(HINT: Remember to solve Formula 9.4 before attempting to solve Formula 9.2. Also, in Formula 9.4, perform the mathematical operations in the proper sequence. First square each sample standard deviation, then divide by N − 1, add the resultant values, and then find the square root of the sum.)*

a.

Sample 1	Sample 2
$\bar{X}_1 = 72.5$	$\bar{X}_2 = 76.0$
$s_1 = 14.3$	$s_2 = 10.2$
$N_1 = 136$	$N_2 = 257$

b.

Sample 1	Sample 2
$\bar{X}_1 = 107$	$\bar{X}_2 = 103$
$s_1 = 14$	$s_2 = 17$
$N_1 = 175$	$N_2 = 200$

9.2 [SOC] Questionnaires were administered to samples of undergraduate students. Among other things, the questionnaires contained a scale that measured attitudes toward interpersonal violence (higher scores indicate greater approval of interpersonal violence). Test the results as reported below for differences in sex and social-class background.

a.

Sample 1 (Males)	Sample 2 (Females)
$\bar{X}_1 = 2.99$	$\bar{X}_2 = 2.99$
$s_1 = 0.88$	$s_2 = 0.91$
$N_1 = 122$	$N_2 = 251$

b.

Sample 1 (White Collar)	Sample 2 (Blue Collar)
$\bar{X}_1 = 2.46$	$\bar{X}_2 = 2.67$
$s_1 = 0.91$	$s_2 = 0.87$
$N_1 = 249$	$N_2 = 97$

c. Summarize your results in terms of the significance and the direction of the differences. Which of these two factors seems to make the biggest difference in attitudes toward interpersonal violence?

9.3 | SOC | Do athletes in different sports vary in terms of intelligence? Below are aptitude test scores of random samples of university varsity hockey and football players. Is there a significant difference? Write a sentence or two explaining the difference.

a.

Sample 1 (Hockey Players)	Sample 2 (Football Players)
$\bar{X}_1 = 460$	$\bar{X}_2 = 442$
$s_1 = 92$	$s_2 = 57$
$N_1 = 102$	$N_2 = 117$

What about male and female university athletes?

b.

Sample 1 (Males)	Sample 2 (Females)
$\bar{X}_1 = 452$	$\bar{X}_2 = 480$
$s_1 = 88$	$s_2 = 75$
$N_1 = 107$	$N_2 = 105$

9.4 | PA | A number of years ago, the fire department in Pearson, Ontario began recruiting females through an employment equity program. In terms of efficiency ratings as compiled by their superiors, how do the employment equity employees rate? The ratings of random samples of both groups were collected, and the results are reported below (higher ratings indicate greater efficiency).

Sample 1 (Employment Equity)	Sample 2 (Regular)
$\bar{X}_1 = 15.2$	$\bar{X}_2 = 15.5$
$s_1 = 3.9$	$s_2 = 2.0$
$N_1 = 97$	$N_2 = 100$

Write a sentence or two of interpretation.

9.5 | SOC | Are middle-class families more likely than working-class families to maintain contact with kin? Write a paragraph summarizing the results of these tests.

a. A sample of middle-class families reported an average of 7.3 visits per year with close kin while a sample of working-class families averaged 8.2 visits. Is the difference significant?

Visits	
Sample 1 (Middle Class)	Sample 2 (Working Class)
$\bar{X}_1 = 7.3$	$\bar{X}_2 = 8.2$
$s_1 = 0.3$	$s_2 = 0.5$
$N_1 = 89$	$N_2 = 55$

b. The middle-class families averaged 2.3 phone calls and 8.7 e-mail messages per month with close kin. The working-class families averaged 2.7 calls and 5.7 e-mail messages per month. Are these differences significant?

Phone Calls	
Sample 1 (Middle Class)	Sample 2 (Working Class)
$\bar{X}_1 = 3$	$\bar{X}_2 = 2.7$
$s_1 = 0.5$	$s_2 = 0.8$
$N_1 = 89$	$N_2 = 55$

E-mail Messages	
Sample 1 (Middle Class)	Sample 2 (Working Class)
$\bar{X}_1 = 8.7$	$\bar{X}_2 = 5.7$
$s_1 = 0.3$	$s_2 = 1.1$
$N_1 = 89$	$N_2 = 55$

9.6 | SOC | Are university students who live in residence significantly more involved in campus life than students who commute to campus? The data below report the average number of hours per week students devote to extracurricular activities. Is the difference between these randomly selected samples of commuter and residential students significant?

Sample 1 (Residential)	Sample 2 (Commuter)
$\bar{X}_1 = 12.4$	$\bar{X}_2 = 10.2$
$s_1 = 2.0$	$s_2 = 1.9$
$N_1 = 158$	$N_2 = 173$

9.7 | SOC | Are senior citizens who live in retirement communities more socially active than those who live in age-integrated communities? Write a sentence or two explaining the results of these tests. *(HINT: Remember to use the proper formulas for small sample sizes.)*

a. A random sample of senior citizens living in a retirement village reported that they had an average of 1.42 face-to-face interactions per day with their neighbours. A random sample of those living in age-integrated communities reported 1.58 interactions. Is the difference significant?

Sample 1 (Retirement Community)	Sample 2 (Age-integrated Neighbourhood)
$\bar{X}_1 = 1.42$	$\bar{X}_2 = 1.58$
$s_1 = 0.10$	$s_2 = 0.78$
$N_1 = 43$	$N_2 = 37$

b. Senior citizens living in the retirement village reported that they had 7.43 telephone calls with friends and relatives each week while those in the age-integrated communities reported 5.50 calls. Is the difference significant?

Sample 1 (Retirement Community)	Sample 2 (Age-integrated Neighbourhood)
$\bar{X}_1 = 7.43$	$\bar{X}_2 = 5.50$
$s_1 = 0.75$	$s_2 = 0.25$
$N_1 = 43$	$N_2 = 37$

9.8 SW As the director of the local Youth Club, you have claimed for years that membership in your club reduces juvenile delinquency. Now, a cynical member of your funding agency has demanded proof of your claim. Fortunately, your local sociology department is on your side and springs to your aid with student assistants, computers, and hand calculators at the ready. Random samples of members and non-members are gathered and interviewed with respect to their involvement in delinquent activities. Each respondent is asked to enumerate the number of delinquent acts he or she has engaged in over the past year. The results are in and reported below (the average number of admitted acts of delinquency). What can you tell the funding agency?

Sample 1 (Members)	Sample 2 (Non-members)
$\bar{X}_1 = 10.3$	$\bar{X}_2 = 12.3$
$s_1 = 2.7$	$s_2 = 4.2$
$N_1 = 40$	$N_2 = 55$

9.9 SOC A survey has been administered to random samples of respondents in each of five nations. For each nation, are men and women significantly different in terms of their reported levels of satisfaction? Respondents were asked: "How satisfied are you with your life as a whole?" Responses varied from 1 (very dissatisfied) to 10 (very satisfied). Conduct a test for the significance of the difference in mean scores for each nation.

Canada	
Males	Females
$\bar{X}_1 = 7.4$	$\bar{X}_2 = 7.7$
$s_1 = .20$	$s_2 = .25$
$N_1 = 1,005$	$N_2 = 1,234$

Nigeria	
Males	Females
$\bar{X}_1 = 6.7$	$\bar{X}_2 = 7.8$
$s_1 = .16$	$s_2 = .23$
$N_1 = 1,825$	$N_2 = 1,256$

China	
Males	Females
$\bar{X}_1 = 7.6$	$\bar{X}_2 = 7.1$
$s_1 = .21$	$s_2 = .11$
$N_1 = 1,400$	$N_2 = 1,200$

Mexico	
Males	Females
$\bar{X}_1 = 8.3$	$\bar{X}_2 = 9.1$
$s_1 = .29$	$s_2 = .30$
$N_1 = 1,645$	$N_2 = 1,432$

Japan	
Males	Females
$\bar{X}_1 = 8.8$	$\bar{X}_2 = 9.3$
$s_1 = .34$	$s_2 = .32$
$N_1 = 1,621$	$N_2 = 1,683$

9.10 For each problem, test the sample statistics for the significance of the difference. *(HINT: In testing proportions, remember to begin with Formula 9.7, then solve Formulas 9.8 and 9.10.)*

a.

Sample 1	Sample 2
$P_{s1} = 0.17$	$P_{s2} = 0.20$
$N_1 = 101$	$N_2 = 114$

b.

Sample 1	Sample 2
$P_{s1} = 0.62$	$P_{s2} = 0.60$
$N_1 = 532$	$N_2 = 478$

9.11 CJ About half of the police officers in Pearson, Ontario have completed a special course in investigative procedures. Has the course increased their efficiency in clearing crimes by arrest? The proportions of cases cleared by arrest for samples of trained and untrained officers are reported below.

Trained	Untrained
$P_{s1} = 0.47$	$P_{s2} = 0.43$
$N_1 = 157$	$N_2 = 113$

9.12 SW A large counselling centre needs to evaluate several experimental programs. Write a paragraph summarizing the results of these tests. Did the new programs work?

a. One program is designed for divorce counselling; the key feature of the program is its counsellors, who are married couples working in teams. About half of all clients have been randomly assigned to this special program and half to the regular program, and the proportion of cases that eventually ended in divorce was recorded for both. The results for random samples of couples from both programs are reported below. In terms of preventing divorce, did the new program work?

Special Program	Regular Program
$P_{s1} = 0.53$	$P_{s2} = 0.59$
$N_1 = 78$	$N_2 = 82$

b. The agency is also experimenting with peer counselling for depressed children. About half of all clients were randomly assigned to peer counselling. After the program had run for a year, a random sample of children from the new program were compared with a random sample of children who did not receive peer counselling. In terms of the percentage who were judged to be "much improved," did the new program work?

Peer Counselling	No Peer Counselling
$P_{s1} = 0.10$	$P_{s2} = 0.15$
$N_1 = 52$	$N_2 = 56$

9.13 SOC At Algebra University, the sociology and psychology departments have been feuding for years about the respective quality of their programs. In an attempt to resolve the dispute, you have gathered data about the graduate school experience of random samples of both groups of majors. The results are presented below: the proportion of majors who applied to graduate schools, the proportion of majors accepted into their preferred programs, and the proportion of these who completed their programs. As measured by these data, is there a significant difference in program quality?

a. Proportion of majors who applied to graduate school:

Sociology	Psychology
$P_{s1} = 0.53$	$P_{s2} = 0.40$
$N_1 = 150$	$N_2 = 175$

b. Proportion accepted by program of first choice:

Sociology	Psychology
$P_{s1} = 0.75$	$P_{s2} = 0.85$
$N_1 = 80$	$N_2 = 70$

c. Proportion completing the programs:

Sociology	Psychology
$P_{s1} = 0.75$	$P_{s2} = 0.69$
$N_1 = 60$	$N_2 = 60$

9.14 CJ The local police chief started a "crimeline" program some years ago and wonders if it's really working. The program publicizes unsolved violent crimes in the local media and offers cash rewards for information leading to arrests. Are "featured" crimes more likely to be cleared by arrest than other violent crimes? Results from random samples of both types of crimes are reported as follows:

Crimeline Crimes Cleared by Arrest	Non-crimeline Crimes Cleared by Arrest
$P_{s1} = 0.35$	$P_{s2} = 0.25$
$N_1 = 178$	$N_2 = 212$

9.15 SOC Some results from a recent social survey administered to a random sample of adults are reported below in terms of differences by sex. Which of these differences, if any, are significant? Write a sentence or two of interpretation for each test.

a. Proportion favouring the legalization of marijuana:

Sample 1 (Males)	Sample 2 (Females)
$P_{s1} = 0.37$	$P_{s2} = 0.31$
$N_1 = 202$	$N_2 = 246$

b. Proportion strongly agreeing that "kids are life's greatest joy":

Sample 1 (Males)	Sample 2 (Females)
$P_{s1} = 0.47$	$P_{s2} = 0.58$
$N_1 = 251$	$N_2 = 351$

c. Proportion voting in the last federal election:

Sample 1 (Males)	Sample 2 (Females)
$P_{s1} = 0.59$	$P_{s2} = 0.47$
$N_1 = 399$	$N_2 = 509$

d. Average hours spent with e-mail each week:

Sample 1 (Males)	Sample 2 (Females)
$\bar{X}_1 = 4.18$	$\bar{X}_2 = 3.38$
$s_1 = 7.21$	$s_2 = 5.92$
$N_1 = 431$	$N_2 = 535$

e. Average number of times religious service attended each month:

Sample 1 (Males)	Sample 2 (Females)
$\bar{X}_1 = 3.19$	$\bar{X}_2 = 3.99$
$s_1 = 2.60$	$s_2 = 2.72$
$N_1 = 641$	$N_2 = 808$

f. Average number of children:

Sample 1 (Males)	Sample 2 (Females)
$\bar{X}_1 = 1.49$	$\bar{X}_2 = 1.93$
$s_1 = 1.50$	$s_2 = 1.50$
$N_1 = 635$	$N_2 = 803$

SPSS for Windows

Using SPSS for Windows to Test the Significance of the Difference between Two Means with the 2004 GSS

The demonstrations and exercises below use the 2004 GSS data set supplied with this text.

SPSS DEMONSTRATION 9.1 Do Men and Women Differ in Social Activity?

SPSS for Windows includes several tests for the significance of the difference between means. In this demonstration, we'll use the **Independent-Samples T Test,** the test we covered in Sections 9.2 and 9.3, to test for the significance of the difference between men and women in how often they go out in the evening to engage in leisure activities such as visiting friends or going to a bar, restaurant, movie, casino, shopping mall, or gym? If there is a statistically significant difference between the sample means for men and women, we can conclude that the populations (all Canadian adult men and women) are different on this variable.

Start SPSS for Windows and load the 2004 GSS database (*GSS.sav*). From the main menu bar, click **Analyze,** then **Compare Means,** and then **Independent-Samples T Test.** The **Independent-Samples T Test** dialog box will open with the usual list of variables on the left. Find and move the cursor over *numevact_c* (average number of evening activities respondent goes out for in a month) and click the top arrow in the middle of the window to move *numevact_c* to the **Test Variable(s)** box. Next, find and highlight *sex* and click the button arrow in the middle of the window to move *sex* to the **Grouping Variable** box. Two question marks will appear in the **Grouping Variable** box, and the **Define Groups** button will become active. SPSS needs to know which cases go in which groups, and in the case at hand, the instructions we need to supply are straightforward. Males (indicated by a score of 1 on *sex*) go into group 1 and females (a score of 2) will go into group 2.

Click the **Define Groups** button, and the **Define Groups** window will appear. The cursor will be blinking in the box beside Group 1—SPSS is asking for the score that will determine which cases go into this group. Type a 1 in this box (for males) and then click the box next to Group 2 and type a 2 (for females). Click **Continue** to return to the **Independent-Samples T Test** window and click **OK** and the output below will be produced.

Group Statistics

	Sex	N	Mean	Std. Deviation	Std. Error Mean
Average number of evening activities respondent goes out for in a month	Male	799	28.06	16.606	.588
	Female	721	23.66	16.421	.612

Independent Samples Test

		Levene's Test for Equality of Variances		*t*-test for Equality of Means						
									95% Confidence interval of the Difference	
		F	Sig.	t	df	Sig. (2-tailed)	Mean Difference	Std. Error Difference	Lower	Upper
Average number of evening activities respondent goes out for in a month.	Equal variances assumed	.020	.888	5.192	1517	.000	4.406	.849	2.742	6.071
	Equal variances not assumed			5.195	1504.855	.000	4.406	.848	2.743	6.070

In the first block of output ("Group Statistics") are some descriptive statistics. There were 799 males in the sample, and they participated in 28.06 activities during the evening in an average month, with a standard deviation of 16.606. The 721 females went out an average of 23.66 times per month with a standard deviation of 23.66.

We can see from this output that the sample means are different and that, on the average, males go out in the evening more often. Is the difference in sample means significant? The results of the test for significance are reported in the next block ("Independent Samples Test") of output.

We will skip over the first two columns of this block for now, which report the results of a test for equality of the population variances. Results in the remaining columns in the row labelled "Equal variances assumed" are based on the same model used in this chapter. To test the significance of the difference between two means we can either manually look up the t value (5.192) in the t table (Appendix B), as practised throughout this chapter, or more conveniently use the "Sig. (2-tailed)" value (.000), where "Sig." means significance. The value of .000 is the alpha level, except it is the *exact probability* of getting the observed difference in sample means if only chance is operating. Thus it is often called the "p" level (see the Reading Statistics 6 box). However, do not interpret .000 as a zero probability. It simply means that the exact probability value is less than .0005. In this example, the exact value is .0000002, which is revealed by double-clicking on the "Sig. (2-tailed)" value in the output, but to save space, SPSS cuts it off at three decimal places, or .000.

Because SPSS provides the exact probability (cut off at three decimal places), there is no need to look up the test statistic in a t table. This value (.000, or more precisely .0000002) is less than .05, our usual indicator of significance, so we reject the null hypothesis and conclude that the difference in means is statistically significant. On the average, men and women do differ significantly in how often they go out in the evening.

These results are based on the assumption that the population variances are equal. In Section 9.3 we noted that this assumption is safe as long as sample sizes are approximately equal, as they are in this case. However, SPSS for Windows provides a *formal* test for equal variances in the population: Levene's Test for Equality of Variances. If the Levene's Test for Equality of Variances is significant (i.e., if the value under the "Sig." column is less than .05, as per our usual indicator of significance), the variances are significantly different. If this is the case, a modified t test should be used, which appears in the row labelled "Equal variances not assumed." A value *greater* than .05 indicates that the assumption of equal variances has been met and that the t test in that row can be used.

The last two columns report the 95% confidence interval for the difference in means. Recall from our discussion in Section 8.8 that a hypothesis test will reject a null hypothesis if a confidence interval does not contain the value of the parameter specified by the null hypothesis, and vice versa. Using the conventional hypothesis test approach, we rejected the null hypothesis that males and females on average go out the same number of times in the population ($\mu_1 - \mu_2 = 0$) as the significance value of .0000002 was less than .05. We make the exact same decision using the 95% confidence interval for the difference in means. Because the interval, with a range of 2.742 to 6.071, does not contain the hypothesized null value, 0, the hypothesis is rejected at the 0.05 level.

SPSS DEMONSTRATION 9.2 The Error Bar Graph

In Demonstration 7.2, we produced an error bar graph for the confidence interval for the mean. As we will demonstrate here, the error bar graph is especially useful when two (or more) groups are being compared because we can quickly assess if there is a statistically significant difference between two means by examining if the two confidence intervals overlap.

It is very important to note, as discussed in Section 9.5, that using the overlap of confidence intervals for *each mean* provides only an approximation of the statistical significance of the difference between sample means. The confidence interval for the *difference in means* illustrated in Demonstration 9.1, on the other hand, provides a precise test for the significance of the difference. The latter is equal to formal hypothesis testing, the former is not.

To produce an error bar graph of the 95% confidence interval of each mean, click **Graphs, Legacy Dialogs,** and then **Error Bar. The Error Bars** dialog box appears, with the **Simple** and **Summaries for Groups of Cases** buttons already highlighted. These are the ones we want, so just click **Define. The Define Simple Error Bar** dialog box appears. Transfer the dependent variable, *numevact_c,* to the **Variable** box and the independent variable, *sex,* to the **Category Axis** box, and then click **OK,** and the following error bars will be produced:

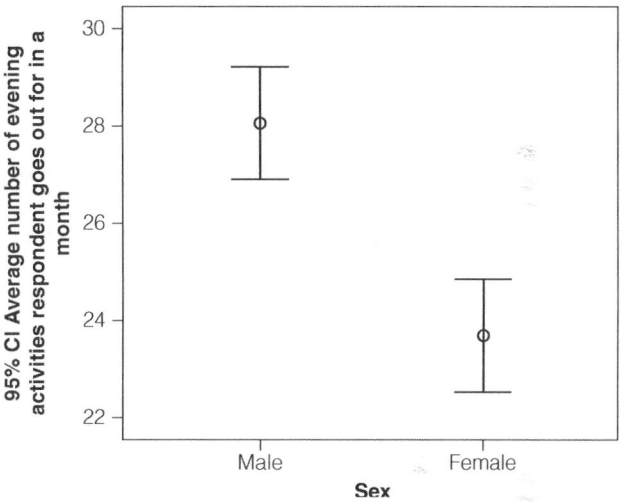

The error bars show that the sample means (marked by the small circles on each bar), are different and that, on the average, males go out in the evening more often than females. Further, the confidence intervals (indicated by the length of each bar) do not overlap, so the two means are significantly different from one another. This is precisely the decision we made in Demonstration 9.1.

SPSS DEMONSTRATION 9.3 Using the COMPUTE Command to Test for Gender Differences in Perception of Criminal Courts

SPSS provides a variety of tools to transform and manipulate variables. One of these tools is the SPSS **Compute** command. Appendix F.5 provides a step-by-step demonstration of the **Compute** command to create a summary scale of perception of criminal courts (*crtscale*) by adding the scores on the three constituent items (*phr_q320, phr_q330,* and *phr_q340*). You can quickly create the *crtscale* variable by following that demonstration.

Here we will test *crtscale* for the significance of the difference by gender. Our question is: Do men and women have different perceptions of the job done by criminal courts? If the difference in the sample means is large enough, we can reject the null hypothesis and conclude that the populations are different.

To answer the question follow the instructions in Demonstration 9.1 for using the **Independent-Samples T Test** command, and move *crtscale* rather than *drr_q120* to the **Test Variable(s)** box. If necessary, repeat the procedure for making *sex* the grouping variable. Your output will be as shown:

Group Statistics

	Sex	N	Mean	Std. Deviation	Std. Error Mean
crtscale	Male	799	5.4540	1.64054	.05805
	Female	721	5.4706	1.57370	.05861

Independent Samples Test

		Levene's Test for Equality of Variances		t-test for Equality of Means							
										95% Confidence Interval of the Difference	
		F	Sig.	t	df	Sig. (2-tailed)	Mean Difference	Std. Error Difference		Lower	Upper
crtscle	Equal variances assumed	1.797	.180	-.201	1517	.841	-.01661	.08267		-.17877	.14556
	Equal variances not assumed			-.201	1511.799	.840	-.01661	.08250		-.17843	.14522

We can assume equal variances because the Levene's Test for Equality of Variances is not significant—the value under the "Sig." column is *greater* than .05. Next, the results show that the sample means are very close in value (5.4540 versus 5.4706) and the test statistic ($t = -.201$) is not significant, as indicated by the "Sig. (2-tailed)" value of .841. There is no significant gender difference in attitude toward criminal courts. We should point out that *crtscale* is only ordinal in level of measurement. Scales like this are often treated as interval-ratio variables, but we should still be cautious in interpreting the results.

Exercises (using *GSS.sav*)

9.1 Do personal safety concerns significantly differ between males and females? Using Demonstration 9.1 as a guide, test for a significant difference in satisfaction with personal safety (variable name *phr_q990*) between males and females. Write a sentence or two summarizing the results of this test.*

---

phr_q990 is ordinal in level of measurement, and while calculation of independent-samples *t* test is not fully justified, such violations are common in social science research. Make sure you understand the coding scheme. See Appendix G to help interpret the values.

9.2 Using Demonstration 9.3 as a guide, construct a summary scale for "perception of police" using *phr_q230, phr_q250,* and *phr_q260* in place of *phr_q320, phr_q330,* and *phr_q340.* Test for the significance of the difference using *sex* as the independent variable. Write a sentence or two summarizing the results of this test.

9.3 What other independent variables might explain differences in the "perception of police scale" constructed in Exercise 9.2? Select three more independent variables besides *sex* and conduct additional *t* tests with this scale as the dependent variable. Write a sentence or two summarizing the results of these tests.[†]

[†]The *t* test requires the independent variable to have only two categories, but you can use a variable with more than two categories (e.g., marital status) and just restrict the *t* test to any two groups (e.g., married versus single, married versus divorced, widowed versus separated, etc.). To do this, open the **Independent-Samples T Test** dialog box, put *marstat* (marital status) in the **Grouping Variable** box, and then click the **Define Groups** button to indicate the two groups you wish to compare (e.g., to compare married and single persons, type the value 1 [married] in the **Group 1** textbox and value 6 [single] in the **Group 2** textbox, or vice-versa as the *t* test results will be exactly the same if you defined single as group 1 and married as group 2).

10

HYPOTHESIS TESTING III
THE ANALYSIS OF VARIANCE

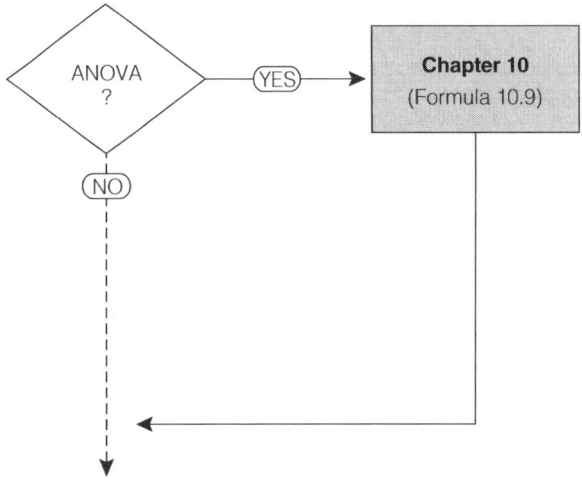

Chapter 10
(Formula 10.9)

LEARNING OBJECTIVES

By the end of this chapter, you will be able to

1. Identify and cite examples of situations in which ANOVA is appropriate.
2. Explain the logic of hypothesis testing as applied to ANOVA.
3. Perform the ANOVA test, using the five-step model as a guide, and correctly interpret the results.
4. Define and explain the concepts of population variance, total sum of squares, sum of squares between, sum of squares within, and mean square estimates.
5. Explain the difference between the statistical significance and the importance of relationships between variables.

10.1 INTRODUCTION

In this chapter, we will examine a very flexible and widely used test of significance called the **analysis of variance** (often abbreviated as **ANOVA**). This test can be used in a number of situations where previously discussed tests are less than optimum or entirely inappropriate. ANOVA is designed to be used with interval-ratio-level dependent variables and is a powerful tool for analyzing the most sophisticated and precise measurements you are likely to encounter.

It is perhaps easiest to think of ANOVA as an extension of the *t* test for the significance of the difference between two sample means, which was presented in Chapter 9. The *t* test can be used only in situations in which our independent variable has exactly two categories (e.g., immigrants and non-immigrants). The analysis of variance, on the other hand, is appropriate for independent variables with more than two categories (e.g., married/common-law, single, widowed, separated, and divorced).

To illustrate, suppose we conducted an experiment in teaching introductory biology at a large university. One section was taught by the traditional "lecture-lab" method, a second was taught by an "all-lab" approach with no lectures, and a third was taught entirely by a series of "videotaped" lectures and demonstrations that the students were free to view at any time and as often as they wanted. Students were randomly assigned to one of three sections, and at the end of the semester, random samples of final exam scores were collected from each section. Is there a significant difference in student performance on the final exam by teaching method? Because the independent variable (teaching method) has three categories and the dependent variable (final exam score) is measured at the interval-ratio level, analysis of variance provides a very useful statistical context in which this question can be addressed.

10.2 THE LOGIC OF THE ANALYSIS OF VARIANCE

For ANOVA, the null hypothesis is that the populations from which the samples are drawn are equal on the characteristic of interest. As applied to our problem, the null hypothesis could be phrased as "Students in the three different sections of introductory biology at the university do not vary in their final exam scores," or symbolically as $\mu_1 = \mu_2 = \mu_3$. (Note that this is an extended version of the null hypothesis for the two-sample t test.) As usual, the researcher will normally be interested in rejecting the null and, in this case, showing that final exam grades are related to teaching method.

If the null hypothesis of "no difference" in the populations is true, then any means calculated from randomly selected samples should be roughly equal in value. The average final exam score for the "lecture-lab" sample should be about the same as the average score for the "all-lab" sample and the "videotaped" sample. Note that the averages are unlikely to be exactly the same value even if the null hypothesis really is true, as we will always encounter some error or chance fluctuations in the measurement process. We are *not* asking: "Are there differences between the samples or categories of the independent variable (or, in our example, the sections of the introductory biology course)?" Rather, we are asking: "Are the differences between the samples large enough to reject the null hypothesis and justify the conclusion that the populations are different?"

Now, consider what kinds of outcomes we might encounter when conducting the teaching method experiment. Of the infinite variety of possibilities, let's focus on two extreme outcomes as exemplified by Tables 10.1 and 10.2. In the first set of hypothetical results (Table 10.1),

TABLE 10.1   FINAL EXAM SCORES BY TEACHING METHOD

	Lecture-Lab	All-Lab	Videotaped
Mean =	70.3	71.0	70.1
Standard Deviation =	12.4	11.9	12.2

TABLE 10.2   FINAL EXAM SCORES BY TEACHING METHOD

	Lecture-Lab	All-Lab	Videotaped
Mean =	84.7	71.3	65.7
Standard Deviation =	12.4	11.9	12.2

we see that the means and standard deviations of the groups are quite similar. The average scores are about the same for every group of students and all three groups exhibit about the same dispersion. These results would be quite consistent with the null hypothesis of no difference. Neither the average score nor the dispersion of the scores changes in any important way by section.

Now consider another set of fictitious results as displayed in Table 10.2. Here we see substantial differences in average score from category to category, with the "Videotaped" group having the lowest average score and the "Lecture-Lab" group having the highest. Also, the standard deviations are low and similar from group to group, indicating that there is not much variation within the groups of students. Table 10.2 shows marked differences *between* groups of students combined with homogeneity *within* groups of students, as indicated by the low values of the standard deviations. In other words, there are marked differences from group to group but little difference within each group. These results would contradict the null hypothesis and support the notion that final exam scores do vary by teaching method.

In principle, ANOVA proceeds by making the kinds of comparisons outlined above. The test compares the amount of variation between categories (e.g., from the "Lecture-Lab" group to the "All-Lab" group to the "Videotaped" group) with the amount of variation within categories (among the "Lecture-Lab" group, among the "All-Lab" group, and among the "Videotaped" group). The greater the differences between categories, relative to the differences within categories, the more likely that the null hypothesis of "no difference" is false and can be rejected. If exam scores truly vary by teaching method, then the sample mean for each group of students should be quite different from the others and dispersion within the groups should be relatively low and similar.

10.3 THE COMPUTATION OF ANOVA

Even though we have been thinking of ANOVA as a test for the significance of the difference between sample means, the computational routine actually involves developing two separate estimates of the population variance, σ^2 (hence the name "analysis of variance"). Recall from Chapter 4 that the variance and standard deviation both measure dispersion and that the variance is simply the standard deviation squared. One estimate of the population variance is based on the amount of variation within each of the categories of the independent variable and the other is based on the amount of variation between categories.

Before constructing these estimates, we need to introduce some new concepts and statistics. The first new concept is the total variation of the scores, which is measured by a quantity called the **total sum of squares,** or **SST**

FORMULA 10.1
$$SST = \sum (X_i - \overline{X})^2$$

To find this quantity, we would take each score, subtract the mean, square the difference, and then add to get the total of the squared differences. If this formula seems vaguely familiar, it's because the same expression appears in the numerator of the formula for the sample variance and the standard deviation (see Chapter 4). This redundancy is not surprising, considering that the SST is also a way of measuring dispersion.

To construct the two separate estimates of the population variance, the total variation (SST) is divided into two components. One of these reflects the pattern of variation within the categories and is called the **sum of squares within (SSW).** The other component is based on the variation between categories and is called the **sum of squares between (SSB).** SSW and SSB are components of SST, as reflected in Formula 10.2:

FORMULA 10.2
$$SST = SSB + SSW$$

The sum of squares within is defined as

FORMULA 10.3
$$SSW = \sum (X_i - \overline{X}_k)^2$$

where SSW = the sum of the squares within the categories
$\overline{X}_k$ = the mean of a category

This formula directs us to take each score, subtract the mean of the category from the score, square the result, and then sum the squared differences. We will do this for each category separately and then sum the squared differences for all categories to find SSW.

The sum of squares between (SSB) reflects the variation between the samples, with the category means serving as summary statistics for each category. Each category mean will be treated as a "case" for purposes of this estimate, and the formula for the sum of squares between (SSB) is

FORMULA 10.4
$$SSB = \sum N_k(\overline{X}_k - \overline{X})^2$$

where SSB = the sum of squares between the categories
N_k = the number of cases in a category
$\overline{X}_k$ = the mean of a category

To find SSB, subtract the overall mean of all scores from each category mean, square the difference, multiply by the number of cases in the category, and add the results across all the categories.

Let's pause for a second to remember what we are after here. If the null hypothesis is true, then there should not be much variation from category to category, relative to the variation within categories, and the two estimates to the population variance based on SSW and SSB should be roughly equal. The larger the difference between the two estimates, the more likely we will be to reject the null hypothesis. If the category means are about the same value, the differences will not be significant. The larger the differences between category means and the more homogeneous the categories, the more likely that the differences are statistically significant.

The next step in the computational routine is to construct the estimates of the population variance. To do this, we will divide each sum of squares by its respective degrees of freedom. To find the degrees of freedom associated with SSW, subtract the number of categories (k) from the number of cases (N). The degrees of freedom associated with SSB are the number of categories minus one. In summary,

FORMULA 10.5
$$\text{dfw} = N - k$$

where dfw = degrees of freedom associated with SSW
N = total number of cases
k = number of categories

FORMULA 10.6
$$\text{dfb} = k - 1$$

where dfb = degrees of freedom associated with SSB
k = number of categories

The actual estimates of the population variance, called the **mean square estimates,** are calculated by dividing each sum of squares by its respective degrees of freedom:

FORMULA 10.7
$$\text{Mean square within} = \frac{\text{SSW}}{\text{dfw}}$$

FORMULA 10.8
$$\text{Mean square between} = \frac{\text{SSB}}{\text{dfb}}$$

The test statistic calculated in step 4 of the five-step model is called the **_F_ ratio,** and its value is determined by the following formula:

FORMULA 10.9
$$F = \frac{\text{Mean square between}}{\text{Mean square within}}$$

As you can see, the value of the F ratio will be a function of the amount of variation between categories to the amount of variation within the categories. The greater the variation between the categories relative to the variation within, the higher the value of the F ratio and the more likely we will reject the null hypothesis.

10.4 A COMPUTATIONAL SHORTCUT

The computational routine for ANOVA, as summarized in the previous section, requires a number of separate steps and different formulas and will surely seem complicated the first time you see it. As is almost always the case, if you proceed systematically from formula to formula (in the correct order, of course), you will see that the computations aren't nearly as formidable as they appear at first glance. Unfortunately, they will still be lengthy and time-consuming. So, at the risk of stretching your patience, let us introduce a way to save some time and computational effort. This will require the introduction of even more formulas, but the eventual savings in time will be worth the effort. Formula 10.10 shows a quicker, more convenient way to calculate SST:

FORMULA 10.10
$$\text{SST} = \sum X^2 - N\overline{X}^2$$

To solve this formula, first find the sum of the squared scores (in other words, square each score and then add up the squared scores). Next, square the overall mean, multiply that value by the total number of cases in the sample (N), and subtract that quantity from the sum of the squared scores.

Once we have the values of SST and SSB, we can find SSW by manipulating Formula 10.2 and doing some simple subtraction:

FORMULA 10.11
$$\text{SSW} = \text{SST} - \text{SSB}$$

The computational routine for ANOVA can be summarized as follows:

1. Find SST by Formula 10.10.
2. Find SSB by Formula 10.4.
3. Find SSW by subtraction (Formula 10.11).
4. Calculate the degrees of freedom (Formulas 10.5 and 10.6).
5. Construct the two mean square estimates to the population variance by dividing SSB and SSW by their respective degrees of freedom (Formulas 10.7 and 10.8).
6. Find the obtained F ratio by dividing the between estimate by the within estimate (Formula 10.9).

These computations and the actual test of significance will be illustrated in the next sections.

10.5 A COMPUTATIONAL EXAMPLE

Continuing with our teaching method problem, let us assume that we have final exam scores (where a score is the percent of correct answers on the final exam) from a random sample of 27 students, equally divided into the three sections. All scores are reported in Table 10.3 along with the squared scores, the category means, and the overall mean.

TABLE 10.3 FINAL EXAM SCORES BY TEACHING METHOD FOR 27 STUDENTS

	Lecture-Lab		All-Lab		Videotaped	
	X	X^2	X	X^2	X	X^2
	55	3,025	56	3,136	50	2,500
	57	3,249	60	3,600	52	2,704
	60	3,600	62	3,844	60	3,600
	63	3,969	67	4,489	61	3,721
	72	5,184	70	4,900	63	3,969
	73	5,329	71	5,041	69	4,761
	79	6,241	82	6,724	71	5,041
	85	7,225	88	7,744	80	6,400
	92	8,464	95	9,025	82	6,724
$\sum X =$	636		651		588	
$\sum X^2 =$		46,286		48,503		39,420
$\overline{X}_k =$	70.67		72.33		65.33	
			$\overline{X} = 1,875/27 = 69.44$			

To organize our computations, we will follow the routine summarized at the end of Section 10.4. We begin by finding SST with Formula 10.10:

$$\text{SST} = \sum X^2 - N\overline{X}^2$$
$$= 134,209 - (27)(69.44)^2$$
$$= 4,017.33$$

The sum of squares between is found by Formula 10.4:

$$\text{SSB} = \sum N_k(\overline{X}_k - \overline{X})^2$$
$$= (9)(70.67 - 69.44)^2 + (9)(72.33 - 69.44)^2$$
$$+ (9)(65.33 - 69.44)^2$$
$$= 13.62 + 75.17 + 152.03$$
$$= 240.82$$

Now SSW can be found by subtraction (Formula 10.11):

$$\text{SSW} = \text{SST} - \text{SSB}$$
$$= 4,017.33 - 240.82$$
$$= 3,776.51$$

To find the degrees of freedom for the two sums of squares, we use Formulas 10.5 and 10.6:

$$\text{dfw} = N - k = 27 - 3 = 24$$
$$\text{dfb} = k - 1 = 3 - 1 = 2$$

Finally, we are ready to construct the mean square estimates to the population variance. For the estimate based on SSW, we use Formula 10.7:

$$\text{Mean square within} = \frac{\text{SSW}}{\text{dfw}} = \frac{3,776.51}{24} = 157.36$$

For the between estimate, we use Formula 10.8:

$$\text{Mean square between} = \frac{\text{SSB}}{\text{dfb}} = \frac{240.82}{2} = 120.41$$

The test statistic, or F ratio, is found by Formula 10.9:

$$F = \frac{\text{Mean square between}}{\text{Mean square within}}$$
$$F = \frac{120.41}{157.36}$$
$$F = 0.77$$

This statistic must still be evaluated for its significance. *(For practice in computing these quantities and solving these formulas, solve any of the end-of-chapter problems.)*

10.6 A TEST OF SIGNIFICANCE FOR ANOVA

In this section, we will see how to test an F ratio for significance and also take a look at some of the assumptions underlying the ANOVA test. As usual, we will follow the five-step model as a convenient way of organizing the decision-making process.

Step 1. Making Assumptions and Meeting Test Requirements.

> Model: Independent random samples
> Level of measurement is interval-ratio
> Populations are normally distributed
> Population variances are equal

The model assumptions are quite stringent and underscore the fact that ANOVA should be used only with dependent variables that have been carefully and precisely measured. However, as long as sample sizes are equal (or nearly so), ANOVA can tolerate some violation of the model assumptions. In situations where you are uncertain or have samples of very different size, it is probably advisable to use an alternative test. (Chi square in Chapter 11 is one option.)

Step 2. Stating the Null Hypothesis. For ANOVA, the null hypothesis always states that the means of the populations from which the samples were drawn are equal. For our example problem, we are concerned with three different populations or categories, so our null hypothesis would be

$$H_0: \mu_1 = \mu_2 = \mu_3$$

where μ_1 represents the mean for students in the "Lecture-Lab" section, μ_2, the mean for students in the "All-Lab" section, and, μ_3, the mean for students in the "Videotaped" section.

The research hypothesis states simply that at least one of the population means is different. The wording here is important. If we reject the null,

ANOVA does not identify which mean or means are significantly different. In the final section of the chapter, we will briefly discuss some advanced tests that can help us identify which pairs of means are significantly different.

(H_1: At least one of the population means is different.)

Step 3. Selecting the Sampling Distribution and Establishing the Critical Region. The sampling distribution for ANOVA is the F distribution, which is summarized in Appendix D. Note that there are separate tables for alphas of .05 and .01, respectively. As with the t table, the value of the critical F score will vary by degrees of freedom. For ANOVA, there are two separate degrees of freedom, one for each estimate of the population variance. The numbers across the top of the table are the degrees of freedom associated with the between estimate (dfb), and the numbers down the side of the table are those associated with the within estimate (dfw). In our example, dfb is $(k - 1)$, or 2, and dfw is $(N - k)$, or 24 (see Formulas 10.5 and 10.6). So, if we set alpha at .05, our critical F score will be 3.40.

Summarizing these considerations:

$$\text{Sampling distribution} = F \text{ distribution}$$
$$\text{Alpha} = .05$$
$$\text{Degrees of freedom (within)} = (N - k) = 24$$
$$\text{Degrees of freedom (between)} = (k - 1) = 2$$
$$F(\text{critical}) = 3.40$$

Taking a moment to inspect the two F tables, you will notice that all the values are greater than 1.00. This is because ANOVA is a one-tailed test, and we are concerned only with outcomes in which there is more variance between categories than within categories. F values of less than 1.00 would indicate that the between estimate was lower in value than the within estimate and, because we would always fail to reject the null in such cases, we simply ignore this class of outcomes.

Step 4. Computing the Test Statistic. This was done in the previous section, where we found an obtained F ratio of 0.77.

Step 5. Making a Decision and Interpreting the Results of the Test. Compare the test statistic with the critical value:

$$F(\text{critical}) = 3.40$$
$$F(\text{obtained}) = 0.77$$

Because the test statistic does not fall into the critical region, our decision would be to fail to reject the null. Student performance does not differ significantly by teaching method, and the variation we observed in the sample means is unimportant.

10.7 AN ADDITIONAL EXAMPLE FOR COMPUTING AND TESTING THE ANALYSIS OF VARIANCE

In this section, we will work through an additional example of the computation and interpretation of the ANOVA test. We will first review matters of computation, then find the obtained F ratio, and then test the statistic for its significance. In the computational section, we will follow the step-by-step guidelines presented at the end of Section 10.4.

We have gathered real data on the life expectancy (the number of years the average citizen can expect to live at birth) for a random sample of 15 nations at three levels of economic development. "Least developed" nations are largely agricultural and have the lowest quality of life, "developed" nations are industrial and the most affluent and modern, and "developing" nations are between these extremes. Is there a significant difference in life expectancy between countries at different levels of development? The data are reported in Table 10.4, which also includes some additional information we will need to complete our calculations.

To find SST by the computational Formula 10.10:

$$SST = \sum X^2 - N\bar{X}^2$$
$$= (113,790.65 + 24,223.23 + 29,578.78) - 15(66.11)^2$$
$$= 67,592.66 - 65,557.98$$
$$= 2,034.68$$

To find SSB by Formula 10.4:

$$SSB = \sum N_k(\bar{X}_k - \bar{X})^2$$
$$= (5)(52.10 - 66.11)^2 + (5)(69.46 - 66.11)^2 + (5)(76.76 - 66.11)^2$$
$$= 981.40 + 56.11 + 567.11$$
$$= 1,604.62$$

TABLE 10.4   LIFE EXPECTANCY BY LEVEL OF DEVELOPMENT

Least Developed			Developing			Developed		
Nation	X	X^2	Nation	X	X^2	Nation	X	X^2
Cambodia	56.8	3,226.24	China	71.6	5,126.56	Belgium	78.0	6,084.00
Mali	47.0	2,209.00	Indonesia	68.3	4,664.89	Canada	79.9	6,384.01
Nepal	58.2	3,387.24	Pakistan	61.5	3,782.25	Japan	80.8	6,528.64
Niger	41.6	1,730.56	Chile	74.7	5,580.09	Russia	67.3	4,529.29
Sudan	56.9	3,237.61	Turkey	71.2	5,069.44	U.K.	77.8	6,052.84
$\sum X =$	260.5			347.3			383.8	
$\sum X^2 =$		13,790.65			24,223.23			29,578.78
$\bar{X}_k =$	52.10			69.46			76.76	
			$\bar{X} = 991.6/15 = 66.11$					

Source: U.S. Bureau of the Census. 2003. *Statistical Abstract of the United States, 2002.*

Now we can find SSW by Formula 10.11:

$$SSW = SST - SSB$$
$$= 2,034.68 - 1,604.62$$
$$= 430.06$$

The degrees of freedom are found by Formulas 10.5 and 10.6:

$$dfw = N - k = 15 - 3 = 12$$
$$dfb = k - 1 = 3 - 1 = 2$$

The estimates to the population variances are found by Formulas 10.7 and 10.8:

$$\text{Mean square within} = \frac{SSW}{dfw} = \frac{430.06}{12} = 35.84$$

$$\text{Mean square between} = \frac{SSB}{dfb} = \frac{1,604.62}{2} = 802.31$$

The F ratio (Formula 10.9) is

$$F(\text{obtained}) = \frac{\text{Mean square between}}{\text{Mean square within}}$$

$$F(\text{obtained}) = \frac{802.31}{35.84}$$

$$F(\text{obtained}) = 22.39$$

And we can now test this value for its significance.

Step 1. Making Assumptions and Meeting Test Requirements.

> Model: Independent random samples
> Level of measurement is interval-ratio
> Populations are normally distributed
> Population variances are equal

The researcher will always be in a position to judge the adequacy of the first two assumptions in the model. The second two assumptions are more problematical, but remember that ANOVA will tolerate some deviation from its assumptions as long as sample sizes are roughly equal.

Step 2. Stating the Null Hypothesis.

> H_0: $\mu_1 = \mu_2 = \mu_3$
> (H_1: At least one of the population means is different.)

Step 3. Selecting the Sampling Distribution and Establishing the Critical Region.

> Sampling distribution = F distribution
> Alpha = .05
> Degrees of freedom (within) = $(N - k) = (15 - 3) = 12$
> Degrees of freedom (between) = $(k - 1) = (3 - 1) = 2$
> $F(\text{critical}) = 3.88$

Step 4. **Computing the Test Statistic**. We found an obtained F ratio of 22.39.

Step 5. **Making a Decision and Interpreting the Results of the Test**. Compare the test statistic with the critical value:

$$F(\text{critical}) = 3.88$$
$$F(\text{obtained}) = 22.39$$

The test statistic is in the critical region, and we would reject the null of no difference. The differences between the three groupings are very unlikely to have occurred by chance alone. There is a significant difference in life expectancy between nations at the three levels of economic development. *(For practice in conducting the ANOVA test, see problems 10.2 to 10.9. Begin with the lower-numbered problems as they have smaller data sets and fewer categories, and, therefore, the simplest calculations.)*

10.8 THE LIMITATIONS OF THE TEST

ANOVA is appropriate whenever you want to test differences between the means of an interval-ratio-level variable across three or more categories of an independent variable. This application is called **one-way analysis of variance,** as it involves the effect of a single variable (e.g., teaching method) on another (e.g., final exam grade). This is the simplest application of ANOVA, and you should be aware that the technique has numerous more advanced and complex forms. For example, you may encounter research projects in which the effects of two separate variables on some third variable were observed. This application is called *two-way analysis of variance.*

One important limitation of ANOVA is that it requires interval-ratio measurement of the dependent variable and roughly equal numbers of cases in each of the categories of the independent variable. The former condition may be difficult to meet with complete confidence for many variables of interest to the social sciences. The latter condition may create problems when the research hypothesis calls for comparisons between groups that are, by their nature, unequal in numbers (e.g., number of people in each province) and may call for some unusual sampling schemes in the data-gathering phase of a research project. Neither of these limitations should be particularly crippling, because ANOVA can tolerate some deviation from its model assumptions, but you should be aware of these limitations in planning your own research as well as in judging the adequacy of research conducted by others.

A second limitation of ANOVA actually applies to all forms of significance testing and was introduced in Section 9.6. These tests are designed to detect non-random differences—differences so large that they are very unlikely to be produced by random chance alone. The problem is that

READING STATISTICS 7: Differences in Attitudes toward Product Expiration Data across Countries

Expiration dates on product labels are integral to consumer safety and product quality. Research shows that consumer attitudes and perceptions toward expiration dates on products vary by sex, age, education, and many other socio-demographic variables within a country. Do attitudes of consumers, however, vary by country? A recent international study by Harcar and Karakaya set out to shed light on this question.

This research team collected information from 243 Canadian, 100 U.S., and 344 Turkish consumers using a questionnaire. The survey contained many questions on attitudes and perceptions of product expiration dates. Table 1 reports the results of a one-way analysis of variance for three of these items: 1) expiration dates on products are reliable; 2) retailers do not sell products past their expiration dates; and 3) fines are justified for companies selling products with expired dates. Each question was based on four-point Likert scale ranging from "do not agree" to "totally agree." The questions, while measured at the ordinal level, were treated as interval-ratio, which is a common approach because it allows researchers to use more flexible and powerful statistics, such as analysis of variance.

Table 1 shows various components of ANOVA results for each of the three questions: sample means for each country, F ratio, and significance-level (alpha) values to reveal statistically significant differences in means between countries. Looking at the first question (attitude toward reliability of product expiration dates) we see that the sample means are very similar across the countries, the F ratio is small, and the significance level is well above the .05 threshold used to reject the null hypothesis of no difference between countries. Consumers in Canada, the U.S., and Turkey have similar perceptions of the reliability of their product expiration dates.

Nationality has an influence on confidence in the retailer, where Canadian and American consumers are more likely than Turkish consumers to agree that retailers do not sell products past their expiration dates: Canadian and American sample means are 1.48 and 1.47 respectively, compared to 1.33 for the Turkish sample. The significance level is less than .05, revealing that countries are significantly different. There are even larger differences between the countries in attitudes toward setting fines for companies selling products with expired dates. The F ratio is 76.57 with a significance level well below .05.

(continued)

differences that are statistically significant are not necessarily important in any other sense. The last two parts of this text will provide statistical techniques that can assess the importance of results directly.

A final limitation of ANOVA relates to the research hypothesis. As you recall, when the null hypothesis is rejected, the research hypothesis is supported. The limitation is that the research hypothesis is not specific; it simply asserts that at least one of the population means is different from the others. Obviously, we would like to know which differences are significant. We can sometimes make this determination by simple inspection. In our problem involving the economic development of nations, for

READING STATISTICS 7: *(continued)*

The significance (alpha) level is actually less than 0.01. In general, country plays a role in consumer attitude toward expiration dates, namely in confidence in the retailer not selling expired product and in justification of fines for those selling expired product.

TABLE 1   DIFFERENCES IN CONSUMER ATTITUDE TOWARD PRODUCT EXPIRATION DATES, BY COUNTRY

	Mean*	F Ratio	Significance Level
Expiration dates on products are reliable		0.91	0.40
Turkey	1.90		
United States	1.91		
Canada	1.97		
Retailers do not sell products past their expiration dates		4.95	0.01
Turkey	1.33		
United States	1.47		
Canada	1.48		
Fines are justified for companies selling products with expired dates		76.57	<0.01
Turkey	1.15		
United States	1.77		
Canada	2.04		

*Higher scores indicate higher levels of agreement with the question.

Source: Harcar, T. and Karakaya, F. 2005. "A Cross-Cultural Exploration of Attitudes toward Product Expiration Dates." *Psychology & Marketing, 22:* 353–371. Copyright © 2005. Reprinted by permission of John Wiley & Sons, Inc.

example, it is pretty clear from Table 10.4 that the "least developed" group is the source of most of the differences. This informal, "eyeball" method can be misleading, however, and you should exercise caution in making conclusions about which means are significantly different. There is a statistical technique called post hoc, or "after the fact" analysis, that can be used to reliably identify which pairs of means are significantly different. The computational routines for post hoc analysis are beyond the scope of this text, but the tests are commonly available in computerized statistical packages such as SPSS.

SUMMARY

1. One-way analysis of variance is a powerful test of significance that is commonly used when comparisons across more than two categories or samples are of interest. It is perhaps easiest to conceptualize ANOVA as an extension of the test for the difference in sample means.

2. ANOVA compares the amount of variation within categories to the amount of variation between categories. If the null of no difference is false, there should be relatively great variation between categories and relatively little variation within categories. The greater the differences from category to category relative to the differences within the categories, the more likely we will be able to reject the null.

3. The computational routine for even simple applications of ANOVA can quickly become quite complex. The basic process is to construct separate estimates to the population variance based on the variation within the categories and the variation between the categories. The test statistic is the *F* ratio, which is based on a comparison of these two estimates. The basic computational routine is summarized at the end of Section 10.4, and this is probably an appropriate time to mention the widespread availability of statistical packages such as SPSS, the purpose of which is to perform complex calculations such as these accurately and quickly. If you haven't yet learned how to use such programs, ANOVA may provide you with the necessary incentive.

4. The ANOVA test can be organized into the familiar five-step model for testing the significance of sample outcomes. Although the model assumptions (step 1) require high-quality data, the test can tolerate some deviation as long as sample sizes are roughly equal. The null takes the familiar form of stating that there is no difference of any importance among the population values, while the research hypothesis asserts that at least one population mean is different. The sampling distribution is the *F* distribution, and the test is always one-tailed. The decision to reject or to fail to reject the null is based on a comparison of the obtained *F* ratio with the critical *F* ratio as determined for a given alpha level and degrees of freedom. The decision to reject the null indicates only that one or more of the population means is different from the others. We can often determine which sample mean(s) account for the difference by inspecting the sample data, but this informal method should be used with caution, and post hoc tests are more reliable indicators of significant differences.

SUMMARY OF FORMULAS

Total sum of squares:

10.1 $$SST = \sum (X_i - \overline{X})^2$$

The two components of the total sum of squares:

10.2 $$SST = SSB + SSW$$

Sum of squares within:

10.3 $$SSW = \sum (X_i - \overline{X}_k)^2$$

Sum of squares between:

10.4 $$SSB = \sum N_k(\overline{X}_k - \overline{X})^2$$

Degrees of freedom for SSW:

10.5 $$dfw = N - k$$

Degrees of freedom for SSB:

10.6 $$dfb = k - 1$$

Mean square within:

10.7 $$\text{Mean square within} = \frac{SSW}{dfw}$$

Mean square between:

10.8 $$\text{Mean square between} = \frac{SSB}{dfb}$$

F ratio:

10.9 $$F = \frac{\text{Mean square between}}{\text{Mean square within}}$$

Computational formula for SST:

10.10 $$SST = \sum X^2 - N\overline{X}^2$$

Finding SSW by subtraction:

10.11 $$SSW = SST - SSB$$

GLOSSARY

Analysis of variance. A test of significance appropriate for situations in which we are concerned with the differences among more than two sample means.

ANOVA. See Analysis of variance.

F ratio. The test statistic computed in step 4 of the ANOVA test.

Mean square estimate. An estimate of the variance calculated by dividing the sum of squares within (SSW) or the sum of squares between (SSB) by the proper degrees of freedom.

One-way analysis of variance. Application of ANOVA in which the effect of a single independent variable on a dependent variable is observed.

Sum of squares between (SSB). The sum of the squared deviations of the sample means from the overall mean, weighted by sample size.

Sum of squares within (SSW). The sum of the squared deviations of scores from the category means.

Total sum of squares (SST). The sum of the squared deviations of the scores from the overall mean.

MULTIMEDIA RESOURCES

http://www.healeystatistics.nelson.com

Visit the companion Web site for the first Canadian edition of *Statistics: A Tool for Social Research* to access a wide range of student resources. Begin by clicking on the Student Resources section of the book's Web site to access review quizzes, flash cards, and other study tools.

PROBLEMS

(NOTE: The number of cases in these problems is very low—a fraction of the sample size necessary for any serious research—in order to simplify computations.)

10.1 Conduct the ANOVA test for each set of scores below. *(HINT: Follow the computational shortcut outlined in Section 10.4 and keep track of all sums and means by constructing computational tables like Table 10.3 or 10.4.)*

a. Category

A	B	C
5	10	12
7	12	16
8	14	18
9	15	20

b. Category

A	B	C
1	2	3
10	12	10
9	2	7
20	3	14
8	1	1

c. Category

A	B	C	D
13	45	23	10
15	40	78	20
10	47	80	25
11	50	34	27
10	45	30	20

10.2 [SOC] What type of person is most involved in the neighbourhood and community? Who is more likely to volunteer for organizations such as Scouts, Big Sisters, or the United Way? A random sample of 15 people have been asked for their number of memberships in community voluntary organizations and some other information. Which differences are significant?

a. Membership by education:

Less Than High School	High School	College/ University
0	1	0
1	3	3
2	3	4
3	4	4
4	5	4

b. Membership by length of residence in present community:

Less Than 2 Years	2–5 Years	More Than 5 Years
0	0	1
1	2	3
3	3	3
4	4	4
4	5	4

c. Membership by extent of television watching:

Little or None	Moderate	High
0	3	4
0	3	4
1	3	4
1	3	4
2	4	5

d. Membership by number of children:

None	One Child	More Than One Child
0	2	0
1	3	3
1	4	4
3	4	4
3	4	5

10.3 [SOC] In a local community, a random sample of 18 couples has been assessed on a scale that measures the extent to which power and decision making are shared (lower scores) or monopolized by one party (higher scores) and on marital happiness (lower scores indicate lower levels of unhappiness). The couples were also classified by type of relationship: traditional (only the husband works outside the home), dual-career (both parties work), and cohabitational (parties living together but not legally married, regardless of work patterns). Does decision making or happiness vary significantly by type of relationship?

a.

	Decision Making	
Traditional	Dual-career	Cohabitational
7	8	2
8	5	1
2	4	3
5	4	4
7	5	1
6	5	2

b.

	Happiness	
Traditional	Dual-career	Cohabitational
10	12	12
14	12	14
20	12	15
22	14	17
23	15	18
24	20	22

10.4 [CJ] Two separate crime-reduction programs have been implemented in the city of Pearson, Ontario. One involves a neighbourhood watch program with citizens actively involved in crime prevention. The second involves officers patrolling the neighbourhoods on foot rather than in patrol cars. In terms of the percentage reduction in crimes reported to the police over a one-year period, were the programs successful? The results are for random samples of 18 neighbourhoods drawn from the entire city.

Neighbourhood Watch	Foot Patrol	No Program
−10	−21	+30
−20	−15	−10
+10	−80	+14
+20	−10	+80
+70	−50	+50
+10	−10	−20

10.5 SOC Are sexually active teenagers any better informed about AIDS and other potential health problems related to sex than teenagers who are sexually inactive? A 15-item test of general knowledge about sex and health was administered to random samples of teens who are sexually inactive, teens who are sexually active but with only a single partner ("going steady"), and teens who are sexually active with more than one partner. Is there any significant difference in the test scores?

Inactive	Active— One Partner	Active— More Than One Partner
10	11	12
12	11	12
8	6	10
10	5	4
8	15	3
5	10	15

10.6 PS Does the rate of voter turnout vary significantly by the type of election? A random sample of electoral districts displays the following pattern of voter turnout by election type. Assess the results for significance.

Municipal	Provincial	Federal
33	35	42
78	56	40
32	35	52
28	40	66
10	45	78
12	42	62
61	65	57
28	62	75
29	25	72
45	47	51
44	52	69
41	55	59

10.7 GER Do older citizens lose interest in politics and current affairs? A brief quiz on recent headline stories was administered to random samples of respondents from each of four different age groups. Is there a significant difference? The data below represent numbers of correct responses.

High School (15–18)	Young Adult (21–30)	Middle-aged (40–55)	Retired (65+)
0	0	2	5
1	0	3	6
1	2	3	6
2	2	4	6
2	4	4	7
2	4	5	7
3	4	6	8
5	6	7	10
5	7	7	10
7	7	8	10
7	7	8	10
9	10	10	10

10.8 SOC A social survey was administered to a random sample of adults. A subsample of these adults, selected randomly, is shown below. Each respondent has been classified as either a city dweller, a suburbanite, or a rural dweller. Are there statistically significant differences by place of residence for any of the variables listed below?

a. Occupational Prestige (higher scores indicate greater prestige)

Urban	Suburban	Rural
32	40	30
45	48	40
42	50	40
47	55	45
48	55	45
50	60	50
51	65	52
55	70	55
60	75	55
65	75	60

b. Number of Children

Urban	Suburban	Rural
1	0	1
1	1	4
0	0	2
2	0	3
1	2	3
0	2	2
2	3	5
2	2	0
1	2	4
0	1	6

c. Monthly Family Income
(in thousands of dollars)

Urban	Suburban	Rural
5	6	5
7	8	5
8	11	11
11	12	10
8	12	9
9	11	6
8	11	10
3	9	7
9	10	9
10	12	8

d. Number of Times Religious Service
Attended per Month

Urban	Suburban	Rural
0	0	1
7	0	5
0	2	4
4	5	4
5	8	0
8	5	4
7	8	8
5	7	8
7	2	8
4	6	5

e. Hours of TV Watching per Day

Urban	Suburban	Rural
5	5	3
3	7	7
12	10	5
2	2	0
0	3	1
2	0	8
3	1	5
4	3	10
5	4	3
9	1	1

10.9 SOC Does support for suicide ("death with dignity") vary by social class? Is this relationship different in different nations? Small samples in three nations were asked if it is ever justified for a person with an incurable disease to take their own lives. Respondents answered in terms of a 10-point scale on which 10 was "always justified" (the strongest support for "death with dignity") and 1 was "never justified" (the lowest level of support). Results are reported below.

Mexico

Lower Class	Working Class	Middle Class	Upper Class
5	2	1	2
2	2	1	4
4	1	3	5
5	1	4	7
4	6	1	8
2	5	2	10
3	7	1	10
1	2	5	9
1	3	1	8
3	1	1	8

Canada

Lower Class	Working Class	Middle Class	Upper Class
7	5	1	5
7	6	3	7
6	7	4	8
4	8	5	9
7	8	7	10
8	9	8	10
9	5	8	8
9	6	9	5
6	7	9	8
5	8	5	9

United States

Lower Class	Working Class	Middle Class	Upper Class
4	4	4	1
5	5	6	5
6	1	7	8
1	4	5	9
3	3	8	9
3	3	9	9
3	4	9	8
5	2	8	6
3	1	7	9
6	1	2	9

Using SPSS for Windows to Conduct Analysis of Variance with the 2001 Census

The demonstrations and exercises below use the shortened version of the 2001 Census data. Start SPSS for Windows and open the *Census.sav* file.

SPSS DEMONSTRATION 10.1 Using the RECODE Command to Test for Regional Differences in Age

SPSS provides several different ways of conducting the analysis of variance test. We'll use the **One-Way ANOVA** procedure, which is the most accessible way to conduct the analysis of variance test, to answer the question "Is there a significant difference in average age by province?"

Before we do the analysis of variance, smaller provinces should be collapsed into groups or regions to create more equal sample sizes. We'll use the SPSS **Recode** command, a commonly used tool to transform and manipulate variables, to collapse *provp* (province) into six regions. (The original scores for *provp* are given in Appendix G, or they can be viewed by clicking **Utilities** and then **Variables** from the SPSS main menu bar.)

First, click **Transform** from the main menu and choose **Recode into Different Variables.** The **Recode into Different Variables** dialog box will open. Highlight *provp* and click on the arrow button to move the variable to the **Input Variable → Output Variable** box. In the **Output Variable** box on the right, click in the **Name** text box and type a name for the new (output) variable: We suggest *region.* Click the **Change** button.

Second, click on the **Old and New Values** button in the middle of the screen to open the **Recode into Different: Old and New Values** dialog box. Read down the left-hand column until you find the **Range** button. Click on the button, and the cursor will move to the small box immediately below. Type 10 into the first **Range** text box and then click on the second text box and type 13. Then, in the **New Value** box in the upper-right-hand corner of the screen, click the **Value** button and then type 1 in the adjacent text box. Finally, click the **Add** button. The expression "10 thru 13 → 1" will appear in the **Old → New** text box. This completes the first recode instruction to SPSS.

For the second recode instruction, click the **Value** button in the **Old Value** box. Move the cursor to the small text box immediately under the **Value** button. Type 24 in the text box. Next, in the **New Value** box, click the **Value** button and type 2 in the adjacent text box. Click the **Add** button. The expression "24 → 2" appears in the **Old → New** box. Continue this sequence of operations until all old values of *provp* have been recoded into new values. The recoding instructions that need to be added in the **Old → New** box should contain all of the following expressions (the order is not important):

$$
\begin{array}{rcl}
10 \text{ thru } 13 & \rightarrow & 1 \\
24 & \rightarrow & 2 \\
35 & \rightarrow & 3
\end{array}
$$

$$46 \text{ thru } 47 \rightarrow 4$$
$$48 \qquad\quad \rightarrow 5$$
$$59 \qquad\quad \rightarrow 6$$

This scheme groups all respondents with: scores 10 (Nfld/Labrador), 11 (PEI), 12 (Nova Scotia), or 13 (New Brunswick) on *provp* together into a score of 1 on *region;* score 24 (Quebec) on *provp* into a score of 2 on *region;* score 35 (Ontario) on *provp* into a score of 3 on *region;* scores 46 (Manitoba) or 47 (Saskatchewan) on *provp* together into a score of 4 on *region;* score 48 (Alberta) on *provp* into a score of 5 on *region;* and score 59 (BC) on *provp* into a score of 6 on *region.*

Third, click the **Continue** button at the bottom of the screen, and you will return to the **Recode into Different Variable** dialog box. Click **OK,** and SPSS will execute the transformation. It is always a good idea to check the frequency distribution of the recoded variable to make sure that the computations were carried out correctly.

We have attached value labels to each score of *region* (1 = Atlantic Canada, 2 = Quebec, etc.) to make the SPSS output easier to read. For more practice using the recode command, including how to add value labels, see Appendix F.5.

To use the **One-Way ANOVA** procedure, click **Analyze, Compare Means,** and then **One-Way ANOVA.** The **One-Way ANOVA** window appears. Find *agep* (age in years) in the variable list on the left and click the arrow to move the variable name into the **Dependent List** box. Next, find *region* (it may appear at the end of the variable list) and click the arrow to move the variable name into the **Factor** box. To request means and standard deviations along with the analysis of variance, click **Options** and then click the checkbox next to **Descriptive** in the **Statistics** section. Click **Continue** and then **OK,** and the output below, slightly edited for clarity, will be produced.

Descriptives: AGE IN YEARS

	N	Mean	Std. Deviation	Std. Error	95% Confidence Interval for Mean Lower Bound	Upper Bound
Atlantic Canada	115	40.71	16.526	1.541	37.66	43.77
Quebec	332	42.17	17.629	.968	40.27	44.08
Ontario	590	41.98	17.677	.728	40.56	43.41
Manitoba/ Saskatchewan	102	47.74	17.337	1.717	44.33	51.14
Alberta	160	41.09	17.363	1.373	38.38	43.80
British Columbia	201	46.26	18.245	1.287	43.72	48.80
Total	1500	42.80	17.694	.457	41.90	43.69

ANOVA: AGE IN YEARS

	Sum of Squares	df	Mean Square	F	Sig.
Between Groups	6377.539	5	1275.508	4.117	.001
Within Groups	462918.255	1494	309.852		
Total	469295.794	1499			

The "Descriptives" report displays various summary statistics. The results indicate that age is distributed differently across the regions. The mean age for the sample as a whole (all provinces) is 42.8 years. Manitobans/ Saskatchewanians tend to be the oldest and Atlantic Canadians the youngest in Canada.

The output box labelled "ANOVA" includes sums of squares, degrees of freedom (*df*), mean square estimates, *F* ratio (4.117), and, at the far right "Sig." value (.001), the exact probability of getting these results if the null hypothesis is true. There is no need to look up the *F* ratio in the *F* table, Appendix D, when the exact probability is provided. Because the value .001 is less than .05, our usual indicator of significance, we reject the null hypothesis. The difference in mean age between the regions is statistically significant.

SPSS DEMONSTRATION 10.2 The Error Bar Graph

ANOVA results, as shown in Demonstration 10.1, tell us if *any* of the group means differ significantly from each other. It does not tell us, however, *which* groups differ significantly from each other. In Demonstration 9.2, the overlap of error bars for individual confidence intervals was used to judge the significance of the difference between two samples. We can use the error bar graph in a similar manner to get an indication of which pairs of means are significantly different.

To produce error bar graphs of the 95% confidence interval of each mean, click **Graphs, Legacy Dialogs,** and then **Error Bar.** The **Error Bars** dialog box appears, with the **Simple** and **Summaries for Groups of Cases** buttons already highlighted. These are the ones we want, so just click **Define.** The **Define Simple Error Bar** dialog box appears. Transfer the dependent variable, *agep,* to the **Variable** box and the independent variable, *region,* to the **Category Axis** box, and click **OK.**

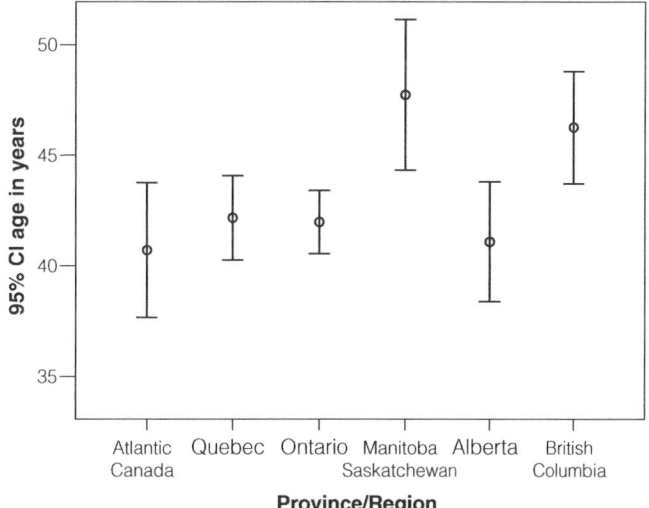

The error bar graph shows the mean age for each region. The 95% confidence interval for each mean is also presented. By "eyeballing" the overlap of confidence intervals for each mean, we can get a sense of which means are significantly different. For example, there appears to be a significant difference in average age between Ontario and Manitoba/Saskatchewan populations, but not between Ontario and Quebec populations. An exact method to determine which pairs of means are significantly different is the post hoc test discussed in Section 10.8. The post hoc test is a multiple comparison test for the significance of the difference between two sample means. It is equivalent to the *t* test covered in Chapter 9, except all possible pairs of sample means are tested. The post hoc test is like performing a series of *t* tests.

Exercises (using *Census.sav*)

10.1 Use the **Recode** command illustrated in Demonstration 10.1 to collapse *provp* into the following three regions: 1) Atlantic Canada and Quebec, 2) Ontario, and 3) Manitoba, Saskatchewan, Alberta, and BC. The recoding instructions that should appear in the **Old → New** box are as follows:

$$10 \text{ thru } 24 \ \rightarrow \ 1$$
$$35 \qquad\qquad \rightarrow \ 2$$
$$46 \text{ thru } 59 \ \rightarrow \ 3$$

Next, use the **One-Way ANOVA** procedure to test for a significant difference between recoded *provp* as the independent variable (factor) and *agep* as the dependent variable. Write a sentence or two summarizing the results of this test.

10.2 Using Demonstration 10.2 as a guide, get an error bar graph for the variables in Exercise 10.1. Write a sentence or two of interpretation for the graph. Which regions appear to differ significantly from each other?

11

HYPOTHESIS TESTING IV
CHI SQUARE

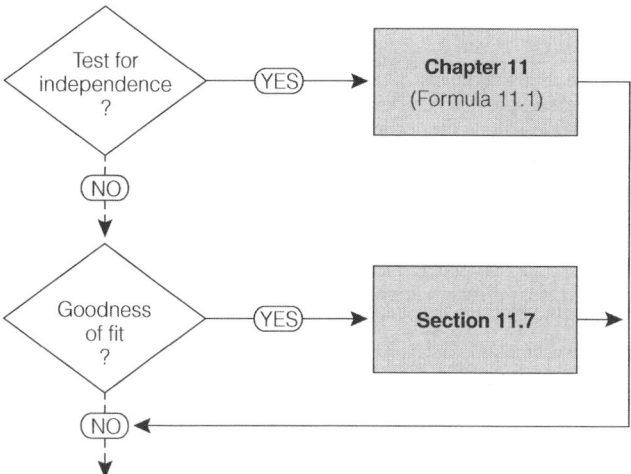

LEARNING OBJECTIVES   By the end of this chapter, you will be able to

1. Identify and cite examples of situations in which the chi square test is appropriate.
2. Explain the structure of a bivariate table and the concept of independence as applied to expected and observed frequencies in a bivariate table.
3. Explain the logic of hypothesis testing as applied to a bivariate table.
4. Perform the chi square test using the five-step model and correctly interpret the results.
5. Explain the limitations of the chi square test and, especially, the difference between statistical significance and importance.

11.1 INTRODUCTION   The **chi square (χ^2) test** has probably been the most frequently used test of hypothesis in the social sciences, a popularity that is due largely to the fact that the assumptions and requirements in step 1 of the five-step model are easy to satisfy. Specifically, the test can be conducted with variables measured at the nominal level (the lowest level of measurement) and, because it is a **non-parametric** or "distribution-free" test, it requires no assumption at all about the shape of the population or sampling distribution. While the Web site for this text provides discussion of other non-parametric tests of significance, the chi square test is the focus of this chapter.

Why is it an advantage to have assumptions and requirements that are easy to satisfy? The decision to reject the null hypothesis (step 5) is not specific: It means only that one statement in the model (step 1) *or* the null hypothesis (step 2) is wrong. Usually, of course, we single out the null hypothesis for rejection. The more certain we are of the model, the greater our confidence that the null hypothesis is the faulty assumption. A "weak" or easily satisfied model means that our decision to reject the null hypothesis can be made with even greater certainty.

Chi square has also been popular for its flexibility. Not only can it be used with variables at any level of measurement, it can be used with variables that have many categories or scores. For example, in Chapter 9, we tested the significance of the difference in the proportions of Americans and Canadians with an unmet health care need due to long waiting times. What if the researcher wished to expand the test to include British persons? The two-sample test would no longer be applicable, but chi square handles the more complex variable easily.

11.2 BIVARIATE TABLES

Chi square is computed from **bivariate tables,** so called because they display the scores of cases on two different variables at the same time. Bivariate tables are used to ascertain if there is a significant relationship between the variables and for other purposes that we will investigate in later chapters. In fact, these tables are very commonly used in research, and a detailed examination of them is in order.

First of all, bivariate tables have (of course) two dimensions. The horizontal (across) dimension is referred to in terms as **rows,** and the vertical dimension (up and down) is referred to in terms of **columns.** Each column or row represents a score on a variable, and the intersections of the row and columns **(cells)** represent the various combined scores on both variables.

Let's use an example to clarify. Suppose a researcher is interested in the relationship between sex and participation in voluntary groups, community-service organizations, and so forth. Is there a difference in the level of involvement in volunteer groups between the sexes? We have two variables here (sex and number of memberships) and, for the sake of simplicity, assume that number of memberships is a simple dichotomy. That is, people have been classified as either male or female and as either high or low in their level of involvement in voluntary associations.

By convention, the independent variable (the variable that is taken to be the cause) is placed in the columns and the dependent variable in the rows. In the example at hand, sex is the causal variable (the question was "is membership *affected by* sex?"), and each column will represent a score on this variable. Each row, on the other hand, will represent a score on level of membership (high or low). Table 11.1 displays the outline of the bivariate table for a sample of 100 people.

Note some further details of the table. First, subtotals have been added to each column and row. These are called the row or column **marginals,** and, in this case, they tell us that 50 members of the sample were male

TABLE 11.1   RATES OF PARTICIPATION IN VOLUNTARY ASSOCIATIONS
BY SEX FOR 100 CITIZENS

	Sex		
Participation Rates	Male	Female	
High			50
Low			50
	50	50	100

and 50 were female (the column marginals) and 50 were rated as high in participation and 50 were rated low (the row marginals). Second, the total number of cases in the sample ($N = 100$) is reported at the intersection of the row and column marginals. Finally, take careful note of the labelling of the table. Each row and column is identified and the table has a descriptive title that includes the names of the variables with the dependent variable listed first. Clear, complete labels and concise titles should be included in *all* tables, graphs, and charts.

As you probably noticed, Table 11.1 lacks one piece of crucial information: the numbers of each sex that rated high or low on the dependent variable. To finish the table, we need to classify each member of the sample in terms of both their sex and their level of participation, keep count of how often each combination of scores occurs, and record these numbers in the appropriate cell of the table. Because each of our variables (sex and participation rates) has two scores, there are four possible combinations of scores, each corresponding to a cell in the table. For example, males with high levels of participation would be counted in the upper-left-hand cell, females with low levels of participation would be counted in the lower-right-hand cell, and so forth. When we are finished counting, each cell will display the number of times each combination of scores occurred.

Finally, note how the bivariate table could be expanded to accommodate variables with more scores. For instance, if we had measured participation rates with three categories (e.g., high, moderate, and low) rather than two, we would simply add an additional row to the table.

11.3 THE LOGIC OF CHI SQUARE

The chi square test has several different uses. Most of this chapter will deal with an application called the chi square test for **independence.** We have encountered the term *independence* in connection with the requirements for the two-sample case (Chapter 9) and for the ANOVA test (Chapter 10). In those situations, we noted that independent random samples are gathered such that the selection of a particular case for one sample has no effect on the probability that any particular case will be selected for the other sample (see Section 9.2).

In the context of chi square, the concept of independence takes on a slightly different meaning because it refers to the relationship between the variables, not the samples. Two variables are independent if the classification of a case into a particular category of one variable has no effect on the probability that the case will fall into any particular category of the second variable. For example, sex and participation in voluntary associations would be independent of each other if the classification of a case as male or female has no effect on the classification of the case as high or low on participation. In other words, the variables would be independent if level of participation and sex were completely unrelated to each other.

Consider Table 11.1 again. If these two variables are truly independent, the cell frequencies will be determined solely by random chance and we would find that, just as an honest coin will show heads about 50% of the time when flipped, about half of the male respondents will rank high on participation and half will rank low. The same pattern would hold for the 50 female respondents and, therefore, each of the four cells would have about 25 cases in it, as illustrated in Table 11.2. This pattern of cell frequencies indicates that the sex of the subjects has no effect on the probability that they would be either high or low in participation. The probability of being classified as high or low would be 0.5 for both males and females, and the variables would therefore be independent.

The null hypothesis for chi square is that the variables are independent. Under the assumption that the null hypothesis is true, the cell frequencies we would expect to find if only random chance were operating are computed. These frequencies, called **expected frequencies** (symbolized f_e), are then compared, cell-by-cell, with the frequencies actually observed in the table (**observed frequencies,** symbolized f_o). If the null hypothesis is true and the variables are independent, then there should be little difference between the expected and observed frequencies. If the null is false, however, there should be large differences between the two. The greater the differences between expected (f_e) and observed (f_o) frequencies, the less likely that the variables are independent and the more likely that we will be able to reject the null hypothesis.

TABLE 11.2 THE CELL FREQUENCIES THAT WOULD BE EXPECTED IF RATES OF PARTICIPATION AND SEX WERE INDEPENDENT

Participation Rates	Sex		
	Male	Female	
High	25	25	50
Low	25	25	50
	50	50	100

11.4 THE COMPUTATION OF CHI SQUARE

As with all tests of hypothesis, with chi square we compute a test statistic, χ^2**(obtained)** from the sample data and then place that value on the sampling distribution of all possible sample outcomes. Specifically, the χ^2(obtained) will be compared with the value of χ^2**(critical)** that will be determined by consulting a chi square table (Appendix C) for a particular alpha level and degrees of freedom. Prior to conducting the formal test of hypothesis, let us take a moment to consider the calculation of chi square, as defined by Formula 11.1.

FORMULA 11.1

$$\chi^2(\text{obtained}) = \sum \frac{(f_o - f_e)^2}{f_e}$$

where f_o = the cell frequencies observed in the bivariate table
f_e = the cell frequencies that would be expected if the variables were independent

We must work on a cell-by-cell basis to solve this formula. To compute chi square, subtract the expected frequency from the observed frequency for each cell, square the result, divide by the expected frequency for that cell, and then sum the resultant values for all cells.

This formula requires an expected frequency for each cell in the table. In Table 11.2, the marginals are the same value for all rows and columns, and the expected frequencies are obvious by intuition: $f_e = 25$ for all four cells. In the more usual case, the expected frequencies will not be obvious, marginals will be unequal, and we must use Formula 11.2 to find the expected frequency for each cell:

FORMULA 11.2

$$f_e = \frac{\text{Row marginal} \times \text{Column marginal}}{N}$$

That is, the expected frequency for any cell is equal to the total number of cases in the row (the row marginal) times the total number of cases in the column (the column marginal) divided by the total number of cases in the table (N).

An example using Table 11.3 should clarify these procedures. A random sample of 100 social work graduates have been classified in terms of whether the Canadian Association of Schools of Social Work (CASSW) has accredited their undergraduate programs (the column or independent variable) and whether they were hired in social work positions within three months of graduation (the row or dependent variable).

Beginning with the upper-left-hand cell (graduates of CASSW-accredited programs who are working as social workers), the expected frequency for this cell, using Formula 11.2, is (40)(55)/100, or 22. For the other cell in this row (graduates of non-accredited programs who are working as social workers), the expected frequency is (40)(45)/100, or 18. For the two cells in the bottom row, the expected frequencies are (60)(55)/100, or 33, and (60)(45)/100, or 27, respectively. The expected frequencies for all four cells are displayed in Table 11.4.

TABLE 11.3   EMPLOYMENT OF 100 SOCIAL WORK GRADUATES BY CASSW-ACCREDITATION STATUS OF UNDERGRADUATE PROGRAM (FICTITIOUS DATA)

Employment Status	Accreditation Status		Totals
	Accredited	Not Accredited	
Working as a social worker	30	10	40
Not working as a social worker	25	35	60
Totals	55	45	100

TABLE 11.4   EXPECTED FREQUENCIES FOR TABLE 11.3

Employment Status	Accreditation Status		Totals
	Accredited	Not Accredited	
Working as a social worker	22	18	40
Not working as a social worker	33	27	60
Totals	55	45	100

TABLE 11.5   COMPUTATIONAL TABLE FOR TABLE 11.3

(1)	(2)	(3)	(4)	(5)
f_o	f_e	$f_o - f_e$	$(f_o - f_e)^2$	$(f_o - f_e)^2 / f_e$
30	22	8	64	2.91
10	18	−8	64	3.56
25	33	−8	64	1.94
35	27	8	64	2.37
$N = 100$	$N = 100$	0	χ^2(obtained) = 10.78	

Note that the row and column marginals as well as the total number of cases in Table 11.4 are exactly the same as those in Table 11.3. The row and column marginals for the expected frequencies must *always* equal those of the observed frequencies, a relationship that provides a convenient way of checking your arithmetic to this point.

The value for chi square for these data can now be found by solving Formula 11.1. It will be helpful to use a computing table, such as Table 11.5, to organize the several steps required to compute chi square. The table lists the observed frequencies (f_o) in column 1 in order from the upper-left-hand cell to the lower-right-hand cell, moving left to right across the table and top to bottom. Column 2 lists the expected frequencies (f_e) in exactly the same order. Double-check to make sure that you have listed the cell frequencies in the same order for both of these columns.

The next step is to subtract the expected frequency from the observed frequency for each cell and list these values in column 3. To complete column 4, square the value in column 3 and then, in column 5, divide the column 4 value by the expected frequency for that cell. Finally, add up column 5. The sum of this column is χ^2(obtained).

$$\chi^2\text{(obtained)} = 10.78$$

Note that the totals for columns 1 and 2 (f_o and f_e) are exactly the same. This will always be the case, and, if the totals do not match, you have probably made a mistake in the calculation of the expected frequencies. Also note that the sum of column 3 will always be zero, another convenient way to check your math to this point.

This sample value for chi square must still be tested for its significance. *(For practice in computing chi square, see problem 11.1.)*

11.5 THE CHI SQUARE TEST FOR INDEPENDENCE

As always, the five-step model for significance testing will provide the framework for organizing our decision making. The data presented in Table 11.3 will serve as our example.

Step 1. **Making Assumptions and Meeting Test Requirements**. Note that we make no assumptions at all about the shape of the sampling distribution.

Model: Independent random samples
Level of measurement is nominal

Step 2. **Stating the Null Hypothesis**. As stated previously, the null hypothesis in the case of chi square states that the two variables are independent. If the null is true, the differences between the observed and expected frequencies will be small. As usual, the research hypothesis directly contradicts the null. Thus, if we reject H_0, the research hypothesis will be supported.

H_0: The two variables are independent
(H_1: The two variables are dependent)

Step 3. **Selecting the Sampling Distribution and Establishing the Critical Region**. The sampling distribution of sample chi squares, unlike the Z and t distributions, is positively skewed, with higher values of sample chi squares in the upper tail of the distribution (to the right). Thus, with the chi square test, the critical region is established in the upper tail of the sampling distribution.

Values for χ^2(critical) are given in Appendix C. This table is similar to the t table, with alpha levels arrayed across the top and degrees of freedom down the side. A major difference, however, is that degrees of freedom (df) for chi square are found by the following formula:

FORMULA 11.3

$$\text{df} = (r - 1)(c - 1)$$

FIGURE 11.1   THE CHI SQUARE DISTRIBUTION, WITH REJECTION REGION FOR ALPHA 0.05, (df = 1) IN SHADE

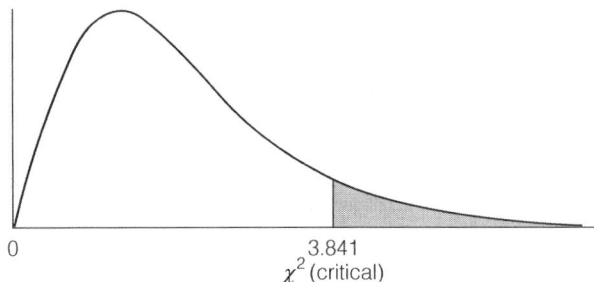

$$0 \qquad\qquad\qquad\qquad \begin{array}{c} 3.841 \\ \chi^2\text{(critical)} \end{array}$$

A table with two rows and two columns (a 2 × 2 table) has one degree of freedom regardless of the number of cases in the sample.* A table with two rows and three columns would have (2 − 1)(3 − 1), or two degrees of freedom. Our sample problem involves a 2 × 2 table with df = 1, so if we set alpha at 0.05, the critical chi square score would be 3.841. Summarizing these decisions, we have

$$\text{Sampling distribution} = \chi^2 \text{ distribution}$$
$$\text{Alpha} = 0.05$$
$$\text{Degrees of freedom} = 1$$
$$\chi^2\text{(critical)} = 3.841$$

The sampling distribution of χ^2 is depicted in Figure 11.1.

Step 4. Computing the Test Statistic. The mechanics of these computations were introduced in Section 11.4. As you recall, we had

$$\chi^2\text{(obtained)} = \sum \frac{(f_o - f_e)^2}{f_e}$$
$$\chi^2\text{(obtained)} = 10.78$$

Step 5. Making a Decision and Interpreting the Results of the Test. Comparing the test statistic with the critical region,

$$\chi^2\text{(obtained)} = 10.78$$
$$\chi^2\text{(critical)} = 3.841$$

---

*Degrees of freedom are the number of values in a distribution that are free to vary for any particular statistic. A 2 × 2 table has one degree of freedom because, for a given set of marginals, once one cell frequency is determined, all other cell frequencies are fixed (i.e., they are no longer free to vary). In Table 11.3, for example, if any cell frequency is known, all others are determined. If the upper-left-hand cell is known to be 30, the remaining cell in that row must be 10, because there are 40 cases total in the row and 40 − 30 = 10. Once the frequencies of the cells in the top row are established, cell frequencies for the bottom row are determined by subtraction from the column marginals. Incidentally, this relationship can be used to good advantage when computing expected frequencies. For example, in a 2 × 2 table, only one expected frequency needs to be computed. The f_e's for all other cells can then be found by subtraction.

we see that the test statistic falls into the critical region and, therefore, we reject the null hypothesis of independence. The pattern of cell frequencies observed in Table 11.3 is unlikely to have occurred by chance alone. The variables are dependent. Specifically, based on these sample data, the probability of securing employment in the field of social work is dependent on the CASSW-accreditation status of the program. *(For practice in conducting and interpreting the chi square test for independence, see problems 11.2 to 11.15.)*

Let's take a moment to stress exactly what the chi square test does and does not tell us. A significant chi square means that the variables are (probably) dependent on each other in the population: CASSW-accreditation status makes a difference in whether or not a person is working as a social worker. Chi square does not give us any detail about the relationship, however. In our example, it does not tell us if it's the graduates of the accredited programs or the non-accredited programs that are more likely to be working as social workers. To compare these two groups, we must perform some additional calculations. We can figure out how the independent variable (CASSW-accreditation status) is affecting the dependent variable (employment as a social worker) by computing *column percents* or by calculating percentages within each column of the bivariate table. This procedure is analogous to calculating percentages for frequency distributions (see Chapter 2).

To calculate column percentages, divide each cell frequency by the total number of cases in the column (the column marginal). For Table 11.3, starting in the upper-left-hand cell, we see that there are 30 cases in this cell and 55 cases in the column. In other words, 30 of the 55 graduates of CASSW-accredited programs are working as social workers. The column percentage for this cell is therefore: $(30/55) \times 100 = 54.55\%$. For the lower-left-hand cell, the column percent is $(25/55) \times 100 = 45.45\%$. For the two cells in the right-hand column (graduates of non-accredited programs), the column percents are $(10/45) \times 100 = 22.22$ and $(35/45) \times 100 = 77.78$. All column percents are displayed in Table 11.6.

Column percents help to make the relationship between the two variables more obvious and we can see easily from Table 11.6 that students from CASSW-accredited programs are more likely to be working as social

TABLE 11.6   COLUMN PERCENTS FOR TABLE 11.3

Employment Status	Accreditation Status		Totals
	Accredited	Not Accredited	
Working as a social worker	54.55%	22.22%	40.00%
Not working as a social worker	45.45%	77.78%	60.00%
Totals	100.00% (55)	100.00% (45)	100.00%

workers. Nearly 55% of these students are working as social workers versus less than 25% of the students from non-accredited programs. We already knew that this relationship is significant (unlikely to be caused by random chance) and now, with the aid of column percents, we know how the two variables are related. According to these results, graduating from a CASSW-accredited program would be a decided advantage for people seeking to enter the social work profession.

Let's highlight two points in summary:

1. Chi square is a test of statistical significance. It tests the null hypothesis that the variables are independent in the population. If we reject the null hypothesis, we are concluding, with a known probability of error (determined by the alpha level), that the variables are dependent on each other in the population. In the terms of our example, this means that CASSW-accreditation status makes a difference in the likelihood of finding work as a social worker. By itself, however, chi square does not tell us the exact nature of the relationship.

2. Computing column percents allows us to examine the bivariate relationship in more detail. By comparing the column percents for the various scores of the independent variable, we can see exactly how the independent variable affects the dependent variable. In this case, the column percents reveal that graduates of CASSW-accredited programs are more likely to find work as social workers. We will explore column percentages more extensively when we discuss bivariate association in Chapters 12 through 14.

11.6 THE CHI SQUARE TEST: AN EXAMPLE

To this point, we have confined our attention to 2 × 2 tables. For purposes of illustration, we will work through the computational routines and decision-making process for larger (4 × 2) tables using data from the World Values Survey. As you will see, larger tables require more computations (because they have more cells); in all other essentials, they are dealt with in the same way as 2 × 2 tables.

The World Values Survey is administered by a network of social scientists about every five years to randomly selected samples of citizens from around the globe. It is designed to allow cross-national comparisons of values and norms on a wide variety of topics including opinions on life, family, work, traditional values, morality, religion, politics, the environment, and other contemporary social issues. World Values Survey data can be downloaded for free on the Internet at http://www.worldvaluessurvey.org.

We will use the World Values Survey to examine the relationship between the respondent's country of residence—the independent variable—and the importance of politics in the life of the respondent—the dependent variable. The analysis is limited to residents of Canada and the United States. Table 11.7 displays the bivariate table for this relationship.

TABLE 11.7 IMPORTANCE OF POLITICS BY COUNTRY

| | Country | | |
Importance of Politics	Canada	U.S.	Totals
Very important	174	188	362
Rather important	609	492	1,101
Not very important	807	421	1,228
Not at all important	333	93	426
Totals	1,923	1,194	3,117

Source: World Values Survey.

The World Values Survey is administered to random samples of individuals selected in accordance with the rules of EPSEM (see Chapter 6), so we can assume that the results apply to the general populations of Canada and U.S.

Our first step in conducting a chi square test is to compute the expected frequency for each cell in the bivariate table. To do so we use Formula 11.2. In the first row, the expected frequency for the left-hand cell is (362)(1,923)/3,117, or 223.3; the expected frequency for the middle cell is (362)(1,194)/3,117, or 138.7. In the second row, the expected frequencies for the left-hand cell is (1,101)(1,923)/3,117, or 679.3; the expected frequency for the middle cell is (1,101)(1,194)/3,117, or 421.7. In the third row, the expected frequency for the left-hand cell is (1,228)(1,923)/3,117, or 757.6; the expected frequency for the middle cell is (1,228)(1,194)/3,117, or 470.4. Finally, for the fourth row, the expected frequency for the left-hand cell is (426)(1,923)/3,117, or 262.8; the expected frequency for the middle cell is (426)(1,194)/3,117, or 163.2. These results are displayed in Table 11.8.

The next step involves solving the formula for χ^2 (obtained) for the bivariate table, being very careful to be certain that we are using the proper f_o's and f_e's for each cell. We use a computational table, Table 11.9, to organize

TABLE 11.8 EXPECTED FREQUENCIES FOR TABLE 11.7

| | Country | | |
Importance of Politics	Canada	U.S.	Totals
Very important	223.33	138.67	362
Rather important	679.25	421.75	1,101
Not very important	757.60	470.40	1,228
Not at all important	262.82	163.18	426
Totals	1,923.00	1,194.00	3,117

TABLE 11.9 COMPUTATIONAL TABLE FOR TABLE 11.7

		Importance of Politics by Country		
(1)	(2)	(3)	(4)	(5)
f_o	f_e	$f_o - f_e$	$(f_o - f_e)^2$	$(f_o - f_e)^2/f_e$
174	223.33	−49.33	2,433.45	10.90
188	138.67	49.33	2,433.45	17.55
609	679.25	−70.25	4,935.06	7.27
492	421.75	70.25	4,935.06	11.70
807	757.60	49.40	2,440.36	3.22
421	470.40	−49.40	2,440.36	5.19
333	262.82	70.18	4,925.23	18.74
931	163.18	−70.18	4,925.23	30.18
$N = 3,117$	$N = 3,117.00$		χ^2 (obtained) = 104.75	

the calculations. We see here, in the total of column 5, that the value of the obtained chi square is 104.75.

In our next step we test the obtained chi square for its statistical significance. The five-step model for significance testing will provide the framework for organizing our decision making.

Step 1. Making Assumptions and Meeting Test Requirements.

Model: Independent random samples
Level of measurement is nominal

Step 2. Stating the Null Hypothesis.

H_0: The two variables are independent
(H_1: The two variables are dependent)

Step 3. Selecting the Sampling Distribution and Establishing the Critical Region.

Sampling distribution = χ^2 distribution
Alpha = 0.05
Degrees of freedom = $(r - 1)(c - 1) = (4 - 1)(2 - 1) = 3$
χ^2(critical) = 7.815

Step 4. Computing the Test Statistic.

$$\chi^2(\text{obtained}) = \sum \frac{(f_o - f_e)^2}{f_e}$$

$$\chi^2(\text{obtained}) = 104.75$$

TABLE 11.10 COLUMN PERCENTS FOR TABLE 11.7

Importance of Politics	Country		Totals
	Canada	U.S.	
Very important	9.05	15.75	11.61
Rather important	31.67	41.21	35.32
Not very important	41.97	35.26	39.40
Not at all important	17.31	7.78	13.67
Totals	100.00%	100.00%	100.00%

Step 5. Making a Decision and Interpreting the Results of the Test. The test statistic, χ^2(obtained) = 104.75, falls into the critical region, which, for alpha = 0.05, df = 3, begins at χ^2(critical) = 7.815. We therefore reject the null hypothesis. The observed frequencies are significantly different from the frequencies we would expect to find if the variables were independent. We can conclude that the importance of politics in peoples' lives is dependent on country or residence.

To complete the analysis, it would be useful to know exactly how the two variables are related. We can determine this by computing and analyzing column percents. The column percents in Table 11.10 show that almost 60% of Americans said that politics are either very or rather important in their lives. Just over 40% of Canadians said the same. We have already concluded that the relationship is significant and now we know the pattern of the relationship: Politics tend to be more important in the lives of Americans than Canadians.

11.7 AN ADDITIONAL APPLICATION OF THE CHI SQUARE TEST: THE GOODNESS-OF-FIT TEST*

To this point we have dealt with the chi square test for independence for situations involving two variables, each of which has two or more categories. Another situation in which the chi square statistic is useful, called the **goodness-of-fit test,** is one in which the distribution of scores on a single variable must be tested for significance. The logic underlying this second research situation is quite similar to that of the test for independence. The chi square statistic will be computed by comparing the actual distribution of a variable against a set of expected frequencies. The greater the difference between the observed distribution of scores and the expected distribution, the more likely that the observed pattern did not occur by random chance alone. If the observed and expected frequencies

---

*This section is optional.

As previously discussed, the World Values Survey collects information on opinions and attitudes on a variety of social issues from people around the globe. Here we will use the data to test the significance of the relationship between support for obedience as a socialization goal and gender using randomly selected samples of respondents from both the United States and Canada. Respondents to the World Values Survey were given a list of possible socialization goals and asked to select the goals they thought were most important. Those that included obedience in their list were coded as "Yes" in the tables that follow.

The relationship for the U.S. sample is:

United States

| Obedience Mentioned? | Gender | | Totals |
	Male	Female	
Yes	727	769	1,496
No	1,395	1,560	2,955
Totals	2,122	2,329	4,451

and chi square is computed with the following table:

(1)	(2)	(3)	(4)	(5)
f_o	f_e	$f_o - f_e$	$(f_o - f_e)^2$	$(f_o - f_e)^2 / f_e$
727	713.21	13.79	190.16	0.27
769	782.79	−13.79	190.16	0.24
1,395	1,408.79	−13.79	190.16	0.14
1,560	1,546.21	13.79	190.16	0.12
$N = 4,451$	$N = 4,451$		χ^2(obtained) = 0.77	

This is a 2 × 2 table, so there is one degree of freedom and the critical chi square is 3.841. The relationship is not significant but we will still look at the pattern of the column percentages:

United States

| Obedience Mentioned? | Gender | | Totals |
	Male	Female	
Yes	34.26	33.02	33.61
No	65.74	66.98	66.39
Totals	100.00	100.00	100.00

Not only is the relationship not significant, there is virtually no difference between U.S. males and females in their support for obedience.

Are the variables related in the Canadian sample? The bivariate table is:

Canada

| Obedience Mentioned? | Gender | | Totals |
	Male	Female	
Yes	350	384	734
No	1,118	1,144	2,262
Totals	1,468	1,528	2,996

and we will use a computing table to get the value of chi square:

(1)	(2)	(3)	(4)	(5)
f_o	f_e	$f_o - f_e$	$(f_o - f_e)^2$	$(f_o - f_e)^2 / f_e$
350	359.65	−9.65	93.12	0.26
384	374.35	9.65	93.12	0.25
1,118	1,108.35	9.65	93.12	0.08
1,144	1,153.65	−9.65	93.12	0.08
$N = 2,996$	$N = 2,996$		χ^2(obtained) = 0.67	

As before, this 2 × 2 table has one degree of freedom and the critical chi square is 3.841. As was the case for the U.S. sample, there is no significant relationship between gender and support for this socialization goal in the Canadian sample.

Looking at the column percentages, we find virtually no difference between Canadian males and females in their support for obedience:

Canada

| Obedience Mentioned? | Gender | | Totals |
	Male	Female	
Yes	23.84	25.13	24.49
No	76.16	74.87	75.51
Totals	100.00	100.00	100.00

Note that although there is no difference between genders in either national sample, the support for obedience in the Canadian sample is about 10 percentage points lower.

Source: World Values Survey.

are similar, it is said that there is a "good fit" (hence the name of this application), and we would conclude that the two distributions were not significantly different.

A major difference in this new application lies in the way in which the expected frequencies are ascertained. Instead of computing these scores, the null hypothesis is used to figure out what the expected frequencies should be. An example may make this process clear. Suppose you were gambling on coin tosses and suspected that a particular coin was biased toward heads. Over a series of tosses, what percentage of heads would you expect to observe from an unbiased coin? In an actual test of significance for this problem, the null hypothesis would be that the coin was unbiased and that half of all tosses should be heads and half tails. Notice what we have just done: We figured out the expected frequencies (half of the flips should be heads) from the null hypothesis (the coin is unbiased), rather than by computing them.

Let's consider another example of a situation in which the goodness-of-fit test is appropriate. Is there a seasonal rhythm to the crime rate? If we gathered monthly crime statistics for a random sample of jurisdictions, what would we expect to find? Given the way in which the problem has been stated, there is only one variable (crime rate), and the focus is on the distribution of that variable over a given set of categories (by month). If the crime rate does *not* vary by month, we would expect that about 1/12 of all crimes committed in a year would be committed in each and every month. Our null hypothesis would be that the crime rate does not vary across time, and our expected frequencies would be calculated by dividing the actual (observed) number of crimes equally by the number of months. (To conserve time and space, we will ignore the slight complexities that would be introduced by taking account of the varying number of days per month.)

In a random sample of jurisdictions, a total of 2,172 crimes were committed last year. The actual distribution of crimes by month is displayed in Table 11.11. The expected distribution of crimes per month would be found by dividing the total number of crimes by 12: $2{,}172/12 = 181$. Note that the expected frequency will be the same for every month. With these values determined, we can calculate chi square by using Formula 11.1.

$$\chi^2(\text{obtained}) = \sum \frac{(f_o - f_e)^2}{f_e}$$

$$\chi^2(\text{obtained}) = \frac{(190 - 181)^2}{181} + \frac{(152 - 181)^2}{181} + \frac{(121 - 181)^2}{181} + \frac{(110 - 181)^2}{181}$$

$$+ \frac{(147 - 181)^2}{181} + \frac{(199 - 181)^2}{181} + \frac{(250 - 181)^2}{181} + \frac{(247 - 181)^2}{181}$$

$$+ \frac{(201 - 181)^2}{181} + \frac{(150 - 181)^2}{181} + \frac{(193 - 181)^2}{181} + \frac{(212 - 181)^2}{181}$$

TABLE 11.11 NUMBER OF CRIMES PER MONTH

Month	Number of Crimes
January	190
February	152
March	121
April	110
May	147
June	199
July	250
August	247
September	201
October	150
November	193
December	212
	2,172

$$\chi^2(\text{obtained}) = \frac{81}{181} + \frac{841}{181} + \frac{3600}{181} + \frac{5041}{181}$$

$$+ \frac{1156}{181} + \frac{324}{181} + \frac{4761}{181} + \frac{4356}{181}$$

$$+ \frac{400}{181} + \frac{961}{181} + \frac{144}{181} + \frac{961}{181}$$

$$\chi^2(\text{obtained}) = 0.45 + 4.65 + 19.89 + 27.85 + 6.39 + 1.79 + 26.30 + 24.07$$
$$+ 2.21 + 5.31 + .80 + 5.31$$

$$\chi^2(\text{obtained}) = 125.02$$

The χ^2 of 125.02 can now be tested for significance in the usual manner.

Step 1. **Making Assumptions and Meeting Test Requirements.**

Model: Random sampling
Level of measurement is nominal

In this application of significance testing, we are assuming that the observed frequencies represent a random sample of all possible frequency distributions.

Step 2. **Stating the Null Hypothesis.**

H_0: There is no difference in the crime rate by month.
(H_1: There is a difference in the crime rate by month.)

Step 3. **Selecting the Sampling Distribution and Establishing the Critical Region.** In the goodness-of-fit test, degrees of freedom are equal to the number of categories minus 1, or df $= k - 1$. In the problem under consideration, there are 12 months or categories and, therefore, 11 degrees of freedom.

$$\text{Sampling distribution} = \chi^2 \text{ distribution}$$
$$\text{Alpha} = .05$$
$$\text{Degrees of freedom} = k - 1 = 12 - 1 = 11$$
$$\chi^2(\text{critical}) = 19.675$$

Step 4. Computing the Test Statistic.

$$\chi^2(\text{obtained}) = 125.02$$

Step 5. Making a Decision and Interpreting the Results of the Test. The test statistic (125.02) clearly falls into the critical region (which begins at 19.675), so we may reject the null. These data suggest that crime rate does vary by month in a nonrandom fashion. *(For practice in conducting and interpreting the chi square goodness-of-fit test, see problems 11.16 and 11.17.)*

11.8 THE LIMITATIONS OF THE CHI SQUARE TEST

Like any other test, chi square has limits, and you should be aware of several potential difficulties. First, even though chi square is very flexible and handles many different types of variables, it becomes difficult to interpret when the variables have many categories. For example, two variables with five categories each would generate a 5 × 5 table with 25 cells—far too many combinations of scores to be easily absorbed or understood. As a very rough rule of thumb, the chi square test is easiest to interpret and understand when both variables have four or fewer scores.

Two further limitations of the test are related to sample size. When sample size is small, it can no longer be assumed that the sampling distribution of all possible sample outcomes is accurately described by the chi square distribution. For chi square, a small sample is defined as one where a high percentage of the cells have expected frequencies (f_e) of 5 or less. Various rules of thumb have been developed to help the researcher decide what constitutes a "high percentage of cells." Probably the safest course is to take corrective action whenever *any* of the cells have expected frequencies of 5 or less.

In the case of 2 × 2 tables, the value of $\chi^2(\text{obtained})$ can be adjusted by applying Yates' correction for continuity, the formula for which is

FORMULA 11.4

$$\chi_c^2 = \sum \frac{(|f_o - f_e| - 0.5)^2}{f_e}$$

where χ_c^2 = corrected chi square
$|f_o - f_e|$ = the absolute values of the difference between the observed and expected frequency for each cell

The correction factor is applied by reducing the absolute value* of the term $(f_o - f_e)$ by .5 before squaring the difference and dividing by the expected frequency for the cell.

---

*Absolute values ignore plus and minus signs.

READING STATISTICS 8: Gender Differences in Health

In this section, we will examine a study on gender and health among Canadian university students. The research was conducted by a group of scholars in the Department of Kinesiology and Physical Education at Wilfrid Laurier University.

The research team selected a sample of 166 male and 472 female undergraduate students. Each student answered questions about their overall health and health-related behaviours during the current school year. The bivariate tables below show relationship between gender and participation in physical activity, hours per day engaged in social activities, and general state of health. Chi square was used to assess each relationship for statistical significance at the 0.05 alpha level. Significant relationships are symbolized as $p < 0.05$ in the tables. This tells us that the relationship would occur by chance alone less than 1 in 20 times, or 5% of the time (see the discussion of the "p" format in Reading Statistics 6).

The first and second bivariate tables reveal that gender is significantly related to both physical and social activity at the 0.05 level. Looking at the column percents, we see how these variables are related. Almost three out of ten (27%) male respondents participated five or more times per week in physical activity. The comparable figure for females is about two out of ten (19%). Males are also more socially active: about 21% spent five to six hours per day in social activity compared to less than 15% of female respondents.

HEALTH BEHAVIOURS AND HEALTH STATUS BY GENDER: Frequencies and Percentages[*]

1. Participation in physical activity	Gender	
	Male	Female
Never	6 (3.6%)	28 (5.9%)
1–2 times/week	48 (29.1%)	198 (41.9%)
3–4 times/week	66 (40.0%)	155 (32.8%)
5+ times/week	45 (27.3%)	91 (19.3%)
Totals	165 (100.0%)	472 (99.9%)
	$\chi^2 = 11.9, p < 0.05$	

2. Hours/day engaged in social activities	Gender	
	Male	Female
0–2	25 (15.2%)	108 (23.0%)
3–4	92 (55.8%)	273 (58.2%)
5–6	35 (21.2%)	67 (14.3%)
6+	13 (7.9%)	21 (4.5%)
Totals	165 (100.1%)	469 (100.0%)
	$\chi^2 = 10.0, p < 0.05$	

3. General state of health	Gender	
	Male	Female
Excellent	53 (32.5%)	104 (22.2%)
Good	96 (58.9%)	320 (68.2%)
Poor/Fair	14 (8.6%)	45 (9.5%)
Totals	163 (100.0%)	469 (99.9%)
	$\chi^2 = 6.9, p < 0.05$	

[*] Percentages may not total to 100% because of rounding error.

Turning to the third bivariate table, we see that the relationship between gender and general health state is statistically significant at the 0.05 level. Further, almost 33% of males in the sample have excellent health compared to 22% of females. According to the authors, the relationship between gender and general health state among Canadian university students reflects differences in disease prevention and health promotion between males and females:

Although Canadian male university students engaged in negative health-related behaviors more frequently than female, this study also revealed that male students were engaging in two key positive and preventive health measures more than their female counterparts. First, male students were engaging more frequently than female students in physical activity. . . . This is important as regular exercise has been identified by numerous health

(continued)

READING STATISTICS 8: *(continued)*

organizations as reducing the risk of cardiovas-
cular illnesses and various cancers, as well as
increasing quality of life. . . . [Second], male students also engaged in significantly greater
amounts of social activity per day than
females. . . . Social activity may serve as a
buffer for college life stress for Canadian male

students and therefore act as a health promot-
ing behavior." (pp. 40–41)

Source: Reproduced with permission from Dawson, K.,
Schneider, M., Fletcher, P., & Bryden, P. 2007. "Examining
Gender Differences in the Health Behaviors of Canadian
University Students." *Journal of the Royal Society for the
Promotion of Health, 127:* 38–44 by permission, Ltd."

For tables larger than 2×2, there is no correction formula for computing χ^2(obtained) for small samples. It may be possible to combine some of
the categories of the variables and thereby increase cell sizes. Obviously,
however, this course of action should be taken only when it is sensible to
do so. In other words, distinctions that have clear theoretical justifications
should not be erased merely to conform to the requirements of a statistical
test. When you feel that categories cannot be combined to build up cell frequencies, and the percentage of cells with expected frequencies of 5 or less
is small, it is probably justifiable to continue with the uncorrected chi square
test as long as the results are regarded with a suitable amount of caution.

A second potential problem related to sample size occurs with large
samples. We pointed out in Chapter 9 that all tests of hypothesis are sensitive
to sample size. That is, the probability of rejecting the null hypothesis increases
as the number of cases increases, regardless of any other factor. It turns out
that chi square is especially sensitive to sample size and that larger samples
may lead to the decision to reject the null when the actual relationship is trivial. In fact, chi square is more responsive to changes in sample size than other
test statistics, because the value of χ^2(obtained) will increase at the same rate
as sample size. That is, if sample size is doubled, the value of χ^2(obtained) will
be doubled. *(For an illustration of this principle, see problem 11.14.)*

Our major purpose in stressing the relationship between sample size
and the value of chi square is really to point out, once again, the distinction
between statistical significance and theoretical importance. On one hand,
tests of significance play a crucial role in research. As long as we are working with random samples, we must know if our research results could have
been produced by mere random chance.

On the other hand, like any other statistical technique, tests of hypothesis are limited in the range of questions they can answer. Specifically, these
tests will tell us whether our results are statistically significant or not. They
will not necessarily tell us if the results are important in any other sense. To
deal more directly with questions of importance, we must use an additional
set of statistical techniques called measures of association. We previewed
these techniques in this chapter when we used column percents, and measures of association will be the subject of Part III of this text.

Application 11.2

There has been a good deal of public debate, particularly in the last decade, over privatization of Canadian health care system. Do attitudes toward privatization of health care vary by region of residence? Is attitude on privatization dependent on region? We will examine this issue with an actual random sample of 394 Canadians from the 2006 Canadian Election Study, and classify respondents by their region of residence—Atlantic Canada, Quebec, Ontario, and Western Canada—and, as a measure of privatization, by whether they favour or oppose having some private hospitals in Canada. (The Canadian Election Study surveyed adults in the 10 provinces only, thus excluding the territories.) The 2 × 4 table below shows these results:

	Region				
Attitude	Atlantic	Quebec	Ontario	Western	Totals
Favour	15	58	46	69	188
Oppose	21	38	65	57	181
Totals	36	96	111	126	369

Source: 2006 Canadian Election Study.

The frequencies we would expect to find if the null hypothesis (H_0: the variables are independent) were true are

	Region				
Attitude	Atlantic	Quebec	Ontario	Western	Totals
Favour	18.34	48.91	56.55	64.19	188.00
Oppose	17.66	47.09	54.45	61.81	181.00
Totals	36.00	96.00	111.00	126.00	369.00

Expected frequencies are found on a cell-by-cell basis by the formula

$$\frac{\text{Row marginal} \times \text{Column marginal}}{N}$$

And, the calculation of chi square will be organized into a computational table.

(1)	(2)	(3)	(4)	(5)
f_o	f_e	$f_o - f_e$	$(f_o - f_e)^2$	$(f_o - f_e)^2/f_e$
15	18.34	−3.34	11.15	0.61
58	48.91	9.09	82.63	1.69
46	56.55	−10.55	111.30	1.97
69	64.19	4.81	23.14	0.36
21	17.66	3.34	11.15	0.63
38	47.09	−9.09	82.63	1.75
65	54.45	10.55	111.30	2.04
57	61.81	−4.81	23.14	0.37
$N = 369$	$N = 369.00$			χ^2 (obtained) = 9.42

Step 1. Making Assumptions and Meeting Test Requirements.
Model: Independent random samples
Level of measurement is nominal

Step 2. Stating the Null Hypothesis.
H_0: The two variables are independent
(H_1: The two variables are dependent)

Step 3. Selecting the Sampling Distribution and Establishing the Critical Region.

Sampling distribution = χ^2 distribution
Alpha = 0.05
Degrees of freedom = (r − 1) (c − 1)
= (2 − 1) (4 − 1) = 3
χ^2 (critical) = 7.815

Step 4. Computing the Test Statistic.

$$\chi^2(\text{ obtained}) = \sum \frac{(f_o - f_e)^2}{f_e}$$
$$\chi^2(\text{obtained}) = 9.42$$

Step 5. Making a Decision and Interpreting the Results of the Test. With an obtained χ^2 of 9.42, we would reject the null hypothesis of independence. For this sample, there is a statistically significant relationship between region of residence and attitude toward health care privatization.

To complete the analysis, it would be useful to know exactly how the two variables are related. We can determine this by computing and analyzing column percents: *(continued)*

Application 11.2 *(continued)*

	Region				
Attitude	Atlantic	Quebec	Ontario	Western	Totals
Favour	41.67	60.42	41.44	54.76	50.95
Oppose	58.33	39.58	58.56	45.24	49.05
Totals	100.00%	100.00%	100.00%	100.00%	100.00%

The column percents show that just 41% of persons from the Atlantic provinces and Ontario favour having some private hospitals in Canada. By comparison, about 55% and 60% of persons from Western Canada and Quebec, respectively, favour the privatization of some hospitals. We have already concluded that the relationship is significant and now we know the pattern of the relationship.

SUMMARY

1. The chi square test for independence is appropriate for situations in which the variables of interest have been organized into table format. The null hypothesis is that the variables are independent or that the classification of a case into a particular category on one variable has no effect on the probability that the case will be classified into any particular category of the second variable.

2. Because chi square is non-parametric and requires only nominally measured variables, its model assumptions are easily satisfied. Furthermore, because it is computed from bivariate tables, in which the number of rows and columns can be easily expanded, the chi square test can be used in many situations in which other tests are inapplicable.

3. In the chi square test, we first find the frequencies that would appear in the cells if the variables were independent (f_e) and then compare those frequencies, cell by cell, with the frequencies actually observed in the cells (f_o). If the null is true, expected and observed frequencies should be quite close in value. The greater the difference between the observed and expected frequencies, the greater the possibility of rejecting the null.

4. The chi square test has several important limitations. It is often difficult to interpret when tables have many (more than four or five) dimensions. Also, as sample size (N) decreases, the chi square test becomes less trustworthy, and corrective action may be required. Finally, with very large samples, we may declare relatively trivial relationships to be statistically significant. As is the case with all tests of hypothesis, statistical significance is not the same thing as "importance" in any other sense. As a general rule, statistical significance is a necessary but not sufficient condition for theoretical or practical importance.

SUMMARY OF FORMULAS

Chi square (obtained):

$$11.1 \qquad \chi^2(\text{obtained}) = \sum \frac{(f_o - f_e)^2}{f_e}$$

Expected frequencies:

$$11.2 \qquad f_e = \frac{(\text{Row marginal} \times \text{Column marginal})}{N}$$

Degrees of freedom, bivariate tables:

$$11.3 \qquad df = (r - 1)(c - 1)$$

Yates' correction for continuity:

$$11.4 \qquad \chi^2_c = \sum \frac{(|f_o - f_e| - 0.5)^2}{f_e}$$

GLOSSARY

Bivariate table. A table that displays the joint frequency distributions of two variables.

Cells. The cross-classification categories of the variables in a bivariate table.

χ^2 (critical). The score on the sampling distribution of all possible sample chi squares that marks the beginning of the critical region.

χ^2 (obtained). The test statistic as computed from sample results.

Chi square test. A non-parametric test of hypothesis for variables that have been organized into a bivariate table.

Column. The vertical dimension of a bivariate table. By convention, each column represents a score on the independent variable.

Expected frequency (f_e). The cell frequencies that would be expected in a bivariate table if the variables were independent.

Goodness-of-fit test. An additional use for chi square that tests the significance of the distribution of a single variable.

Independence. The null hypothesis in the chi square test. Two variables are independent if, for all cases, the classification of a case on one variable has no effect on the probability that the case will be classified in any particular category of the second variable.

Marginals. The row and column subtotals in a bivariate table.

Non-parametric. A "distribution-free" test. These tests do not assume a normal sampling distribution.

Observed frequency (f_o). The cell frequencies actually observed in a bivariate table.

Row. The horizontal dimension of a bivariate table, conventionally representing a score on the dependent variable.

MULTIMEDIA RESOURCES

 http://www.healeystatistics.nelson.com

Visit the companion Web site for the first Canadian edition of *Statistics: A Tool for Social Research* to access a wide range of student resources. Begin by clicking on the Student Resources section of the book's Web site to access review quizzes, flash cards, and other study tools.

PROBLEMS

11.1 For each table below, calculate the obtained chi square. *(HINT: Calculate the expected frequencies for each cell with Formula 11.2. Double-check to make sure you are using the correct row and column marginals for each cell. It may be helpful to record the expected frequencies in table format as well—see Tables 11.2, 11.4, and 11.8. Next, use a computational table to organize the calculation for Formula 11.1—see Tables 11.5 and 11.9. For each cell, subtract expected frequency from observed frequency and record the result in column 3. Square the value in column 3 and record the result in column 4, and then divide the value in column 4 by the expected frequency for that cell and record the result in column 5. Remember that the sum of column 5 in the computational table is obtained chi square. As you proceed, double-check to make sure that you are using the correct values for each cell.)*

a.
20	25	45
20	25	45
45	45	90

b.
10	15	25
20	30	50
30	45	75

a.
20	25	45
30	30	60
55	45	100

b.
10	15	25
20	30	50
35	65	25

11.2 SOC A sample of 25 cities have been classified as high or low on their homicide rates and on the number of guns sold within the city limits. Is there a relationship between these two variables? Explain your results in a sentence or two.

Volume of Gun Sales	Homicide Rate		
	Low	High	Totals
High	8	5	13
Low	4	8	12
Totals	12	13	25

11.3 SW A local politician is concerned that a program for the homeless in her city is discriminating against females. The data below were taken from a random sample of female and male homeless people.

Received Services?	Sex		
	Female	Male	Totals
Yes	6	7	13
No	4	9	13
Totals	10	16	26

a. Is there a statistically significant relationship between sex and whether the person has received services from the program?
b. Compute column percents for the table to determine the pattern of the relationship. Which group was more likely to get services?

11.4 PS Is there a "gender gap" in support of the Liberal Party of Canada among university faculty? To answer this question, a sample of university faculty has been asked about their political party preference.

Party Preference	Sex		
	Male	Female	Totals
Liberal	10	15	25
Other	15	10	25
Totals	25	25	50

a. Is there a statistically significant relationship between sex and party preference?
b. Compute column percents for the table to determine the pattern of the relationship. Which sex is more likely to prefer the Liberals?

11.5 PA Is there a relationship between salary levels and unionization for public employees? The data below represent this relationship for fire departments in a random sample of 100 cities of roughly the same size. Salary data have been dichotomized at the median. Summarize your findings.

Salary	Status		
	Union	Non-union	Totals
High	21	29	50
Low	14	36	50
Totals	35	65	100

a. Is there a statistically significant relationship between these variables?
b. Compute column percents for the table to determine the pattern of the relationship. Which group was more likely to get high salaries?

11.6 SOC A program of pet therapy has been running at a local nursing home. Are the participants in the program more alert and responsive than non-participants? The results, drawn from a random sample of residents, are reported below.

Alertness	Status		
	Participants	Non-participants	Totals
High	23	15	38
Low	11	18	29
Totals	34	33	67

a. Is there a statistically significant relationship between participation and alertness?
b. Compute column percents for the table to determine the pattern of the relationship. Which group was more likely to be alert?

11.7 SOC The provincial Ministry of Education has rated a sample of local school boards for compliance with province-mandated guidelines for quality. Is the quality of a school board significantly related to the affluence of the community as measured by per capita income?

	Per Capita Income		
Quality	Low	High	Totals
Low	16	8	24
High	9	17	26
Totals	25	25	50

a. Is there a statistically significant relationship between these variables?

b. Compute column percents for the table to determine the pattern of the relationship. Are high- or low-income communities more likely to have high-quality schools?

11.8 CJ A local judge has been allowing some individuals convicted of "driving under the influence" to work in a hospital emergency room as an alternative to fines, suspensions, and other penalties. A random sample of offenders has been drawn. Do participants in this program have lower rates of recidivism for this offence?

	Status		
Recidivist?	Participants	Non-participants	Totals
Yes	60	123	183
No	55	108	163
Totals	115	231	346

a. Is there a statistically significant relationship between these variables?

b. Compute column percents for the table to determine the pattern of the relationship. Which group is more likely to be arrested again for driving under the influence?

11.9 SOC Is there a relationship between length of marriage and satisfaction with marriage? The necessary information has been collected from a random sample of 100 respondents drawn from a local community.

	Length of Marriage (in years)			
Satisfaction	Less than 5	5–10	More than 10	Totals
Low	10	20	20	50
High	20	20	10	50
Totals	30	40	30	100

a. Is there a statistically significant relationship between these variables? Write a sentence or two explaining your decision.

b. Compute column percents for the table to determine the pattern of the relationship. Which group is more likely to be highly satisfied?

11.10 PS Is there a relationship between political ideology and class standing? Are upperclass persons significantly different from lowerclass individual on this variable? The table below reports the relationship between these two variables for a random sample of 267 adult Canadians.

Political Ideology	Class Standing		
	Lowerclass	Upperclass	Totals
Liberal	43	40	83
Moderate	50	50	100
Conservative	40	44	84
Totals	133	134	267

a. Is there a statistically significant relationship between these variables?

b. Compute column percents for the table to determine the pattern of the relationship. Which group is more likely to be conservative?

11.11 SOC At a large urban university, about half of the students live off campus in various arrangements, and the other half live in residence on campus. Is academic performance dependent on living arrangements? The results based on a random sample of 300 students are presented below.

	Residential Status			
GPA	Off Campus with Roommates	Off Campus with Parent	On Campus	Totals
Low	22	20	48	90
Moderate	36	40	54	130
High	32	10	38	80
Totals	90	70	140	300

a. Is there a statistically significant relationship between these variables?

b. Compute column percents for the table to determine the pattern of the relationship. Which group is more likely to have a high GPA?

11.12 SOC An urban sociologist has built up a database describing a sample of the neighbourhoods in her city and has developed a scale by which each area can be rated for the "quality of life" (this includes measures of pollution, noise, open space, services available, and so on). She has also asked samples of residents of these areas about their level of satisfaction with their neighbourhoods.

	Quality of Life			
Satisfaction	Low	Moderate	High	Totals
Low	21	15	6	42
Moderate	12	25	21	58
High	8	17	32	57
Totals	41	57	59	157

a. Is there significant agreement between the sociologist's objective ratings of quality and the respondents' self-reports of satisfaction?

b. Compute column percents for the table to determine the pattern of the relationship. Which group is most likely to say that their satisfaction is high?

11.13 SOC Does support for the legalization of marijuana vary by region of Canada? The table displays the relationship between the two variables for a random sample of 1,020 adult Canadians.

	Region				
Legalize?	Atlantic	Central	Western	Northern	Totals
Yes	60	65	42	78	245
No	245	200	180	150	775
Totals	305	265	222	228	1,020

a. Is there a statistically significant relationship between these variables?

b. Compute column percents for the table to determine the pattern of the relationship. Which region is most likely to favour the legalization of marijuana?

11.14 SOC A researcher is concerned with the relationship between attitudes toward violence and violent behaviour. If attitudes "cause" behaviour (a very debatable proposition), then people who have positive attitudes toward violence should have high rates of violent behaviour. A pretest was conducted on 70 respondents and, among other things, the respondents were asked, "Have you been involved in a violent incident of any kind over the past six months?" The researcher established the following relationship:

	Attitude toward Violence		
Involvement	Favourable	Unfavourable	Totals
Yes	16	19	35
No	14	21	35
Totals	30	40	70

The chi square calculated on these data is .23, which is not significant at the .05 level (confirm this conclusion with your own calculations). Undeterred by this result, the researcher proceeded with the project and gathered a random sample of 7,000. In terms of percentage distributions, the results for the full sample were exactly the same as for the pretest:

	Attitude toward Violence		
Involvement	Favourable	Unfavourable	Totals
Yes	1,600	1,900	3,500
No	1,400	2,100	3,500
Totals	3,000	4,000	7,000

However, the chi square obtained is a very healthy 23.4 (confirm with your own calculations). Why is the full-sample chi square significant when the pretest was not? What happened? Do you think that the second result is important?

11.15 SOC Some results from a survey given to a random sample of Canadians are presented below. For each table, conduct the chi square test of significance and compute column percents. Write a sentence or two of interpretation for each test.

a. Support for the same-sex marriage by age:

	Age			
Support?	Younger than 30	30–49	50 and Older	Totals
Yes	154	360	213	727
No	179	441	429	1,049
Totals	333	801	642	1,776

b. Support for gun control by age:

	Age			
Support?	Younger than 30	30–49	50 and Older	Totals
Favour	361	867	675	1,903
Oppose	144	297	252	693
Totals	505	1,164	927	2,596

c. Fear of walking alone at night by age:

	Age			
Fear?	Younger than 30	30–49	50 and Older	Totals
Yes	147	325	300	772
No	202	507	368	1,077
Totals	349	832	668	1,849

d. Support for legalizing marijuana by age:

	Age			
Legalize?	Younger than 30	30–49	50 and Older	Totals
Should	128	254	142	524
Should not	224	534	504	1,262
Totals	352	788	646	1,786

e. Support for suicide when a person has an incurable disease by age:

	Age			
Support?	Younger than 30	30–49	50 and Older	Totals
Yes	225	537	367	1,129
No	107	270	266	643
Totals	332	807	633	1,772

11.16* SOC The director of athletics at the local high school wonders if the sports program is getting a proportional amount of support from each of the four grades. If there are roughly equal numbers of students in each grade, what does the following breakdown of attendance figures from a random sample of students in attendance at a recent basketball game suggest?

Grade	Frequencies
Nine	200
Ten	150
Eleven	120
Twelve	110
Totals	580

11.17* SOC A small town has roughly equal numbers of young, middle-age, and older residents. Are the three groups equally represented at town meetings? The attendance figures for a random sample drawn from those attending a meeting were

Group	Frequencies
Young	74
Middle-age	55
Older	53
Totals	182

Is there a statistically significant pattern here?

*This problem is optional.

Using SPSS for Windows to Conduct the Chi Square Test with the 2004 GSS

The demonstrations and exercises below use the 2004 GSS data set supplied with this text.

SPSS DEMONSTRATION 11.1 Does Criminal Victimization Vary by Sex?

The **Crosstabs** procedure in SPSS produces bivariate tables and a wide variety of statistics. This procedure is commonly used in social science research at all levels, and you will see many references to **Crosstabs** in chapters to come. We will introduce the command here, and we will return to it often in later sessions.

In this demonstration we ask two questions: "Is sex significantly related to criminal victimization?" and, if so, "Which sex is most likely to be a victim of crime?" We can answer these questions, at least for the 2004 GSS sample, by constructing a bivariate table to display the relationship between *sex* and *lifevict* (ever been a victim of crime). We will also request a chi square test for the table.

Start SPSS for Windows and load the 2004 GSS database (*GSS.sav*). From the main menu bar, click **Analyze, Descriptive Statistics,** and then **Crosstabs.** The **Crosstabs** dialog box will appear with the variables listed in a box on the left. Highlight *lifevict* and click the arrow to move the variable name into the **Row(s)** box, and then highlight *sex* and move it into the **Column(s)** box. Click the **Statistics** button at the top of the window and click the box next to **Chi-square.** Click **Continue.** Then, click the **Cells** button and check the boxes next to "**Expected**" in the **Counts** box and "**Column**" in the **Percentages** box. This will generate the expected frequencies and column percents, respectively, for the table. Click **Continue** and **OK,** and the output below will be produced. (Note, the output has been slightly edited for clarity, and will not exactly match the output on your screen.)

EVER BEEN A VICTIM OF CRIME * SEX CROSSTABULATION

			Sex		
			Male	Female	Total
Ever been a victim of crime	Yes	Count	530	414	944
		Expected Count	496.2	447.8	944.0
		% within Sex	66.3%	57.4%	62.1%
	No	Count	269	307	576
		Expected Count	302.8	273.2	576.0
		% within Sex	33.7%	42.6%	37.9%
Total			799	721	1,520
			100.0%	100.0%	100.0%

Chi-Square Tests

	Value	df	Asymp. Sig. (2-sided)
Pearson Chi-Square	12.792[†]	1	.000
Continuity Correction[*]	12.416	1	.000
Likelihood Ratio	12.795	1	.000
Linear-by-Linear Association	12.784	1	.000
N of Valid Cases	1520		

*Computed only for a 2 3 2 table.
†Zero cells (.0%) have expected count less than 5.

The crosstabulation table is small (2 × 2), and the information is straightforward. Let's begin with the cells. Each cell displays the observed frequency, or the number of cases, in the cell ("Count") and the column percent for that cell ("% within Sex"). For example, there were 530 respondents who were male and who had answered "yes" to being a victim of crime, and these were 66.3% of all male respondents. By contrast, there were 414 female respondents, or 57.4%, who reported being a victim. Males are generally more likely than females to have been a victim of crime at some point in the past.

The table also displays the expected frequency for each cell. The greater the differences between expected frequencies ("Expected Count") and observed frequencies ("Count"), the less likely that the variables are independent and the more likely that we will be able to reject the null hypothesis. The results of the chi square test are formally reported in the output block that follows the crosstabulation table.

The value of chi square (obtained) is found in the row "Pearson Chi-Square." The value of the obtained chi square is 12.792, the degree of freedom is 1, and the exact significance of the chi square is .000 (i.e., the exact probability of getting these results if only random chance is operating). Recall that when the exact probability value is less than .0005, SPSS cuts it off at three decimal places, or .000, to save space.

To test if there is a significant relationship between the variables we can manually compare the value of chi square (obtained) to the value of chi square (critical), determined by consulting the chi square table in Appendix C for a particular alpha level and degrees of freedom as we have practised throughout this chapter. Because SPSS provides the exact probability, there is no need to look up the test statistic in the chi-square table. The exact probability value, .000, is well below the standard indicator of a significant result (alpha = .05), so we reject the null hypothesis that the variables are independent and conclude that there is a statistically significant relationship between sex and victimization. Being a victim of crime is dependent on sex, and males are more likely to be a victim. In exercise 11.1, you will have the opportunity to investigate other variables that might be significantly related to victimization.

As a final note, the number of the cells with expected frequencies less than five is provided at the bottom of the "Chi-Square Tests" output box. Yates' correction for continuity, labelled "Continuity Correction," should be used in any 2 × 2 table where one or more cells have expected counts less than five. When this is the case for tables larger than 2 × 2, consider collapsing categories of the variables to increase cell sizes.

SPSS DEMONSTRATION 11.2 Does Perception of Crime Vary by Community Size?

In this demonstration we will examine the relationship between community size and perception of crime. Specifically, "Is the perception of crime higher in urban or rural communities?" Run the **Crosstabs** procedure again with *phr_q110* (compared to other areas in Canada, do you think your neighbourhood has a higher amount of crime, about the same or a lower amount of crime) as the row variable and *luc_rst* (Urban/Rural indicator) as the column variable. Don't forget to request chi square, expected frequencies, and column percents. The output, slightly edited for clarity, is shown below.

YOUR NEIGHBOURHOOD HAS_CRIME THAN OTHER * Urban/Rural indicator
Crosstabulation

| | | | Urban/Rural indicator | | |
			Urban	Rural	Total
Your neighbourhood has_crime than other	Higher	Count	122	10	132
		Expected Count	106.0	26.0	132.0
		% within Urban/Rural	10.0%	3.3%	8.7%
	Same	Count	449	69	518
		Expected Count	416.1	101.9	518.0
		% within Urban/Rural	36.8%	23.1%	34.1%
	Lower	Count	650	220	870
		Expected Count	698.9	171.1	870.0
		% within Urban/Rural	53.2%	73.6%	57.2%
Total			1221	299	1520
			100.0%	100.0%	100.0%

Chi-Square Tests

	Value	df	Asymp. Sig.(2-sided)
Pearson Chi-Square	42.809[*]	2	.000
Likelihood Ratio	45.951	2	.000
Linear-by-Linear Association	41.292	1	.000
N of Valid Cases	1520		

*Zero cells (.0%) have expected count less than 5.

Chi square is 42.809, degrees of freedom are 2, and the exact probability of getting this pattern of cell frequencies by random chance alone is .000. There is a significant relationship between the variables. The column percents show that perception of crime decreases from urban to rural communities. Focusing on the bottom row, we see that 73.6% of respondents living in rural areas thought crime was "lower" in their neighbourhood compared to other neighbourhoods. Just 53.2% of urban respondents said the same. Exercise 11.2 provides an opportunity to look at other variables that might be significantly related to *phr_q110*.

Exercises (using *GSS.sav*)

11.1 For a follow-up to Demonstration 11.1, find two more variables that might be related to *lifevict*. Run the **Crosstabs** procedure with *lifevict* as the row variable and your other variables as the column variables.* Write a paragraph summarizing the results of these two tests. Which relationships are significant at the .05 alpha level?

11.2 As a follow-up to Demonstration 11.2, find two more variables that might be related to *phr_q110*. Use the **Crosstabs** procedure to see if any of your variables have a significant relationship with *phr_q110*.* Which of the variables had the most significant relationship?

---

*If necessary, use the recode procedure shown in Appendix F.5 to reduce the number of categories in the independent (column) variables.

PART II CUMULATIVE EXERCISES

1. Conduct the appropriate test of significance for each research situation. Problems are stated in no particular order and include research situations from each chapter in Part II. (Use alpha = 0.05 throughout.)

a. Is there a gender gap in use of the Internet? Random samples of men and women have been questioned about the average number of minutes they spend each week on the Internet for any purpose. Is the difference significant?

Women	Men
$\bar{X}_1 = 55$	$\bar{X}_2 = 60$
$s_1 = 2.5$	$s_2 = 2.0$
$N_1 = 520$	$N_2 = 515$

b. For high school students, is there a relationship between social class and involvement in activities such as clubs and sports? Data have been gathered for a random sample of students. Is the relationship significant?

	Class		
Involvement	Higher	Lower	Totals
High	11	19	30
Moderate	19	21	40
Low	8	12	20
Totals	38	52	90

c. A social survey was administered to a random sample of adults. One question asked respondents how many total sex partners they have had over their lifetimes. The data for a subsample of 23 of these respondents are shown below. Does the number vary significantly by educational level?

Less than High School	High School	At Least Some College/University
1	1	2
1	2	1
2	3	5
1	8	9
9	10	11
2	5	2
9	4	1
	3	1

d. A sample of Canadians selected at random was asked how many times they had moved since they were 18 years of age. The results are presented below. On the average, how many times do Canadians move?

$$\bar{X} = 3.5$$
$$s = 0.4$$
$$N = 1,450$$

    e. On the average, school boards in a province receive budget support from the provincial government of $623 per student. A random sample of 107 rural schools reports that they received an average of $605 per pupil. Is the difference significant?

$$\mu = 623 \qquad \overline{X} = 605$$
$$s = \ \ 74$$
$$N = 107$$

2. Below are a number of research questions that can be answered by the techniques presented in Chapters 7 through 11. For each question, select the most appropriate test, compute the necessary statistics, and state your conclusions.

    In order to complete some problems, you must first calculate the sample statistics (for example, means or proportions) that are used in the test of hypothesis. Use alpha = 0.05 throughout. The questions are presented in random order. There is at least one problem for each chapter, but we have not included a research situation for every statistical procedure covered in the chapters.

    In selecting tests and procedures, you need to consider the question, the number of samples or categories being compared, and the level of measurement of the variables. These problems are based on social survey data, shown below, collected from a random sample of 25 Canadian adults, and you may have to violate some assumptions about sample size in order to complete this exercise. Abbreviated versions of the survey questions along with the meanings of the codes are also presented.

    a. Is there a statistically significant difference in average hours of TV watching by income level? By sex?

    b. Is there a statistically significant relationship between age and happiness?

    c. Estimate the average number of hours spent watching TV for the entire population.

    d. If Canadians currently average 2.3 children, is this sample representative of the population?

    e. Are the educational levels of political conservatives and political liberals significantly different?

    f. Does average hours of TV watching vary by level of happiness?

    g. Based on the sample data, estimate the proportion of female Canadians in the population.

SURVEY ITEMS

1. How many children have you ever had? Scores are actual numbers.
2. Respondent's educational level
    0. Less than high school
    1. High school
    2. At least some college or university
3. Sex
    1. Male
    2. Female
4. Age
    1. Younger than 35
    2. 35 and older

5. Number of hours of TV watched per day. Values are actual number of hours.
6. What is your political ideology?
    1. Liberal
    2. Conservative
7. Respondent's income
    1. $24,999 or less
    2. $25,000 or more
8. Respondent's overall level of happiness
    1. Very happy
    2. Pretty happy
    3. Not too happy

Case	No. of Children	Educational Level	Sex	Age	TV Hours	Political Ideology	Income	Happiness
1	3	1	1	1	3	1	1	2
2	2	0	1	1	1	1	2	3
3	4	2	1	2	3	1	1	1
4	0	2	1	1	2	1	1	1
5	5	1	1	1	2	1	2	2
6	1	1	1	2	3	1	2	1
7	9	0	1	1	6	1	1	1
8	6	1	1	2	4	1	1	2
9	4	2	1	1	2	2	2	2
10	2	1	1	1	1	1	2	3
11	2	0	1	2	4	1	1	3
12	4	1	2	1	5	2	1	2
13	0	1	1	2	2	2	1	2
14	2	1	1	2	2	1	1	2
15	3	1	2	2	4	1	1	1
16	2	0	1	2	2	1	2	1
17	2	1	1	2	2	1	2	3
18	0	2	1	2	2	1	2	1
19	3	0	1	2	5	2	1	1
20	2	1	2	1	10	1	1	3
21	2	1	1	2	4	1	2	1
22	1	0	1	2	5	1	2	1
23	0	2	1	1	2	2	1	1
24	0	1	1	2	0	2	2	1
25	2	2	1	1	1	2	2	1

Part III Bivariate Measures of Association

The four chapters in this section cover the computation and analysis of a class of statistics known as measures of association. These statistics are extremely useful in scientific research and commonly reported in the professional literature. They provide, in a single number, an indication of the strength and—if applicable—direction of a bivariate relationship.

It is important to remember the difference between statistical significance, covered in Part II, and association, the topic of this section. Tests for statistical significance provide answers to certain questions: Were the differences or relationships observed in the sample caused by mere random chance? What is the probability that the sample results reflect patterns in the population(s) from which the sample(s) was selected? Measures of association address a different set of questions: How strong is the relationship between the variables? What is the direction or pattern of the relationship?

Thus, measures of association provide information complementary to tests of significance. Association and significance are two different things and, while the most satisfying results are those that are *both* statistically significant and strong, it is common to find mixed results: relationships that are statistically significant but weak, not statistically significant but strong, and so forth.

Chapter 12 introduces the basic ideas behind the analysis of association in terms of bivariate tables and column percentages. The remaining chapters are organized by level of measurement. Chapter 13 presents measures of association designed for use with nominal-level variables, Chapter 14 presents measures of association for variables measured at the ordinal level, and Chapter 15 presents Pearson's *r*, the most important measure of association and the only one designed for interval-ratio-level variables.

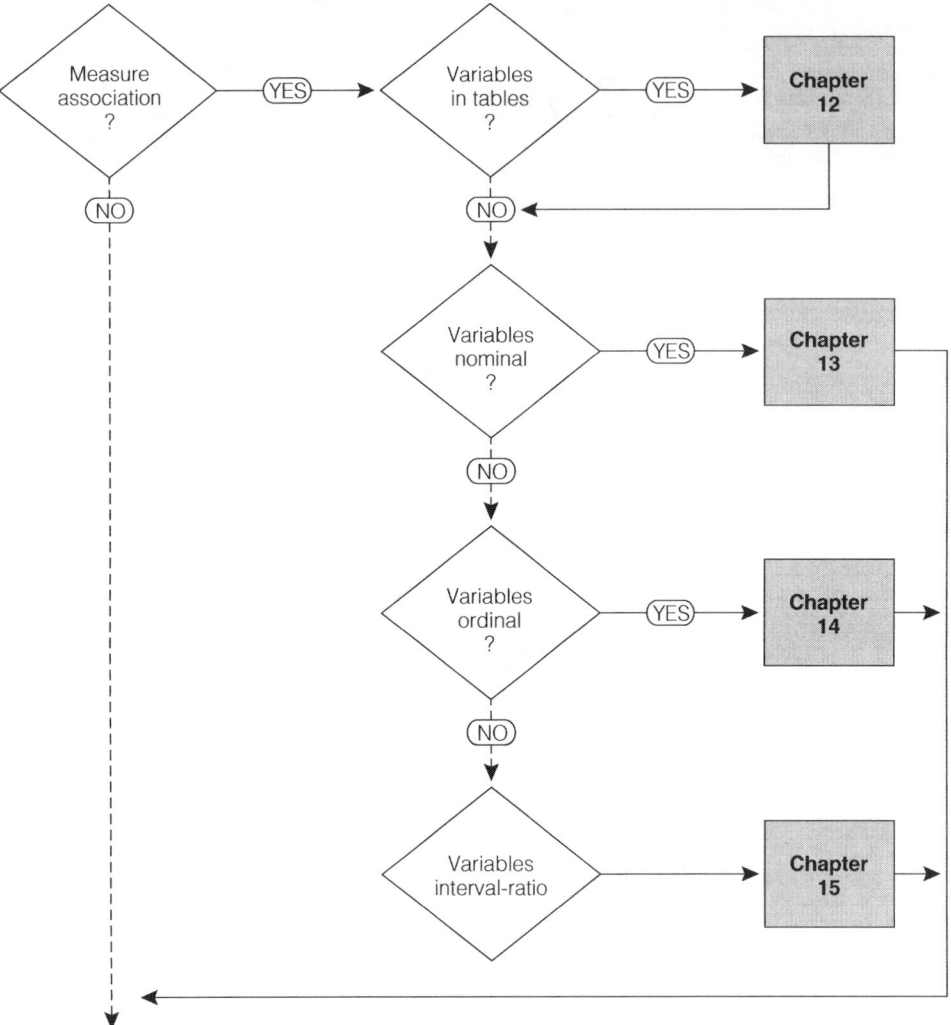

12

BIVARIATE ASSOCIATION
INTRODUCTION AND
BASIC CONCEPTS

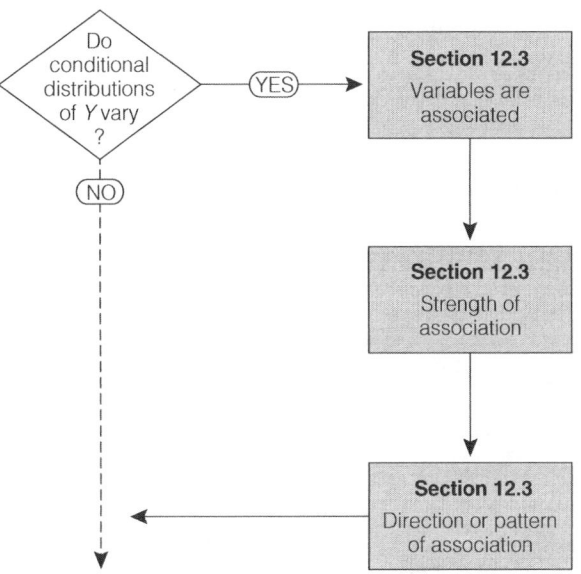

LEARNING OBJECTIVES

By the end of this chapter, you will be able to

1. Explain how we can use measures of association to describe and analyze the importance of relationships (versus their statistical significance).
2. Define "association" in the context of bivariate tables and in terms of changing conditional distributions.
3. List and explain the three characteristics of a bivariate relationship: existence, strength, and pattern or direction.
4. Investigate a bivariate association by properly calculating percentages for a bivariate table and interpreting the results.

12.1 STATISTICAL SIGNIFICANCE AND THEORETICAL IMPORTANCE

As we have seen over the past several chapters, tests of statistical significance are extremely important in social science research. As long as social scientists must work with random samples rather than populations, these tests are indispensable for dealing with the possibility that our research results are the products of mere random chance. However, tests of significance are often merely the first step in the analysis of research results. These tests do have limitations, and statistical significance is not necessarily the same thing as relevance or importance. Furthermore, all tests of significance are affected by sample size; tests performed on large samples may result in decisions to reject the null hypothesis when, in fact, the observed differences are quite minor.

Beginning with this chapter, we will be working with **measures of association.** Whereas tests of significance detect non-random relationships, measures of association provide information about the strength and direction of relationships, information that is more directly relevant for assessing the importance of relationships and testing the power and validity of our theories. The theories that guide scientific research are almost always stated in cause-and-effect terms (e.g., "variable *X* causes variable *Y*"). As an example, recall our discussion of the materialistic hypothesis in Chapter 1. In that theory, the causal (or independent) variable was social class and the effect (or dependent) variable was health status. The theory asserts that social class *causes* health. Measures of association help us trace causal relationships among variables, and they are our most important and powerful statistical tools for documenting, measuring, and analyzing cause-and-effect relationships.

As useful as they are, measures of association, like any class of statistics, do have their limitations. Most importantly, these statistics cannot *prove* that two variables are causally related. Even if there is a strong (and significant) statistical association between two variables, we cannot necessarily conclude that one variable is a cause of the other. We will explore causation in more detail in Part IV, but for now you should keep in mind that causation and association are two different things. We can use a statistical association between variables as evidence for a causal relationship, but association by itself is not proof that a causal relationship exists.

Another important use for measures of association is prediction. If two variables are associated, we can predict the score of a case on one variable from the score of that case on the other variable. For example, if social class and health are associated, we can predict that people who have high social class will be healthier than those with low social class. Note that prediction and causation can be two separate matters. If variables are associated, we can predict from one to the other even if the variables are not causally related.

This chapter will introduce the concept of **association** between variables in the context of bivariate tables and will stress the use of percentages to analyze associations between variables. In the chapters that follow, we will concentrate on the logic, calculation, and interpretation of the various measures of association. Finally, in Part IV, we will extend some of these ideas to the multivariate (more than two variables) case.

12.2 ASSOCIATION BETWEEN VARIABLES AND THE BIVARIATE TABLE

Most generally, two variables are said to be associated if the distribution of one of them changes under the various categories or scores of the other. For example, suppose that an industrial sociologist was concerned with the relationship between job satisfaction and productivity for assembly-line workers. If these two variables are associated, then scores on productivity will change under the different conditions of satisfaction. Highly satisfied workers will have different scores on productivity than workers who are low on satisfaction, and levels of productivity will vary by levels of satisfaction.

This relationship will become clearer with the use of bivariate tables. As you recall (see Chapter 11), bivariate tables display the scores of cases on two different variables. By convention, the **independent** or **X variable** (i.e., the variable taken as causal) is arrayed in the columns, and the **dependent** or **Y variable** in the rows (for the sake of brevity, we will often refer to the independent variable as X and the dependent variable as Y in the material that follows). Each column of the table (the vertical dimension) represents a score or category of the independent variable (X), and each row (the horizontal dimension) represents a score or category of the dependent variable (Y).*

Table 12.1 displays a relationship between productivity and job satisfaction for a fictitious sample of 173 factory workers. We focus on the columns to detect the presence of an association between variables displayed in table format. Each column shows the pattern of scores on the dependent variable for each score on the independent variable. For example, the left-hand column indicates that 30 of the 60 workers who were low on job satisfaction were low on productivity, 20 were moderately productive, and 10 were high on productivity. The middle column shows that 21 of the 61 moderately satisfied workers were low on productivity, 25 were moderately productive, and 15 were high on productivity. Of the 52 workers who are highly satisfied (the right-hand column), 7 were low on productivity, 18 were moderate, and 27 were high.

By inspecting the table from column to column we can observe the effects of the independent variable on the dependent variable (provided, of course, that the table is constructed with the independent variable in the columns). These "within-column" frequency distributions are called the **conditional distributions of Y;** they display the distribution of scores on the dependent variable for each condition (or score) of the independent variable.

Table 12.1 indicates that productivity and satisfaction are associated: The distribution of scores on Y (productivity) changes across the various conditions of X (satisfaction). For example, half of the workers who were low on satisfaction were also low on productivity (30 out of 60), and over half of the workers who were high on satisfaction were high on productivity (27 out of 52).

---

*While it is conventional to construct a bivariate table in this format, the opposite is equally acceptable where the columns are scores of the dependent variable and rows are scores of the independent variable.

TABLE 12.1 PRODUCTIVITY BY JOB SATISFACTION (frequencies)

Productivity (Y)	Job Satisfaction (X)			Totals
	Low	Moderate	High	
Low	30	21	7	58
Moderate	20	25	18	63
High	10	15	27	52
Totals	60	61	52	173

Although it is intended to be a test of significance, the chi square statistic provides another way to detect the existence of an association between two variables that have been organized into table format. Any non-zero value for obtained chi square indicates that the variables are associated. For example, the obtained chi square for Table 12.1 is 24.2, a value that affirms our previous conclusion, based on the conditional distributions of Y, that an association of some sort exists between job satisfaction and productivity.

Often, the researcher will have already conducted a chi square test before considering matters of association. In such cases, it will not be necessary to inspect the conditional distributions of Y to ascertain whether or not the two variables are associated. If the obtained chi square is zero, the two variables are independent and not associated. Any value other than zero indicates some association between the variables. Remember, however, that statistical significance and association are two different things. It is perfectly possible for two variables to be associated (as indicated by a non-zero chi square) but still independent (if we fail to reject the null hypothesis).

In this section, we have defined, in a general way, the concept of association between two variables. We have also shown two different ways to detect the presence of an association. In the next section, we will extend the analysis beyond questions of the mere presence or absence of an association and, in a systematic way, show how additional very useful information about the relationship between two variables can be developed.

12.3 THREE CHARACTERISTICS OF BIVARIATE ASSOCIATIONS

Bivariate associations possess three different characteristics, each of which must be analyzed for a full investigation of the relationship. Investigating these characteristics may be thought of as a process of finding answers to three questions:

1. Does an association exist?
2. If an association does exist, how strong is it?
3. What is the pattern and/or the direction of the association?

We will consider each of these questions separately.

Does an Association Exist?   We have already discussed the general definition of association, and we have seen that we can detect an association by observing the conditional distributions of Y in a table or by using chi square. In Table 12.1, we know that the two variables are associated to some extent because the conditional distributions of productivity (Y) are different across the various categories of satisfaction (X) and because the chi square statistic is a non-zero value.

Comparisons from column to column in Table 12.1 are relatively easy to make because the column totals are roughly equal. This will not usually be the case and it is helpful to compute percentages to control for varying column totals. These **column percentages,** introduced in Chapter 11, are computed within each column separately and make the pattern of association more visible.

The general procedure for detecting association with bivariate tables is to compute percentages within the columns (vertically or down each column) and then compare column to column across the table (horizontally or across the rows). Table 12.2 presents column percentages calculated from the data in Table 12.1. Note that this table reports the row and column marginals in parentheses. Besides controlling for any differences in column totals, tables in percentage form are usually easier to read because changes in the conditional distributions of Y are easier to detect.

In Table 12.2, we can see that the largest cell changes position from column to column. For workers who are low on satisfaction, the single largest cell is in the top row (low on productivity). For the middle column (moderate on satisfaction), the largest cell is in the middle row (moderate on productivity), and, for the right-hand column (high on satisfaction), it is in the bottom row (high on productivity). Even a cursory glance at the conditional distributions of Y in Table 12.2 reinforces our conclusion that an association does exist between these two variables.

If two variables are not associated, then the conditional distributions of Y will not change across the columns. The distribution of Y would be the same for each condition of X. Table 12.3 illustrates a "perfect nonassociation"

TABLE 12.2   PRODUCTIVITY BY JOB SATISFACTION (percentages)

Productivity (Y)	Job Satisfaction (X)			Totals
	Low	Moderate	High	
Low	50.00%	34.43%	13.46%	33.53%
Moderate	33.33%	40.98%	34.62%	36.42%
High	16.67%	24.59%	51.92%	30.05%
Totals	100.00%	100.00%	100.00%	100.00%
	(60)	(61)	(52)	(173)

Application 12.1

Early retirement from the workforce is more common today than it was a few decades ago, with the average Canadian retiring at about age 62. Many Canadians, however, feel that they will not be able to afford to retire early. We would expect that persons with lower levels of education, who tend to have lower earnings and are less likely to have a private pension plan, are more likely to believe that early retirement will not happen for them, compared to those with higher education.

This section will examine the association between highest level of education completed and age at which one plans to retire. The following table reports the joint frequency distributions of education and planned retirement age in percentages for a sample of 1,426 Canadians from the Survey of Financial Security, a survey administered by Statistics Canada to collect information on the economic well-being of Canadians.

PLANNED RETIREMENT AGE BY LEVEL OF EDUCATION (percentages)

	Education		
Age	< High School	High School	College/University
65+	69	52	46
60–64	19	27	30
<60	12	21	24
	100%	100%	100%
	(215)	(325)	(886)

Source: Statistics Canada, 2005 Survey of Financial Security, PUMF.

Conditional distributions of planned retirement age (Y) change across the values of education (X), so these variables are associated. The clustering of cases in the diagonal from upper left to lower right suggests a substantial relationship in the predicted direction. People who are low on education are more likely to plan for retirement at age 65 or later, and people who are high on education are more likely to plan for early retirement (i.e., plan to retire before the age of 65). Because the maximum difference in column percentages in the table is 23 (in the top row), the relationship can be characterized as moderate. The results support our causal argument that better-educated people feel that they will have the financial security necessary to facilitate an early retirement from the workforce (X causes Y).

---

between height and productivity. Table 12.3 is only one of many patterns that indicate "no association." The important point is that the conditional distributions of Y are the same. Levels of productivity do not change at all for the various heights and, therefore, no association exists between these variables. Also, the obtained chi square computed from this table would have a value of zero, again indicating no association.

How Strong Is the Association? Once we establish the existence of the association, we need to develop some idea of how strong the association is. This is essentially a matter of determining the amount of change in the

TABLE 12.3   PRODUCTIVITY BY HEIGHT (an illustration of no association)

	Height (X)		
Productivity (Y)	Short	Medium	Tall
Low	33.33%	33.33%	33.33%
Moderate	33.33%	33.33%	33.33%
High	33.33%	33.33%	33.33%
	100.00%	100.00%	100.00%

TABLE 12.4   PRODUCTIVITY BY HEIGHT (an illustration of perfect association)

	Height (X)		
Productivity (Y)	Short	Medium	Tall
Low	0%	0%	100%
Moderate	0%	100%	0%
High	100%	0%	0%
	100%	100%	100%

conditional distributions of Y. At one extreme, of course, there is the case of "no association" where the conditional distributions of Y do not change at all (see Table 12.3). At the other extreme is a perfect association, the strongest possible relationship. In general, a perfect association exists between two variables if each value of the dependent variable is associated with one and only one value of the independent variable.* In a bivariate table, all cases in each column would be located in a single cell and there would be no variation in Y for a given value of X (see Table 12.4).

A perfect relationship would be taken as very strong evidence of a causal relationship between the variables, at least for the sample at hand. In fact, the results presented in Table 12.4 would indicate that, for this sample, height is the sole cause of productivity. Also, in the case of a perfect relationship, predictions from one variable to the other could be made without error. If we knew that a particular worker was short, for example, we could be sure that he or she is highly productive.

Of course, the huge majority of relationships will fall somewhere between the two extremes of no association and perfect association. We need to

---

*Each measure of association that will be introduced in the following chapters incorporates its own definition of a "perfect association," and these definitions vary somewhat, depending on the specific logic and mathematics of the statistic. That is, for different measures computed from the same table, some measures will possibly indicate perfect relationships when others will not. We will note these variations in the mathematical definitions of a perfect association at the appropriate times.

It is very common for societies to be male dominated but the status of women relative to men is also highly variable, ranging from abject oppression to relative equality (and, on a few indicators for a few nations, higher status than men). Is the relative status of women related to a nation's religiosity? Because many religions sanction the lower status of women, are women in the most religious nations at a comparative disadvantage? To examine this question, a study of 47 nations, selected from all levels of development and all parts of the world, has been completed. Each nation has been rated on women's status relative to men in schooling, occupational prestige, politics, health care, and in several areas of social life. Nations have been scored as high (women have high status relative to men) or low (women have low status relative to men). Nations have also been characterized as high or low on religiosity. The table below presents the results of the comparison in both frequencies and column percentages.

STATUS OF WOMEN BY RELIGIOSITY FOR 47 NATIONS: Frequencies and (*Percentages*)

Women's Status	Religiosity		Totals
	Low	High	
Low	8 (*36.36%*)	17 (*68.00%*)	25
High	14 (*63.64%*)	8 (*32.00%*)	22
Totals	22 (*100.00%*)	25 (*100.00%*)	47

Analyzing this table step by step, we see that the column percentages vary, so the variables are related. The size of the difference from column to column is substantial and the maximum difference is 68.00% − 36.36% = 31.64%, so this is a moderate to strong relationship. (Note that, in a 2 × 2 table, the maximum difference will be the same for either row.) Looking at the pattern of the relationship, we see that women tend to have low status in nations that are high on religiosity and high status in less religious nations. This is a negative relationship: As religiosity increases, the status of women relative to men decreases.

What other factors might be related to the status of women? Another possibility is that more industrialized nations will raise the status of women as they upgrade the quality of the workforce and the literacy of the population. More traditional agricultural societies can function without an educated or literate workforce but industrial, "high-tech" societies cannot. The same 47 nations have been rated as "LDCs" (least developed countries or nations that are largely agricultural), developed (fully industrialized), or developing (nations between the more agricultural LDCs and the fully industrialized nations). The table below shows the relationship between the two variables.

STATUS OF WOMEN BY LEVEL OF DEVELOPMENT FOR 47 NATIONS: Frequencies and (*Percentages*)

Women's Status	Level of Development			Totals
	LDCs	Developing	Developed	
Low	13 (*81.25%*)	8 (*53.33%*)	4 (*25.00%*)	25 (*53.19%*)
High	3 (*18.75%*)	7 (*46.67%*)	12 (*75.00%*)	22 (*46.81%*)
Totals	16 (*100.00%*)	15 (*100.00%*)	16 (*100.00%*)	47 (*100.00%*)

Analyzing the table step-by-step, we see that these variables are related because there is a very substantial change in the column percentages across the table. The maximum difference is 81.25% − 25.00% = 56.25%, indicating a strong relationship. This is a positive relationship: Women's status increases as level of development increases. Only 18.75% of the LDC's are high on women's status versus 75% of the developed nations. In sum, there is a strong, positive relationship between the status of women and the development level of a nation.

develop some way of describing these intermediate relationships consistently and meaningfully. For example, Tables 12.1 and 12.2 show that there is an association between productivity and job satisfaction. How could this relationship be described in terms of strength? How close is the relationship to perfect? How far away from no association?

To answer these questions, researchers rely on statistics called measures of association, a variety of which are presented in Chapters 13 through 15. Measures of association provide precise, objective indicators of the strength of a relationship. Virtually all of these statistics are designed so that they have a lower limit of 0.00 and an upper limit of 1.00 (± 1.00 for ordinal and interval-ratio measures of association). A measure that equals 0.00 indicates no association between the variables (the conditional distributions of Y do not vary), and a measure of 1.00 (± 1.00 in the case of ordinal and interval-ratio measures) indicates a perfect relationship. The exact meaning of values between 0.00 and 1.00 varies from measure to measure, but for all measures, the closer the value is to 1.00, the stronger the relationship (the greater the change in the conditional distributions of Y).

Although researchers rely heavily on measures of association, there is a less formal way of assessing the strength of a relationship, which is based on comparing column percentages across the rows and called the **maximum difference.** This technique is best regarded as a "quick and easy" method for assessing the strength of a relationship: easy to apply but limited in its usefulness. To use this technique, compute the column percentages as usual and then skim the table across each of the rows to find the largest difference—in any row—between column percentages. For example, the largest difference in column percentages in Table 12.2 is in the top row between the "Low" column and the "High" column: 50.00% − 13.46% = 36.54%. The maximum difference in the middle row is between "moderates" and "lows" (40.98% − 33.33% = 7.65%), and in the bottom row, it is between "highs" and "lows" (51.92% − 16.67% = 35.25%). Both of these values are less than the maximum difference in the top row.

Once you have found the maximum difference in the table, the scale presented in Table 12.5 can be used to describe the strength of the relationship. Using this scale, we can describe the relationship between productivity and job satisfaction in Table 12.2 as strong.

TABLE 12.5   THE RELATIONSHIP BETWEEN THE MAXIMUM DIFFERENCE AND THE STRENGTH OF THE RELATIONSHIP

Maximum Difference	Strength
If the maximum difference is:	*The strength of the relationship is:*
between 0 and 10 percentage points	weak
between 11 and 30 percentage points	moderate
more than 30 percentage points	strong

The conventions for constructing and interpreting bivariate tables presented in this text are commonly but not universally followed in the professional literature. Tables will usually be constructed with the independent variable in the columns, the dependent variable in the rows, and percentages calculated in the columns. However, you should be careful to check the format of every table you attempt to read to see if these conventions have been observed. If the table is presented with the independent variable in the rows, for example, you will have to reorient your analysis (or redraw the table) to account for this. Above all, you should convince yourself that the percentages have been calculated in the correct direction. Even skilled professionals occasionally calculate percentages incorrectly and misinterpret the data.

Once you have assured yourself that the table is properly presented, you can apply the analytical techniques developed in this chapter. By comparing the conditional distributions of the dependent variable, you can ascertain for yourself if the variables are associated and check the strength and pattern of the association. You may then compare your conclusions with those of the researchers. As an aid in the interpretation of bivariate tables, researchers will usually compute and report other statistics in addition to percentages. We'll talk about these statistics in Reading Statistics 10 and 11 in Chapters 13 and 14.

Statistics in the Professional Literature

Studies in Canada and elsewhere have found that men and women differ in health status—women tend to report poorer health than men (see Reading Statistics 8 in Chapter 11). There are various explanations of sex differences in health. One theory, the differential exposure hypothesis, states that women report poorer health because they are more likely to have (to be *exposed* to) lower socio-economic status, work outside the home while caring for family, sedentary lifestyles, and higher levels of stress given their gender and marital roles. Collectively, these social, material, and stress variables are referred to as the social determinants of health.

To test the differential exposure hypothesis, sociologists Margaret Denton, Steven Prus, and Vivienne Walters used both bivariate and multivariate measures of association. Multivariate measures are discussed in Chapters 16 and 17. This section reports their bivariate findings. The bivariate tables below show the joint frequency distribution of gender and work activity, level of exercise, and stress in percentages for a random sample of 14,279 Canadian adults (6,785 males and 7,494 females).

Overall, the conditional distribution for each health determinant is different for males and females, so the variables are associated. The first bivariate table reveals that the association between gender and work activity is strong, as predicted, and statistically significant ($p < 0.05$). Almost one-fifth of adult women (19.4%) work both full-time in the labour force and at home as the family's primary caregiver. Only 10.8% of men work a "double day." More than six out of every ten men (61.3%) indicate that their primary activity is full-time work, compared to just 24.9% of women—a difference of more than 30 percentage points. The second and third bivariate tables show that the relationships between gender and exercise and stress are weaker, but their patterns are as predicted, and they are significant at the 0.05 alpha level.

DETERMINANTS OF HEALTH BY SEX (percentages)*

	Sex	
1. Work Activity	Male	Female
Work full-time and care for family	10.8%	19.4%
Work part-time and care for family	0.5	10.1
Caring for family	0.8	19.4
Work full-time	61.3	24.9
Other (work part-time, retired, etc.)	26.6	26.2
	100.0%	100.0%
	(6,785)	(7,494)
	$p < 0.05$[†]	

(continued)

READING STATISTICS 9: *(continued)*

	Sex	
2. Level of Exercise	Male	Female
Active	19.4%	14.0%
Moderate	22.5	21.4
Inactive	58.1	64.5
	100.0%	100.0%
	(6,785)	(7,494)
	$p < 0.05$[†]	

	Sex	
3. Personal Stress	Male	Female
Yes	56.4%	62.2%
No	43.6	37.8
	100.0%	100.0%
	(6,785)	(7,494)
	$p < 0.05$[†]	

[*] Percentages may not total to 100% because of rounding error.
[†] Statistical significance based on chi square test.

Denton and her colleagues point out that these bivariate findings offer convincing but indirect evidence in support of the differential exposure hypothesis. Men and women are differentially exposed to the determinants of health. However, this does not tell us per se if differential exposure contributes to differences in health between men and women. Multivariate techniques are needed to formally test the hypothesis and probe for a causal relationship between gender and health.

Source: Reprinted from Denton, M., Prus, S. & Walters, V. 2004. "Gender Differences in Health: A Canadian Study of the Psychosocial, Structural and Behavioural Determinants of Health." *Social Science & Medicine, 58:* 2585–2600 with permission from Elsevier.

You should be aware that the relationships between the size of the maximum difference and the descriptive terms (weak, moderate, and strong) in Table 12.5 are arbitrary and approximate. We will get more precise and useful information when we compute and analyze the measures of association that will be presented in Chapters 13 through 15. Also, maximum differences are easiest to find and most useful for smaller tables. In large tables, with many (say, more than three) columns and rows, it can be cumbersome to find the high and low percentages and it is advisable to consider only measures of association as indicators of the strength for these tables. Finally, note that the maximum difference is based on only two values (the high and low column percentages within any row). Like the range (see Chapter 4), this statistic can give a misleading impression of the overall strength of the relationship. Within these limits, however, the maximum difference can provide a useful, quick, and easy way of characterizing the strength of relationships (at least for smaller tables).

As a final caution, do not mistake chi square as an indicator of the strength of a relationship. Even very large values for chi square do not necessarily mean that the relationship is strong. Remember that significance and association are two separate matters, and chi square, by itself, is not a measure of association. While a non-zero value indicates that there is some association between the variables, the magnitude of chi square bears no particular relationship to the strength of the association. Chapter 13 will introduce some ways to transform chi square into other statistics that do measure the strength of the association between two variables. *(For practice in computing percentages and judging the existence and strength of an association, see any of the problems at the end of this chapter.)*

What Is the Pattern and/or the Direction of the Association?   Investigating the pattern of the association requires that we ascertain which values or categories of one variable are associated with which values or categories of the other. We have already remarked on the pattern of the relationship between productivity and satisfaction. Table 12.2 indicates that low scores on satisfaction are associated with low scores on productivity, moderate satisfaction with moderate productivity, and high satisfaction with high productivity.

When both variables are at least ordinal in level of measurement, the association between the variables may also be described in terms of direction.* The direction of the association can be either positive or negative. An association is positive if the variables vary in the same direction. That is, in a **positive association,** high scores on one variable are associated with high scores on the other variable, and low scores on one variable are associated with low scores on the other. In a positive association, as one variable increases in value, the other also increases; and as one variable decreases, the other also decreases. Table 12.6 displays, with fictitious data, a positive relationship between education and use of public libraries. As education increases (as you move from left to right across the table), library use also increases (the percentage of "high" users increases). The association between job satisfaction and productivity, as displayed in Tables 12.1 and 12.2, is also a positive association.

In a **negative association,** the variables vary in opposite directions. High scores on one variable are associated with low scores on the other, and increases in one variable are accompanied by decreases in the other. Table 12.7 displays a negative relationship, again with fictitious data,

TABLE 12.6   LIBRARY USE BY EDUCATION (an illustration of a positive relationship)

Library Use	Education		
	Low	Moderate	High
Low	60%	20%	10%
Moderate	30	60	30
High	10	20	60
Total	100%	100%	100%

TABLE 12.7   AMOUNT OF TELEVISION VIEWING BY EDUCATION (an illustration of a negative relationship)

Television Viewing	Education		
	Low	Moderate	High
Low	10%	20%	60%
Moderate	30	60	30
High	60	20	10
Total	100%	100%	100%

*Variables measured at the nominal level have no numerical order to them (by definition). Therefore, associations including nominal-level variables, while they may have a pattern, cannot be said to have a direction.

between education and television viewing. The amount of television viewing decreases as education increases. In other words, as you move from left to right across the top of the table (as education increases), the percentage of heavy viewers decreases.

Measures of association for ordinal and interval-ratio variables are designed so that they will take on positive values for positive associations and negative values for negative associations. Thus, a measure of association preceded by a plus sign indicates a positive relationship between the two variables, with the value +1.00 indicating a perfect positive relationship. A negative sign indicates a negative relationship, with −1.00 indicating a perfect negative relationship. *(For practice in determining the pattern of an association, see any of the end-of-chapter problems. For practice in determining the direction of a relationship, see problems 12.1, 12.6, 12.7, 12.8, 12.9, 12.10, and 12.11.)*

SUMMARY

1. Analyzing the association between variables provides information that is complementary to tests of significance. The latter are designed to detect non-random relationships, whereas measures of association are designed to quantify the importance or strength of a relationship.

2. Relationships between variables have three characteristics: the existence of an association, the strength of the association, and the direction or pattern of the association. These three characteristics can be investigated by calculating percentages for a bivariate table in the direction of the independent variable (vertically) and then comparing in the opposite direction (horizontally). It is often useful (as well as quick and easy) to assess the strength of a relationship by finding the maximum difference in column percentages in any row of the table.

3. Tables 12.1 and 12.2 can be analyzed in terms of these three characteristics. Clearly, a relationship does exist between job satisfaction and productivity, because the conditional distributions of the dependent variable (productivity) are different for the three different conditions of the independent variable (job satisfaction). Even without a measure of association, we can see that the association is substantial in that the change in Y (productivity) across the three categories of X (satisfaction) is marked. The maximum difference of 36.54% confirms that the relationship is substantial (moderate to strong).

Furthermore, the relationship is positive in direction. Productivity increases as job satisfaction rises, and workers who report high job satisfaction tend also to be high on productivity. Workers with little job satisfaction tend to be low on productivity.

4. Given the nature and strength of the relationship, it could be predicted with fair accuracy that highly satisfied workers tend to be highly productive ("happy workers are busy workers"). These results might be taken as evidence of a causal relationship between these two variables, but they cannot, by themselves, prove that a causal relationship exists: Association is not the same thing as causation. In fact, although we have presumed that job satisfaction is the independent variable, we could have argued the reverse causal sequence ("busy workers are happy workers"). The results presented in Tables 12.1 and 12.2 are consistent with both causal arguments.

5. The analysis of the association between variables produces systematic evidence for (or against) a causal relationship between two variables. Ultimate proof that variables have a causal relationship depends less on statistics and more on logic, theory, and methodology (actually proving causation is a rather difficult task). As we shall see in Part IV, some of the multivariate techniques are quite useful for probing possible causal relationships, and we will return to some of these concerns at that point.

GLOSSARY

Association. The relationship between two (or more) variables. Two variables are said to be associated if the distribution of one variable changes for the various categories or scores of the other variable.

Column percentages. Percentages computed within each column of a bivariate table.

Conditional distribution of Y. The distribution of scores on the dependent variable for a specific score or category of the independent variable when the variables have been organized into table format.

Dependent variable. In a bivariate relationship, the variable that is taken as the effect.

Independent variable. In a bivariate relationship, the variable that is taken as the cause.

Maximum difference. A way to assess the strength of an association between variables that have been organized into a bivariate table. The maximum

difference is the largest difference between column percentages for any row of the table.

Measures of association. Statistics that quantify the strength of the association between variables.

Negative association. A bivariate relationship where the variables vary in opposite directions. As one variable increases, the other decreases, and high scores on one variable are associated with low scores on the other.

Positive association. A bivariate relationship where the variables vary in the same direction. As one variable increases, the other also increases, and high scores on one variable are associated with high scores on the other.

X. Symbol used for any independent variable.

Y. Symbol used for any dependent variable.

MULTIMEDIA RESOURCES

   http://www.healeystatistics.nelson.com

Visit the companion Web site for the first Canadian edition of *Statistics: A Tool for Social Research* to access a wide range of student resources. Begin by clicking on the Student Resources section of the book's Web site to access review quizzes, flash cards, and other study tools.

PROBLEMS

12.1 PA Various supervisors in the municipal government of Pearson, Ontario, have been rated on the extent to which they practise authoritarian styles of leadership and decision making. The efficiency of each department has also been rated, and the results are summarized below. Calculate percentages for the table so that it shows the effect of leadership style on efficiency. Is there an association between these two variables? Describe the strength and direction of the relationship.

| | Authoritarianism | | |
Efficiency	Low	High	Totals
Low	10	12	22
High	17	5	22
Totals	27	17	44

12.2 SOC The administration of a university has proposed an increase in the mandatory student fee inorder to finance an upgrading of the varsity football program. A sample of the faculty has completed a survey on the issue. Is there any association between support for raising fees and the sex, discipline, or tenured status of the faculty? Describe the strength and direction of the association.

a. Support for raising fees by sex:

| | Sex | | |
Support	Males	Females	Totals
For	12	8	20
Against	15	12	27
Totals	27	20	47

b. Support for raising fees by discipline:

Discipline

Support	Social Sciences & Arts	Science & Business	Totals
For	6	13	19
Against	14	14	28
Totals	20	27	47

c. Support for raising fees by tenured status:

Status

Support	Tenured	Non-tenured	Totals
For	15	4	19
Against	18	10	28
Totals	33	14	47

12.3 PS How consistent are people in their voting habits? Do the same people vote from election to election? Below are the results of a poll in which people were asked if they had voted in each of the last two federal elections. Assess the strength of this relationship.

2006 Election	2004 Election Voted	2004 Election Didn't Vote	Totals
Voted	117	23	140
Didn't Vote	17	178	195
Totals	134	201	335

12.4 SOC A needs assessment survey has been distributed in a large retirement community. Residents were asked to check off the services or programs they thought should be added. Is there any association between sex and the perception of a need for more social occasions? Write a few sentences describing the relationship in terms of pattern and strength of the association.

More Parties?	Sex Male	Sex Female	Totals
Yes	321	426	747
No	175	251	426
Totals	496	677	1,173

12.5 Below are problems 11.3–11.5 from Chapter 11. In that chapter, you tested these relationships for their significance (the chi square test) and, now, you will test the relationships to determine the existence, strength, and pattern or direction of

the relationship. Find column percentages and the maximum difference for each table and write a short paragraph summarizing the relationship.

a. Services by sex for a sample of the homeless:

Received Services?	Sex Female	Male	Totals
Yes	6	7	13
No	4	9	13
Totals	10	16	26

b. Party preference by sex for a sample of university faculty:

Party Preference	Sex Male	Female	Totals
Liberal	10	15	25
Other	15	10	25
Totals	25	25	50

c. Salary level by unionization status for 100 workplaces:

Salary	Status Union	Non-union	Totals
High	21	29	50
Low	14	36	50
Totals	35	65	100

12.6 SW As the provincial director of mental health programs, you note that some local mental health facilities have very high rates of staff turnover. You believe that part of this problem is a result of the fact that some of the local directors have very little training in administration and poorly developed leadership skills. Before implementing a program to address this problem, you collect some data to make sure that your beliefs are supported by the facts. Is there a relationship between staff turnover and the administrative experience of the directors? Describe the relationship in terms of pattern and strength of the association.

Turnover	Director Experienced? No	Yes	Totals
Low	4	9	13
Moderate	9	8	17
High	15	5	20
Totals	28	22	50

12.7 CJ About half the neighbourhoods in a large city have instituted programs to increase citizen involvement in crime prevention. Do these areas experience less crime? Write a few sentences describing the relationship in terms of pattern and strength of the association.

Crime Rate	Program		
	No	Yes	Totals
Low	29	15	44
Moderate	33	27	60
High	52	45	97
Totals	114	87	201

12.8 SOC What types of people are most concerned about the future of the environment? The World Values Survey includes an item asking people if they would agree to an increase in taxes if the extra money was used to prevent environmental damage. The tables below show the relationship between this variable and income for Canada, the United States, and Mexico. Income has been collapsed into three levels based on the relative income of each nation. Compute column percentages and find the maximum difference for each table. Is there a relationship between income and concern for the environment? Describe the strength and direction of the relationship for each nation. Does the relationship between these variables change from nation to nation? How?

a. Canada:

Support Higher Tax to Help the Environment?	Income			
	Low	Moderate	High	Totals
Yes	157	380	281	818
No	90	222	117	429
	247	602	398	1,247

b. United States:

Support Higher Tax to Help the Environment?	Income			
	Low	Moderate	High	Totals
Yes	330	655	631	1,616
No	263	405	360	1,028
	593	1,060	991	2,644

c. Mexico:

Support Higher Tax to Help the Environment?	Income			
	Low	Moderate	High	Totals
Yes	695	627	236	1,558
No	531	400	96	1,027
	1,226	1,027	332	2,585

Source: World Values Survey.

12.9 SOC The latest fad to sweep university campuses is streaking to panty raids while swallowing live goldfish. A researcher is interested in how closely the spread of this bizarre behaviour is linked to the amount of coverage and publicity provided by local campus newspapers. For a sample of 25 universities, the researcher has rated the amount of press coverage (as extensive, moderate, or no coverage) and how much the student body was involved in this new fad. The data for each campus are reported below. Organize the data into a properly labelled table in percentage form. Does the table indicate an association between press coverage and fad behaviour?

Campus	Amount of Press Coverage	Extent of Student Involvement
1	Extensive	Extensive
2	Extensive	Some
3	Moderate	Some
4	Moderate	Some
5	Moderate	Extensive
6	Extensive	Some
7	Extensive	Extensive
8	Moderate	Some
9	None	Some
10	Moderate	None
11	None	None
12	Extensive	Extensive
13	None	Some
14	Extensive	Extensive
15	Moderate	None
16	Moderate	Some
17	Moderate	Extensive
18	Moderate	None
19	None	None
20	Extensive	Some
21	None	Extensive
22	Moderate	None
23	None	None
24	Extensive	Extensive
25	Moderate	Extensive

12.10 In any social science journal, find an article that includes a bivariate table. Inspect the table and the related text carefully and answer the following questions:

  a. Identify the variables in the table. What values (categories) does each possess? What is the level of measurement for each variable?

  b. Is the table in percentage form? In what direction are the percentages calculated? Are comparisons made between columns or rows?

  c. Is one of the variables identified by the author as independent? Are the percentages in the direction of the independent variable?

  d. How is the relationship characterized by the author in terms of the strength of the association? In terms of the direction (if any) of the association?

  e. Find the measure of association (if any) calculated for the table. What is the numerical value of the measure? What is the sign (if any) of the measure?

12.11 │SOC│ If a person's political ideology (liberal, moderate, or conservative) is known, can we predict their position on issues? If liberals are generally progressive and conservatives are generally traditional (with moderates in between), what relationships would you expect to find between political ideology and these issues?

  a. Support for same-sex marriage
  b. The death penalty
  c. The legal right to commit suicide for people with incurable disease
  d. Support for traditional gender roles
  e. Support for the legalization of marijuana

The tables below show the results of a recent public opinion survey. For each table, compute column percentages and the maximum difference. Summarize the strength and direction of each relationship in a brief paragraph. Were your expectations confirmed?

  a. Support for same-sex marriage by political ideology:

| Supports Same-sex Marriage? | Political Ideology | | | |
	Liberal	Moderate	Conservative	Totals
Favour	309	234	154	697
Oppose	211	360	419	990
Totals	520	594	573	1,687

  b. Support for capital punishment by political ideology:

| Supports Capital Punishment? | Political Ideology | | | |
	Liberal	Moderate	Conservative	Totals
Favour	440	693	693	1,826
Oppose	265	214	186	665
Totals	705	907	879	2,491

  c. Support for the right of people with an incurable disease to commit suicide by political ideology:

| Supports the Right to Suicide? | Political Ideology | | | |
	Liberal	Moderate	Conservative	Totals
Favour	381	394	319	1,094
Oppose	120	229	261	610
Totals	501	623	580	1,704

  d. Support for traditional gender roles by political ideology:

| Supports Traditional Gender Roles? | Political Ideology | | | |
	Liberal	Moderate	Conservative	Totals
Favour	59	90	108	257
Oppose	454	548	484	1,486
Totals	513	8	592	1,743

  e. Support for legalizing marijuana by political ideology.

| Should Marijuana Be Legalized? | Political Ideology | | | |
	Liberals	Moderates	Conservatives	Totals
Favour	132	78	52	262
Oppose	101	87	109	297
Totals	233	165	161	559

Using SPSS for Windows to Analyze Bivariate Association with the 2004 GSS

The demonstrations and exercises below use the 2004 GSS data set supplied with this text. Start SPSS for Windows and open the *GSS.sav* file.

SPSS DEMONSTRATION 12.1 Does Health Vary by Income?

What's the relationship between income and health? To answer this question we'll run a **Crosstabs** on *incmhsd* (total household income) and *hlthstat* (state of health). We must first recode *incmhsd* because it has too many (12) categories (see Appendix G) to be used in a bivariate table. We will provide only a brief review here; a detailed guide on recoding *incmhsd*, including adding labels to the values of the recoded variable, is given in Appendix F.5.

Click **Transform** from the main menu and choose **Recode into Different Variables.** Next, move the variable *incmhsd* to the **Input Variable → Output Variable** box, then type a name—we suggest *income4*—in the **Output Variable** box. Click the **Change** button. Next, click on the **Old and New Values** button. We have decided to collapse the values of *incmhsd* into four categories. The recoding instructions that should appear in the **Old → New** dialog box are:

$$1 \text{ thru } 6 \rightarrow 1$$
$$7 \text{ thru } 9 \rightarrow 2$$
$$10 \text{ thru } 11 \rightarrow 3$$
$$12 \rightarrow 4$$

Click **Continue,** and then **OK** after inputting these recode instructions.

We will also recode state of health, *hlthstat.* As a rule of thumb, it is best to collapse a variable into logical groups. We decided to collapse *hlthstat* into a dichotomized variable: good health versus poor health. Click **Transform** and then **Recode into Different Variables.** Next, click the **Reset** button to reset all specifications in the dialog and sub-dialog boxes to their default state. Move the variable *hlthstat* to the **Input Variable → Output Variable** box. Give the recoded variable a new name in the **Output Variable** box (we used *health*), then click the **Change** button. Click **Old and New Values** button, and follow these recoding instructions:

$$1 \text{ thru } 3 \rightarrow 1$$
$$4 \text{ thru } 5 \rightarrow 2$$

Click **Continue,** and then **OK.** Scores 1 (excellent), 2 (very good), or 3 (good) on *hlthstat* are grouped together into a score of 1 on *health,* and scores 4 (fair) or 5 (poor) on *hlthstat* into a score of 2 on *health.*

We highly recommend that both new variables be added to the permanent data file because they will be used in future SPSS demonstrations and exercises. To do so, click **Save** from the **File** menu, and the updated data set with *income4* and *health* added will be saved to disk. If you are using the student version of SPSS, remember that your data set is limited to 50 variables.

To examine the effect of *income4* on *health,* click **Analyze, Descriptive Statistics,** and **Crosstabs,** and then put *health* as the row variable and *income4* as the column variable. Click the **Cells** button and request column percentages by clicking the box next to **Column** in the **Percentages** box. With the dependent variable in the rows and the independent variable in the columns and with percentages calculated within columns, we will be able to read the table by following the rules developed in this chapter. Click the **Continue** button to return to the **Crosstabs** dialog box. Also, request chi square by clicking the **Statistics** button. Click **Continue,** and then **OK,** and the following output will be produced. (The output has been modified slightly, including adding labels to the values of *income4* and *health* as illustrated in Appendix F.5, to improve readability.)

HEALTH * INCOME4 Cross tabulation

		Income4				Total
		1 (<$30,000)	2 ($30,000- 59,999)	3 ($60,000- 99,999)	4 ($100,000+)	
Health	1 (Good)	198	396	355	239	1188
		82.5%	90.4%	94.2%	95.2%	91.0%
	2 (Poor)	42	42	22	12	118
		17.5%	9.6%	5.8%	4.8%	9.0%
Total		240	438	377	251	1306
		100.0%	100.0%	100.0%	100.0%	100.0%

Chi-Square Tests

	Value	df	Asymp. Sig. (2-sided)
Pearson Chi-Square	31.310[*]	3	.000
Likelihood Ratio	28.894	3	.000
Linear-by-Linear Association	26.832	1	.000
N of Valid Cases	1306		

[*]Zero cells (.0%) have expected count less than 5.

Inspecting the table column by column, you will see that there is a relationship, and that it is moderate in strength. The maximum difference in the bottom row, poor health, is between the lowest and highest income groups: 17.5% − 4.8% = 12.7%.

Both variables are measured at the ordinal level, so we also can describe the direction. Is this relationship positive or negative? Remember that in a positive association, high scores on one variable will be associated with high scores on the other and low scores will be associated with low. In a negative relationship, high scores on one variable are associated with low scores on the other. Looking at the table again, we see that the relationship is negative: As income increases, poor health decreases.

The exact probability value of chi square, .000, is well below the standard indicator of a significant result, .05, so we reject the null hypothesis that the variables are independent and conclude that there is a statistically significant relationship between income and health.

As a final point, let us direct your attention to the "Total" (or total number of cases) column in the "Crosstabulation" output. There are a total of 1,306 people in the analysis. The original sample included over 1,500 people. What happened to all those "missing cases"? These missing cases are respondents who did not provide information on income. All statistics produced by the crosstabs command apply to only those that provide information on both variables; all other cases are deleted from the analysis. This is called *pairwise* deletion of missing data as only those cases that have non-missing values for *both* variables are included in the crosstab. The phenomenon of diminishing sample size is a common problem in survey research that, at some point, may jeopardize the integrity of the inquiry.

SPSS DEMONSTRATION 12.2 Does Disability Vary by Age?

Let's take another look at a relationship between two ordinal-level variables: *hal_q120* (any difficulty hearing, seeing, walking, etc.) as the dependent variable and *agegr5* (age) as the independent variable. The latter has too many categories (15) to be used in a bivariate table (see Appendix G), so we must first recode the variable. We have decided to collapse the values of *agegr5* into three categories.

Click **Transform** and **Recode into Different Variables.** Next, move the variable *agegr5* to the **Input Variable → Output Variable** box, then type a name—we suggest *age3*—in the **Output Variable** box. Click the **Change** button. Next, click on the **Old and New Values** button. The recoding instructions that should appear in the **Old → New** box of the **Recode into Different Variables: Old and New Values** window should be:

$$1 \text{ thru } 6 \rightarrow 1$$
$$7 \text{ thru } 10 \rightarrow 2$$
$$11 \text{ thru } 15 \rightarrow 3$$

Click **Continue,** and then **OK** after inputting these recode instructions. This scheme groups all respondents with scores 1 thru 6 on *agegr5* (15–39) together into a score of 1 on *age3,* scores 7 thru 10 on *agegr5* (40–59) together into a score of 2 on *age3,* and scores 11 thru 15 on *agegr5* (60+) together into a score of 3 on *age3.*

Again, we highly recommend that this variable be added to the permanent data file as it will be used in subsequent demonstrations and exercises. Click **Save** from the **File** menu, and the updated data set with *age3* added will be saved to disk. Remember that your data set is limited to 50 variables in the SPSS student version.

Run the **Crosstabs** procedure (see Demonstration 12.1) with *hal_q120* as the row variable and *age3* as the column variable. Click the **Cells** button and make sure that the button next to **Columns** under **Percentages** is checked. (If you wish, click the **Statistics** button and request a chi square test) Click **Continue,** and then **OK.** The bivariate table, which has again been modified slightly to improve readability, for these two variables is shown below.

HAL_Q120* AGE3 Crosstabulation

| | | Age | | | |
		1 (15–39)	2 (40–59)	3 (60+)	Total
Any difficulty hearing/seeing/ walking/etc.)	1 (Yes, often)	39	56	56	151
		5.3%	10.0%	25.3%	9.9%
	2 (Yes, sometimes)	38	36	34	108
		5.1%	6.5%	15.4%	7.1%
	3 (No)	663	466	131	1260
		89.6%	83.5%	59.3%	82.9%
Total		740	558	221	1519
		1 00.0%	100.0%	100.0%	100.0%

Chi-Square Tests

	Value	df	Asymp. Sig. (2-sided)
Pearson Chi- Square	113.532*	4	.000
Likelihood Ratio	97.590	4	.000
Linear-by-Linear Association	70.775	1	.000
N of Valid Cases	1519		

* Zero cells (.0%) have expected count less than 5.

Looking at changes in the conditional distributions of Y or *hal_q120* from column to column or from age group to age group, we see that there is a relationship. The relationship is also strong. The maximum difference is in the bottom row ("No") between the youngest (15–39) and oldest (60+) age groups: 89.6% − 59.3% = 30.3%.

Is this relationship positive or negative? Find the single largest cell in each column in the table and see if you can detect the pattern. The lowest score (youngest age group = 1, or 15–39) on *age3* is in the left-hand column. For this age group, the most common score (89.6% of this age group) on *hal_q120* is 3 ("No"). In other words, the vast majority of the youngest respondents reported having no disability (i.e., no difficulty with hearing, seeing, walking, etc.). Conversely, looking at the top row of the table ("Yes, often" has difficulty with hearing, seeing, walking, and so on), we see the percentage of cases is highest in the oldest age group: 25.3% of respondents 60 years of age and older report that they often experience disability. In conclusion, being free of disability decreases as age increases—the variables change in the opposite direction, so the relationship is negative.

Exercises (using *GSS.sav*)

12.1 As long as *hlthstat* has already been recoded, examine the relationship between recoded *hlthstat* as dependent or row variable and *luc_rst* (urban/ rural indicator) as the independent or column variable using the **Crosstabs**

procedure. Be sure to request column percentage in the cells and the chi square test. Write a paragraph summarizing the results. Describe the relationships in terms of strength and pattern.

12.2 Continue to assess the theme of urban/rural differences in health, and examine the relationships between *actlimit* (long-term health problem) and *hal_q120* (any difficulty with hearing, seeing, walking, etc.) as dependent variables and *luc_rst* as the independent variable. Be sure to request column percentage in the cells and the chi square test for each table. Write a paragraph describing each relationship. Describe each relationship in terms of pattern and strength of the association. Which of these two "health measures" is most influenced by *luc_rst*?

13

ASSOCIATION BETWEEN VARIABLES MEASURED AT THE NOMINAL LEVEL

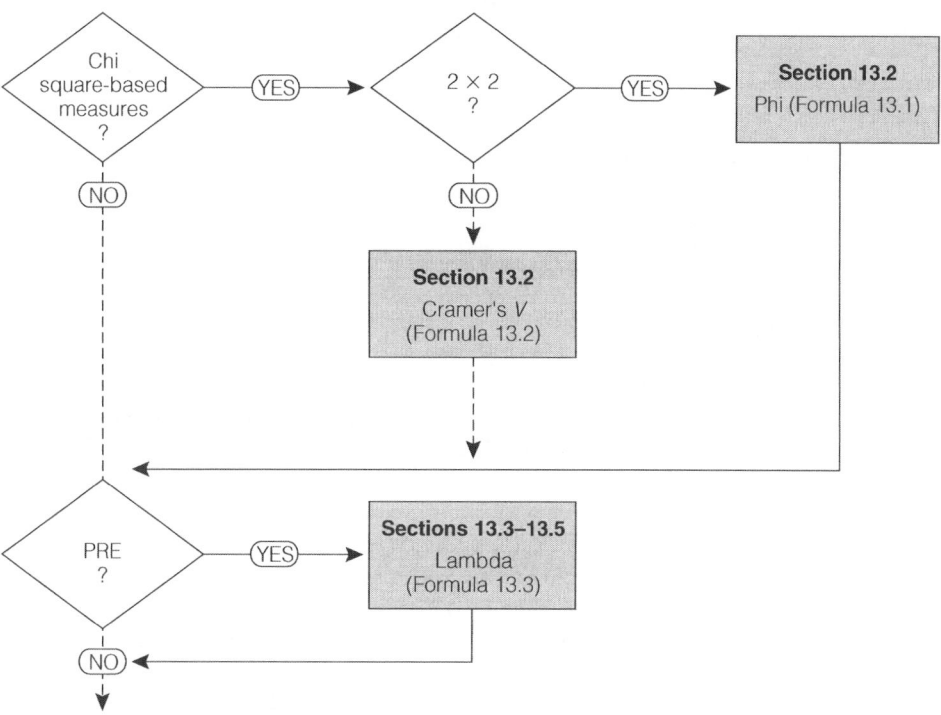

LEARNING OBJECTIVES

By the end of this chapter, you will be able to

1. Calculate and interpret phi, Cramer's *V*, and lambda.
2. Explain the logic of proportional reduction in error in terms of lambda.
3. Use any of the three measures of association to analyze and describe a bivariate relationship in terms of the three questions introduced in Chapter 12.

13.1 INTRODUCTION

Measures of association are descriptive statistics that summarize the overall strength of the association between two variables. Because they represent that relationship in a single number, these statistics are more efficient methods of expressing an association than conditional distributions, column percentages, and the maximum difference. As with any summarizing technique, however, a certain amount of information (detail and nuance) about the relationship will be lost if the researcher considers only the measure of association. Always make it a habit to inspect the patterns of cell frequencies or percentages in the table along with the summary measure of association in order to maximize the amount of information you have about the relationship. You should do this regardless of the level of measurement of the data or the specific measure that has been calculated.

As we shall see, there are many measures of association. In this text, these statistics have been organized according to the level of measurement for which they are most appropriate. In this chapter, we will consider measures appropriate for nominally measured variables. You will note that several of the research situations used as examples involve variables measured at different levels (for example, one nominal-level variable and one ordinal-level variable). The general procedure in the situation of "mixed levels" is to be conservative and select measures of association appropriate for the lower of the two levels of measurement.

13.2 CHI SQUARE–BASED MEASURES OF ASSOCIATION

Over the years, social science researchers have relied heavily on measures of association based on the value of chi square. When the value of chi square is already known, these measures are easy to calculate. To illustrate, let us reconsider Table 11.3, which displayed, with fictitious data, a relationship between CASSW (Canadian Association of Schools of Social Work) accreditation and employment for social work graduates. For the sake of convenience, this table is reproduced here as Table 13.1.

We saw in Chapter 11 that this relationship is statistically significant ($\chi^2 = 10.78$, which is significant at $\alpha = .05$), but the question now concerns the *strength* of the association. A brief glance at Table 13.1 shows that the conditional distributions of employment status do change, so the variables are associated. To emphasize this point, it is always helpful to calculate column percentages, as in Table 13.2.

So far, we know that the relationship between these two variables is statistically significant and that there is an association of some kind between CASSW accreditation and employment. To assess the strength of the association, we will compute a **phi (ϕ).** This statistic is a frequently

TABLE 13.1 EMPLOYMENT STATUS OF 100 SOCIAL WORK GRADUATES BY CASSW-ACCREDITATION STATUS OF UNDERGRADUATE PROGRAM

Employment Status	Accreditation Status		Totals
	Accredited	Not Accredited	
Working as a social worker	30	10	40
Not working as a social worker	25	35	60
Totals	55	45	100

TABLE 13.2 EMPLOYMENT STATUS BY CASSW-ACCREDITATION STATUS (percentages)

| | Accreditation Status | | |
Employment Status	Accredited	Not Accredited	Totals
Working as a social worker	54.55%	22.22%	40.00%
Not working as a social worker	45.45%	77.78%	60.00%
	100.00%	100.00%	100.00%

used chi square–based measure of association appropriate for 2 × 2 tables (i.e., tables with two rows and two columns).

It will be helpful to have some general guidelines for interpreting the value of measures of association, similar to the guidelines we used for interpreting the maximum difference in column percentages in Chapter 12. For phi and the other measures introduced in this chapter, the general relationship between the value of the statistic and the strength of the relationship is presented in Table 13.3. As was the case for Table 12.5, the relationships in Table 13.3 are arbitrary and meant as general guidelines only. Measures of association generally have mathematical definitions that yield interpretations more meaningful and exact than these.

One of the attractions of phi is that it is easy to calculate. Simply divide the value of the obtained chi square by N and take the square root of the result. Expressed in symbols, the formula for phi is

FORMULA 13.1

$$\phi = \sqrt{\frac{\chi^2}{N}}$$

For the data displayed in Table 13.1, the chi square was 10.78. Therefore, phi is

$$\phi = \sqrt{\frac{\chi^2}{N}}$$

$$\phi = \sqrt{\frac{10.78}{100}}$$

$$\phi = 0.33$$

TABLE 13.3 THE RELATIONSHIP BETWEEN THE VALUE OF NOMINAL-LEVEL MEASURES OF ASSOCIATION AND THE STRENGTH OF THE RELATIONSHIP

Value	Strength
If the value is	*The strength of the relationship is*
between 0.00 and 0.10	weak
between 0.11 and 0.30	moderate
greater than 0.30	strong

For a 2 × 2 table, phi ranges in value from 0 (no association) to 1.00 (perfect association). The closer to 1.00, the stronger the relationship; the closer to 0.00, the weaker the relationship. For Table 13.1, we already knew that the relationship was statistically significant at the 0.05 level. Phi, as a measure of association, adds information about the strength of the relationship: There is a moderate to strong relationship between these two variables. As for the pattern of the association, the column percentages in Table 13.2 show that graduates of CASSW-accredited programs were more often employed as social workers.

For tables larger than 2 × 2 (specifically, for tables with more than two columns and more than two rows), the upper limit of phi can exceed 1.00. This makes phi difficult to interpret, and a more general form of the statistic called **Cramer's V** must be used. The formula for Cramer's V is

FORMULA 13.2

$$V = \sqrt{\frac{\chi^2}{(N)(\min\ r - 1,\ c - 1)}}$$

where (min $r - 1$, $c - 1$) = the minimum value of $r - 1$ (number of rows minus 1) or $c - 1$ (number of columns minus 1)

In words: To calculate V, find the lesser of the number of rows minus 1 ($r - 1$) or the number of columns minus 1 ($c - 1$), multiply this value by N, divide the result into the value of chi square, and then find the square root. Cramer's V has an upper limit of 1.00 for any size table and will be the same value as phi if the table has either two rows or two columns. Like phi, Cramer's V can be interpreted as an index that measures the strength of the association between two variables.

To illustrate the computation of V, suppose you had gathered the data displayed in Table 13.4, which shows the relationship between membership in student clubs or organizations and academic achievement for a sample of university students. The obtained chi square for this table is 31.5, a value that is significant at the .05 level. Cramer's V is

$$V = \sqrt{\frac{\chi^2}{(N)(\min\ r - 1,\ c - 1)}}$$

TABLE 13.4 ACADEMIC ACHIEVEMENT BY STUDENT-CLUB MEMBERSHIP (fictitious data)

Academic Achievement	Club Membership			Totals
	Varsity or Intramural Sports Club	Non-Sports Club	No Membership	
Low	4	4	17	25
Moderate	15	6	4	25
High	4	16	5	25
Totals	23	26	26	75

$$V = \sqrt{\frac{31.50}{(75)(2)}}$$

$$V = \sqrt{\frac{31.50}{150}}$$

$$V = \sqrt{0.21}$$

$$V = 0.46$$

Because Table 13.4 has the same number of rows and columns, we may use either $(r - 1)$ or $(c - 1)$ in the denominator. In either case, the value of the denominator is N multiplied by $(3 - 1)$, or 2. The computed value of V of .46 means that there is a strong association between club membership and academic achievement. Column percentages are presented in Table 13.5 to help identify the pattern of this relationship. Members of sports clubs tend to be moderate, members of non-sports clubs tend to be high, and non-members tend to be low in academic achievement.

One limitation of phi and Cramer's V is that they are only general indicators of the strength of the relationship. Of course, the closer these measures are to 0.00, the weaker the relationship, and the closer to 1.00, the stronger the relationship. Values between 0.00 and 1.00 can be described as weak, moderate, or strong according to the general convention introduced earlier but have no direct or meaningful interpretation. On the other hand, phi and V are easy to calculate (once the value of chi square has been obtained) and are commonly used indicators of the importance of an association. Two other chi square–based measures of association, Tschuprow's T^2 and C (the contingency coefficient), are also occasionally used. Both of these measures have serious limitations. T^2 has an upper limit of 1.00 only for tables with an equal number of rows and columns, and the upper limit of C varies depending on the dimensions of the table. These characteristics make these measures more difficult to interpret and thus less useful than phi or Cramer's V. (*For practice in computing phi and Cramer's V, see any of the problems at the end of this chapter or at the*

TABLE 13.5   ACADEMIC ACHIEVEMENT BY STUDENT-CLUB MEMBERSHIP (percentages)

Academic Achievement	Club Membership			Totals
	Varsity or Intramural Sports Club	Non-Sports Club	No Membership	
Low	17.39	15.38	65.38	33.33
Moderate	65.22	23.08	15.39	33.33
High	17.39	61.54	19.23	33.33
Totals	100.00	100.00	100.00	100.00

end of Chapter 12. To minimize computations, however, use problems from the end of Chapter 11 for which you already have a value for chi square. Otherwise, use the problems based on 2 × 2 tables. Remember that for tables that have either two rows or two columns, phi and Cramer's V will have the same value.)

13.3 PROPORTIONAL REDUCTION IN ERROR (PRE)

In recent years, a group of measures based on a logic known as **proportional reduction in error (PRE)** have been developed to complement the older chi square–based measures of association. Most generally stated, the logic of these measures requires us to make two different predictions about the scores of cases. In the first prediction, we ignore information about the independent variable and, therefore, make many errors in predicting the score on the dependent variable. In the second prediction, we take account of the score of the case on the independent variable to help predict the score on the dependent variable. If there is an association between the variables, we will make fewer errors when taking the independent variable into account. PRE measures of association express the proportional reduction in errors between the two predictions. Applying these general thoughts to the case of nominal-level variables will make the logic clearer.

For nominal-level variables, we first predict the category into which each case will fall on the dependent variable (Y) while ignoring the independent variable (X). Because we would, in effect, be predicting blindly in this case, we would make many errors (i.e., we would often incorrectly predict the category of a case on the dependent variable).

The second prediction allows us to take the independent variable into account. If the two variables are associated, the additional information supplied by the independent variable will reduce our errors of prediction (i.e., we should misclassify fewer cases). The stronger the association between the variables, the greater the reduction in errors. In the case of a perfect association, we would make no errors at all when predicting the score on Y from the score on X. But when there is no association between the variables, knowledge of the independent variable will not improve the accuracy of our predictions. We would make just as many errors of prediction with knowledge of the independent variable as we would without knowledge of the independent variable.

An illustration should make these principles clearer. Suppose you were placed in the rather unusual position of having to predict whether each of the next 100 people you meet will be shorter or taller than 5 feet 9 inches under the condition that you would have no knowledge of these people at all. With absolutely no information about these people, your predictions will be wrong quite often (you will frequently misclassify a tall person as short and vice versa).

Now assume that you must go through this ordeal twice, but on the second round, you know the sex of the person whose height you must predict. Because height is associated with sex and females are, on the average, shorter than males, the optimal strategy would be to predict that all females are short and all males are tall. Of course, you will still make errors on this second round, but if the variables are associated, the number of errors on the second round will be less than the number of errors on the first. That is, using information about the independent variable will reduce the number of errors (if, of course, the two variables are related). How can these unusual thoughts be translated into a useful statistic?

13.4 A PRE MEASURE FOR NOMINAL-LEVEL VARIABLES: LAMBDA

One hundred individuals have been categorized by gender and height, and the data are displayed in Table 13.6. It is clear, even without percentages, that the two variables are associated. To measure the strength of this association, a PRE measure called **lambda** (symbolized by the Greek letter λ) will be calculated. Following the logic introduced in the previous section, we must find two quantities. First, the number of prediction errors made while ignoring the independent variable (gender) must be found. Then, we will find the number of prediction errors made while taking gender into account. These two sums will then be compared to derive the statistic.

First, the information given by the independent variable (gender) can be ignored, in effect, by working only with the row marginals. Two different predictions can be made about height (the dependent variable) by using these marginals. We can predict either that all subjects are tall or that all subjects are short.* For the first prediction (all subjects are tall), 48 errors will be made. That is, for this prediction, all 100 cases would be placed in the first row. Because only 52 of the cases actually belong in this row, this prediction would result in $(100 - 52)$, or 48, errors. If we had predicted that all subjects were short, on the other hand, we would have made 52 errors

TABLE 13.6   HEIGHT BY GENDER

Height	Gender		Totals
	Male	Female	
Tall	44	8	52
Short	6	42	48
Totals	50	50	100

*Other predictions are, of course, possible, but these are the only two permitted by lambda.

$(100 - 48 = 52)$. We will take the *lesser* of these two numbers and refer to this quantity as $\boldsymbol{E_1}$ for the number of errors made while ignoring the independent variable. So, $E_1 = 48$.

In the second step in the computation of lambda, we predict score on Y (height) again but this time we take X (gender) into account. To do this, follow the same procedure as in the first step but this time move from column to column. Because each column is a category of X, we thus take X into account in making our predictions. For the left-hand column (males), we predict that all 50 cases will be tall and make six errors $(50 - 44 = 6)$. For the second column (females), our prediction is that all females are short, and eight errors will be made. By moving from column to column, we have taken X into account and have made a total of 14 errors of prediction, a quantity we will label $\boldsymbol{E_2}$ $(E_2 = 6 + 8 = 14)$.

If the variables are associated, we will make fewer errors under the second procedure than under the first. In other words, E_2 will be smaller than E_1. In this case, we made fewer errors of prediction while taking gender into account $(E_2 = 14)$ than while ignoring gender $(E_1 = 48)$, so gender and height are clearly associated. Our errors were reduced from 48 to only 14. To find the *proportional* reduction in error, use Formula 13.3:

FORMULA 13.3
$$\lambda = \frac{E_1 - E_2}{E_1}$$

For the sample problem, the value of lambda would be

$$\lambda = \frac{E_1 - E_2}{E_1}$$

$$\lambda = \frac{48 - 14}{48}$$

$$\lambda = \frac{34}{48}$$

$$\lambda = 0.71$$

The value of lambda ranges from 0.00 to 1.00. Of course, a value of 0.00 means that the variables are not associated at all (E_1 is the same as E_2) and a value of 1.00 means that the association is perfect (E_2 is zero and scores on the dependent variable can be predicted without error from the independent variable). Unlike phi or V, however, the numerical value of lambda between the extremes of 0.00 and 1.00 has a precise meaning: It is an index of the extent to which the independent variable (X) helps us to predict (or, more loosely, understand) the dependent variable (Y). When multiplied by 100, the value of lambda indicates the strength of the association in terms of the percentage reduction in error. Thus, the lambda above would be interpreted by concluding that knowledge of gender improves our ability to predict height by 71%. Or, we are 71% better off knowing gender when attempting to predict height.

Application 13.1

A random sample of students from the Canadian Internet Use Survey, conducted by Statistics Canada to measure the extent and scope to which Canadians use the Internet, was asked about using the Internet to play games in the last year. The table below displays the actual data for this variable by sex of respondent. Is online gaming related to sex?

Online Gaming	Sex		Totals
	Male	Female	
Yes	407	438	845
No	253	590	843
Totals	660	1,028	1,688

Because this is a 2 × 2 table, we can compute phi as a measure of association. The chi square for the table is 58.41, so phi is

$$\phi = \sqrt{\frac{\chi^2}{N}}$$

$$\phi = \sqrt{\frac{58.41}{1,688}}$$

$$\phi = \sqrt{0.035}$$

$$\phi = 0.19$$

which indicates a moderate relationship between the two variables.

A lambda can also be computed as an additional measure of association:

$$E_1 = 1,688 - 845 = 843$$

$$E_2 = (660 - 407) + (1,028 - 590)$$

$$= 253 + 438 = 691$$

$$\lambda = \frac{E_1 - E_2}{E_1}$$

$$\lambda = \frac{843 - 691}{843}$$

$$\lambda = \frac{152}{843}$$

$$\lambda = 0.18$$

A lambda of 0.18 indicates that we would make 18% fewer errors in predicting use of the Internet to play games (Y) from sex (X), as opposed to predicting use of the Internet to play games while ignoring sex. The association is moderate and, by inspection of the table, we can see that male students are more likely to play games online (62%), and female students are more likely not to use the Internet to play games (57%).

Source: Statistics Canada, 2005 Canadian Internet Use Survey, PUMF.

13.5 THE COMPUTATION OF LAMBDA

In this section, we will work through another example, based on actual data, to state the computational routine for lambda in more general terms. Implemented in 1994, the North American Free Trade Agreement (NAFTA) removed most barriers to trade, and increased cross-border trade among the United States, Canada, and Mexico. Since that time, public opinion on NAFTA in Canada has been mixed. We will use data from the 2006 Canadian Election Study, shown in Table 13.7, to examine whether public opinion toward free trade varies by region. (The Canadian Election Study surveyed adults in the 10 provinces only, thus excluding the territories). To make the number of

TABLE 13.7 OPINION TOWARD FREE TRADE* BY REGION

| | Region | | | | |
Opinion on Free Trade	Atlantic	Quebec	Ontario	Western	Totals
Somewhat/Strongly Disagree	10	40	29	60	139
Somewhat Agree	21	33	48	43	145
Strongly Agree	10	19	40	26	95
Totals	41	92	117	129	379

*Based on the question, "Do you strongly agree, somewhat agree, somewhat disagree, or strongly disagree that, overall, free trade with the U.S. has been good for the Canadian economy?"
Source: 2006 Canadian Election Study.

cases in this example more manageable, yet still representative, we randomly selected about 10% of cases (or 379 respondents) from the full sample of about 4,000 respondents.

Step 1. To find E_1, the number of errors made while ignoring X (region, in this case), subtract the largest row total from N. For Table 13.7, E_1 will be

$$E_1 = N - (\text{Largest row total})$$
$$E_1 = 379 - 145$$
$$E_1 = 234$$

Thus, we will misclassify 234 cases on opinion toward free trade while ignoring region.

Step 2. Next, E_2—the number of errors made when taking the independent variable into account—must be found. For each column, subtract the largest cell frequency from the column total and then add the subtotals together. For the data presented in Table 13.7:

$$\text{For Atlantic Canada: } 41 - 21 = 20$$
$$\text{For Quebec: } 92 - 40 = 52$$
$$\text{For Ontario: } 117 - 48 = 69$$
$$\text{For Western Canada: } 129 - 60 = 69$$
$$E_2 = 210$$

A total of 210 errors are made when predicting opinion toward free trade while taking region into account.

Application 13.2

In Application 12.2, we examined the relationships between the status of women and two different independent variables—religiosity and level of development—for a sample of 47 nations. We found a moderate to strong relationship between religiosity and the status of women and a strong relationship between level of development and the status of women. In this application, we'll use the measures of association introduced in this chapter to verify these characterizations of the strength of the relationship.

STATUS OF WOMEN BY RELIGIOSITY FOR 47 NATIONS: Frequencies and (*Percentages*)

Women's Status	Religiosity		Totals
	Low	High	
Low	8 (*36.36%*)	17 (*68.00%*)	25
High	14 (*63.64%*)	8 (*32.00%*)	22
Totals	22 (*100.00%*)	25 (*100.00%*)	47

We have already examined the conditional distributions and the maximum difference for both tables, so we can proceed to the measures of association. For the relationship between the status of women and religiosity, chi square is 4.7, so phi is

$$\phi = \sqrt{\frac{\chi^2}{N}}$$

$$\phi = \sqrt{\frac{4.7}{47}}$$

$$\phi = \sqrt{0.10}$$

$$\phi = 0.32$$

Lambda is

$$E_1 = 47 - 25 = 22$$

$$E_2 = (22 - 14) + (25 - 17)$$

$$= (8 + 8) = 16$$

$$\lambda = \frac{E_1 - E_2}{E_1}$$

$$\lambda = \frac{22 - 16}{22}$$

$$\lambda = \frac{6}{22}$$

$$\lambda = 0.27$$

A lambda of 0.27 indicates that we would make 27% fewer errors using the independent variable (religiosity) to predict women's status. According to the guidelines suggested in Table 13.3, both measures of association indicate that the relationship is on the borderline between moderate and strong.

(continued next page)

Step 3. In step 1, 234 errors of prediction were made as compared to 210 errors in step 2. Because the number of errors has been reduced, the variables are associated. To find the proportional reduction in error, the values for E_1 and E_2 can be directly substituted into Formula 13.3:

$$\lambda = \frac{234 - 210}{234}$$

$$\lambda = \frac{24}{234}$$

$$\lambda = 0.10$$

Application 13.2: *(continued)*

STATUS OF WOMEN BY LEVEL OF DEVELOPMENT FOR 47 NATIONS: Frequencies and (*Percentages*)

Women's Status	Level of Development			Totals
	LDCs	Developing	Developed	
Low	13 (*81.25%*)	8 (*53.33%*)	4 (*25.00%*)	25
High	3 (*18.75%*)	7 (*46.67%*)	12 (*75.00%*)	22
Totals	16 (*100.00%*)	15 (*100.00%*)	16 (*100.00%*)	47

Turning to the relationship between level of development and the status of women, the chi square is 10.17, so phi is

$$\phi = \sqrt{\frac{\chi^2}{N}}$$

$$\phi = \sqrt{\frac{10.17}{47}}$$

$$\phi = \sqrt{0.22}$$

$$\phi = 0.47$$

The lambda is

$$E_1 = 47 - 25 = 22$$
$$E_2 = (16 - 13) + (15 - 8) + (16 - 12)$$
$$\quad = (3 + 7 + 4) = 14$$

$$\lambda = \frac{E_1 - E_2}{E_1}$$

$$\lambda = \frac{22 - 14}{22}$$

$$\lambda = \frac{8}{22}$$

$$\lambda = 0.36$$

A lambda of 0.36 means that we will make 36% fewer errors of prediction using information from the independent variable (level of development) to predict scores on the dependent variable (women's status). Using the guidelines suggested in Table 13.3, both phi (0.47) and lambda (0.36) indicate that this is a strong relationship.

Using our conventional labels, we would call this a weak to moderate relationship. Using PRE logic, we can add more detail to the characterization: When attempting to predict opinion toward free trade, we would make 10% fewer errors by taking region into account. Knowledge of a respondent's region of residence improves the accuracy of our predictions by a factor of 10%. The weak to moderate strength of lambda indicates that factors other than region are associated with the dependent variable.

READING STATISTICS 10: Bivariate Tables and Associated Statistics

In this chapter and the next one, our primary concern is with measures of association for bivariate tables. These statistics are very useful for summarizing the strength and—as we will see in Chapter 14—the direction of relationships. The statistics associated with any bivariate table will usually be reported directly below the table itself. This information would include the name of the measure of association and its value. Also, if the research involves a random sample, the results of the chi square test or a test for the significance of the measure itself (as we will see in Section 14.7) will be reported. Thus, the information would look something like this:

$$\lambda = 0.47$$
$$\chi^2 = 13.23 \ (2df, \ p < 0.05)$$

Note that the alpha level is reported in the "$p <$" format, which we discussed in Reading Statistics 6.

Besides reporting the value of these statistics, researchers also interpret them in the text of their studies. The preceding statistics might be characterized by the following statement: "The association between the variables is statistically significant and strong." Again, we see that researchers will avoid our rather wordy (but more careful) style of presenting results. Where we might say "a lambda of 0.47 indicates that we will reduce our errors of prediction by 47% when predicting the dependent variable from the independent variable, as opposed to predicting the dependent while ignoring the independent," the researcher will simply report the value of lambda and characterize that value in a word or two (e.g., "The association is strong"). The researcher assumes that his or her audience is statistically literate and can make the more detailed interpretations themselves.

However, the first step in examining a bivariate table for a relationship is to apply the techniques introduced in Chapter 12. Column percentages and conditional distributions will give you more detail about the relationship than measures of association. As useful as they are, the latter should be regarded as summary statements rather than analysis in depth. In this installment of Reading Statistics we will review a study that looks at the relationship between ethnicity and politics using both sets of techniques.

Statistics in the Professional Literature

Heterogeneity in ethnicity and culture is a growing characteristic of Canadian society. Many aspects of Canadian society reflect this ethnocultural diversity. Yet as Tossutti and Najem (2002) highlight, there is a considerable gap between ethnocultural minorities in the general population and their representation in federal politics.

Tossutti and Najem look specifically at the association between federal political party affiliation and ethnocultural origin of political candidates. Party affiliation is categorized as follows: Liberal Party, Canadian Alliance, Progressive Conservative Party (PC), New Democratic Party (NDP), and Bloc Québécois (BQ). Ethnocultural origin is divided into two categories: those who trace their origins to the Aboriginal, French, and British founding groups ("non-minority") and those who do not ("minority"). Tossutti and Najem examine a number of relationships between politics and ethnocultural origin.

We focus here on two of these relationships, based on data from the 2000 federal election. Both bivariate tables are constructed in conventional format, with the independent variable in the columns, the dependent variable in the rows, and percentages calculated in the columns. The Cramer's *V* associated with each table is reported directly below it.

Table 1 shows the relationship between federal election candidates' party affiliation (independent variable) and ethnocultural origin (dependent variable). A Cramer's *V* of 0.11 indicates a weak

(continued)

READING STATISTICS 10:   *(continued)*

moderate association. The column percentages show that political parties differed in minority candidate recruitment in the 2000 federal election, with the Liberals fielding the most and the BQ the least minority candidates in the election, yet the Alliance was not far behind the Liberals. This was an unexpected finding, the authors note, given the Alliance's perceived "anti-immigrant" image versus the Liberal's image of openness to minorities.

TABLE 1   PARTY AFFILIATION AND ETHNOCULTURAL ORIGIN OF CANDIDATES IN THE 2000 FEDERAL ELECTION, PERCENTAGES (*N*'S IN PARENTHESES)

Ethnocultural Origin	Party Affiliation				
	Liberal	Alliance	PC	NDP	BQ
Minority	26.6	23.5	19.2	24.7	6.7
Non-minority	73.4	76.5	80.8	75.3	93.3
Totals	100.0	100.0	100.0	100.0	100.0
	(301)	(298)	(292)	(300)	(75)

Cramer's $V = 0.11$

Looking at minority candidates only, Table 2 examines the relationship between party affiliation (independent variable) and election success of candidates (dependent variable) in the 2000 federal election. Cramer's V (0.52) indicates a strong association. Conditional distributions show that minority candidates representing the Liberals, followed by the Alliance, had the highest success rates at the ballot box. PC, NDP, and BQ minority candidates had the lowest election victory rates. If you want to learn more about this study, the reference is provided at the end of this box.

TABLE 2   PARTY AFFILIATION AND VICTORY RATES OF ETHNIC MINORITY CANDIDATES IN THE 2000 FEDERAL ELECTION, PERCENTAGES (*N*'S IN PARENTHESES)

Election Success	Party Affiliation				
	Liberal	Alliance	PC	NDP	BQ
Elected	57.0	28.6	1.8	5.5	0.0
Not elected	43.0	71.4	98.2	94.5	100.0
Totals	100.0	100.0	100.0	100.0	100.0
	(80)	(70)	(56)	(74)	(5)

Cramer's $V = 0.52$

Source: Tossutti L. and Najem T. 2002. "Minorities and Elections in Canada's Four Party System: Macro and Micro Constraints and Opportunities." *Canadian Ethnic Studies, 34:* 84–111.

13.6 THE LIMITATIONS OF LAMBDA

As a measure of association, lambda has two characteristics that should be stressed. First, lambda is asymmetric. This means that the value of the statistic will vary, depending on which variable is taken as independent. For example, in Table 13.7, the value of lambda would be about 0.07 if opinion toward free trade had been taken as the independent variable (verify this with your own computation). Thus, you should exercise some caution in the designation of an independent variable. If you consistently follow the convention of arraying the independent variable in the columns and compute lambda as outlined above, the asymmetry of the statistic should not be confusing.

Second, when one of the row totals is much larger than the others, lambda can be misleading. It can be 0.00 even when other measures of association are greater than 0.00 and the conditional distributions for the table indicate that there is an association between the variables. This anomaly is a function of the way lambda is calculated and suggests that great caution should be exercised in the interpretation of lambda when the row marginals are very unequal. In fact, in the case of very unequal row marginals, a chi square–based measure of association would be the preferred measure of association. *(For practice in computing lambda, see any of the problems at the end of this chapter, Chapter 12, or Chapter 11. As with phi and Cramer's V, it's probably a good idea to start with small samples and 2 × 2 tables.)*

SUMMARY

1. Three measures of association—phi, Cramer's *V*, and lambda—were introduced. Each is used to summarize the overall strength of the association between two variables that have been organized into a bivariate table.
2. Phi and Cramer's *V* are chi square–based measures of association and have the advantage of being easy to compute (once the value of chi square is found). Phi is used for 2 × 2 tables; Cramer's *V* can be used for any size table. Both indicate the strength of the relationship, but values between 0.00 and 1.00 have no direct interpretation.

3. Lambda is a PRE-based measure and provides a more direct interpretation for values between the extremes of 0.00 and 1.00. Lambda indicates the improvement in predicting the dependent variable with knowledge of the independent, compared to predicting the dependent without knowledge of the independent. Because of the meaningfulness of values between the extremes, lambda is often preferred over the more traditional chi square–based measures (except when row totals are very unequal).

SUMMARY OF FORMULAS

Phi	13.1	$\phi = \sqrt{\dfrac{\chi^2}{N}}$
Cramer's *V*	13.2	$V = \sqrt{\dfrac{\chi^2}{(N)(\min r - 1, c - 1)}}$
Lambda	13.3	$\lambda = \dfrac{E_1 - E_2}{E_1}$

GLOSSARY

Cramer's V. A chi square–based measure of association. Appropriate for nominally measured variables that have been organized into a bivariate table of any number of rows and columns.

E_1. For lambda, the number of errors of prediction made when predicting which category of the dependent variable cases will fall into while ignoring the independent variable.

E_2. For lambda, the number of errors of prediction made when predicting which category of the dependent variable cases will fall into while taking account of the independent variable.

Lambda (λ). A measure of association appropriate for nominally measured variables that have been organized into a bivariate table. Lambda is based on the logic of proportional reduction in error (PRE).

Phi (ϕ). A chi square–based measure of association. Appropriate for nominally measured variables that have been organized into a 2 × 2 bivariate table.

Proportional reduction in error (PRE). The logic that underlies the definition and computation of lambda. The statistic compares the number of errors made when predicting the dependent variable while ignoring the independent variable (E_1) with the number of errors made while taking the independent variable into account (E_2).

MULTIMEDIA RESOURCES

http://www.healeystatistics.nelson.com

Visit the companion Web site for the first Canadian edition of *Statistics: A Tool for Social Research* to access a wide range of student resources. Begin by clicking on the Student Resources section of the book's Web site to access review quizzes, flash cards, and other study tools.

PROBLEMS

13.1 SOC Who is most likely to be victimized by crime? A small sample of city residents has been asked if they were the victims of burglary or robbery over the past year. The tables below report relationships between several variables and victimization. Compute phi and lambda for each table. Which relationship is strongest?

a. Victimization by sex of respondent:

	Sex		
Victimized?	Male	Female	Totals
Yes	10	12	22
No	15	18	33
Totals	25	30	55

b. Victimization by age of respondent:

	Age		
Victimized?	21 or Younger	22 or Older	Totals
Yes	12	10	22
No	15	18	33
Totals	27	28	55

c. Victimization by area of residence of respondent:

	Area		
Victimized?	Urban	Suburban	Totals
Yes	9	13	22
No	6	27	33
Totals	15	40	55

13.2 Compute a phi and a lambda for problems 12.1 to 12.4. Compare the value of the measure of association with your impressions of the strength of the relationships based solely on the percentages you calculated in Chapter 12.

13.3 | SOC | There is concern that suicides are motivated, in part, by imitation. Especially among young people, it may be that "epidemics" of self-destructive behaviours follow publication of suicides in local media. A number of cities have been classified by rate of suicide and by whether or not they experienced a publicized suicide within the past year. Is there an association between these two variables? Summarize your conclusions in a sentence or two.

Suicide Rate	Publicized Suicide?		Totals
	Yes	No	
Low	15	20	35
High	15	10	25
Totals	30	30	60

13.4 | SW | The director of a shelter for battered women has noticed that many of the women who are referred to the shelter eventually return to their violent husbands even when there is every indication that the husband will continue the pattern of abuse. The director suspects that the women who return to their husbands do so because they have no place else to go—for example, no close relatives in the area with whom the women could reside. Do the data below support the director's suspicion? (Data are from the case files of former clients.)

Return to Husband?	Relatives Nearby?		Totals
	Yes	No	
Yes	10	23	33
No	50	17	67
Totals	60	40	100

13.5 | PA | Traditionally, bus ridership in your town has been confined to lower-income and blue-collar patrons. As head of transportation planning for the city, you believe that ridership from white-collar, middle-income neighbourhoods can be increased if bus routes linking these neighbourhoods to the downtown area (where most people work) are increased. A survey is conducted, and the results are displayed below. Is willingness to ride the bus related to job location? What is the pattern of the relationship (if any)?

Potential Ridership	Job Location		Totals
	Downtown	Other	
Would use bus	55	20	75
Would not use bus	15	21	36
Totals	70	41	111

13.6 | GER | A survey of senior citizens who live in either a housing development specifically designed for retirees or an age-integrated neighbourhood has been conducted. Is type of living arrangement related to sense of social isolation?

Sense of Isolation	Living Arrangement		Totals
	Housing Development	Integrated Neighbourhood	
Low	80	30	110
High	20	120	140
Totals	100	150	250

13.7 | SOC | Is there an association between the sex of university instructors and the teaching effectiveness ratings they receive from students? Write a few sentences summarizing your findings.

Teaching Effectiveness	Sex		Totals
	Female	Male	
High	115	241	356
Low	54	113	167
Totals	169	354	523

13.8 | SOC | A researcher has conducted a survey on sexual attitudes for a sample of 317 teenagers. The respondents were asked whether they considered premarital sex to be "always wrong" or "OK under certain circumstances." The tables below summarize the relationship between responses to this item and several other variables. For each table, assess the strength and pattern of the relationship and write a paragraph interpreting these results.

a. Attitudes toward premarital sex by sex:

	Sex		
Premarital Sex	Female	Male	Totals
Always wrong	90	105	195
Not always wrong	65	57	122
Totals	155	162	317

b. Attitudes toward premarital sex by courtship status:

	Ever "Gone Steady"?		
Premarital Sex	No	Yes	Totals
Always wrong	148	47	195
Not always wrong	42	80	122
Totals	190	127	317

c. Attitudes toward premarital sex by social class:

	Social Class		
Premarital Sex	Blue Collar	White Collar	Totals
Always wrong	72	123	195
Not always wrong	47	75	122
Totals	119	198	317

13.9 SOC Algebra University has a problem with attrition. A sizable number of non-graduating students do not return to classes each semester. Is attrition importantly related to sex, status, or age? For each table below, how strong is the association (if any) between each of the independent variables and attrition? Does the relationship have a pattern? (Calculating percentages for the table will help to answer the second question.) Write a paragraph summarizing the results presented in these three tables.

a. Attrition by sex for 532 students enrolled in fall semester:

	Sex		
Attrition	Male	Female	Totals
Returned spring semester	280	100	380
Did not return	105	47	152
Totals	385	147	532

b. Attrition by status for 532 students enrolled in fall semester:

	Status		
Attrition	Part-time	Full-time	Totals
Returned spring semester	60	320	380
Did not return	65	87	152
Totals	125	407	532

c. Attrition by age for 532 students enrolled in fall semester:

	Age		
Attrition	18–24	25 and Older	Totals
Returned spring semester	315	65	380
Did not return	64	88	152
Totals	379	153	532

13.10 SOC A sociologist is researching public attitudes toward crime and has asked a sample of residents of his city if they think that the crime rate in their neighbourhoods is rising. Is there a relationship between sex and perception of the crime rate? Between immigration status and perception of the crime rate? What is the pattern of the relationship? Write a paragraph summarizing the information presented in these tables.

a. Perception of crime rate by sex:

Crime Rate Is	Sex		
	Male	Female	Totals
Rising	200	225	425
Stable	175	150	325
Falling	125	125	250
Totals	500	500	1,000

b. Perception of crime rate by immigration status:

Crime Rate Is	Immigration Status		
	Non-immigrant	Immigrant	Totals
Rising	300	125	425
Stable	230	95	325
Falling	170	80	250
Totals	700	300	1,000

13.11 [PS] You are running for mayor of Pearson, Ontario, and realize that, if you are to win, you must win the support of blue-collar voters. (You already have strong support in the white-collar neighbourhoods.) You have a very limited advertising budget and wonder how best to reach your intended audience. An aide has found the data below, which show the relationship between social class and "main source of news" for a sample of residents from Pearson, Ontario. Will this information help you make a decision?

Main Source of News	Social Class		Totals
	Blue Collar	White Collar	
Television	140	200	340
Radio	25	40	65
Newspapers	85	100	185
Totals	250	340	590

13.12 Problem 12.11 analyzed some bivariate relationships taken from a recent public-opinion survey. Political ideology was used as the independent variable for five different dependent variables and, using only percentages, you were asked to characterize the relationships in terms of strength and direction. Now, with the aid of measures of association, these characterizations should be easier to develop. Compute a Cramer's V and a lambda for each table in problem 12.11. Compare the measures of association with your characterizations based on the percentages.

Below are the same five dependent variables cross-tabulated against sex as an independent variable. Compare the strength of these relationships with those for political ideology. Which independent variable has the stronger associations?

a. Support for same-sex marriage by sex:

Same-sex Marriage?	Sex		Totals
	Male	Female	
Favour	310	418	728
Oppose	432	618	1,050
Totals	742	1,036	1,778

b. Support for capital punishment by sex:

Capital Punishment?	Sex		Totals
	Male	Female	
Favour	908	998	1,906
Oppose	246	447	693
Totals	1,154	1,445	2,599

c. Approval of suicide for people with incurable disease by sex:

Right to Suicide?	Sex		Totals
	Male	Female	
Favour	524	608	1,132
Oppose	246	398	644
Totals	770	1,006	1,776

d. Support for traditional gender roles by sex:

Traditional Gender Roles?	Sex		Totals
	Male	Female	
Favour	116	164	280
Oppose	669	865	1,534
Totals	785	1,029	1,814

e. Support for legalizing marijuana by sex:

Legalize Marijuana?	Sex		Totals
	Male	Female	
Favour	685	900	1,585
Oppose	102	134	236
Totals	787	1,034	1,821

Using SPSS for Windows to Produce Nominal-Level Measures of Association with the 2004 GSS

The demonstrations and exercises below use the 2004 GSS data set supplied with this text.

SPSS DEMONSTRATION 13.1 Does Criminal Victimization Vary by Sex? Another Look

In Demonstration 11.1, we used the **Crosstabs** procedure to examine the relationship between *lifevict* (ever been a victim of crime) and *sex*. We saw that the relationship was statistically significant, and that males were more likely than females to have been a victim of crime. In this demonstration, we will re-examine the relationship and have SPSS compute some measures of association.

Start SPSS for Windows and load the 2004 GSS database (*GSS.sav*). Click **Analyze,** then **Descriptive Statistics,** and then **Crosstabs.** Move *lifevict* into the **Row(s)** box and *sex* into the **Column(s)** box. Click the **Cells** button and request column percentages. Click the **Statistics** button and request chi square, phi, Cramer's V, and lambda. Click **Continue,** and then **OK,** and the following output, slightly edited to improve readability, will be produced.

EVER BEEN A VICTIM OF CRIME * SEX Crosstabulation

		SEX		Total
		MALE	FEMALE	
EVER BEEN A VICTIM OF CRIME	Yes	530	414	944
		66.3%	57.4%	62.1%
	No	269	307	576
		33.7%	42.6%	37.9%
Total		799	721	1520
		100.0%	100.0%	100.0%

Chi-Square Tests

	Value	df	Asymp. Sig. (2-sided)
Pearson Chi-Square	12.792*	1	.000
Continuity Correction†	12.416	1	.000
Likelihood Ratio	12.795	1	.000
Fisher's Exact Test			
Linear-by-Linear Association	12.784	1	.000
N of Valid Cases	1520		

*Zero cells (.0%) have expected count less than 5. The minimum expected count is 273.22.
†Computed only for a 2 × 2 table.

Directional Measures

			Value	Asymp. Std. Error*	Approx. $t^{\dagger}$	Approx. Sig.
Nominal by Nominal	Lambda	Symmetric	.029	.018	1.585	.113
		Ever been a victim of crime dependent	.000	.000	.‡	.‡
		Sex dependent	.053	.032	1.585	.113
	Goodman and Kruskal tau	Ever been a victim of crime dependent	.008	.005		.000§
		Sex dependent	.008	.005		.000§

*Not assuming the null hypothesis.
†Using the asymptotic standard error assuming the null hypothesis.
‡Cannot be computed because the asymptotic standard error equals zero.
§Based on chi-square approximation.

Symmetric Measures

		Value	Approx. Sig.
Nominal by Nominal	Phi	.092	.000
	Cramer's V	.092	.000
N of Valid Cases		1520	

The measures of association are reported below the output for the chi square tests. Three values for lambda are reported in the "Directional Measures" output block. Remember that lambda is asymmetric and will change value depending on which variable is taken as dependent. (Symmetric lambda is more or less an average of the two asymmetric lambda values.) In this case, *lifevict* (ever been a victim of crime) is the dependent variable, so lambda is .000, a value that indicates no relationship between the variables. Looking at the first block in the output "Crosstabulation," we see, however, that the conditional distributions do change, indicating that there actually is a relationship. The problem here is that the row totals are very unequal, and lambda is misleading and should be disregarded (see Section 13.6). (Goodman and Kruskal tau is similar to lambda, and is based on the logic of proportional reduction in error. It is also an asymmetric measure of association.)

Phi and Cramer's *V* are reported in the "Symmetric Measures" output block. The statistics are identical in value, .092, as they will be whenever the table has either two rows or two columns. The measures reveal an association between the variables, albeit a weak one.

The significance value of chi square, .000, reported in the "Chi-Square Tests" output block, is lower than .05, so we reject the null hypothesis and conclude that the relationship between sex and victimization is statistically significant. Even though Phi and Cramer's *V* tell us that the relationship between sex and victimization is rather weak, chi square indicates that it is statistically significant. This reminds us once again that association and statistical significance are two different things.

SPSS DEMONSTRATION 13.2 Do Demographic Variables Affect Criminal Victimization?

Let's see if we can do any better in "explaining" criminal victimization with some other commonly used independent variables. As you are no doubt aware, victimization is often associated with various demographic variables. In keeping with our focus on the nominal level of measurement, let's investigate relationships between *lifevict* and *dwelc* (dwelling type), *luc_rst* (urban/rural indicator), and *marstat* (marital status). Incorporating a number of potential independent variables, although quite common in social science research, generates a large volume of output, and we will abbreviate the actual output from SPSS in this demonstration.

	Percent Victimized	Significance of Chi Square	Phi	Lambda
dwelc		.703	.03	.000
Single detached house	62.3			
Low-rise apartment	61.3			
High-rise apartment	56.8			
Other	63.8			
luc_rst		.001	.084	.000
Larger urban centres	64.1			
Rural and small town	53.8			
marstat		.000	.127	.023
Married	61.6			
Living common-law	73.3			
Widowed	33.3			
Separated	70.3			
Divorced	65.4			
Single	60.4			

Using phi as a guide, we see that *lifevict* is related to each variable, yet the strength of the relationships are weak to moderate in range, with *marstat* having the strongest relationship. Because the rows are very unequal, lambda should be disregarded.

Exercises (using *GSS.sav*)

13.1 Following up on Demonstrations 13.1 and 13.2, select two more variables that you think might be related to *lifevict*. Run the **Crosstabs** procedure with *lifevict* as dependent or row variable and your other variables as the independent or column variables. Be sure to request column percentage in the cells, as well as phi and lambda. Write a few sentences describing each relationship.

13.2 Run the tables you did for Exercise 12.2 again with a request for phi and lambda. Do the measures of association help you interpret the relationships?

14 ASSOCIATION BETWEEN VARIABLES MEASURED AT THE ORDINAL LEVEL

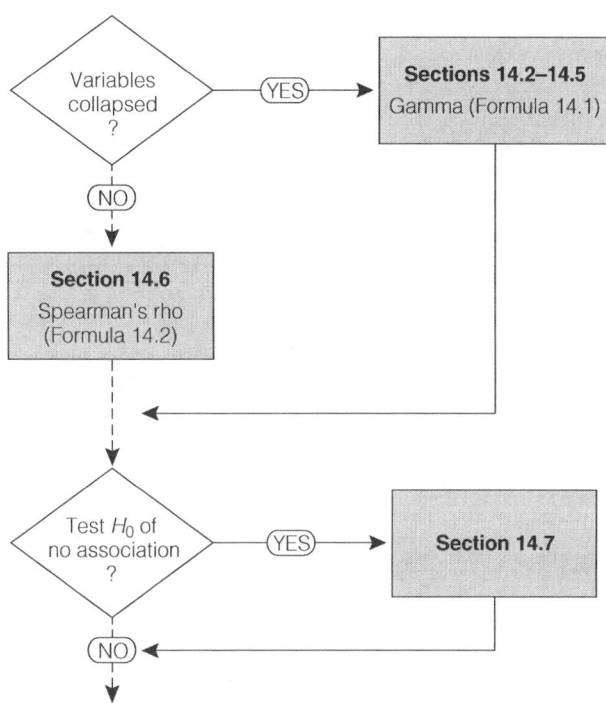

LEARNING OBJECTIVES

By the end of this chapter, you will be able to

1. Calculate and interpret gamma and Spearman's rho.
2. Explain the logic of proportional reduction in error in terms of gamma.
3. Use gamma and Spearman's rho to analyze and describe a bivariate relationship in terms of the three questions introduced in Chapter 12.
4. Test gamma and Spearman's rho for significance.

14.1 INTRODUCTION

There are two common types of ordinal-level variables. Some have many possible scores and look, at least at first glance, like interval-ratio-level variables. We will call these "continuous ordinal variables." An attitude scale that incorporated many different items and, therefore, had many possible values would produce this type of variable.

The second type, which we will call a "collapsed ordinal variable," has only a few (no more than five or six) values or scores and can be created either by collecting data in collapsed form or by collapsing a continuous ordinal scale. For example, we would produce collapsed ordinal variables by measuring social class as upper, middle, or lower or by reducing the scores on an attitude scale into just a few categories (such as high, moderate, and low).

A number of measures of association have been invented for use with collapsed ordinal-level variables. Rather than attempt a comprehensive coverage of all of these statistics, we will concentrate on **gamma (G).** Other measures suitable for collapsed ordinal-level data (Somer's *d* and Kendall's tau-*b*) are covered at the website for this text. For "continuous" ordinal variables, a statistic called **Spearman's rho (r_s)** is commonly used, and we will cover this measure of association toward the end of this chapter.

This chapter will expand your understanding of how bivariate associations can be described and analyzed, but it is important to remember that we are still trying to answer the three questions raised in Chapter 12: Are the variables associated? How strong is the association? What is the direction of the association?

14.2 PROPORTIONAL REDUCTION IN ERROR (PRE)

For nominal-level variables, the logic of PRE was based on two different "predictions" of the scores of cases on the dependent variable (Y): one that ignored the independent variable (X) and a second that took the independent variable into account. The value of lambda showed the extent to which taking the independent variable into account improved accuracy when predicting the score of the dependent variable (see Section 13.4). The PRE logic for variables measured at the ordinal level is similar, and gamma, like lambda, measures the proportional reduction in error gained by predicting one variable while taking the other into account. The major difference lies in the way predictions are made.

In the case of gamma, we predict the order of pairs of cases rather than a score on the dependent variable. That is, we predict whether one case will have a higher or lower score than the other. First, we predict the order of a pair of cases on one variable while ignoring their order on the other. Second, we predict the order on one variable while taking order on the other variable into account.

As an illustration, assume that a researcher is concerned about the causes of "burnout" (i.e., demoralization and loss of commitment) among elementary school teachers and wonders about the relationship between levels of burnout and years of service. One way to state the research question would be to ask if teachers with more years of service have higher levels of burnout. Another way to ask the same question is: Do teachers who *rank higher* on years of service also *rank higher* on burnout? If we knew that teacher A had more years of service than teacher B, would we be able to predict that teacher A is also more "burned out" than teacher B? That is, would knowledge of the order of this pair of cases on one variable help us predict their order on the other?

If the two variables are associated, we will reduce our errors when our predictions about one of the variables are based on knowledge of the other. Furthermore, the stronger the association, the fewer the errors we will make. When there is no association between the variables, gamma will be 0.00, and knowledge of the order of a pair of cases on one variable will not improve our ability to predict their order on the other. A gamma of ± 1.00 denotes a perfect relationship: The order of all pairs of cases on one variable would be predictable without error from their order on the other variable.

With nominal-level variables, we analyzed the pattern of the relationship between the variables. That is, we looked to see which value on one variable (e.g., "male" on the variable gender) was associated with which value on the other variable (e.g., "tall" on the variable height). Recall that a defining characteristic of variables measured at the ordinal level is that the scores or values can be rank ordered from high to low or from more to less (see Chapter 1). This means that relationships between ordinal-level variables can have a direction as well as a pattern. In terms of the logic of gamma, the overall relationship between the variables is *positive* if cases tend to be ranked in the same order on both variables. For example, if Case A is ranked above Case B on one variable, it would also be ranked above Case B on the second variable. The relationship suggested above between years of service and burnout would be a positive relationship. In a *negative* relationship, the order of the cases would be reversed between the two variables. If Case A ranked above Case B on one variable, it would tend to rank below Case B on the second variable. If there is a negative relationship between sexism and education and Case A was more educated than Case B (or, ranked above Case B on education), then Case A would be less sexist (or, would rank below Case B on sexism).

14.3 THE COMPUTATION OF GAMMA

Table 14.1 summarizes the relationship between "length of service" and "burnout" for a fictitious sample of 100 teachers. To compute gamma, two sums are needed. First, we must find the number of pairs of cases that are

TABLE 14.1 BURNOUT BY LENGTH OF SERVICE (fictitious data)

Burnout	Length of Service			Totals
	Low	Moderate	High	
Low	20	6	4	30
Moderate	10	15	5	30
High	8	11	21	40
Totals	38	32	30	100

Application 14.1

A group of 40 nations have been rated as high or low on religiosity (based on the percentage of a random sample of citizens that described themselves as "a religious person") and as high or low in their support for single mothers (based on the percentage of a random sample of citizens who said they would approve of a woman choosing to be a single parent). Are more religious nations less approving of single mothers?

	Religiosity		
Approval	Low	High	Totals
Low	4	9	13
High	11	16	27
Totals	15	25	40

The number of pairs of cases ranked in the same order on both variables (N_s) would be

$$N_s = 4(16) = 64$$

The number of pairs of cases ranked in different order on both variables (N_d) would be

$$N_d = 9 (11) = 99$$

Gamma is

$$G = \frac{N_s - N_d}{N_s + N_d} = \frac{64 - 99}{64 + 99} = \frac{-35}{163} = -0.21$$

A gamma of -0.21 means that, when predicting the order of pairs of cases on the dependent variable (approval of single mothers), we would make 21% fewer errors by taking the independent variable (religiosity) into account. There is a moderate to weak, negative association between these two variables. As religiosity increases, approval decreases (or, more religious nations are less approving of single mothers).

---

ranked the same on both variables (we will label this N_s) and then the number of pairs of cases ranked differently on the variables (N_d). We find these sums by working with the cell frequencies.

To find the number of pairs of cases ranked the same (N_s), begin with the cell containing the cases that were ranked the lowest on both variables. In Table 14.1, this would be the upper-left-hand cell. (NOTE: Not all tables are constructed with values increasing from left to right across the columns and from top to bottom across the rows. When using other tables, always be certain that you have located the proper cell.) The 20 cases in the upper-left-hand cell all rank low on both burnout and length of service, and we will refer to these cases as "low-lows," or "LLs."

Now, form a pair of cases by selecting one case from this cell and one from any other cell—for example, the middle cell in the table. All 15 cases in this cell are moderate on both variables and, following our practice above, can be labelled moderate-moderates, or MMs. Any pair of cases formed between these two cells will be ranked the same on both variables. That is, all LLs are lower than all MMs on both variables (on X, low is less than moderate, and on Y, low is less than moderate). The total number of pairs of cases is given by multiplying the cell frequencies. So, the contribution of these two cells to the total N_s is (20)(15), or 300.

FIGURE 14.1   COMPUTING N_s IN A 3 × 3 TABLE

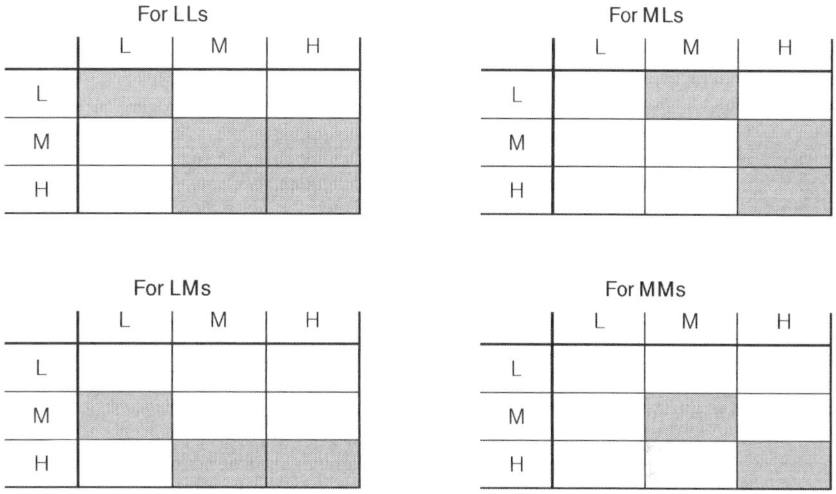

For LLs

	L	M	H
L			
M			
H			

For MLs

	L	M	H
L			
M			
H			

For LMs

	L	M	H
L			
M			
H			

For MMs

	L	M	H
L			
M			
H			

Gamma ignores all pairs of cases that are tied on either variable. For example, any pair of cases formed between the LLs and any other cell in the top row (low on burnout) or the left-hand column (low on length of service) will be tied on one variable. Also, any pair of cases formed within any cell will be tied on both X and Y. Gamma ignores all pairs of cases formed within the same row, column, or cell. Practically, this means that, in computing N_s, we will work with only the pairs of cases that can be formed between each cell and the cells below and to the right of it.

In summary: To find the total number of pairs of cases ranked the same on both variables (N_s), multiply the frequency in each cell by the total of all frequencies below and to the right of that cell. Repeat this procedure for each cell and add the resultant products. The total of these products is N_s. This procedure is displayed below for each cell in Table 14.1. Note that none of the cells in the bottom row or the right-hand column can contribute to N_s because they have no cells below and to the right of them. Figure 14.1 shows the direction of multiplication for each of the four cells that, in a 3 × 3 table, can contribute to N_s. Computing N_s for Table 14.1, we find that a total of 1,831 pairs of cases are ranked the same on both variables.

	Contribution to N_s
For LLs, $20(15 + 5 + 11 + 21) = 1,040$	
For MLs, $6(21 + 5)$ $= 156$	
For HLs, $4(0)$ $= 0$	
For LMs, $10(11 + 21)$ $= 320$	

(*continued next page*)

(*continued*)

	Contribution to N_s
For MMs, 15(21)	= 315
For HMs, 5(0)	= 0
For LHs, 8(0)	= 0
For MHs, 11(0)	= 0
For HHs, 21(0)	= 0
	$N_s = 1{,}831$

Our next step is to find the number of pairs of cases ranked differently (N_d) on both variables. To find the total number of pairs of cases ranked in different order on the variables, multiply the frequency in each cell by the total of all frequencies below and to the left of that cell. Note that the pattern for computing N_d is the reverse of the pattern for N_s. This time, we begin with the upper-right-hand cell (high-lows, or HLs) and multiply the number of cases in the cell by the total frequency of cases below and to the left. The four cases in the upper-right-hand cell are low on Y and high on X; if a pair is formed with any case from this cell and any cell below and to the left, the cases will be ranked differently on the two variables. For example, if a pair is formed between any HL case and any case from the middle cell (moderate-moderates, or MMs), the HL case would be less than the MM case on Y ("low" is less than "moderate") but more than the MM case on X ("high" is greater than "moderate"). The computation of N_d is detailed below and shown graphically in Figure 14.2. In the computations, we have omitted cells that cannot contribute to N_d because they have no cells below and to the left of them.

	Contribution to N_d
For HLs, $4(10 + 15 + 8 + 11)$	= 176
For MLs, $6(10 + 8)$	= 108
For HMs, $5(8 + 11)$	= 95
For MMs, 15(8)	= 120
	$N_d = 499$

Table 14.1 has 499 pairs of cases ranked in different order and 1,831 pairs of cases ranked in the same order. The formula for computing gamma is

FORMULA 14.1
$$G = \frac{N_s - N_d}{N_s + N_d}$$

where N_s = the number of pairs of cases ranked the same on both variables
N_d = the number of pairs of cases ranked differently on the two variables

Application 14.2

There is no age at which individuals are immune to stress. However, do levels of stress vary by age? Are younger Canadians more stressed out than older Canadians? We examine the relationship between age and stress using an actual random sample of 1,000 respondents from the Canadian Mental Health and Well-being Survey. Age has been grouped as 15 to 44 years of age, 45 to 64 years of age, and 65 years of age and older. Stress was measured in the survey with the following question, "Thinking about the amount of stress in your life, would you say that most days are: not stressful ('low' stress) or stressful ('high' stress)?"

Stress	Age			
Level	15–44	45–64	65+	Totals
Low	154	121	125	600
High	346	179	75	400
Totals	500	300	200	1,000

Because both variables are ordinal in level of measurement, we will compute a gamma to summarize the strength and direction of the association. The number of pairs of cases ranked in the same order on both variables (N_s) would be

$$N_s = 154(179 + 75) + 121(75) = 39,116 + 9,075$$
$$= 48,191$$

The number of pairs of cases ranked in different order on both variables (N_d) would be

$$N_d = 125(179 + 346) + 121(346) = 65,625$$
$$+ 41,866 = 107,491$$

Gamma is

$$G = \frac{N_s - N_d}{N_s + N_d}$$

$$G = \frac{48,191 - 107,491}{48,191 + 107,491}$$

$$G = \frac{-59,300}{155,682}$$

$$G = -0.38$$

A gamma of −0.38 means that, when predicting the order of pairs of cases on stress level, we would make 38% fewer errors by taking age into account, as opposed to ignoring the latter variable. There is a moderate, negative association between these two variables. As age increases, stress level decreases: Older Canadians are less likely to report high levels of stress.

Source: Statistics Canada, 2002 Mental Health and Well-being, Canadian Community Health Survey, PUMF.

For Table 14.1, the value of gamma would be

$$G = \frac{N_s - N_d}{N_s + N_d}$$

$$G = \frac{1,831 - 499}{1,831 + 499}$$

$$G = \frac{1,332}{2,330}$$

$$G = 0.57$$

A gamma of 0.57 indicates that we would make 57% fewer errors if we predicted the order of pairs of cases on one variable from the order of pairs of cases on the other (as opposed to predicting order while ignoring the other

FIGURE 14.2 COMPUTING N_d IN A 3 × 3 TABLE

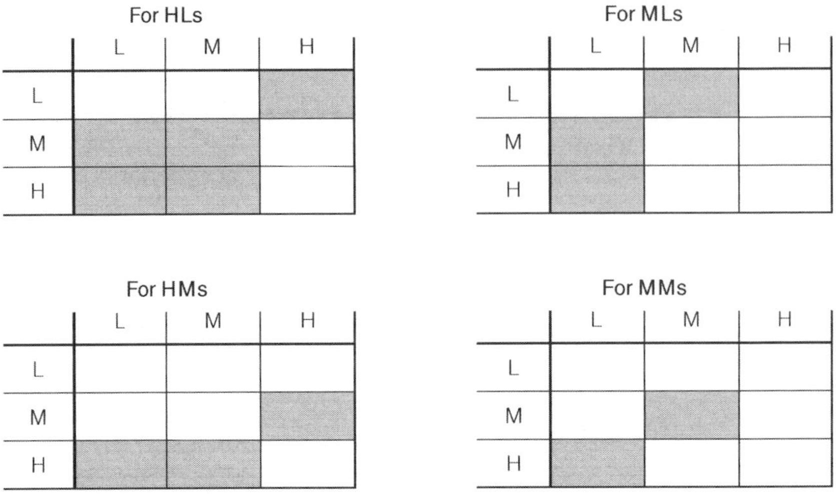

For HLs

	L	M	H
L			
M			
H			

For MLs

	L	M	H
L			
M			
H			

For HMs

	L	M	H
L			
M			
H			

For MMs

	L	M	H
L			
M			
H			

variable). Length of service is associated with degree of burnout, and the relationship is positive. Knowing the respective rankings of two teachers on length of service (Case A is higher on length of service than Case B) will help us predict their ranking on burnout (we would predict that Case A will also be higher than Case B on burnout).

Table 14.2 provides some additional assistance for interpreting gamma in a format similar to Tables 12.5 and 13.3. So, a gamma of 0.57 indicates a moderate association between length of service and burnout. We should point out that the strength of a relationship is independent of its direction. That is, a gamma of −0.57 would be exactly as strong as a gamma of +0.57 but opposite in direction. As before, the relationship between the values and the descriptive terms is arbitrary, so the outline presented in Table 14.2 is intended as a general guideline only. We further note that when calculating the strength of association between the same two variables, gamma will tend to be higher than other measures of association used for tabular data. Gamma ignores tied pairs of cases, and is based only on pairs (N_s and N_d) that inherently reflect a relationship between the variables. The tendency for gamma to "exaggerate"

TABLE 14.2 THE RELATIONSHIP BETWEEN THE VALUE OF GAMMA
AND THE STRENGTH OF THE RELATIONSHIP

Value	Strength
If the value is	*The strength of the relationship is*
between 0.00 and 0.30	weak
between 0.31 and 0.60	moderate
greater than .60	strong

the actual strength of association is compensated by the higher gamma thresholds for classifying weak, moderate, and strong relationships in Table 14.2. Alternatively, other ordinal measures that take ties into account, such as Somer's *d* and Kendall's tau-*b*, may also be used. These measures of association are just versions of gamma that additionally incorporate the number of tied pairs of cases in different ways. See the website for this text for more information on calculating Somer's *d* and Kendall's tau-*b*.

To use the computational routine for gamma presented above, you must arrange the table in the manner of Table 14.1, with the column variable increasing in value as you move from left to right and the row variable increasing from top to bottom. Be careful to construct your tables according to this format. If you are working with data already in table format, you may have to rearrange the table or rethink the direction of patterns. Gamma is a symmetrical measure of association; that is, the value of gamma will be the same regardless of which variable is taken as independent. *(To practise computing and interpreting gamma, see problems 14.1 to 14.10 and 14.15. Begin with some of the smaller, 2 × 2 tables until you are comfortable with these procedures.)*

14.4 DETERMINING THE DIRECTION OF RELATIONSHIPS

Nominal measures of association, like phi and lambda, measure only the strength of a bivariate association. Ordinal measures of association, like gamma, are more sophisticated and add information about the overall direction of the relationship (positive or negative). In one way, it is easy to determine direction: If the sign of the statistic is a plus, the direction is positive; a minus sign indicates a negative relationship. Often, however, direction is confusing when working with ordinal-level variables and it will be helpful if we focus on the matter specifically. We'll discuss positive relationships first and then relationships in the negative direction.

With gamma, a positive relationship means that the scores of cases tend to be ranked in the same order on both variables. In more general terms, a positive relationship means that the variables change in the same direction. That is, as scores on one variable increase (or decrease), scores on the other variable also increase (or decrease). Cases tend to have scores in the same range on both variables (i.e., low scores go with low scores, moderate with moderate, and so forth). Table 14.3 illustrates the general shape of a positive relationship. In a positive relationship, cases tend to fall along a diagonal from upper left to lower right (assuming, of course, that tables have been constructed with the column variable increasing from left to right and the row variable from top to bottom).

Table 14.4 presents an example of a positive relationship with actual data. The sample consists of 186 pre-industrial societies from around the globe. Each has been rated in terms of their degree of stratification and the type of political institution they have. In the societies that are the lowest in stratification, there are virtually no differences between people in terms of wealth and power and the degree of inequality in the society increases from left to right across the columns of the table. In "stateless" societies there is

TABLE 14.3 A GENERALIZED POSITIVE RELATIONSHIP

Variable Y	Variable X		
	Low	Moderate	High
Low	X		
Moderate		X	
High			X

TABLE 14.4 STATE STRUCTURE BY DEGREE OF STRATIFICATION

State	Degree of Stratification		
	Low	Medium	High
Stateless	77	5	0
Semi-state	28	15	4
State	12	19	26
	117	39	30

Source: The Standard Cross-Cultural Sample.

no formal political institution and the political institution becomes more elaborate and stronger as you move down the rows from top to bottom.

The gamma for this table is 0.86, so the relationship is strong and positive. By inspection, we can see that most cases fall in the diagonal from upper left to lower right and, even without percentages, it is clear that societies with little inequality tend to be stateless and that the political institution becomes more elaborate as inequality increases. The great majority of the least stratified societies had no political institution and none of the highly stratified societies were stateless.

Negative relationships are the opposite of positive relationships. Low scores on one variable are associated with high scores on the other and high scores with low scores. This pattern means that the cases will tend to fall along a diagonal from lower left to upper right (at least for all tables in this text). Table 14.5 illustrates a generalized negative relationship. The cases with higher scores on variable X tend to have lower scores on variable Y, and scores on Y decrease as scores on X increase.

Table 14.6 presents an example of a negative relationship from an actual random sample of 315 adult Canadians from the 2005 Canadian Internet Use Survey, conducted by Statistics Canada to measure the extent and scope to

TABLE 14.5 A GENERALIZED NEGATIVE RELATIONSHIP

Variable Y	Variable X		
	Low	Moderate	High
Low			X
Moderate		X	
High	X		

TABLE 14.6 HOURS SPENT ON THE INTERNET AT HOME PER WEEK BY AGE

Hours of Internet Use	Age			Totals
	18–24	25–34	35+	
<5	8	19	128	155
5–9	14	30	47	91
10+	20	11	38	69
	42	60	213	315

Source: Statistics Canada, 2005 Canadian Internet Use Survey, PUMF.

which Canadians use the Internet. The independent variable is age and the dependent variable is average weekly hours spent on the Internet at home. In the table, age increases from left to right and Internet use from top to bottom.

The pattern is again obvious without the aid of percentages. Adults aged 18 to 24 were most likely to use the Internet at home on average for 10 or more hours per week, adults aged 25 to 35 were most likely to use it for 5 to 9 hours, and adults 35 and over were most likely to use it less than 5 hours per week. As age increases, Internet use tends to decrease. The gamma for this table is −0.47, indicating a moderate, negative relationship between age and Internet use.

You should be aware of an additional complication. The coding for ordinal-level variables is arbitrary, and a higher score may mean "more" or "less" of the variable being measured. For example, if we measured social class as upper, middle, and lower, we could assign scores to the categories in either of two ways:

A	B
(1) Upper	(3) Upper
(2) Middle	(2) Middle
(3) Lower	(1) Lower

While coding scheme "B" might seem preferable (because higher scores go with higher class position), *both* schemes are perfectly legitimate and the direction of a relationship will change, depending on which scheme is selected. Using scheme "B," we would find positive relationships between social class and education: As education increased, so would class.

Using scheme "A," however, the same relationship would appear to be negative because the numerical scores (1, 2, 3) are coded in reverse order: The highest social class is assigned the lowest score, and so forth. If you don't check the coding scheme, you might conclude that the negative gamma means that class decreases as education increases when, actually, the opposite is true.

Unfortunately, this source of confusion cannot be avoided when working with ordinal-level variables. Coding schemes will always be arbitrary for these variables and you need to exercise additional caution when interpreting the direction of ordinal-level variables.

14.5 INTERPRETING ASSOCIATION WITH BIVARIATE TABLES: WHAT ARE THE SOURCES OF VOLUNTEERISM IN CANADA?

In this section, we will examine an important feature of Canadian life: community participation and civic engagement. We will look specifically at what kind of person is most engaged in volunteerism. Put differently, what factors are related to volunteerism?

We will use data from the 2004 Canada Survey of Giving, Volunteering and Participating (CSGVP) to answer this question. The CSGVP, which began in 1997, is conducted every few years by Statistics Canada to collect information on how and why Canadians donate their money, time, and other resources to

READING STATISTICS 11: Examining the Relationship between Gender and Religious Service Attendance

Studies show that in industrial nations, including Canada, women are more religious than men. One popular explanation of this phenomenon relates to differences in labour force participation of men and women. Canadian sociologist Ellen Gee (1991) writes that "religious involvement declines with participation in the modern material world with its emphasis on logic and reason as explanations for life and the cosmos. Women are less likely to be fully a part of the ongoing social world, at least in terms of outside-the-home employment; they are, thus, less secularized (more religious) than men" (267). In other words, women are more religious than men due to their lower levels of labour force participation. Hence, men and women with similar levels of labour force involvement should have similar levels of religious involvement.

Gee (1991) tested the labour force hypothesis using data from the Canadian General Social Survey. She examined the relationship between gender and religious involvement (regular religious service attendance versus non-regular attendance) using bivariate tables with computed gammas. The relationship was examined within three categories of labour force participation: full-time workers, part-time workers, and non-workers (including the unemployed and persons not in the labour force). Even though gender is a nominal variable, Gee uses gamma as it allows the reader to access the pattern of the relationship quickly. In her bivariate tables, a "negative" gamma indicates that *women are more frequent* religious service attendees.

The findings below partially confirm the labour force hypothesis. The bivariate table for full-time workers supports for the hypothesis: A gamma of −0.03 indicates a non-existent relationship between gender and religious service attendance, which is also not statistically significant ($p > 0.05$). On the other hand, the

hypothesis is not supported within the other two labour-force categories. Among part-time workers there is a "negative" and significant association between the variables (gamma = −0.33, $p < 0.05$). Women working part-time are more likely to be regular religious service attendees than men working part-time. Similarly, the relationship between gender and religious service attendance is "negative" and significant for non-workers (gamma = −0.19, $p < 0.05$).

RELIGIOUS SERVICE ATTENDANCE BY SEX, FOR THREE CATEGORIES OF LABOUR FORCE PARTICIPATION

1. Full-Time Workers

Attendance	Gender	
	Male	Female
Regular	53.5%	54.9%
Non-regular	46.5%	55.1%
Totals	100.0%	100.0%

Gamma = −0.03, $p > 0.05$

2. Part-Time Workers

Attendance	Gender	
	Male	Female
Regular	45.7%	62.3%
Non-regular	54.3%	37.7%
Totals	100.0%	100.0%

Gamma = −0.33, $p < 0.05$

3. Non-Workers

Attendance	Gender	
	Male	Female
Regular	58.9%	67.6%
Non-regular	41.1%	32.4%
Totals	100.0%	100.0%

Gamma = −0.19, $p < 0.05$

Source: Gee, E. 1991. "Gender Differences in Church Attendance in Canada: The Role of Labor Force Participation." *Review of Religious Research, 32:* 267–273. © Religious Research Association, Inc. All rights reserved.

charitable and non-profit organizations. The 2004 CSGVP was administered to a randomly selected sample of approximately 21,000 adult Canadians.

To measure volunteerism (the dependent variable), we used a series of variables that asked people whether they had engaged, without pay on behalf of a group(s) or an organization(s), over the past 12 months in the following activities: canvassing, fundraising, committee membership, mentoring, event organization, administrative duties, coaching, counselling, health care support, food collection, facilities/grounds maintenance, volunteer driving, first aid, conservation, or other unpaid activities. We created a composite variable that counted the number of activities undertaken by each respondent. Their level of volunteerism was then rated as high, moderate, or low. People rated as low had been engaged in no activities in the previous year, and those rated as moderate had volunteered for one or two activities. Individuals volunteering for three or more activities in the past year were coded as high.

This simple variable will not be a perfectly accurate measurement of volunteerism. For example, people might help others directly on their own (e.g., visiting the elderly or unpaid babysitting) or be involved in the daily life of their community but not actually belong to any formal groups or organizations. This kind of "informal" volunteering will not be captured by the variable we created. Or, some people might be involved in many volunteer activities but actually spend very little time (e.g., just a few hours once or twice a year) on each activity. These people will be classified as highly involved on the variable we created, even though their involvement is actually minimal. Like almost all variables of interest to the social sciences, volunteerism is complex and subtle and cannot be adequately captured with a single measurement. Nonetheless, we should be able to develop some insight into the issue, even if the variable is not perfect. Researchers typically have to settle for partial or incomplete measurement of their concepts.

What should we use as independent variables? In other words, what factors might have causal relationships with volunteerism? In this section, we investigate three possibilities. First, we predict that health has a positive impact on volunteerism as good health facilitates one's ability to do volunteer work. Second, because studies show that education is positively related to job performance, we predict that it has a similar relationship with volunteer work. Finally, we argue that religiosity, measured by frequency of religious service attendance, is an important predictor of charitable activity because most religious faiths and organizations encourage—and provide the mechanisms for—volunteering, altruistic giving, and civic participation.

The level of measurement of each of these independent variables, as well as the dependent variable, is ordinal; the categories can be distinguished in terms of "more or less." We will use tables, column percentages, and gamma to examine which of these arguments has support and to compare the strength and direction of each relationship.

TABLE 14.7 VOLUNTEERISM BY HEALTH STATUS*

| | Health Status | | |
Volunteerism	Poor	Good	Totals
Low	1,685 (55.4%)	5,640 (32.8%)	7,325 (36.2%)
Moderate	679 (22.3%)	4,802 (27.9%)	5,481 (27.1%)
High	675 (22.2%)	6,770 (39.3%)	7,445 (36.8%)
Totals	3,039 (99.9%)	17,212 (100.0%)	20,251 (100.1%)

Gamma = 0.378, $p < 0.05$
*Percentages may not total to 100% because of rounding error.
Source: Statistics Canada, 2004 Canada Survey of Giving, Volunteering and Participating, PUMF.

Table 14.7 shows that the relationship between health status and volunteering is moderate in strength and positive in direction (gamma = 0.378), and is statistically significant ($p < 0.05$). The column percentages in the table show that volunteerism increases as health status increases: Only 22.2% of people with poor health are highly involved in volunteer activities compared to 39.3% of people with good health.

The relationship between volunteering and education in Table 14.8 is significant at the 0.05 level, moderate to weak in strength, and in the predicted direction. Looking at the bottom row of the table, we see that the percentage of each education group that is highly involved in volunteer activities increases as education increases. The column percents show that just 23.7% of respondents with less than a high school education are high on volunteerism versus 51.0% of those with a university education.

Table 14.9 shows the relationship between volunteering and religiosity. The relationship is significant, and changes in the column percentages are

TABLE 14.8 VOLUNTEERISM BY EDUCATION*

| | Education | | | | |
Volunteerism	Less Than High School	High School	Other Post-Secondary	University	Totals
Low	1,719 (51.0%)	1,330 (40.2%)	2,833 (34.2%)	1,010 (22.3%)	6,892 (35.4%)
Moderate	852 (25.3%)	958 (28.9%)	1,416 (27.8%)	1,212 (26.7%)	5,319 (27.3%)
High	799 (23.7%)	1,022 (30.9%)	3,144 (38.0%)	2,310 (51.0%)	7,275 (37.3%)
Totals	3,370 (100.0%)	3,310 (100.0%)	8,274 (100.0%)	4,532 (100.0%)	19,486 (100.0%)

Gamma = 0.270, $p < 0.05$
*Percentages may not total to 100% because of rounding error.
Source: Statistics Canada, 2004 Canada Survey of Giving, Volunteering and Participating, PUMF.

TABLE 14.9   VOLUNTEERISM BY RELIGIOUS SERVICE ATTENDANCE*

| Volunteerism | Religious Service Attendance | | | Totals |
	Never	Yearly or Monthly	Daily or Weekly	
Low	2,097 (47.1%)	1,539 (38.0%)	1,822 (25.5%)	5,458 (34.9%)
Moderate	1,198 (26.9%)	1,117 (27.6%)	1,951 (27.3%)	4,266 (27.2%)
High	1,159 (26.0%)	1,396 (34.5%)	3,380 (47.3%)	5,935 (37.9%)
Totals	4,454 (100.0%)	4,052 (100.1%)	7,153 (100.1%)	15,659 (100.0%)

Gamma = 0.290, $p < 0.05$
*Percentages may not total to 100% because of rounding error.
Source: Statistics Canada, 2004 Canada Survey of Giving, Volunteering and Participating, PUMF.

rather large. Persons that attend religious service daily or weekly are more likely to be highly involved in volunteer activities (47.3%) than those that never attend (26.0%). As indicated by gamma, this is a positive relationship (as frequency of religious service attendance increases, volunteering increases) that is more or less moderate in strength.

In summary, we can see that people in good health, those with higher education, and frequent attendees of religious services are more actively involved in volunteer activities. Health, education, and religiosity seem to be relatively important causes of volunteerism. While these bivariate results cannot show which variable is cause and which is effect (remember that correlation is not the same thing as causation), they are worthy of additional investigation. The multivariate techniques discussed in Chapter 16 might be a logical next step in the process of analyzing each of the relationships.

14.6 SPEARMAN'S RHO (r_s)   To this point, we have considered ordinal variables that have a limited number of categories (possible values) and are presented in tables. However, many ordinal-level variables have a broad range of scores and many distinct values. Such data may be collapsed into a few broad categories (such as high, moderate, and low), organized into a bivariate table, and analyzed with gamma. Collapsing scores in this manner may be beneficial and desirable in many instances, but some important distinctions between cases may be obscured or lost as a consequence.

For example, suppose a researcher wished to test the claim that jogging is beneficial not only physically but also psychologically. Do joggers have an enhanced sense of self-esteem? To deal with this issue, 10 female joggers are measured on two scales, the first measuring involvement in jogging and the other measuring self-esteem. Scores are reported in Table 14.10.

TABLE 14.10 THE SCORES OF 10 SUBJECTS ON INVOLVEMENT IN JOGGING AND A MEASURE OF SELF-ESTEEM

Joggers	Involvement in Jogging (X)	Self-esteem (Y)
Wendy	18	15
Debbie	17	18
Alicia	15	12
Ava	12	16
Evelyn	10	6
Camille	9	10
Tori	8	8
Isabel	8	7
Maxine	5	5
Lynn	1	2

These data could be collapsed and a bivariate table produced. We could, for example, dichotomize both variables to create only two values (high and low) for both variables. Although collapsing scores in this way is certainly legitimate and often necessary,* two difficulties with this practice must be noted. First, the scores seem continuous, and there are no obvious or natural division points in the distribution that would allow us to distinguish, in a non-arbitrary fashion, between high scores and low ones. Second, and more important, grouping these cases into broader categories will cause us to lose information. That is, if both Wendy and Debbie are placed in the category "high" on involvement, the fact that they had different scores on the variable would be obscured. If differences like this are important and meaningful, then we should opt for a measure of association that permits the retention of as much detail and precision in the scores as possible.

Spearman's rho (r_s) is a measure of association for ordinal-level variables that have a broad range of many different scores and few ties between cases on either variable. Scores on ordinal-level variables cannot, of course, be manipulated mathematically except for judgments of "greater than" or "less than." To compute Spearman's rho, cases are first ranked from high to low on each variable and then the ranks (not the scores) are manipulated to produce the final measure. Table 14.11 displays the original scores and the rankings of the cases on both variables.

To rank the cases, first find the highest score on each variable and assign it rank 1. Wendy has the high score on X (18) and is thus ranked number 1. Debbie, on the other hand, is highest on Y and is ranked first on that variable. All other cases are then ranked in descending order of scores. If

---

*For example, collapsing scores may be advisable when the researcher is not sure that fine distinctions between scores are meaningful.

TABLE 14.11   COMPUTING SPEARMAN'S RHO

	Involvement (X)	Rank	Self-Image (Y)	Rank	D	D^2
Wendy	18	1	15	3	−2	4
Debbie	17	2	18	1	1	1
Alicia	15	3	12	4	−1	1
Ava	12	4	16	2	2	4
Evelyn	10	5	6	8	−3	9
Camille	9	6	10	5	1	1
Tori	8	7.5	8	6	1.5	2.25
Isabel	8	7.5	7	7	.5	.25
Maxine	5	9	5	9	0	0
Lynn	1	10	2	10	0	0
					$\Sigma D = 0$	$\Sigma D^2 = 22.50$

any cases have the same score on a variable, assign them the average of the ranks they would have used up had they not been tied. Tori and Isabel have identical scores of 8 on involvement. Had they not been tied, they would have used up ranks 7 and 8. The average of these two ranks is 7.5, and this average of used ranks is assigned to all tied cases. (For example, if Maxine had also had a score of 8, three ranks—7, 8, and 9—would have been used, and all three tied cases would have been ranked eighth.)

The formula for Spearman's rho is

FORMULA 14.2

$$r_s = 1 - \frac{6 \Sigma D^2}{N(N^2 - 1)}$$

where ΣD^2 = the sum of the differences in ranks, the quantity squared

To compute ΣD^2, the rank of each case on Y is subtracted from its rank on X (D is the difference between rank on Y and rank on X). A column has been provided in Table 14.11 so that these differences may be recorded on a case-by-case basis. Note that the sum of this column (ΣD) is 0. That is, the negative differences in rank are equal to the positive differences, as will always be the case, and you should find the total of this column as a check on your computations to this point. If the ΣD is not equal to 0, you have made a mistake either in ranking the cases or in subtracting the differences.

In the column headed D^2, each difference is squared to eliminate negative signs. The sum of this column is ΣD^2 and this quantity is entered directly into the formula. For our sample problem:

$$r_s = 1 - \frac{6 \Sigma D^2}{N(N^2 - 1)}$$

$$r_s = 1 - \frac{6(22.5)}{10(100 - 1)}$$

Application 14.3

The Human Development Index (HDI) is a measure of a country's "human development" achievements in health (life expectancy), literacy (educational attainment), and standard of living (income). United Nations member states are ranked annually according to their computed HDI score. The higher the HDI score, the higher the level of "human development" in a country. The table below lists the top five ranked (i.e., most developed) countries in 2008 according to the HDI (note that only ranks, not actual HDI scores, are provided in the table). Canada, for example, ranked fourth out of the 177 countries in 2008.

The table also shows how these five countries rank *among themselves* according to the United Nations' Gender Empowerment Measure (GEM) index, which measures the level of gender equality

in countries (i.e., percent of seats in a country's national legislative body held by females, percent of female legislators and senior officials, percent of females in professional jobs, and ratio of female to male earnings). The higher the GEM score, the higher the level of gender equality in country. Again, we only show how these five nations ranked among themselves, not their actual GEM scores or ranking among all nations.

Overall, the HDI and GEM provide powerful measures of human well-being. However, are they related? Do countries with higher human development have more gender equality? We have the ranks of the HDI and GEM scores for each country, so we will compute Spearman's rho to summarize the strength and direction of the association.

Country	HDI Rank	GEM Rank	D	D^2
Iceland	1	2	-1	1
Norway	2	1	1	1
Australia	3	3	0	0
Canada	4	4	0	0
Ireland	5	5	0	0
			$\sum D = 0$	$\sum D^2 = 2$

Spearman's rho for these variables is

$$r_s = 1 - \frac{6 \sum D^2}{N(N^2 - 1)}$$

$$r_s = 1 - \frac{(6)(2)}{5(25 - 1)}$$

$$r_s = 1 - \left(\frac{12}{120}\right)$$

$$r_s = 1 - 0.1$$

$$r_s = 0.90$$

For these five countries, the variables have a strong, positive association. The higher the human development, the greater the gender equality within a country. The value of r_s^2 is 0.81 ($0.90^2 = 0.81$), which indicates that we will make 81% fewer errors when predicting rank on one variable from rank on the other, as opposed to ignoring rank on the other variable, for these five nations.

Source: United Nations, 2008. http://hdr.undp.org/en/statistics/.

$$r_s = 1 - \frac{135}{990}$$

$$r_s = 1 - 0.14$$

$$r_s = 0.86$$

Spearman's rho is an index of the strength of association between the variables; it ranges from 0 (no association) to ±1.00 (perfect association). A perfect positive association ($r_s = +1.00$) would exist if there were no disagreements in ranks between the two variables (if cases were ranked in exactly the same order on both variables). A perfect negative relationship ($r_s = -1.00$) would exist if the ranks were in perfect disagreement (if the case ranked highest on one variable were lowest on the other, and so forth). A Spearman's rho of 0.86 indicates a strong, positive relationship between these two variables. The respondents who were highly involved in jogging also ranked high on self-image. These results are supportive of claims regarding the psychological benefits of jogging.

Spearman's rho is an index of the relative strength of a relationship, and values between 0 and ±1.00 have no direct interpretation. However, if the value of rho is squared, a PRE interpretation is possible. Rho squared (r_s^2) represents the proportional reduction in errors of prediction when predicting rank on one variable from rank on the other variable, as compared to predicting rank while ignoring the other variable. In the example above, r_s was 0.86 and r_s^2 would be 0.74. Thus, our errors of prediction would be reduced by 74% if, when predicting the rank of a subject on self-image, the rank of the subject on involvement in jogging were taken into account. *(For practice in computing and interpreting Spearman's rho, see problems 14.11 to 14.14. Problem 14.11 has the fewest number of cases and is probably a good choice for a first attempt at these procedures.)*

14.7 TESTING THE NULL HYPOTHESIS OF "NO ASSOCIATION" WITH GAMMA AND SPEARMAN'S RHO

Whenever a researcher is working with EPSEM, or random, samples, he or she will need to ascertain if the sample findings can be generalized to the population. In Part II of this text, we considered various ways that information taken from samples—for example, the difference between two sample means—could be generalized to the populations from which the samples were drawn. A test of the null hypothesis, regardless of the form or specific test used, asks essentially if the patterns (or differences, or relationships) that have been observed in the samples can be assumed to exist in the population. Measures of association can also be tested for significance. When data have been collected from a random sample, we will not only need to measure the existence, strength, and direction of the association, but we will also want to know if we can assume that the variables are related in the population.

For nominal-level variables, the statistical significance of a relationship is usually judged by the chi square test. Chi square tests could also be conducted on tables displaying the relationship between ordinal-level variables. However, chi square tests deal with the probability that the observed cell frequencies occurred by chance alone and are therefore not a direct test of the significance of the measure of association (gamma or Spearman's rho) itself.

When testing gamma and Spearman's rho for statistical significance, the null hypothesis will state that there is no association between the variables in the population and that, therefore, the population value for the measure is 0.00. Population values will be denoted by the Greek letters gamma (γ) and rho (ρ_s). For both measures, the test procedures will be organized around the familiar five-step model (see Chapter 8).

Testing Gamma for Significance   To illustrate the test of significance for gamma, we will use Table 14.1, where gamma was 0.57.

Step 1. Making Assumptions and Meeting Test Requirements. When sample size is greater than 10, the sampling distribution of all possible sample gammas can be assumed to be normal in shape.

> Model: Random sampling
> Level of measurement is ordinal
> Sampling distribution is normal

Step 2. Stating the Null Hypothesis.

$$H_0: \gamma = 0.0$$
$$(H_1: \gamma \neq 0.0)$$

Step 3. Selecting the Sampling Distribution and Establishing the Critical Region. For samples of 10 or more, the Z distribution (Appendix A) can be used to find areas under the sampling distribution:

> Sampling distribution = Z distribution
> Alpha = .05
> Z(critical) = ± 1.96

Step 4. Computing the Test Statistic.

FORMULA 14.3

$$Z(\text{obtained}) = G\sqrt{\frac{N_s + N_d}{N(1 - G^2)}}$$

$$Z(\text{obtained}) = G\sqrt{\frac{N_s + N_d}{N(1 - G^2)}} = 0.57\sqrt{\frac{1831 + 499}{100(1 - 0.33)}} = 0.57\sqrt{\frac{2330}{100(0.67)}}$$

$$Z(\text{obtained}) = 0.57\sqrt{34.78} = 3.36$$

Step 5. Making a Decision and Interpreting the Results of the Test. Comparing the Z (obtained) with the Z (critical):

$$Z(\text{obtained}) = 3.36$$
$$Z(\text{critical}) = \pm 1.96$$

We see that the null hypothesis can be rejected. The sample gamma is unlikely to have occurred by chance alone, and we may conclude that these variables are related in the population from which the sample was drawn. *(For practice in conducting and interpreting the test of significance for gamma, see problems 14.2, 14.4, 14.7, 14.10, and 14.15.)*

Testing Spearman's Rho for Significance   When testing Spearman's rho, the null hypothesis states that the population value (ρ_s) is actually 0 and, therefore, that the value of the sample Spearman's rho (r_s) is the result of mere random chance. When the number of cases in the sample is 10 or more, the sampling distribution of Spearman's rho approximates the t distribution, and we will use this distribution to conduct the test. To illustrate, the Spearman's rho computed in Section 14.6 will be used.

Step 1. Making Assumptions and Meeting Test Requirements.

> Model: Random sampling
> Level of measurement is ordinal
> Sampling distribution is normal

Step 2. Stating the Null Hypothesis.

$$H_0: \rho_s = 0.0$$
$$(H_1: \rho_s \neq 0.0)$$

Step 3. Selecting the Sampling Distribution and Establishing the Critical Region.

> Sampling distribution = t distribution
> Alpha = .05
> Degrees of freedom = $N - 2 = 8$
> t (critical) = ± 2.306

Step 4. Computing the Test Statistic.

FORMULA 14.4

$$t\text{ (obtained)} = r_s\sqrt{\frac{N-2}{1-r_s^2}}$$

$$t\text{ (obtained)} = r_s\sqrt{\frac{N-2}{1-r_s^2}} = 0.86\sqrt{\frac{8}{1-0.74}} = 0.86\sqrt{\frac{8}{0.26}}$$

$$t\text{(obtained)} = 0.86\sqrt{30.77} = (0.86)(5.55) = 4.77$$

Step 5. Making a Decision and Interpreting the Results of the Test. Comparing the test statistic with the critical region:

$$t\text{ (obtained)} = 4.77$$
$$t\text{ (critical)} = \pm 2.306$$

We see that the null hypothesis can be rejected. We may conclude, with a .05 chance of making an error, that the variables are related in the population from which the samples were drawn. *(For practice in conducting and interpreting the test of significance for Spearman's rho, see problems 14.11 to 14.14.)*

SUMMARY

1. A measure of association for variables with collapsed ordinal scales (gamma) was covered along with a measure (Spearman's rho) appropriate for "continuous" ordinal variables. Both measures summarize the overall strength and direction of the association between the variables.

2. Gamma is a PRE-based measure that shows the improvement in our ability to predict the order of pairs of cases on one variable from the order of pairs of cases on the other variable, as opposed to ignoring the order of the pairs of cases on the other variable.

3. Spearman's rho is computed from the ranks of the scores of the cases on two "continuous" ordinal variables and, when squared, can be interpreted by the logic of PRE.

4. Both gamma and Spearman's rho should be tested for their statistical significance when computed for a random sample drawn from a defined population. The null hypothesis is that the variables are not related in the population, and the test can be organized by using the familiar five-step model.

SUMMARY OF FORMULAS

Gamma	14.1	$G = \dfrac{N_s - N_d}{N_s + N_d}$
Spearman's rho	14.2	$r_s = 1 - \dfrac{6 \sum D^2}{N(N^2 - 1)}$
Z (obtained) for gamma	14.3	$Z(\text{obtained}) = G\sqrt{\dfrac{N_s + N_d}{N(1 - G^2)}}$
t (obtained) for Spearman's rho	14.4	$t(\text{obtained}) = r_s\sqrt{\dfrac{N - 2}{1 - r_s^2}}$

GLOSSARY

Gamma (G). A measure of association appropriate for variables measured with "collapsed" ordinal scales that have been organized into table format; G is the symbol for any sample gamma, γ is the symbol for any population gamma.

N_d. The number of pairs of cases ranked in different order on two variables.

N_s. The number of pairs of cases ranked in the same order on two variables.

Spearman's rho (r_s). A measure of association appropriate for ordinally measured variables that are "continuous" in form; r_s is the symbol for any sample Spearman's rho; ρ_s is the symbol for any population Spearman's rho.

MULTIMEDIA RESOURCES

http://www.healeystatistics.nelson.com

Visit the companion Web site for the first Canadian edition of *Statistics: A Tool for Social Research* to access a wide range of student resources. Begin by clicking on the Student Resources section of the book's Web site to access review quizzes, flash cards, and other study tools.

PROBLEMS

For problems 14.1 to 14.10 and 14.15 calculate percentages for the bivariate tables as described in Chapter 12. Use the percentages to help analyze the strength and direction of the association.

14.1 $\boxed{\text{SOC}}$ A small sample of immigrants to Canada, none of whom speak either of the nation's two official languages, has been interviewed about their level of adjustment. Is the pattern of adjustment affected by length of residence in Canada? For each table compute gamma and summarize the relationship in terms of strength and direction. *(HINT: In 2 × 2 tables, only two cells can contribute to N_s or N_d. To compute N_s, multiply the number of cases in the upper-left-hand cell by the number of cases in the lower-right-hand cell. For N_d, multiply the number of cases in the upper-right-hand cell by the number of cases in the lower-left-hand cell.)*

a. Facility in English or French:

| English /French Facility | Length of Residence | | |
	Less than Five Years (Low)	More than Five Years (High)	Totals
Low	20	10	30
High	5	15	20
Totals	25	25	50

b. Total family income:

| Income | Length of Residence | | |
	Less than Five Years (Low)	More than Five Years (High)	Totals
Below national average (1)	18	8	26
Above national average (2)	7	17	24
Totals	25	25	50

c. Extent of contact with country of origin:

| Contact | Length of Residence | | |
	Less than Five Years (Low)	More than Five Years (High)	Totals
Rare (1)	5	20	25
Frequent (2)	20	5	25
Totals	25	25	50

14.2 Compute gamma for the tables presented in problems 11.2, 11.6, 11.7, 11.9, 11.10, and 11.12. Because these tables are based on random samples, test the gammas you computed for significance.

14.3 Compute gamma for the table presented in problem 12.1. If you computed a nominal measure of association for this table in problem 13.2, compare the measures of association. Are they similar in value? Do they characterize the strength for the association in the same way? What information about the relationship does gamma provide that is not available from nominal measures of association?

14.4 [CJ] A random sample of 150 cities has been classified as small, medium, or large by population and as high or low on crime rate. Is there a relationship between city size and crime rate?

Crime Rate	City Size			Totals
	Small	Medium	Large	
Low	21	17	8	46
High	29	33	42	104
Totals	50	50	50	150

a. Describe the strength and direction of the relationship.

b. Is the relationship significant?

14.5 [SOC] Some research has shown that families vary by how they socialize their children to sports, games, and other leisure-time activities. In middle-class families, such activities are carefully monitored by parents and are, in general, dominated by adults (e.g., minor league hockey). In working-class families, children more often organize and initiate such activities themselves, and parents are much less involved (for example, sandlot or playground baseball games). Are the data below consistent with these findings? Summarize your conclusions in a few sentences.

As a Child, Did You Play Mostly Organized or Sandlot Sports?	Social Class Background		Totals
	White-collar	Blue-collar	
Organized	155	123	278
Sandlot	101	138	239
Totals	256	261	517

14.6 Is support for sexual freedom related to age? Is the relationship between the variables different for different nations? The World Values Survey has been administered to random samples drawn from Canada, the United States, and Mexico. Respondents were asked if they agree or disagree that "individuals should have the chance to enjoy complete sexual freedom without being restricted." Compute gamma for each table. Is there a relationship? Describe the strength and direction of the relationship. Which age group is most supportive of sexual freedom? How does the relationship change from nation to nation?

a. Canada

"People Should Enjoy Sexual Freedom"	Age			Totals
	18–34	35–54	55+	
Agree	378	174	66	618
Neither agree nor disagree	626	710	586	1,922
Disagree	163	101	74	338
Totals	1,167	985	726	2,878

b. United States

"People Should Enjoy Sexual Freedom"	Age			Totals
	18–34	35–54	55+	
Agree	583	288	147	1,018
Neither agree nor disagree	877	982	1,061	2,920
Disagree	113	72	53	238
Totals	1,573	1,342	1,261	4,176

c. Mexico

"People Should Enjoy Sexual Freedom"	Age			Totals
	18–34	35–54	55+	
Agree	780	284	61	1,125
Neither agree nor disagree	1,300	847	275	2,422
Disagree	317	148	43	508
Totals	2,397	1,279	379	4,055

Source: World Values Survey.

14.7 [PA] All applicants for municipal jobs in Pearson, Ontario, are given an aptitude test, but the test has never been evaluated to see if test scores are in any way related to job performance. The following table reports aptitude test scores and job performance ratings for a random sample of 75 city employees.

Efficiency Ratings	Test Scores			
	Low	Moderate	High	Totals
Low	11	6	7	24
Moderate	9	10	9	28
High	5	9	9	23
Totals	25	25	25	75

a. Are these two variables associated? Describe the strength and direction of the relationship in a sentence or two.
b. Is gamma statistically significant?
c. Should the aptitude test continue to be administered? Why or why not?

14.8 SW A sample of children has been observed and rated for symptoms of depression. Their parents have been rated for authoritarianism. Is there any relationship between these variables? Write a few sentences stating your conclusions.

Symptoms of Depression	Authoritarianism			
	Low	Moderate	High	Totals
Few	7	8	9	24
Some	15	10	18	43
Many	8	12	3	23
Totals	30	30	30	90

14.9 SOC Are levels of stress and education related? State your conclusion in a few sentences.

Stress Level	Level of Education				
	Less than High School	High School	Some College/ University	College/ University Graduate	Totals
Low	48	50	61	42	201
High	45	43	33	27	148
Totals	93	93	94	69	349

14.10 SOC In a recent survey, a random sample of respondents was asked to indicate how happy they were with their situations in life. Are their responses related to income level?

Happiness	Income			
	Low	Moderate	High	Totals
Not happy	101	82	36	219
Pretty happy	40	227	100	367
Very happy	216	198	203	617
Totals	357	507	339	1203

a. Describe the strength and direction of the relationship.
b. Is the relationship significant?

14.11 SOC A random sample of 11 neighbourhoods in Pearson, Ontario, have been rated by an urban sociologist on a "quality-of-life" scale (which includes measures of affluence, availability of medical care, and recreational facilities) and a social cohesion scale. The results are presented below in scores. Higher scores indicate higher "quality of life" and greater social cohesion.

Neighbourhood	Quality of Life	Social Cohesion
Queens Lake	17	8.8
North End	40	3.9
Mountaintop	47	4.0
Lakeside	90	3.1
Blossom Park	35	7.5
Kingswood	52	3.5
Cambridge Shores	23	6.3
Windsor Forest	67	1.7
College Park	65	9.2
Uplands	63	3.0
Riverview	100	5.3

a. Are the two variables associated? What is the strength and direction of the association? Summarize the relationship in a sentence or two. (*HINT: Don't forget to square the value of Spearman's rho for a PRE interpretation.*)
b. Conduct a test of significance for this relationship. Summarize your findings.

14.12 SW Several years ago, a job-training program began, and a team of social workers screened the candidates for suitability for employment. Now the screening process is being evaluated, and the actual work performance of a sample of hired candidates has been rated. Did the screening process work? Is there a relationship between the original scores and performance evaluation on the job?

Case	Original Score	Performance Evaluation
A	17	78
B	17	85
C	15	82
D	13	92
E	13	75
F	13	72
G	11	70
H	10	75
I	10	92
J	10	70
K	9	32
L	8	55
M	7	21
N	5	45
O	2	25

14.13 SOC Below are the scores of a sample of 15 countries on a measure of ethnic diversity (the higher the number, the greater the diversity) and a measure of economic inequality (the higher the score, the greater the inequality). Are these variables related? Are ethnically diverse countries more economically unequal?

Country	Diversity	Inequality
A	91	29.7
B	87	58.4
C	83	57.5
D	75	31.5
E	72	48.4
F	69	32.7
G	65	32.0
H	63	41.0
I	57	30.1
J	50	50.3
K	44	32.5
L	31	33.7
M	16	25.6
N	4	35.9
O	3	27.2

14.14 A random sample of foreign-born and non-foreign-born citizens from 20 countries were

rated on a Social Distance Scale. Lower scores represent less social distance and less prejudice. How similar are these rankings? Is the relationship statistically significant?

Country	Average Social Distance Scale Score	
	Non-foreign Born	Foreign Born
A	1.2	2.6
B	1.4	2.9
C	1.5	3.6
D	1.6	3.6
E	1.8	3.9
F	1.9	3.3
G	2.0	3.8
H	2.1	2.7
I	2.2	3.0
J	2.3	3.3
K	2.4	4.2
L	2.4	1.3
M	2.8	3.5
N	2.9	3.4
O	3.4	3.7
P	3.7	5.1
Q	3.9	3.9
R	3.9	4.1
S	4.2	4.4
T	5.3	5.4

14.15 In problems 12.11 and 13.12, we looked at the relationships between five dependent variables and, respectively, political ideology and sex. In this exercise, we'll use income as an independent variable and assess its relationship with this set of variables. For each table, calculate percentages and gamma. Describe the strength, direction, and statistical significance of each relationship in a few sentences. *Be careful in interpreting direction.*

a. Support for same-sex marriage by income:

Same-sex Marriage?	Income			Totals
	Less than $24,900	$24,900 to $50,000	More than $50,000	
Favour	220	218	226	664
Oppose	366	299	250	915
Totals	586	517	476	1,579

b. Support for capital punishment by income:

	Income			
Capital Punishment?	Less than $24,900	$24,900 to $50,000	More than $50,000	Totals
Favour	567	574	552	1,693
Oppose	270	183	160	613
Totals	837	757	712	2,306

d. Support for traditional gender roles by income:

	Income			
Traditional Gender Roles?	Less than $24,900	$24,900 to $50,000	More than $50,000	Totals
Favour	130	71	39	240
Oppose	448	479	461	1,388
Totals	578	550	500	1,628

c. Approval of suicide for people with an incurable disease by income:

	Income			
Right to Suicide?	Less than $24,900	$24,900 to $50,000	More than $50,000	Totals
Favour	343	341	338	1,022
Oppose	227	194	147	568
Totals	570	535	485	1,590

e. Support for legalizing marijuana by income:

	Income			
Legalize Marijuana?	Less than $24,900	$24,900 to $50,000	More than $50,000	Totals
Favour	492	478	451	1,421
Oppose	85	68	53	206
Totals	577	546	504	1,627

SPSS for Windows

Using SPSS for Windows to Produce Ordinal-Level Measures of Association with the 2004 GSS

The demonstrations and exercise below use the 2004 GSS data set supplied with this text. Start SPSS for Windows and open the *GSS.sav* file.

SPSS DEMONSTRATION 14.1 Interpreting the Direction of Relationships— Another Look at Income and Health

In Demonstration 12.1, we used percentages to look at the relationship between recoded *hlthstat* (state of health) and recoded *incmhsd* (total household income). Let's re-examine this relationship and find out whether gamma can add any new information. We will use the **Crosstabs** program with *income4* (recoded *incmhsd*) as the independent (column) variable and *health* (recoded *hlthstat*) as the dependent (row) variable. If you no longer have access to the recoded version of these variables, follow the directions in Demonstration 12.1.

In the **Crosstabs** dialog box, click the **Statistics** button and request gamma. Don't forget to click the **Cells** button and request column percentages. Click **OK,** and the output (slightly edited for readability) should look like this:

HEALTH * INCOME4 Crosstabulation

		INCOME4				Total
		1 (<$30,000)	2 ($30,000–59,999)	3 ($60,000–99,999)	4 ($100,000+)	
HEALTH	1 (Good)	198 82.5%	396 90.4%	355 94.2%	239 95.2%	1188 91.0%
	2 (Poor)	42 17.5%	42 9.6%	22 5.8%	12 4.8%	118 9.0%
Total		240 100.0%	438 100.0%	377 100.0%	251 100.0%	1306 100.0%

Symmetric Measures

		Value	Asymp. Std. Error	Approx. t	Approx. Sig.
Ordinal by Ordinal	Gamma	−.373	.068	−4.940	.000
N of Valid Cases		1306			

A gamma of −.373 indicates a moderate, negative relationship. So, the higher the income, the lower the health, right? Wrong. Look at the codes for *health.* A *low* score indicates a *high* level of health. The negative sign for gamma is telling us that higher scores on *income4* are associated with a low score (a score of 1 or good) on *health.* Despite the negative sign, this is really a "positive" relationship in the sense that health improves with income. Always inspect tables carefully to make sure that you are interpreting the direction of the relationship properly.

SPSS DEMONSTRATION 14.2 Does Disability Vary by Age? Another Look

Let's also re-examine with gamma the relationship between *hal_q120* (any difficulty hearing, seeing, walking, and so on) and recoded *agegr5* from Demonstration 12.2. Use **Crosstabs** once again with *age3* (recoded *agegr5*) as the independent (column) variable. (If needed, see the recode instructions in Demonstration 12.2.) The dependent variable *hal_q120* will go in the rows. Request gamma and column percentages. The output, slightly edited for readability, should look like this:

hal_q120 * age3 Crosstabulation

			AGE3			
			1 (15–39)	2 (40–59)	3 (60+)	Total
hal_q120 (any difficulty hearing, seeing, walking, and so on)	1 (Yes, often)		39 5.3%	56 10.0%	56 25.3%	151 9.9%
	2 (Yes, sometimes)		38 5.1%	36 6.5%	34 15.4%	108 7.1%
	3 (No)		663 89.6%	466 83.5%	131 59.3%	1260 82.9%
Total			740 100.0%	558 100.0%	221 100.0%	1519 100.0%

Symmetric Measures

		Value	Asymp. Std. Error*	Approx. $t^\dagger$	Approx. Sig.
Ordinal by Ordinal	Gamma	−.459	.046	−8.227	.000
N of Valid Cases		1519			

*Not assuming the null hypothesis.
†Using the asymptotic standard error, assuming the null hypothesis.

A gamma of −0.459 indicates a moderate, negative relationship. Older respondents (a score of 3 on *age3*) had the highest percentage who reported "Yes, often" (has difficulty with hearing, seeing, walking, and so on), and younger respondents had the highest percentage who reported "No" (difficulty with hearing, seeing, walking, and so on). As age increases, being free of disability (the percentage who say "No") decreases. Thus we can say the same about this relationship as we did about the relationship in Demonstration 14.1. A negative gamma means that the numerical scores of the variables *age3* and *hal_q120* are inversely related, but the underlying relationship is truly "positive" (i.e., disability increases with age).

Exercise (using *GSS.sav*)

14.1 Use gamma to analyze and describe the relationship between any two ordinal-level variables.* Summarize the strength and direction of the relationship in a few sentences.

14.2 Follow up on Demonstration 14.2 with two new ordinal-level independent variables. What other factors might affect *hal_q120*? As a suggestion, try *drr_q110* and *drr_q120* as independent variables.* Summarize the strength and direction of the relationships in a few sentences. Are these relationships stronger or weaker than those with recoded *agegr5*? Be careful in interpreting the direction of the relationships.

---

*If necessary, use the **Recode** command illustrated in Appendix F.5 to reduce the number of categories in your variables.

15

ASSOCIATION BETWEEN VARIABLES MEASURED AT THE INTERVAL-RATIO LEVEL

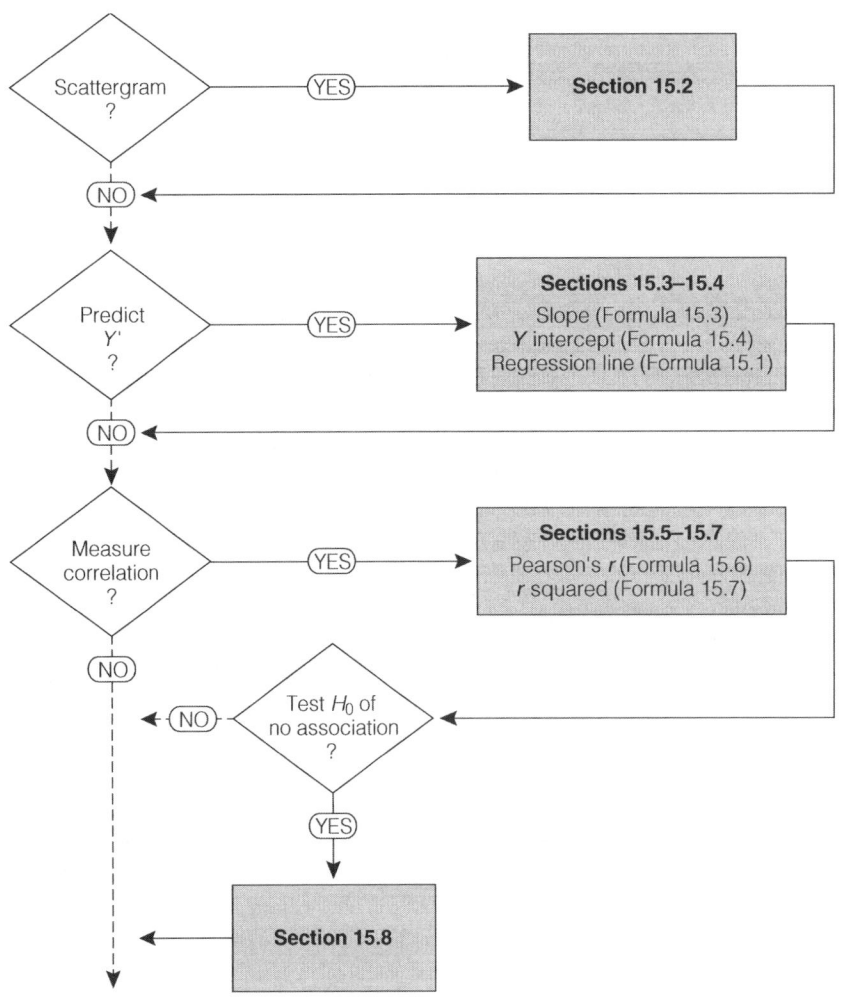

LEARNING OBJECTIVES   By the end of this chapter, you will be able to

1. Interpret a scattergram.
2. Calculate and interpret slope (b), Y intercept (a), and Pearson's r and r^2.
3. Find and explain the least-squares regression line and use it to predict values of Y.
4. Explain the concepts of total, explained, and unexplained variance.

5. Use regression and correlation techniques to analyze and describe a bivariate relationship in terms of the three questions introduced in Chapter 12.

6. Test Pearson's *r* for significance.

15.1 INTRODUCTION

This chapter presents a set of statistical techniques for analyzing the association or correlation between variables measured at the interval-ratio level.* As we shall see, these techniques are rather different in their logic and computation from those covered in Chapters 13 and 14. Let us stress at the outset, therefore, that we are still asking the same three questions: Is there a relationship between the variables? How strong is the relationship? What is the direction of the relationship? You might become preoccupied with some of the technical details and computational routines in this chapter, so remind yourself occasionally that our ultimate goals are unchanged: We are trying to understand bivariate relationships, explore possible causal ties between variables, and improve our ability to predict scores.

15.2 SCATTERGRAMS

As we have seen over the past several chapters, properly percentaged tables provide important information about bivariate associations between nominal- and ordinal-level variables. In addition to measures of association like phi or gamma, the conditional distributions and patterns of cell frequency almost always provide useful information and a better understanding of the relationship between variables.

By the same token, the usual first step in analyzing a relationship between interval-ratio variables is to construct and examine a **scattergram.** Like bivariate tables, these graphs allow us to quickly identify several important features of the relationship. An example will illustrate the construction and use of scattergrams. Suppose a researcher is interested in analyzing how dual-wage-earner families (i.e., families where both husband and wife have jobs outside the home) cope with housework. Specifically, the researcher wonders if the number of children in the family is related to the amount of time the husband contributes to housekeeping chores. The relevant data for a sample of 12 dual-wage-earner families are displayed in Table 15.1.

A scattergram, like a bivariate table, has two dimensions. The scores of the independent (X) variable are arrayed along the horizontal axis, and the scores of the dependent (Y) variable along the vertical axis. Each dot on the scattergram represents a case in the sample and is located at a point determined by the scores of the case. Figure 15.1 shows a scattergram displaying the relationship between "number of children" and "husband's housework" for the sample of 12 families presented in Table 15.1. Family A has a score

---

*The term *correlation* is commonly used instead of *association* when discussing the relationship between interval-ratio variables. We will use the two terms interchangeably.

TABLE 15.1 NUMBER OF CHILDREN AND HUSBAND'S CONTRIBUTION TO HOUSEWORK (fictitious data)

Family	Number of Children	Hours per Week Husband Spends on Housework
A	1	1
B	1	2
C	1	3
D	1	5
E	2	3
F	2	1
G	3	5
H	3	0
I	4	6
J	4	3
K	5	7
L	5	4

FIGURE 15.1 HUSBAND'S HOUSEWORK BY NUMBER OF CHILDREN

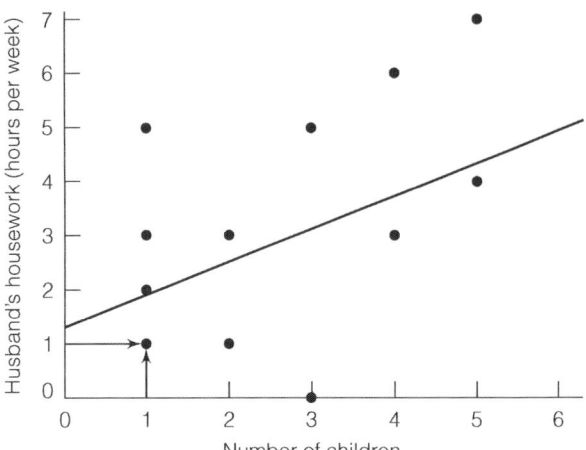

of 1 on the X variable (number of children) and 1 on the Y variable (husband's housework) and is represented by the dot above the score of 1 on the X axis and directly to the right of the score of 1 on the Y axis. All 12 cases are similarly represented by dots on Figure 15.1. Also note that, as always, the scattergram is clearly titled and both axes are labelled.

The overall pattern of the dots or cases summarizes the nature of the relationship between the two variables. The clarity of the pattern can be enhanced by drawing a straight line through the cluster of dots such that the line touches every dot or comes as close to doing so as possible. In Section 15.3, a precise technique for fitting this line to the pattern of the dots will be explained. For now, an "eyeball" approximation will suffice. This summarizing line is called the **regression line** and has already been added to the scattergram.

Scattergrams, even when they are crudely drawn, can be used for a variety of purposes. They provide at least impressionistic information about the existence, strength, and direction of the relationship and can also be used to check the relationship for linearity (i.e., how well the pattern of dots can be approximated with a straight line). Finally, the scattergram can be used to predict the score of a case on one variable from the score of that case on the other variable. We will briefly examine each of these uses.

To ascertain the existence of a relationship, we can return to the basic definition of an association stated in Chapter 12. Two variables are associated if the distributions of Y (the dependent variable) change for the various conditions of X (the independent variable). In Figure 15.1, scores on X (number of children) are arrayed along the horizontal axis. The dots above each score on X are the scores (or conditional distributions) of Y. That is, the dots represent scores on Y for each value of X. Figure 15.1 shows that there is a relationship between these variables because these conditional distributions of Y (the dots above each score on X) change as X changes.

The existence of an association is further reinforced by the fact that the regression line lies at an angle to the X axis. If these two variables had not been associated, the conditional distributions of Y would not have changed, and the regression line would have been parallel to the horizontal axis.

The strength of the bivariate association can be judged by observing the spread of the dots around the regression line. In a perfect association, all dots would lie on the regression line. The more the dots are clustered around the regression line, the stronger the association.

The direction of the relationship can be detected by observing the angle of the regression line. Figure 15.1 shows a positive relationship: As X (number of children) increases, husband's housework (Y) also increases. Husbands in families with more children tend to do more housework. If the relationship had been negative, the regression line would have sloped in the opposite direction to indicate that high scores on one variable were associated with low scores on the other.

To summarize these points about the existence, strength, and direction of the relationship, Figure 15.2 shows a perfect positive and a perfect negative relationship and a "zero relationship," or "non-relationship," between two variables.

One key assumption underlying the statistical techniques to be introduced later in this chapter is that the two variables have an essentially **linear relationship.** In other words, the observation points or dots in the scattergram must form a pattern that can be approximated with a straight line. Significant departures from linearity would require the use of statistical techniques beyond the scope of this text. Examples of some common curvilinear relationships are

FIGURE 15.2   POSITIVE, NEGATIVE, AND ZERO RELATIONSHIPS

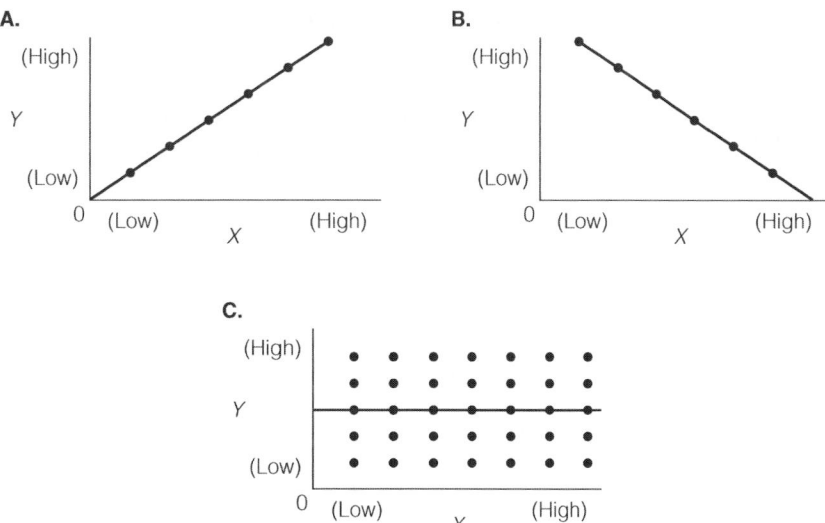

FIGURE 15.3   SOME NON-LINEAR RELATIONSHIPS

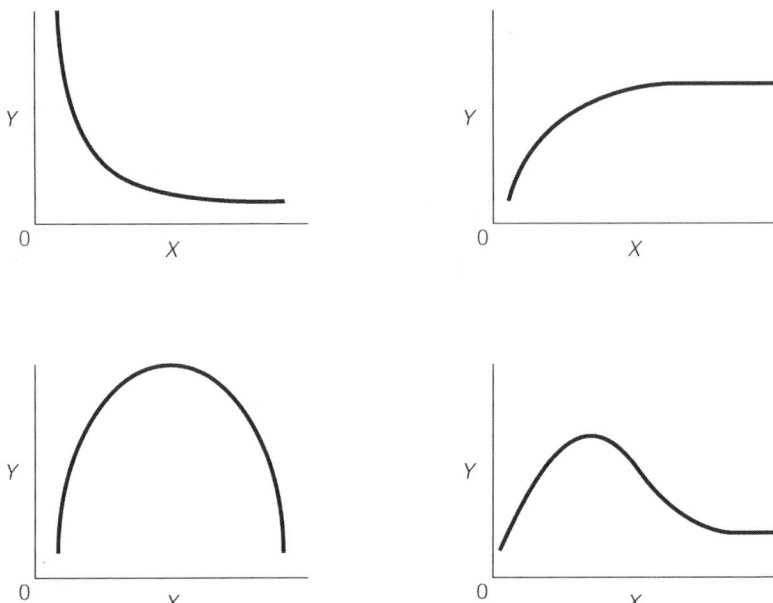

presented in Figure 15.3. If the scattergram shows that the variables have a non-linear relationship, the techniques described in this chapter should be used with great caution or not at all. Checking for the linearity of the relationship is perhaps the most important reason for constructing at least a crude, hand-drawn scattergram before proceeding with the statistical analysis. If the relationship is non-linear, you might need to treat the variables as if they were ordinal rather than interval-ratio in level of measurement. *(For practice in constructing and interpreting scattergrams, see problems 15.1 to 15.5.)*

15.3 REGRESSION AND PREDICTION

A final use of the scattergram is to predict scores of cases on one variable from their score on the other. To illustrate, suppose that, based on the relationship between number of children and husband's housework displayed in Figure 15.1, we wish to predict the number of hours of housework a husband with a family of six children would do each week. The sample has no families with six children, but if we extend the axes and regression line in Figure 15.1 to incorporate this score, a prediction is possible. Figure 15.4 reproduces the scattergram and illustrates how the prediction would be made.

The predicted score on Y—which is symbolized as Y' to distinguish predictions of Y from actual Y scores—is found by first locating the relevant score on X ($X = 6$ in this case) and then drawing a straight line from that point to the regression line. From the regression line, another straight line parallel to the X axis is drawn across to the Y axis. The predicted Y score (Y') is found at the point where the line crosses the Y axis. In our example,

FIGURE 15.4   PREDICTING HUSBAND'S HOUSEWORK

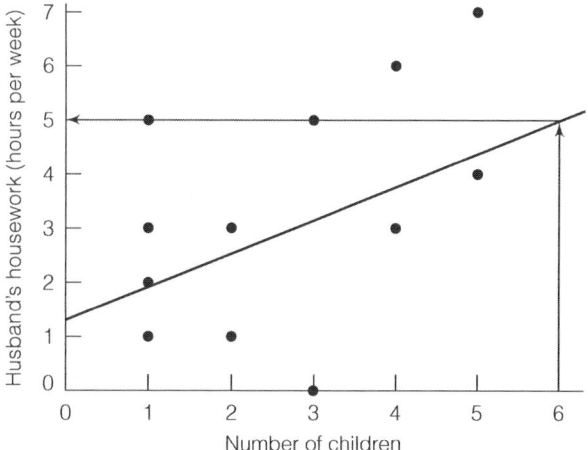

we would predict that, in a dual-wage-earner family with six children, the husband would devote about five hours per week to housework.

Of course, this prediction technique is crude, and the value of Y' can change depending on how accurately the freehand regression line is drawn. One way to eliminate this source of error would be to find the straight line that most accurately summarizes the pattern of the observation points and so best describes the relationship between the two variables. Is there such a "best-fitting" straight line? If there is, how is it defined?

Recall that our criterion for the freehand regression line was that it touch all the dots or come as close to doing so as possible. Also, recall that the dots above each value of X can be thought of as conditional distributions of Y, the dependent variable. Within each conditional distribution of Y, the mean is the point around which the variation of the scores is at a minimum. In Chapter 3, we noted that the mean of any distribution of scores is the point around which the variation of the scores, as measured by squared deviations, is minimized:

$$\sum (X_i - \overline{X})^2 = \text{minimum}$$

Thus, if the regression line is drawn so that it touches each **conditional mean of Y,** it would be the straight line that comes as close as possible to all the scores.

Conditional means are found by summing all Y values for each value of X and then dividing by the number of cases. For example, four families had one child ($X = 1$), and the husbands of these four families devoted 1, 2, 3, and 5 hours per week to housework. Thus, for $X = 1$, $Y = 1, 2, 3,$ and 5, and the conditional mean of Y for $X = 1$ is 2.75 (11/4 = 2.75). Husbands in families with one child worked an average of 2.75 hours per week doing housekeeping chores. Conditional means of Y are computed in the same way for each value of X displayed in Table 15.2 and plotted in Figure 15.5.

FIGURE 15.5   CONDITIONAL MEANS OF *Y*

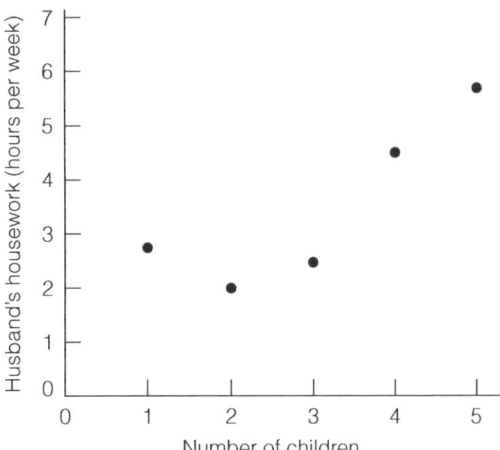

TABLE 15.2   CONDITIONAL MEANS OF *Y*
(husband's housework) FOR VARIOUS VALUES OF *X*
(number of children)

Number of Children (*X*)	Husband's Housework (*Y*)	Conditional Means of *Y*
1	1,2,3,5	2.75
2	3,1	2.00
3	5,0	2.50
4	6,3	4.50
5	7,4	5.50

Let us quickly remind ourselves of the reason for these calculations. We are seeking the single best-fitting regression line for summarizing the relationship between *X* and *Y*, and we have seen that a line drawn through the conditional means of *Y* will minimize the spread of the observation points. It will come as close to all the scores as possible and will therefore be the single best-fitting regression line.

Now, a line drawn through the points on Figure 15.5 (the conditional means of *Y*) will be the best-fitting line we are seeking, but you can see from the scattergram that the line will not be straight. In fact, only rarely (when there is a perfect relationship between *X* and *Y*) will conditional means fall in a perfectly straight line. Because we still must meet the condition of linearity, let us revise our criterion and define the regression line as the unique straight line that touches all conditional means of *Y* or comes as close to doing so as possible. Formula 15.1 defines the "least-squares" regression line, or the single straight regression line that best fits the pattern of the data points.

FORMULA 15.1
$$Y = a + bX$$

where Y = score on the dependent variable
   a = the *Y* intercept or the point where the regression line crosses the *Y* axis
   b = the slope of the regression line or the amount of change produced in *Y* by a unit change in *X*
   X = score on the independent variable

The formula introduces two new concepts. First, the **Y intercept (a)** is the point at which the regression line crosses the vertical, or *Y*, axis. This means that the intercept is equal to the value *Y* when *X* is zero. Second, the **slope (b)** of the least-squares regression line is the amount of change produced in the dependent variable (Y) by a unit change in the independent variable (X). Think of the slope of the regression line as a measure of the effect of the X variable on the Y variable. If the variables have a strong association, then changes in the value of X will be accompanied by substantial changes in the value of Y, and the slope (b) will have a high value. The weaker the effect of X on Y (the weaker the association between the variables), the lower the value of the slope (b). If the two variables are unrelated, the least-squares regression line would be parallel to the X axis, and b would be 0.00 (the line would have no slope). As a final point, the intercept and the slope are both expressed in the *units* of the dependent variable (e.g., number of *hours* per week the husband spends on housework), and thus provide a direct and intuitive interpretation.

With the least-squares formula (Formula 15.1), we can predict values of Y in a much less arbitrary and impressionistic way than through mere eyeballing. This will be so, remember, because the least-squares regression line as defined by Formula 15.1 is the single straight line that best fits the data because it comes as close as possible to all of the conditional means of Y. To see how predictions of Y can be made, however, we must first calculate a and b. *(For practice in using the regression line to predict scores on Y from scores on X, see problems 15.1 to 15.3 and 15.5)*

Before doing so, we want to briefly discuss *logistic regression*, a technique related to least-squares regression. Logistic regression has many similarities to linear regression. The logistic regression equation has coefficients that correspond to the Y intercept (a) and slope (b) of the least-squares regression equation, and can be used to predict the values of Y. However, logistic regression is used when the dependent variable is nominal or ordinal (e.g., pass or fail an exam) and the independent variable is of any level of measurement.

In logistic regression, the dependent variable is transformed into odds (more technically, the natural logarithm of the odds), such as the odds of passing an exam or the odds of failing an exam, and the method of maximum likelihood estimation is used to calculate the logistic regression equation, in contrast to the least-squares method used to calculate the linear regression equation. Logistic regression makes very few assumptions of the data, making it a very practical and commonly used method in the social sciences. The computational routines for logistic regression are beyond the scope of this text, but logistic regression is available in most computerized statistical packages such as SPSS.

15.4 THE COMPUTATION OF *a* AND *b*

Because the value of b is needed to solve for a, we will begin with the computation of the slope of the least-squares regression line. The definitional formula for the slope is

FORMULA 15.2

$$b = \frac{\Sigma(X - \overline{X})(Y - \overline{Y})}{\Sigma(X - \overline{X})^2}$$

The numerator of this formula is called the *covariation* of X and Y. It is a measure of how X and Y vary together, and its value will reflect both the direction and strength of the relationship. These days, of course, computers and statistical packages like SPSS are used to compute complex statistics like b. However, for smaller samples (and for the end-of-chapter problems in this text), b is sometimes still calculated using handheld calculators. In these situations, Formula 15.2 is awkward to use and the following computational formula, which can be derived from Formula 15.2, can be used instead:

FORMULA 15.3

$$b = \frac{N \sum XY - (\sum X)(\sum Y)}{N \sum X^2 - (\sum X)^2}$$

where b = the slope
N = the number of cases
$\sum XY$ = the summation of the crossproducts of the scores
$\sum X$ = the summation of the X scores
$\sum Y$ = the summation of the Y scores
$\sum X^2$ = the summation of the squared scores on X

Admittedly, this formula appears formidable at first glance, but it can be solved without too much difficulty if computations are organized into table format. The computing table displayed in Table 15.3 has a column for each of the four quantities needed to solve the formula. The data are from the dual-wage-earner family sample (see Table 15.1).

In Table 15.3, the first two columns list the original X and Y scores for each case. The third column contains the squared scores on X, and the

TABLE 15.3 COMPUTATION OF THE SLOPE (b)

X	Y	X^2	Y^{2}*	XY
1	1	1	1	1
1	2	1	4	2
1	3	1	9	3
1	5	1	25	5
2	3	4	9	6
2	1	4	1	2
3	5	9	25	15
3	0	9	0	0
4	6	16	36	24
4	3	16	9	12
5	7	25	49	35
5	4	25	16	20
$\sum X = 32$	$\sum Y = 40$	$\sum X^2 = 112$	$\sum Y^2 = 184$	$\sum XY = 125$

$$\bar{X} = \frac{32}{12} = 2.67$$

$$\bar{Y} = \frac{40}{12} = 3.33$$

*The quantity $\sum Y^2$ is not used in the computation of b. We will need it later, however, when we compute Pearson's r (see Section 15.5).

fourth lists the squared scores on Y. The fifth column lists the crossproducts of the scores for each case. In other words, the entries in the last column are determined by multiplying both scores for each case. We can now replace the symbols in Formula 15.3 with the proper sums:

$$b = \frac{N \sum XY - (\sum X)(\sum Y)}{N \sum X^2 - (\sum X)^2}$$

$$b = \frac{(12)(125) - (32)(40)}{(12)(112) - (32)^2}$$

$$b = \frac{(1,500 - 1,280)}{(1,344 - 1,024)}$$

$$b = \frac{220}{320}$$

$$b = 0.69$$

A slope of 0.69 indicates that, for each unit change in X, there is an increase of .69 units in Y. For our example, the addition of each child (an increase of one unit in X) results in an increase of .69 hour of housework being done by the husband (an increase of .69 units—or hours—in Y).

Once the slope has been calculated, finding the intercept (a) is relatively easy. To compute the mean of X and the mean of Y, divide the sums of columns 1 and 2 of Table 15.3 by N and enter these figures into Formula 15.4:

FORMULA 15.4
$$a = \overline{Y} - b\overline{X}$$

For our sample problem, the value of a would be

$$a = \overline{Y} - b\overline{X}$$
$$a = 3.33 - (0.69)(2.67)$$
$$a = 3.33 - 1.84$$
$$a = 1.49$$

Thus, the least-squares regression line will cross the Y axis at the point where Y equals 1.49.

The full least-squares regression line for our sample data can now be specified:

$$Y = a + bX$$
$$Y = (1.49) + (0.69)X$$

This formula can be used to estimate or predict scores on Y for any value of X. In Section 15.3, we used the freehand regression line to predict a score on Y (husband's housework) for a family with six children ($X = 6$). Our prediction was that, in families of six children, husbands would contribute about five hours per week to housekeeping chores. By using the least-squares regression line, we can see how close our impressionistic, eyeball prediction was.

$$Y' = a + bX$$
$$Y' = (1.49) + (0.69)(6)$$

$$Y' = (1.49) + (4.14)$$
$$Y' = 5.63$$

Based on the least-squares regression line, we would predict that in a dual-wage-earner family with six children, husbands would devote 5.63 hours a week to housework. What would our prediction of husband's housework be for a family of seven children ($X = 7$)?

Note that our predictions of Y scores are basically "educated guesses." We will be unlikely to predict values of Y exactly except in the (relatively rare) case where the bivariate relationship is perfect and perfectly linear. Note also, however, that the accuracy of our predictions will increase as relationships become stronger. This is because the dots are more clustered around the least-squares regression line in stronger relationships. *(The slope and Y intercept may be computed for any problem at the end of this chapter, but see problems 15.1 to 15.5 in particular. These problems have smaller data sets and will provide good practice until you are comfortable with these calculations.)*

15.5 THE CORRELATION COEFFICIENT (PEARSON'S *r*)

We pointed out in Section 15.4 that the slope (*b*) of the least-squares regression line is a measure of the effect of X on Y. Because the slope is the amount of change produced in Y by a unit change in X, *b* will increase in value as the relationship increases in strength. However, *b* does not vary between zero and one and is therefore awkward to use as a measure of association. Instead, researchers rely heavily (almost exclusively) on a statistic called **Pearson's *r*,** or the correlation coefficient, to measure association between interval-ratio variables. Like the ordinal measures of association discussed in Chapter 14, Pearson's *r* varies from 0.00 to ±1.00, with 0.00 indicating no association and +1.00 and −1.00 indicating perfect positive and perfect negative relationships, respectively. The definitional formula for Pearson's *r* is

FORMULA 15.5

$$r = \frac{\Sigma(X - \bar{X})(Y - \bar{Y})}{\sqrt{[\Sigma(X - \bar{X})^2][\Sigma(Y - \bar{Y})^2]}}$$

Note that the numerator of this formula is the covariation of X and Y, as was the case with Formula 15.2. When computing with a handheld calculator, computational Formula 15.6 is preferred over the definitional formula.

FORMULA 15.6

$$r = \frac{N\Sigma XY - (\Sigma X)(\Sigma Y)}{\sqrt{[N\Sigma X^2 - (\Sigma X)^2][N\Sigma Y^2 - (\Sigma Y)^2]}}$$

A computing table such as Table 15.3 is strongly recommended as a way of organizing the quantities needed to solve this equation. For our sample problem involving dual-wage-earner families, the quantities displayed in Table 15.3 can be substituted directly into Formula 15.6:

$$r = \frac{(12)(125) - (32)(40)}{\sqrt{[(12)(112) - (32)^2][(12)(184) - (40)^2]}}$$

$$r = \frac{1,500 - 1,280}{\sqrt{(1,344 - 1,024)(2,208 - 1,600)}}$$

$$r = \frac{220}{\sqrt{194,560}}$$

$$r = 0.50$$

An r value of 0.50 indicates a moderately strong, positive linear relationship between the variables. As the number of children in the family increases, the hourly contribution of husbands to housekeeping duties also increases. *(Every problem at the end of this chapter requires the computation of Pearson's r. It is probably a good idea to practise with smaller data sets and easier computations first—see problem 15.1 in particular.)*

15.6 INTERPRETING THE CORRELATION COEFFICIENT: r^2

Pearson's r is an index of the strength of the linear relationship between two variables. While a value of 0.00 indicates no linear relationship and a value of ± 1.00 indicates a perfect linear relationship, values between these extremes have no direct interpretation. We can, of course, describe relationships in terms of how closely they approach the extremes (e.g., coefficients approaching 0.00 can be described as "weak" and those approaching ± 1.00 as "strong"), but this description is somewhat subjective. Also, we can use the guidelines stated in Table 14.2 for gamma to attach descriptive words to the specific values of Pearson's r. In other words, values between 0.00 and 0.30 would be described as weak, values between 0.31 and 0.60 would be moderate, and values greater than 0.60 would be strong. Remember, of course, that these labels are arbitrary guidelines and will not be appropriate or useful in all possible research situations.

Fortunately, we can develop a less arbitrary, more direct interpretation of r by calculating an additional statistic called the **coefficient of determination.** This statistic, which is simply the square of Pearson's r (r^2), can be interpreted with a logic akin to proportional reduction in error (PRE). As you recall, the logic of PRE measures of association is to predict the value of the dependent variable under two different conditions. First, Y is predicted while ignoring the information supplied by X and, second, the independent variable is taken into account. With r^2, both the method of prediction and the construction of the final statistic are somewhat different and require the introduction of some new concepts.

Application 15.1

Five students were randomly selected from a larger sample of 1,500 students in the Student Financial Survey, a comprehensive study on the financial circumstances of Canadian post-secondary students sponsored by the Canada Millennium Scholarship Foundation. The table below shows data for these five students on their GPA (grade point average) and the average number of hours worked per week in the last semester. (While the data in this application are real, the number of cases is far too small to draw any serious conclusions, and thus, this is intended only for purposes of illustration and to simplify computations.) Are these variables associated? Columns have been added for all necessary sums.

Student	Hours Worked (per week) (X)	GPA (Y)	X^2	Y^2	XY
1	25	61	625	3,721	1,525
2	20	72	400	5,184	1,440
3	15	82	225	6,724	1,230
4	8	87	64	7,569	696
5	0	67	0	4,489	0
	68	369	1,314	27,687	4,891

The slope (b) is

$$b = \frac{N \sum XY - (\sum X)(\sum Y)}{N \sum X^2 - (\sum X)^2}$$

$$b = \frac{(5)(4,891) - (68)(369)}{(5)(1,314) - (68)^2}$$

$$b = \frac{-637}{1,946}$$

$$b = -0.33$$

A slope of −0.33 means that for every unit change in X (for every 1 hour increase in work per week), there was a change of −0.33 units in Y (grade point average decreased by 0.33, or by one-third of a point). The Y intercept (a) is

$$a = \overline{Y} - b\overline{X}$$

$$a = \frac{369}{5} - (-0.33)\left(\frac{68}{5}\right)$$

$$a = 73.8 - (-0.33)(13.6)$$

$$a = 73.8 + 4.5$$

$$a = 78.3$$

The least-squares regression equation is

$$Y = a + bX = 78.3 + (-0.33)X$$

The correlation coefficient is

$$r = \frac{N \sum XY - (\sum X)(\sum Y)}{\sqrt{[N \sum X^2 - (\sum X)^2][N \sum Y^2 - (\sum Y)^2]}}$$

$$r = \frac{(5)(4,891) - (68)(369)}{\sqrt{[(5)(1,314) - (68)^2][(5)(27,687) - (369)^2]}}$$

$$r = \frac{-637}{\sqrt{(1,946)(2,274)}}$$

$$r = \frac{-637}{\sqrt{442,5204}}$$

$$r = \frac{-637}{2,103.62}$$

$$r = -0.30$$

For these five students, GPA and hours worked have a weak to moderate, negative relationship. Grade point average decreases as the number of hours worked per week increases. The coefficient of determination, r^2, is $(-0.30)^2$, or 0.09. This indicates that 9% of the variance in GPA is explained by hours worked for this sample of five students.

Source: Canada Millennium Scholarship Foundation, 2001–2002 Student Financial Survey.

When working with variables measured at the interval-ratio level, the predictions of the Y scores under the first condition (while ignoring X) will be the mean of Y. Given no information on X, this prediction strategy will be optimal because we know that the mean of any distribution is closer to all the scores than any other point in the distribution. We remind you of the principle of minimized variation introduced in Chapter 3 and expressed as

$$\sum(Y - \overline{Y})^2 = \text{minimum}$$

The scores of any variable vary less around the mean than around any other point. If we predict the mean of Y for every case, we will make fewer errors of prediction than if we predict any other value for Y.

Of course, we will still make many errors in predicting Y even if we faithfully follow this strategy. The amount of error is represented in Figure 15.6, which displays the relationship between number of children and husband's housework with the mean of Y noted. The vertical lines from the actual scores to the predicted score represent the amount of error we would make when predicting Y while ignoring X.

We can define the extent of our prediction error under the first condition (while ignoring X) by subtracting the mean of Y from each actual Y score and squaring and summing these deviations. The resultant figure, which can be noted as $\sum(Y - \overline{Y})^2$, is called the **total variation** in Y. We now have a visual representation (Figure 15.6) and a method for calculating the error we incur by predicting Y without knowledge of X. As we shall see below, we do not need to actually calculate the total variation to find the value of the coefficient of determination, r^2.

Our next step will be to determine the extent to which knowledge of X improves our ability to predict Y. If the two variables have a linear relationship, then predicting scores on Y from the least-squares regression equation

FIGURE 15.6   PREDICTING Y WITHOUT X (dual-career families)

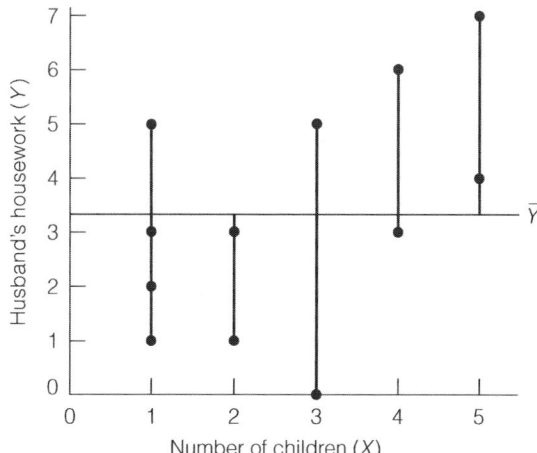

FIGURE 15.7   PREDICTING *Y* WITH *X* (dual-career families)

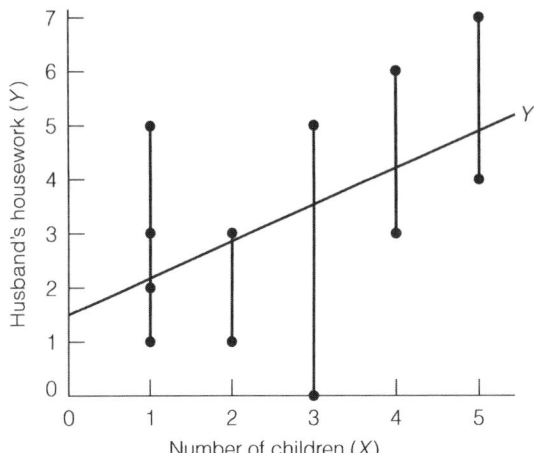

will incorporate knowledge of *X* and reduce our errors of prediction. So, under the second condition, our predicted *Y* score for each value of *X* will be

$$Y' = a + bX$$

Figure 15.7 displays the data from the dual-career families with the regression line, as determined by the above formula, drawn in. The vertical lines from each data point to the regression line represent the amount of error in predicting *Y* that remains even after *X* has been taken into account.

As was the case under the first condition, we can precisely define the reduction in error that results from taking *X* into account. Specifically, two different sums can be found and then compared with the total variation of *Y* to construct a statistic that will indicate the improvement in prediction. The first sum, called the **explained variation,** represents the improvement in our ability to predict *Y* when taking *X* into account. This sum is found by subtracting $\overline{Y}$ (our predicted *Y* score without *X*) from the score predicted by the regression equation (Y', or the *Y* score predicted with knowledge of *X*) for each case and then squaring and summing these differences. These operations can be summarized as $\Sigma(Y' - \overline{Y})^2$ and the resultant figure could then be compared with the total variation in *Y* to ascertain the extent to which our knowledge of *X* improves our ability to predict *Y*. Specifically, it can be shown mathematically that

FORMULA 15.7

$$r^2 = \frac{\Sigma(Y' - \overline{Y})^2}{\Sigma(Y - \overline{Y})^2} = \frac{\text{Explained variation}}{\text{Total variation}}$$

Thus, the coefficient of determination, or r^2, is the proportion of the total variation in *Y* attributable to or explained by *X*. Like other PRE measures, r^2 indicates precisely the extent to which *X* helps us predict, understand, or explain *Y*.

Above, we refer to the improvement in predicting Y with X as the explained variation. The use of this term suggests that some of the variation in Y will be "unexplained" or not attributable to the influence of X. In fact, the vertical lines in Figure 15.7 represent the **unexplained variation,** or the difference between our best prediction of Y with X and the actual scores. The unexplained variation is thus the scattering of the actual scores around the regression line and can be found by subtracting the predicted Y scores from the actual Y scores for each case and then squaring and summing the differences. These operations can be summarized as $\Sigma(Y - Y')^2$ and the resultant sum would measure the amount of error in predicting Y that remains even after X has been taken into account. The proportion of the total variation in Y unexplained by X can be found by subtracting the value of r^2 from 1.00. Unexplained variation is usually attributed to the influence of some combination of other variables, measurement error, and random chance.

As you may have recognized by this time, the explained and unexplained variations bear a reciprocal relationship with each other. As one of these sums increases in value, the other decreases. Furthermore, the stronger the linear relationship between X and Y, the greater the value of the explained variation and the lower the unexplained variation. In the case of a perfect relationship ($r = \pm 1.00$), the unexplained variation would be 0 and r^2 would be 1.00. This would indicate that X explains or accounts for all the variation in Y and that we could predict Y from X without error. On the other hand, when X and Y are not linearly related ($r = 0.00$), the explained variation would be 0 and r^2 would be 0.00. In such a case, we would conclude that X explains none of the variation in Y and does not improve our ability to predict Y.

Relationships intermediate between these two extremes can be interpreted in terms of how much X increases our ability to predict or explain Y. For the dual-career families, we calculated an r of 0.50. Squaring this value yields a coefficient of determination of 0.25 ($r^2 = 0.25$), which indicates that number of children (X) explains 25% of the total variation in husband's housework (Y). When predicting the number of hours per week that husbands in such families would devote to housework, we will make 25% fewer errors by basing the predictions on number of children and predicting from the regression line, as opposed to ignoring this variable and predicting the mean of Y for every case. Also, 75% of the variation in Y is unexplained by X and presumably due to some combination of the influence of other variables, measurement error, and random chance. *(For practice in the interpretation of r^2, see any of the problems at the end of this chapter.)*

15.7 THE CORRELATION MATRIX

Social science research projects usually include many variables and the data analysis phase of a project often begins with the examination of a correlation matrix, a table that shows the relationships between all possible pairs of variables. The correlation matrix gives a quick, easy-to-read overview of the interrelationships in the data set and may suggest strategies or "leads" for

TABLE 15.4 A CORRELATION MATRIX SHOWING INTERRELATIONSHIPS FOR FIVE VARIABLES ACROSS 161 NATIONS

	(1) GDP per Capita	(2) Inequality	(3) Unemployment Rate	(4) Literacy	(5) Voter Turnout
(1) GDP per Capita	1.00	−0.43	−0.34	0.46	0.28
(2) Inequality	−0.43	1.00	0.33	−0.15	−0.36
(3) Unemployment Rate	−0.34	0.33	1.00	−0.48	−0.28
(4) Literacy	0.46	−0.15	−0.48	1.00	0.40
(5) Voter Turnout	0.28	−0.36	−0.28	0.40	1.00

VARIABLES:

(1) *GDP per Capita:* Gross Domestic Product (the total value of all goods and services) divided by population size. This variable is an indicator of the level of affluence and prosperity in the society. Higher scores mean greater prosperity.
(2) *Inequality:* An index of income inequality. Higher scores mean greater inequality.
(3) *Unemployment Rate:* The annual rate of joblessness.
(4) *Literacy:* Number of people over age 15 able to read and write per 1,000 population.
(5) *Voter Turnout:* Percentage of eligible voters who participated in the most recent election.

further analysis. These tables are commonly included in the professional research literature and it will be useful to have some experience reading them.

An example of a correlation matrix, using cross-national data, is presented in Table 15.4. The matrix uses variable names as rows and columns and the cells in the table show the bivariate correlation (usually a Pearson's *r*) for each combination of variables. Note that the row headings duplicate the column headings. To read the table, begin with GDP per capita, the variable in the far left-hand column (column 1) and top row (row 1). Read down column 1 or across row 1 to see the correlations of this variable with all other variables, including the correlation of GDP per capita with itself (1.00) in the top cell. To see the relationships between other variables, move from column to column or row to row.

Note that the diagonal from upper left to lower right of the matrix presents the correlation of each variable with itself. Values along this diagonal will always be exactly 1.00 and, because this information is not useful, it could easily be deleted from the table.

Also note that the cells below and to the left of the diagonal are redundant with the cells above and to the right of the diagonal. For example, look at the second cell down (row 2) in column 1. This cell displays the correlation between GDP per capita and inequality, as does the cell in the top row (row 1) of column 2. In other words, the lower-left-hand part of the table is a mirror image of the upper-right-hand part. Commonly, research articles in the professional literature will delete the redundant cells in order to make the table more readable.

What does this matrix tell us? Starting at the upper left of the table (column 1), we can see that GDP per capita has a moderate negative

Application 15.2

Are nations that have more educated populations more tolerant? Are more educated nations therefore less likely to see homosexuality as wrong? Random samples from 10 nations have been asked if they agree that homosexuality is "never acceptable."

Information has also been gathered on the average years of school completed for people over 25 in each nation. How are these variables related? The data are presented in the table below. Columns have been added for all necessary sums.

Nation	Average Years of Schooling (X)	Percent Agreeing that Homosex- uality Is "Always Wrong" (Y)	X^2	Y^2	XY
China	6	88	36	7,744	528
Brazil	5	56	25	3,136	280
United States	12	45	144	2,025	540
Japan	10	42	100	1,764	420
Mexico	7	55	49	3,025	385
India	5	77	25	5,929	385
South Africa	6	61	36	3,721	366
Finland	10	37	100	1,369	370
Canada	11	26	121	676	286
Germany	10	15	100	225	150
Totals	82	502	736	29,614	3,710

Source: World Values Survey and United Nations Human Development Report.

(*continued next page*)

relationship with inequality and unemployment rate, which means that more affluent nations tend to have less inequality and lower rates of joblessness. GDP per capita also has a moderate positive relationship with literacy (more affluent nations have higher levels of literacy) and a weak to moderate positive relationship with voter turnout (more affluent nations tend to have higher levels of participation in the electoral process).

To assess the other relationships in the data set, move from column to column and row to row, one variable at a time. For each subsequent variable, there will be one less cell of new information. For example, consider inequality, the variable in column 2 and row 2. We have already noted its moderate negative relationship with GDP per capita and, of course, we can ignore the correlation of the variable with itself. This leaves only three new

Application 15.2: *(continued)*

The slope (*b*) is

$$b = \frac{N \sum XY - (\sum X)(\sum Y)}{N \sum X^2 - (\sum X)^2}$$

$$b = \frac{(10)(3,710) - (82)(502)}{(10)(736) - (82)^2}$$

$$b = \frac{37,100 - 41,164}{7,360 - 6,724}$$

$$b = \frac{-4,064}{636}$$

$$b = -6.39$$

A slope of −6.39 means that for every increase in years of education (a unit change in *X*), there is a decrease of 6.39 points in the percentage of people who feel that homosexuality is never justified.

The *Y* intercept (*a*) is

$$a = \overline{Y} - b\overline{X}$$

$$a = \frac{502}{10} - (-6.39)\left(\frac{82}{10}\right)$$

$$a = 50.2 - (-6.39)(8.2)$$

$$a = 50.2 + 52.4$$

$$a = 102.6$$

The least-squares regression equation is

$$Y = a + bX = 102.6 + (-6.39)X$$

The correlation coefficient is

$$r = \frac{N \sum XY - (\sum X)(\sum Y)}{\sqrt{[N \sum X^2 - (\sum X)^2][N \sum Y^2 - (\sum Y)^2]}}$$

$$r = \frac{(10)(3,710) - (82)(502)}{\sqrt{[(10)(736) - (82)^2][(10)(29,614) - (502)^2]}}$$

$$r = \frac{37,100 - 41,164}{\sqrt{(7,360 - 6,724)(296,140 - 252,004)}}$$

$$r = \frac{-4,064}{\sqrt{(636)(44,136)}}$$

$$r = \frac{-4,064}{\sqrt{28,070,7496}}$$

$$r = \frac{-4,064}{5,298.16}$$

$$r = -0.77$$

For these 10 nations, education and disapproval of homosexuality have a strong, negative relationship. Disapproval of homosexuality decreases as education increases. The coefficient of determination, r^2, is $(0.77)^2$, or 0.59. This indicates that 59% of the variance in attitude toward homosexuality is explained by education for this sample of 10 nations.

relationships, which can be read by moving down column 2 or across row 2. Inequality has a moderate positive relationship with unemployment (the greater the inequality, the greater the unemployment), a weak negative relationship with literacy (nations with more inequality tend to have lower literacy rates), and a moderate negative relationship with voter turnout (the greater the inequality, the lower the turnout).

For unemployment, the variable in column 3, there are only two new relationships: a moderate negative correlation with literacy (the higher the unemployment, the lower the literacy) and a weak to moderate negative relationship with voter turnout (the higher the unemployment rate, the lower the turnout). For literacy, the variable in column 4, there is only one new relationship. Literacy has a moderate positive relationship with voter turnout (turnout increases as literacy goes up).

In closing, we should note that the cells in a correlation matrix will often include other information in addition to the bivariate correlations. It is common, for example, to include the number of cases on which the correlation is based and, if relevant, an indication of the statistical significance of the relationship.

15.8 TESTING PEARSON'S r FOR SIGNIFICANCE

When the relationship measured by Pearson's r is based on data from a random sample, it will usually be necessary to test r for its statistical significance. That is, we will need to know if a relationship between the variables can be assumed to exist in the population from which the sample was drawn. To illustrate this test, the r of .50 from the dual-wage-earner family sample will be used. As was the case when testing gamma and Spearman's rho, the null hypothesis states that there is no linear association between the two variables in the population from which the sample was drawn. The population parameter is symbolized as ρ (rho), and the appropriate sampling distribution is the t distribution.

To conduct this test, we need to make a number of assumptions in step 1. Most should be quite familiar, but several are new. First, we must assume that both variables are normal in distribution **(bivariate normal distributions).** Second, we must assume that the relationship between the two variables is roughly linear in form.

The third assumption involves a new concept: **homoscedasticity.** Basically, a homoscedastic relationship is one where the variance of the Y scores is uniform for all values of X. That is, if the Y scores are evenly spread above and below the regression line for the entire length of the line, the relationship is homoscedastic.

A visual inspection of the scattergram will usually be sufficient to appraise the extent to which the relationship conforms to the assumptions of linearity and homoscedasticity. As a rule of thumb, if the data points fall in a roughly symmetrical, cigar-shaped pattern, whose shape can be approximated with a straight line, then it is appropriate to proceed with this test of significance. Any significant evidence of non-linearity or marked departures from homoscedasticity may indicate the need for an alternative measure of association and thus a different test of significance.

Step 1. Making Assumptions and Meeting Test Requirements.

> Model: Random sampling
> Level of measurement is interval-ratio
> Bivariate normal distributions
> Linear relationship
> Homoscedasticity
> Sampling distribution is normal

Step 2. Stating the Null Hypothesis.

$$H_0: \rho = 0.0$$
$$(H_1: \rho \neq 0.0)$$

Step 3. Selecting the Sampling Distribution and Establishing the Critical Region. With the null of "no relationship" in the population, the sampling distribution of all possible sample r's is approximated by the t distribution. Degrees of freedom are equal to $(N - 2)$.

$$\text{Sampling distribution} = t \text{ distribution}$$
$$\text{Alpha} = 0.05$$
$$\text{Degrees of freedom} = N - 2 = 10$$
$$t(\text{critical}) = \pm 2.28$$

Step 4. Computing the Test Statistic. The formula for computing the test statistic is given in Formula 15.8.

FORMULA 15.8
$$t(\text{obtained}) = r\sqrt{\frac{N - 2}{1 - r^2}}$$

Substituting the values into the formula, we would have:

$$t(\text{obtained}) = (0.50)\sqrt{\frac{12 - 2}{1 - (0.50)^2}}$$

$$t(\text{obtained}) = (0.50)\sqrt{\frac{10}{0.75}}$$

$$t(\text{obtained}) = (0.50)(3.65)$$

$$t(\text{obtained}) = 1.83$$

Step 5. Making a Decision and Interpreting the Results of the Test. Because the test statistic does not fall into the critical region as marked by $t(\text{critical})$, we fail to reject the null hypothesis. We do not have sufficient evidence to conclude that the variables are related in the population. The test indicates that the sample value of $r = 0.50$ could have occurred by chance alone if the null hypothesis is true and the variables are unrelated in the population. *(For practice in conducting and interpreting tests of significance with Pearson's r, see problems 15.1, 15.2, 15.4, 15.6, 15.8, and 15.9.)*

15.9 INTERPRETING STATISTICS: THE CORRELATES OF CRIME

What causes crime? Sociologists have been researching this question since the discipline was founded. While we cannot contribute to this voluminous body of work in a text devoted to statistical analysis, we can investigate some of the relationships and correlations that are of continuing interest to criminologists.

One school of criminological thought argues that crime is related to poverty. A central proposition of this approach might be phrased as: "Crime rates will be highest among the most disadvantaged and impoverished groups, those with the highest rates of unemployment and the lowest levels of 'economic viability' (job skills, levels of education) in the legitimate economy." In this installment of Interpreting Statistics, we will take a look at the empirical relationship between a measure of criminality and a measure of poverty in Canada.

The units of analysis will be Canada's largest cities, called CMAs or Census Metropolitan Areas. A CMA is defined as an area consisting of one or more adjacent municipalities surrounding a major urban core with a population of at least 100,000. To make the data comparable, only those CMAs with populations of 500,000 and over are examined.

We will use the police-reported crime rate (i.e., criminal offences reported to police per 100,000 population) in the year 2000 as an indicator of criminal activity. Police-reported crime data are gathered by the Uniform Crime Reporting survey of the Canadian Centre for Justice Statistics at Statistics Canada. The reader should note that police-reported crime is not a perfect measure of crime. Victimization surveys usually produce higher rates of criminal activity than police-reported statistics. This is because victimization surveys collect crime information directly from the population, whether or not it has been reported to police. (There are various reasons why victims of criminal incidents do not report incidents to the police, including the seriousness of the incident, the victim's reluctance to get police involved, the belief that police cannot or will not do much, and fear of reprisals.) As the independent variable of our exercise, we will use the percent of the population living below the poverty line in the year 2000.

The scores and basic descriptive statistics for the variables are reported in Table 15.5. On crime, cities range from a high of 11,210 offences per 100,000 population in Vancouver to a low of 5,108 per 100,000 population in Quebec City. Poverty rates range from a high of 22.3% in Montreal to a low of 14.3% in Calgary.

The first step in assessing an association between interval-ratio-level variables is to produce a scattergram. Figure 15.8 plots the crime rate on the vertical

TABLE 15.5   SCORES ON POVERTY AND CRIME FOR NINE CANADIAN CITIES, WITH DESCRIPTIVE STATISTICS

City	Crime Rate[1] (Y)	Poverty Rate[2] (X)
Calgary	7,115	14.3
Edmonton	8,377	16.5
Hamilton	6,565	17.0
Montreal	7,234	22.3
Ottawa	5,680	15.0
Quebec	5,108	18.9
Toronto	5,290	16.7
Vancouver	11,210	20.8
Winnipeg	10,377	19.8
Mean	7,449	17.9
Standard Deviation	2,173	2.7
Range	6,102	8.0

[1]Number of criminal offences per 100,000 population, 2000.
[2]Percent of population living below the poverty line, 2000.
Source: Statistics Canada. 2001. *Crime Statistics in Canada, 2000.* Catalogue no. 85-002-XIE (Crime rate) and Statistics Canada, 2001 Canadian Census, individual PUMF (Poverty rate).

FIGURE 15.8   CRIME RATE BY POVERTY RATE FOR NINE CANADIAN CITIES

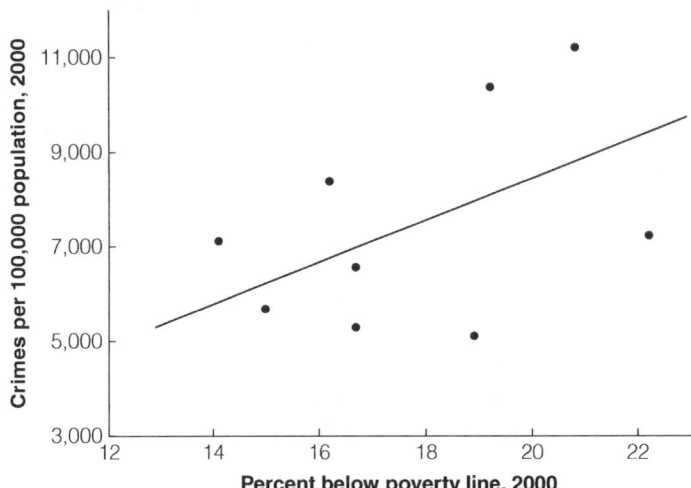

or *Y* axis and the poverty rate along the horizontal or *X* axis. What can we say about this relationship? The regression line is not horizontal, so there is a relationship between these variables. The dots (cities) are fairly well scattered around the regression line, and we can see immediately that this will be, at best, a moderately strong relationship. The regression line slopes up from left to right, so this is a positive relationship: Cities that have higher poverty rates tend to have higher crime rates (or, crime rates tend to increase as poverty rates increase).

The second step in assessing this relationship is to specify the regression line. We will skip the mechanics of computation here and simply report the values for the regression coefficients (*a* and *b*).

$$Y = a + bX$$
$$Y = 744 + (374)X$$

The regression line will cross the *Y* axis at the point where *Y* = 744. In other words, when the poverty rate is 0%, the number of criminal offences per 100,000 population is 744. The slope of the regression, *b,* is 374. That is, every unit (i.e., percent) increase in *X* (poverty rate) increases the number of criminal offences by 374 per 100,000 population.

Next, we will calculate and interpret Pearson's *r*. Again, we will skip the details of the computation and report that *r* = 0.47, which reinforces the impression that there is a moderately strong relationship between crime and poverty rates. The coefficient of determination (r^2) is about 0.22, which means that poverty rate, by itself, explains about 22% of the variation in the crime rate.

In sum, the linear regression equation, the correlation coefficient, and the coefficient of determination suggest that there is a moderately strong relationship between inequality and crime. The amount of unexplained variation (78%) suggests that many other variables besides poverty have an influence on the crime rate.

We should also note two other limitations of this simple test. First, correlation is not the same thing as causation. Just because two variables are correlated does not mean that they have a causal relationship. Second, a related point, a criminal offence is by definition an individual act of behaviour, but the data we used in this test was collected from cities. Just because there is an association between the variables at the macro (city) level does not necessarily mean that the variables are related in the same way at the micro (individual) level. (This problem is called the *ecological fallacy*.) All we know from our analysis is that cities with higher rates of poverty tend to have higher rates of crime. Our theory would lead us to assume that it is the victims of poverty (poor people) who are the offenders, but this conclusion is not proven by this analysis. It may also be the wealthier residents of the poorer cities who are committing the crimes. We would need much more information—on both the micro and macro levels—before we develop final conclusions on the relation between poverty and crime.

SUMMARY

This summary is based on the example used throughout the chapter.

1. We began with a question: Is the number of children in dual-wage-earner families related to the number of hours per week husbands devote to housework? We presented the observations in a scattergram (Figure 15.1), and our visual impression was that the variables were associated in a positive direction. The pattern formed by the observation points in the scattergram could be approximated with a straight line, thus, the relationship was roughly linear.

2. Values of Y can be predicted with the freehand regression line, but predictions are more accurate if the least-squares regression line is used. The least-squares regression line is the line that best fits the data by minimizing the variation in Y. Using the formula that defines the least-squares regression line ($Y = a + bX$), we found a slope (b) of .69, which indicates that each additional child (a unit change in X) is accompanied by an increase of .69 hour of housework per week for the husbands. We also predicted, based on this formula, that in a dual-wage-earner family with six children ($X = 6$), husbands would contribute 5.63 hours of housework a week ($Y' = 5.63$ for $X = 6$).

3. Pearson's r is a statistic that measures the overall linear association between X and Y. Our impression from the scattergram of a substantial positive relationship was confirmed by the computed r of .50. We also saw that this relationship yields an r^2 of .25, which indicates that 25% of the total variation in Y (husband's housework) is accounted for or explained by X (number of children).

4. Assuming that the 12 families represented a random sample, we tested the Pearson's r for its statistical significance and found that, at the .05 level, we could not assume that these two variables were also related in the population.

5. We acquired a great deal of information about this bivariate relationship. We know the strength and direction of the relationship and have also identified the regression line that best summarizes the effect of X on Y. We know the amount of change we can expect in Y for a unit change in X. In short, we have a greater volume of more precise information about this association between interval-ratio variables than we ever did about associations between ordinal or nominal variables. This is possible, of course, because the data generated by interval-ratio measurement are more precise and flexible than those produced by ordinal or nominal measurement techniques.

SUMMARY OF FORMULAS

Least-squares regression line:

15.1 $Y = a + bX$

Definitional formula for the slope:

15.2 $b = \dfrac{\Sigma(X - \bar{X})(Y - \bar{Y})}{\Sigma(X - \bar{X})^2}$

Computational formula for the slope:

15.3 $b = \dfrac{N\Sigma XY - (\Sigma X)(\Sigma Y)}{N\Sigma X^2 - (\Sigma X)^2}$

Y intercept:

15.4 $a = \bar{Y} - b\bar{X}$

Definitional formula for Pearson's r:

15.5 $r = \dfrac{\Sigma(X - \bar{X})(Y - \bar{Y})}{\sqrt{[\Sigma(X - \bar{X})^2][\Sigma(Y - \bar{Y})^2]}}$

Computational formula for Pearson's r:

15.6 $r = \dfrac{N\Sigma XY - (\Sigma X)(\Sigma Y)}{\sqrt{[N\Sigma X^2 - (\Sigma X)^2][N\Sigma Y^2 - (\Sigma Y)^2]}}$

Coefficient of determination:

15.7 $r^2 = \dfrac{\Sigma(Y' - \bar{Y})^2}{\Sigma(Y - \bar{Y})^2}$

15.8 $t(\text{obtained}) = r\sqrt{\dfrac{N - 2}{1 - r^2}}$

GLOSSARY

Bivariate normal distributions. The model assumption in the test of significance for Pearson's r that both variables are normally distributed.

Coefficient of determination (r^2). The proportion of all variation in Y that is explained by X. Found by squaring the value of Pearson's r.

Conditional means of Y. The mean of all scores on Y for each value of X.

Explained variation. The proportion of all variation in Y that is attributed to the effect of X. Equal to $\Sigma(Y' - \bar{Y})^2$.

Homoscedasticity. The model assumption in the test of significance for Pearson's r that the variance of the Y scores is uniform across all values of X.

Linear relationship. A relationship between two variables in which the observation points (dots) in the scattergram can be approximated with a straight line.

Pearson's r (r). A measure of association for variables that have been measured at the interval-ratio level; ρ (Greek letter rho) is the symbol for the population value of Pearson's r.

Regression line. The single best-fitting straight line that summarizes the relationship between two variables. Regression lines are fitted to the data points by the least-squares criterion, whereby the line touches all conditional means of Y or comes as close to doing so as possible.

Scattergram. Graphic display device that depicts the relationship between two variables.

Slope (b). The amount of change in one variable per unit change in the other; b is the symbol for the slope of a regression line.

Total variation. The spread of the Y scores around the mean of Y. Equal to $\Sigma(Y - \bar{Y})^2$.

Unexplained variation. The proportion of the total variation in Y that is not accounted for by X. Equal to $\Sigma(Y - Y')^2$.

Y intercept (a). The point where the regression line crosses the Y axis.

Y'. Symbol for predicted score on Y.

MULTIMEDIA RESOURCES

http://www.healeystatistics.nelson.com

Visit the companion Web site for the first Canadian edition of *Statistics: A Tool for Social Research* to access a wide range of student resources. Begin by clicking on the Student Resources section of the book's Web site to access review quizzes, flash cards, and other study tools.

PROBLEMS

15.1 [PS] Why does voter turnout vary from election to election? For municipal elections in five different cities, information has been gathered on the percent of eligible voters who actually voted, unemployment rate, average years of education for the city, and the percentage of all political ads that used "negative campaigning" (personal attacks, negative portrayals of the opponent's record, etc). For each relationship:

a. Draw a scattergram and a freehand regression line.

b. Compute the slope (*b*) and find the *Y* intercept (*a*). *(HINT: Remember to compute b before computing a. A computing table such as Table 15.3 is highly recommended.)*

c. State the least-squares regression line and predict the voter turnout for a city in which the unemployment rate was 12, a city in which the average years of schooling was 11, and an election in which 90% of the ads were negative.

d. Compute *r* and *r²*. *(HINT: A computing table such as Table 15.3 is highly recommended. If you constructed one for computing b, you already have most of the quantities you will need to solve for r.)*

e. Assume these cities are a random sample and conduct a test of significance for each relationship.

f. Describe the strength and direction of the relationships in a sentence or two. Which

(if any) relationships were significant? Which factor had the strongest effect on turnout?

TURNOUT AND UNEMPLOYMENT

City	Turnout	Unemployment Rate
A	55	5
B	60	8
C	65	9
D	68	9
E	70	10

TURNOUT AND LEVEL OF EDUCATION

City	Turnout	Average Years of School
A	55	11.9
B	60	12.1
C	65	12.7
D	68	12.8
E	70	13.0

TURNOUT AND NEGATIVE CAMPAIGNING

City	Turnout	% of Negative Advertisements
A	55	60
B	60	63
C	65	55
D	68	53
E	70	48

15.2 [SOC] Occupational prestige scores (higher scores indicate greater prestige) for a sample of fathers and their oldest son and oldest daughter are shown in the table.

Family	Father's Prestige	Son's Prestige	Daughter's Prestige
A	80	85	82
B	78	80	77
C	75	70	68
D	70	75	77
E	69	72	60
F	66	60	52
G	64	48	48
H	52	55	57

Analyze the relationship between father's and son's prestige and the relationship between father's and daughter's prestige. For each relationship:

a. Draw a scattergram and a freehand regression line.

b. Compute the slope (b) and find the Y intercept (a).

c. State the least-squares regression line. What prestige score would you predict for a son whose father had a prestige score of 72? What prestige score would you predict for a daughter whose father had a prestige score of 72?

d. Compute r and r^2.

e. Assume these families are a random sample and conduct a test of significance for both relationships.

f. Describe the strength and direction of the relationships in a sentence or two. Does the occupational prestige of the father have an impact on his children? Does it have the same impact for daughters as it does for sons?

15.3 GER The residents of a housing development for senior citizens have completed a survey whereon they indicated how physically active they are and how many visitors they receive each week. Are these two variables related for the 10 cases reported on the following table? Draw a scattergram and compute r and r^2. Find the least-squares regression line. What would be the predicted number of visitors for a person whose level of activity was a 5? How about a person who scored 18 on level of activity?

Case	Level of Activity	Number of Visitors
A	10	14
B	11	12
C	12	10
D	10	9
E	15	8
F	9	7
G	7	10
H	3	15
I	10	12
J	9	2

15.4 PS The variables below were collected for a random sample of 10 electoral districts during the last federal election. Draw scattergrams and compute r and r^2 for each combination of variables and test the correlations for their significance. Write a paragraph interpreting the relationship between these variables.

District	Percent Working-class	Unemployment Rate	Voter Turnout
A	50	10	56
B	45	12	55
C	56	8	52
D	78	15	60
E	13	5	89
F	85	20	25
G	62	18	64
H	33	9	88
I	25	0	42
J	49	9	36

15.5 SOC/CJ The table below presents the scores of 10 randomly selected Canadian cities on each of six variables: three measures of criminal activity and three measures of population structure. Crime rates are the number of incidents per 100,000 population. For each combination of crime rate and population characteristic:

a. Draw a scattergram and a freehand regression line.

b. Compute the slope (b) and find the Y intercept (a).

c. State the least-squares regression line. What homicide rate would you predict for a city with a growth rate of -1? What robbery rate would you predict for a city with a population density of 250? What auto theft rate would you predict for a city in which 50% of the population lived in urban areas?

	Crime Rates			Population		
City	Homicide	Robbery	Auto Theft	Growth[1]	Density[2]	Urbanization[3]
A	1	19	104	3.8	41.7	52.6
B	5	214	286	5.5	402.7	92.1
C	4	138	344	4.7	277.8	81.2
D	2	37	184	5.4	52.3	45.3
E	6	89	252	14.4	181.5	78.1
F	5	81	230	9.6	102.3	48.8
G	6	145	447	22.8	81.5	84.8
H	7	146	842	40.0	46.7	88.2
I	3	99	594	21.1	90.0	83.1
J	6	178	537	13.6	221.2	96.7

[1]Percentage change in population over the last 10 years.
[2]Population per square kilometre of land area.
[3]Percent of population living in urban core.

d. Compute r and r^2.

e. Since these cities come from a random sample, conduct a test of significance for both relationships.

f. Describe the strength and direction of each of these relationships in a sentence or two.

15.6 $\boxed{\text{SOC}}$ Data on three variables have been collected for 15 nations. The variables are fertility rate (average number of children born to each woman), average education for females (expressed as a percentage of average education for men), and maternal mortality (death rate for mothers per 100,000 live births). On female education, a value of 100 means that men and women have equal levels of education, values over 100 mean that women have more education and values less than 100 mean that women have less education than men.

Nation	Fertility	Education of Females	Maternal Mortality
Niger	7.2	50	590
Cambodia	4.8	74	470
Guatemala	4.7	86	190
Ghana	4.0	46	210
Bolivia	3.7	60	390
Egypt	3.2	41	170
Dominican Republic	3.0	87	230
Mexico	2.7	96	55
Vietnam	2.5	59	130
Turkey	2.2	49	130
United States	2.1	102	8

(continued in next column)

(continued)

Nation	Fertility	Education of Females	Maternal Mortality
China	1.8	60	55
Canada	1.7	102	7
Japan	1.4	98	8
Italy	1.2	99	7

a. Compute r and r^2 for each combination of variables.

b. Summarize these relationships in terms of strength and direction.

15.7 $\boxed{\text{SOC}}$ The basketball coach at a university believes that his team plays better and scores more points in front of larger crowds. The number of points scored and attendance for all home games last season are reported below. Do these data support the coach's argument?

Game	Points Scored	Attendance
1	54	378
2	57	350
3	59	320
4	80	478
5	82	451
6	75	250
7	73	489
8	53	451
9	67	410
10	78	215
11	67	113
12	56	250
13	85	450
14	101	489
15	99	472

15.8 SOC The table below presents the scores of 15 large Canadian cities on three variables. Compute r and r^2 for each combination of variables. Assume that these 15 cities are a random sample of Canada's 50 largest cities and test the correlations for their significance. Write a paragraph interpreting the relationship among these three variables.

City	Per Capita Expenditures on Education	Percent High School Graduates[1]	Rank in Per Capita Income
A	1,102	82	48
B	1,339	90	7
C	1,907	88	1
D	1,171	84	25
E	1,621	86	9
F	1,276	88	24
G	1,159	81	45
H	1,412	86	5
I	1,487	86	18
J	1,041	80	50
K	1,194	90	22
L	1,262	88	6
M	1,163	79	32
N	1,223	86	15
O	1,549	90	20

[1] Based on percentage of population age 25 and older.

15.9 SOC A social survey was administered to a random sample of adults. Fifteen individuals were then randomly selected from the sample. Their scores on five of the variables in the survey are reproduced below. Is there a relationship between occupational prestige (higher scores indicate greater prestige) and age? Between number of times religious service attended (per month) and number of children? Between number of children and hours of TV watching (per day)? Between age and hours of TV watching? Between age and number of children? Between hours of TV watching and occupational prestige? Which of these relationships are significant?

Occupational Prestige	Number of Children	Age	Religious Service Attendance per month	Hours of TV per Day
32	3	34	3	1
50	0	41	0	3
17	0	52	7	2
69	3	67	0	5
17	0	40	0	5
52	0	22	2	3
32	3	31	0	4
50	0	23	8	4
19	9	64	1	6
37	4	55	0	2
14	3	66	5	5
51	0	22	6	0
45	0	19	3	7
44	0	21	4	1
46	4	58	2	0

Using SPSS for Windows to Produce Pearson's *r* and the Regression Line with the 2001 Census

The demonstrations and exercises below use the shortened version of the 2001 Census data. Start SPSS for Windows and open the *Census.sav* file.

SPSS DEMONSTRATION 15.1 The Scattergram

The scattergram provides a convenient look at the relationship between two variables. Here we will examine the effect of *unitsp* (household size) on *valuep* (value of dwelling) with the scattergram. Click **Graphs, Legacy Dialogs,** and then **Scatter/Dot.** The **Scatter/Dot** dialog box appears with five choices. We want the **Simple Scatter,** so highlight this option and click **Define.** The **Simple Scatterplot** dialog box appears. Transfer the dependent variable, *valuep,* to the Y Axis box, and the independent variable, *unitsp,* to the X **Axis** box. Click **OK,** and the following scattergram will be produced.

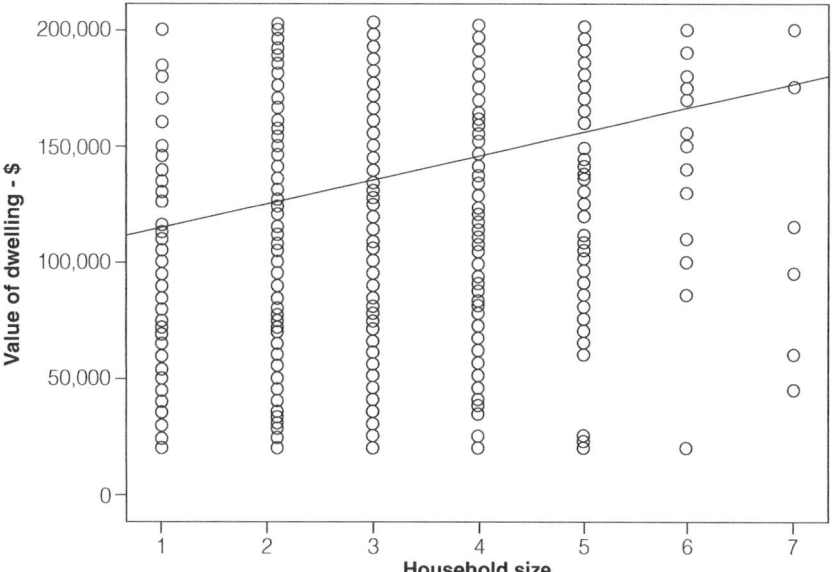

We added the least-squares regression line to the scattergram to provide a better sense of the relationship between the variables. To do this, double-click on any part of the scattergram to open the **Chart Editor** window. Then, click the **Elements** menu and choose **Fit Line at Total.** Close the **Chart Editor** window to return to the **Output** window.

The regression line tells us that a relationship exists, and that it is positive in direction. As household size increases, house value increases. However, the strength and linearity (whether the data points approximate a straight line) of this relationship are more difficult to detect because the overall pattern of the dots around the regression line is obscured by overlapping data points (respondents with identical values on both the independent and dependent variable).

It is difficult to eliminate completely the problem of overplotting. One way to reduce the problem is to "jitter" the data, that is, to subtract or add a small random quantity to each value of the independent and dependent variable. Data points will be separated by this quantity, reducing the overlap and making it easier to assess the strength and linearity of the relationship in the scattergram. Jittering disentangles overlapping data points and, in many cases, makes it possible to assess the nature of a relationship.

A second and more practical way to reduce overlap and assess the strength and linearity of a relationship is to take a random sample from the larger sample, and then get a scattergram from that sample. This will greatly reduce the number of cases and make the scattergram easier to read. To do this, click **Data** from the menu bar of the **Data Editor** window and click **Select Cases.** Next, click the **Random sample of cases** button and then the **Sample** button. Request a 2% random sample by typing 2 into the box on the first line. (You can request a smaller or larger sample, but 2% should work well in most cases.) Click **Continue,** and then

OK to draw the random sample. Then, use the **Simple Scatter** procedure once again, and the output will look similar to this:

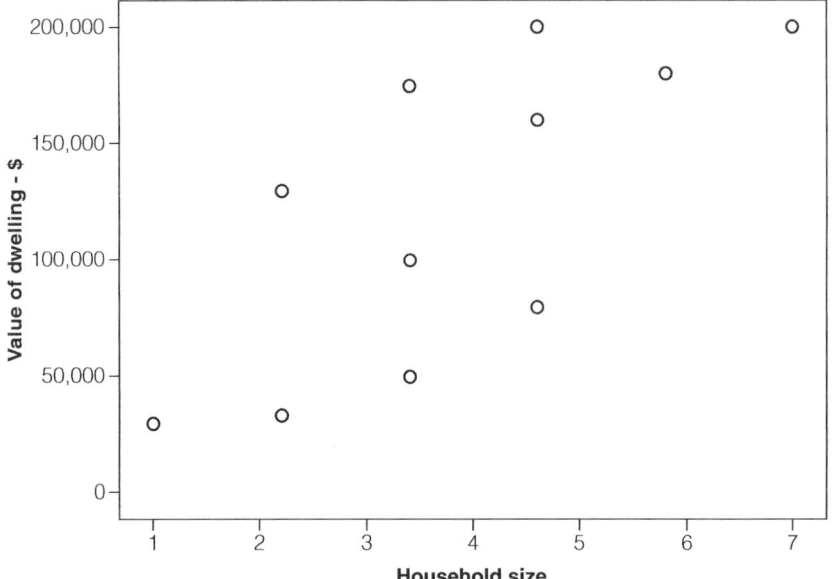

The nature of the relationship between the two variables is now exposed. The pattern of dots on the scattergram indicates a moderate, positive linear relationship between the value of the house and the number of people residing in a house. The scores of *Y* are also evenly spread at each value of *X*, indicating the relationship is homoscedastic.

If you carry out this demonstration, your output will be based on a different set of randomly selected cases, so your scattergram will look slightly different. You may wish to repeat the steps above several times to get a better sense of the nature of the relationship; each time you want to produce a new random sample and scatterplot, go back to the **Select Cases** dialog box and click the **OK** button.

SPSS DEMONSTRATION 15.2 Assessing the Effect of Household Size on the Value of a House with Linear Regression

After assessing the nature and verifying the linearity of the relationship with the scattergram, we can proceed to find the slope (*b*) and the *Y* intercept (*a*) of the least-squares regression line. In this demonstration, we will continue to examine the relationship between household size and house price. (Make sure that the random sample filter is turned off by clicking the **Reset** button and then OK in the **Select Cases** dialog box.) Click **Analyze, Regression,** and **Linear.** In the **Linear Regression** window, move *valuep* into the **Dependent** box and *unitsp* into the **Independent(s)** box. Click **OK,** and the following output will appear.

Model Summary

Model	R	r Square	Adjusted r Square	Std. Error of the Estimate
1	.250*	.062	.062	56065.669

*Predictors: (Constant), *unitsp*

ANOVA*

Model		Sum of Squares	df	Mean Square	F	Sig.
1	Regression	2.243E11	1	2.243E11	71.349	.000†
	Residual	3.370E12	1,072	3.143E9		
	Total	3.594E12	1,073			

*Dependent variable: *valuep*
†Predictors: (Constant), *unitsp*

Coefficients*

Model		Unstandardized Coefficients		Standardized Coefficients	t	Sig.
		B	Std. Error	Beta		
1	(Constant)	103921.607	4332.740		23.985	.000
	unitsp	10288.421	1218.022	.250	8.447	.000

*Dependent variable: *valuep*

The "Model Summary" block reports Pearson's *r* (.250) and *r* square (.062). The "ANOVA" output block shows the significance of the relationship (Sig. = .000). Recall that when the exact probability value is less than .0005, SPSS cuts it off at three decimal places, or .000, to save space. Because we have the exact probability, there is no need to look up the test statistic in a table. The exact probability value, .000, is well below the standard indicator of a significant result (alpha = .05), so we reject the null hypothesis and conclude that there is a statistically significant relationship between household size and house value. (See Demonstration 7.1 for an explanation about why some values in the output contain numbers with the letter "E".)

So far, we know that the independent variable explains 6.2% of the variance in *valuep* and that this result is statistically significant. In the last output block, we see the slope (*B*) is 10,288.421 and the *Y* intercept (labelled as Constant) is 103,921.607. A slope of 10,288.421 means that for every increase of one person in household size, the average price of a house increases by $10,288. Accordingly, the value of a two-person house is worth on average $10,288 more than a one-person house, the value of a three-person house is worth on average $10,288 more than a two-person house, and so on. The *Y* intercept tells us that the average value of a house is $103,922 when household size is zero. *Y* intercept has no meaningful interpretation because household size cannot be zero. Finally, we can use the least-squares regression line $Y = a + bX$, or $Y = (103,922) + (10,288)X$, to predict scores on *valuep* for any value of *unitsp.*

SPSS DEMONSTRATION 15.3 Producing the Correlation Matrix

Do sources of income change with level of education? It seems reasonable to assume that people with higher education are less reliant on the government and more reliant on the labour market for income. We can investigate these issues by examining the relationship between *totschp* (total years of schooling) and each income source: *tgovtp* (total government transfer payments) and *wagesp* (wages and salaries). By comparing the strength and direction of these bivariate correlations, we may be able to make some judgment about how income sources change with education. (Note that *totschp* is measured at the ordinal level, yet it is common for variables like *totschp,* which have a wide range of scores, to be treated as interval-ratio variables.)

To request Pearson's *r,* click **Analyze, Correlate,** and **Bivariate.** The **Bivariate Correlations** window appears with the variable list on the left. Find *totschp, tgovtp,* and *wagesp* in the list and click the arrow to move them into the **Variables** box. If you wish, you can get descriptive statistics for each variable by clicking the **Options** button and requesting means and standard deviations. Unless you request otherwise, the program will conduct two-tailed tests of significance on the correlations. Note that Spearman's rho (see Chapter 14) is also an option. Click **OK,** and your output will look like this:

Correlations

		TOTSCHP TOTAL YEARS OF SCHOOLING	TGOVTP TOTAL GOV TRANSFER PAYMENTS $	WAGESP WAGES AND SALARIES $
TOTSCHP TOTAL YEARS OF SCHOOLING	Pearson Correlation	1	-.324*	.312*
	Sig. (2-tailed)		.000	.000
	N	1500	1500	1500
TGOVTP TOTAL GOV TRANSFER PAYMENTS $	Pearson Correlation	-.324*	1	-.344*
	Sig. (2-tailed)	.000		.000
	N	1500	1500	1500
WAGESP WAGES AND SALARIES $	Pearson Correlation	.312*	-.344*	1
	Sig. (2-tailed)	.000	.000	
	N	1500	1500	1500

**Correlation is significant at the 0.01 level (2-tailed).

The output is in the form of a correlation matrix showing the relationships between all variables, including the correlation of a variable with itself. For each possible relationship, Pearson's *r* is reported in the top row, the results of the test of significance in the second row, and sample size in the third row.

The correlation matrix gives a quick, easy-to-read overview of the relationships between all possible pairs of variables. For our question, we need only the correlations in the first column (or row), excluding the correlation of *totschp* with itself. Overall, the relationships are statistically significant at the .05 level, and in the direction that we expected.

Let's start with the relationship between *totschp* and *tgovtp*. Its Pearson's *r* value (−.324) indicates a moderate, negative linear relationship. As education increases, government benefits decrease. Next, the *r* value for *totschp* and *wagesp* is .312, revealing a moderate, positive linear association. Better-educated persons tend to have more labour-market income than less-educated persons. So, these correlations seem to support the idea that Canadians become less reliant on public sources and more on private sources of income with increased education.

Exercises (using *Census.sav*)

15.1 Run the analyses in Demonstrations 15.1 and 15.2 again, but substitute *grosrtp* (price of rent) for *valuep*. Examine the relationship with the scatter-gram and least-squares regression line. Summarize the nature (linearity, strength, and direction) of the relationship. Does household size have an effect on *grosrtp* as it did with *valuep?* Write up your results.

15.2 Using Demonstration 15.3 as a guide, produce a correlation matrix showing the relationships between *agep* (age), *invstp* (investment income), and *retirp* (retirement pensions). Summarize the strength and direction of the relationships in a few sentences.

1. For each situation, compute and interpret the appropriate measure of association. Also, compute and interpret percentages for bivariate tables. Describe relationships in terms of the strength and pattern or direction.

a. For 10 Canadian cities data has been gathered on rates of property crime (theft, breaking and entering, fraud) per 100,000 population and the percentage of people who are new immigrants (arrived in Canada within the past five years). Are the variables related?

City	Property Crime Rate	Percent Immigrants
A	1,500	10
B	1,200	18
C	2,000	9
D	1,700	11
E	1,600	15
F	1,000	20
G	1,700	9
H	1,300	22
I	900	10
J	700	15

b. There is some evidence that people's involvement in their communities (membership in voluntary organizations, participation in local politics, and so forth) has been declining, and television has been cited as the cause. Do the data below support the idea that TV is responsible for the decline?

Hours of Community Service	Television Viewing			Totals
	Low	Moderate	High	
Low	5	10	18	33
Moderate	10	12	10	32
High	15	8	7	30
Totals	30	30	35	95

c. An international magazine has rated countries in terms of "quality of life" (a scale that includes health care, availability of leisure facilities, unemployment rate, and a number of other variables) and quality of the system of higher education. Both scales range from 1 (low) to 20 (high). Is there a correlation between these two variables for the 10 countries listed below?

Country	Quality of Life	Quality of Higher Education
A	10	10
B	12	13
C	15	18

(continued next page)

(*continued*)

Country	Quality of Life	Quality of Higher Education
D	18	20
E	10	15
F	9	11
G	11	12
H	8	6
I	13	9
J	6	8

d. The number of Canadian employees doing telework—scheduled work from home—has grown sharply over the last decade, with advancements in information technology and telecommunications. The table below shows the relationship between marital status and telework arrangement, if any, for a random sample of Canadian employees. Is there a relationship between these variables?

Do You Work from Home?	Marital Status			Totals
	Married/ Common-law	Separated/ Divorced/ Widowed	Single	
Yes, but not regularly	2	0	3	5
Yes, 1–2 days each week	8	4	0	12
Yes, 3 or more days each week	0	3	3	6
No	10	8	4	22
Totals	20	15	10	45

2. A number of research questions are stated below. Each can be answered by at least one of the techniques presented in Chapters 12 through 15. For each research situation, use the social survey data collected from 25 respondents shown below to compute the most appropriate measure of association and write a sentence or two of response to the question. The questions are presented in random order. In selecting a measure of association, you need to consider the number of possible values and the level of measurement of the variables.

a. Are scores on "number of sex partners over the past year" associated with education or age? Compute a measure of association, assuming that the variables are interval-ratio in level of measurement.

b. Is fear of walking alone at night associated with sex? Is it associated with marital status?

c. Is support for spanking associated with religious service attendance? Is it associated with marital status?

Survey Items:

1. Marital status of respondent:
   1. Married
   2. Not married (includes widowed, divorced, etc.)

2. How often do you attend religious service?
   0. Never
   1. Rarely
   2. Often
3. Age.
4. Respondent's years of education.
5. Sex:
   1. Male
   2. Female
6. It is sometimes necessary to discipline a child with a spanking:
   1. Support
   2. Oppose
7. Fear of walking alone at night:
   1. Yes
   2. No
8. Number of sex partners over the past year.

Case	Marital Status	Religious Service Attendance	Age	Education	Sex	Spanking	Fear	Number of Sex Partners
1	2	0	22	12	2	1	2	5
2	1	0	52	13	1	1	2	2
3	1	2	44	16	1	2	1	3
4	1	0	56	10	1	1	2	1
5	1	2	61	8	2	2	2	0
6	1	0	28	19	2	1	2	5
7	2	1	59	9	1	2	1	0
8	1	1	69	11	1	2	2	5
9	2	0	23	4	1	1	2	6
10	2	2	31	20	2	1	1	6
11	1	2	67	21	2	2	1	1
12	1	1	46	9	1	1	1	2
13	2	0	19	10	2	1	1	5
14	1	2	34	11	1	2	2	2
15	2	0	29	18	2	1	1	4
16	1	1	31	16	1	1	1	5
17	2	1	88	6	2	2	2	1
18	1	0	24	15	2	1	1	4
19	2	2	69	11	1	1	1	2
20	1	2	60	14	1	2	2	3
21	1	1	29	12	2	1	2	4
22	1	2	43	13	2	2	1	2
23	1	0	35	20	1	1	1	4
24	2	2	38	9	2	2	2	4
25	2	0	83	19	1	2	1	0

Part IV Multivariate Techniques

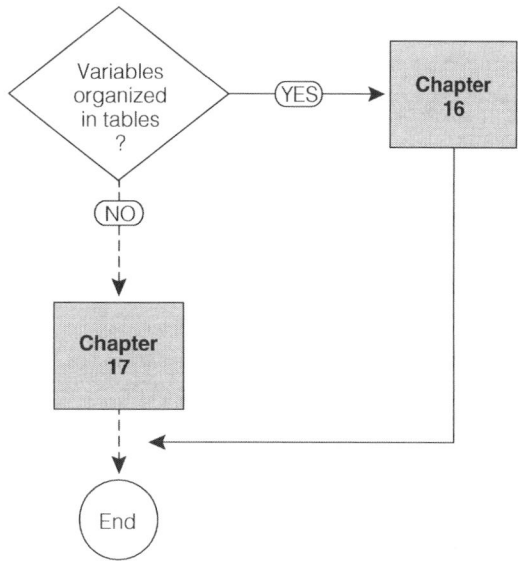

The two chapters in this section introduce multivariate analytical techniques or statistics that allow us to analyze the relationships among more than two variables at a time. These statistics are extremely useful for probing possible causal relationships between variables and are commonly reported in the professional literature. In particular, Chapter 17 introduces regression analysis, which is the basis for many of the most popular and powerful statistical techniques in use today.

Chapter 16 covers multivariate analysis for nominal- and ordinal-level variables that have been organized in table format. The chapter discusses the logic and procedures for analyzing the effect of third (or control) variables on the relationship between independent and dependent variables. The possible outcomes of controlling for a third variable are introduced and analyzed one at a time, and the discussion is summarized in Table 16.5.

Chapter 17 introduces partial and multiple correlation and regression for variables measured at the interval-ratio level of measurement. Partial correlation is analogous to controlling for a third variable with bivariate tables, as presented in Chapter 16. Several references are made to the concepts presented in the earlier chapter and to Table 16.5. However, it is not necessary to cover all of Chapter 16 in order to understand the process and logic of partial correlation. Furthermore, the section on partial correlation has been divided into clearly labelled subsections to distinguish the basic concepts of partial correlation from matters of computation.

Multiple regression and correlation are some of the most powerful and useful statistical techniques available to social science researchers. The mathematics underlying these statistics can become very complicated, and the chapter focuses on the simplest possible applications. Again, clearly labelled subsections divide the presentation of basic concepts and interpretation from computation.

16

ELABORATING
BIVARIATE TABLES

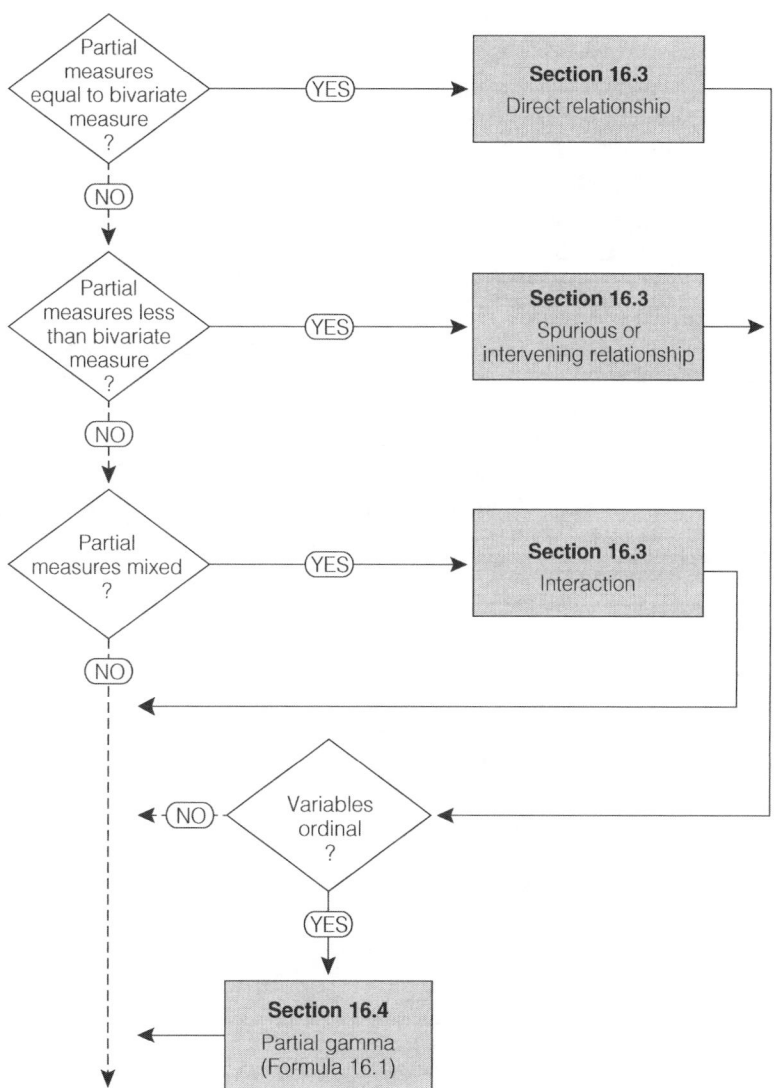

LEARNING OBJECTIVES   By the end of this chapter, you will be able to

1. Explain the purpose of multivariate analysis in terms of observing the effect of a control variable.

2. Construct and interpret partial tables.

3. Compute and interpret partial measures of association.
4. Recognize and interpret direct, spurious or intervening, and interactive relationships.
5. Compute and interpret partial gamma.
6. Cite and explain the limitations of elaborating bivariate tables.

16.1 INTRODUCTION

Few questions can be answered by a statistical analysis of only two variables, and therefore, the typical research project will include many variables. In Chapters 12 through 15, we saw how various statistical techniques can be applied to bivariate relationships. In this chapter and the next, we will see how some of these techniques can be extended to probe the relationships among three or more variables. This chapter will present some multivariate techniques appropriate for variables that have been measured at the nominal or ordinal level and organized into table format. Chapter 17 will present some techniques that can be used when the variables have been measured at the interval-ratio level.

Before considering the techniques themselves, we should consider why they are important and what they might be able to tell us. There are two general reasons for utilizing multivariate techniques. First, and most fundamental, is the goal of simply gathering additional information about a specific bivariate relationship by observing how that relationship is affected (if at all) by the presence of a third variable (or a fourth or a fifth variable). Multivariate techniques will increase the amount of information we have on the basic bivariate relationship and (we hope) enhance our understanding of that relationship.

A second and very much related rationale for multivariate statistics involves the issue of causation. While multivariate statistical techniques cannot prove the existence of causal connections between variables, they can provide valuable evidence in support of causal arguments and are very important tools for testing and revising theory.

16.2 CONTROLLING FOR A THIRD VARIABLE

For variables arrayed in tables, multivariate analysis proceeds by observing the effects of other variables on the bivariate relationship. That is, we observe the relationship between the independent (X) and dependent (Y) variables after a third variable (which we will call $\mathbf{Z}$) has been controlled. We do this by reconstructing the relationship between X and Y for each value or score of Z. If the control variable has an effect, the relationship between X and Y will change under the various conditions of Z.*

---

*For the sake of brevity, we will focus on the simplest application of multivariate statistical analysis, the case where the relationship between an independent (X) and dependent (Y) variable is analyzed in the presence of a single control variable (Z). Once the basic techniques are grasped, they can be readily expanded to situations involving more than one control variable.

TABLE 16.1   SATISFACTION WITH UNIVERSITY BY NUMBER OF MEMBERSHIPS
IN STUDENT ORGANIZATIONS

	Memberships (X)		
Satisfaction (Y)	None	At Least One	Totals
Low	57 (54.3%)	56 (33.9%)	113
High	48 (45.7%)	109 (66.1%)	157
Totals	105 (100%)	165 (100%)	270
	Gamma = 0.40		

To illustrate, suppose that a researcher wishes to analyze the relationship between how well an individual is integrated into a group or organization and that individual's level of satisfaction with the group. The researcher has decided to focus on students and their level of satisfaction with the university as a whole. The necessary information on satisfaction (Y) is gathered from a sample of 270 students, and all are asked to list the student clubs or organizations to which they belong. Integration (X) is measured by dividing the students into two categories: The first includes students who are not members of any organizations (non-members), and the second includes students who are members of at least one organization (members). The researcher suspects that membership and satisfaction are positively related and that students who are members of at least one organization will report higher levels of satisfaction than students who are non-members. The relationship between these two variables is displayed in Table 16.1.

Inspection of the table suggests that these two variables are associated. The conditional distributions of satisfaction (Y) change across the two conditions of membership (X), and membership in at least one organization is associated with high satisfaction, whereas non-membership is associated with low satisfaction. The existence and direction of the relationship are confirmed by the computation of a gamma of $+.40$ for this table.* In short, Table 16.1 strongly suggests the existence of a relationship between integration and morale, and these results can be taken as evidence for a causal or direct relationship between the two variables. The causal relationship is summarized symbolically in Figure 16.1, where the arrow represents the effect of X on Y.

FIGURE 16.1 A DIRECT RELATIONSHIP BETWEEN TWO VARIABLES

$X \longrightarrow Y$

The researcher recognizes, of course, that membership is not the sole factor associated with satisfaction (if it were, the gamma noted above would be $+1.00$). Other variables may alter this relationship, and the researcher

---

*We will not display the computation of gamma here. See Chapter 14 for a review of this measure of association.

will need to consider the effects of these third variables (Z's) in a systematic and logical way. By doing so, the researcher will accumulate further information and detail about the bivariate relationship and can further probe the possible causal connection between X and Y.

For example, perhaps levels of satisfaction are affected by the rewards received by students from the university. Perhaps the most significant reward the university can dispense is recognition of academic achievements (i.e., grades). Perhaps students who are more highly rewarded (have higher grade point averages) are more satisfied with the university and are also more likely to participate actively in the life of the campus by joining student organizations. How can the effects of this third variable on the bivariate relationship be investigated?

Consider Table 16.1 again. This table provides information about the distribution of 270 cases on two variables. By analyzing the table, we can see that 165 students hold at least one membership, that 48 students are both nonmembers and highly satisfied, that the majority of the students are highly satisfied, and so forth. What the bivariate table cannot show us, of course, is the distribution of these students on GPA. For all we know at this point, the 109 highly satisfied members could all have high GPAs, low GPAs, or any combination of scores on this third variable. GPA is "free to vary" in this table, because the distribution of the cases on this variable is not accounted for.

We control for the effect (if any) of third variables by fixing their distributions so that they are no longer free to vary. We do this by sorting all cases in the sample according to their score on the third variable (Z) and then observing the relationship between X and Y for each value (or score) of Z. In the example at hand, we will construct separate tables displaying the relationship between membership and satisfaction for each category of GPA. The tables so produced are called **partial tables** and are displayed in Table 16.2. The students have been classified as "high" or "low" on GPA, and there are exactly 135 students in each category. Within each category of GPA, students have been reclassified by membership (X) and satisfaction (Y) in order to produce the two partial tables.

This type of multivariate analysis is called **elaboration** because the partial tables present the original bivariate relationship in a more detailed or elaborate form. The cell frequencies in the partial tables are subdivisions of the cell frequencies reported in Table 16.1. For example, if the frequencies of the cells in the partial tables are added together, the original frequencies of Table 16.1 will be reproduced.*

---

*The total of the cell frequencies in the partial tables will always equal the corresponding cell frequencies in the bivariate table except when, as often happens in "real life" research situations, the researcher is missing scores on the third variable for some cases. These cases must be deleted from the analysis and, as a consequence, the partial tables will have fewer cases than the bivariate table.

TABLE 16.2 SATISFACTION BY MEMBERSHIP, CONTROLLING FOR GPA

A. High GPA

Satisfaction (*Y*)	Memberships (*X*)		Totals
	None	At Least One	
Low	29 (54.7%)	28 (34.1%)	57
High	24 (45.3%)	54 (65.9%)	78
Totals	53 (100%)	82 (100%)	135

Gamma = 0.40

B. Low GPA

Satisfaction (*Y*)	Memberships (*X*)		Totals
	None	At Least One	
Low	28 (53.8%)	28 (33.7%)	56
High	24 (46.2%)	55 (66.3%)	79
Totals	52 (100%)	83 (100%)	135

Gamma = 0.39

Also note how this method of controlling for other variables can be extended. In our example, the control variable (grades) had two categories and, thus, there were two partial tables, one for each value of the control variable. Had the control variable had more than two categories, we would have had more partial tables. By the same token, we can control for more than one variable at a time by sorting the cases on all scores of all control variables and producing partial tables for each combination of scores on the control variables. Thus, if we had controlled for both GPA and gender, we would have had four partial tables to consider. There would have been one partial table for males with low GPAs, a second for males with high GPAs, and two partial tables for females with high and low GPAs.

To summarize, for nominal and ordinal variables, multivariate analysis begins by constructing partial tables or tables that display the relationship between *X* and *Y* for each value of *Z*. The next step is to trace the effect of *Z* by comparing the partial tables with each other and with the original bivariate table. By analyzing the partial tables, we can observe the effects (if any) of the control variable on the original bivariate relationship.

16.3 INTERPRETING PARTIAL TABLES

The cell frequencies in the partial tables may follow a variety of forms, but we will concentrate on three basic patterns. The patterns, determined by comparing the partial tables with each other and with the original bivariate table, are

1. **Direct relationships:** The relationship between X and Y is the same in all partial tables and in the bivariate table.
2. **Spurious relationships** or **intervening relationships:** The relationship between X and Y is the same in all partial tables but much weaker than in the bivariate table.
3. **Interaction:** Each partial table and the bivariate table all show different relationships between X and Y.

Each pattern has different implications for the relationships among the variables and for the subsequent course of the statistical analysis. We will now describe each pattern in detail and then summarize our discussion in Table 16.5.

Direct Relationships. This pattern is often called **replication** because the partial tables reproduce (or replicate) the bivariate table; the pattern of cell frequencies is the same in the partial tables and the bivariate table. Measures of association calculated on the partial tables have the same value as the measure of association calculated for the bivariate table.

This outcome indicates that the control variable (Z) has no effect on the relationship between X and Y. Table 16.2 provides an example of this outcome. In this table, the relationship between membership (X) and satisfaction (Y) was investigated with GPA (Z) controlled. Table 16.2A shows the relationship for high-GPA students, and Table 16.2B shows the relationship for low-GPA students. The partial tables show the same conditional distributions of Y: For both high- and low-GPA students, about 45% of the non-members are highly satisfied, versus about 66% of the members. This same pattern was observed in the bivariate table (Table 16.1). Thus, the conditional distributions of Y are the same in each partial table as they were in the bivariate table.

The pattern of the cell frequencies will be easier to identify if you calculate measures of association. Working from the cell frequencies presented in Table 16.2, the gamma for high-GPA students is .40, and the gamma for low-GPA students is .39. The bivariate gamma (from Table 16.1) is .40, and the essential equivalence of these gammas reinforces our finding that the relationship between X and Y is the same in the partial tables and the bivariate table.

This pattern of outcomes indicates that the control variable has no important impact on the bivariate relationship (if it did, the pattern in the partial tables would be different from the bivariate table) and may be ignored in any further analysis. In terms of the original research problem, the researcher may conclude that students who are members are more likely to express high satisfaction with the university regardless of their GPA. The level of rewards dispensed to students by the institution (as measured by GPA) has no effect on the relationship between membership and satisfaction. Low-GPA students who are members of at least one organization are just as likely to report high satisfaction as high-GPA students who are

Application 16.1

Seventy-eight teenage males in a sample have been classified as high or low on a scale that measures involvement in delinquency. Also, each subject has been classified, using school records, as either a good or poor student. The following table displays a strong relationship between these two variables for this sample ($G = -0.69$).

Delin-quency	Academic Record		Totals
	Poor	Good	
Low	13 (27.1%)	20 (66.7%)	33 (42.3%)
High	35 (72.9%)	10 (33.3%)	45 (57.7%)
Totals	48 (100.0%)	30 (100.0%)	78 (100.0%)

Gamma = −0.69

Judging by the column percentages and the gamma, it is clear that teenage males with poor academic records are especially prone to delinquency. Is this relationship between delinquency and academic record affected by whether the subject resides in an urban or non-urban area?

Urban areas:

Delin-quency	Academic Record		Totals
	Poor	Good	
Low	10 (27.8%)	3 (30.0%)	13 (28.3%)
High	26 (72.2%)	7 (70.0%)	33 (71.7%)
Totals	36 (100.0%)	10 (100.0%)	46 (100.0%)

Gamma = −0.05

Non-urban areas:

Delin-quency	Academic Record		Totals
	Poor	Good	
Low	3 (25.0%)	17 (85.0%)	20 (62.5%)
High	9 (75.0%)	3 (15.0%)	12 (37.5%)
Totals	12 (100.0%)	20 (100.0%)	32 (100.0%)

Gamma = −0.89

For urban teenage males, the relationship between academic record and delinquency disappears. The gamma for this table is −0.05, and the column percentages are very similar. For this group, delinquency is not associated with experience in school.

For non-urban males, on the other hand, there is a very strong relationship between the two variables. Gamma is −.89, and there is a dramatic difference in the column percentages. Poor students living in non-urban areas are especially prone to delinquency.

Comparing the partial tables with each other and with the bivariate table reveals an interactive relationship. Although urban teenage males are more delinquent than non-urban males (71.7% of the urban males were highly delinquent, as compared to 37.5% of the non-urban males), their delinquency is not associated with academic record. For non-urban males, academic record is very strongly associated with delinquency. Urban males are more delinquent than non-urban males but not because of their experience in school. Non-urban males who are also poor students are especially likely to become involved in a misdeed.

members of at least one organization. *(For practice in dealing with direct relationships, see Problems 16.1 and 16.2.)*

Spurious or Intervening Relationships.   In this pattern, the relationship between X and Y is much weaker in the partial tables than in the bivariate table but the same across all partials. Measures of association for the partial tables are much lower in value (perhaps even dropping to 0.00) than the measure computed for the bivariate table. This outcome is consistent with two different causal relationships among the three variables. The first is called a spurious relationship or **explanation;** in this situation, Z is conceptualized as being antecedent to both X and Y (i.e., Z is thought to occur before the other two variables in time). In this pattern, Z is a common cause of both X and Y, and the original bivariate relationship is said to be spurious. The apparent bivariate relationship between X and Y is explained by or due to the effect of Z. Once Z is controlled, the association between X and Y disappears, and the value of the measures of association for the partial tables is dramatically lower than the measure of association for the bivariate table.

To illustrate, suppose that the researcher in our example had also controlled for year of study by dividing the sample into upper years (third-year and fourth-year students) and lower years (first-year and second-year students). The reasoning of the researcher might be that upper-year students, as a function of simple longevity, display higher levels of satisfaction with the university than do lower-year students. Self-selection processes may be operating, and dissatisfied students may have transferred to another university or dropped out before they attained upper-year standing. Students who have been on campus longer will be more likely to locate an organization of sufficient appeal or interest to join. This might especially be the case for organizations based on major field (such as the Criminology Club), which lower-year students are less likely to join, or organizations for which lower-year students are unlikely to qualify.

These thoughts about the possible relationships among these variables are expressed in diagram form in Figure 16.2. The absence of an arrow from membership (X) to satisfaction (Y) indicates that these variables are not truly associated with each other but rather are both caused by year of study (Z). If this causal diagram is a correct description of the relationship between these three variables (if the association between X and Y is spurious), then the association between membership and satisfaction should disappear once year of study has been controlled. That is, even though the bivariate gamma was .40 (Table 16.1), the gammas computed on the partial tables will approach 0. Table 16.3 displays the partial tables generated by controlling for year of study.

The partial tables indicate that, once year of study is controlled, membership is no longer related to satisfaction. Upper-year students are likely to express high satisfaction and lower-year students are likely to express low satisfaction regardless of their number of memberships. In the partial tables, the distributions of Y no longer vary by the conditions of X, and the gammas computed on the partial tables are virtually 0. These results indicate that the bivariate association is spurious and that X and Y have no direct relationship. Year of study (Z) is a key factor in accounting for varying levels of satisfaction, and the analysis must be reoriented with year of study as an independent variable.

This outcome (partial measures much weaker than the original measure but equal to each other) is consistent with another conception of the causal links among the variables. In addition to a causal scheme wherein Z is

FIGURE 16.2 A SPURIOUS RELATIONSHIP

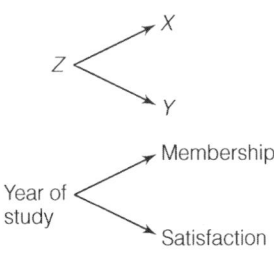

TABLE 16.3   SATISFACTION BY MEMBERSHIP, CONTROLLING FOR YEAR OF STUDY

A. Upper-year Students

| Satisfaction (Y) | Memberships (X) | | Totals |
	None	At Least One	
Low	8 (25.0%)	32 (24.8%)	40
High	24 (75.0%)	97 (75.2%)	121
Totals	32 (100%)	129 (100%)	161

Gamma = 0.01

B. Lower-year Students

| Satisfaction (Y) | Memberships (X) | | Totals |
	None	At Least One	
Low	49 (67.1%)	24 (66.7%)	73
High	24 (32.9%)	12 (33.3%)	36
Totals	73 (100%)	36 (100%)	109

Gamma = 0.01

FIGURE 16.3   AN INTERVENING RELATIONSHIP

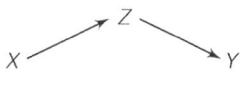

antecedent to both X and Y, Z may also intervene between the two variables. This pattern is also called **interpretation** and is illustrated in Figure 16.3, where X is causally linked to Z, which is in turn linked to Y. This pattern indicates that, although X and Y are related, they are associated primarily through the control variable Z. This pattern of outcomes does not allow the researcher to distinguish between spurious relationships (Figure 16.2) and intervening relationships (Figure 16.3). The differentiation between these two types of causal patterns may be made on temporal or theoretical grounds, but not on statistical grounds. *(For practice in dealing with spurious or intervening relationships, see problem 16.6.)*

Interaction.   In this pattern, also called **specification,** the relationship between X and Y changes markedly for the different values of the control variable. The partial tables differ from each other and from the bivariate table. Interaction can be manifested in various ways in the partial tables. One possible pattern, for example, is for one partial table to display a stronger relationship between X and Y than that displayed in the bivariate table, while the relationship between X and Y drops to 0 in a second partial table. Symbolically, this

FIGURE 16.4   AN INTERACTIVE RELATIONSHIP

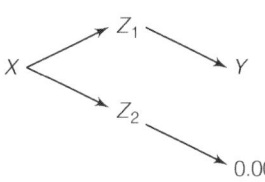

outcome could be represented as in Figure 16.4, which would indicate that X and the first category of Z (Z_1) have strong effects on Y but, for the second category of Z (Z_2), there is no association between X and Y.

Interaction might be found, for example, in a situation in which *all* employees of a corporation were required to attend a program (X) designed to reduce ageism (prejudice, discrimination, and stereotyping against older people in the workplace) (Y). Such a program would be likely to have stronger effects on younger employees (Z_1) than older employees (Z_2). That is, the program would have an effect on prejudice only for certain categories of subjects. The partial tables for younger employees (Z_1) might show a strong relationship between program attendance and reduction in prejudice, whereas the partial tables for older employees showed no relationship. Older employees, being unprejudiced against themselves in the first place, would be less affected by the program.

Interaction can take other forms. For example, the relationship between X and Y can vary not only in strength but also in direction between the partial tables. This causal relationship is symbolically represented in Figure 16.5, which indicates a situation where X and Y are positively related for the first category of Z (Z_1) and negatively related for the second category of Z (Z_2).

The researcher investigating the relationship between club membership and satisfaction with university life establishes a final control for sex and divides the sample into male and female students. The partial tables are displayed in Table 16.4 and show an interactive relationship. The relationship between membership and satisfaction is different for male students (Z_1) and for female students (Z_2), and each partial table is different from the bivariate table. For male students, the relationship is positive and stronger than in the bivariate table. Male students who are also members are much more likely to express high overall satisfaction with the university, as indicated by both the percentage distribution (83% of the male students who are members are highly satisfied) and the measure of association (gamma = +.67 for male students).

For female students, the relationship between membership and satisfaction is very different—nearly the reverse of the pattern shown by male students. The

FIGURE 16.5 AN INTERACTIVE RELATIONSHIP

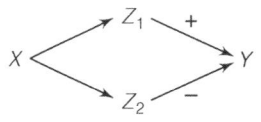

TABLE 16.4 SATISFACTION BY MEMBERSHIP, CONTROLLING FOR SEX

A. Male Students

Satisfaction (Y)	Memberships (X) None	At Least One	Totals
Low	40 (50.0%)	20 (16.7%)	60
High	40 (50.0%)	100 (83.3%)	140
Totals	80 (100%)	120 (100%)	200
	Gamma = 0.67		

B. Female Students

Satisfaction (Y)	Memberships (X) None	At Least One	Totals
Low	17 (68.0%)	36 (80.0%)	53
High	8 (32.0%)	9 (20.0%)	17
Totals	25 (100%)	45 (100%)	70
	Gamma = −0.31		

great majority (80%) of the female students who are members report low satisfaction, and the gamma for this partial table is negative ($-.31$). Thus, for male students, satisfaction increases with membership, whereas, for female students, satisfaction decreases with membership. Based on these results, one might conclude that the social meanings and implications of joining student clubs and organizations vary by sex and that the function of joining has different effects for female students. It may be, for example, that female students join different kinds of organizations than do male students. If the female students belonged primarily to a female student association that had an antagonistic relationship with the university, then belonging to such an organization could increase dissatisfaction with the university as it increased awareness of sexism on campus. *(For practice in dealing with interaction, see problem 16.4.)*

In closing this section, let us stress that, for the sake of clarity, the examples presented here have been unusually "clean." In any given research project, the results of controlling for third variables will probably be considerably more ambiguous and open to varying interpretation (as an example, see Section 16.7). In the case of spurious relationships, for example, the measures of association computed for the partial tables will probably not actually drop to zero, even though they may be dramatically lower than the bivariate measure. (The pattern where the partial measures are roughly equivalent and much lower than the bivariate measure, but not zero, is sometimes called attenuation.) It is probably best to consider the examples above as ideal types against which any given empirical result can be compared.

Table 16.5 summarizes this discussion by outlining guidelines for decision making for each of the three outcomes discussed in this section. Because your own results will probably be more ambiguous than the ideal types presented here, you should regard this table as a set of suggestions and not as a substitute for your own creativity and sensitivity to the problem under consideration.

TABLE 16.5   A SUMMARY OF THE POSSIBLE RESULTS OF CONTROLLING FOR THIRD VARIABLES

Partial Tables (compared with bivariate table) Show	Pattern	Implications for Further Analysis	Likely Next Step in Statistical Analysis	Theoretical Implications
Same relationship between X and Y	Direct relationship, replication	Disregard Z	Analyze another control variable	Theory that X causes Y is supported
Weaker relationship between X and Y	Spurious relationship	Incorporate Z	Focus on relationship between Z and Y	Theory that X causes Y is not supported
	Intervening relationship	Incorporate Z	Focus on relationships between X, Y, and Z	Theory that X causes Y is partially supported but must be revised to take Z into account
Mixed	Interaction	Incorporate Z	Analyze subgroups (categories of Z) separately	Theory that X causes Y is partially supported but must be revised to take Z into account

16.4 PARTIAL GAMMA (G_p)

When the results of controlling for a third variable indicate a direct, spurious, or intervening relationship, it is often useful to compute an additional measure that indicates the overall strength of the association between X and Y after the effects of the control variable (Z) have been removed. This statistic, called **partial gamma (G_p),** is somewhat easier to compare with the bivariate gamma than are the gammas computed on the partial tables separately. G_p is computed across all partial tables by Formula 16.1:

FORMULA 16.1

$$G_p = \frac{\Sigma N_s - \Sigma N_d}{\Sigma N_s + \Sigma N_d}$$

where N_s = the number of pairs of cases ranked the same across all partial tables
N_d = the number of pairs of cases ranked differently across all partial tables

In words, ΣN_s is the total of all N_s's from the partial tables, and ΣN_d is the total of all N_d's from all partial tables. (See Chapter 14 to review the computation of N_s and N_d.)

To illustrate the computation of G_p, let us return to Table 16.2, which showed the relationship between satisfaction and membership while controlling for GPA. The gammas computed on the partial tables were essentially equal to each other and to the bivariate gamma. Our conclusion was that the control variable had no effect on the relationship, and this conclusion can be confirmed by also computing partial gamma.

From Table 16.2A High GPA	From Table 16.2B Low GPA
$N_s = (29)(54) = 1{,}566$	$N_s = (28)(55) = 1{,}540$
$N_d = (28)(24) = \quad 672$	$N_d = (28)(24) = \quad 672$

$$\Sigma N_s = 1{,}566 + 1{,}540 = 3{,}106$$
$$\Sigma N_d = 672 + 672 = 1{,}344$$

$$G_p = \frac{\Sigma N_s - \Sigma N_d}{\Sigma N_s + \Sigma N_d}$$

$$G_p = \frac{3{,}106 - 1{,}344}{3{,}106 + 1{,}344}$$

$$G_p = \frac{1{,}762}{4{,}450}$$

$$G_p = 0.40$$

The partial gamma measures the strength of the association between X and Y once the effects of Z have been removed. In this instance, the partial gamma is the same value as the bivariate gamma ($G_p = G = 0.40$) and indicates that GPA has no effect on the relationship between satisfaction and membership.

When year of study was controlled (Table 16.3), clear evidence of a spurious relationship was found, because the gammas computed on the partial tables dropped almost to zero. Let us see what the value of partial gamma (G_p) would be for this second control:

From Table 16.3A Upper-year Students	From Table 16.3B Lower-year Students
$N_s = (8)(97) = 776$	$N_s = (49)(12) = 588$
$N_d = (32)(24) = 768$	$N_d = (24)(24) = 576$

$$\Sigma N_s = 776 + 588 = 1{,}364$$
$$\Sigma N_d = 768 + 576 = 1{,}344$$

$$G_p = \frac{\Sigma N_s - \Sigma N_d}{\Sigma N_s + \Sigma N_d}$$

$$G_p = \frac{1{,}364 - 1{,}344}{1{,}364 + 1{,}344}$$

$$G_p = \frac{20}{2{,}708}$$

$$G_p = 0.01$$

Once the effects of the control variable are removed, there is no relationship between X and Y. The very low value of G_p confirms our previous conclusion that the bivariate relationship between membership and satisfaction is spurious and actually due to the effects of year of study.

In a sense, G_p tells us no more about the relationships than we can see for ourselves from a careful analysis of the percentage distributions of Y in the partial tables or by a comparison of the measures of association computed on the partial tables. The advantage of G_p is that it tells us, in a single number (that is, in a compact and convenient way), the precise effects of Z on the relationship between X and Y. While G_p is no substitute for the analysis of the partial tables per se, it is a convenient way of stating our results and conclusions when working with direct or spurious relationships.

Although G_p can be calculated in cases of interactive relationships (see Table 16.4), it is rather difficult to interpret in these instances. If substantial interaction is found in the partial tables, this indicates that the control variable has a profound effect on the bivariate relationship. Thus, we should not attempt to separate the effects of Z from the bivariate relationship and, because G_p involves exactly this kind of separation, it should not be computed.

16.5 WHERE DO CONTROL VARIABLES COME FROM?

In one sense, this question is quite easy to answer. Although control variables can arise from various sources, they arise especially from theory. Social research proceeds in many different ways and is begun in response to a variety of problems. However, virtually all research projects are guided by a more-or-less-explicit theory or by some question about the relationship between two or more variables. The ultimate goal of social research is to develop defensible generalizations that improve our understanding of the variables under consideration and link back to theory at some level.

Thus, research projects are anchored in theory, and the concepts of interest, which will later be operationalized as variables, are first identified and their interrelationships first probed at the theoretical level. Because the social world is exceedingly complex, very few theories attempt to encompass that world in only two variables. Theories are, almost by definition, multivariate even when they focus on a bivariate relationship. Thus, to the extent that a research project is anchored in theory, the theory itself will suggest the control variables that need to be incorporated into the analysis. In the example used throughout this chapter, we tried to suggest that any researcher attempting to probe the relationship between involvement in an organization and satisfaction would, in the course of thinking over the possibilities, identify a number of additional variables that needed to be explicitly incorporated into the analysis.

Of course, textbook descriptions of the research process are oversimplified and tend to imply that research flows smoothly from conceptualization to operationalization to quantification to generalization. In reality, research is full of surprises, unexpected outcomes, and unanticipated results. Research in "real life" is more loosely structured and requires more imagination and creativity than textbooks can fully convey. Our point is that the control variables that might be appropriate to incorporate in the data-analysis phase will be suggested or implied in the theoretical backdrop of the research project. They will flow from the researcher's imagination and sensitivity to the problem being addressed as much as from any other source.

These considerations have taken us well beyond the narrow realm of statistics and back to the planning stages of the research project. At this early time the researcher must make decisions about which variables to measure during the data-gathering phase and, thus, which variables might be incorporated as potential controls. Careful thinking and an extended consideration of possible outcomes at the planning stage will pay significant dividends during the data-analysis phase. Ideally, all relevant control variables will be incorporated and readily available for statistical analysis.

Thus, control variables come from the theory underlying the research project and from creative and imaginative thinking and planning during the early phases of the project. Nonetheless, it is not unheard of for a researcher to realize during data analysis that the control variable now so obviously relevant was never measured during data gathering and is thus unavailable for statistical analysis.

16.6 THE LIMITATIONS OF ELABORATING BIVARIATE TABLES

The basic limitation of this technique involves sample size. Elaboration is a relatively inefficient technique for multivariate analysis because it requires that the researcher divide the sample into a series of partial tables. If the control variable has more than two or three possible values, or if we attempt to control for more than one variable at a time, many partial tables will be produced. The greater the number of partial tables, the more likely we are to run out of cases to fill all of the cells. Empty or small cells, in turn, can create serious problems in terms of generalizability and confidence in our findings.

To illustrate, the example used throughout this chapter began with two dichotomized variables and a four-cell table (Table 16.1). Each of the control variables was also dichotomized, and we never confronted more than two partial tables with four cells each, or eight cells for each control variable. If we had used a control variable with three values, we would have had 12 cells to fill up, and if we had attempted to control for two dichotomized variables, we would have had 16 cells in four different partial tables. Clearly, as control variables become more elaborate and/or as the process of controlling becomes more complex, the phenomenon of empty or small cells will increasingly become a problem.

Two potential solutions to this dilemma immediately suggest themselves. The easy solution is to reduce the number of cells in the partial tables by collapsing categories within variables. If all variables are dichotomized, for example, the number of cells will be kept to a minimum. The best solution is to work with only very large samples so that there will be plenty of cases to fill up the cells. Unfortunately, the easy solution will often violate common sense (collapsed categories are more likely to group dissimilar elements together), and the best solution is not always feasible (mundane matters of time and money rear their ugly heads).

A third solution to the problem of empty cells requires the (sometimes risky) assumption that the variables of interest are measured at the interval-ratio level. At that level the techniques of partial and multiple correlation and regression, to be introduced in Chapter 17, are available. These multivariate techniques are more efficient than elaboration because they utilize all cases simultaneously and do not require that the sample be divided among the various partial tables.

16.7 INTERPRETING STATISTICS: ANALYZING VOLUNTEERISM

In Chapter 14, we analyzed the sources of volunteerism using data from the Canada Survey of Giving, Volunteering and Participating. In this section, we will analyze how the bivariate relationship behaves after controlling for a third variable. As you recall from Chapter 14, volunteerism was measured with a composite variable that ranked people as high, moderate, or low in their number of volunteer activities through charitable and non-profit organizations. We analyzed the relationship between this variable and three different independent variables: health status, education, and religiosity. To keep the number of tables manageable, we will now concentrate on the bivariate relationship between religiosity and volunteerism while controlling for country of birth and age. The bivariate relationship is reproduced here as Table 16.6. Because both variables are ordinal in level of measurement, we will focus on gamma as our measure of the strength and direction of the relationship.

TABLE 16.6 VOLUNTEERISM BY RELIGIOUS SERVICE ATTENDANCE*

| | Religious Service Attendance | | | |
Volunteerism	Never	Yearly or Monthly	Daily or Weekly	Totals
Low	2,097 (47.1%)	1,539 (38.0%)	1,822 (25.5%)	5,458 (34.9%)
Moderate	1,198 (26.9%)	1,117 (27.6%)	1,951 (27.3%)	4,266 (27.2%)
High	1,159 (26.0%)	1,396 (34.5%)	3,380 (47.3%)	5,935 (37.9%)
Totals	4,454 (100.0%)	4,052 (100.1%)	7,153 (100.1%)	15,659 (100.0%)
		Gamma = 0.29		

*Percentages may not total to 100% because of rounding error.
Source: Statistics Canada, 2004 Canada Survey of Giving, Volunteering and Participating, PUMF.

The original theory investigated in Chapter 14 was that religiosity increases volunteerism. The gamma of 0.29 indicates a weak to moderate, positive association between the variables. There is a relationship between the variables, and the relationship is in the direction predicted by the theory. Also, the pattern of column percentages is largely what would be expected if the theory is true (e.g., people who attend religious service more frequently are more involved in volunteer activities). This pattern is consistent with the idea that religiosity leads to higher levels of volunteerism.

Will this relationship retain its strength and direction after controlling for other variables? Table 16.7 presents the partial tables and gammas after controlling for country of birth (Canadian-born versus foreign-born), and Table 16.8 does the same for age (under the age of 35 years and age 35 years and over) as a control variable. We will analyze the partial tables separately and then come to some conclusions about the original bivariate relationship.

Religious service attendance has a stronger relationship with volunteer activity for Canadian-born respondents than for foreign-born respondents. For respondents born outside Canada (Part A of Table 16.7), the relationship is still positive but weaker ($G = 0.22$) than the bivariate relationship ($G = 0.29$). For respondents born inside Canada (Part B of Table 16.7), the relationship is also positive but stronger ($G = 0.31$) than the bivariate relationship. Using Table 16.5 as a guide, we see that these partial tables, compared to the bivariate table, show a "mixed" pattern, so there is an interactive relationship between these three variables.

To know more about this pattern, scan the bottom row of the table ("high") for Canadian-born persons, and you will see that those who never or moderately attend religious service are much less engaged in volunteer activities than high attendees. The maximum difference (see Chapter 12) for that row is between the Canadian-born who are non-attendees and the Canadian-born who are high on religious service attendance (49.0% − 26.0% = 23.0%). The maximum difference in the same row for the foreign-born is

TABLE 16.7   VOLUNTEERISM BY RELIGIOUS SERVICE ATTENDANCE, CONTROLLING FOR COUNTRY OF BIRTH*

A. Foreign-born

| Volunteerism | Religious Service Attendance | | | Totals |
	Never	Yearly or Monthly	Daily or Weekly	
Low	261 (51.0%)	183 (42.1%)	370 (32.1%)	814 (38.8%)
Moderate	115 (22.5%)	127 (29.2%)	339 (29.5%)	581 (27.7%)
High	136 (26.6%)	125 (28.7%)	442 (38.4%)	703 (33.5%)
Total	512 (100.1%)	435 (100.0%)	1,151 (100.0%)	2,098 (100.0%)

Gamma = 0.22

B. Canadian-born

| Volunteerism | Religious Service Attendance | | | Totals |
	Never	Yearly or Monthly	Daily or Weekly	
Low	1,831 (46.5%)	1,349 (37.4%)	1,445 (24.2%)	4,625 (34.2%)
Moderate	1,081 (27.5%)	990 (27.4%)	1,606 (26.8%)	3,677 (27.2%)
High	1,023 (26.0%)	1,270 (35.2%)	2,931 (49.0%)	5,224 (38.6%)
Totals	3,935 (100.0%)	3,609 (100.0%)	5,982 (100.0%)	13,526 (100.0%)

Gamma = 0.31

*Percentages may not total to 100% because of rounding error.
Source: Statistics Canada, 2004 Canada Survey of Giving, Volunteering and Participating, PUMF.

38.4% − 26.6% = 11.8% (between high and non-attendees), a lower value than for those born inside of Canada. These patterns reinforce the idea that religiosity makes a bigger difference (is more closely related to volunteerism) for the Canadian-born group.

What can we conclude? As is often the case in social science research, the evidence is somewhat ambiguous and open to varying interpretations. There is some interaction in these relationships, as the gammas show a weaker relationship for the foreign-born and a slightly stronger relationship for the Canadian-born. On the other hand, the results do not precisely match the pattern we would expect in an interactive relationship between three variables as described in Figure 16.4 and Figure 16.5. It may be alternatively concluded that the gammas for the partial tables are fairly close in value to the bivariate gamma, which would indicate a direct relationship between religious service attendance and volunteerism.

Considering all the evidence, we could argue that the original theory (i.e., religiosity increases volunteerism) is, at least, partially supported. The differences between the three gammas are relatively small, indicating that the interaction is mild, and the percentage patterns are consistent with the theory.

TABLE 16.8   VOLUNTEERISM BY RELIGIOUS SERVICE ATTENDANCE, CONTROLLING FOR AGE*

A. Under age 35

Volunteerism	Religious Service Attendance			Totals
	Never	Yearly or Monthly	Daily or Weekly	
Low	514 (43.3%)	461 (35.8%)	347 (21.9%)	1,322 (32.6%)
Moderate	345 (29.0%)	380 (29.5%)	450 (28.5%)	1,175 (29.0%)
High	329 (27.7%)	445 (34.6%)	784 (49.6%)	1,558 (38.4%)
Totals	1,188 (100.0%)	1,286 (99.9%)	1,581 (100.0%)	4,055 (100.0%)
		Gamma = 0.29		

B. Age 35 and over

Volunteerism	Religious Service Attendance			Totals
	Never	Yearly or Monthly	Daily or Weekly	
Low	1,583 (48.5%)	1,078 (39.0%)	1,475 (26.5%)	4,136 (35.6%)
Moderate	853 (26.1%)	737 (26.6%)	1,501 (26.9%)	3,091 (26.6%)
High	830 (25.4%)	951 (34.4%)	2,596 (46.6%)	4,377 (37.7%)
Totals	3,266 (100.0%)	2,766 (100.0%)	5,572 (100.0%)	11,604 (99.9%)
		Gamma = 0.30		

*Percentages may not total to 100% because of rounding error.
Source: Statistics Canada, 2004 Canada Survey of Giving, Volunteering and Participating, PUMF.

Table 16.8 presents the results of controlling for age. The relationship for younger respondents (under the age of 35) is almost exactly the same as the relationship in the bivariate table both in terms of the pattern of column percentages and in terms of gamma. For older respondents (35 years of age and older), the overall relationship is roughly the same ($G = 0.30$) as in the bivariate table as are the column percentages.

We can conclude that this is a direct relationship: The gammas for the partial tables are about the same as the bivariate gamma, and age does not have much effect on the relationship between volunteerism and religiosity. As an additional step in the analysis, we can compute G_p for Table 16.8. We will not show the calculations here but simply report that $G_p = 0.29$, the same value as the bivariate gamma.

In conclusion, we can say that the results of controlling for country of birth and age generally support the original theory, although we found some ambiguity when controlling for country of birth. Our likely next step would be to analyze the effect of additional control variables (e.g., sex and education) to improve our knowledge about the bivariate relationship and more evidence for (or against) the idea that religiosity and volunteerism are causally related.

SUMMARY

1. Most research questions require the analysis of the interrelationship among many variables, even when the researcher is primarily concerned with a specific bivariate relationship. Multivariate statistical techniques provide the researcher with a set of tools by which additional information can be gathered about the variables of interest and by which causal interrelationships can be probed.

2. When variables have been organized in bivariate tables, multivariate analysis proceeds by controlling for a third variable. Partial tables are constructed and compared with each other and with the original bivariate table. Comparisons are made easier if appropriate measures of association are computed for all tables.

3. A direct relationship exists between the independent (X) and dependent (Y) variables if, after controlling for the third variable (Z), the relationship between X and Y is the same across all partial tables and the same as in the bivariate table. This pattern suggests a causal relationship between X and Y.

4. If the relationship between X and Y is the same across all partial tables but much weaker than in the bivariate table, the relationship is either spurious (Z causes both X and Y) or intervening (X causes Z, which causes Y). Either pattern suggests that Z must be explicitly incorporated into the analysis.

5. Interaction exists if the relationship between X and Y varies across the partial tables and between each partial and the bivariate table. This pattern suggests that no simple or direct causal relationship exists between X and Y and that Z must be explicitly incorporated into the causal scheme.

6. Partial gamma (G_p) is a useful summary statistic that measures the strength of the association between X and Y after the effects of the control variable (Z) have been removed. Partial gamma should not be computed when an analysis of the partial tables shows substantial interaction.

7. Potential control variables must be identified before the data-gathering phase of the research project. The theoretical backdrop of the research project, along with creative thinking and some imagination, will suggest the variables that should be controlled for and measured.

8. Controlling for third variables by constructing partial tables is inefficient in that the cases must be spread out across many cells. If the variables have many categories and/or the researcher attempts to control for more than one variable simultaneously, "empty cells" may become a problem. It may be possible to deal with this problem by either collapsing categories or gathering very large samples. If interval-ratio level of measurement can be assumed, the multivariate techniques presented in the next chapter will be preferred, because they do not require the partitioning of the sample.

SUMMARY OF FORMULAS

Partial gamma	16.1	$G_p = \dfrac{\sum N_s - \sum N_d}{\sum N_s + \sum N_d}$

GLOSSARY

Direct relationship. A multivariate relationship in which the control variable has no effect on the bivariate relationship.

Elaboration. The basic multivariate technique for analyzing variables arrayed in tables. Partial tables are constructed to observe the bivariate relationship in a more detailed or elaborate format.

Explanation. See **spurious relationship.**

Interaction. A multivariate relationship wherein a bivariate relationship changes across the categories of the control variable.

Interpretation. See **intervening relationship.**

Intervening relationship. A multivariate relationship wherein a bivariate relationship becomes substantially weaker after a third variable is controlled for. The independent and dependent variables are linked primarily through the control variable.

Partial gamma (G_p). A statistic that indicates the strength of the association between two variables after the effects of a third variable have been removed.

Partial tables. Tables produced when controlling for a third variable.

Replication. See **direct relationship.**

Specification. See **interaction.**

Spurious relationship. A multivariate relationship in which a bivariate relationship becomes substantially weaker after a third variable is controlled for. The independent and dependent variables are not causally linked. Rather, both are caused by the control variable.

Z. Symbol for any control variable.

MULTIMEDIA RESOURCES

 http://www.healeystatistics.nelson.com

Visit the companion Web site for the first Canadian edition of *Statistics: A Tool for Social Research* to access a wide range of student resources. Begin by clicking on the Student Resources section of the book's Web site to access review quizzes, flash cards, and other study tools.

PROBLEMS

16.1 SOC Problem 14.1 examined the adjustment of a small sample of immigrants. One table showed the relationship between length of residence in Canada and facility with the English or French language (where Gamma = 0.71), as follows

Length of Residence

English/ French Facility	Less than Five Years (Low)	More than Five Years (High)	Totals
Low	20	10	30
High	5	15	20
Totals	25	25	50

a. Is the relationship between residence and language affected by the sex of the immigrant? Partial tables showing the bivariate relationship for males and females are provided below. To answer the question, compute and then compare the column percentages and gamma of the partial tables with each other and with the bivariate table.

A. Males:

Length of Residence

English/ French Facility	Less than Five Years (Low)	More than Five Years (High)	Totals
Low	10	5	15
High	2	8	10
Totals	12	13	25

B. Females:

Length of Residence

English/ French Facility	Less than Five Years (Low)	More than Five Years (High)	Totals
Low	10	5	15
High	3	7	10
Totals	13	12	25

b. Is the relationship between residence and language affected by the "age at which a person immigrated" to Canada? Partial tables showing the bivariate relationship for those that immigrated before the age of 45 and those that immigrated at 45 years of age or older are provided below. To answer the question compute and then compare the column percentages and gamma of the partial tables with each other and with the bivariate table.

A. Immigrated before age 45:

| | Length of Residence | | |
English/ French Facility	Less than Five Years (Low)	More than Five Years (High)	Totals
Low	8	4	12
High	2	5	7
Totals	10	9	19

B. Immigrated at age 45+:

| | Length of Residence | | |
English/ French Facility	Less than Five Years (Low)	More than Five Years (High)	Totals
Low	12	6	18
High	3	10	13
Totals	15	16	31

16.2 SOC Data on suicide rates, age structure, and unemployment rates have been gathered for 100 cities. Suicide and unemployment rates have been dichotomized at the median so that each city could be rated as high or low. Age structure is measured in terms of the percentage of the population age 65 and older. This variable has also been dichotomized, and cities have been rated as high or low. The tables below display the bivariate relationship between suicide rate and age structure and the same relationship controlling for unemployment.

Suicide Rate	Population 65 and Older (%)		
	Low	High	Totals
Low	45	20	65
High	10	25	35
Totals	55	45	100

a. Calculate percentages and gamma for the bivariate table. Describe the bivariate relationship in terms of strength and direction.

Suicide rate by age, controlling for unemployment:

A. High unemployment:

Suicide Rate	Population 65 and Older (%)		
	Low	High	Totals
Low	23	10	33
High	5	12	17
Totals	28	22	50

B. Low unemployment:

Suicide Rate	Population 65 and Older (%)		
	Low	High	Totals
Low	22	10	32
High	5	13	18
Totals	27	23	50

b. Calculate percentages and gamma for each partial table. Compare the partial tables with each other and with the bivariate table. Compute partial gamma (G_p). Summarize the results of the control. Does unemployment rate have any effect on the relationship between age and suicide rate? Describe the effect of the control variable in terms of the pattern of percentages, the value of the gammas, and the possible causal relationships among these variables.

16.3 SW Do long-term patients in mental health facilities become more withdrawn and reclusive over time? A sample of 608 institutionalized patients was rated by a standard "reality orientation scale." Is there a relationship with length of institutionalization? Does sex have any effect on the relationship?

Reality orientation by length of institutionalization:

Reality Orientation	Length of Institutionalization		Totals
	Less than 5 Years	More than 5 Years	
Low	200	213	413
High	117	78	195
Totals	317	291	608

Reality orientation by length of institutionalization, controlling for sex:

A. Females:

Reality Orientation	Length of Institutionalization		Totals
	Less than 5 Years	More than 5 Years	
Low	95	120	215
High	60	37	97
Totals	155	157	312

B. Males:

Reality Orientation	Length of Institutionalization		Totals
	Less than 5 Years	More than 5 Years	
Low	105	93	198
High	57	41	98
Totals	162	134	296

16.4 SOC Is there a relationship between attitudes on sexuality and age? Are older people more conservative with respect to questions of sexual morality? A national sample of 925 respondents has been questioned about attitudes on premarital sex. Responses have been collapsed into two categories: those who believe that premarital sex is "always wrong" and those who believe it is not wrong under certain conditions ("sometimes wrong").

These responses have been cross-tabulated by age, and the results are reported below:

Attitude toward premarital sex by age:

Premarital Sex Is	Age		Totals
	Younger than 35	35 or Older	
Always wrong	90	235	325
Sometimes wrong	420	180	600
Totals	510	415	925

a. Calculate percentages and gamma for the table. Is there a relationship between these two variables? Describe the bivariate relationship in terms of its strength and direction.

b. Below, the bivariate relationship is reproduced after controlling for the sex of the respondent. Summarize the results of this control. Does sex have any effect on the relationship between age and attitude? If so, describe the effect of the control variable in terms of the pattern of percentages, the value of the gammas, and the possible causal interrelationships among these variables.

Attitude toward premarital sex by age, controlling for sex:

A. Males:

Premarital Sex Is	Age		Totals
	Younger than 35	35 or Older	
Always wrong	70	55	125
Sometimes wrong	190	80	270
Totals	260	135	395

B. Females:

Premarital Sex Is	Age		Totals
	Younger than 35	35 or Older	
Always wrong	20	180	200
Sometimes wrong	230	100	330
Totals	250	280	530

16.5 SOC A job-training centre is trying to justify its existence to its funding agency. To this end, data on four variables have been collected for each of the 403 trainees served over the past three years: (1) whether the trainee completed the program, (2) whether the trainee got and held a job for at least a year after training, (3) the age of the trainee, and (4) the sex of the trainee. Is employment related to completion of the program? Is the relationship between completion and employment affected by age or sex?

Employment by training:

Held Job for at Least One Year?	Training Completed?		
	Yes	No	Totals
Yes	145	60	205
No	72	126	198
Totals	217	186	403

Employment by training, controlling for age:
A. Younger than 25:

Held Job for at Least One Year?	Training Completed?		
	Yes	No	Totals
Yes	85	33	118
No	38	47	85
Totals	123	80	203

B. 25 or older:

Held Job for at Least One Year?	Training Completed?		
	Yes	No	Totals
Yes	60	27	87
No	34	79	113
Totals	94	106	200

Employment by training, controlling for sex:
C. Males:

Held Job for at Least One Year?	Training Completed?		
	Yes	No	Totals
Yes	73	30	103
No	36	62	98
Totals	109	92	201

D. Females:

Held Job for at Least One Year?	Training Completed?		
	Yes	No	Totals
Yes	72	30	102
No	36	64	100
Totals	108	94	202

16.6 SOC What are the social sources of support for the environmental movement? A recent survey gathered information on level of concern for such issues as global warming and acid rain. Is concern for the environment related to level of education? What effects do the control variables have? Write a paragraph summarizing your conclusions.

Concern for the environment by level of education:

Concern	Level of Education		
	Low	High	Totals
Low	27	35	62
High	22	48	70
Totals	49	83	132

Concern for the environment by level of education, controlling for sex:
A. Males:

Concern	Level of Education		
	Low	High	Totals
Low	14	17	31
High	11	22	33
Totals	25	39	64

B. Females:

Concern	Level of Education		
	Low	High	Totals
Low	13	18	31
High	11	26	37
Totals	24	44	68

Concern for the environment by level of education, controlling for "level of trust in the nation's leadership":

A. Low levels of trust:

Concern	Level of Education		Totals
	Low	High	
Low	6	22	28
High	10	40	50
Totals	16	62	78

B. High levels of trust:

Concern	Level of Education		Totals
	Low	High	
Low	21	13	34
High	12	8	20
Totals	33	21	54

Concern for the environment by level of education, controlling for age:

A. Younger than 45:

Concern	Level of Education		Totals
	Low	High	
Low	19	11	30
High	18	44	62
Totals	37	55	92

B. 45 or older:

Concern	Level of Education		Totals
	Low	High	
Low	8	24	32
High	4	4	8
Totals	12	28	40

16.7 In problem 14.15, we investigated the relationships between income and five dependent variables. Let's return to two of those relationships and see if sex has any effect on the bivariate relationships. The bivariate and partial tables are presented below along with the bivariate gammas that were computed in the previous exercise. Compute percentages for the bivariate table and percentages and gammas for each of the partial tables and state your conclusions. Does controlling for sex have any effect?

a. Support for same-sex marriage by income (from problem 14.15a):

Same-sex Marriage?	Income			Totals
	Less than $24,900	$24,900 to $50,000	More than $50,000	
Favour	220	218	226	664
Oppose	366	299	250	915
Totals	586	517	476	1,579

Gamma = −.14

(HINT: Note that the higher score on the variable that measures support for same-sex marriage is associated with "OPPOSE." The negative sign on the gamma means that as score on income increases, score on the dependent variable decreases. In other words, people with higher incomes were more supportive of same-sex marriage (more likely to say "FAVOUR").

Support for same-sex marriage by income, controlling for sex:

A. Males:

Same-sex Marriage?	Income			Totals
	Less than $24,900	$24,900 to $50,000	More than $50,000	
Favour	89	96	100	285
Oppose	130	141	122	393
Totals	219	237	222	678

B. Females:

Same-sex Marriage?	Income			Totals
	Less than $24,900	$24,900 to $50,000	More than $50,000	
Favour	131	122	126	379
Oppose	236	158	128	522
Totals	367	280	254	901

b. Support for the right to commit suicide for people with an incurable disease by income (from problem 14.15c):

Right to Suicide?	Income			Totals
	Less than $24,900	$24,900 to $50,000	More than $50,000	
Favour	343	341	338	1,022
Oppose	227	194	147	568
Totals	570	535	485	1,590

Gamma = −.14

Approval of suicide for people with an incurable disease by income, controlling for sex:

A. Males:

Right to Suicide?	Income			Totals
	Less than $24,900	$24,900 to $50,000	More than $50,000	
Favour	140	165	170	475
Oppose	82	80	61	223
Totals	222	245	231	698

B. Females:

Right to Suicide?	Income			Totals
	Less than $24,900	$24,900 to $50,000	More than $50,000	
Favour	203	176	168	547
Oppose	145	114	86	345
Totals	348	290	254	892

16.8 In problem 14.6, we analyzed the relationship between support for sexual freedom and age for three different nations. The bivariate relationships for Canada and the United States are reproduced here along with the bivariate gamma. For both nations, there is a weak to moderate positive relationship between age and opinion about sexual freedom. Given the way the dependent variable is scored (higher scores mean *less* approval), we can say that support for sexual freedom decreases with age. Are the bivariate relationships affected by sex? For each partial table, find gamma and write a paragraph of analysis comparing the partial tables with each other and with the bivariate table.

a. Support for sexual freedom by age (Canada)

"People should enjoy sexual freedom"	Age			Totals
	18–34	35–54	55+	
(1) Agree	378	174	66	618
(2) Neither agree nor disagree	625	710	596	1,931
(3) Disagree	163	100	74	337
Totals	1,166	984	736	2,886

Gamma = 0.20

b. Support for sexual freedom by age (United States)

"People should enjoy sexual freedom"	Age			Totals
	18–34	35–54	55+	
(1) Agree	583	288	147	1,018
(2) Neither agree nor disagree	877	982	1,061	2,920
(3) Disagree	113	72	53	238
Totals	1,573	1,342	1,261	4,176

Gamma = 0.28

c. Support for sexual freedom by age, controlling for sex (Canada)

A. Males:

"People should enjoy sexual freedom"	Age			Totals
	18–34	35–54	55+	
(1) Agree	230	101	39	370
(2) Neither agree nor disagree	273	339	282	894
(3) Disagree	82	37	38	157
Totals	585	477	359	1,421

B. Females:

"People should enjoy sexual freedom"	Age			Totals
	18–34	35–54	55+	
(1) Agree	148	73	27	248
(2) Neither agree nor disagree	352	371	314	1,037
(3) Disagree	81	63	36	180
Totals	581	507	377	1,465

d. Support for sexual freedom by age, controlling for sex (United States)

A. Males:

"People should enjoy sexual freedom"	Age			Totals
	18–34	35–54	55+	
(1) Agree	302	169	87	558
(2) Neither agree nor disagree	393	451	470	1,314
(3) Disagree	49	39	29	117
Totals	744	659	586	1,989

B. Females:

"People should enjoy sexual freedom"	Age			Totals
	18–34	35–54	55+	
(1) Agree	277	116	57	450
(2) Neither agree nor disagree	483	525	583	1,591
(3) Disagree	64	31	24	119
Totals	824	672	664	2,160

Source: World Values Survey.

SPSS for Windows

Using SPSS for Windows to Elaborate Bivariate Tables with the 2004 GSS

The demonstrations and exercises below use the 2004 GSS data set supplied with this text. Start SPSS for Windows and open the *GSS.sav* file.

SPSS DEMONSTRATION 16.1 Analyzing the Effects of Age and Sex on Disability

Because we have been concerned with bivariate tables in this chapter, it will come as no surprise to find that we will once again make use of the **Crosstabs** procedure. To control for a third variable with **Crosstabs,** add the name of the control variable to the box at the bottom of the **Crosstabs** window. In other words, on the **Crosstabs** window, place the name of your dependent variable(s) in the top (row) box, the name of your independent variable(s) in the middle (column) box, and the name of your control variable(s) in the box at the bottom of the screen.

To illustrate, in Demonstrations 12.2 and 14.2 we looked at the relationship between *hal_q120* (any difficulty hearing, seeing, walking, and so on) and recoded *agegr5*, what we named *age3* (see Demonstration 12.2 for the recoding scheme). We found a moderate to strong negative relationship: being free of disability decreases with age.

Now, let's see if gender has any effect on this bivariate relationship. That is, are older men more likely to have difficulty (with hearing, seeing, walking, and so on) than older women? On the **Crosstabs** window, *hal_q120* should be in the top box (**Row(s)**), recoded *agegr5* (*age3*) in the middle box (**Column(s)**), and *sex* in the box at the bottom (**Layer**). Make sure you request **Gamma** in **Statistics** dialog box and **Column** percentages in **Cell Display** dialog box. The output will consist of two partial tables, one for males and one for females, and gammas computed for each of these partial tables. To conserve space, the partial tables are not reproduced here. Instead, we will concentrate on the gammas. The results of the test are presented in the following summary table:

	Gamma
For the bivariate table (*hal_q120 by age3*)	−0.459
Controlling for gender (*sex*)	
Males	−0.506
Females	−0.414

Recall that we found a bivariate gamma of −0.459 in Demonstration 14.2. In the present demonstration after controlling for gender, we get a gamma of −0.506 for males and −0.414 for females. So is the relationship between age and disability affected by the gender of the respondent? Yes and no!

No, in the sense that the gammas for the partial tables (−0.506 and −0.414) are fairly close in value to the bivariate gamma (−0.459), which would indicate a direct relationship between age and disability: being free of disability decreases with age regardless of sex. Yes, in the sense that the gammas show a slightly weaker relationship for females and a stronger relationship for males, a pattern that is consistent with an interactive relationship between the three variables.

These results are somewhat ambiguous and do not precisely match the pattern we would expect in either a direct relationship or an interactive relationship, so we would probably conclude that this relationship is closer to a direct than to an interactive relationship. The difference between the gammas for the partial tables is certainly worthy of note but is not dramatic enough to call this a case of interaction. We would probably eliminate gender from further analysis and select another control variable (e.g., marital status or visible minority status) to test the relationship between age and disability further.

SPSS DEMONSTRATION 16.2   Another Look at Sex as a Control Variable

We recoded and then looked at the relationship between state of health and income in Demonstrations 12.1 and 14.1. Let's re-examine that relationship with *sex* as a control variable.

Run the **Crosstabs** procedure and move *health* (recoded *hlthstat*) into the **Row(s)** box, *income4* (recoded *incmhsd*) into the **Column(s)** box, and *sex* into the bottom box (**Layer**). (If you no longer have access to the recoded version of these variables, follow the directions in Demonstration 12.1.) Don't forget gamma and column percents. We will again concentrate on gamma and not reproduce the partial tables here:

	Gamma
For the bivariate table (*health by income4*)	−0.373
Controlling for gender (*sex*)	
Males	−0.366
Females	−0.359

The bivariate gamma of −0.373 (see Demonstration 14.1) indicates that people with higher income have better health. Recall that *health* was recoded so that higher scores indicate poorer health. Further, the control variable (*sex*) has no effect on the relationship between *income4* and *health.* The gammas for males and females, −0.366 and −0.359, are essential equivalent to the bivariate gamma of −0.373. The relationship between health and income does not vary by gender, so this is clearly a direct relationship.

Exercises (using *GSS.sav*)

16.1 Run the analysis in Demonstration 16.1 again but replace *sex* with any control variable of your choice. (It is best to select a control variable with two categories. If necessary, use the **Recode** command illustrated in Appendix F.5 to reduce the number of categories on a control variable.) Summarize the results in a paragraph.

16.2 Use Demonstration 16.2 as a guide and analyze the relationship between *income4* and *health* using the control variable from Exercise 16.1. Summarize the results in a paragraph.

17

PARTIAL CORRELATION AND MULTIPLE REGRESSION AND CORRELATION

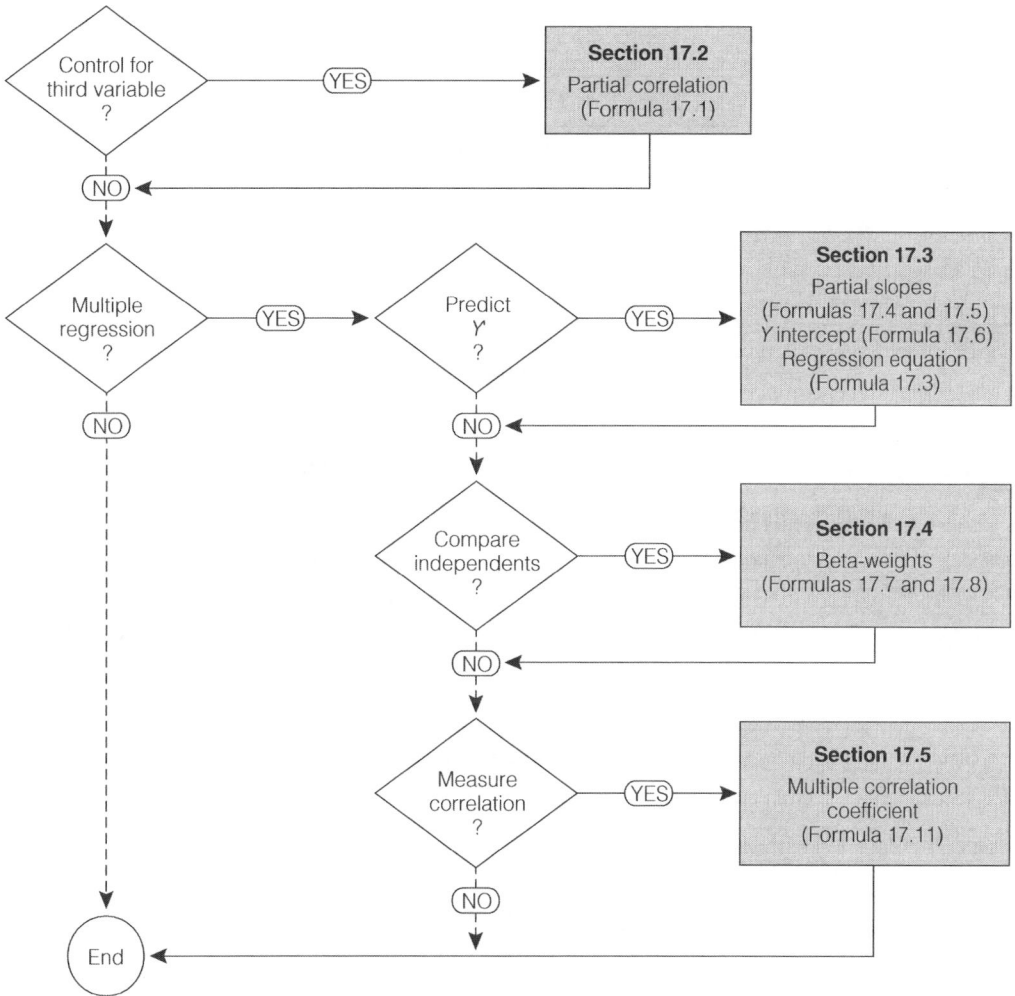

LEARNING OBJECTIVES   By the end of this chapter, you will be able to

1. Compute and interpret partial correlation coefficients.
2. Find and interpret the least-squares multiple regression equation with partial slopes.

3. Calculate and interpret the multiple correlation coefficient (R^2).

4. Explain the limitations of partial and multiple regression analysis.

17.1 INTRODUCTION

In Chapter 16, we made the point that very few (if any) worthwhile research questions can be answered through a statistical analysis of only two variables. Social science research is, by nature, multivariate and often involves the simultaneous analysis of scores of variables. Some of the most powerful and widely used statistical tools for multivariate analysis are introduced in this chapter. We will cover techniques that are used to analyze causal relationships and to make predictions, both crucial endeavours in any science.

These techniques are based on Pearson's r (see Chapter 15). They are generally more flexible than the techniques presented in Chapter 16, produce more information, and provide a wider variety of ways of disentangling the interrelationships among the variables.

We will first consider partial correlation analysis, a technique analogous to controlling for a third variable by constructing partial tables (see Chapter 16). The second technique involves multiple regression and correlation and allows the researcher to assess the effects, separately and in combination, of more than one independent variable on the dependent variable.

Throughout this chapter, we will focus our attention on research situations involving three variables. This is the least complex application of these techniques but extensions to situations involving four or more variables are relatively straightforward. To deal efficiently with the computations required by the more complex applications, we refer you to any of the computerized statistical packages (such as SPSS) probably available at your local computer centre.

17.2 PARTIAL CORRELATION

The technique of **partial correlation** can be used when a researcher wishes to observe how a specific bivariate relationship behaves in the presence of a third variable. By observing the partial correlation coefficients, we can identify direct or spurious and intervening relationships (see Chapter 16 and Table 16.5). Compared with the techniques covered in Chapter 16, partial correlation is more efficient because it does not require us to spread the cases across partial tables and inspect the bivariate relationship separately for each category of the control variable. However, for this same reason, partial correlation will not reveal interactive relationships among the variables (that is, relationships where the bivariate relationship changes across the categories of the control variable).

Terminology and Formula.   The formula for partial correlation requires some new terminology. We will be dealing with more than one bivariate relationship and need to differentiate them by using subscripts for the various correlations. Thus, the symbol r_{yx} will refer to the correlation coefficient between variable Y and variable X, r_{yz} will refer to the correlation coefficient between Y and Z, and r_{xz} to the correlation coefficient between X and Z. Correlation coefficients calculated for bivariate relationships are often referred to as **zero-order correlations.**

Partial correlation coefficients, when controlling for a single variable, are called first-order partials and are symbolized as $r_{yx.z}$. The variable to the right of the dot is the control variable. Thus, $r_{yx.z}$ refers to the partial correlation coefficient that measures the relationship between variables X and Y while controlling for variable Z. The formula for the first-order partial is

FORMULA 17.1

$$r_{yx.z} = \frac{r_{yx} - (r_{yz})(r_{xz})}{\sqrt{1 - r_{yz}^2}\sqrt{1 - r_{xz}^2}}$$

Note that you must first calculate the zero-order coefficients between all possible pairs of variables (variables X and Y, X and Z, and Y and Z) before solving this formula.

Computation.   To illustrate the computation of a first-order partial, we will return to the problem introduced in Chapter 15 that examined the relationship between number of children (X) and husband's contribution to housework (Y) for 12 dual-career families. The zero-order r between these two variables ($r_{yx} = 0.50$) indicated a moderate, positive relationship. Suppose the researcher wished to investigate the possible effects of socioeconomic status (SES) on the bivariate relationship. The original data (from Table 15.1) and the scores of the 12 families on the new variable of SES (measured by the years of education completed by the husband) are presented in Table 17.1.

TABLE 17.1   SCORES ON THREE VARIABLES FOR 12 DUAL-WAGE-EARNER FAMILIES

Family	Husband's Housework (Y)	Number of Children (X)	Husband's Years of Education (Z)
A	1	1	12
B	2	1	14
C	3	1	16
D	5	1	16
E	3	2	18
F	1	2	16
G	5	3	12
H	0	3	12
I	6	4	10
J	3	4	12
K	7	5	10
L	4	5	16

TABLE 17.2   ZERO-ORDER CORRELATIONS

	Husband's Housework (Y)	Number of Children (X)	Husband's Years of Education (Z)
Husband's Housework (Y)	1.00	0.50	−0.30
Number of Children (X)		1.00	−0.47
Husband's Years of Education (Z)			1.00

The zero-order correlations, as presented in Table 17.2, indicate that the husband's contribution to housework is positively related to number of children ($r_{yx} = 0.50$), that husbands in higher-SES families tend to do less housework ($r_{yz} = -0.30$), and that higher-SES families have fewer children ($r_{xz} = -0.47$).

Is the relationship between husband's housework and number of children affected by SES? Substituting the zero-order correlations into Formula 17.1, we would have

$$r_{yx.z} = \frac{r_{yx} - (r_{yz})(r_{xz})}{\sqrt{1 - r_{yz}^2}\ \sqrt{1 - r_{xz}^2}}$$

$$r_{yx.z} = \frac{(0.50) - (-0.30)(-0.47)}{\sqrt{1 - (-0.30)^2}\ \sqrt{1 - (0.47)^2}}$$

$$r_{yx.z} = \frac{(0.50) - (0.14)}{\sqrt{1 - 0.09}\ \sqrt{1 - 0.22}}$$

$$r_{yx.z} = \frac{0.36}{\sqrt{0.91}\ \sqrt{0.78}}$$

$$r_{yx.z} = \frac{0.36}{(0.95)(0.88)}$$

$$r_{yx.z} = \frac{0.36}{0.84}$$

$$r_{yx.z} = 0.43$$

Direct Relationships.   The first-order partial ($r_{yx.z} = 0.43$) is lower in value than the zero-order coefficient ($r_{yx} = 0.50$), but the difference in the two values is not great. This result suggests a direct relationship between variables X and Y (see Section 16.3). That is, when controlling for SES, the statistical relationship between husband's housework and number of children is essentially unchanged. Regardless of SES, husband's hours of housework increase with the number of children.

Our next step in statistical analysis would probably be to discard this control variable (SES) and select another (see Table 16.5). The more the bivariate relationship retains its strength across a series of controls for third variables (Z's), the stronger the evidence for a direct relationship between X and Y.

Spurious and Intervening Relationships. In addition to direct relationships, there are two other possible relationships between the partial and zero-order correlation coefficients. If the partial correlation coefficient is much lower in value than the zero-order coefficient ($r_{yx.z} < r_{yx}$), the bivariate relationship between X and Y is spurious or intervening. That is, there is no direct association between X and Y, and the zero-order relationship is due mainly to the effects of Z. In a spurious relationship, X and Y are both caused by Z, whereas an intervening relationship means that X and Y are linked by Z (see Figures 16.2 and 16.3). In either case, the relationship between X and Y disappears once the effect of Z is controlled, and the next step in the statistical analysis would be to incorporate the control variable into the analysis as an independent variable (see Table 16.5). Note that partial correlation cannot distinguish between situations in which the control variable is antecedent (where Z causes both X and Y) and situations in which the control variable intervenes between X and Y (when X causes Z, which in turn causes Y). Judgments about possible causal relationships must be made on the grounds of temporal ordering among the variables and/or theory.

A third possible outcome of the application of partial correlation is for the partial correlation coefficient to be greater in value than the zero-order coefficient ($r_{yx.z} > r_{yx}$). This outcome would be consistent with a causal model in which the variable taken as independent and the control variable each had a separate effect on the dependent variable and were uncorrelated with each other. This relationship is depicted in Figure 17.1. The absence of an arrow between X and Z indicates that they have no mutual relationship.

This pattern means that both X and Z should be treated as independent variables, and the next step in the statistical analysis would probably involve multiple correlation and regression. As we shall see in Sections 17.3 and 17.4, these techniques enable the researcher to isolate the separate effects of several independent variables on the dependent variable and thus to make judgments about which independent has the stronger effect on the dependent. *(For practice in computing and interpreting partial correlation coefficients, see problems 17.1 to 17.3.)*

FIGURE 17.1 A POSSIBLE CAUSAL RELATIONSHIP AMONG THREE VARIABLES

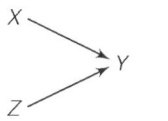

17.3 MULTIPLE REGRESSION: PREDICTING THE DEPENDENT VARIABLE

In Chapter 15, the least-squares regression line was introduced as a way of describing the overall linear relationship between two interval-ratio variables and of predicting scores on Y from scores on X. This line was the best-fitting line to summarize the bivariate relationship and was defined by the formula:

FORMULA 17.2

$$Y = a + bX$$

where a = the Y intercept
b = the slope

The least-squares regression line can be modified to include (theoretically) any number of independent variables. This technique is called **multiple regression.** For ease of explication, we will confine our attention to the case involving two independent variables. The least-squares multiple regression equation is

FORMULA 17.3

$$Y = a + b_1X_1 + b_2X_2$$

where b_1 = the partial slope of the linear relationship between the first independent variable and Y
b_2 = the partial slope of the linear relationship between the second independent variable and Y

Some new notation and some new concepts are introduced in this formula. First, while the dependent variable is still symbolized as Y, the independent variables are differentiated by subscripts. Thus, X_1 identifies the first independent variable and X_2 the second. The symbol for the slope (b) is also subscripted to identify the independent with which it is associated.

Partial Slopes.   A major difference between the multiple and bivariate regression equations concerns the slopes (b's). In the case of multiple regression, the b's are called **partial slopes,** and they show the amount of change in Y for a unit change in the independent while controlling for the effects of the other independents in the equation. The partial slopes are thus analogous to partial correlation coefficients (see Section 17.2) and represent the direct effect of the associated independent variable on Y.

Computing Partial Slopes.   The partial slopes for the independent variables are determined by Formulas 17.4 and 17.5:[*]

FORMULA 17.4

$$b_1 = \left(\frac{s_y}{s_1}\right)\left(\frac{r_{y1} - r_{y2}r_{12}}{1 - r_{12}^2}\right)$$

---

[*]Partial slopes can be computed from zero-order slopes but Formulas 17.4 and 17.5 are somewhat easier to use.

FORMULA 17.5

$$b_2 = \left(\frac{s_y}{s_2}\right)\left(\frac{r_{y2} - r_{y1}r_{12}}{1 - r_{12}^2}\right)$$

where b_1 = the partial slope of X_1 on Y
b_2 = the partial slope of X_2 on Y
s_y = the standard deviation of Y
s_1 = the standard deviation of the first independent variable (X_1)
s_2 = the standard deviation of the second independent variable (X_2)
r_{y1} = the bivariate correlation between Y and X_1
r_{y2} = the bivariate correlation between Y and X_2
r_{12} = the bivariate correlation between X_1 and X_2

To illustrate the computation of the partial slopes, we will assess the combined effects of number of children (X_1) and SES (X_2) on husband's contribution to housework. All the relevant information can be calculated from Table 17.1 and is reproduced below:

Husband's Housework	Number of Children	SES
$\overline{Y} = 3.3$	$\overline{X}_1 = 2.7$	$\overline{X}_2 = 13.7$
$s_y = 2.1$	$s_1 = 1.5$	$s_2 = 2.6$

Zero-order correlations

$r_{y1} = 0.50$
$r_{y2} = -0.30$
$r_{12} = -0.47$

The partial slope for the first independent variable (X_1) is

$$b_1 = \left(\frac{s_y}{s_1}\right)\left(\frac{r_{y1} - r_{y2}r_{12}}{1 - r_{12}^2}\right)$$

$$b_1 = \left(\frac{2.1}{1.5}\right)\left(\frac{0.50 - (-0.30)(-0.47)}{1 - (-0.47)^2}\right)$$

$$b_1 = (1.4)\left(\frac{0.50 - 0.14}{1 - 0.22}\right)$$

$$b_1 = (1.4)\left(\frac{0.36}{0.78}\right)$$

$$b_1 = (1.4)(0.46)$$

$$b_1 = 0.65$$

For the second independent variable, SES or X_2, the partial slope is

$$b_2 = \left(\frac{s_y}{s_2}\right)\left(\frac{r_{y2} - r_{y1}r_{12}}{1 - r_{12}^2}\right)$$

$$b_2 = \left(\frac{2.1}{2.6}\right)\left(\frac{-0.30 - (-0.24)}{1 - 0.22}\right)$$

$$b_2 = (0.81)\left(\frac{-0.30 + 0.24}{0.78}\right)$$

$$b_2 = (0.81)\left(\frac{-0.06}{0.78}\right)$$

$$b_2 = (0.81)(-0.08)$$

$$b_2 = -0.07$$

Finding the Y Intercept. Now that partial slopes have been determined for both independent variables, the Y intercept (a) can be found. Note that a is calculated from the mean of the dependent variable (symbolized as $\overline{Y}$) and the means of the two independent variables $(\overline{X}_1$ and $\overline{X}_2)$.

FORMULA 17.6

$$a = \overline{Y} - b_1\overline{X}_1 - b_2\overline{X}_2$$

Substituting the proper values for the example problem at hand, we would have

$$a = \overline{Y} - b_1\overline{X}_1 - b_2\overline{X}_2$$

$$a = 3.3 - (0.65)(2.7) - (-0.07)(13.7)$$

$$a = 3.3 - (1.8) - (-1.0)$$

$$a = 3.3 - 1.8 + 1.0$$

$$a = 2.5$$

The Least Squares Multiple Regression Line and Predicting Y′. For our example problem, the full least-squares multiple regression equation would be

$$Y = a + b_1X_1 + b_2X_2$$

$$Y = 2.5 + (0.65)X_1 + (-0.07)X_2$$

As was the case with the bivariate regression line, this formula can be used to predict scores on the dependent variable from scores on the independent variables. For example, what would be our best prediction of husband's housework (Y') for a family of four children $(X_1 = 4)$ where the husband had completed 11 years of schooling $(X_2 = 11)$? Substituting these values into the least-squares formula, we would have

$$Y' = 2.5 + (0.65)(4) + (-0.07)(11)$$

$$Y' = 2.5 + 2.6 - 0.8$$

$$Y' = 4.3$$

Our prediction would be that this husband would contribute 4.3 hours per week to housework. This prediction is, of course, a kind of "educated guess," which is unlikely to be perfectly accurate. However, we will make fewer errors of prediction using the least-squares line (and, thus, incorporating information from the independent variables) than we would using any other method of prediction (assuming, of course, that there is a linear association between the independent and the dependent variables). *(For practice in predicting Y scores and in computing slopes and the Y intercept, see problems 17.1 to 17.6.)*

17.4 MULTIPLE REGRESSION: ASSESSING THE EFFECTS OF THE INDEPENDENT VARIABLES

The least-squares multiple regression equation (Formula 17.3) is used to isolate the separate effects of the independents and to predict scores on the dependent variable. However, in many situations, using this formula to determine the relative importance of the various independent variables will be awkward—especially when the independent variables differ in terms of units of measurement (e.g., number of children vs. years of education). When the units of measurement differ, a comparison of the partial slopes will not necessarily tell us which independent variable has the strongest effect and is thus the most important. Comparing the partial slopes of variables that differ in units of measurement is a little like comparing apples and oranges.

The comparability of the independent variables can be increased by converting all variables in the equation to a common scale and thereby eliminating variations in the values of the partial slopes that are solely a function of differences in units of measurement. We can, for example, standardize all distributions by changing the scores of all variables to Z scores. Each distribution of scores would then have a mean of 0 and a standard deviation of 1 (see Chapter 5), and comparisons between the independent variables would be much more meaningful.

Beta-weights.   To standardize the variables to the normal curve, we could actually convert all scores into the equivalent Z scores and then recompute the slopes and the Y intercept. This would require a good deal of work, and, fortunately, a shortcut is available for directly computing the slopes of the standardized scores. These **standardized partial slopes** are called **beta-weights** and are symbolized b^*. The beta-weights show the amount of change in the standardized scores of Y for a one-unit change in the standardized scores of each independent variable while controlling for the effects of all other independent variables.

Formulas and Computation for Beta-weights.   When we have two independent variables, the beta-weight for each is found by using Formula 17.7 and Formula 17.8:

Application 17.1

Five recently divorced men have been asked to rate subjectively the success of their adjustment to single life on a scale ranging from 5 (very successful adjustment) to 1 (very poor adjustment). Is adjustment related to the length of time married? Is adjustment related to socio-economic status as measured by yearly income?

Case	Adjustment (Y)	Years Married (X_1)	Income (dollars) (X_2)
A	5	5	30,000
B	4	7	45,000
C	4	10	25,000
D	3	2	27,000
E	1	15	17,000

$$\overline{Y} = 3.4 \qquad \overline{X}_1 = 7.8 \qquad \overline{X}_2 = 28,800.00$$
$$s = 1.4 \qquad s = 4.5 \qquad s = 9,173.88$$

The zero-order correlations among these three variables are

	Years Married (X_1)	Income (X_2)
Adjustment (Y)	−.62	.62
Years married (X_1)		−.49

These results suggest strong but opposite relationships between each independent and adjustment. Adjustment decreases as years married increases, and increases as income increases.

To find the multiple regression equation, we must find the partial slopes.

For years married (X_1):

$$b_1 = \left(\frac{s_y}{s_1}\right)\left(\frac{r_{y1} - r_{y2}r_{12}}{1 - r_{12}^2}\right)$$

$$b_1 = \frac{1.4}{4.5}\left(\frac{(-0.62) - (0.62)(-0.49)}{1 - (-0.49)^2}\right)$$

$$b_1 = (0.31)\left(\frac{(-0.62) - (-0.30)}{1 - 0.24}\right)$$

$$b_1 = (0.31)\left(\frac{-0.32}{0.76}\right)$$

$$b_1 = (0.31)(-0.42)$$

$$b_1 = -0.13$$

For income (X_2):

$$b_2 = \left(\frac{s_y}{s_2}\right)\left(\frac{r_{y2} - r_{y1}r_{12}}{1 - r_{12}^2}\right)$$

$$b_2 = \left(\frac{1.4}{9173.88}\right)\left(\frac{(0.62) - (-0.62)(-0.49)}{1 - (-0.49)^2}\right)$$

$$b_2 = (0.00015)\left(\frac{(0.62) - (0.30)}{1 - 0.24}\right)$$

$$b_2 = (0.00015)\left(\frac{0.32}{0.76}\right)$$

$$b_2 = (0.00015)(0.42)$$
$$b_2 = 0.000063$$

(*continued next page*)

FORMULA 17.7

$$b_1^* = b_1\left(\frac{s_1}{s_y}\right)$$

FORMULA 17.8

$$b_2^* = b_2\left(\frac{s_2}{s_y}\right)$$

We can now compute the beta-weights for our sample problem to see which of the two independents has the stronger effect on the dependent. For the first independent variable, number of children (X_1):

Application 17.1: (*continued*)

The Y intercept would be

$$a = \overline{Y} - b_1\overline{X_1} - b_2\overline{X_2}$$
$$a = 3.4 - (-0.13)(7.8) - (0.000063)(28,800)$$
$$a = 3.4 - (-1.01) - (1.81)$$
$$a = 3.4 + 1.01 - 1.81$$
$$a = 2.60$$

The multiple regression equation is

$$Y = a + b_1X_1 + b_2X_2$$
$$Y = 2.60 + (-0.13)X_1 + (0.000063)X_2$$

What adjustment score could we predict for a male who had been married 30 years ($X_1 = 30$) and had an income of \$50,000 ($X_2 = 50,000$)?

$$Y' = 2.60 + (-0.13)(30) + (0.000063)(50,000)$$
$$Y' = 2.60 + (-3.9) + (3.15)$$
$$Y' = 1.85$$

To assess which of the two independents has the stronger effect on adjustment, the standardized partial slopes must be computed.
    For years married (X_1):

$$b_1^* = b_1\left(\frac{s_1}{s_y}\right)$$

$$b_1^* = (-0.13)\left(\frac{4.5}{1.4}\right)$$

$$b_1^* = -0.42$$

For income (X_2):

$$b_2^* = b_2\left(\frac{s_2}{s_y}\right)$$

$$b_2^* = (0.000063)\left(\frac{9173.88}{1.4}\right)$$

$$b_2^* = 0.41$$

The standardized regression equation is

$$Z_y = b_1^*Z_1 + b_2^*Z_2$$
$$Z_y = (-0.42)Z_1 + (0.41)Z_2$$

and the independents have nearly equal but opposite effects on adjustment. To assess the combined effects of the two independents on adjustment, the coefficient of multiple determination must be computed.

$$R^2 = r_{y1}^2 + r_{y2.1}^2(1 - r_{y1}^2)$$
$$R^2 = (-0.62)^2 + (0.46)^2(1 - (-0.62)^2)$$
$$R^2 = 0.38 + (0.21)(1 - 0.38)$$
$$R^2 = 0.38 + (0.21)(0.62)$$
$$R^2 = 0.38 + 0.13$$
$$R^2 = 0.51$$

The first independent, years married, explains 38% of the variation in adjustment by itself. To this quantity, income explains an additional 13% of the variation in adjustment. Taken together, the two independents explain a total of 51% of the variation in adjustment.

$$b_1^* = b_1\left(\frac{s_1}{s_y}\right)$$

$$b_1^* = (0.65)\left(\frac{1.5}{2.1}\right)$$

$$b_1^* = (0.65)(0.71)$$

$$b_1^* = 0.46$$

Application 17.2

The table below presents information on three variables for a small sample of eight nations. We will take abortion rate as the dependent variable and examine its relationship with two variables: One measures women's status and power and the other measures religiosity. In this analysis, we will focus on R^2 and the beta-weights only.

Our expectation is that the rate of abortion will have a positive relationship with women's status ("abortion rate will increase as women's power and freedom of choice increases") and a negative relationship with religiosity ("the greater the strength of traditional value systems, including religion, the lower the rate of abortion").

Nation	Abortion Rate[1] (Y)	Women's Status[2] (X_1)	Religiosity[3] (X_2)
Canada	165	.76	74
Chile	10	.45	93
Denmark	400	.71	48
Germany	208	.75	67
Italy	389	.54	82
Japan	379	.52	87
U.K.	207	.67	67
U.S.	428	.74	90

(continued next column)

(continued)

Nation	Abortion Rate[1] (Y)	Women's Status[2] (X_1)	Religiosity[3] (X_2)
Mean =	273.25	.64	76.00
Standard Deviation =	138.86	.11	14.11

[1] Number of abortions per 1,000 live births.
[2] This variable is a measure of the status of women relative to men across a variety of areas including politics and education. The higher the score, the higher the status of women.
[3] The percentage of respondents who say they pray "at least sometimes."

The zero-order correlations for these variables are given in the correlation matrix below.

	Abortion Rate	Women's Status	Religiosity
Abortion Rate	1.00	0.22	−0.17
Women's Status		1.00	−0.56
Religiosity			1.00

Consistent with our expectations, there is a positive—but fairly weak—relationship between abortion rate and women's status. The relationship between abortion rate and religiosity is negative, as expected, and

(continued next page)

For the second independent variable, SES (X_2):

$$b_2^* = b_2\left(\frac{s_2}{s_y}\right)$$

$$b_2^* = (-0.07)\left(\frac{2.6}{2.1}\right)$$

$$b_2^* = (-0.07)(1.24)$$

$$b_2^* = -0.09$$

Application 17.2: (*continued*)

also weak. The relationship between the two independent variables—women's status and religiosity—is moderate to strong and negative, indicating that women in more religious nations tend to have lower status.

The combined effect of women's status and religiosity on abortion rate is found by computing R^2:

$$R^2 = r_{y1}^2 + r_{y2.1}^2(1 - r_{y1}^2)$$
$$R^2 = (0.22)^2 + (-0.06)^2(1 - 0.22)^2$$
$$R^2 = 0.05 + (0.0036)(0.95)$$
$$R^2 = 0.05 + (0.003)$$
$$R^2 = 0.053$$

By itself, women's status explains 5% of the variance in abortion rates. To this, religiosity adds another .3%—a very minimal amount—for a total of 5.3%. This leaves about 95% of the variance unexplained, a sizable proportion but not unusually large in social science research.

To assess the separate effects of the two independent variables, the beta-weights must be calculated. We need values for the unstandardized partial slopes to compute beta-weights, and we will simply report the values as 229.52 for X_1 and -0.67 for X_2.

For the first independent variable (women's status):

$$b_1^* = b_1\left(\frac{s_1}{s_y}\right)$$

$$b_1^* = (229.52)\left(\frac{0.11}{138.86}\right)$$

$$b_1^* = (229.52)(0.00079)$$

$$b_1^* = 0.18$$

For the second independent variable (religiosity):

$$b_2^* = b_2\left(\frac{s_2}{s_y}\right)$$

$$b_2^* = (-0.67)\left(\frac{14.11}{138.86}\right)$$

$$b_2^* = (-0.67)(0.102)$$

$$b_2^* = -0.07$$

Recall that the beta-weights show the effect of each independent variable on the dependent variable while controlling for the other independent variables in the equation. In this case, women's status has the stronger effect and the relationship is positive. The effect of religiosity is negative.

In summary, for these eight nations, abortion rate has weak relationships with women's status and with religiosity. Taken together, the independent variables explain 5.3% of the variation in abortion rates. As expected, abortion rates increase as women gain status and power and decrease as religiosity increases.

Comparing the value of the beta-weights, we see that number of children has a stronger effect than SES on husband's housework. Furthermore, the net effect (after controlling for the effect of SES) of the first independent variable is positive while the net effect of the second independent variable is negative.

The Standardized Least-Squares Regression Line.   Using standardized scores, the least-squares regression equation can be written as

FORMULA 17.9

$$Z_y = a_z + b_1^* Z_1 + b_2^* Z_2$$

where Z indicates that all scores have been standardized to the normal curve

The standardized regression equation can be further simplified by dropping the term for the Y intercept; this term will always be zero when scores have been standardized. This value is the point where the regression line crosses the Y axis and is equal to the mean of Y when all independents equal 0. This relationship can be seen by substituting 0 for all independent variables in Formula 17.6:

$$a = \overline{Y} - b_1\overline{X}_1 - b_2\overline{X}_2$$
$$a = \overline{Y} - b_1(0) - b_2(0)$$
$$a = \overline{Y}$$

Because the mean of any standardized distribution of scores is zero, the mean of the standardized Y scores will be zero and the Y intercept will also be zero ($a = \overline{Y} = 0$). Thus, Formula 17.9 simplifies to

FORMULA 17.10
$$Z_y = b_1^* Z_1 + b_2^* Z_2$$

The standardized regression equation, with beta-weights noted, would be

$$Z_y = (0.46)Z_1 + (-0.09)Z_2$$

and it is immediately obvious that the first independent variable has a much stronger direct effect on Y than the second independent variable.

Summary. Multiple regression analysis permits the researcher to summarize the linear relationship among two or more independents and a dependent variable. The unstandardized regression equation (Formula 17.3) permits values of Y to be predicted from the independent variables in the original units of the variables. The standardized regression equation (Formula 17.10) allows the researcher to easily assess the relative importance of the various independent variables by comparing the beta-weights. *(For practice in computing and interpreting beta-weights, see any of the problems at the end of this chapter. It is probably a good idea to start with problem 17.1 as it has the smallest data set and the least complex computations.)*

17.5 MULTIPLE CORRELATION

We use the multiple regression equations to disentangle the separate direct effects of each independent variable on the dependent. Using **multiple correlation** techniques, we can also ascertain the combined effects of all independents on the dependent variable. We do so by computing the **multiple correlation coefficient (R)** and the **coefficient of multiple determination (R^2).** The value of the latter statistic represents the proportion of the variance in Y that is explained by all the independent variables combined.

In terms of zero-order correlation, we have seen that "number of children" (X_1) explains a proportion of .25 of the variance in Y ($r_{y1}^2 = (.50)^2 = .25$) by itself and that SES explains a proportion of .09 of the variance in Y ($r_{y2}^2 = (-.30)^2 = .09$). The two zero-order correlations cannot be simply added together to ascertain their combined effect on Y, because the two independents are also correlated with each other and, therefore, they will "overlap" in their effects on Y and explain some of the same variance. This overlap is eliminated in Formula 17.11:

FORMULA 17.11
$$R^2 = r_{y1}^2 + r_{y2.1}^2(1 - r_{y1}^2)$$

where R^2 = the multiple correlation coefficient
r_{y1}^2 = the zero-order correlation between Y and X_1, the quantity squared
$r_{y2.1}^2$ = the partial correlation of Y and X_2, while controlling for X_1, the quantity squared

The first term in this formula (r_{y1}^2) is the coefficient of determination for the relationship between Y and X_1. It represents the amount of variation in Y explained by X_1 by itself. To this quantity we add the amount of the variation remaining in Y (given by $1 - r_{y1}^2$) that can be explained by X_2 after the effect of X_1 is controlled ($r_{y2.1}^2$). Basically, Formula 17.11 allows X_1 to explain as much of Y as it can and then adds in the effect of X_2 after X_1 is controlled (thus eliminating the "overlap" in the variance of Y that X_1 and X_2 have in common).

Computing and Interpreting R and R^2. To observe the combined effects of number of children (X_1) and SES (X_2) on husband's housework (Y), we need two quantities. The correlation between X_1 and Y (r_{y1} = .50) has already been found. Before we can solve Formula 17.11, we must first calculate the partial correlation of Y and X_2 while controlling for X_1 ($r_{y2.1}$):

$$r_{y2.1} = \frac{r_{y2} - (r_{y1})(r_{12})}{\sqrt{1 - r_{y1}^2}\ \sqrt{1 - r_{12}^2}}$$

$$r_{y2.1} = \frac{(-0.30) - (0.50)(-0.47)}{\sqrt{1 - (0.50)^2}\ \sqrt{1 - (-0.47)^2}}$$

$$r_{y2.1} = \frac{(-0.30) - (-0.24)}{\sqrt{0.75}\ \sqrt{0.78}}$$

$$r_{y2.1} = \frac{-0.06}{0.77}$$

$$r_{y2.1} = -0.08$$

Formula 17.11 can now be solved for our sample problem:

$$R^2 = r_{y1}^2 + r_{y2.1}^2(1 - r_{y1}^2)$$
$$R^2 = (0.50)^2 + (-0.08)^2(1 - 0.50^2)$$
$$R^2 = 0.25 + (0.006)(1 - 0.25)$$
$$R^2 = 0.25 + 0.005$$
$$R^2 = 0.255$$

The first independent variable (X_1), number of children, explains 25% of the variance in Y by itself. To this total, the second independent (X_2), SES, adds only a half a percent, for a total explained variance of 25.5%. In combination, the two independents explain a total of 25.5% of the variation in the dependent variable. *(For practice in computing and interpreting R and R^2, see any of the problems at the end of this chapter. It is probably a good idea to start with problem 17.1 as it has the smallest data set and the least complex computations.)*

17.6 INTERPRETING STATISTICS: ANOTHER LOOK AT THE CORRELATES OF CRIME

In Chapter 15, we assessed the association between poverty and crime. We found a moderate to strong and positive relationship ($r = 0.47$) between a measure of poverty and the crime rate for Canada's largest cities, an indication that there is an important relationship between these two variables. In this installment of Interpreting Statistics, we will return to this relationship and add several independent variables to the analysis.[*]

Our first new independent variable is a measure of age: the percentage of the population less than 25. The rates for some crimes are strongly related to age: They are highest for people in their teens and twenties but decline dramatically as age rises. Thus, we can expect that there will be a substantial positive relationship between this measure of age and the crime rate (the higher the proportion of younger people in a population, the higher the crime rate).

Our second new independent variable comes from research showing that crime rates follow a regional pattern in Canada, rising from east to west.[†] Thus, we should expect to find higher rates of crime in western cities (Calgary, Edmonton, Winnipeg, and Vancouver) compared to eastern cities (Hamilton, Montreal, Ottawa, Quebec, and Toronto).

Although it is reasonable to include region in this analysis, we must first confront an important problem. Region is a nominal-level variable but regression analysis requires that all variables be interval-ratio in level of measurement. We can resolve this problem by treating region as a "dummy variable," a variable that can be treated as interval-ratio regardless of its actual level of measurement.

Dummy variables have exactly two categories, one coded as a score of zero and the other as a score of one. Treated this way, nominal-level variables such as gender (e.g., with males coded as 0 and females coded as 1) or immigration status (e.g., Canadian-born coded as 0 and foreign-born coded as 1) are commonly included as independent variables in regression equations. In this case, we will create a variable that is coded so that western cities are scored as "1" and non-western cities as "0." Coded this way, region

---

[*] This analysis considers the effects of three independent variables, one more than was included in previous examples in this chapter. As you will see, the addition of an independent variable will not complicate interpretation and analysis unduly. However, the mathematics underlying multiple regression with three independent variables is complex and should be performed with the aid of a computerized statistics packages such as SPSS. We will not show the underlying computations in this analysis.

[†] Source: Statistics Canada. 2001. *Crime comparisons between Canada and the United States.* Catalogue no. 85-002-XPE.

should have a positive relationship with crime—as region "increases" (as we increase from a score of 0, non-western cities, to a score of 1, western cities), the crime rate also increases.

It is important to note that we could have as easily coded eastern cities as "1" and non-eastern cities as "0," with identical results. Correlation coefficients, slopes, and R^2 values would be the same regardless of what region we coded as 1 and 0. The only difference would be the direction of the relationship. If we instead decided to score eastern cities as "1" and non-eastern cities as "0," we would expect region to have a negative relationship (i.e., correlation coefficients and slopes would be negative) with crime. Coding of dummy variables is therefore a subjective decision made by the researcher.

Before beginning the multivariate analysis, we should examine the correlation coefficients between all possible pairs of variables. Zero-order correlations, and the scores used in computing them, for the variables are reported in Table 17.3. As we saw in Chapter 15, there is a moderate to strong, positive relationship between poverty and crime: Cities with higher rates of poverty have higher rates of crime. Crime rate has a weak, positive relationship with age: Cities with younger populations tend to have slightly higher crime

TABLE 17.3   SCORES ON POVERTY, AGE, REGION, AND CRIME FOR NINE CANADIAN CITIES AND ZERO-ORDER CORRELATIONS

Scores

City	Crime[1]	Poverty[2]	Age[3]	Region[4]
Calgary	7,115	14.3	34.1	1
Edmonton	8,377	16.5	35.5	1
Hamilton	6,565	17.0	32.4	0
Montreal	7,234	22.3	31.4	0
Ottawa	5,680	15.0	32.9	0
Quebec	5,108	18.9	30.0	0
Toronto	5,290	16.7	32.8	0
Vancouver	11,210	20.8	30.9	1
Winnipeg	10,377	19.8	33.4	1

Zero-order correlations

	Crime	Poverty	Age	Region
Crime	1.00	0.47	0.12	0.80
Poverty		1.00	−0.60	−0.03
Age			1.00	0.49
Region				1.00

[1]Number of criminal offences per 100,000 population, 2000.
[2]Percent of population living below the poverty line, 2000.
[3]Percent of population under age 25, 2000.
[4]Western cities coded as 1; non-western cities coded as 0.
Source: Statistics Canada. 2001. *Crime Statistics in Canada, 2000*. Catalogue no. 85-002-XIE (Crime rate) and Statistics Canada, 2001 Canadian Census, individual PUMF (Age and Poverty rate).

TABLE 17.4 MULTIPLE REGRESSION ANALYSIS OF THE CRIME RATE

Variable	b	b*
Poverty	403	0.50
Age	35	0.03
Region	3,278	0.80
Intercept (a)	−2,367	
	$R^2 = 0.87$	

b = partial slope
b* = standardized partial slopes

rates. Finally, crime rate has a very strong, positive relationship with region: Western Canadian cities have higher rates of crime than non-western cities.

The results of the multivariate analysis are provided in Table 17.4. Looking at the unstandardized partial slopes (*b*), we see that the number of criminal offences per 100,000 people increases on average by 403 for each percentage increase in the poverty rate, while controlling for the effects of age and region. The slope for age is also positive—cities with younger populations tend to have higher crime rates. Crime also increases with region. On an average, western Canadian cities experience 3,278 more criminal offences per 100,000 people compared to eastern Canadian cities, controlling for poverty and age. The standardized partial slopes (*b*) in Table 17.4 tell us that crime is more affected by region than poverty or age. In fact, the effect of region on crime is 1.6 times that of poverty (0.80/0.50 = 1.6).

By itself, poverty explains 22% (*r* = 0.47, so $(0.47)^2 = 0.22$) of the variance in crime rates among the cities (Table 17.3). To this, age and region add another 65% for a total of 87% ($R^2 = 0.87$). These three variables, together, account for over 80% of the variation in crime rates from city to city. This is a very substantial percentage, with only 13% of the variation remaining unaccounted for or unexplained. We might be able to raise the value of R^2 by adding more independent variables to the equation. However, it is common to find that additional independent variables will explain smaller and smaller proportions of the variance and have a diminishing effect on R^2. This phenomenon can be caused by many factors including the fact that the independent variables will usually be correlated with each other (e.g., see the relationship between region and age in Table 17.3) and will overlap in their effect on the dependent variable.

In summary, the multivariate analysis indicates that poverty and region have important, positive effects on crime rate. The effect of age is positive, but of little importance. The standardized partial slopes show that region is clearly the most important of the three independent variables in understanding crime rates. Taken together, the three variables account for 87% of the variance in crime rate from city to city. However, with only nine cases (cities) in this analysis, we must be particularly cautious in interpreting and drawing conclusions from these findings.

READING STATISTICS 12: Multiple Regression and Partial Correlation

Research projects that analyze the interrelationships among many variables are particularly likely to employ multiple regression and correlation as central statistical techniques. The results of these projects will typically be presented in summary tables that report the multiple correlations, slopes, and, if applicable, the significance of the results. The zero-order correlations are often presented in the form of a matrix that displays the value of Pearson's r for every possible bivariate relationship in the data set. An example of such a matrix can be found in Section 17.6.

Usually, tables that summarize the multivariate analysis will report R^2 and the slope for each independent variable in the regression equation. An example of this kind of summary table would look like this:

Independent Variables	Multiple R^2	Beta-weights
X_1	.17	.47
X_2	.23	.32
X_3	.27	.16
$\vdots$	$\vdots$	$\vdots$

This table reports that the first independent variable, X_1, has the strongest direct relationship with the dependent variable and explains 17% of the variance in the dependent by itself ($R^2 = 0.17$). The second independent, X_2, adds 6% to the explained variance ($R^2 = 0.23$ after X_2 is entered into the equation). The third independent, X_3, adds 4% to the explained variance of the dependent

($R^2 = 0.27$ after X_3 is entered into the equation). Table 17.4 provides an alternative example of how the results of a multiple regression analysis may be reported.

In addition to multiple regression, partial correlation is also frequently used in research. As we will now see, partial correlation allows researchers to observe how a bivariate relationship behaves in the presence of a third variable.

Statistics in the Professional Literature

There are a great number of cross-national comparative studies on the topic of income inequality and population health. Reviews of the literature reveal that the majority of international studies support the hypothesis that income inequality has a negative effect on population health. In other words, the greater the dispersion of income in a country, the lower its life expectancy. According to this hypothesis, the U.S. would have a lower life expectancy than Canada, for example, because the former has more income inequality than the latter.

Income inequality as a determinant of population health, however, has become an increasingly contentious issue. It is argued that evidence of a population-level association between income inequality and health is slowly dissipating. To shed light on this issue, Canadian social scientists Rob Brown and Steven Prus tested the income inequality–population health hypothesis with the most currently available data at the time of their publication—data from the year 2000.

(continued)

17.7 THE LIMITATIONS OF MULTIPLE REGRESSION AND CORRELATION

Multiple regression and correlation are very powerful tools for analyzing the interrelationships among three or more variables. The techniques presented in this chapter permit the researcher to predict scores on one variable from two or more other variables, to distinguish between independent variables in terms of the importance of their direct effects on a dependent variable, and to ascertain the total effect of a set of independent variables on a dependent variable. In terms of the flexibility of the techniques and the

READING STATISTICS 12: (*continued*)

TABLE 1 CORRELATION COEFFICIENT FOR INCOME INEQUALITY (GINI) AND LIFE EXPECTANCY FOR 18 COUNTRIES, BY SEX, BEFORE AND AFTER CONTROLLING FOR AVERAGE POPULATION INCOME.*

	Zero-order Correlation	Partial Correlation
	r	*r*
Male	−.603[†]	−.207
Female	−.605[†]	.024

*These countries are Australia, Austria, Belgium, Canada, Denmark, Finland, France, Germany, Greece, Ireland, Israel, Netherlands, Norway, Spain, Sweden, Switzerland, the United Kingdom, and the United States.
[†] $p < .01$
Source: From Prus, S. and R. Brown. 2008. "Age-specific Income Inequality and Life Expectancy: New Evidence," 2008 Living to 100 Symposium Monograph, The Society of Actuaries. Copyright 2008 by the Society of Actuaries, Schaumburg Illinois. Reprinted with permission.

The correlation coefficient was used to examine the relationship between income inequality (Gini coefficient) and life expectancy, separately for males and females. The Gini coefficient, introduced in Chapter 4, is a measure of inequality that ranges from 0 to 1. If everyone in a given country had the same income, there would be no income inequality, and the Gini coefficient would be 0. If one individual held all income in a given country, the Gini coefficient would be equal to 1. So, the Gini coefficient increases as inequality increases. Life expectancy is the expected number of years to be lived at birth in a given country.

The correlation coefficient was calculated before (zero-order) and after (partial) controlling for average income of the entire population to gauge the extent to which average population income changes the original relationship between income inequality and life expectancy. The results of their multivariate analysis are reported in Table 1.

Brown and Prus found that life expectancy is negatively and significantly related to income inequality regardless of sex. The zero-order correlation coefficients for males and females are approximately −0.60. That is, as income inequality increases, life expectancy decreases.

After controlling for average population income, the partial correlations are noticeably weaker and statistically insignificant compared to the zero-order correlations. The coefficients are reduced to −0.207 for males and 0.024 for females after removing the effect of average population income. This outcome weakens the hypothesis that there is a direct causal relationship between income inequality and life expectancy. Brown and Prus conclude that the zero-order relationship is spurious and due to the effects of average population income rather than income inequality itself.

volume of information they can supply, multiple regression and correlation represent some of the most powerful statistical techniques available to social science researchers.

Powerful tools are not cheap. They demand high-quality data, and measurement at the interval-ratio level is difficult to accomplish at this stage in the development of the social sciences. Furthermore, these techniques assume that the interrelationships among the variables follow a particular form. First, they assume that each independent variable has a linear relationship with the dependent variable. How well a given set of variables meets this assumption can be quickly checked with scattergrams.

Second, the techniques presented in this chapter assume that there is no interaction among the variables in the equation. If there is interaction among the variables, it will not be possible to accurately estimate or predict the dependent variable by simply adding the effects of the independents. There are techniques for handling interaction among the variables in the set, but these techniques are beyond the scope of this text.

Third, the techniques of multiple regression and correlation assume that the independent variables are uncorrelated with each other. Strictly speaking, this condition means that the zero-order correlation among all pairs of independents should be zero, but practically, we act as if this assumption has been met if the intercorrelations among the independents are low.

To the extent that these assumptions are violated, the regression coefficients (especially partial and standardized slopes) and the coefficient of multiple determination (R^2) become less and less trustworthy and the techniques less and less useful. If the assumptions of the model cannot be met, the alternative might be to turn to the multivariate techniques described in Chapter 16. Unfortunately, those techniques, in general, supply a lower volume of less precise information about the interrelationships among the variables.

Finally, we should note that we have covered only the simplest applications of partial correlation and multiple regression and correlation. In terms of logic and interpretation, the extensions to situations involving more variables are relatively straightforward. However, the computations for these situations are extremely complex. If you are faced with a situation involving more than three variables, turn to one of the computerized statistical packages that are commonly available on university campuses (e.g., SPSS). These programs require minimal computer literacy and can handle complex calculations in, literally, the blink of an eye. Efficient use of these packages will enable you to avoid drudgery and will free you to do what social scientists everywhere enjoy doing most: pondering the meaning of your results and, by extension, the nature of social life.

SUMMARY

1. Partial correlation involves controlling for third variables in a manner analogous to that introduced in the previous chapter. Partial correlations permit the detection of direct and spurious or intervening relationships between X and Y.

2. Multiple regression includes statistical techniques by which predictions of the dependent variable from more than one independent variable can be made (by using partial slopes and the multiple regression equation) and by which we can disentangle the relative importance of the independent variables (by using standardized partial slopes).

3. The multiple correlation coefficient (R^2) summarizes the combined effects of all independents on the dependent variable in terms of the proportion of the total variation in Y that is explained by all of the independent variables.

4. Partial correlation and multiple regression and correlation are some of the most powerful tools available to the researcher and demand high-quality measurement and relationships among the variables that are linear and noninteractive. Further, correlations among the independents must be low (preferably zero). Although the price is high, these techniques pay considerable dividends in the volume of precise and detailed information they generate about the interrelationships among the variables.

SUMMARY OF FORMULAS

Partial correlation coefficient:

$$17.1 \qquad r_{yx.z} = \frac{r_{yx} - (r_{yz})(r_{xz})}{\sqrt{1 - r_{yz}^2}\,\sqrt{1 - r_{xz}^2}}$$

Least-squares regression line (bivariate):

$$17.2 \qquad Y = a + bX$$

Least-squares multiple regression line:

$$17.3 \qquad Y = a + b_1X_1 + b_2X_2$$

Partial slope for X_1:

$$17.4 \qquad b_1 = \left(\frac{s_y}{s_1}\right)\left(\frac{r_{y1} - r_{y2}r_{12}}{1 - r_{12}^2}\right)$$

Partial slope for X_2:

$$17.5 \qquad b_2 = \left(\frac{s_y}{s_2}\right)\left(\frac{r_{y2} - r_{y1}r_{12}}{1 - r_{12}^2}\right)$$

Y intercept:

$$17.6 \qquad a = \overline{Y} - b_1\overline{X}_1 - b_2\overline{X}_2$$

Standardized partial slope (beta-weight) for X_1:

$$17.7 \qquad b_1^* = b_1\left(\frac{s_1}{s_y}\right)$$

Standardized partial slope (beta-weight) for X_2:

$$17.8 \qquad b_2^* = b_2\left(\frac{s_2}{s_y}\right)$$

Standardized least-squares regression line:

$$17.9 \qquad Z_y = a_z + b_1^*Z_1 + b_2^*Z_2$$

Standardized least-squares regression line (simplified):

$$17.10 \qquad Z_y = b_1^*Z_1 + b_2^*Z_2$$

Coefficient of multiple determination:

$$17.11 \qquad R^2 = r_{y1}^2 + r_{y2.1}^2(1 - r_{y1}^2)$$

GLOSSARY

Beta-weights (b^*). Standardized partial slopes.

Coefficient of multiple determination (R^2). A statistic that equals the total variation explained in the dependent variable by all independent variables combined.

Multiple correlation. A multivariate technique for examining the combined effects of more than one independent variable on a dependent variable.

Multiple correlation coefficient (R). A statistic that indicates the strength of the correlation between a dependent variable and two or more independent variables.

Multiple regression. A multivariate technique that breaks down the separate effects of the independent variables on the dependent variable; used to make predictions of the dependent variable.

Partial correlation. A multivariate technique for examining a bivariate relationship while controlling for other variables.

Partial correlation coefficient. A statistic that shows the relationship between two variables while controlling for other variables; $r_{yx.z}$ is the symbol for the partial correlation coefficient when controlling for one variable.

Partial slopes. In a multiple regression equation, the slope of the relationship between a particular independent variable and the dependent variable while controlling for all other independents in the equation.

Standardized partial slopes (beta-weights). The slope of the relationship between a particular independent variable and the dependent when all scores have been normalized.

Zero-order correlations. Correlation coefficients for bivariate relationships.

MULTIMEDIA RESOURCES

http://www.healeystatistics.nelson.com

Visit the companion Web site for the first Canadian edition of *Statistics: A Tool for Social Research* to access a wide range of student resources. Begin by clicking on the Student Resources section of the book's Web site to access review quizzes, flash cards, and other study tools.

PROBLEMS

17.1 PS In problem 15.1 data regarding voter turnout in five cities were presented. For the sake of convenience, the data for three of the variables are presented again here along with descriptive statistics and zero-order correlations.

City	Turnout	Unemployment Rate	% Negative Ads
A	55	5	60
B	60	8	63
C	65	9	55
D	68	9	53
E	70	10	48
Mean =	63.6	8.2	55.8
S =	5.5	1.7	5.3

	Unemployment	Negative Ads
Turnout	.95	−0.87
Unemployment		−0.70

a. Compute the partial correlation coefficient for the relationship between turnout (Y) and unemployment (X) while controlling for the effect of negative advertising (Z). What effect does this control variable have on the bivariate relationship? Is the relationship between turnout and unemployment direct? *(HINT: Use Formula 17.1 and see Section 17.2.)*

b. Compute the partial correlation coefficient for the relationship between turnout (Y) and negative advertising (X) while controlling for the effect of unemployment (Z). What effect does this have on the bivariate relationship? Is the relationship between turnout and negative advertising direct? *(HINT: Use Formula 17.1 and see Section 17.2. You will need this partial correlation to compute the multiple correlation coefficient.)*

c. Find the unstandardized multiple regression equation with unemployment (X_1) and negative ads (X_2) as the independent variables. What turnout would be expected in a city in which the unemployment rate was 10% and 75% of the campaign ads were negative? *(HINT: Use Formulas 17.4 and 17.5 to compute the partial slopes and then use Formula 17.6 to find a, the Y intercept. The regression line is stated in Formula 17.3. Substitute 10 for X_1 and 75 for X_2 to compute predicted Y.)*

d. Compute beta-weights for each independent variable. Which has the stronger impact on turnout? *(HINT: Use Formulas 17.7 and 17.8 to calculate the beta-weights.)*

e. Compute the multiple correlation coefficient (R) and the coefficient of multiple determination (R^2). How much of the variance in voter turnout is explained by the two independent variables? *(HINT: Use Formula 17.11. You calculated $r^2_{y2.1}$ in part b of this problem.)*

f. Write a paragraph summarizing your conclusions about the relationships among these three variables.

17.2 | SOC | A scale measuring support for increases in the national defence budget has been administered to a sample. The respondents have also been asked to indicate how many years of school they have completed and how many years, if any, they served in the Canadian military. Take "support" as the dependent variable.

Case	Support	Years of School	Years of Service
A	20	12	2
B	15	12	4
C	20	16	20
D	10	10	10
E	10	16	20
F	5	8	0
G	8	14	2
H	20	12	20
I	10	10	4
J	20	16	0

a. Compute the partial correlation coefficient for the relationship between support (Y) and years of school (X) while controlling for the effect of years of service (Z). What effect does this have on the bivariate relationship? Is the relationship between support and years of school direct?

b. Compute the partial correlation coefficient for the relationship between support (Y) and years of service (X) while controlling for the effect of years of school (Z). What effect does this have on the bivariate relationship? Is the relationship between support and years of service direct? *(HINT: You will need this partial correlation to compute the multiple correlation coefficient.)*

c. Find the unstandardized multiple regression equation with school (X_1) and service (X_2) as the independent variables. What level of support would be expected in a person with 13 years of school and 15 years of service?

d. Compute beta-weights for each independent variable. Which has the stronger impact on support?

e. Compute the multiple correlation coefficient (R) and the coefficient of multiple determination (R^2). How much of the variance in support is explained by the two independent variables? *(HINT: You calculated $r^2_{y2.1}$ in part b of this problem.)*

f. Write a paragraph summarizing your conclusions about the relationships among these three variables.

17.3 | SOC | Data on civil strife (number of incidents), unemployment, and urbanization have been gathered for 10 nations. Take civil strife as the dependent variable. Compute the zero-order correlations among all three variables.

Number of Incidents of Civil Strife	Unemployment Rate	Percentage of Population Living in Urban Areas
0	5.3	60
1	1.0	65
5	2.7	55
7	2.8	68
10	3.0	69
23	2.5	70
25	6.0	45
26	5.2	40
30	7.8	75
53	9.2	80

a. Compute the partial correlation coefficient for the relationship between strife (Y) and unemployment (X) while controlling for the effect of urbanization (Z). What effect does this have on the bivariate relationship? Is the relationship between strife and unemployment direct?

b. Compute the partial correlation coefficient for the relationship between strife (Y) and urbanization (X) while controlling for the effect of unemployment (Z). What effect does this have on the bivariate relationship? Is the relationship between strife and urbanization direct? *(HINT: You will need this partial correlation to compute the multiple correlation coefficient.)*

c. Find the unstandardized multiple regression equation with unemployment (X_1) and urbanization (X_2) as the independent variables. What level of strife would be expected in a nation in which the unemployment rate was 10% and 90% of the population lived in urban areas?

d. Compute beta-weights for each independent variable. Which has the stronger impact on strife?

e. Compute the multiple correlation coefficient (R) and the coefficient of multiple determination (R^2). How much of the variance in strife is explained by the two independent variables?

f. Write a paragraph summarizing your conclusions about the relationships among these three variables.

17.4 SOC/CJ In problem 15.5, crime and population data were presented for each of 10 Canadian cities. The data are reproduced here.

b. Make a prediction for each crime variable for a city with a 5% growth rate and a population that is 90% urbanized.

c. Compute beta-weights for each independent variable in each equation and compare their relative effect on each dependent.

d. Compute R and R^2 for each crime variable, using the population variables as independent variables.

e. Write a paragraph summarizing your findings.

17.5 PS Problem 15.4 presented data on 10 electoral districts. The information is reproduced here.

District	Percent Working-class	Unemployment Rate	Voter Turnout
A	50	10	56
B	45	12	55
C	56	8	52
D	78	15	60
E	13	5	89
F	85	20	25
G	62	18	64
H	33	9	88
I	25	0	42
J	49	9	36

City	Crime Rate			Population		
	Homicide	Robbery	Car Theft	Growth	Density	Urban
A	1	19	104	3.8	41.7	52.6
B	5	214	286	5.5	402.7	92.1
C	4	138	344	4.7	277.8	81.2
D	2	37	184	5.4	52.3	45.3
E	6	89	252	14.4	181.5	78.1
F	5	81	230	9.6	102.3	48.8
G	6	145	447	22.8	81.5	84.8
H	7	146	842	40.0	46.7	88.2
I	3	99	594	21.1	90.0	83.1
J	6	178	537	13.6	221.2	96.7

Source: U.S. Bureau of the Census, Statistical Abstracts of the United States 2001. Washington DC, 2002.

Take the three crime variables as the dependent variables (one at a time) and

a. Find the multiple regression equations (unstandardized) with growth and urbanization as independent variables.

Take voter turnout as the dependent variable and

a. Find the multiple regression equations (unstandardized).

b. What turnout would you expect for a district in which 0% of the voters were working-class and 5% were unemployed?

c. Compute beta-weights for each independent variable and compare their relative effect on turnout. Which was the more important factor?

d. Compute R and R^2.

e. Write a paragraph summarizing your findings.

17.6 SW Twelve families have been referred to a counsellor, and she has rated each of them on a cohesiveness scale. Also, she has information on family income and number of children currently living at home. Take family cohesion as the dependent variable.

Family	Cohesion Score	Family Income	Number of Children
A	10	30,000	5
B	10	70,000	4
C	9	35,000	4
D	5	25,000	0
E	1	55,000	3
F	7	40,000	0
G	2	60,000	2
H	5	30,000	3
I	8	50,000	5
J	3	25,000	4
K	2	45,000	3
L	4	50,000	0

a. Find the multiple regression equations (unstandardized).

b. What level of cohesion would be expected in a family with an income of $20,000 and 6 children?

c. Compute beta-weights for each independent variable and compare their relative effect on cohesion. Which was the more important factor?

d. Compute R and R^2.

e. Write a paragraph summarizing your findings.

17.7 Problem 15.8 presented per capita expenditures on education for 15 large Canadian cities, along with rank on income per capita and the percentage of the population that has graduated from high school. The data are reproduced below. Take educational expenditures as the dependent variable.

a. Compute beta-weights for each independent variable and compare their relative effect on expenditures. Which was the more important factor?

City	Per Capita Expenditures on Education	Percent High School Graduates	Rank in per Capita Income
A	1,102	82	48
B	1,339	90	7
C	1,907	88	1
D	1,171	84	25
E	1,621	86	9
F	1,276	88	24
G	1,159	81	45
H	1,412	86	5
I	1,487	86	18
J	1,041	80	50
K	1,194	90	22
L	1,262	88	6
M	1,163	79	32
N	1,223	86	15
O	1,549	90	20

b. Compute R and R^2.

c. Write a paragraph summarizing your findings.

17.8 SOC The scores on four variables for 20 individuals are reported below: hours of TV (number of hours of TV viewing each day), occupational prestige (higher scores indicate greater prestige), number of children, and age. Take TV viewing as the dependent variable and select two of the remaining variables as independents.

Hours of TV	Occupational Prestige	Number of Children	Age
4	50	2	43
3	36	3	58
3	36	1	34
4	50	2	42
2	45	2	27
3	50	5	60
4	50	0	28
7	40	3	55
1	57	2	46
3	33	2	65
1	46	3	56
3	31	1	29
1	19	2	41
0	52	0	50
2	48	1	62
4	36	1	24
3	48	0	25
1	62	1	87
5	50	0	45
1	27	3	62

a. Compute beta-weights for each of the independent variables you selected and compare their relative effect on the hours of television watching. Which was the more important factor?

b. Compute R and R^2.

c. Write a paragraph summarizing your findings.

SPSS for Windows

Using SPSS for Windows for Regression Analysis with the 2001 Census

The demonstration and exercise below use the shortened version of the 2001 Census data. Start SPSS for Windows and open the *Census.sav* file.

SPSS DEMONSTRATION 17.1 What Are the Effects of Education and Sex on Income?

We will use the **Linear Regression** procedure to examine the effects of education (*totschp*) and sex (*sexp*) on total annual income (*totincp*). The **Linear Regression** procedure permits the user to control many aspects of the regression formula, and it can produce a much greater volume of output than the **Correlate** procedure. This demonstration represents a very sparing use of the power of the regression command and an extremely economical use of all the options available. We urge you to explore some of the variations and capabilities of this powerful data-analysis procedure.

Ideally, the independent variables in a linear regression analysis should be interval-ratio in level of measurement, but ordinal variables with a broad range of scores such as *totschp* will work as well. Sex is a nominal-level variable, and its inclusion in a regression procedure may be surprising. However, nominal variables with only two categories—sometimes called "dummy variables"—are commonly used in regression (see Section 17.6).

With the 2001 Census loaded, click **Analyze, Regression,** and **Linear,** and the **Linear Regression** window will appear. Move *totincp* into the **Dependent** box and *totschp* and *sexp* into the **Independent(s)** box. If you wish, you can click the **Statistics** button and then click **Descriptives** to get zero-order correlations, means, and standard deviations for the variables. Click **Continue,** and then **OK,** and the following output will appear (descriptive information about the variables and the zero-order correlations are omitted here to conserve space).

Model Summary

Model	R	R Square	Adjusted R Square	Std. Error of the Estimate
1	.380[*]	.144	.143	24734.363

[*]Predictors: (Constant), *sexp* (sex), *totschp* (total years of schooling)

ANOVA[†]

Model		Sum of Squares	df	Mean Square	F	Sig.
1	Regression	1.546E11	2	7.729E10	126.335	.000[*]
	Residual	9.158E11	1497	6.118E8		
	Total	1.070E12	1499			

[*] Predictors: (Constant), *sexp* (sex), *totschp* (total years of schooling)
[†] Dependent variable: *totincp* (total income $)

Coefficients*

Model		Unstandardized Coefficients B	Std. Error	Standardized Coefficients Beta	t	Sig.
1	(Constant)	−14766.173	2708.137		−5.453	.000
	Totschp (Total years of schooling)	3459.140	293.278	.282	11.795	.000
	Sexp (sex)	14049.951	1280.270	.262	10.974	.000

*Dependent Variable: totincp total income $

The "Model Summary" output block reports the multiple R (.380) and R square (.144), which indicates that the independent variables combined account for 14.4% of the variation in total annual income. The "ANOVA" block shows the relationship between the variables is statistically significance (Sig. = .000). (See Demonstration 7.1 for an explanation about why some values in the output contain numbers with the letter "E.")

In the last output block, we see the slopes (B) of the independent variables on *totincp*, the standardized partial slopes (Beta), and the Y intercept (reported as a constant of −14,766.173). The slope for education indicates that income increases by $3,459 on average as we move up one education category to the next category while controlling for the effects of sex. The slope for sex is also positive (14,049.951). In other words, income increases as sex "increases," that is, income is higher for people with the "higher" score on sex. Because a female is coded as 1 and a male as 2, the average income for males is $14,049 higher than the average income for females, even after controlling for education. From this information, we can build a regression equation to predict scores on *totincp*.

The beta for *totschp* (.282) is slightly larger than the beta for *sexp* (.262). What does this mean? At least for this sample, a person's income is more affected by education than by sex.

Exercise (using *Census.sav*)

17.1 Conduct the analysis in Demonstration 17.1 again with *selfip* (self-employment income) as the dependent variable. Compare and contrast with the analysis of *totincp*.

PART IV CUMULATIVE EXERCISES

1. Two research questions that can be answered by one of the techniques presented in Chapters 16 and 17 are stated below. For each research situation, choose either the elaboration technique or regression analysis. The level of measurement of the variables should have a great deal of influence on your decision.

a. For a sample of recently graduated students planning to go into a master's degree program, did having a job during the school year interfere with academic success? For 20 students, data have been gathered on overall undergraduate GPA, the average number of hours the student worked each week, and Graduate Record Examinations (GRE) score (a measure of preparedness for graduate-level work). Take GPA as the dependent variable.

b. Only about half of this sample graduated within four years (1 = yes, 2 = no). Was their progress affected by their level of social activity (1 = low, 2 = high)? Is the relationship between these variables the same for both males (1) and females (2)?

GPA	Hours Worked per Week	GRE	Graduated in 4 Years	Social Activity	Sex
3.14	13	550	1	1	1
2.00	20	375	1	2	2
2.11	22	450	1	1	2
3.00	10	575	1	2	1
3.75	0	600	1	1	1
3.11	21	650	1	1	2
3.22	7	605	1	2	1
2.75	25	630	1	1	2
2.50	30	680	1	1	1
2.10	32	610	1	1	2
2.45	20	580	2	2	2
2.01	40	590	2	1	1
3.90	0	675	2	2	2
3.45	0	650	2	2	1
2.30	25	550	2	2	1
2.20	18	470	2	1	2
2.60	25	600	2	2	1
3.10	15	525	2	2	1
2.60	27	480	2	1	2
2.20	20	500	2	2	1

2. A research project has been conducted on the audiences of religious television programs. Several hypotheses have been developed with regard to the following variables:

How many hours per week do you watch religious programs on television? (actual hours)

What is your age? (in years)

How many years of formal schooling have you completed? _____
Have you ever donated money to a religious television program?
_____ 1. Yes
_____ 2. No
What is your marital status?
_____ 1. Married
_____ 2. Not married
What is your sex
_____ 1. Female
_____ 2. Male

a. The amount of time devoted to religious television will increase with age and decrease with education, but age will have the strongest effect.
b. Married individuals will be more likely to donate money. Married females will be especially likely to donate money.

Do the data support these hypotheses?

Hours Watching Religious TV	Age	Education	Ever Donate?	Marital Status	Sex
14	52	10	1	1	1
10	45	12	1	1	2
8	18	12	1	1	1
5	45	12	1	1	1
10	57	10	1	1	2
14	65	8	2	1	1
3	23	12	1	1	1
12	47	11	2	1	1
2	30	14	2	1	2
1	20	16	2	1	2
21	60	16	1	2	1
15	55	12	1	2	2
12	47	9	2	2	1
8	32	14	1	2	2
15	50	12	1	2	1
10	45	10	2	2	2
20	72	16	1	2	1
12	40	16	2	2	2
14	42	14	2	2	2
10	38	12	1	2	1

Appendix A   Area under the Normal Curve

Column (a) lists *Z* scores from 0.00 to 4.00. Only positive scores are displayed, but because the normal curve is symmetrical, the areas for negative scores will be exactly the same as areas for positive scores. Column (b) lists the proportion of the total area between the *Z* score and the mean. Figure A.1 displays areas of this type. Column (c) lists the proportion of the area beyond the *Z* score, and Figure A.2 displays this type of area.

FIGURE A.1   AREA BETWEEN MEAN AND Z

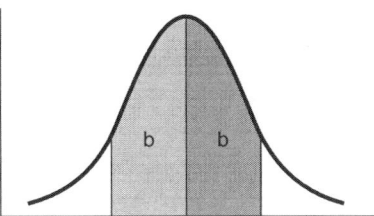

FIGURE A.2   AREA BEYOND Z

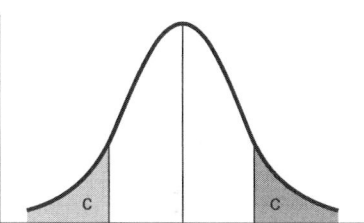

(a) Z	(b) Area between Mean and Z	(c) Area beyond Z	(a) Z	(b) Area between Mean and Z	(c) Area beyond Z
0.00	0.0000	0.5000	0.27	0.1064	0.3936
0.01	0.0040	0.4960	0.28	0.1103	0.3897
0.02	0.0080	0.4920	0.29	0.1141	0.3859
0.03	0.0120	0.4880	0.30	0.1179	0.3821
0.04	0.0160	0.4840			
0.05	0.0199	0.4801	0.31	0.1217	0.3783
0.06	0.0239	0.4761	0.32	0.1255	0.3745
0.07	0.0279	0.4721	0.33	0.1293	0.3707
0.08	0.0319	0.4681	0.34	0.1331	0.3669
0.09	0.0359	0.4641	0.35	0.1368	0.3632
0.10	0.0398	0.4602	0.36	0.1406	0.3594
			0.37	0.1443	0.3557
0.11	0.0438	0.4562	0.38	0.1480	0.3520
0.12	0.0478	0.4522	0.39	0.1517	0.3483
0.13	0.0517	0.4483	0.40	0.1554	0.3446
0.14	0.0557	0.4443			
0.15	0.0596	0.4404	0.41	0.1591	0.3409
0.16	0.0636	0.4364	0.42	0.1628	0.3372
0.17	0.0675	0.4325	0.43	0.1664	0.3336
0.18	0.0714	0.4286	0.44	0.1700	0.3300
0.19	0.0753	0.4247	0.45	0.1736	0.3264
0.20	0.0793	0.4207	0.46	0.1772	0.3228
			0.47	0.1808	0.3192
0.21	0.0832	0.4168	0.48	0.1844	0.3156
0.22	0.0871	0.4129	0.49	0.1879	0.3121
0.23	0.0910	0.4090	0.50	0.1915	0.3085
0.24	0.0948	0.4052			
0.25	0.0987	0.4013	0.51	0.1950	0.3050
0.26	0.1026	0.3974	0.52	0.1985	0.3015

(a) Z	(b) Area between Mean and Z	(c) Area beyond Z	(a) Z	(b) Area between Mean and Z	(c) Area beyond Z
0.53	0.2019	0.2981	1.05	0.3531	0.1469
0.54	0.2054	0.2946	1.06	0.3554	0.1446
0.55	0.2088	0.2912	1.07	0.3577	0.1423
0.56	0.2123	0.2877	1.08	0.3599	0.1401
0.57	0.2157	0.2843	1.09	0.3621	0.1379
0.58	0.2190	0.2810	1.10	0.3643	0.1357
0.59	0.2224	0.2776	1.11	0.3665	0.1335
0.60	0.2257	0.2743	1.12	0.3686	0.1314
0.61	0.2291	0.2709	1.13	0.3708	0.1292
0.62	0.2324	0.2676	1.14	0.3729	0.1271
0.63	0.2357	0.2643	1.15	0.3749	0.1251
0.64	0.2389	0.2611	1.16	0.3770	0.1230
0.65	0.2422	0.2578	1.17	0.3790	0.1210
0.66	0.2454	0.2546	1.18	0.3810	0.1190
0.67	0.2486	0.2514	1.19	0.3830	0.1170
0.68	0.2517	0.2483	1.20	0.3849	0.1151
0.69	0.2549	0.2451	1.21	0.3869	0.1131
0.70	0.2580	0.2420	1.22	0.3888	0.1112
0.71	0.2611	0.2389	1.23	0.3907	0.1093
0.72	0.2642	0.2358	1.24	0.3925	0.1075
0.73	0.2673	0.2327	1.25	0.3944	0.1056
0.74	0.2703	0.2297	1.26	0.3962	0.1038
0.75	0.2734	0.2266	1.27	0.3980	0.1020
0.76	0.2764	0.2236	1.28	0.3997	0.1003
0.77	0.2794	0.2206	1.29	0.4015	0.0985
0.78	0.2823	0.2177	1.30	0.4032	0.0968
0.79	0.2852	0.2148	1.31	0.4049	0.0951
0.80	0.2881	0.2119	1.32	0.4066	0.0934
0.81	0.2910	0.2090	1.33	0.4082	0.0918
0.82	0.2939	0.2061	1.34	0.4099	0.0901
0.83	0.2967	0.2033	1.35	0.4115	0.0885
0.84	0.2995	0.2005	1.36	0.4131	0.0869
0.85	0.3023	0.1977	1.37	0.4147	0.0853
0.86	0.3051	0.1949	1.38	0.4162	0.0838
0.87	0.3078	0.1922	1.39	0.4177	0.0823
0.88	0.3106	0.1894	1.40	0.4192	0.0808
0.89	0.3133	0.1867	1.41	0.4207	0.0793
0.90	0.3159	0.1841	1.42	0.4222	0.0778
0.91	0.3186	0.1814	1.43	0.4236	0.0764
0.92	0.3212	0.1788	1.44	0.4251	0.0749
0.93	0.3238	0.1762	1.45	0.4265	0.0735
0.94	0.3264	0.1736	1.46	0.4279	0.0721
0.95	0.3289	0.1711	1.47	0.4292	0.0708
0.96	0.3315	0.1685	1.48	0.4306	0.0694
0.97	0.3340	0.1660	1.49	0.4319	0.0681
0.98	0.3365	0.1635	1.50	0.4332	0.0668
0.99	0.3389	0.1611	1.51	0.4345	0.0655
1.00	0.3413	0.1587	1.52	0.4357	0.0643
1.01	0.3438	0.1562	1.53	0.4370	0.0630
1.02	0.3461	0.1539	1.54	0.4382	0.0618
1.03	0.3485	0.1515	1.55	0.4394	0.0606
1.04	0.3508	0.1492	1.56	0.4406	0.0594

(a) Z	(b) Area between Mean and Z	(c) Area beyond Z	(a) Z	(b) Area between Mean and Z	(c) Area beyond Z
1.57	0.4418	0.0582	2.09	0.4817	0.0183
1.58	0.4429	0.0571	2.10	0.4821	0.0179
1.59	0.4441	0.0559	2.11	0.4826	0.0174
1.60	0.4452	0.0548	2.12	0.4830	0.0170
1.61	0.4463	0.0537	2.13	0.4834	0.0166
1.62	0.4474	0.0526	2.14	0.4838	0.0162
1.63	0.4484	0.0516	2.15	0.4842	0.0158
1.64	0.4495	0.0505	2.16	0.4846	0.0154
1.65	0.4505	0.0495	2.17	0.4850	0.0150
1.66	0.4515	0.0485	2.18	0.4854	0.0146
1.67	0.4525	0.0475	2.19	0.4857	0.0143
1.68	0.4535	0.0465	2.20	0.4861	0.0139
1.69	0.4545	0.0455	2.21	0.4864	0.0136
1.70	0.4554	0.0446	2.22	0.4868	0.0132
1.71	0.4564	0.0436	2.23	0.4871	0.0129
1.72	0.4573	0.0427	2.24	0.4875	0.0125
1.73	0.4582	0.0418	2.25	0.4878	0.0122
1.74	0.4591	0.0409	2.26	0.4881	0.0119
1.75	0.4599	0.0401	2.27	0.4884	0.0116
1.76	0.4608	0.0392	2.28	0.4887	0.0113
1.77	0.4616	0.0384	2.29	0.4890	0.0110
1.78	0.4625	0.0375	2.30	0.4893	0.0107
1.79	0.4633	0.0367	2.31	0.4896	0.0104
1.80	0.4641	0.0359	2.32	0.4898	0.0102
1.81	0.4649	0.0351	2.33	0.4901	0.0099
1.82	0.4656	0.0344	2.34	0.4904	0.0096
1.83	0.4664	0.0336	2.35	0.4906	0.0094
1.84	0.4671	0.0329	2.36	0.4909	0.0091
1.85	0.4678	0.0322	2.37	0.4911	0.0089
1.86	0.4686	0.0314	2.38	0.4913	0.0087
1.87	0.4693	0.0307	2.39	0.4916	0.0084
1.88	0.4699	0.0301	2.40	0.4918	0.0082
1.89	0.4706	0.0294	2.41	0.4920	0.0080
1.90	0.4713	0.0287	2.42	0.4922	0.0078
1.91	0.4719	0.0281	2.43	0.4925	0.0075
1.92	0.4726	0.0274	2.44	0.4927	0.0073
1.93	0.4732	0.0268	2.45	0.4929	0.0071
1.94	0.4738	0.0262	2.46	0.4931	0.0069
1.95	0.4744	0.0256	2.47	0.4932	0.0068
1.96	0.4750	0.0250	2.48	0.4934	0.0066
1.97	0.4756	0.0244	2.49	0.4936	0.0064
1.98	0.4761	0.0239	2.50	0.4938	0.0062
1.99	0.4767	0.0233	2.51	0.4940	0.0060
2.00	0.4772	0.0228	2.52	0.4941	0.0059
2.01	0.4778	0.0222	2.53	0.4943	0.0057
2.02	0.4783	0.0217	2.54	0.4945	0.0055
2.03	0.4788	0.0212	2.55	0.4946	0.0054
2.04	0.4793	0.0207	2.56	0.4948	0.0052
2.05	0.4798	0.0202	2.57	0.4949	0.0051
2.06	0.4803	0.0197	2.58	0.4951	0.0049
2.07	0.4808	0.0192	2.59	0.4952	0.0048
2.08	0.4812	0.0188	2.60	0.4953	0.0047

(a)	(b) Area between Mean and Z	(c) Area beyond Z	(a)	(b) Area between Mean and Z	(c) Area beyond Z
Z			Z		
2.61	0.4955	0.0045	3.11	0.4991	0.0009
2.62	0.4956	0.0044	3.12	0.4991	0.0009
2.63	0.4957	0.0043	3.13	0.4991	0.0009
2.64	0.4959	0.0041	3.14	0.4992	0.0008
2.65	0.4960	0.0040	3.15	0.4992	0.0008
2.66	0.4961	0.0039	3.16	0.4992	0.0008
2.67	0.4962	0.0038	3.17	0.4992	0.0008
2.68	0.4963	0.0037	3.18	0.4993	0.0007
2.69	0.4964	0.0036	3.19	0.4993	0.0007
2.70	0.4965	0.0035	3.20	0.4993	0.0007
2.71	0.4966	0.0034	3.21	0.4993	0.0007
2.72	0.4967	0.0033	3.22	0.4994	0.0006
2.73	0.4968	0.0032	3.23	0.4994	0.0006
2.74	0.4969	0.0031	3.24	0.4994	0.0006
2.75	0.4970	0.0030	3.25	0.4994	0.0006
2.76	0.4971	0.0029	3.26	0.4994	0.0006
2.77	0.4972	0.0028	3.27	0.4995	0.0005
2.78	0.4973	0.0027	3.28	0.4995	0.0005
2.79	0.4974	0.0026	3.29	0.4995	0.0005
2.80	0.4974	0.0026	3.30	0.4995	0.0005
2.81	0.4975	0.0025	3.31	0.4995	0.0005
2.82	0.4976	0.0024	3.32	0.4995	0.0005
2.83	0.4977	0.0023	3.33	0.4996	0.0004
2.84	0.4977	0.0023	3.34	0.4996	0.0004
2.85	0.4978	0.0022	3.35	0.4996	0.0004
2.86	0.4979	0.0021	3.36	0.4996	0.0004
2.87	0.4979	0.0021	3.37	0.4996	0.0004
2.88	0.4980	0.0020	3.38	0.4996	0.0004
2.89	0.4981	0.0019	3.39	0.4997	0.0003
2.90	0.4981	0.0019	3.40	0.4997	0.0003
2.91	0.4982	0.0018	3.41	0.4997	0.0003
2.92	0.4982	0.0018	3.42	0.4997	0.0003
2.93	0.4983	0.0017	3.43	0.4997	0.0003
2.94	0.4984	0.0016	3.44	0.4997	0.0003
2.95	0.4984	0.0016	3.45	0.4997	0.0003
2.96	0.4985	0.0015	3.46	0.4997	0.0003
2.97	0.4985	0.0015	3.47	0.4997	0.0003
2.98	0.4986	0.0014	3.48	0.4997	0.0003
2.99	0.4986	0.0014	3.49	0.4998	0.0002
3.00	0.4986	0.0014	3.50	0.4998	0.0002
3.01	0.4987	0.0013	3.60	0.4998	0.0002
3.02	0.4987	0.0013	3.70	0.4999	0.0001
3.03	0.4988	0.0012	3.70	0.4999	0.0001
3.04	0.4988	0.0012	3.80	0.4999	0.0001
3.05	0.4989	0.0011	3.90	0.4999	<0.0001
3.06	0.4989	0.0011	3.90	0.4999	<0.0001
3.07	0.4989	0.0011	4.00	0.4999	<0.0001
3.08	0.4990	0.0010			
3.09	0.4990	0.0010			
3.10	0.4990	0.0010			

Appendix B Distribution of *t*

Degrees of Freedom (df)	Level of Significance for One-tailed Test					
	.10	.05	.025	.01	.005	.0005
	Level of Significance for Two-tailed Test					
	.20	.10	.05	.02	.01	.001
1	3.078	6.314	12.706	31.821	63.657	636.619
2	1.886	2.920	4.303	6.965	9.925	31.598
3	1.638	2.353	3.182	4.541	5.841	12.941
4	1.533	2.132	2.776	3.747	4.604	8.610
5	1.476	2.015	2.571	3.365	4.032	6.859
6	1.440	1.943	2.447	3.143	3.707	5.959
7	1.415	1.895	2.365	2.998	3.499	5.405
8	1.397	1.860	2.306	2.896	3.355	5.041
9	1.383	1.833	2.262	2.821	3.250	4.781
10	1.372	1.812	2.228	2.764	3.169	4.587
11	1.363	1.796	2.201	2.718	3.106	4.437
12	1.356	1.782	2.179	2.681	3.055	4.318
13	1.350	1.771	2.160	2.650	3.012	4.221
14	1.345	1.761	2.145	2.624	2.977	4.140
15	1.341	1.753	2.131	2.602	2.947	4.073
16	1.337	1.746	2.120	2.583	2.921	4.015
17	1.333	1.740	2.110	2.567	2.898	3.965
18	1.330	1.734	2.101	2.552	2.878	3.922
19	1.328	1.729	2.093	2.539	2.861	3.883
20	1.325	1.725	2.086	2.528	2.845	3.850
21	1.323	1.721	2.080	2.518	2.831	3.819
22	1.321	1.717	2.074	2.508	2.819	3.792
23	1.319	1.714	2.069	2.500	2.807	3.767
24	1.318	1.711	2.064	2.492	2.797	3.745
25	1.316	1.708	2.060	2.485	2.787	3.725
26	1.315	1.706	2.056	2.479	2.779	3.707
27	1.314	1.703	2.052	2.473	2.771	3.690
28	1.313	1.701	2.048	2.467	2.763	3.674
29	1.311	1.699	2.045	2.462	2.756	3.659
30	1.310	1.697	2.042	2.457	2.750	3.646
40	1.303	1.684	2.021	2.423	2.704	3.551
60	1.296	1.671	2.000	2.390	2.660	3.460
120	1.289	1.658	1.980	2.358	2.617	3.373
∞	1.282	1.645	1.960	2.326	2.576	3.291

Source: Table III of Fisher & Yates: *Statistical Tables for Biological, Agricultural and Medical Research*, published by Longman Group Ltd., London (1974), 6th edition (previously published by Oliver & Boyd Ltd., Edinburgh). Reprinted by permission of Pearson Education Limited.

Appendix C   Distribution of Chi Square

df	.99	.98	.95	.90	.80	.70	.50	.30	.20	.10	.05	.02	.01	.001
1	.000	.001	.004	.016	.064	.148	.455	1.074	1.642	2.706	3.841	5.412	6.635	10.827
2	.0201	.0404	.103	.211	.446	.713	1.386	2.408	3.219	4.605	5.991	7.824	9.210	13.815
3	.115	.185	.352	.584	1.005	1.424	2.366	3.665	4.642	6.251	7.815	9.837	11.341	16.268
4	.297	.429	.711	1.064	1.649	2.195	3.357	4.878	5.989	7.779	9.488	11.668	13.277	18.465
5	.554	.752	1.145	1.610	2.343	3.000	4.351	6.064	7.289	9.236	11.070	13.388	15.086	20.517
6	.872	1.134	1.635	2.204	3.070	3.828	5.348	7.231	8.558	10.645	12.592	15.033	16.812	22.457
7	1.239	1.564	2.167	2.833	3.822	4.671	6.346	8.383	9.803	12.017	14.067	16.622	18.475	24.322
8	1.646	2.032	2.733	3.490	4.594	5.527	7.344	9.524	11.030	13.362	15.507	18.168	20.090	26.125
9	2.088	2.532	3.325	4.168	5.380	6.393	8.343	10.656	12.242	14.684	16.919	19.679	21.666	27.877
10	2.558	3.059	3.940	4.865	6.179	7.267	9.342	11.781	13.442	15.987	18.307	21.161	23.209	29.588
11	3.053	3.609	4.575	5.578	6.989	8.148	10.341	12.899	14.631	17.275	19.675	22.618	24.725	31.264
12	3.571	4.178	5.226	6.304	7.807	9.034	11.340	14.011	15.812	18.549	21.026	24.054	26.217	32.909
13	4.107	4.765	5.892	7.042	8.634	9.926	12.340	15.119	16.985	19.812	22.362	25.472	27.688	34.528
14	4.660	5.368	6.571	7.790	9.467	10.821	13.339	16.222	18.151	21.064	23.685	26.873	29.141	36.123
15	5.229	5.985	7.261	8.547	10.307	11.721	14.339	17.322	19.311	22.307	24.996	28.259	30.578	37.697
16	5.812	6.614	7.962	9.312	11.152	12.624	15.338	18.418	20.465	23.542	26.296	29.633	32.000	39.252
17	6.408	7.255	8.672	10.085	12.002	13.531	16.338	19.511	21.615	24.769	27.587	30.995	33.409	40.790
18	7.015	7.906	9.390	10.865	12.857	14.440	17.338	20.601	22.760	25.989	28.869	32.346	34.805	42.312
19	7.633	8.567	10.117	11.651	13.716	15.352	18.338	21.689	23.900	27.204	30.144	33.687	36.191	43.820
20	8.260	9.237	10.851	12.443	14.578	16.266	19.337	22.775	25.038	28.412	31.410	35.020	37.566	45.315
21	8.897	9.915	11.591	13.240	15.445	17.182	20.337	23.858	26.171	29.615	32.671	36.343	38.932	46.797
22	9.542	10.600	12.338	14.041	16.314	18.101	21.337	24.939	27.301	30.813	33.924	37.659	40.289	48.268
23	10.196	11.293	13.091	14.848	17.187	19.021	22.337	26.018	28.429	32.007	35.172	38.968	41.638	49.728
24	10.856	11.992	13.848	15.659	18.062	19.943	23.337	27.096	29.553	33.196	36.415	40.270	42.980	51.179
25	11.524	12.697	14.611	16.473	18.940	20.867	24.337	28.172	30.675	34.382	37.652	41.566	44.314	52.620
26	12.198	13.409	15.379	17.292	19.820	21.792	25.336	29.246	31.795	35.563	38.885	42.856	45.642	54.052
27	12.879	14.125	16.151	18.114	20.703	22.719	26.336	30.319	32.912	36.741	40.113	44.140	46.963	55.476
28	13.565	14.847	16.928	18.939	21.588	23.647	27.336	31.391	34.027	37.916	41.337	45.419	48.278	56.893
29	14.256	15.574	17.708	19.768	22.475	24.577	28.336	32.461	35.139	39.087	42.557	46.693	49.588	58.302
30	14.953	16.306	18.493	20.599	23.364	25.508	29.336	33.530	36.250	40.256	43.773	47.962	50.892	59.703

Source: Table IV of Fisher & Yates: *Statistical Tables for Biological, Agricultural and Medical Research,* published by Longman Group Ltd., London (1974), 6th edition (previously published by Oliver & Boyd Ltd., Edinburgh). Reprinted by permission of Pearson Education Limited.

Appendix D Distribution of *F*

$$p = .05$$

n_1 n_2	1	2	3	4	5	6	8	12	24	∞
1	161.4	199.5	215.7	224.6	230.2	234.0	238.9	243.9	249.0	254.3
2	18.51	19.00	19.16	19.25	19.30	19.33	19.37	19.41	19.45	19.50
3	10.13	9.55	9.28	9.12	9.01	8.94	8.84	8.74	8.64	8.53
4	7.71	6.94	6.59	6.39	6.26	6.16	6.04	5.91	5.77	5.63
5	6.61	5.79	5.41	5.19	5.05	4.95	4.82	4.68	4.53	4.36
6	5.99	5.14	4.76	4.53	4.39	4.28	4.15	4.00	3.84	3.67
7	5.59	4.74	4.35	4.12	3.97	3.87	3.73	3.57	3.41	3.23
8	5.32	4.46	4.07	3.84	3.69	3.58	3.44	3.28	3.12	2.93
9	5.12	4.26	3.86	3.63	3.48	3.37	3.23	3.07	2.90	2.71
10	4.96	4.10	3.71	3.48	3.33	3.22	3.07	2.91	2.74	2.54
11	4.84	3.98	3.59	3.36	3.20	3.09	2.95	2.79	2.61	2.40
12	4.75	3.88	3.49	3.26	3.11	3.00	2.85	2.69	2.50	2.30
13	4.67	3.80	3.41	3.18	3.02	2.92	2.77	2.60	2.42	2.21
14	4.60	3.74	3.34	3.11	2.96	2.85	2.70	2.53	2.35	2.13
15	4.54	3.68	3.29	3.06	2.90	2.79	2.64	2.48	2.29	2.07
16	4.49	3.63	3.24	3.01	2.85	2.74	2.59	2.42	2.24	2.01
17	4.45	3.59	3.20	2.96	2.81	2.70	2.55	2.38	2.19	1.96
18	4.41	3.55	3.16	2.93	2.77	2.66	2.51	2.34	2.15	1.92
19	4.38	3.52	3.13	2.90	2.74	2.63	2.48	2.31	2.11	1.88
20	4.35	3.49	3.10	2.87	2.71	2.60	2.45	2.28	2.08	1.84
21	4.32	3.47	3.07	2.84	2.68	2.57	2.42	2.25	2.05	1.81
22	4.30	3.44	3.05	2.82	2.66	2.55	2.40	2.23	2.03	1.78
23	4.28	3.42	3.03	2.80	2.64	2.53	2.38	2.20	2.00	1.76
24	4.26	3.40	3.01	2.78	2.62	2.51	2.36	2.18	1.98	1.73
25	4.24	3.38	2.99	2.76	2.60	2.49	2.34	2.16	1.96	1.71
26	4.22	3.37	2.98	2.74	2.59	2.47	2.32	2.15	1.95	1.69
27	4.21	3.35	2.96	2.73	2.57	2.46	2.30	2.13	1.93	1.67
28	4.20	3.34	2.95	2.71	2.56	2.44	2.29	2.12	1.91	1.65
29	4.18	3.33	2.93	2.70	2.54	2.43	2.28	2.10	1.90	1.64
30	4.17	3.32	2.92	2.69	2.53	2.42	2.27	2.09	1.89	1.62
40	4.08	3.23	2.84	2.61	2.45	2.34	2.18	2.00	1.79	1.51
60	4.00	3.15	2.76	2.52	2.37	2.25	2.10	1.92	1.70	1.39
120	3.92	3.07	2.68	2.45	2.29	2.17	2.02	1.83	1.61	1.25
∞	3.84	2.99	2.60	2.37	2.21	2.09	1.94	1.75	1.52	1.00

Values of n_1 and n_2 represent the degrees of freedom associated with the between and within estimates of variance, respectively.

Source: Table V of Fisher and Yates: *Statistical Tables for Biological, Agricultural and Medical Research,* published by Longman Group Ltd., London (1974), 6th edition (previously published by Oliver and Boyd Ltd., Edinburgh). Reprinted by permission of Pearson Education Limited.

$p = .01$

n_1 n_2	1	2	3	4	5	6	8	12	24	∞
1	4052	4999	5403	5625	5764	5859	5981	6106	6234	6366
2	98.49	99.01	99.17	99.25	99.30	99.33	99.36	99.42	99.46	99.50
3	34.12	30.81	29.46	28.71	28.24	27.91	27.49	27.05	26.60	26.12
4	21.20	18.00	16.69	15.98	15.52	15.21	14.80	14.37	13.93	13.46
5	16.26	13.27	12.06	11.39	10.97	10.67	10.27	9.89	9.47	9.02
6	13.74	10.92	9.78	9.15	8.75	8.47	8.10	7.72	7.31	6.88
7	12.25	9.55	8.45	7.85	7.46	7.19	6.84	6.47	6.07	5.65
8	11.26	8.65	7.59	7.01	6.63	6.37	6.03	5.67	5.28	4.86
9	10.56	8.02	6.99	6.42	6.06	5.80	5.47	5.11	4.73	4.31
10	10.04	7.56	6.55	5.99	5.64	5.39	5.06	4.71	4.33	3.91
11	9.65	7.20	6.22	5.67	5.32	5.07	4.74	4.40	4.02	3.60
12	9.33	6.93	5.95	5.41	5.06	4.82	4.50	4.16	3.78	3.36
13	9.07	6.70	5.74	5.20	4.86	4.62	4.30	3.96	3.59	3.16
14	8.86	6.51	5.56	5.03	4.69	4.46	4.14	3.80	3.43	3.00
15	8.68	6.36	5.42	4.89	4.56	4.32	4.00	3.67	3.29	2.87
16	8.53	6.23	5.29	4.77	4.44	4.20	3.89	3.55	3.18	2.75
17	8.40	6.11	5.18	4.67	4.34	4.10	3.79	3.45	3.08	2.65
18	8.28	6.01	5.09	4.58	4.25	4.01	3.71	3.37	3.00	2.57
19	8.18	5.93	5.01	4.50	4.17	3.94	3.63	3.30	2.92	2.49
20	8.10	5.85	4.94	4.43	4.10	3.87	3.56	3.23	2.86	2.42
21	8.02	5.78	4.87	4.37	4.04	3.81	3.51	3.17	2.80	2.36
22	7.94	5.72	4.82	4.31	3.99	3.76	3.45	3.12	2.75	2.31
23	7.88	5.66	4.76	4.26	3.94	3.71	3.41	3.07	2.70	2.26
24	7.82	5.61	4.72	4.22	3.90	3.67	3.36	3.03	2.66	2.21
25	7.77	5.57	4.68	4.18	3.86	3.63	3.32	2.99	2.62	2.17
26	7.72	5.53	4.64	4.14	3.82	3.59	3.29	2.96	2.58	2.13
27	7.68	5.49	4.60	4.11	3.78	3.56	3.26	2.93	2.55	2.10
28	7.64	5.45	4.57	4.07	3.75	3.53	3.23	2.90	2.52	2.06
29	7.60	5.42	4.54	4.04	3.73	3.50	3.20	2.87	2.49	2.03
30	7.56	5.39	4.51	4.02	3.70	3.47	3.17	2.84	2.47	2.01
40	7.31	5.18	4.31	3.83	3.51	3.29	2.99	2.66	2.29	1.80
60	7.08	4.98	4.13	3.65	3.34	3.12	2.82	2.50	2.12	1.60
120	6.85	4.79	3.95	3.48	3.17	2.96	2.66	2.34	1.95	1.38
∞	6.64	4.60	3.78	3.32	3.02	2.80	2.51	2.18	1.79	1.00

Values of n_1 and n_2 represent the degrees of freedom associated with the between and within estimates of variance, respectively.

Appendix E Using Statistics: Ideas for Research Projects

This appendix presents outlines for four research projects, each of which requires the use of SPSS to analyze the 2001 Census or the 2004 GSS data used throughout this text, though most of the projects can be done with other data sets that may be available to your instructor. The research projects should be completed at various intervals during the course, and each project permits a great deal of choice on the part of the student. The first project stresses description and should be done after completing Chapters 2–4. The second involves estimation and should be completed in conjunction with Chapter 7. The third project uses inferential statistics and should be done after completing Part II, and the fourth combines inferential statistics with measures of association (with an option for multivariate analysis) and should be done after Part III (or IV).

**PROJECT 1—
DESCRIPTIVE
STATISTICS**

1. From either the 2001 Census (short version, *Census.sav*, or full version, *CensusFull.sav*) or the 2004 GSS (*GSS.sav*) data set, select five variables and use the **Frequencies** command to get frequency distributions and summary statistics. *(NOTE: Select at least one variable from each level of measurement.)* Click the **Statistics** button and request the mean, median, mode, standard deviation, and range. See Demonstrations 3.1 and 4.1 for guidelines and examples. Make a note of all relevant information when it appears on screen or make a hard copy. See Appendix G for a list of variables available in the Census and GSS.

2. For each variable, get bar or line charts to summarize the overall shape of the distribution of the variable. See Demonstration 2.2 for guidelines and examples.

3. Inspect the frequency distributions and graphs and choose appropriate measures of central tendency and, for ordinal- and interval-ratio-level variables, dispersion. Also, for interval-ratio and ordinal variables with many scores, check for skew both by using the line chart and by comparing the mean and median (see Sections 3.6 and 3.7). Write a sentence or two of description for each variable, being careful to include a description of the overall shape of the distribution (see Chapter 2), the central tendency (Chapter 3), and the dispersion (Chapter 4).

4. Below are examples of *minimal* summary sentences, using fictitious data:

   For a nominal-level variable (e.g., marital status), report the mode and some detail about the overall distribution. For example:

"Most respondents were married (57.5%), but divorced (17.4%) and single (21.3%) individuals were also common."

For an ordinal-level variable (e.g., occupational prestige), use the median (and, perhaps, the mode) and the range.

"The median prestige score was 44.3, and the range extended from 34 to 87. The most common score was 42."

For an interval-ratio level variable (e.g., population density for 124 nations), use the mean (and, perhaps, the median or mode) and the standard deviation (and, perhaps, the range).

"For these nations, population density (population per square kilometre) ranged from a low of 4.00 to a high of 12,000. The standard deviation was 1,000. The nations averaged 351 people per square kilometre, and the median density was 193. The distribution is positively skewed, and some nations have very high population density."

PROJECT 2—ESTIMATION In this exercise, you will use the 2001 Census (short version: *Census.sav*) sample to estimate the characteristics of the Canadian population. You will use SPSS to generate the sample statistics to find the confidence interval and state each interval in words.

A. Estimating Means

1. There are relatively few interval-ratio variables in the 2001 Census, and for this part of the project, you may use ordinal variables that have *at least* three categories or scores. Choose a total of three variables that fit this description *other than* the variables you used in Exercise 7.1. *(NOTE: Your instructor may specify a different number of variables.)*

2. Use the **Explore** command to get the 95% confidence interval for the first of your variables. Repeat this procedure for the remaining variables.

3. For each variable, write a summary sentence reporting the variable, the interval itself, the confidence level, and sample size. Write in plain English, as if you were reporting results in a newspaper. Most importantly, you should make it clear that you are estimating characteristics of the entire Canadian population. For example, a summary sentence might look like this:

"Based on a random sample of 1,500, I estimate at the 95% level that Canadian drivers average between 98.46 and 102.22 kilometres per hour when driving on highways."

B. Estimating Proportions

1. Choose three variables that are nominal or ordinal with *two or three* categories *other than* the variables you used in Exercise 7.3. *(NOTE: Your instructor may specify a different number of variables.)*

2. Use the **Frequencies** command to get the percentage of the sample in the various categories of each variable. Change the percentages (remember to use the "valid percents" column) to find proportions and construct confidence intervals for one category of each variable (e.g., the % female for *sex*) using Formula 7.3.

3. For each variable, write a summary sentence reporting the variable, the interval, the confidence level, and sample size. Write in plain English, as if you were reporting results in a newspaper. Remember to make it clear that you are estimating a characteristic of the Canadian population.

4. For any one of the intervals you constructed, identify each of the following concepts and terms and briefly explain their role in estimation: sample, population, statistic, parameter, EPSEM, representative, confidence level.

**PROJECT 3 —
SIGNIFICANCE TESTING**

Use the 2001 Census (short version: *Census.sav*) data set for this project.

A. Two-Sample *T* Test (Chapter 9)

1. Choose two different dependent variables from the interval-ratio or ordinal variables that have three or more scores. Choose independent variables that might logically be a cause of your dependent variables. Remember that, for a *t* test, independent variables can have *only* two categories. Independent variables can be any level of measurement, and you may use the same independent variable for both tests.

2. Click **Analyze, Compare Means,** and then **Independent Samples T Test.** Put your dependent variable(s) in the **Test Variable(s)** box and your independent variable in the **Grouping Variable** box. You will also need to specify the scores used to define the groups on the independent variable. See SPSS Demonstration 9.1 for an example. Make a note of the test results (group means, obtained *t* score, significance, sample size) or keep a hard copy. Repeat the procedure for the second dependent variable.

3. Write up the results of the test. See Reading Statistics 6 for some ideas about how to report results. At a minimum, your report should clearly identify the independent and dependent variables, the sample statistics, the value of the test statistic (step 4), the results of the test (step 5), and the alpha level you used.

B. Analysis of Variance (Chapter 10)

1. Choose two different dependent variables from the interval-ratio or ordinal variables that have three or more scores. Choose independent variables that might logically be a cause of your dependent variables and that have between three and five categories. You may use the same independent variables for both tests.

2. Click **Analyze, Compare Means,** and then **One-way Anova.** The **One-way Anova** window will appear. Find your dependent variable in the variable list on the left and click the arrow to move the variable name into the **Dependent List** box. Note that you can request more than one dependent variable at a time. Next, find the name of your independent variable and move it to the **Factor** box. Click **Options** and then click the box next to **Descriptive** in the **Statistics** box to request means and standard deviations. Click **Continue** and **OK.** Make a note of the test results or keep a hard copy. Repeat, if necessary, for your second dependent variable.

3. Write up the results of the test. At a minimum, your report should clearly identify the independent and dependent variables, the sample statistics (category means), the value of the test statistic (step 4), the results of the test (step 5), the degrees of freedom, and the alpha level you used.

C. Chi Square (Chapter 11)

1. Choose two different dependent variables of any level of measurement that have five or fewer (preferably 2–3) scores. For each dependent variable, choose an independent variable that might logically be a cause. Independent variables can be any level of measurement as long as they have five or fewer (preferably 2–3) categories. Output will be easier to analyze if you use variables with few categories. You may use the same independent variable for both tests.

2. Click **Analyze, Descriptive Statistics,** and then **Crosstabs.** The **Crosstabs** dialog box will appear. Highlight your first dependent variable and move it into the **Rows** box. Next, highlight your independent variable and move it into the **Columns** box. Click the **Statistics** button at the bottom of the window and click the box next to **Chi square.** Click **Continue** and **OK.** Make a note of the results or keep a hard copy. Repeat for your second dependent variable.

3. Write up the results of the test. At a minimum, your report should clearly identify the independent and dependent variables, the value of the test statistic (step 4), the results of the test (step 5), the degrees of freedom, and the alpha level you used. It is almost always desirable to also report the column percentages (see Section 11.5).

PROJECT 4—ANALYZING THE STRENGTH AND SIGNIFICANCE OF RELATIONSHIPS

A. Using Bivariate Tables

1. From the 2004 GSS data set (*GSS.sav*), select either

    a. One dependent variable and three independent variables (possible causes)

or **b.** One independent variable and three possible dependent variables (possible effects).

Variables can be from any level of measurement but must have only a few (2–5) categories or "scores." Develop research questions or hypotheses about the relationships between variables. Make sure that the causal links you suggest are sensible and logical.

2. Use the **Crosstabs** procedure to generate bivariate tables. See any of the Demonstrations at the end of Chapters 12, 13, or 14 for examples. Click **Analyze, Descriptive Statistics,** and **Crosstabs** and place your dependent variable(s) in the rows and independent variable(s) in the columns. On the **Crosstabs** dialog box, click the **Statistics** button and choose chi square, phi or V, and gamma for every table you request. On the **Crosstabs** dialog box, click the **Cells** button and get column percentages for every table you request. Make a note of results as they appear on the screen or get hard copies.

3. Write a report that presents and analyzes these relationships. Be clear about which variables are dependent and which are independent. For each combination of variables, report the test of significance and measure of association. In addition, for each relationship, report and discuss column percentages, pattern or direction of the relationship, and strength of the relationship.

4. *OPTIONAL MULTIVARIATE ANALYSIS:* Pick one of the bivariate relationships you produced in step 2 and find a logical control variable for this relationship. Run **Crosstabs** for the bivariate relationship again while controlling for the third variable. Compare the partial tables with each other and with the bivariate table. Is the original bivariate relationship direct? Is there evidence of a spurious or intervening relationship? Do the variables have an interactive relationship? Write up the results of this analysis and include them in your summary paper for this project.

B. Using Interval-Ratio Variables

1. From the 2001 Census (short version: *Census.sav;* or full version: *CensusFull.sav*), select either

    a. One dependent variable and three independent variables (possible causes) or **b.** One independent variable and three possible dependent variables (possible effects).

Variables should be interval-ratio in level of measurement, but you may use ordinal-level variables as long as they have more than (preferably many more than) two scores. Develop research questions or hypotheses about the relationships between variables. Make sure that the causal links you suggest are sensible and logical.

2. Use the **Regression** and **Scatterplot** (click **Graphs, Legacy Dialogs,** then **Scatter/Dot**) procedures to analyze the bivariate relationships. Make a note of results (including r, r^2, slope, beta-weights, and a) as they appear on the screen or get hard copies.

3. Write a report that presents and analyzes these relationships. Be clear about which variables are dependent and which are independent. For each combination of variables, report the significance of the relationship (if relevant) and the strength and direction of the relationship. Include r, r^2, and the beta-weights in your report.

4. *OPTIONAL MULTIVARIATE ANALYSIS:* Pick one of the bivariate relationships you produced in step 2 and find another logical independent variable. Run **Regression** again with both independent variables and analyze the results. How much improvement is there in the explained variance after the second independent variable is included? Write up the results of this analysis and include them in your summary paper for this project.

Appendix F   An Introduction to SPSS for Windows

Computers have affected virtually every aspect of human society, and, as you would expect, their impact on the conduct of social research has been profound. Researchers routinely use computers to organize data and compute statistics—activities that humans often find dull, tedious, and difficult but which computers accomplish with accuracy and ease. This division of labour allows social scientists to spend more time on analysis and interpretation—activities that humans typically enjoy but which are beyond the power of computers (so far, at least).

These days, the skills needed to use computers successfully are quite accessible, even for people with little or no experience. This appendix will prepare you to use a statistics program called SPSS for Windows (SPSS stands for "Statistical Package for the Social Sciences"). We use Version 16, though Versions 10 to 17 of SPSS are completely compatible with the information and instructions presented here and throughout the text. If you have used a mouse to "point and click" and run a computer program, you are ready to learn how to use this program. Even if you are completely unfamiliar with computers, you will find this program accessible. After you finish this appendix, you will be ready to do the exercises found at the end of most chapters of this text.

A word of caution before we begin: This appendix is intended only as an *introduction* to SPSS. It will give you an overview of the program and enough information so that you can complete the assignments in the text. It is unlikely, however, that this appendix will answer all your questions or provide solutions to all the problems you might encounter. So, this is a good place to tell you that SPSS has an extensive and easy-to-use "help" facility that will provide assistance as you request it. You should familiarize yourself with this feature and use it as needed. To get help, simply click on the **Help** command on the toolbar across the top of the screen.

SPSS is a **statistical package** (or **statpak**), a set of computer programs that work with data and compute statistics as requested by the user (you). Once you have entered the data for a particular group of observations, you can easily and quickly produce an abundance of statistical information without doing any computations yourself. Also, you can access the power of the computer without having to write computer programs yourself.

Why bother to learn this technology? The truth is that the labour-saving capacity of computers is sometimes exaggerated, and there are research situations in which they are unnecessary. If you are working with a small number of observations or need only a few, uncomplicated statistics, then statistical packages are probably not going to be helpful. However, as the number of cases increases and as your requirements for statistics become more sophisticated, computers and statpaks will become more and more useful.

An example should make this point clearer. Suppose you have gathered a sample of 150 respondents and the *only* thing you want to know about these people is their average age. To compute an average, as you know, you add the scores and divide by the total number of cases. How long do you think it would take you to add 150 two-digit numbers (ages) with a hand calculator? (Don't even think about doing it by hand.) If you entered the scores at the (pretty fast) rate of one per second, or sixty scores a minute, it would take about three or four minutes to enter the ages and get the average. Even if you worked slowly and carefully and did the addition a second and third time to check your math, you could probably complete all calculations in less than 20 minutes. If this were all the information you needed, computers and statpaks would not save you any time.

Such a simple research project is not very realistic, however. Typically, researchers deal with not one but scores or even hundreds of variables, and samples have hundreds or thousands of cases. While you could add 150 numbers in perhaps three or four minutes, how long would it take to add the scores for 1,500 cases? What are the chances of processing 1,500 numbers without making significant errors of arithmetic? The more complex the research situation, the more valuable and useful statpaks become. SPSS can produce statistical information in a few keystrokes or clicks of the mouse that might take you minutes, hours, or even days to produce with a hand calculator.

Clearly, this is technology worth mastering by any social researcher. With SPSS, you can avoid the drudgery of mere computation, spend more time on analysis and interpretation, and conduct research projects with very large data sets. Mastery of this technology might be very handy indeed in your upper-level courses, in a wide variety of jobs, or in graduate school.

F.1 GETTING STARTED— DATABASES AND COMPUTER FILES

Before statistics can be calculated, SPSS must first have some data to process. A **database** is an organized collection of related information such as the responses to a survey. For purposes of computer analysis, a database is organized into a **file,** a collection of information that is stored under the same name in the memory of the computer; on a diskette, CD-ROM, or DVD-ROM; or in some other medium. Words as well as numbers can be saved in files. If you've ever used a word processing program to type a letter or term paper, you probably saved your work in a file so that you could update or make corrections at a later time. Data can be stored in files indefinitely. Because it can take months to conduct a thorough data analysis, the ability to save a database is another advantage of using computers.

For the SPSS exercises in this text, we will use data from two well-established Canadian social surveys, the Census of Canada and the Canadian General Social Survey (GSS). Both surveys contain questions on a large variety of issues from a sample of Canadians. The Census and GSS are conducted regularly and have been the basis for hundreds of research projects by professional social researchers. The GSS is a rich source of information about public opinion in Canada and includes data on everything from attitudes about crime to self-evaluation of one's health. The Census provides information on the demographic, social, and economic characteristics of Canadians.

The Census and GSS are especially valuable because the respondents are chosen so that the samples as a whole are representative of the entire Canadian population. A representative sample reproduces, in miniature form, the characteristics of the population from which it was taken (see Chapters 6 and 7). So, when you analyze either the Census or GSS database, you are in effect analyzing Canadian society. The data are real, and the relationships you will analyze reflect some of the most important and sensitive issues in Canadian life.

The 2001 and 2004 versions of the Census and General Social Survey, respectively, are provided with this text. The complete 2001 Census and 2004 GSS databases each contain hundreds of items of information for thousands of respondents. Some of you will be using a student version of SPSS for Windows, which is limited in the number of cases and variables it can process. To accommodate these limits, we have reduced the databases to about 50 items of information and 1,500 respondents.

The 2001 Census and 2004 GSS data files are summarized in Appendix G. Please turn to this appendix and familiarize yourself with it. Note that the variables are listed alphabetically by their variable names. In many cases, the variable names (e.g., *sex*) are easy to figure out. In other cases, variable names (like *msvic*) are not so obvious. Appendix G also shows the wording of the item that generated the variable. For example, the *msvic* variable consists of responses to a question about victimization: What is the most serious *victimization* (reported by respondent) in the past 12 months? Note that the variable name is formed from the question: *most* serious *victimization* reported by the respondent? Appendix G is a code book; it lists all the codes (or scores) for each survey item along with their meanings.

It's important that you understand the difference between a statpak (SPSS) and a database (like the Census or GSS) and what we are ultimately after here. A database consists of information. A statpak organizes the information in the database and produces statistics. Our goal is to apply the statpak to the database to produce output (e.g., statistics and graphs) that we can analyze and use to answer questions. The process might be diagrammed as in Figure F.1.

FIGURE F.1   THE DATA ANALYSIS PROCESS

Database	$\rightarrow$	**Statpak**	$\rightarrow$	**Output**	$\rightarrow$	**Analysis**
(raw information)		(computer programs)		(statistics and graphs)		(interpretation)

Statpaks like SPSS are general research tools that can be used to analyze databases of all sorts; they are not limited to the 2001 Census or 2004 GSS. In the same way, the 2001 Census or 2004 GSS could be analyzed with statpaks other than those used in this text. Other widely used statpaks include Microcase, SAS, and Stata—each of which may be available on your campus.

F.2 STARTING SPSS FOR WINDOWS AND LOADING THE 2004 GSS

If you are using the complete, professional version of SPSS for Windows, you will probably be working in a computer lab, and you can begin running the program immediately. If you are using the student version of the program on your personal computer, the first thing you need to do is install the software. Follow the instructions that came with the program and return to this appendix when installation is complete.

To start SPSS for Windows, find the icon (or picture) on the screen of your monitor that has an "SPSS" label attached to it. Use the computer mouse to move the arrow on the monitor screen over this icon and then double-click the left button on the mouse. This will start up the SPSS program.

After a few seconds the SPSS for Windows screen will appear and ask, in the middle of the screen, "What would you like to do?" Of the choices listed, the button next to "Open an existing data source" will be checked (or pre-selected), and there will probably be a number of data sets listed in the window at the bottom of the screen. Find the 2004 General Social Survey data set, labelled *GSS.sav,* which we will work with in the remainder of this appendix. If you have the data set on a diskette or other medium, you will need to specify the correct drive. Check with your instructor to make sure that you know where to find the 2004 GSS.

Once you've located the data set, click on the name of the file with the left-hand button on the mouse, and SPSS will load the data. The next screen you will see is the SPSS Data Editor screen.

Note that there is a list of commands across the very top of the screen. These commands begin with **File** at the far left and end with **Help** at the far right. This is the main menu bar for SPSS. When you click any of these words, a **menu** of commands and choices will drop down. Basically, you tell SPSS what to do by clicking on your desired choices from these menus. Sometimes, submenus will appear, and you will need to specify your choices further.

SPSS provides the user with a variety of options for displaying information about the data file and output on the screen. We highly recommend that you tell the program to display lists of variables by name (e.g., *actlimit*) rather than labels (e.g., Long-term health problem limits activity). Lists displayed this way will be easier to read and compare to Appendix G. To do this, click **Edit** on the main menu bar and then click **Options** from the drop-down submenu. A dialog box labelled "Options" will appear with a series of "tabs" along the

TABLE F.1   SUMMARY OF COMMANDS

To start SPSS for Windows	Click the SPSS icon on the screen of the computer monitor
To open a data file	Double-click on the data file name
To set display options for lists of variables	Click **Edit** from the main menu bar, then click **Options.** On the "General" tab make sure that "Display names" and "Alphabetical" are selected and then click **OK.**

top. The "General" options should be displayed but, if not, click on this tab. On the "General" screen, find the box labelled "Variable Lists" and, if they are not already selected, click "Display names" and "Alphabetical" and then click **OK.** If you make changes, a message may appear on the screen that tells you that changes will take effect the next time a data file is opened.

In this section, you learned how to start up SPSS for Windows, load a data file, and set some of the display options for this program. These procedures are summarized in Table F.1.

F.3 WORKING WITH THE 2004 GSS DATABASE

Note that in the SPSS Data Editor window the data are organized into a two-dimensional grid with columns running up and down (vertically) and rows running across (horizontally). Each column is a variable or item of information from the survey. The names of the variables are listed at the tops of the columns. Remember that you can find the meaning of these variable names in the GSS 2004 code book in Appendix G.

Another way to decipher the meaning of variable names is to click **Utilities** on the menu bar and then click **Variables.** The Variables window opens. This window has two parts. On the left is a list of all variables in the database arranged in alphabetical order with the first variable highlighted. On the right is the Variable Information window with information about the highlighted variable. The second variable listed, for example, is *actlimit.* The Variable Information window displays a fragment of the question that was actually asked during the survey ("Long-term health problem limits activity") and shows the possible scores on this variable (a score of 1 = yes and a score of 2 = no) along with some other information.

The same information can be displayed for any variable in the data set. For example, find the variable *sex* in the list. You can do this by using the arrow keys on your keyboard or the slider bar on the right of the variable list window. You can also move through the list by typing the first letter of the variable name you are interested in. For example, type "s" and you will be moved to the first variable name in the list that begins with that letter. Now you can see that the variable measures sex and that a score of "1" indicates that the respondent is male and "2" is female. What do *relig6* and *marstat* measure? Close this window by clicking the **Close** button at the bottom of the window.

TABLE F.2   SUMMARY OF COMMANDS

To move around in the Data window	1. Click the cell you want to highlight or 2. Use the arrow keys on your keyboard or 3. Move the slider buttons or 4. Click the arrows on the right-hand and bottom margins
To get information about a variable	1. From the menu bar, click **Utilities** and then click **Variables.** Scroll through the list of variable names until you highlight the name of the variable in which you are interested. Variable information will appear in the window on the right 2. See Appendix G

Examine the window displaying the 2004 GSS a little more. Each row of the window (reading across or from left to right) contains the scores of a particular respondent on all the variables in the database. Note that the upper-left-hand cell is highlighted (shaded a darker colour than the other cells). This cell contains the score of respondent #1 on the first variable. The second row contains the scores of respondent #2, and so forth. You can move around in this window with the arrow keys on your keyboard. The highlight moves in the direction of the arrow, one cell at a time.

In this section, you learned to read information in the Data Editor window and to decipher the meaning of variable names and scores. These commands are summarized in Table F.2, and we are now prepared to actually perform some statistical operations with the 2004 GSS database.

F.4 PUTTING SPSS TO WORK ON THE 2004 GSS DATABASE: PRODUCING STATISTICS

At this point, the database on the screen is just a mass of numbers with little meaning for you. That's okay because you will not have to actually read any information from this screen. Virtually all of the statistical operations you will conduct will begin by clicking the **Analyze** (or **Statistics** for version 8.0 or earlier) command from the menu bar, selecting a procedure and statistics, and then naming the variable or variables you would like to process.

To illustrate, let's have SPSS for Windows produce a frequency distribution for the variable *sex*. Frequency distributions are tables that display the number of times each score of a variable occurred in the sample (see Chapter 2). So, when we complete this procedure, we will know the number of males and females in the 2004 GSS sample.

With the 2004 GSS loaded, begin by clicking the **Analyze** command on the menu bar. From the menu that drops down, click **Descriptive Statistics** and then **Frequencies.** The Frequencies window appears with the variables listed in alphabetical order in the box on the left. The first variable (*acmyr*) will be highlighted. Use the slider button or the arrow keys on the right-hand margin of this box to scroll through the variable list until you highlight the variable *sex,* or type "s" to move to the approximate location.

Once the variable you want to process has been highlighted, click the arrow button in the middle of the screen to move the variable name to the

TABLE F.3 AN EXAMPLE OF SPSS OUTPUT (RESPONDENTS' SEX)

		Frequency	Percent	Valid Percent	Cumulative Percent
Valid	Male	799	52.6	52.6	52.6
	Female	721	47.4	47.4	100.0
	Total	1,519	100.0	100.0	

box on the right-hand side of the screen. SPSS will produce frequency distributions for all variables listed in this box, but, for now, we will confine our attention to *sex*. Click the **OK** button in the upper-right-hand corner of the Frequencies window and, in seconds, a frequency distribution will be produced.

SPSS sends all tables and statistics to the Output window or SPSS viewer. This window is now "closest" to you, and the Data Editor window is "behind" the Output window. If you wanted to return to the Data Editor, click on any part of it if it is visible, and it will move to the "front" and the Output window will be "behind" it. To display the Data Editor window if it is not visible, minimize the Output window by clicking the "-" box in the upper-right-hand corner.

Frequencies The output from SPSS, slightly modified, is reproduced as Table F.3. What can we tell from this table? The score labels (male and female) are printed at the left with the number of cases (frequency) in each category of the variable one column to the right. As you can see, there are 799 males and 721 females in the sample. The next two columns give information about percentages and the last column to the right displays cumulative percentages. We will defer a discussion of this last column until a later exercise.

One of the percentage columns is labelled Percent and the other is labelled Valid Percent. The difference between these two columns lies in the handling of missing values. The Percent column is based on all cases, including people who did not respond to the item and people who said they did not have the requested information. The Valid Percent column excludes all missing scores. Because we will almost always want to ignore missing scores, we will pay attention only to the Valid Percent column. Note that for sex, there are no missing scores (gender was determined by the interviewer), and the two columns are identical.

F.5 COMPUTING, RECODING, AND LABELLING VARIABLES

SPSS provides a variety of ways to transform and manipulate variables. This section demonstrates how to use SPSS to create and recode variables. We will use the SPSS compute command to create a *new* variable and the SPSS recode command to transform the values of an *existing* variable. We will also demonstrate how to add labels to make variables more meaningful.

Creating a New Variable with the Compute Command   In this demonstration, we will use the SPSS **Compute** command to create new variables and summary scales. Let's begin by considering three of the questions from the 2004 GSS that measure perception of criminal courts in Canada: *phr_q320, phr_q330,* and *phr_q340.* Each item examines a unique aspect of attitude toward criminal courts. Specifically, the questions ask about the type of job that courts are doing in helping victims (*phr_q320*), determining guilt (*phr_q330*), and ensuring a fair trial (*phr_q340*). Because these three situations are distinct, each item should be analyzed in its own right. Suppose, however, that you wanted to create a summary scale that indicated a person's *overall* feelings about Canadian criminal courts.

One way to do this would be to add the scores on the three variables together. This would create a new variable, which we will call *crtscale,* with nine possible scores since each of the three variables contain three scores (1, 2, and 3).

A respondent that consistently answered "good job" (coded as "1") to all three items would receive a score of 3 on the new summary variable. We might label this as a "highly positive" view of the overall job done by criminal courts. A score of 4 would occur when a respondent answered "good job" to any two items and "average job" (coded as "2") to the remaining item, and would indicate an overall "positive" perception. The other scores on this scale would be 5, 6, 7, 8, and 9, the highest possible score which is given to a respondent that answered "poor job" (coded as "3") to all items. This would be consistent with a "highly negative" perception of the overall work done by criminal courts. Once created, *crtscale* could be analyzed, transformed, and manipulated exactly like a variable actually recorded in the data file.

To create this scale, use the **Compute** command. Click **Transform** and then **Compute Variable** from the main menu. The **Compute Variable** window will appear. Find the **Target Variable** box in the upper-left-hand corner of this window. The first thing we need to do is assign a name to the new variable we are about to compute (*crtscale*) and type that name in this box.

Next, we need to tell SPSS how to compute the new variable. In this case, *crtscale* will be computed by adding the scores of *phr_q320, phr_q330,* and *phr_q340.* Find *phr_q320* in the variable list on the left and click the arrow button in the middle of the screen to transfer the variable name to the **Numeric Expression** box. Next, click the plus sign (+) on the calculator pad under the **Numeric Expression** box, and the sign will appear next to *phr_q320.* Then, highlight *phr_q330* in the variable list and click the arrow button to transfer the variable name to the **Numeric Expression** box. Again click the plus sign (+). Finally highlight and transfer the last variable, *phr_q340,* into the **Numeric Expression** box.

The expression in the **Numeric Expression** box should now read *phr_q320* + *phr_q330* + *phr_q340*. Click **OK,** and *crtscale* will be created and added to the data set. If you want to keep this new variable permanently, click **Save** from the **File** menu, and the updated data set with *crtscale* added will be saved to disk. If you are using the student version of SPSS, remember that your data set is limited to 50 variables.

We now have a new variable that measures perception of criminal courts—a more general, summary item that was created from three existing items related to specific aspects of the work done by criminal courts. It is always a good idea to check the frequency distribution for computed and recoded variables to make sure that the computations were carried out correctly. Use the **Frequencies** procedure (click **Analyze, Descriptive Statistics,** and **Frequencies**) to get tables for *phr_q320, phr_q330, phr_q340,* and *crtscale.* Your output will look like this:

Criminal courts help victims

		Frequency	Percent	Valid Percent	Cumulative Percent
Valid	Good job	354	23.3	23.3	23.3
	Average job	716	47.1	47.1	70.4
	Poor job	450	29.6	29.6	100.0
	Total	1,519	100.0	100.0	

Criminal courts good at sentencing

		Frequency	Percent	Valid Percent	Cumulative Percent
Valid	Good job	486	32.0	32.0	32.0
	Average job	785	51.6	51.6	83.6
	Poor job	249	16.4	16.4	100.0
	Total	1,519	100.0	100.0	

Criminal courts ensure a fair trial

		Frequency	Percent	Valid Percent	Cumulative Percent
Valid	Good job	805	53.0	53.0	53.0
	Average job	585	38.5	38.5	91.5
	Poor job	129	8.5	8.5	100.0
	Total	1,519	100.0	100.0	

crtscale

		Frequency	Percent	Valid Percent	Cumulative Percent
Valid	3.00 (highly positive)	216	14.2	14.2	14.2
	4.00	248	16.3	16.3	30.5
	5.00	269	17.7	17.7	48.3
	6.00	407	26.8	26.8	75.1
	7.00	230	15.2	15.2	90.2
	8.00	81	5.3	5.3	95.5
	9.00 (highly negative)	68	4.5	4.5	100.0
	Total	1,519	100.0	100.0	

Looking at the first three tables we see that the level of approval varies by item. Only about 23% of respondents feel that criminal courts do a good job at helping victims, while more than half (53%) feel that criminal courts do a good job at ensuring a fair trial.

The new variable, *crtscale* shown in the final table above, summarizes each respondent's overall position on the issue. (Note, as a convenience we added labels to the first and last values to improve the readability of this table. We will demonstrate how to add labels at the end of this section.)

We see that about 14% of the sample believe that the courts do a good job in all three areas (scored 3), while less than 5% believe the courts do a poor job (scored 9). Thus, there are many more Canadians who have a "highly positive" view of the overall job done by criminal courts than there those that have a "highly negative" perception. Most Canadians, however, fall somewhere in between these two extremes. In fact, about 27% of the sample scored a 6, meaning that they approved of the work done in some situations but not in all cases.

Notice that the total number of respondents (1,519) is equal for all three questions, and therefore, this number is equal to the number of cases included in the combined scale *crtscale*. This means there are no missing values in the variables measured. In most practical settings, however, researchers encounter missing values in some or all of their questions. Let's assume such a situation. If, for example, only 1,000 respondents answered the question about "criminal courts ensuring a fair trial" but all 1,519 respondents answered the other two questions, the number of cases included in the computed scale, *crtscale,* would be 1,000. That is, when SPSS executes a **Compute** statement, it automatically eliminates any cases that are missing scores on any of the constituent items. If these cases were not eliminated, a variety of errors and misclassifications could result.

Collapsing Categories with the Recode Command   We often need to make a variable more compact by collapsing its scores into fewer categories. SPSS provides a number of ways to change the scores of a variable, and one of the most useful of these is the **Recode** command.

As an example of using this command, we will create a new version of the variable *incmhsd* (total household income) that has fewer categories and is more suitable for display in a frequency distribution. When we are finished, we will have two different versions of the same variable in the data set: the original version and a new version with collapsed categories. We recommend that the new version be added to the permanent data file because it will be used in future demonstrations.

We have decided to collapse the values of *incmhsd* into four categories. We begin by collapsing all respondents with values 1 (no income) through 6 ($20,000–$29,999) on *incmhsd* into a value of $\underline{1}$. Hence, this collapsed category includes all respondents with total household incomes of $29,999 or less. The next recodes involve collapsing values 7 ($30,000–$39,999) through 9 ($50,000–$59,999) on *incmhsd* into a value of $\underline{2}$, values 10 ($60,000–$79,999) through 11 ($80,000–$99,999) on *incmhsd* into a value of $\underline{3}$, and finally a value 12 ($100,000 or more) on *incmhsd* into a value of $\underline{4}$. As you will see, recoding requires many small steps, so please be patient and execute the commands as they are discussed.

1. In the **SPSS Data Editor** window, click **Transform** from the menu bar where you can find two types of recode command: **Recode into Same Variables** and **Recode into Different Variables.** If we choose the former (**Recode into Same Variables**), the new version of the variable will replace the old version—the original version of *incmhsd* (total household income) would disappear. We definitely do not want this to happen, so we will choose (click on) **Recode into Different Variables.** This option will allow us to keep both the old and new versions of the variable.

2. The **Recode into Different Variables** dialog box will open. A list box containing an alphabetical list of variables is on the left. Use your mouse to highlight *incmhsd* and then click on the arrow button to move the variable to the **Input Variable → Output Variable** box. The input variable is the old version of *incmhsd,* and the output variable is the new, recoded version we will soon create.

3. In the **Output Variable** box on the right, click in the **Name** text box and type a name for the new (output) variable. We suggest *income4* (total household income grouped into four categories) for the new variable, but you can assign any name as long as it does not duplicate the name of some other variable in the data set. Click the **Change** button and the expression *incmhsd → income4* will appear in the **Input Variable → Output Variable** box.

4. Click on the **Old and New Values** button in the middle of the screen, and a new dialog box will open.

5. Read down the left-hand column in the **Old Value** box until you find the **Range** button. Click on the button, and the cursor will move to the small text box immediately below. Type 1 into the first **Range** text box and then click on the second text box and type 6. In the **New Value** box in the upper-right-hand corner of the screen, click the **Value** button. Type 1 in the **Value** text box and then click the **Add** button directly below. The expression "1 thru 6 → 1" will appear in the **Old → New** dialog box. This completes the first recode instruction to SPSS.

   Note, alternatively, for the first category, you can choose the **Range, LOWEST through value** button. The cursor will move to the small box immediately below. Then type 6 in the text box. Do not forget to type 1 in the **New Value** box and click the **Add** button. The expression "Lowest thru 6 → 1" appears in the **Old → New** box.

6. Continue recoding by returning to the **Range** text boxes on the left. Type 7 in the first box under the **Range** option and 9 in the second box, and then click the Value button in the **New Values** box. Type 2 in the **Value** text box and then click the **Add** button. The expression "7 thru 9 → 2" appears in the **Old → New** box.

7. Return again to the **Range** text boxes, and specify the low and high points of next interval. Type 10 in the first box under the **Range** option and 11 in the second box and then click the **Value** button in the **New Values** box. Type 3 in the **Value** text box and then click the **Add** button. The expression "10 thru 11 → 3" appears in the **Old → New** box.

8. For the last recode, click the **Value** button on the left-hand column in the **Old Value** box. The cursor will move to the small text box immediately below. Type 12 in the text box. Next, click the **Value** button in the **New Values** box. Type 4 in the **Value** text box and then click the **Add** button. The expression "12 → 4" will appear in the **Old → New** dialog box. This completes the last recode instruction to SPSS.

   Note, the values 98 and 99 are defined as missing in the original variable *incmhsd,* and are automatically redefined during the recode procedure as missing and re-labeled as "." [period] in the new variable *income4.* Because this is done automatically by SPSS, these cases are referred to as "system" missing values.

9. Now click the **Continue** button at the bottom of the screen, and you will return to the **Recode into Different Variable** dialog box. Click **OK,** and SPSS will execute the transformation.

You now have a data set with one more variable named *income4* (or whatever name you gave the recoded variable). SPSS adds the new variable to the data set, and you can find it in the last column to the right in the data window. You can make the new variable a permanent part of the data set by saving the data file at the end of the session. If you do not wish to save the new, expanded data file, click **No** when you are asked if you want to save the data file. Remember that if you are using the student version of SPSS for Windows you are limited to a maximum of 50 variables, and you will not be able to save more than two new variables (unless you delete other variables to make space) because there are already 48 variables in the 2004 GSS data set.

Finally, to make sure that no mistakes were made in the recoding process, produce a frequency distribution for *income4* using the **Frequencies** command. The table should look like this:

income4

		Frequency	Percent	Valid Percent	Cumulative Percent
Valid	1	240	15.8	18.4	18.4
	2	437	28.8	33.5	51.9
	3	377	24.8	28.9	80.8
	4	251	16.5	19.2	100.0
	Total	1,305	85.9	100.0	
Missing	System	215	14.1		
Total		1,519	100.0		

The sample is particularly clustered around categories 2 and 3, or between $30,000 and $59,999 and $60,000 and $99,999—over 60% of the sample is in these categories. There are fewer respondents at the income extremes, categories 1 and 4, or <$30,000 and $100,000+.

Adding Labels   This table can be made easier to read and more meaningful by attaching labels. There are two types of labels that can be attached to a variable.

First, a "variable label" provides a description of the variable. For example we may decide to label our new variable *income4* "recode version of total household income." To do this, click the **Variable View** tab located at the bottom of the SPSS Data Editor screen. The first column, **Name,** in the variable view window contains the names of the variables in the data file. Scroll up or down this window until you locate the variable name *income4,* which will be in the last row. Next, click on the cell in the **Label** column and type: recode version of total household income (or any other label that you wish to provide the variable). SPSS output for this variable will now display both the name and label.

Second, labels can be applied to the values of a variable. Thus, whereas a "variable label" provides a description of the entire variable, a "value label" describes the meaning of each value of a variable. To add value labels to *income4,* click the **Variable View** tab located at the bottom of the SPSS Data Editor screen, and scroll to the row containing the variable name (*income4*). Next, click on the cell in the **Values** column, which initially indicates "**None**" of the values has been labelled, then click on the button with the three dots in it. The **Value Labels** dialog box will open. Type the first value (1) into the **Value** text box and its label into the **Value Label** text box (<$30,000, or any other label that you wish to provide the value). Then click **Add.** Next, enter the second value (2) into the **Value** text box and its label into the **Value Label** text box ($30,000–$59,999). Repeat this exercise for each value, making sure to click **Add** after each entry. (You can fix or delete any entry by highlighting it in the large display box and clicking **Change** or **Remove.**) Click **OK** after all values labels have been added.

SPSS output will now display all labels. For example, the **Frequencies** command will produce a frequency distribution for *income4* as follows:

income4

recode version of total household income

		Frequency	Percent	Valid Percent	Cumulative Percent
Valid	<$30,000	240	15.8	18.4	18.4
	$30,000–$59,999	437	28.8	33.5	51.9
	$60,000–$99,999	377	24.8	28.9	80.8
	$100,000+	251	16.5	19.2	100.0
	Total	1,305	85.9	100.0	
Missing	System	215	14.1		
Total		1,519	100.0		

F.6 EDITING OUTPUT

SPSS output can be edited directly in the **Output** window. To edit a table, double-click on any part of the table. Next, double-click the exact area of the table to be edited, and make the appropriate revision. To edit a graph, double-click on any part of the graph in the **Output** window and the SPSS **Chart Editor** window will appear. This window gives you a wide array of options for the final appearance of the chart.

For example, if you want to change the colour of some elements (e.g., bars or background) in the chart, you need first to click on the elements to be highlighted, then click on the **Edit** menu and choose **Properties.** (Alternatively, you can directly open the **Properties** dialog box by right clicking anywhere on the highlighted elements then choosing **Properties**

Window.) The **Properties** dialog box will appear where you can find different options under each tap. For example, the options for changing the colour of the elements is the **Fill & Border** tab. Explore these options at your leisure using the **Help** button at the bottom of the window as necessary. You need to close the **SPSS Chart Editor** window and return to the **Output** window to see the changes you have made.

F.7 PRINTING, SAVING, PASTING, AND EXPORTING OUTPUT

Once you've gone to the trouble of producing statistics, a table, or a graph, you will probably want to keep a permanent record. There are three ways to do this. First, you can print a copy of the contents of the SPSS Viewer to take with you. To do this, click on **File** and then click **Print** from the **File** menu. Alternatively, find the icon of a printer (third from the left) in the row of icons just below the menu bar and click on it.

The second way to create a permanent record of SPSS output is to save the window to the computer's memory or to a diskette or other medium. To do this, click **Save** from the **File** menu. The Save dialog box opens. Give the output a name (some abbreviation such as "freqsex" might do) and, if necessary, specify the name of the drive in which your diskette is located. Click **OK,** and the table will be permanently saved.

Third, tables and charts in the Output window can be used in many applications, including word processors. Specifically, SPSS output tables and charts can be pasted into a word processing document. Formats are retained and can be edited in the word processor. (Note that charts are pasted in graph format and tables in table format.)

To paste, click on any part of the table or chart in the SPSS Output window, then click **Copy** from the **Edit** menu. Next, open your word processor, and click **Paste** from the **Edit** menu. Repeat this process separately for each table or chart that you want to paste into the word processor document.

Alternatively, SPSS output tables and charts can be exported to a document. From the SPSS Output window, click **Export** from the **File** menu. Next, select **Word/RTF file (*.doc)** from the **File Type** drop-down list, and click **OK**. Then, open your word processor, click **Open** from the **Edit** menu, and double-click the file name to open it. You may have to change the folder specification to locate the file. By default, SPSS names the file OUTPUT and saves it in the SPSS program folder.

F.8 ENDING YOUR SPSS FOR WINDOWS SESSION

Once you have saved or printed your work, you may end your SPSS session. Click on **File** from the menu bar and then click **Exit.** If you haven't already done so, you will be asked if you want to save the contents of the Output window. You may save the frequency distribution at this point if you wish. Otherwise, click **NO.** The program will close, and you will be returned to the screen from which you began.

Appendix G　Information and Code Books for the 2001 Census and 2004 General Social Survey

G.1 INTRODUCTION TO CENSUS AND GSS

Three data sets from two social surveys, the 2001 Census of Canada and the 2004 Canadian General Social Survey (GSS), are provided on the Web site for the text. The data sets are named *CensusFull.sav, Census.sav,* and *GSS.sav.* SPSS uses the file extension ".sav" as a saved data format. These files will load easily into most versions of SPSS.

The Census and GSS are conducted by Statistics Canada. The GSS is a public-opinion poll that has been conducted annually since 1985 on representative samples of Canadians aged 15 years and older living in private households in the 10 provinces. The content and focus of the survey change each year. The 2004 GSS contained items on the nature and extent of criminal victimization in Canada, as well as demographic and background characteristics of the respondents.

The Census, on the other hand, is an enumeration of the entire Canadian population, and is conducted every five years. It collects information on the demographic, social, and economic characteristics of Canadians.

The Census data set that is supplied with this text is based on a random sample, called the Public Use Microdata File for individuals, or PUMF, of all persons in the population enumerated in the 2001 Census. The 2001 Census PUMF for individuals contains 140 variables, including family composition, labour-force activity, and income. Because many of these variables are not applicable to younger Canadians, we restricted the sample to adults (i.e., persons 15 and over).

G.2 CENSUS AND GSS DATA SETS

The original Census and GSS data sets each contain dozens of variables on a sample of thousands of cases. We have shortened the Census (*Census.sav*) and GSS (*GSS.sav*) data sets to about 50 variables and 1,500 randomly selected cases to be compatible with the student version of SPSS. (SPSS Student Version, created for classroom instruction, is in essence the full version of the SPSS base software but limited to a maximum of 50 variables and 1,500 cases.) These shortened data sets are used for all of the end-of-chapter exercises.

For those using the full, professional version of SPSS for Windows, we additionally provide the complete Census data set (*CensusFull.sav*). It includes the original random sample of 640,526 cases for the variables in the shortened Census data set. It was not possible to provide the complete version of the GSS for distribution with the text due to licensing issues.

Variables in the Census and GSS data sets were selected to best meet the objectives of this text, and to provide students with the ability to examine issues of current and emerging interest. The code book for the Census and GSS data sets are provided below. The variable names, shown in the left margin, are those used in the data file to identify the variables. A description or the exact question as it was asked on the Census and GSS questionnaires for each variable is provided. The numbers beside each response are the scores recorded in each data set.

The Web site for the text provides further information on the Census and GSS. Detailed descriptions and frequency distributions for all variables in the full sample, as well as information on other issues such as sampling design and data collection, are contained in the files named Census.pdf and GSS.pdf on the Web site.

In sum, the three data sets provided with, and used throughout, this text are:

1. *CensusFull.sav*. The full (complete sample) version of the 2001 Census of Canada.
2. *Census.sav*. The short (1,500 randomly selected cases) version of the 2001 Census of Canada.
3. *GSS.sav*. The short (1,500 randomly selected cases) version of the 2004 General Social Survey (GSS).

G.3 SPSS STUDENT VERSION

The SPSS Student Version (available for Windows only) may be purchased and downloaded directly online at http://www.spss.com/vertical_markets/ education/online.htm. Alternatively, many Canadian university and college bookstores stock this software. There is also a version of this textbook that is bundled with the SPSS Student Version, with an increased price tag to cover the fee of including the studentware.

G.4 MISSING DATA AND SAMPLE DESIGN IN THE CENSUS AND GSS

It is important to comment on two features of the data sets. First, social survey data like the Census and GSS typically contain "missing data." Missing data occur when a respondent did not (e.g., refused to) or could not (e.g., lacked the information to) answer a specific question. Most variables in the original Census and GSS data sets had relatively few missing cases. The missing cases for these variables were simply excluded from the data files supplied with this text.

On the other hand, a few other variables (e.g., income) contained significantly more missing cases. Deleting these cases may produce biased data and results, so for these variables, missing data were retained but defined as missing in data sets. For example, missing cases for the variable *incm* (annual personal income) in the GSS data set were assigned the numeric values of 98 and 99, and then defined as missing. These missing data will be automatically eliminated from all statistical analysis, unless SPSS is commanded to do otherwise. Missing data are a common problem in survey research that, if significant in number, may jeopardize the integrity of the inquiry.

Second, the sample data in the Census file were selected according to the principles of EPSEM as discussed in Chapter 6. The GSS, like the vast majority of Statistics Canada surveys, uses a "complex" sampling design that is ultimately based on the principle of EPSEM. It is said to be "complex" as opposed to "simple" (as in "simple" random sampling) because of the types and combinations of sampling methods used—the GSS uses a stratified, multi-stage cluster design with probability sampling at all stages to select a representative sample of persons 15 years of age and older in Canada (excluding residents of the Yukon, Northwest Territories, Nunavut, and full-time residents of institutions).

However, the GSS uses an *unequal* probability of selection method. That is, it under- and over-samples various groups of individuals to ensure that subpopulations of interest to the survey, such as persons 65 and older, are represented in the sample. Because individuals do not have an equal probability of selection, it is necessary to "weight" (correct) the sample to approximate an EPSEM sample. A weight variable, called *wght_per,* was calculated by Statistics Canada. It is included in the GSS data file, and once you open the *GSS.sav* file in SPSS, the weight variable is automatically "turned on" to correct for this bias. With the weight turned on, the sample of 1,500 cases actually converts to a sample size of 1,519.

G.5 GSS CODE BOOK

acmyr

Main activity of the respondent in the last 12 months.
1. Working at a paid job or business
2. Looking for paid work
3. Going to school
4. Caring for children
5. Household work
6. Retired
7. Maternity/paternity leave
8. Long term illness
9. Other
10. Volunteer work

actlimit

Are you limited in the amount or kind of activity you can do at home, at work, or at school or in other activities because of a long-term physical or mental condition or health problem?
1. Yes
2. No

agegr5   Age group of the respondent.

1. 15 to 17	2. 18 to 19
3. 20 to 24	4. 25 to 29
5. 30 to 34	6. 35 to 39
7. 40 to 44	8. 45 to 49
9. 50 to 54	10. 55 to 59
11. 60 to 64	12. 65 to 69
13. 70 to 74	14. 75 to 79
15. 80 years and over	

discrim   Respondent has been a victim of discrimination (because of his/her sex, ethnicity, race, religion, sexual orientation, age, disability, or language) in the past five years.
   1. Yes
   2. No

drr_q110   In the past month, how often did you drink alcoholic beverages? Was it:
   1. ...every day
   2. ...4 to 6 times a week
   3. ...2 to 3 times a week
   4. ...once a week
   5. ...once or twice in the past month
   6. ...never in the past month
   7. ...never drinks

drr_q120   How many times in the past month have you had 5 or more drinks on the same occasion?
   97 Not asked: never drinks or did not drink *(defined as missing in the data set)*

dwelc   Dwelling type of the respondent.
   1. Single detached house
   2. Low-rise apartment (<5 stories)
   3. High-rise apartment (5+ stories)
   4. Other

dwellown   Dwelling owned by a member of the household?
   1. Yes
   2. No

edu10   Highest level of education obtained by the respondent—10 groups.
   1. Doctorate/masters/some graduate
   2. Bachelor's degree
   3. Diploma/certificate from community college
   4. Diploma/certificate from trade/technical
   5. Some university
   6. Some community college/CEGEP/nursing
   7. Some trade/technical

8. High school diploma
9. Some secondary/high school
10. Elementary school/no schooling

famtype   Respondent's type of family structure.
1. Couple only
2. Intact family
3. Stepfamily with common child
4. Stepfamily without a common child
5. Lone-parent family
7. Not asked; no spouse/partner or children in household

hal_q120   Do you have any difficulty hearing, seeing, communicating, walking, climbing stairs, bending, learning or doing any similar activities?
1. Yes, often
2. Yes, sometimes
3. No

hlthstat   State of health of the respondent.
1. Excellent?
2. Very good?
3. Good?
4. Fair?
5. Poor?

hsdsizec   Household size of respondent.
1. One household member
2. Two household members
3. Three household members
4. Four household members
5. Five household members
6. Six household members or more

incm   Annual personal income of the respondent
1. No income
2. Less than $5,000
3. $5,000 to $9,999
4. $10,000 to $14,999
5. $15,000 to $19,999
6. $20,000 to $29,999
7. $30,000 to $39,999
8. $40,000 to $49,999
9. $50,000 to $59,999
10. $60,000 to $79,999
11. $80,000 to $99,999
12. $100,000 or more
98. Not stated *(defined as missing in the data set)*
99. Don't know *(defined as missing in the data set)*

incmhsd	Total household income.

        1. No income or loss
        2. Less than $5,000
        3. $5,000 to $9,999
        4. $10,000 to $14,999
        5. $15,000 to $19,999
        6. $20,000 to $29,999
        7. $30,000 to $39,999
        8. $40,000 to $49,999
        9. $50,000 to $59,999
        10. $60,000 to $79,999
        11. $80,000 to $99,999
        12. $100,000 or more
        98. Not stated *(defined as missing in the data set)*
        99. Don't know *(defined as missing in the data set)*

lanhsdc	Respondent's household language.

        1. English only
        2. French only
        3. Other language

lifevict	Victim of crime—lifetime.

        1. Yes
        2. No

live_neigh	Length of time respondent has lived in current neighbourhood.

        1. Less than 6 months
        2. 6 months to less than 1 year
        3. 1 year to less than 3 years
        4. 3 years to less than 5 years
        5. 5 years to less than 10 years
        6. 10 years and over

luc_rst	Urban/rural indicator.

        1. Larger urban centres (CMA/CA)
        2. Rural and small town (non-CMA/CA, including all residents of Prince Edward Island)

marstat	Marital status of the respondent.

        1. Married
        2. Living common-law
        3. Widowed
        4. Separated
        5. Divorced
        6. Single (Never married)

med_depress   Medication of respondent—to help you get out of depression.
1. Yes
2. No

msvic   Most serious victimization reported by respondent in the past 12 months—excludes spousal and ex-spousal abuse.
101. Sexual assault
202. Robbery
203. Attempted robbery
304. Assault
405. Break and enter
406. Attempted break and enter
507. Motor vehicle theft
508. Attempted motor vehicle theft
609. Theft of personal property
610. Attempted theft of personal property
711. Theft of household property
712. Attempted theft of household property
813. Vandalism
997. Not applicable (No crime reported)

numevact_c   Average number of evening activities respondent goes out for in a month.
62. 62 and more

phr_q110   Compared to other areas in Canada, do you think your neighbourhood has a higher amount of crime, about the same, or a lower amount of crime?
1. Higher
2. About the same
3. Lower

phr_q120   During the last 5 years, do you think that crime in your neighbourhood has increased, decreased, or remained about the same?
1. Increased
2. Decreased
3. About the same

phr_q130   How safe do you feel from crime walking ALONE in your area after dark? Do you feel:
1. very safe?   2. reasonably safe?
3. somewhat unsafe? 4. very unsafe?
5. does not walk alone

phr_q190   When alone in your home in the evening or at night, do you feel:
1. ... very worried?
2. ... somewhat worried?
3. ... not at all worried about your safety from crime?
4. ... never alone

phr_q230   Do you think your local police force does a good job, an average job, or a poor job: ... of being approachable and easy to talk to?
1. Good job
2. Average job
3. Poor job

phr_q250   Do you think your local police force does a good job, an average job, or a poor job: ... of ensuring the safety of the citizens in your area?
1. Good job
2. Average job
3. Poor job

phr_q260   Do you think your local police force does a good job, an average job, or a poor job: ... of treating people fairly?
1. Good job
2. Average job
3. Poor job

phr_q320   Are the Canadian criminal courts doing a good job, an average job, or a poor job: ... of helping the victim?
1. Good job
2. Average job
3. Poor job

phr_q330   Are the Canadian criminal courts doing a good job, an average job, or a poor job: ... of determining whether the accused or the person charged is guilty or not?
1. Good job
2. Average job
3. Poor job

phr_q340   Are the Canadian criminal courts doing a good job, an average job, or a poor job: ... of ensuring a fair trial for the accused?
1. Good job
2. Average job
3. Poor job

phr_q400   In general, would you say that sentences handed down by the courts are too severe, about right, or not severe enough?
1. Too severe
2. About right
3. Not severe enough

phr_q410   Do you think that the prison system does a good job, an average job, or a poor job: ... of supervising and controlling prisoners while in prison?
1. Good job
2. Average job
3. Poor job

phr_q420   Do you think that the prison system does a good job, an average job, or a poor job: ... of helping prisoners become law-abiding citizens?
1. Good job
2. Average job
3. Poor job

phr_q510   Do you think that the parole system does a good job, an average job, or a poor job: ... of releasing offenders who are not likely to commit another crime?
1. Good job
2. Average job
3. Poor job

phr_q520   Do you think that the parole system does a good job, an average job, or a poor job: ... of supervising offenders on parole?
1. Good job
2. Average job
3. Poor job

phr_q990   In general, how satisfied are you with your personal safety from crime? Are you:
1. ... very satisfied?
2. ... somewhat satisfied?
3. ... somewhat dissatisfied?
4. ... very dissatisfied?

prv   Province of residence of the respondent.
10. Newfoundland and Labrador
11. Prince Edward Island
12. Nova Scotia
13. New Brunswick
24. Quebec
35. Ontario
46. Manitoba
47. Saskatchewan
48. Alberta
59. British Columbia

relig6   Religion of respondent. In six categories.
1. No religion   2. Roman Catholic
3. United Church   4. Protestant
5. Other

rl_q105   How important are your religious or spiritual beliefs to the way that you live your life? Would you say it is:
1. ... very important?
2. ... somewhat important?
3. ... not very important?
4. ... not at all important?

sex   Sex of the respondent.
1. Male
2. Female

stalking   Respondent has reported stalking incident(s).
1. Yes
2. No

vismin   Visible minority status.
1. Visible minority
2. Non–visible minority

wght_per   Person Weight

wkwehr_c   Number of hours usually worked at all jobs in a week.
0. Not asked (Not working at a paid job or business)
75. 75 and more hours

yrarri   Range of years when the respondent came to live permanently in Canada.
1. Before 1946
2. 1946 to 1959
3. 1960 to 1964
4. 1965 to 1969
5. 1970 to 1974
6. 1975 to 1979
7. 1980 to 1984
8. 1985 to 1989
9. 1990 to 1994
10. 1995 to 2004
97. Not asked; Born in Canada/Canadian citizen by birth

G.6 CENSUS CODE BOOK

agep   Age of the respondent.
85. 85 years+

citizenp   Legal citizenship status of the respondent.
1. Canadian, by birth
2. Canadian naturalization
3. Not Canadian citizen

cmap   Area (census metropolitan area or CMA) of residence of the respondent.
205. Halifax
421. Quebec
462. Montreal
499. Sherbrooke/Trois-Rivières

505. Ottawa/Hull
532. Oshawa
535. Toronto
537. Hamilton
539. St. Catharines/Niagara
541. Kitchener
555. London
559. Windsor
599. Sudbury/Thunder Bay
602. Winnipeg
799. Regina/Saskatoon
825. Calgary
835. Edmonton
933. Vancouver
935. Victoria
999. Not applicable (Persons not living in selected CMAs)

dgmfsp   Refers to the predominant discipline or area of learning or training of a person's highest postsecondary degree, certificate or diploma.
1. Education, recreational services
2. Fine and applied arts
3. Humanities
4. Social sciences
5. Business and commerce
6. Financial management
7. Industrial/institutional management
8. Marketing, sales ...
9. Office administration
10. Agriculture, food sciences
11. Engineer, applied sciences
12. Building technology
13. Data/computer technology
14. Electronic technology
15. Other engineering technology
16. Nursing
17. Alternative medicine
18. Math, computer sciences
19. All other
20. No post-secondary

distp   Refers to the distance, in kilometres, between the respondent's residence and his or her usual workplace location
1. Less than 5 km
2. 5 to 9.9 km
3. 10 to 14.9 km
4. 15 to 19.9 km

5. 20 to 24.9 km
6. 25 to 29.9 km
7. 30 km or more
9. Not in the Labour Force or Work at Home

ethnicr
Refers to the ethnic or cultural group(s) to which the respondent's ancestors belong.
1. British Isles
2. French
3. Other European
4. African
5. Arab
6. West Asian
7. South Asian
8. East and Southeast
9. Latin, Central, South America
10. Caribbean
11. Aboriginal
12. Canadian
13. Provincial
14. Other single origins
15. Multi British Isles
16. British and French
17. British and Canadian
18. British and other
19. British, Canadian, and other
20. Multi French
21. French and Canadian
22. French and other
23. French, Canadian, and other
24. Canadian and other
25. British, French, and Canadian
26. British, French, and other
27. British, French, Canadian, and other
28. Other multi origins

fptwkp
Refers to persons who worked for pay or in self-employment in 2000.
1. FT weeks in 2000
2. PT weeks in 2000
9. Not in the Labour Force

genstpob
Generation status of the respondent.
1. 1st generation
2. 2nd: Parents not born in Canada
3. 2nd: One parent born in Canada
4. 3rd over

grosrtp   Refers to the total average monthly payments paid by tenant households to secure shelter.

      99. Monthly rent under $100
      1100. Monthly rent $1,100 or over
      9999. Persons in owner occupied dwellings *(defined as missing in the data set)*

hhincp   Refers to the total income of a household (i.e., sum of the total incomes of all members of that household).

1. Loss	2. No income
3. $1 to $1,999	4. $2,000 to $4,999
5. $5,000 to $7,999	6. $8,000 to $9,999
7. $10,000 to $14,999	8. $15,000 to $19,999
9. $20,000 to $24,999	10. $25,000 to $29,999
11. $30,000 to $34,999	12. $35,000 to $39,999
13. $40,000 to $44,999	14. $45,000 to $49,999
15. $50,000 to $54,999	16. $55,000 to $59,999
17. $60,000 to $64,999	18. $65,000 to $69,999
19. $70,000 to $74,999	20. $75,000 to $84,999
21. $85,000 to $99,999	22. $100,000 to $119,999
23. $120,000 or more	

hlosp   Refers to the highest grade or year of elementary or secondary (high) school attended, or to the highest year of university or college education completed.

      1. Less than Grade 5
      2. Grades 5 to 8
      3. Grades 9 to 13
      4. High school graduate
      5. Trades certificate/diploma
      6. College, no trades
      7. College w/trades
      8. College w/college certificate
      9. University no certificate
      10. University w/certificate
      11. University w/BA
      12. University above BA
      13. University masters'
      14. University doctorate

hrswkp   Refers to the actual number of hours that persons worked for pay or in self-employment at all jobs held in the week (Sunday to Saturday) prior to Census Day (May 15, 2001).

      0. Not in the Labour Force
      100. 100 hrs +

htypep   Type of household.
1. Married couple
2. Married w/others
3. Married w/children
4. Married w/kids & others
5. Common-law
6. Common-law w/others
7. Common-law w/children
8. Common-law w/kids and others
9. Lone-parent
10. Lone-parent w/others
11. Multiple family
12. One person only
13. 2+ people not related

incstp   The income status of the respondent in relation to Statistics Canada's low income cut-offs (LICOs) (i.e., poverty line).
1. ABOVE LICO
2. BELOW LICO

invstp   Refers to interest or other investment income received during calendar year 2000 by the respondent.

lfactp   Refers to the labour market activity of the respondent in the week (Sunday to Saturday) prior to Census Day (May 15, 2001).
1. Employed: worked
2. Employed: absent
3. Laid off: not looking
4. Laid off: look FT
5. Laid off: look PT
6. New job: not look
7. New job: look FT
8. New job: look PT
9. Unemployed: look FT
10. Unemployed: look PT
11. Not in the Labour Force: last work 2001
12. Not in the Labour Force: last work 2000
13. Not in the Labour Force: last work <2000
14. Not in the Labour Force: never worked

marsthp   Marital status of the respondent.
1. Divorced
2. Married, including common-law
3. Separated
4. Single
5. Widowed

modep	Refers to the mode of transportation to work by the respondent.

    1. Car as driver
    2. Car as passenger
    3. Public transit
    4. Walk
    5. Bicycle
    6. Motorcycle
    7. Taxicab
    8. Other method
    9. Not in the Labour Force or Work at Home

mtnpa   Refers to the first language learned at home in childhood and still understood by the individual at the time of the census.

    1. English
    2. French
    3. English and French
    4. Aboriginal languages
    5. German
    6. Netherlandic
    7. Italian
    8. Spanish
    9. Portuguese
    10. Polish
    11. Ukrainian
    12. Greek
    13. Chinese
    14. Austro-Asiatic languages
    15. Arabic
    16. Punjabi
    17. Other Indo-Iranian
    18. Other non-official
    99. Not applicable *(defined as missing in the data set)*

naicsp   Refers to the general nature of the business carried out in the establishment where the person worked.

    1. Agriculture ...
    2. Mining/oil/gas
    3. Utilities
    4. Construction
    5. Manufacturing
    6. Wholesale trade
    7. Retail trade
    8. Transport/warehouse
    9. Information/cultural industries
    10. Finance, insurance
    11. Real estate

12. Science/tech services
13. Company management
14. Administrative, waste management
15. Educational services
16. Health care/social assistance
17. Arts, entertainment
18. Accommodations
19. Other services
20. Public administration
99. Not in the Labour Force

nocs01p   Refers to the kind of work persons were doing during the reference week, as determined by their kind of work and the description of the main activities in their job.

1. Senior management
2. Other management
3. Professional business
4. Financial/administration
5. Clerical
6. Natural/applied sciences
7. Health: professionals
8. Health: tech, assisting
9. Social sciences, government, religion
10. Teachers
11. Art, culture, sport
12. Real estate, buyer ...
13. Retail, cashiers
14. Chefs, food service
15. Protective services
16. Childcare/home support
17. Service supervisors
18. Contractors
19. Construction trades
20. Other trades
21. Transport/equipment operator
22. Construction, transportation
23. Primary industries
24. Manufacturing
25. Processing, manufacturing
99. Not in the Labour Force

ompp   Refers to the total average monthly payments made by owner of households to secure shelter.

99. Owner's major payments are under $100
1100. Owner's major payments are $1,100 and over

9999. Persons in tenant occupied dwellings *(defined as missing in the data set)*

otincp
Refers to all regular cash income received during calendar year 2000 and not reported in any of the other sources listed in the data set.

provp
Province or territory of residence of the respondent.
    10. Newfoundland and Labrador
    11. Prince Edward Island
    12. Nova Scotia
    13. New Brunswick
    24. Quebec
    35. Ontario
    46. Manitoba
    47. Saskatchewan
    48. Alberta
    59. British Columbia
    60. Yukon Territory, Northwest Territories, and Nunavut

religrpa
Refers to the specific religious denominations, groups or bodies as well as other religiously defined communities or systems of belief.
    1. Catholic
    2. Protestant
    3. Christian Orthodox
    4. Christian
    5. Muslim
    6. Jewish
    7. Buddhist
    8. Hindu
    9. Sikh
    10. Eastern religions
    11. All other religions
    12. No affiliation
    99. Not applicable *(defined as missing in the data set)*

retirp
Refers to all regular income received by the respondent during calendar year 2000 as the result of having been a member of a pension plan of one or more employers.

schattp
Refers to either full-time or part-time (day or evening) attendance at school, college or university during the nine-month period between September 2000 and May 15, 2001.
    1. Not in school
    2. School full time
    3. School part time

selfip
Refers to the total income received by respondent during calendar year 2000 as net income from self-employment.

sexp

Gender of the respondent.
1. Female
2. Male

tenurp

Refers to whether some member of the household owns or rents the dwelling.
1. Owned
2. Rented

tgovtp

Refers to total income from all transfer payments received from federal, provincial or municipal governments by respondent during calendar year 2000.

totincp

Refers to the total money income received from the following sources during calendar year 2000 by the respondent.

totschp

Refers to the total sum of the years (or grades) of schooling at the elementary, high school, university and college levels.

1. Less than Grade 5	2. 5 to 8 yrs
3. 9 years	4. 10 years
5. 11 years	6. 12 years
7. 13 years	8. 14 to 17 years
9. 18 or more years	

unitsp

Number of persons in a household.

1. 1 person	2. 2 persons
3. 3 persons	4. 4 persons
5. 5 persons	6. 6 persons
7. 7+ persons	

uphwkp

Refers to the number of hours persons spent doing unpaid housework, yard work or home maintenance in the week (Sunday to Saturday) prior to Census Day (May 15, 2001).

0. None	1. Less than 5 hours
2. 5 to 14 hours	3. 15 to 29 hours
4. 30 to 59 hours	5. 60 hours or more

upkidp

Refers to the number of hours persons spent looking after children without pay in the week (Sunday to Saturday) prior to Census Day (May 15, 2001).

0. None	1. Less than 5 hours
2. 5 to 14 hours	3. 15 to 29 hours
4. 30 to 59 hours	5. 60 hours or more

upsrp

Refers to the number of hours persons spent providing unpaid care or assistance to seniors in the week (Sunday to Saturday) prior to Census Day (May 15, 2001).

0. None	1. Less than 5 hours
2. 5 to 9 hours	3. 10 to 19 hours
4. 20 hours or more	

valuep   The dollar amount expected by the owner if the dwelling were to be sold.
      199999. 199,999 or less
      200000. 200,000 +
      999999. Persons in tenant occupied dwellings ***(defined as missing in the data set)***

visminp   Refers to whether the person is a member of a visible minority in Canada.
      1. Chinese   2. South Asian
      3. Black   4. Other visible minority
      5. Not visible minority

wagesp   Refers to gross wages and salaries before deductions by the respondent.

wkswkp   Refers to the number of weeks in 2000 during which persons worked for pay or in self-employment at all jobs held.
      0. Not in the Labour Force

yrimmig   The year in which landed immigrant status was first obtained.
      1. Before 1961
      2. 1961–1970
      3. 1971–1980
      4. 1981–1990
      5. 1991–1995
      6. 1996–2001
      9. Canadian citizens by birth

Appendix H   Basic Mathematics Review

H.1 OF ARITHMETIC, CALCULATORS, AND COMPUTERS

You will probably be relieved to hear that first courses in statistics are not particularly mathematical and do not stress computation per se. While you will encounter many numbers to work with and numerous formulas to use, the major emphasis will be on understanding the role of statistics in research and the logic by which we attempt to answer research questions empirically. You will also find that, at least in this text, the example problems and many of the homework problems have been intentionally simplified so that the computations will not unduly distract you from the task of understanding the statistics themselves.

On the other hand, you may regret to learn that there is, inevitably, some arithmetic that you simply cannot avoid if you want to master this material. It is likely that some of you haven't had any math in a long time, others have convinced themselves that they just cannot do math under any circumstances, and still others are just rusty and out of practice. All of you will find that even the most complex and intimidating operations and formulas can be broken down into simple steps. If you have forgotten how to cope with some of these steps or are unfamiliar with these operations, this appendix is designed to ease you into the skills you will need to do all of the computation in this textbook.

Before we begin the review, let us point out that a calculator is a virtual necessity for this text. While you could do all the arithmetic by hand, the calculator will save you time and effort and is definitely worth the small investment. Incidentally, you do not need to invest in any of the sophisticated, more expensive models you might see for sale. A square root function is the only extra feature you really need. Of course, if you want the additional features, such as memories and preprogrammed functions, by all means spend the extra money and learn how to use them. However, a simple, inexpensive calculator will work fine for all of the problems in this text.

Along the same lines, many of you probably have access to computers and statistical packages. If so, take the time now to learn how to use them, because they will eventually save you time and effort. This text includes a guide to a statistical package called SPSS, but many other programs are available that will accomplish the goals of saving time and avoiding drudgery while generating precise and accurate results.

In summary, you should find a way at the beginning of this course—with a calculator, a computer, or both—to minimize the tedium and hassle of mere computing. This will permit you to devote maximum effort to the truly important goal of increasing your understanding of the meaning of statistics in particular and social research in general.

H.2 VARIABLES AND SYMBOLS

Statistics are a set of techniques by which we can describe, analyze, and manipulate **variables.** A variable is a trait that can change value from case to case or from time to time. Examples of variables would include height, weight, level of prejudice, and political party preference. The possible values associated with a given variable might be numerous (e.g., income) or relatively few (e.g., gender). We will often use symbols, usually the letter X, to refer to variables in general or to a specific variable.

Sometimes we will need to refer to a specific value or set of values of a variable. This is usually done with the aid of subscripts. So, the symbol X_1 (read "X-sub-one") would refer to the first score in a set of scores, X_2 ("X-sub-two") to the second score, and so forth. Also, we will use the subscript i to refer to all the scores in a set. Thus, the symbol X_i ("X-sub-eye") refers to all of the scores associated with a given variable (e.g., the test grades of a particular class).

H.3 OPERATIONS

You are all familiar with the four basic mathematical operations of addition, subtraction, multiplication, and division and the standard symbols ($+$, $-$, $\times$, $\div$) used to denote them. Some of you may not be aware, however, that the latter two operations can be symbolized in a variety of ways. For example, the operation of multiplying some number a by some number b may be symbolized in (at least) six different ways:

$$a \times b$$
$$a \cdot b$$
$$a * b$$
$$ab$$
$$a(b)$$
$$(a)(b)$$

In this text, we will commonly use the "adjacent symbols" format (i.e., ab), the conventional times sign ($\times$), or adjacent parentheses to indicate multiplication. On most calculators and computers, the asterisk ($*$) is the symbol for multiplication.

The operation of division can also be expressed in several different ways. In this text, we will use either of these two methods:

$$a/b \quad \text{or} \quad \frac{a}{b}$$

Several of the formulas with which we will be working require us to find the square of a number. To do this, simply multiply the number by itself. This operation is symbolized as X^2 (read "X squared"), which is the same thing as $(X)(X)$. If X has a value of 4, then

$$X^2 = (X)(X) = (4)(4) = 16$$

or we could say that "4 squared is 16."

The square root of a number is the value that, when multiplied by itself, results in the original number. So the square root of 16 is 4 because $(4)(4)$ is 16. The operation of finding the square root of a number is symbolized as

$$\sqrt{X}$$

Be sure that you have access to a calculator with a built-in square root function.

A final operation with which you should be familiar is summation, or the addition of the scores associated with a particular variable. When a formula requires the addition of a series of scores, this operation is usually symbolized as $\sum X_i$. The symbol $\sum$ is the uppercase Greek letter sigma and stands for "the summation of." So the combination of symbols $\sum X_i$ means "the summation of all the scores" and directs us to add the value of all the scores for that variable. If four people had family sizes of 2, 4, 5, and 7, then the summation of these four scores for this variable could be symbolized as

$$\sum X_i = 2 + 4 + 5 + 7 = 18$$

The symbol $\sum$ is an operator, just like the $+$ or $\times$ signs. It directs us to add all of the scores on the variable indicated by the X symbol.

There are two other common uses of the summation sign and, unfortunately, the symbols denoting these uses are not, at first glance, sharply different from each other or from the symbol used above. A little practice and some careful attention to these various meanings should minimize the confusion. The first set of symbols is $\sum X_i^2$, which means "the sum of the squared scores." This quantity is found by *first* squaring each of the scores and *then* adding the squared scores together. A second common set of symbols will be $(\sum X_i)^2$, which means "the sum of the scores, squared." This quantity is found by *first* summing the scores and *then* squaring the total.

These distinctions might be confusing at first, so let's see if an example helps to clarify the situation. Suppose we had a set of three scores: 10, 12, and 13. So,

$$X_i = 10, 12, 13$$

The sum of these scores would be indicated as

$$\sum X_i = 10 + 12 + 13 = 35$$

The sum of the squared scores would be

$$\sum X_i^2 = (10)^2 + (12)^2 + (13)^2 = 100 + 144 + 169 = 413$$

Take careful note of the order of operations here. First, the scores are squared one at a time and then the squared scores are added. This is a completely different operation from squaring the sum of the scores:

$$\left(\sum X_i \right)^2 = (10 + 12 + 13)^2 = (35)^2 = 1,225$$

To find this quantity, first the scores are summed and then the total of all the scores is squared. The value of the sum of the scores squared (1,225) is not the same as the value of the sum of the squared scores (413). In summary, the operations associated with each set of symbols are:

Symbols	Operations
$\sum X_i$	Add the scores
$\sum X_i^2$	First square the scores and then add the squared scores
$(\sum X_i)^2$	First add the scores and then square the total

H.4 OPERATIONS WITH NEGATIVE NUMBERS

A number can be either positive (if it is preceded by a + sign or by no sign at all) or negative (if it is preceded by a − sign). Positive numbers are greater than zero, and negative numbers are less than zero. It is very important to keep track of signs because they will affect the outcome of virtually every mathematical operation. This section will briefly summarize the relevant rules for dealing with negative numbers. First, adding a negative number is the same as subtraction. For example,

$$3 + (-1) + 4 = 3 - 1 + 4 = 2 + 4 = 6$$

Second, subtraction changes the sign of a negative number:

$$3 - (-1) - 4 = 3 + 1 - 4 = 4 - 4 = 0$$

Note the importance of keeping track of signs here. It would be relatively easy for an inexperienced person to forget to change the sign of the negative number in the expression above and arrive at the wrong answer.

For multiplication and division, there are various combinations of negative and positive numbers you should be aware of. For purposes of this text, you will rarely have to multiply or divide more than two numbers at a time, and we will confine our attention to this situation. Ignoring the case of all positive numbers, this leaves several possible combinations. A negative number times a positive number results in a negative value:

$$(-3)(4) = -12$$

or

$$(3)(-4) = -12$$

A negative number times a negative number is always positive:

$$(-3)(-4) = 12$$

Division follows the same patterns. If there is a single negative number in the calculations, the answer will be negative. If both numbers are negative, the answer will be positive. So,

$$(-4)/(2) = -2$$

and

$$(4)/(-2) = -2$$

but

$$(-4)/(-2) = 2$$

Negative numbers do not have square roots, because multiplying a number by itself cannot result in a negative value. Squaring a negative number always results in a positive value (see the multiplication rules above).

H.5 ACCURACY AND ROUNDING OFF

A possible source of confusion in computation involves the issues of accuracy and rounding off. People work at different levels of accuracy and precision and, for this reason alone, may arrive at different answers to problems. This is important because, if you work at one level of precision and we (or your instructor or your study partner) work at another, we will often arrive at solutions that are at least slightly different. You may sometimes think you've gotten the wrong answer when all you've really done is round off at a different place in the calculations or in a different way.

There are two issues here: when to round off and how to round off. In this text, we have followed the convention of working in as much accuracy as our calculator or statistics package will allow and then rounding off to two places of accuracy (two places beyond the decimal point) at the very end. If a set of calculations is lengthy and requires the reporting of intermediate sums or subtotals, we will round the subtotals off to two places also.

In terms of how to round off, begin by looking at the digit immediately to the right of the last digit you want to retain. If you want to round off to 100ths (two places beyond the decimal point), look at the digit in the 1000ths place (three places beyond the decimal point). If that digit is greater than 5, round up. For example, 23.346 would round off to 23.35. If the digit to the right is less than 5, round down. So, 23.343 would become 23.34. If the digit to the right is 5, round up if the digit immediately to the left is even and round down if the digit is odd. So, 23.345 would become 23.35 and 23.355 would round to 23.35.

Let's look at some more examples of how to follow the rounding rules stated above. If you are calculating the mean value of a set of test scores and your calculator shows a final value of 83.459067, and you want to round off to two places beyond the decimal point, look at the digit three places beyond the decimal point. In this case the value is 9 (greater than 5), so we would round the second digit beyond the decimal point up and report the mean as 83.46. If the value had been 83.453067, we would have reported our final answer as 83.45. A value of 83.455067 would round to 83.45, and a value of 83.445067 would be 83.45.

H.6 FORMULAS, COMPLEX OPERATIONS, AND THE ORDER OF OPERATIONS

A mathematical formula is a set of directions, stated in general symbols, for calculating a particular statistic. To "solve a formula" means that you must replace the symbols with the proper values and then manipulate the values through a series of calculations. Even the most complex formula can be rendered manageable if it is broken down into smaller steps. Working through these steps requires some knowledge of general procedure and the rules of precedence of mathematical operations. This is because the order in which you perform calculations may affect your final answer. Consider the following expression:

$$2 + 3(4)$$

Note that if you do the addition first, you will evaluate the expression as

$$5(4) = 20$$

but if you do the multiplication first, the expression becomes

$$2 + 12 = 14$$

Obviously, it is crucial to complete the steps of a calculation in the correct order.

The basic rules of precedence are to find all squares and square roots first, then do all multiplication and division, and finally complete all addition and subtraction. So the following expression:

$$8 + 2 \times 2^2/2$$

would be evaluated as

$$8 + 2 \times 4/2 = 8 + 8/2 = 8 + 4 = 12$$

The rules of precedence may be overridden when an expression contains parentheses. Solve all expressions within parentheses before applying the rules stated above. For most of the complex formulas in this text, the order of calculations will be controlled by the parentheses. Consider the following expression:

$$(8 + 2) - 4(3)^2/(8 - 6)$$

Resolving the parenthetical expressions first, we would have

$$(10) - 4 \times 9/(2) = 10 - 36/2 = 10 - 18 = -8$$

Without the parentheses, the same expression would be evaluated as

$$8 + 2 - 4 \times 3^2/8 - 6$$
$$= 8 + 2 - 4 \times 9/8 - 6$$
$$= 8 + 2 - 36/8 - 6$$
$$= 8 + 2 - 4.5 - 6$$
$$= 10 - 10.5$$
$$= -.5$$

A final operation you will encounter in some formulas in this text involves denominators of fractions that themselves contain fractions. In this situation, solve the fraction in the denominator first and then complete the division. For example,

$$15 - 9/6/2$$

would become

$$15 - 9/3 = 6/3 = 2$$

When you are confronted with complex expressions such as these, don't be intimidated. If you're patient with yourself and work through them step by step, beginning with the parenthetical expression, even the most imposing formulas can be managed.

H.7 EXERCISES

You can use the problems below as a "self-test" on the material presented in this review. If you can handle these problems, you're ready to do all of the arithmetic in this text. If you have difficulty with any of these problems, please review the appropriate section of this appendix. You might also want to use this section as an opportunity to become more familiar with your calculator. Answers are given on the next page, along with some commentary and some reminders.

1. Complete each of the following:
   a. $17 \times 3 =$
   b. $17(3) =$
   c. $(17)(3) =$
   d. $17/3 =$
   e. $(42)^2 =$
   f. $\sqrt{113} =$

2. For the set of scores (X_i) of 50, 55, 60, 65, and 70, evaluate each of the expressions below:
   $\Sigma X_i =$
   $\Sigma X_i^2 =$
   $\Sigma (X_i)^2 =$

3. Complete each of the following:
   a. $17 + (-3) + (4) + (-2) =$
   b. $15 - 3 - (-5) + 2 =$

c. $(-27)(54) =$
d. $(113)(-2) =$
e. $(-14)(-100) =$
f. $-34/-2 =$
g. $322/-11 =$
h. $\sqrt{-2} =$
i. $(-17)^2 =$

4. Round off each of the following to two places beyond the decimal point:
  a. 17.17532
  b. 43.119
  c. 1,076.77337
  d. 32.4651152301
  e. 32.4751152301

5. Evaluate each of the following:
  a. $(3 + 7)/10 =$
  b. $3 + 7/10 =$
  c. $((4 - 3) + (7 + 2))/((4 + 5)(10)) =$
  d. $\sqrt{(7(5 - 3)^2)/((17/3)(4))} =$
  e. $22 + 44/15 =$

H.8 ANSWERS

1. a. 51   **b.** 51   **c.** 51
(The obvious purpose of these first three problems is to remind you that there are several different ways of expressing multiplication.)
d. 5.67 (Note the rounding off.)   **e.** 1,764   **f.** 10.63

2. The first expression translates to "the sum of the scores," so this operation would be

$$\sum X_i = 50 + 55 + 60 + 65 + 70 = 300$$

The second expression is the "sum of the squared scores." So

$$\sum X_i^2 = (50)^2 + (55)^2 + (60)^2 + (65)^2 + (70)^2$$

$$\sum X_i^2 = 2{,}500 + 3{,}025 + 3{,}600 + 4{,}225 + 4{,}900$$

$$\sum X_i^2 = 18{,}250$$

The third expression is "the sum of the scores, squared":

$$\left(\sum X_i\right)^2 = (50 + 55 + 60 + 65 + 70)^2$$

$$\left(\sum X_i\right)^2 = (300)^2$$

$$\left(\sum X_i\right)^2 = 90{,}000$$

Remember that $\sum X_i^2$ and $(\sum X_i)^2$ are two completely different expressions with very different values.

3. a. 16   **b.** 19 (Remember to change the sign of -5.)   **c.** $-1,458$
   d. -226 **e.** 1,400   **f.** 17   **g.** -29.27
   h. Your calculator probably gave you some sort of error message for this problem, because negative numbers do not have square roots.
   i. 289

4. a. 17.17   **b.** 43.12   **c.** 1,076.77
   d. 32.47   **e.** 32.47

5. a. 1   **b.** 3.7 (Note again the importance of parentheses.)   **c.** 0.11
   d. Whoa!—this looks complicated and should be worked out carefully, step by step. Note that complex expressions such as this are solved from the "inside out." That is, we begin within the innermost parentheses, follow the rules of precedence until we have resolved the numbers under the square root sign into a single number, and the *final* thing we do is take the square root:

$$\sqrt{(7(5-3)^2)/((17/3)(4))} = 7(2)^2/(5.6666667)(4)$$
$$= 7(4)/22.666667$$
$$= 28/22.666667$$
$$= 1.2352941$$
$$= 1.11143790 \text{ or, rounded off} = 1.11$$

   e. 24.93

Answers to Odd-Numbered Computational Problems

In addition to answers, this section suggests some problem-solving strategies and provides examples of how to interpret the numerical answers. You should try to solve and interpret the problems on your own before consulting this section.

In solving these problems, we let our calculators or computers do most of the work. We worked with whatever level of precision these devices permitted and, generally, didn't round off until the end or until we had to record an intermediate sum. We always rounded off to two places of accuracy (or, two places beyond the decimal point, or to 100ths). If you follow these same conventions, your answers will almost always match our answers. However, there is no guarantee that our answers will always be exact matches, and you should be aware that small discrepancies might occur and that they are almost always trivial. If the difference between your answer and our answer doesn't seem trivial, you should double-check to make sure you haven't made an error or solve the problem again using a greater degree of precision.

Finally, please allow us a brief disclaimer about mathematical errors in this section. Let us assure you, first of all, that we know how important this section is for most students and that we worked hard to be certain that these answers are correct. Human fallibility being what it is, however, we know that we cannot make absolute guarantees. Should you find any errors, please let us know so we can make corrections in the future.

Chapter 2

2.1 **a.** Complex A: $(5/20) \times 100 = 25.00\%$
Complex B: $(10/20) \times 100 = 50.00\%$
b. Complex A: $4:5 = 0.80$
Complex B: $6:10 = 0.60$
c. Complex A: $(0/20) = 0.00$
Complex B: $(1/20) = 0.05$
d. $(6/(4 + 6)) = (6/10) = 60.00\%$
e. Complex A: $8:5 = 1.60$
Complex B: $2:10 = 0.20$

2.3 Bank robbery rate $=$
$(47/211,732) \times 100,000 = 22.20$
Homicide rate $= (13/211,732) \times 100,000 = 6.14$
Auto theft rate $= (23/211,732) \times 100,000 = 10.86$

Chapter 3

3.1 "Region of birth" is a nominal-level variable, "support for legalization" and "opinion of food" are ordinal, and "expenses" and "number of movies" are interval-ratio. The mode, the most common score, is the only measure of central tendency available for nominal-level variables. For the ordinal-level variables, *don't forget to array the scores from high to low* before locating the median. There are ten lower-year students (N is even), so the median will be the score halfway between the scores of the two middle cases. There are 11 upper-year students (N is odd), so the median will be the score of the middle case. To find the mean for the interval-ratio variables, add the scores and divide by the number of cases.

Variable:	Lower Year:	Upper Year:
Region of birth:	Mode = Atlantic	Mode = Atlantic
Legalization:	Median = 3	Median = 5
Expenses:	Mean = 48.50	Mean = 63.00
Movies:	Mean = 5.8	Mean = 5.18
Food:	Median = 6	Median = 4

3.3

Variable	Level of Measurement	Measure of Central Tendency
Sex	Nominal	Mode = male
Social class	Ordinal	Median = "medium" (the middle case is in this category)
Number of years in the party	I-R	Mean = 26.15
Education	Ordinal	Median = high school
Marital status	Nominal	Mode = married
Number of children	I-R	Mean = 2.39

3.5

Variable	Level of Measurement	Measure of Central Tendency
Marital status	Nominal	Mode = married
Sex	Nominal	Mode = female
Age	I-R	Mean = 27.53
Attitude on legalization of marijuana	Ordinal	Median = 7

3.7

Variable	Level of Measurement	Measure of Central Tendency
Sex	Nominal	There are 10 males and 10 females so this distribution is bimodal (Mode = male and female)
Marital status	Nominal	Mode = single
Satisfaction	Ordinal	Median = 3
Age	I-R	Mean = 20.05

3.9 Attitude and opinion scales almost always generate ordinal-level data, so the appropriate measure of central tendency would be the median. For the students, the median is 9 and, for the neighbours, the median is 2. Incidentally, the means are 7.80 for the students and 4.00 for the neighbours.

3.11 Mean = 40.25, Median = 44.5. The lower value for the mean indicates a negative skew or a few very *low* scores. For this small group of nations, the skew is caused by the score of Mexico (10), which is much lower than the scores of the other seven nations (which are grouped between 37 and 51).

3.13 To find the median, the scores for both groups first must be ranked from high to low. Both groups have 25 cases (N = odd), so the median is the score of the 13th case. For first-year students, the median is 35 and, for final-year students, the median is 30. The mean score for first-year students is 31.72. For final-year students, the mean is 28.60.

Chapter 4

4.1

Complex	IQV
A	0.89
B	0.99
C	0.71
D	0.74

Complex B has the highest IQV and is the most heterogeneous. Complex C is the least heterogeneous.

4.3 The high score is 50 and the low score is 10 so the range is 50 − 10 or 40. The standard deviation is 12.28.

4.5

Statistic	2000	2005
Mean	654.6	703
Median	654	703
Standard deviation	40.86	29.46
Range	142	89

In this time period, the mean and median increase. The distributions for both years are symmetrical (the mean and the median are the same in 2005 and nearly identical in 2000). The standard deviation and range become smaller over the time period. This indicates that the dispersion in the group (the differences in income from province to province) decreased.

4.7

Variable	Statistic	Males	Females
Labour force participation	Mean	77.60	58.40
	Standard deviation	2.73	6.73
% High school graduate	Mean	69.20	70.20
	Standard deviation	5.38	4.98
Mean income	Mean	33,896.60	29,462.40
	Standard deviation	4,443.16	4,597.93

Males and females are very similar in terms of educational level, but females are less involved in the labour force and, on the average, earn almost $4,500 less than males per year. The females in these 10 cities are much more variable in their labour force participation but are similar to males in dispersion on the other two variables. See Section 9.7 for more on this topic.

4.9 $s = 12.29$

4.11 $R = 53 - 3 = 50$, $s = 13.03$. Because the score for Montreal (53) is much higher than the other scores (the next highest score is 33), removing this score would reduce the variation in the data set. The standard deviation of the scores without Montreal would be lower in value.

4.13

Division	Range	Standard Deviation
A:	$R = 18$	$s = 5.32$
B:	$R = 8$	$s = 2.37$
C:	$R = 3$	$s = 1.02$
D:	$R = 25$	$s = 7.87$

Chapter 5

5.1

X_i	Z score	% Area Above	% Area Below
5	−1.67	95.25	4.75
6	−1.33	90.82	9.18
7	−1.00	84.13	15.87
8	−.67	74.86	25.14
9	−.33	62.93	37.07
11	.33	37.07	62.93
12	.67	25.14	74.86
14	1.33	9.18	90.82
15	1.67	4.75	95.25
16	2.00	2.28	97.72
18	2.67	.38	99.62

5.3

	Z scores	Area
a.	.10 & 1.10	32.45%
b.	.60 & 1.10	13.86%
c.	.60	27.43%
d.	.90	18.41%
e.	.60 & −.40	38.11%
f.	.10 & −.40	19.52%
g.	.10	53.98%
h.	.30	61.79%
i.	.60	72.57%
j.	1.10	86.43%

5.5

X_i	Z Score	Number of Students Above	Number of Students Below
60	−2.00	195	5
57	−2.50	199	1
55	−2.83	199	1
67	−0.83	159	41
70	−0.33	126	74
72	0.00	100	100
78	1.00	32	168
82	1.67	10	190
90	3.00	1	199
95	3.83	1	199

Note: Number of students (a discrete variable) has been rounded off to the nearest whole number.

5.7

	Z score	Area
a.	−2.20	1.39%
b.	1.80	96.41%
c.	−0.20 & 1.80	54.34%
d.	0.80 & 2.80	20.93%
e.	−1.20	88.49%
f.	0.80	21.19%

5.9

	Z score	Area
a.	−1.00 & 1.50	.7745
b.	0.25 & 1.50	.3345
c.	1.50	.0668
d.	0.25 & −2.25	.5865
e.	−1.00 & −2.25	.1465
f.	−1.00	.1587

5.11 Yes. The raw score of 110 translates into a Z score of $+2.88$. 99.80% of the area lies below this score, so this individual was in the top 1% on this test.

5.13 For the first event, the probability is .0919 and, for the second, the probability is .0655. The first event is more likely.

Part I Cumulative Exercises

1. The level of measurement is the most important criteria for selecting descriptive statistics. The table below presents all relevant statistics for each variable. Statistics which are not appropriate for a variable are noted with an "X."

Religion is nominal so the only statistics available are the mode and the IQV. For the two ordinal-level variables ("strength" and "comfort"), the median and the range are the appropriate choices. However, for ordinal-level variables like "strength," which have a wide range of scores, it is common for social science researchers to report the standard deviation and mean. For interval-ratio variables like "pray" and "age," the mean and standard deviation are the preferred summary statistics.

Level of measurement:	Religion Nominal	Strength Ordinal	Pray I-R	Comfort Ordinal	Age I-R
Mode	Protestant				
Median	X	7		1	
Mean	X	6.07	1.40		41.53
IQV	0.95				
Range	X	9	9	4	49
Stnd. dev.	X	2.77	1.62		12.54

3. As always, the level of measurement is the primary guideline for choosing descriptive statistics and the most appropriate statistics are noted in the table below. Statistics which are not appropriate for a variable are noted with an "X."

Level of measurement:	Children I-R	School Ordinal	Sex Nominal	Spanking Ordinal	TV I-R	Age Ordinal
Mode			Male			
Median		1.00	X	2		1
Mean	2.44		X		3.08	
IQV			0.64			
Range	9	4	X	3	10	2
Stnd. dev.	2.06		X		2.04	

Chapter 7

7.1 **a.** 5.2 ± 0.11 **b.** 100 ± 0.71
c. 20 ± 0.40 **d.** $1{,}020 \pm 5.41$
e. 7.3 ± 0.23 **f.** 33 ± 0.80

7.5 **a.** 2.30 ± 0.04 **b.** 2.10 ± 0.01, $0.78 \pm .07$
c. 6.00 ± 0.37

7.7 **a.** 178.23 ± 1.97 The estimate is that students spent between \$176.26 and \$180.20 on books.
b. $1.5 \pm .04$ The estimate is that students visited the clinic between 1.46 and 1.54 times on the average.
c. $2.8 \pm .13$ **d.** $3.5 \pm .19$

7.9. $14 \pm .07$ The estimate is that between 7% and 21% of the population consists of unmarried couples living together.

7.11 **a.** $P_s = (823/1{,}496) = .55$
Confidence interval: $.55 \pm .02$
Between 53% and 57% of the population agrees with the statement.
b. $P_s = (650/1{,}496) = .44$
Confidence interval: $.44 \pm .02$
c. $P_s = (375/1{,}496) = .25$
Confidence interval: $.25 \pm .02$
d. $P_s = (1{,}023/1{,}496) = .68$
Confidence interval: $.68 \pm .02$
e. $P_s = (800/1{,}496) = .54$
Confidence interval: $.54 \pm .02$

7.13

Alpha (α)	Confidence Level	Confidence Interval
0.10	90%	100 ± 0.74
0.05	95%	100 ± 0.88
0.01	99%	100 ± 1.16
0.001	99.9%	100 ± 1.47

7.15 The confidence interval is .51 ± .05. The estimate would be that between 46% and 56% of the population prefer candidate A. The population parameter (P_u) is equally likely to be anywhere in the interval (i.e., it's just as likely to be 46% as it is to be 56%), so a winner cannot be predicted.

7.17 The confidence interval is 0.23 ± 0.08. At the 95% confidence level, the estimate would be that between 240 (15%) and 496 (31%) of the 1,600 incoming students would be extremely interested. The estimated numbers are found by multiplying N (1,600) by the upper (.31) and lower (.15) limits of the interval.

7.19 a. 43.87 ± 0.49
   b. 2.86 ± 0.08
   c. 1.81 ± 0.06
   d. 0.29 ± 0.02
   e. 0.18 ± 0.02
   f. 0.36 ± 0.02
   g. 0.81 ± 0.02

Chapter 8

8.3 a. Z (obtained) = −41.00
   b. Z (obtained) = 29.09

8.5 Z (obtained) = 6.04

8.7 a. Z (obtained) = −13.66
   b. Z (obtained) = 25.50

8.9 t (obtained) = 4.50

8.11 Z (obtained) = 3.06

8.13 Z (obtained) = −1.48

8.15 a. Z (obtained) = −0.74
   b. Z (obtained) = 2.19
   c. Z (obtained) = −8.55
   d. Z (obtained) = −18.07
   e. Z (obtained) = 2.09
   f. Z (obtained) = −53.33

8.17 t (obtained) = −1.14

Chapter 9

9.1 a. σ = 1.39, Z (obtained) = −2.52
   b. σ = 1.61, Z (obtained) = 2.49

9.3 a. Z (obtained) = 1.70
   b. Z (obtained) = −2.48

9.5 a. σ = 0.08 Z (obtained) = 11.25
   b. Phone calls: σ = 0.12 Z (obtained) = −3.33
   E-mail messages: σ = 0.15 Z (obtained) = 20.00

9.7 These are small samples (combined N's of less than 100), so be sure to use Formulas 9.5 and 9.6 in step 4.
   a. σ = 0.12, t (obtained) = −1.33
   b. σ = 0.13, t (obtained) = 14.85

9.9 a. (Canada) σ = 0.0095, Z (obtained) = −31.58
   b. (Nigeria) σ = 0.0075, Z (obtained) = −146.67
   c. (China) σ = 0.0065, Z (obtained) = 76.92
   d. (Mexico) σ = 0.0107, Z (obtained) = −74.77
   e. (Japan) σ = 0.012, Z (obtained) = −41.67

The large values for the Z scores indicate that the differences are significant at very low alpha levels (i.e., they are extremely unlikely to have been caused by random chance alone). Note that women are significantly happier than men in every nation except China where men are significantly happier.

9.11 P_u = .45, σ_p = .06, Z (obtained) = 0.67

9.13 a. P_u = .46, σ_p = 0.06, Z (obtained) = 2.17
   b. P_u = .80, σ_p = 0.07, Z (obtained) = −1.43
   c. P_u = .72, σ_p = 0.08, Z (obtained) = 0.75

9.15 a. Z (obtained) = 1.50
   b. Z (obtained) = −2.75
   c. Z (obtained) = 4.00
   d. Z (obtained) = 1.86
   e. Z (obtained) = −5.71
   f. Z (obtained) = −5.50

Chapter 10

10.1

Prob- lem	Grand Mean	SST	SSB	SSW	F ratio
a.	12.17	231.67	173.17	58.5	13.32
b.	6.87	455.73	78.53	377.20	1.25
c.	31.65	8,362.55	5,053.35	3,309.2	8.14

10.3

Problem	Grand Mean	SST	SSB	SSW	F ratio
a.	4.39	86.28	45.78	40.50	8.48
b.	16.44	332.44	65.44	267.00	1.84

For problem 10.3a, with alpha = 0.05 and df = 2, 15, the critical F ratio would be 3.68. We would reject the null hypothesis and conclude that decision making *does* vary significantly by type of relationship. By inspection of the group means, it seems that the "cohabitational" category accounts for most of the differences.

10.5 SST = 213.61, SSB = 2.11, SSW = 211.50
F (obtained) = .08

10.7 SST = 429.48, SSB = 124.06, SSW = 305.42
F (obtained) = 5.96

10.9

Nation	Grand Mean	SST	SSB	SSW	F ratio
Mexico	3.78	300.98	154.08	146.90	12.59
Canada	6.88	156.38	20.08	136.30	1.78
United States	5.13	286.38	135.28	151.10	10.74

At alpha = 0.05 and df = 3, 36, the critical F ratio is 2.92. There is a significant difference in support for suicide by class in Mexico and the United States but not in Canada. The category means for Mexico suggest that the upper class accounts for most of the differences. For the United States, there is more variation across the category means and the working class seems to account for most of the differences. Going beyond the ANOVA test and comparing the grand means, support is highest in Canada and lowest in Mexico.

Chapter 11

11.1 **a.** 1.11   **b.** 0.00   **c.** 1.52   **d.** 1.46

11.3 A computing table is highly recommended as a way of organizing the computations for chi square:

Computational Table for Problem 11.3

(1)	(2)	(3)	(4)	(5)
f_o	f_e	$f_o - f_e$	$(f_o - f_e)^2$	$(f_o - f_e)^2/ f_e$
6	5	1	1	.20
7	8	−1	1	.13
4	5	−1	1	.20
9	8	1	1	.13
$N = 26$	$N = 26$	0		χ^2 (obtained) = 0.65

There is 1 degree of freedom in a 2 × 2 table. With alpha set at 0.05, the critical value for the chi square would be 3.841. The obtained chi square is 0.65, so we fail to reject the null hypothesis of independence between the variables. There is no statistically significant relationship between sex and services received.

11.5

Computational Table for Problem 11.5

(1)	(2)	(3)	(4)	(5)
f_o	f_e	$f_o - f_e$	$(f_o - f_e)^2$	$(f_o - f_e)^2/ f_e$
21	17.5	3.5	12.25	.70
29	32.5	−3.5	12.25	.38
14	17.5	−3.5	12.25	.70
36	32.5	3.5	12.25	.38
$N = 100$	$N = 100.0$	0		χ^2 (obtained) = 2.15

With 1 degree of freedom and alpha set at 0.05, the critical region will begin at 3.841. The obtained chi square of 2.15 does not fall within this area, so the null hypothesis cannot be rejected. There is no statistically significant relationship between unionization and salary.

11.7 The obtained chi square is 5.12, which is significant (df = 1, alpha = .05).

11.9 The obtained chi square is 6.67.

11.11 The obtained chi square is 12.59.

11.13 The obtained chi square is 19.33.

11.15

Problem	Chi Square	Significant at $\alpha = 0.05$?
a.	25.19	Yes
b.	1.80	No
c.	5.23	No
d.	28.43	Yes
e.	14.17	Yes

Part II Cumulative Exercises

1. One of the challenges of empirical research is to make reasonable decisions about which statistical test to use in which situation. You can minimize the confusion and ambiguity by approaching the decision systematically. We'll use the first problem of this exercise to consider some ways in which reasonable decisions can be made. The situation calls for a test of hypothesis ("Is the difference significant?"), so our choice of procedures will be limited to Chapters 8–11. Next, determine the types of variables you are working with. Number of minutes is an interval-ratio-level variable, and gender is nominal and has only two categories. Which test should we use? The techniques in Chapter 8 (one-sample tests) and Chapter 10 (tests involving more than two samples or categories) are not relevant. Chi square (Chapter 11) won't work unless we collapse the scores on Internet use into a few categories. This leaves Chapter 9. A test of sample means fits the situation, and we have a large sample (combined N's greater than 100), so it looks like we're going to wind up in Section 9.2.

Another way to approach test selection would be to use the flowcharts presented at the beginning of each part and chapter. The flowcharts would quickly lead to Chapter 9, where we would answer: YES, we want to test for the significance of the difference between means, and YES, sample size is large. These answers will also lead to Section 9.2.

a. $\sigma = .14$, Z (obtained) $= -35.71$
The difference in Internet minutes is significant. Men, on the average, use this technology more frequently.

b. The table format is a sure tip-off that the chi square test is appropriate. The obtained chi square is 0.87, which is not significant at the .05 level. There is no statistically significant relationship between involvement and social class.

c. "Number of partners" sounds like an interval-ratio-level variable, and education has three categories. Analysis of variance is an appropriate test for this situation. The F ratio is .13—not at all significant—so we must conclude that this dimension of sexuality does not vary by level of education.

d. The problem asks for a characteristic of a population ("how many times do adult Canadians move?") but gives information only for a "random sample." The estimation procedures presented in Chapter 7 fit the situation and, because the information is presented in the form of a mean, you should use Formula 7.2 to form the estimate. At an alpha level of .05, the confidence interval would be 3.5 ± 0.02.

e. The research question focuses on the difference between a single sample and a population, so Chapter 8 is relevant. Because the population standard deviation is unknown, and we have a large sample, Sections 8.1–8.5 and Formula 8.1 will be relevant. Z (obtained) is -2.50, which would be significant at alpha $= .05$. The sample is significantly different from the population—rural school districts are different from the universe of school districts in this province.

Chapter 12

Tables display conditional distributions (or column percentages).

12.1

Efficiency	Authoritarianism	
	Low	High
Low	37.04	70.59
High	62.96	29.41
Totals	100.00	100.00

The conditional distributions change, so there is a relationship between the variables. The change from column to column is quite large and the maximum difference is $(70.59 - 37.04) = 33.55$. Using Table 12.5 as a guideline, we can say that this relationship is strong. From inspection of the percentages, we can see that efficiency decreases as authoritarianism increases—workers with dictatorial bosses are less productive (or, maybe, bosses become more dictatorial when workers are inefficient), so this relationship is negative in direction.

12.3

| 2006 Election | 2004 Election | |
	Voted	Didn't Vote
Voted	87.31	11.44
Didn't Vote	12.69	88.56
Totals	100.00	100.00

The maximum difference for this table is (87.31 − 11.44) or 75.87. This is a very strong relationship. People are very consistent in their voting habits.

12.5 a.

| Received Services? | Sex | |
	Female	Male
Yes	60.00	43.75
No	40.00	56.25
Totals	100.00	100.00

The maximum difference is (60.00 − 43.75) or 16.25. This is a moderate relationship and females were more likely to receive services.

12.7

| Crime Rate | Program | |
	No	Yes
Low	25.44	17.24
Moderate	28.95	31.03
High	45.61	51.72
Totals	100.00	100.00

The maximum difference is (25.44 − 17.24) or 8.2. This is a weak relationship but a higher percentage of the cities with the program have high crime rates.

12.9   Student Involvement by Extent of Press Coverage

| Involvement | Coverage | | | Totals |
	None	Moderate	Extensive	
None	3 (50.00%)	4 (36.36%)	0 (00.00%)	7 (28.00%)
Some	2 (33.33%)	4 (36.36%)	3 (37.50%)	9 (36.00%)
Extensive	1 (16.67%)	3 (27.27%)	5 (62.50%)	9 (36.00%)
Totals	6 (100.00%)	11 (99.99%)	8 (100.00%)	25 (100.00%)

The conditional distributions change so there is a relationship between these two variables. The maximum difference is (50.00 − 00.00) = 50 so the relationship is strong. Campuses with extensive coverage had more extensive involvement and campuses with no coverage tended to have no involvement. This is a positive relationship: the greater the coverage, the more extensive the involvement.

12.11 a.

| Supports Same-sex Marriage? | Political Ideology | | |
	Liberal	Moderate	Conservative
Favour	59.42	39.39	26.88
Oppose	40.58	60.31	73.12
Totals	100.00	100.00	100.00

The maximum difference of 32.54 indicates a strong relationship. Liberals support same-sex marriage, conservatives are opposed, and moderates are intermediate.

Chapter 13

13.1   **a.** $\phi = 0.00$, $\lambda = 0.00$
b. $\phi = 0.09$, $\lambda = 0.00$
c. $\phi = 0.25$, $\lambda = 0.14$

13.3 $\phi = .17$, $\lambda = .00$

13.5 $\phi = .31$, $\lambda = 0.03$

13.7 $\phi = .00$, $\lambda = .00$

13.9   **a.** $\phi = .05$, $\lambda = .00$
b. $\phi = .29$, $\lambda = .03$
c. $\phi = .41$, $\lambda = .15$

Note that phi is greater than lambda for all three tables. This is a reflection of the much larger number of cases in the top row. Even though they differ in value, the two statistics rank the relationships consistently: sex has the weakest effect on attrition followed by status and then age. Using phi, we can conclude that sex is not an important correlate of attrition. Status and age have moderate to strong relationships with the dependent variable.

13.11 Cramer's $V = .05$, $\lambda = .00$

Chapter 14

14.1 a. $G = 0.71$ **b.** $G = 0.69$ **c.** $G = -0.88$
These relationships are strong. Facility in English/French and income increase with length of residence. Use the percentages to help interpret the direction of a relationship. In the first table, 80% of recent immigrants were "Low" in English/French facility while 60% of long-term immigrants were "High." In this relationship, low scores on one variable are associated with low scores on the other, and scores increase together (as one increases, the other increases), so this is a positive relationship. In contrast, contact with country of origin decreases with length of residence (-0.88). Most recent immigrants have higher levels of contact, and most long-term immigrants have lower levels.

14.3 $G = -0.61$ This is a strong negative relationship. As authoritarianism increases, efficiency decreases.

14.5 $G = 0.27$ Be careful interpreting the direction of this relationship. The positive sign of gamma means that cases tend to fall along the diagonal from upper left to lower right. In this case, white-collar families are more associated with organized sports and blue-collar families with sandlot sports. Computing percentages will help you identify the direction of the relationship.

14.7 $G = 0.22$, Z (obtained) $= 0.92$

14.9 $G = -0.14$

14.11 $r_s = -0.46$, t (obtained) $= -1.55$

14.13 $r_s = 0.33$
For these nations, there is a moderate positive relationship between diversity and inequality. The greater the diversity, the greater the inequality.

14.15 a. $G = -0.14$ **b.** $G = -0.17$
c. $G = -0.14$ **d.** $G = 0.39$
e. $G = -0.13$
Income has weak negative relationships with the first three and the last dependent variables. Be careful in interpreting direction for these tables and remember that a negative gamma means that cases tend to be clustered along the diagonal from lower left to upper right. Computing percentages will clarify direction. For example, for the first table, low income is associated with opposition to same-sex marriage (62% of the people in this column said "Oppose") and high income is associated with support (47% of the people in this column said "Favour" and this is the highest percentage of support across the three income groups).

Income has a moderate positive relationship with support for traditional gender roles. Note the way in which the dependent variable is coded: "Favour" means support for traditional gender roles. A positive relationship means that cases tend to fall along the diagonal from upper left to lower right. In this case, favouring is greater for low income and declines as income increases. Is this truly a "positive" relationship? As always, percentages will help clarify the direction of the relationship.

Chapter 15

15.1 (*HINT: When finding the slope, remember that "Turnout" is the dependent or Y variable.*)

	For Turnout (Y) and		
	Unemployment	Education	Neg. Campaigning
Slope (b)	3.00	12.67	−0.90
Y intercept (a)	39.00	−94.73	114.01
Reg. Eq.	$Y = (39) + (3)X$	$Y = (−94.73) + (12.67)X$	$Y = (114.01) + (−0.90)X$
r	0.95	0.98	−0.87
r^2	0.90	0.96	0.76
t (obtained)	5.00	9.05	−3.08

15.3 *(HINT: When finding the slope, remember that "Number of visitors" is the dependent or Y variable.)*

Slope (b)	−0.37
Y intercept (a)	13.42
r	−0.31
r^2	0.09

15.5

Dependent Variables		Independent Variables		
		Density	Growth	Urbanization
Car theft	a	417.08	135.47	−215.46
	b	−0.23	17.50	7.96
	r	−0.13	0.89	0.67
	r^2	0.02	0.79	0.45
Robbery	a	59.97	94.38	−96.71
	b	0.37	1.44	2.81
	r	0.72	0.27	0.87
	r^2	0.52	0.07	0.76
Homicide	a	3.87	3.01	−0.58
	b	0.00	0.11	0.07
	r	0.26	0.62	0.65
	r^2	0.07	0.38	0.42

c. For a growth rate of −1, the predicted homicide rate would be 2.90. For a population density of 250, the predicted robbery rate would be 152.47. For a city with 50% urbanization, the predicted rate of auto theft would be 182.54.

15.7 $b = 0.05$, $a = 53.18$, $r = 0.40$, $r^2 = 0.16$

15.9

Relationship	r	r^2	t (obtained)
Prestige and age	−0.30	0.09	−1.13
Attendance and number of children	−0.39	0.15	−1.53
Number of children and hours of TV	0.18	0.03	0.66
Age and hours of TV	0.16	0.03	0.58
Age and number of children	0.67	0.45	3.25
Hours of TV and prestige	−0.19	0.04	0.70

Part III Cumulative Exercises

1. a. Assuming that crime rates and "percent immigrant" are both measured at the interval-ratio level, Pearson's r would be the appropriate measure of association. This is a moderate negative relationship ($r = −0.47$) and percentage of immigrants explains 22% of the variation in crime rate for these 10 cities. As the percentage of immigrants increases, the crime rate decreases.

b. These variables are ordinal in level of measurement, so gamma would be the appropriate measure of association. Gamma is −0.43, indicating a moderate negative relationship. As TV viewing increases, involvement decreases.

c. The appropriate measure for these variables is Spearman's rho, which is 0.74. This is a strong positive relationship and countries with higher quality of life have superior systems of higher education.

d. Marital status is a nominal-level variable, and the table is larger than 2 × 2. Cramer's V is .40, indicating a strong relationship between the variables. Because of the uneven row totals, lambda is zero even though there is an association between these variables.

Chapter 16

16.1 Bivariate Gamma   0.71

Partial Gammas		
Controlling for		
Sex	Male	0.78
	Female	0.65
Age at Immigration	Immigrated before age 45	0.67
	Immigrated at age 45+	0.74

The bivariate relationship is strong and positive. The longer the residence, the greater the facility in

English/French. The bivariate relationship is not affected by the sex or age at immigration of the immigrants. These results would be taken as strong evidence of a direct (causal) relationship between length of residence and English/French facility.

16.3

Bivariate Gamma		−0.23

Partial Gammas		
Controlling for Sex	Female	−0.34
	Male	−0.10

This is an interactive relationship. Length of institutionalization has a greater effect on the reality orientation of females than of males.

16.5

Bivariate Gamma		0.62

Partial Gammas		
Controlling for		
Age	Younger than 25	0.52
	25 or older	0.68
	$G_p =$	0.60
Sex	Males	0.62
	Females	0.62
	$G_p =$	0.62

The bivariate relationship is strong and positive. Completion of the training program is closely associated with holding a job for at least one year. There is some interaction with age. The training has less impact for younger trainees than for older trainees. Older trainees who did not complete the training were less likely than younger ones to have held a job for at least one year. Sex has no impact at all on the relationship. Overall, there is a direct relationship between completion of the training and holding a job for at least a year, though there is some interaction with age.

16.7

Support for Same-sex Marriage

Bivariate Gamma		−0.14

Partial Gammas		
Controlling for Sex	Males	−0.06
	Females	−0.19
	$G_p =$	−0.15

Support for the Right to Suicide

Bivariate Gamma		−0.14

Partial Gammas		
Controlling for Sex	Males	−0.16
	Females	−0.11
	$G_p =$	−0.13

Chapter 17

17.1 a. For turnout (Y) and unemployment (X) while controlling for negative advertising (Z), $r_{yx.z} = 0.95$. The relationship between X and Y is not affected by the control variable Z.
  b. For turnout (Y) and negative advertising (X) while controlling for unemployment (Z), $r_{yx.z} = -0.89$. The bivariate relationship is not affected by the control variable.
  c. Turnout $(Y) = 70.25 + (2.09)$ unemployment $(X_1) + (-0.43)$ negative advertising (X_2). For unemployment $(X_1) = 10$ and negative advertising $(X_2) = 75$, turnout $(Y) = 58.90$.
  d. For unemployment (X_1): $b_1^* = 0.66$. For negative advertising (X_2): $b_2^* = -0.41$. Unemployment has a stronger effect on turnout than negative advertising. Note that the independent variables' effect on turnout is in opposite directions.
  e. $R^2 = 0.98$

17.3 a. For strife (Y) and unemployment (X), controlling for urbanization (Z), $r_{yx.z} = 0.79$.
  b. For strife (Y) and urbanization (X), controlling for unemployment (Z), $r_{yx.z} = 0.20$.
  c. Strife $(Y) = (-14.60) + (4.94)$ unemployment $(X_1) + (0.16)$ urbanization (X_2). With unemployment $= 10$ and urbanization $= 90$, strife (Y') would be 49.19.
  d. For unemployment (X_1): $b_1^* = 0.78$. For urbanization (X_2): $b_2^* = 0.13$.
  e. $R^2 = 0.65$

17.5 a. Turnout $(Y) = 83.80 + (-1.16)$ working-class $(X_1) + (2.89)$ unemployment (X_2).
  b. For $X_1 = 0$ and $X_2 = 5$, $Y' = 98.25$
  c. $Z_y = (-1.27)Z_1 + (.84)Z_2$
  d. $R^2 = 0.51$

17.7 a. $Z_y = (-0.001)$ HS grads $(Z_1) + (-0.71)$ Rank (Z_2)

   b. $R^2 = 0.51$

Part IV Cumulative Exercises

1. a. The choice of multivariate procedures will depend on level of measurement and the number of possible scores for each variable. Regression analysis is appropriate for interval-ratio, continuous variables. In this situation, we have three variables: GPA, hours of work, and GRE score, each measured at the interval-ratio level. GPA is the dependent variable, and the zero-order correlation with "hours worked" is -0.83, a strong and negative relationship, which indicates that having a job did interfere with academic success for this sample. The zero-order correlation between GPA and GRE score is 0.55, a relationship that is consistent with the idea that GRE scores predict success in university.

The results of the regression analysis with "hours worked" (X_1) and GRE score (X_2) as independents:

$$Y = 1.71 + (-0.04)X_1 + (0.003)X_2$$
$$Z_y = (-0.75)Z_1 + (0.43)Z_2$$
$$R^2 = 0.86$$

The beta-weights indicate that "hours worked" has a stronger direct effect on GPA than GRE score. Even for students who were well prepared for graduate school and had high GRE scores, having a job had a negative impact on GPA. The high value for R^2 means that only a small percentage of the variance in GPA (14%) is left unexplained by these two independent variables.

   b. In this situation, we have three dichotomous variables, two ordinal-level and one nominal. With the limited variation possible, the elaboration technique is appropriate to analyze these relationships. The bivariate table shows that there is a relationship between graduating and level of social activity for this sample: 70% of the students with low levels of social activity graduated in four years vs. only 30% of the students with high levels. Bivariate gamma is 0.69, indicating a strong relationship.

Controlling for sex reveals some interaction. The gamma for males (0.77) is stronger than the bivariate gamma, and the gamma for females (0.60) is weaker. In other words, while level of social activity has an effect on graduation rates, the effect is stronger for males than for females. This suggests that sex should be incorporated into the analysis with a view to developing an understanding of why it would have different effects for males and females.

Glossary

Each entry includes a brief definition and notes the chapter in which the term was introduced.

Alpha error. See *Type I error.* Chapter 8

Alpha level (α). In inferential statistics, the probability of error. (1) In estimation, the probability that a confidence interval does not contain the population value. Chapter 7 (2) In hypothesis testing, the proportion of the area under the sampling distribution that contains unlikely sample outcomes if the null is true. The probability of Type I error. Chapter 8

Analysis of variance. A test of significance appropriate when testing for the differences among more than two sample means. Chapter 10

ANOVA. See *Analysis of variance.* Chapter 10

Arrow keys. When using SPSS, the keys used to move the cursor around the screen. Appendix F

Association. The relationship between two (or more) variables. Two variables are said to be associated if the distribution of one variable changes for the various categories or scores of the other variable. Chapter 12

Average deviation. The average of the absolute deviations of the scores around the mean. Chapter 4

Bar chart. A graphic display device for nominal- and ordinal-level variables. Chapter 2

Beta error. See *Type II error.* Chapter 8

Beta-weights (b^*). Standardized partial slopes. Chapter 17

Bias. A criterion used to select sample statistics for estimation procedures. A statistic is unbiased if the mean of its sampling distribution is equal to the population value of interest. Chapter 7

Bivariate normal distributions. The model assumption in the test of significance for Pearson's r that both variables are normally distributed. Chapter 15

Bivariate table. A table that displays the joint frequency distribution of two variables. Chapters 11 and 12

Boxplot. A graphic display device based on the median, interquartile range, and range. It is used to display the centre, dispersion, and overall range of scores in a distribution. Chapter 4

Cells. The cross-classification categories of the variables in a bivariate table. Chapter 11

Central Limit Theorem. A theorem that specifies the mean, standard deviation, and shape of the sampling distribution, given that the sample is large. Chapter 6

χ^2(critical). The chi square score that marks the beginnings of the critical region of the chi square sampling distribution. Chapter 11

χ^2(obtained). The test statistic computed in step 4 of the five-step model. Chapter 11

Chi square test. A non-parametric test of hypothesis for variables organized in a bivariate table. Chapter 11

Class intervals. The categories used in frequency distributions for interval-ratio-level variables. Chapter 2

Cluster sampling. A method of EPSEM sampling that is based on selecting groups, such as geographical areas, rather than cases from a list of the population. Chapter 6

Coefficient of determination (r^2). The proportion of all variation in Y that is explained by X. Chapter 15

Coefficient of multiple determination (R^2). A statistic that equals the total variation explained in the dependent variable by all independent variables combined. Chapter 17

Column. The vertical dimension of a bivariate table. Chapter 11

Column percentages. Percentages computed within each column of a bivariate table. Chapters 11 and 12

Conditional distribution of Y. The distribution of scores on the dependent variable for a specific score or category of the independent variable. Chapter 12

Conditional means of Y. The mean of all scores on Y for each value of X. Chapter 15

Confidence interval. An estimate of a population value in which a range of values is specified. Chapter 7

Confidence level. An alternative way to express alpha, the probability that a confidence interval will not contain the population value. Chapter 7

Continuous variable. A variable with a unit of measurement that can be subdivided infinitely. Chapter 1

Cramer's V. A chi square–based measure of association. Chapter 13

Critical region (region of rejection). The area under the sampling distribution that includes all unlikely sample outcomes. Chapter 8

Cumulative frequency. A column in a frequency distribution that displays the number of cases in an interval and all preceding intervals. Chapter 2

Cumulative percentage. A column in a frequency distribution that displays the percentage of cases in an interval and all preceding intervals. Chapter 2

Data. In social science research, information that is represented by numbers. Chapter 1

Database. An organized collection of related information. Appendix F

Data reduction. Summarizing many scores with a few statistics. Chapter 1

Deciles. The points that divide a distribution of scores into tenths. Chapter 3

Dependent variable. A variable that is identified as an effect, result, or outcome variable. The dependent variable is thought to be caused by the independent variable. Chapters 1 and 12

Descriptive statistics. The branch of statistics concerned with (1) summarizing the distribution of a single variable or (2) measuring the relationship between two or more variables. Chapter 1

Deviations. The distances between the scores and the mean. Chapter 4

Direct relationship. A multivariate relationship in which a control variable has no effect on the bivariate relationship. Chapter 16

Discrete variable. A variable with a basic unit of measurement that cannot be subdivided. Chapter 1

Dispersion. The amount of variety or heterogeneity in a distribution of scores. Chapter 4

E_1. For lambda, the number of errors of prediction made when predicting which category of the dependent variable cases will fall into while ignoring the independent variable. Chapter 13

E_2. For lambda, the number of errors of prediction made when predicting which category of the dependent variable cases will fall into while taking the independent variable into account. Chapter 13

Efficiency. The extent to which sample outcomes are clustered around the mean of the sampling distribution. Chapter 7

Elaboration. The basic multivariate technique for analyzing variables arrayed in tables. Partial tables are constructed to observe the bivariate relationship in a more detailed or elaborated format. Chapter 16

EPSEM. Equal probability of selection method. A technique for selecting samples in which every element or case in the population has an equal probability of being selected for the sample. Chapter 6

Error bar. A graphic display device used to illustrate the confidence interval of a sample mean. Chapter 7

Expected frequency (f_e). The cell frequencies that would be expected in a bivariate table if the variables were independent. Chapter 11

Explained variation. The proportion of all variation in Y that is attributed to the effect of X. Chapter 15

Explanation. See *Spurious relationship*. Chapter 16

F ratio. For the analysis of variance, the test statistic computed in step 4 of the five-step model. Chapter 10

File. A database (or any other information) that is stored under the same name in the memory of the computer or other storage media. Appendix F

Five-step model. A step-by-step guideline for conducting tests of hypotheses. Chapter 8

Frequency distribution. A table that displays the number of cases in each category of a variable. Chapter 2

Frequency polygon (line chart). A graphic display device for interval-ratio variables. Chapter 2

Gamma (G). A measure of association for ordinal variables organized in table format. Chapter 14

Goodness-of-fit test. An additional use for chi square that tests the significance of the distribution of a single variable. Chapter 11

Histogram. A graphic display device for interval-ratio variables. Chapter 2

Homoscedasticity. The model assumption in the test of significance for Pearson's r that the variance of the Y scores is uniform across all values of X. Chapter 15

Hypothesis. A statement about the relationship between variables that is derived from a theory. Hypotheses are more specific than theories, and all terms and concepts are fully defined. Chapter 1

Hypothesis testing. Statistical tests that estimate the probability of sample outcomes if assumptions about the population (the null hypothesis) are true. Chapter 8

Independence. The null hypothesis in the chi square test. Two variables are independent if the classification of a case on one variable has no effect on the probability that the case will be classified in any particular category of the second variable. Chapter 11

Independent random samples. Random samples gathered so that the selection of a case for one sample has no effect on the probability that any particular case will be selected for the other samples. Chapter 9

Independent variable. A variable that is identified as a causal variable. The independent variable is thought to cause the dependent variable. Chapters 1 and 12

Index of qualitative variation (IQV). A measure of dispersion for variables that have been organized into frequency distributions. Chapter 4

Inferential statistics. The branch of statistics concerned with making generalizations from samples to populations. Chapter 1

Interaction. A multivariate relationship in which a bivariate relationship changes across the categories of the control variable. Chapter 16

Interpretation. See *Intervening relationship.* Chapter 16

Interquartile range (Q). The distance from the third quartile to the first. Chapter 4

Interval estimate. See *Confidence interval.* Chapter 7

Intervening relationship. A multivariate relationship in which the independent and dependent variables are linked primarily through the control variable. Chapter 16

Lambda (λ). A measure of association for nominal-level variables that have been organized into a bivariate table. Lambda is based on the logic of PRE. Chapter 13

Level of measurement. The mathematical characteristics of a variable as determined by the measurement process. A major criterion for selecting statistical techniques. Chapter 1

Linear relationship. A relationship between two variables in which the observation points (dots) in the scattergram can be approximated with a straight line. Chapter 15

Line chart. See *Frequency polygon.*

Marginals. The row and column subtotals of a bivariate table. Chapter 11

Margin of error. The size of a confidence interval for a sample mean or sample proportion. It is also called the margin of sampling error, or just sampling error. Chapter 7

Maximum difference. The largest difference between column percentages for any row of a bivariate table. A way to assess the strength of the association, most useful for smaller tables. Chapter 12

Mean ($\overline{X}$ or M). The arithmetic average of the scores; $\overline{X}$ represents the mean of a sample, and M represents the mean of a population. Chapter 3.

Mean square. In the analysis of variance, an estimate of the variance calculated by dividing the sum of squares within (SSW) or the sum of squares between (SSB) by the appropriate degrees of freedom. Chapter 10

Measures of association. Statistics that summarize the strength and direction of the relationship between variables. Chapters 1 and 12

Measures of central tendency. Statistics that summarize a distribution of scores by reporting the most typical, average, or central value of the distribution. Chapter 3

Measures of dispersion. Statistics that indicate the amount of variety or heterogeneity in a distribution of scores. Chapter 4

Median (Md). The point in a distribution of scores above and below which half of the cases fall. Chapter 3

Menu. A list of options in a statistical package. Appendix F

Midpoint. The point halfway between the upper and lower limits of a class interval. Chapter 2

Mode. The most common value in a distribution or the largest category of a variable. Chapter 3

Multiple correlation. A multivariate technique for examining the combined effects of more than one independent variable on a dependent variable. Chapter 17

Multiple correlation coefficient (R). A statistic that indicates the strength of the correlation between a dependent variable and two or more independent variables. Chapter 17

Multiple regression. A multivariate technique that breaks down the separate effects of the independent variables on the dependent variable. Chapter 17

Negative association. A bivariate relationship in which the variables vary in opposite directions. As one variable increases, the other decreases, and high scores on one variable are associated with low scores on the other. Chapter 12

Nonparametric test. A type of significance test in which no assumptions about the shape of the sampling distribution are made. Chapter 11

Normal curve. A theoretical distribution of scores that is symmetrical, unimodal, and bell shaped. The standard normal curve always has a mean of 0 and a standard deviation of 1. Chapter 5

Normal curve table. Appendix A; a detailed description of the area between a Z score and the mean of a standardized normal distribution. Chapter 5

Null hypothesis (H_0). A statement of "no difference." The specific form varies from test to test. Chapter 8

Observed frequency (f_o). The cell frequencies actually observed in a bivariate table. Chapter 11

One-tailed test. A type of hypothesis test that can be used when (1) the direction of the difference can be predicted or (2) concern is focused on only one tail of the sampling distribution. Chapter 8

One-way analysis of variance. An application of ANOVA in which the effect of a single variable on another is observed. Chapter 10

Parameter. A characteristic of a population. Chapter 6

Partial correlation. A multivariate technique for examining a bivariate relationship while controlling for other variables. Chapter 17

Partial correlation coefficient. A statistic that shows the relationship between two variables while controlling for other variables; $r_{yx.z}$ is the symbol for the partial correlation coefficient when controlling for one variable. Chapter 17

Partial gamma (G_p). A statistic that indicates the strength of the association between two variables after the effects of a third variable have been removed. Chapter 16

Partial slopes. In a multiple regression equation, the slope of the relationship between a particular independent variable and the dependent variable while controlling for all other independents in the equation. Chapter 17

Partial tables. Tables produced when controlling for a third variable. Chapter 16

Pearson's r (r). A measure of association for variables that have been measured at the interval-ratio level. Chapter 15

Percentage (%). The number of cases in a category divided by the number of cases in all categories, the entire quantity multiplied by 100. Chapter 2

Percentage change. A way of measuring how much a variable has changed over time. Chapter 2

Percentile. The point in a distribution of scores below which a specific percentage of the cases fall. Chapter 3

Phi (ϕ). A chi square–based measure of association. Chapter 13

Pie chart. A graphic display device for nominal- and ordinal-level variables. Chapter 2

Point estimate. An estimate of a population value in which a single value is specified. Chapter 7

Pooled estimate. An estimate of the standard deviation of the sampling distribution of the difference in sample means based on the standard deviations of both samples. Chapter 9

Population. The total collection of all cases in which the researcher is interested. Chapter 1

Positive association. A bivariate relationship in which the variables vary in the same direction. As one variable increases, the other also increases, and high scores on one variable are associated with high scores on the other. Chapter 12

Proportion (p). The number of cases in a category divided by the number of cases in all categories. Chapter 2

Proportional reduction in error (PRE). The logic that underlies the definition and computation of several different measures of association. Statistics are derived by comparing the number of errors made in predicting the dependent variable while ignoring the independent variable with the number of errors made while taking the independent variable into account. Chapter 13

Quartiles. The points in a distribution of scores that divide the distribution into quarters. Chapter 3

Random samples. See *EPSEM.* Chapter 6

Range (R). A measure of variation in a set of scores. The range is equal to the highest score minus the lowest score. Chapter 4

Rate. The number of actual occurrences divided by the number of possible occurrences per some unit of time. Chapter 2

Ratio. The number of cases in one category divided by the number of cases in another category. Chapter 2

Real class limits. The upper and lower limits of an interval in a frequency distribution when the variable is treated as continuous. Chapter 2

Region of rejection. See *Critical region.* Chapter 8

Regression line. The best-fitting straight line that summarizes the relationship between two variables. The regression line is fitted to the data points by the least-squares criterion whereby the line touches all conditional means of Y or comes as close to doing so as possible. Chapter 15

Replication. See *Direct relationship.* Chapter 16

Representative. A characteristic of a random sample or a sample drawn according to the rule of EPSEM. A sample that accurately reproduces the major characteristics of the population from which it was drawn is said to be representative of the population. Chapter 6

Research. Any process of gathering information systematically and carefully to answer questions or test theories. Statistics are useful for research projects in which the information is represented in numerical form or as data. Chapter 1

Research hypothesis (H_1). A statement that contradicts the null hypothesis. The specific form varies from test to test. Chapter 8

Row. The horizontal dimension of a table. Chapter 11

Sample. A subset of a population. In inferential statistics, information is gathered from random or EPSEM samples and then generalized to populations. Chapters 1 and 6

Sampling distribution. The distribution of all possible sample outcomes of a given statistic. Chapter 6

Scattergram. A graphic display device that depicts the relationship between two variables. Chapter 15

Significance testing. See *Hypothesis testing.* Chapter 8

Simple random sample. A sample drawn from a population so that every case has an equal chance of being included. Chapter 6

Skew. The extent to which a distribution of scores has a few cases that are extremely high (positive skew) or extremely low (negative skew). Chapter 3

Slope (b). The amount of change in a variable per unit change in the other variable. Chapter 15

SPSS for Windows. A statistical package designed for the analysis of social science data. Appendix F

Spearman's rho (r_s). A measure of association for ordinal variables that are in "continuous" format. Chapter 14

Specification. See *Interaction.* Chapter 16

Spurious relationship. A multivariate relationship in which both the independent and dependent variables are actually caused by the control variable. The independent and dependent are not causally related. Chapter 16

Standard deviation (s or σ). The square root of the squared deviations of the scores around the mean, divided by N. The most commonly used measure of dispersion; s represents the standard deviation of a sample, and σ represents the standard deviation of a population. Chapter 4

Standard error of the mean. The standard deviation of a sampling distribution of sample means. Chapter 6

Standardized partial slopes (beta-weights). The slope of the relationship between a particular independent variable and the dependent when all scores are expressed as Z scores. Chapter 17

Stated class limits. The class intervals of a frequency distribution when stated as discrete categories. Chapter 2

Statistical package (statpak). A set of computer programs designed to manipulate and statistically analyze data. Appendix F

Statistics. A set of mathematical techniques for organizing and analyzing data. Chapter 1

Stem-and-Leaf Plot. A graphic display device for interval-ratio variables. Class intervals are represented by rows of digits of equal width (equal to the class limits), the length of each corresponding to the number of cases in the interval. Chapter 2

Stratified random sample. A random sample drawn from a population by selecting cases from sublists of groups in proportion to the representation of the groups in the population. Chapter 6

Student's t distribution. A distribution used to find the critical region for tests of sample means when σ is unknown and sample size is small. Chapter 8

Sum of squares between (SSB). The sum of the squared deviations of the sample means from the overall mean, weighted by sample size. Chapter 10

Sum of squares total (SST). The sum of the squared deviations of the scores from the overall mean. Chapter 10

Sum of squares within (SSW). The sum of the squared deviations from the category means. Chapter 10

Systematic random sample. A sample selected by choosing the first case from a list of the population randomly and then choosing every kth case. Chapter 6

t(critical). The t score that marks the beginnings of the critical region of a t distribution. Chapter 8

t distribution. A distribution used to find the critical region for tests of sample means when N is small and is unknown. Chapter 8

t(obtained). The test statistic computed in step 4 of the five-step model for tests of sample means when

N is small and population standard deviation is unknown. Chapter 8

Test statistic. The value computed in step 4 of the five-step model that places the sample outcome on the sampling distribution. Chapter 8

Theory. A generalized explanation of the relationship between two or more variables. Chapter 1

Total variation. The spread of the Y scores around the mean of Y. Chapter 15

Two-tailed test. A type of hypothesis test that can be used when (1) the direction of the difference cannot be predicted or (2) concern is focused on both tails of the sampling distribution. Chapter 8

Type I error (alpha error). The probability of rejecting a null hypothesis that is true. Chapter 8

Type II error (beta error). The probability of failing to reject a null hypothesis that is false. Chapter 8

Unexplained variation. The proportion of the total variation in Y that is not accounted for by X. Chapter 15

Variable. Any trait that can change values from case to case. Chapter 1

Variance (s^2 or σ^2). The squared deviations of the scores around the mean, divided by N. A measure of dispersion used in inferential statistics and in regression techniques; s^2 represents the variance of a sample, and σ^2 represents the variance of a population. Chapter 4

Y intercept (a). The point where the regression line crosses the Y axis. Chapter 15

Z(critical). The Z score that marks the beginnings of the critical region of a Z distribution. Chapter 8

Z(obtained). The test statistic computed in step 4 of the five-step model. Chapter 8

Z scores. Standard scores; the way scores are expressed after they have been standardized to the theoretical normal curve. Chapter 5

Zero-order correlations. Correlation coefficients for bivariate relationships. Chapter 17

Index

CHAPTER 2

Proportion

$$p = \frac{f}{N}$$

Percentage

$$\% = \left(\frac{f}{N}\right) \times 100$$

CHAPTER 3

Mean

$$\overline{X} = \frac{\Sigma(X_i)}{N}$$

CHAPTER 4

Standard deviation

$$s = \sqrt{\frac{\Sigma(X_i - \overline{X})^2}{N}}$$

CHAPTER 5

Z scores

$$Z_i = \frac{X_i - \overline{X}}{s}$$

CHAPTER 7

Confidence interval for a sample mean

$$\text{c.i.} = \overline{X} \pm Z\left(\frac{s}{\sqrt{N-1}}\right)$$

Confidence interval for a sample proportion

$$\text{c.i.} = P_s \pm Z\sqrt{\frac{P_u(1 - P_u)}{N}}$$

CHAPTER 8

Means

$$Z\,(\text{obtained}) = \frac{\overline{X} - \mu}{s/\sqrt{N-1}}$$

Proportions

$$Z\,(\text{obtained}) = \frac{P_s - P_u}{\sqrt{P_u(1 - P_u)/N}}$$

CHAPTER 9

Means

$$Z\,(\text{obtained}) = \frac{(\overline{X}_1 - \overline{X}_2)}{\sigma_{\overline{x} - \overline{x}}}$$

Standard deviation of the sampling distribution for sample means

$$\sigma_{\overline{x} - \overline{x}} = \sqrt{\frac{s_1^2}{N_1 - 1} + \frac{s_2^2}{N_2 - 1}}$$

Pooled estimate of population proportion

$$P_u = \frac{N_1 P_{s1} + N_2 P_{s2}}{N_1 + N_2}$$

Standard deviation of the sampling distribution for sample proportions

$$\sigma_{p-p} = \sqrt{P_u(1 - P_u)}\,\sqrt{(N_1 + N_2)/N_1 N_2}$$

Proportions

$$Z\,(\text{obtained}) = \frac{(P_{s1} - P_{s2})}{\sigma_{p-p}}$$

CHAPTER 10

Total sum of squares

$$\text{SST} = \sum X^2 - N\overline{X}^2$$

Sum of squares between

$$\text{SSB} = \sum N_k(\overline{X}_k - \overline{X})^2$$

Sum of squares within

$$\text{SSW} = \text{SST} - \text{SSB}$$

Degrees of freedom for SSW

$$\text{dfw} = N - k$$

Degrees of freedom for SSB

$$\text{dfb} = k - 1$$

Mean square within

$$MSW = \frac{SSW}{dfw}$$

Mean square between

$$MSB = \frac{SSB}{dfb}$$

F ratio

$$F = \frac{MSB}{MSW}$$

CHAPTER 11

Chi square

$$\chi^2 \text{ (obtained)} = \sum \frac{(f_o - f_e)^2}{f_e}$$

CHAPTER 13

Phi

$$\phi = \sqrt{\frac{\chi^2}{N}}$$

Cramer's V

$$V = \sqrt{\frac{\chi^2}{(N)(\text{Minimum of } r - 1, c - 1)}}$$

Lambda

$$\lambda = \frac{E_1 - E_2}{E_1}$$

CHAPTER 14

Gamma

$$G = \frac{N_s - N_d}{N_s + N_d}$$

Spearman's rho

$$r_s = 1 - \frac{6 \sum D^2}{N(N^2 - 1)}$$

CHAPTER 15

Least-squares regression line

$$Y = a + bX$$

Slope

$$b = \frac{N \sum XY - (\sum X)(\sum Y)}{N \sum X^2 - (\sum X)^2}$$

Y intercept

$$a = \overline{Y} - b\overline{X}$$

Pearson's r

$$r = \frac{N \sum XY - (\sum X)(\sum Y)}{\sqrt{[N \sum X^2 - (\sum X)^2][N \sum Y^2 - (\sum Y)^2]}}$$

CHAPTER 17

Partial correlation coefficient

$$r_{yx.z} = \frac{r_{yx} - (r_{yz})(r_{xz})}{\sqrt{1 - r_{yz}^2} \sqrt{1 - r_{xz}^2}}$$

Least-squares multiple regression line

$$Y = a + b_1 X_1 + b_2 X_2$$

Partial slope for X_1

$$b_1 = \left(\frac{s_y}{s_1}\right) \left(\frac{r_{y1} - r_{y2} r_{12}}{1 - r_{12}^2}\right)$$

Partial slope for X_2

$$b_2 = \left(\frac{s_y}{s_2}\right) \left(\frac{r_{y2} - r_{y1} r_{12}}{1 - r_{12}^2}\right)$$

Y intercept

$$a = \overline{Y} - b_1 \overline{X}_1 - b_2 \overline{X}_2$$

Beta-weight for X_1

$$b_1^* = b_1 \left(\frac{s_1}{s_y}\right)$$

Beta-weight for X_2

$$b_2^* = b_2 \left(\frac{s_2}{s_y}\right)$$

Standardized least-squares regression line

$$Z_y = b_1^* Z_1 + b_2^* Z_2$$

Coefficient of multiple determination

$$R^2 = r_{y1}^2 + r_{y2.1}^2 (1 - r_{y1}^2)$$

GLOSSARY OF SYMBOLS

The number in parentheses indicates the chapter in which the symbol is introduced.

a	Point at which the regression line crosses the Y axis (15)
ANOVA	The analysis of variance (10)
b	Slope of the regression line (15)
b_i	Partial slope of the linear relationship between the ith independent variable and the dependent variable (17)
b_i^*	Standardized partial slope of the linear relationship between the ith independent variable and the dependent variable (17)
df	Degrees of freedom (8)
f	Frequency (2)
F	The F ratio (10)
f_e	Expected frequency (11)
f_o	Observed frequency (11)
G	Gamma for a sample (14)
G_p	Partial gamma (16)
H_0	Null hypothesis (8)
H_1	Research or alternate hypothesis (8)
IQV	Index of qualitative variation (4)
Md	Median (3)
Mo	Mode (3)
N	Number of cases (2)
N_d	Number of pairs of cases ranked in different order on two variables (14)
N_s	Number of pairs of cases ranked in the same order on two variables (14)

%	Percentage (2)
P	Proportion (2)
P_s	A sample proportion (7)
P_u	A population proportion (7)
PRE	Proportional reduction in error (13)
Q	Interquartile range (4)
r	Pearson's correlation coefficient for a sample (15)
r^2	Coefficient of determination (15)
R	Range (4)
r_s	Spearman's rho for a sample (14)
$r_{xy.z}$	Partial correlation coefficient (17)
R^2	Multiple correlation coefficient (17)
s	Sample standard deviation (4)
SSB	The sum of squares between (10)
SST	The total sum of squares (10)
SSW	The sum of squares within (10)
s^2	Sample variance (4)
t	Student's t score (8)
V	Cramer's V (13)
X	Any independent variable (12)
$\overline{X}$	Mean of a sample (3)
X_i	Any score in a distribution (3)
Y	Any dependent variable (12)
Y'	A predicted score on Y (15)
Z scores	Standard scores (5)
Z	A control variable (16)

GREEK LETTERS

α Probability of Type I error (8)

β Probability of Type II error (8)

γ Gamma for a population (14)

λ Lambda (13)

μ Mean of a population (3)

μ_p Mean of a sampling distribution of sample proportions (6)

$\mu_{\bar{X}}$ Mean of a sampling distribution of sample means (6)

ρ Pearson's correlation coefficient for a population (15)

ρ_s Spearman's rho for a population (14)

σ Population standard deviation (4)

σ_p Standard deviation of a sampling distribution of sample proportions (6)

σ_{p-p} Standard deviation of the sampling distribution of difference in sample proportions (9)

$\sigma_{\bar{X}}$ Standard deviation of a sampling distribution of sample means (6)

$\sigma_{\bar{X}-\bar{X}}$ Standard deviation of the sampling distribution of the difference in sample means (9)

σ^2 Population variance (4)

Σ "Summation of" (3)

ϕ Phi (13)

χ^2 Chi square statistic (11)

χ_c^2 Chi square corrected by Yates' correction (11)

GLOSSARY OF SYMBOLS

The number in parentheses indicates the chapter in which the symbol is introduced.

a Point at which the regression line crosses the Y axis (15)

ANOVA   The analysis of variance (10)

b Slope of the regression line (15)

b_i Partial slope of the linear relationship between the ith independent variable and the dependent variable (17)

b_i^* Standardized partial slope of the linear relationship between the ith independent variable and the dependent variable (17)

df   Degrees of freedom (8)

f Frequency (2)

F The F ratio (10)

f_e Expected frequency (11)

f_o Observed frequency (11)

G Gamma for a sample (14)

G_p Partial gamma (16)

H_0 Null hypothesis (8)

H_1 Research or alternate hypothesis (8)

IQV   Index of qualitative variation (4)

Md   Median (3)

Mo   Mode (3)

N Number of cases (2)

N_d Number of pairs of cases ranked in different order on two variables (14)

N_s Number of pairs of cases ranked in the same order on two variables (14)

$\%$ Percentage (2)

P Proportion (2)

P_s A sample proportion (7)

P_u A population proportion (7)

PRE   Proportional reduction in error (13)

Q Interquartile range (4)

r Pearson's correlation coefficient for a sample (15)

r^2 Coefficient of determination (15)

R Range (4)

r_s Spearman's rho for a sample (14)

$r_{xy.z}$ Partial correlation coefficient (17)

R^2 Multiple correlation coefficient (17)

s Sample standard deviation (4)

SSB   The sum of squares between (10)

SST   The total sum of squares (10)

SSW   The sum of squares within (10)

s^2 Sample variance (4)

t Student's t score (8)

V Cramer's V (13)

X Any independent variable (12)

$\overline{X}$ Mean of a sample (3)

X_i Any score in a distribution (3)

Y Any dependent variable (12)

Y' A predicted score on Y (15)

Z scores   Standard scores (5)

Z A control variable (16)